UNTOUCHABLE CHANDALS OF INDIA: THE DEMOCRATIC MOVEMENT

UNTOUCHABLE CHANDALS OF INDIA
The Democratic Movement

S.K. BISWAS

GYAN

ISBN: 978-81-212-1197-0

Price: ₹ 1125

First Published 2013

Published by

Gyan Publishing House
23, Main Ansari Road, Daryaganj,
New Delhi - 110002
Phones : 23282060, 23261060
Fax : (011) 23285914
E-mail: books@gyanbooks.com
website: gyanbooks.com

Laser Typesetting: Rajender Vashist, Delhi
Printed at: G. Print Process, Delhi

Cataloging in Publication Data--DK
Courtesy: D.K. Agencies (P) Ltd. <docinfo@dkagencies.com>

Biswas, S. K.
Untouchable Chandal of India : the democratic movement / S.K. Biswas.
p. cm.
Includes bibliographical references and index.
ISBN 9788121211970

1. Caṇḍālas--Political activity--History. 2. Caṇḍālas--Social conditions. 3. Democracy--India--History. I. Title.

DDC 305.800954 23

Dedicated

to

Manyawar Kanshiram

who desired such a book by me

Contents

Preface

A number of my friends and learned persons had posed the same question, 'why have you written on the Chandals now?' It is, indeed, not only a very interesting question but also a very relevant question. Such a question was obvious to come. Practically, the book is the answer to the query.

It were the Chandals who for the first time paved the path of democracy by denouncing Hinduism and declaring a new faith, Matuaism in 1835. Without such an act the natives of India, the 'Mulniwasis', that way entire India, were disqualified by religious sanctions to aspire for any human rights that the modern world ushered. It were the Chandals who for the first time paved the path of democracy by rejecting Hinduism which according to Dr Ambedkar 'is a menace to liberty, equality and fraternity. On that account it is incompatible with democracy.' Being the unconscious tools in the hands of history, rather destiny, it is the Chandals of Bengal, the Chandals of the East helped the British East India Company establish the British Raj in India. It were they who formed the British army in India and 'the native army organised and trained by the British Drill Sergeants was the *sin-qua-non* of Indian self-emancipation and of India ceasing to be the prey of the first foreign intruders' as was assessed by Karl Marx. It is they who fought and won the battle of Palassay in 1757 against the Muslim-Hindu combine army of Nawab Sirajuddula. They for the first time, started '*sarva-siksha andolon*' or the movement for education for all, right from 1880 in the rural Bengal. Since 1882 social-democracy was initiated by these Chandals of the East by refusing the hereditary caste hierarchy and joining voting system. They raised the banner of political-democracy since 1891 and made it a national movement shortly before 1921 when their representatives entered in the Legislature in Bengal. I felt my indebtedness towards my country for putting the saga of the untold history of the Chandals and their democratic movement on record.

S.K. Biswas

Introduction

Indians being born non-human, i.e., Brahmins and Sudras did not know about franchise. The process of enfranchisement of the Indian subjects is found to have started in right perspective by the British Government under the sun-shine of 'Rule of Laws' enacted in the Parliament of Great Britain as a part of the democratisation scheme of Indian Polity during the first quarter of the 20th Century. The process was, however, initiated by Lord Ripon, a 'true Liberal of the Gladstonian era, with a strong belief in the virtues of peace, *laiseez faire*, and self-government.' His plan as embodied in a Government Resolution of 1882 envisaged local boards with smaller areas and laid emphasis on the elective principle. In rural areas, he set up a system of District Boards and Local Boards known as '*Tahasil*' or '*Taluk*' boards. Wherever possible, the representatives were to be elected by rate-payers rather than nominated by the Government. The jurisdiction of the order included the areas in rural Bengal where untouchables were immense majority. The British were the rulers of India who for the first time utilised the services of the untouchables of the country while conquering the territorial battles. With the help of an army composed of the untouchables they conquered all battles right from Plassey in Bengal in 1757 to the battle of Koregaon in Pune in 1818 in India. Thus the century's deprived people came under the process of enfranchisement. This march of democratisation through enfranchisement continued without break for four decades. The vast Untouchable producer classes officially known as the Depressed Classes got a better deal in the 'Franchise Committee' better known as the Southborough Committee that was constituted in pursuance of the Montagu-Chelmsford Reforms to enact the Government of India Act 1919.

The history of modern Europe is nothing but the history of successive civil wars. It is not gain said that the series of peasant-revolts starting with the fall of Bastille in Paris in 1789; birth of nationalism and growth of socialist activities that followed in Europe embossed their obvious impacts in the growth and shaping of colonial history in the World. Soon after the Communists established Paris Commune as the free government of the people or of the proletariat in Paris. It was crushed in 1871 by the combine forces of European imperialists. England played a leading role in it. Undaunted were the Socialists groups in Europe; the Communist International was founded by Karl Marx. Finally, the Bolshevik revolution of October 1917 in Russia vanquished the mighty Czarist regime. The colonial forces tackled two devastating World Wars from 1914 to 1941. Even before all these, the revolts of American colonies during 1773 onwards and declaration of their constitution in 1789 shuttered the ruling colonial forces of the world. It gave birth to a republican democratic country in the world called USA which has been a countruy without a monarch or a king or that culture. 'The political development in America established the right to protest against injustice and right to fight for freedom and independence.' Sitting in such precarious fire circle, the British colonial forces with utmost political sagacity adopted all these populous and democratic steps in India to retain their rule.

Initially the British East India Company and finally the British Crown introduced for the first time a form of Government called Democracy in India. Democracy is the form of Government where the immense majority 'govern' rule the country. In Republic the country belongs to the subjects. In such circumstances, the British statesmen gradually dragged even the illiterate and pauper untouchables in the affairs of the governance. They started empowering the Untouchables with education and political rights to elect their own representatives in the Legislature. This became totally contrary to the Hindu spirituality and was diametrically detrimental to the interests of supercilious Brahmins. Bengal was the seat of power and Calcutta was political capital of India since Warren Hastings. Untouchables formed 58 per cent of the Hindu population besides, 55 per cent Muslim subjects of the then large and rich Bengal. The untouchables, especially powerful Chandals played a crucial role in democratic power game. Advent of Guruchand Thakur in the rural Bengal as the deliverer of the subdued untouchable people coincided with the period of Lord Ripon in every respect. History seems to have played her invisible role.

The creamy-layer caste-Hindus on the one hand became happy with the prospect of getting handles of power in their hands in the Parliamentary Democracy and to avoid Muslim or Christian rule. On the other hand they simultaneously opposed the same process of political empowerment of the Untouchable masses with democratic rights. The British had the similar situation. On the one side they were to transfer power in democratic polity to the subjects; on the other hand they were to perpetuate their colonial market and interests intact. British authority enrolled the untouchables in their army and schools and eventually in politics. Thus, the Brahmin and British ruling-class had to start a cunning game called disenfranchisement of the Untouchables after sanctioning them with voting rights.

Despite all out opposition of the Brahmins, the immense majority autochthons (*Mulniwasis*) the Untouchables in particular started successfully gaining their franchise rights in Bengal since 1882 onwards (Lord Ripon's scheme) by dint of their own strenuous struggles. The creamy-layer-ruling castes also adopted well calculated method to disenfranchise these unfortunate lots through official and unofficial modes. The educated creamy layer-elite Hindus were in advantageous position as they were in administration and were holding wealth. As a result, officially at least three times, within a span of period of a century i.e. from 1903 to 2003 it went under such a process. First time, it was the Poona Pact of 1932 that disenfranchised them. They got disenfranchised once again when India was vivisected in 1947 into three parts. The hat-trick has been achieved in 2003 with the enactment of the Citizenship Bill 2003 which simultaneously granted Indian citizenship to the Green Card Holders and snatched away the citizenship right of more than 10 million Indians who came to India after the partition in 1947 from East-Bengal and are residing in different places scattered all over India without break. This has been done in complete rupture of the provisions of Charter of Human Rights by which the UNO promises to assure citizenship to all and each human being. Thus in India, the Hindu Rule under the Brahmanical hegemony got ensured and established. The Untouchables and the Sudras (Backwards) are en-caged in the servile-condition even in the parlor of Democracy. The history of this process of nation-fixing remained untold.

The creamy-layer-Hindus, therefore, started opposing the system and corrupting the British personnel. And Bengal became the 1st victim of this game and in a latter period the Punjab fell in line with Bengal. This disenfranchisement process was not necessary in any other province. According to the 1911 Census Report in the Bombay and Sindh Province untouchables were enumerated only 6,00,000 souls (0.6 million) or 3 per cent of the total population of 19.5 million (1,95,00,000) people. The tribe of the Untouchables increased in Bombay Province satisfactorily in the next decade and they formed 8 per cent of the total population. In 1941 Census they increased to be enumerated as 18,55,148 and that formed 8.9 per cent of the total population of Bombay when Muslims formed another 9.2 per cent population. As a result, enfranchised or disenfranchised it was meaningless in the Bombay Province.

But the position in Bengal and in the Punjab was quite different. According to the 1911 Census 99,00,000 were the Untouchables (9.9 millions) or 22.4 per cent out of the total population of 4,50,00,000 (45.0 millions). When, the Muslim population was around 55.2 per cent. The Hindus (including Backwards) were abject minority. During the next decennials census 1931, the untouchable formed 24.7 per cent and the Muslims remained to 54.9 per cent. The Hindus were enumerated 18.3 per cent only. Next decade the untouchable population according to the same Census Report declined to only 12.6 per cent with a total of 73,78,970 souls. Around 35 Lakhs of untouchable population were just manipulated to evaporate from the surface of the region. The decline was around 50 per cent. These untouchable masses lived in heavy concentration and in social consolidation over only 8 or nine Districts or in around 30 Sub-divisions of Eastern and Western Bengal. The position in the Punjab was not less serious or challenging. Hindus in 1931 Census Report formed only 15.1 per cent of the total population. Untouchables were 13.5 per cent and Muslims formed 56.5 per cent and Sikhs 13 per cent. In the circumstances the balls of 'Enfranchisement' and 'Disenfranchisement' of the population of India in the dance of Democracy rolled and rocked simultaneously.

Manyawar Kanshi Ramji while inaugurating the "2nd Dalit History Congress" in December 2000, at the ISI, New Delhi appealed to the *Dalit*-Historians to concentrate their research work on her past history not beyond 600 years from now. He lamented that the history of Modern time has not yet been written and that needs to be written. Once sometimes during 2002, he asked me, "Mr. Jogendra Nath Mandal flew back to India from Pakistan (without submitting his resignation as Law Minister there) in 1950 and Babasheb expired in 1956. This six years time was very long as well as very crucial but why these *Chela* and *Guru* never came together, never met, never telephoned once, never sent any correspondence, and never planned any united movement? Why? Who betrayed whom?" Since then I enquired and sounded many possible sources but failed to give him any reply. The answer is historical. It is to be understood. Kanshi Ramji is no more and I complete the untold history of India. The answer is perhaps here. I record here with deep gratitude for Bhusan Phooljule, an Executive Engineer with ONGC, Gujarat for his remarkable contribution in proof reading and editing entire manuscript.

S.K. Biswas
1.1.2009

1

India, That is Bharat: Its Society

India is a vast country. It is a sub-continent. Its length from the eastern end of West Bengal to the western border of Gujarat is 3,000 kms. From the Himalayan peaks of Kashmir in the north to the sea-shores of Indian-Ocean on the down south to Kanyakumari it spans 3200 kms. The near square shaped country that exists between the longitude 8.5° to 37.8° and latitude 68.7° to 97.25° stands as the fifth largest country with 12,63,000 square miles (32,87,240 square km.) after Russia, Canada, China and Brazil. From the standpoint of population, it is second only to China. According to the Census Report of 2001 its total population is 102,86,10328; female population per 1000 is 933. The latest 2011 Report reveals total population as 121,01,93,422; female per 1000 is 940. 18,740 is the number of categories of Scheduled Castes and Tribes listed by the last Census held in 2001. 1,963 is the number of castes in the Central list of OBCs, which includes 4000 sub-castes. Each state has its own list of OBCs.[1]

The name of the country is found to have been *Bharat* as evidenced in its ancient language and literature. In the Vedic hymns the autochthons of the land, on several occasions have been addressed as "*Aa Bharati Bharatibhi....*" '*O Bharati*!', 'hallo, the man of *Bharat*'.[2] In 1949, on the eve of finalizing the Constitution of India the Chairman of the Constituent Assembly, Dr Rajendra Prasad proposed to name the country, *Bharat*. Pandit Jawaharlal Nehru opposed this move. He argued that the foreigners knew the country as India. And it would be embarrassing for the foreigners with this new nomenclature. He, therefore, did not want to embarrass the foreigners' lobby. "I do not want to put India in an absurd position internationally," said Nehru. In the disputing situation, Dr Ambedkar, the Chairman of the Drafting Committee, made a compromise between these two views and finally recorded in the Constitution, "India that is Bharat".[3] Dr Rajendra Prasad still resolved to maintain his stand after becoming the first President of the country.

Consequently, in the Rastrapati Bhavan he made all the employees to have the armband embroidered with the word '*Bharat*'. The armband tradition continues.[4]

Pandit Nehru in his book, 'Discovery of India' recorded that he had faced two different countries in this land. When he addressed meetings of small gatherings of two to three hundred persons in the sophisticated halls in the cities they called the country India. And when he visited countryside to address crowds of rural people they shouted, 'Bharat Mata Ki Jai'. 'Bharat' and 'India' of early Nehru age still continues as distinctly separate even in the third millennium. Priya Sahgal writes, "There is an India that continues to be feted at global high tables as a regional power blessed with a robust civil society.... Then there is other India, that infernal land without justice, where your identity is defined not by your profession or your talent but by your caste. India is a country of thousand castes, and they are the foundation on which social structures are built, certainly in the countryside.'[5]

Nature is abundantly bountiful to the country. In the north, the snow-capped Himalayan ranges with her enchanting beauty and grandeur make all the nations adore her profusely. It is the first line of natural defence of India. In the south the storming waves of the Indian Ocean being flanked by Arabian Sea and by the Bay of Bengal provide along with other wealth a natural privilege of coastal security. Dozens of streams of furious long rivers water and help irrigate the country, and remain as the invaluable source of hydro-electricity and easy means of pollution-free transport system. The vast alluvial plains, forest ranges and small mountains of the country are profusely showered with monsoon rains. She is endowed with the source of unending solar-energy. Entire surface of the country remains flooded with scorching sunlight all the days. It is cool and it shines with moonlit during nights. There remains limitless deposit of mineral ores under the crust of the Earth. The moderate temperature keeps its dwellers, the huge man-power in comfort, contentment and good mood. Innumerable and varieties of cattle and fowls along with wild animals are the matchless sources of milk and protein in the dense forests and deep jungles. Supply of seas, rivers and pond-fish is abundant.

People of the vast country, though maintain ancient heritage, instead of being united are not only diverse but they are also divided even in hostile ethnic and cultural groups. Eventually the country is claimed to have maintained its unity in diversity. It is divided into Tribes and Clans. Creeds and Religions, Castes and Castes. The country and its society continue to be a conglomeration of different linguistic zones. The society actually displays a disloyal disposition of disintegrated and degraded humanity that remains engaged in an internecine quarrel all through the ages. The four international religions like Buddhism, Christianity, Islam and Zoroastrianism as well as Hinduism, Sikhism, Jainism play their paradoxical role as major religions of the country. Apart from these, different ethnic, semi-Hinduised people numbering billions devoutly follow many other religious faiths rooted in the soil of the country. Innumerable Indian autochthons known as Tribes being aloof and afar from the so-called main-stream or official society follow their ancient religious faiths, language-scripts and distinct culture. Many of the tribes (*Adivasis*) in eastern India still follow the mysterious faith and languages that prevailed in pre-Aryan Indus valley regions.[6]

Hinduism appears to have grown in course of time, taking foreign and indigenous elements in it. The Vedic Aryans never claimed themselves as Hindus. The term Hindu came to existence only in the post-Islamic period in India. In 2001 Census, the Hindus are enumerated as 827,587,868 souls. This figure includes semi-Hinduised Untouchables and Tribes of India. After being Hinduised the Untouchables are now called contemptuously as Scheduled Castes or S.Cs. Tribes or non-Hinduised autochthons who generally do not declare their institutionalised religion are also included in the figure. Muslims are counted 138,101,896; Christians 240,80016; Sikhs 192,15,730; Buddhists 79,55,207. The Parsis or the Zoroastrians, though very dominant in finance-market and politics their population remains around eighty thousand only. Their population is diminishing gradually. The Jains are fabulously wealthy but small in number. Around 27 per cent of the total population are recorded to be inter-state migrants, they have all (including more than 1.8 million population who are enumerated under the term 'generics') been counted as Hindus and not as SC/STs.

With a view to obliging constitutional requirements the SCs (new terms for the untouchables since 1935) and the Tribal population have been enumerated separately also and their number has been shown as 16,66,35700 (16.2 per cent) and 8,43,26240 (8.2 per cent) respectively. For some political reasons that arise out of democratic movement, their number does not grow in record. Otherwise, they are prolific; neither infertile nor declared as an endangered species.

The concentration and distribution of such different groups vary from regions to regions. This situation obviously affected the growth and influence of the democratic movement that was ignited by the British ruling-class during the last quarter of the nineteenth century India. Such peculiarity in demography, also help building diverse and complex social character and economic growth in the country. The density of Muslims, Sikhs, Tribals, Buddhists, Jains and the Untouchable population are not uniform all over the Indian Territory. I 'he undivided India, until the year 1946 the Punjab, Sindh, Assam and Bengal had a deep concentration of Muslim population. It was around 55 to 59 per cent of the total population. Bengal, Bihar, Assam, Uttar Pradesh, Orissa, Madras and the Punjab had the maximum concentration of Untouchable population. In the eastern part of India, the Untouchables composed not less than 25 per cent of the total population. In 1921 Census, the Untouchables in Bengal were enumerated more than 15 million and 24.7 per cent of the total population of Bengal. In the Bombay province, as per the Census Report of 1911 there were only 6 lakhs or 3.2 per cent (of total population) Untouchables. In 1921, they increased to 17 lakhs and formed 8.2 per cent of the total population. Their number in the Bombay province increased phenomenally in each decade thereafter. In 2001 they have been enumerated 50,63,062 out of a total population of 9,68,78,627 souls. It forms 6.1 per cent. A substantial number of them had converted to Buddhism after 1956.

On the map of India the areas with high concentration of Tribal people has formed a geographic-shape of a belt. It is called the Tribal belt. This Tribal-belt stretches through the central Indian Territory starting from Gujarat to Southern Bengal of Santhal Parganas, Birbhum, Manbhum etc. through Bhilwara of Rajasthan and Madhya Pradesh. High density of Tribal people is also found in Gondwana-land, Chota Nagpur and in the North East Region of Assam, Meghalaya, Manipur, Nagaland, etc. Sikhs are predominantly found in the Punjab state only.

Around 70 per cent of 9 million Buddhists in India today reside in Maharashtra. A good number of them are found in West Bengal and Bihar. A large number of untouchables got converted to Buddhism along with Dr Ambedkar since 14th October 1956 in Maharashtra. According to the 2001 Census there were 58,38,710 Buddhists in Maharashtra. They formed 6.5 per cent of the total population. During the last 40 years their number just doubled. In 1961 they were enumerated 27,89,501 souls. In Bengal too the number of Buddhists during the same period simply doubled. However, the maximum speed of expansion of Buddhist population has been recorded in Karnakaka. In 1961 they were 9,770 only. In 2001 their tribe increased by 44 folds and touched the total number to 3,93,300 persons.

India is a land of contrast in every respect. India is the source of the most ancient scripts, language and literature in the world. The script (Astric) found in use in the Indus-region, appears to have been widely in use four millenniums ago. The scripts available in the Asokan Edicts of 250 B.C. belong to the Indus family of scripts. The linguists after thorough examinations have also concluded that these Asokan scripts originated out of the Indus scripts. The Buddhist Pali literature and the Vedic Sanskrit literature are regarded to be the ancient literature in the annals of World literature. India holds the distinction of having Universities like Nalanda, Vikramsila, Odantapuri and Vallabhi. These Alma maters of tens of thousands of students from all over the contemporary advanced countries were the most ancient in the World. The citizens were so vastly literate that the Buddhist Emperor, Asoka the great had the wisdom to circulate his official and other instructions to his Governors as well as to the ordinary subjects by engraving the edicts on roadside rocks and on finely polished monolithic large pillars in places of pilgrimages, markets and offices. The most literate nation, in course of time has, however, reduced to the country of most populous with maximum illiterate population of the world. Despite the best efforts of the British Colonial Government and afterwards the pressure from the World Bank authority, the literacy rate in the country as per the 2001 Census is found to be only 64.8 per cent (male-75.3 per cent and female 53.5 per cent). In 1901 Census the literacy rate was 1.1 per cent only.

The ancient country that always maintained favourable balance of trade until the Mughal period, now glitters in the panel of the names of the poorest countries in the World. As per the World Bank report, in 2001 to 2005, around 79 per cent of the total population of India remains under the poverty level and 'in distressing condition'. At the same time, the richest man and many others amongst top 20 billionaires of the World belong to India. 'India has no Middle Class', commented F. Barnier, the court physician of the Mughal Emperor, Aurangzeb in his famous 'Travels in Mughal India' in the last decade of A.D. 17th century. During the medieval period the Indian rich, the *Amirs*, *Omrahas* and their associates rolled in reckless festivities with wanton wealth and women. The poor, the toiling masses, the peasantry and artisans used to remain almost naked and on empty stomach under the tree-shed or in the thatched roofs. 'The glittering pearls and diamonds in the crowns of the Emperor are the crystallised blood oozing out of the tearful eyes of the peasants', described Barnier in his account. The situation had hardly changed during the following periods with the changing of political grips from one hand to the other.

Noted economist Nancy Birdsall, president of the Centre for global Development, has proposed a new definition of the middle class for the developing countries in the forthcoming World Bank Publication in 2010, Equality in globalising World. Birdsall defines the middle class for developing world to include people with income above $10 day, but excluding the top 5 per cent of that country. By this definition, India even urban India alone has no middle class; everyone at over $10 a day is in the top 5 per cent of the country. This is a combination of both the depth of India's poverty and its inequality[7] throughout the ages. These 95 per cent poor are the autochthons (*Mulnivasis*) and known as the Tribals, Sudras, the Untouchables and their proselytes.

However, the watchdogs and evergreen creamy-layer intellectuals of India did not shy to blame the poor or the Dalits for help build such a misleading dada to show the bad-face of the country. The Creamy-layer surveyors and Government sponsored researchers expect the 'Dalits' or the poor, instead of being truthful lying for incentive for which they are prone to, to be patriots in their empty stomach and boast in behalf of the super-rich of India who donate million dollars to their American alma-maters. The people in distressing condition, instead of remaining illiterate and ignorant must know about the super rich who construct personal living houses spending 9000 Crores of rupees for a family of four or the village Jats who spend more than the marriage party of Buckingham Palace. According to the report, it is the poor who have a fascination to magnify their pecuniary bad condition and their wants in pains. They always cry, always hungry and eat all food-grains of the World-granary to create universal crisis. Swaminathan S Ankeleswariaya, therefore, writes in his regular column: "I agree that the poverty data are wrong, but not because they have been fudged. Rather, poor people are increasingly lying to surveyors about their true living standards, and this is inflating apparent poverty."[8] The far-flanged wings of corruption in India have even eaten up the vitals of the nation by means of breaking bounds of the intellectual dishonesty. It is really surprising! Why the poor want to stay ever poor and pauper? Why the illiterate want to stay in perpetual state of illiteracy to blacken the face of the country internationally? Let us not forget that India was a rich country where there used to be the singing birds of gold and silver where the Roman exchequer used to lose 550 million Sesterces (gold coin) every year.[9]

India, one of the six ancient civilisations: The world had produced six civilisations in ancient age. At least such have been discovered so far. Chronologically they are (i) the 'Catal Hayuk' (7000 to 6000 B.C) on the bank of Charsamba river of Anatolia in present day Turkey; (ii) the 'Summer Akkad' and 'Babylonian' 'Assyrian-civilisation' in the cities of Assur and Nineveh on the river bank of Eufretis and Tigris, (this is known also as Austric civilisation) (iii) the Persian Assura Civilisation in the Middle East; (iv) the 'Egyptian' civilisation on the bank of river Nile, (v) 'Chinese' civilisation on the bank of Hoang-Ho, the sorrow of China, and the (vi) Indian Assura civilisation in the opulent metropolis of Harappa, Mohenjodaro on the bank of river Indus and many other parts of ancient India. This Indian civilisation was developed by the 'Assura-rulers', Kings and Emperors of the country during 2500 B.C. Indian *Assura* civilisation continued till it was razed to ground along with its basic rather economic-structure of production and distribution. This was the most developed urban civilisation till it was vanquished by the 'first foreign' vandal 'intruders',[10] the Aryan Brahmins during 1500 B.C.

The country, from remote antiquity, is found to have been the seat of rich tradition of '*Shramana Sanskriti*' that is the culture of dignity of labour, peace, *laissez faire* and rationality. Her diligent people earned their livelihood by the sweat of their brow. With the most ancient Universities of repute in the contemporary world, India played the centre of letters, learning and international brotherhood. Her coasts were studded with ports and docks which were the hubs of thalassic commerce. These international maritime activities were supported by inter-state trade-mobility of the powerful bankers and *Sresthis.* People developed a rich heritage of peace and socio-economic structure on the basis of agro-cottage industry.

Being colonised by the Aryan-Brahmins, paradoxically the country got clouded with the darkest spots of human behavioural pattern in the following Vedic period which lasted unchallenged and unabated for around a millennium. The society in the Vedic period is found to have started a culture of graded hatred towards its fellow human beings. Discriminatory inter-human-relations, total exploitation of the servile classes and atrocities on the humanity became sacred sanctum of social order. The most inhuman system of social-interaction that a man can imagine got developed in India, during this period, in the name of spirituality called '*Chatur Varnasharm Dharma*'.

Since 1400 B.C. *Arya Devatas* or the Brahmins held the *Brahman*-culture in prominence in diametric opposition to the earlier, vanquished *Shramana*-culture.[11] The Barbaric and warmonger Aryans did not know the art of recording or writing. *Brahman*-culture being bereft of scripts, letters and learning remained negative to the further advance of the civilisation. Besides, being disdained by the governing class the producer classes lost their impetus to discover and bring forth new methods for material advance in economic structure of the society and culture. The avaricious nomadic tribe was averse to any kind of productive work as their mode of subsistence was food-gathering, hunting and capturing. Food hunting, gathering, looting and exploitation of others surplus were their means of subsistence. Any type of menial-work they avoided and considered doing it below their dignity. They loved to live on others' earnings like social parasites. After vanquishing the *Assura* rulers of *Shramana* culture they ingeniously developed an engine of exploitation called *Varnashram-dharma*. This system, above all, ensured resistance-less extortion of all means of production from the society.

Man and money, '*Manus*' and '*Mudra*' are the two-sides of the same coin. No other species on the Earth are concerned with currency. Necessity for survival or the greed for more wealth and more privileges and the imbibed human tendency or desire to aggrandize power in individual handled the avaricious human beings to usher in a domain of 'Slave-dom'. Thus, they eventually, created a stratified society. As a natural corollary, slaves and masters, placed on different strata of society are found to have been engaged in a ceaseless struggle, called class-struggle since the beginning of the human civilisation. No species other than human beings have experienced the state of co-existence of the 'Masters' and 'Slaves'. Human society has enslaved or domesticated even animals even for exploitation. Surplus labour of various animals under harness and of fellow human beings are exploited in an equally natural process. Therefore, the history of all hitherto existing society but the Hindu society is nothing but the history of a ceaseless class struggle. The Hindu society, though hierarchical is, therefore, bereft of class-struggle and have no social mobility either vertical or horizontal. There is no class-struggle. There has been fight between Shraman and brahman culture.[12]

Society Stratified in Thousands of Castes: Indian Hindu society like all other human societies, is composed of masters and slaves. The masters, at the apex remained the microscopic minority while the slaves formed the immense majority and the lowest stratum of the society. It is formed through natural class struggle. The Hindu social order and its stratification, however, is constitutional. It is fixed and claimed to be systematised by the divinity or scriptural injunctions. These divine covenants are executed by the temporal rules. Its social hierarchies are unalterably static and without mobility. The socio-economic structural arrangement are claimed to have been a result and will of the supreme Divinity. Therefore, it was treated as an irrevocable natural product. Violation or even deviation from this hierarchical arrangement is an offence against the state, and blasphemous sins against the God as such are liable for punishment in both, this world and the next. Even the reign will come under peril if the potentate fails to resist caste contamination and its purity.[13] It is known as 'Caste-system' or '*Varnashram-Dharma*'. According to the scripture, it is four fold. But in reality castes are found in thousands. Whatever the scriptures may say, caste is a hereditary system of fixing occupation. Hardly anything is spiritual in it. Even the English men established 'Caste *Cacharies*' in 1721.

Consequently, almost each set of occupational group has eventually been termed as a distinct caste unfit to interact mutually. Indian slaves as well the masters are therefore, found to have got further stratified in different varieties of water-tight compartments called castes, sub-castes in a specifically prescribed job-world. Indian society thus, 'transformed a self-developing social state into never changing natural destiny, and thus brought about a brutalizing worship of nature, exhibiting its degeneration in the fact that man, the sovereign of nature, fell down on his knees in adoration of Hanuman, the monkey-god, and *Sabala*, the holy-cow'[14]

The Orthodox Hindus are generally scrupulous in meticulously maintaining caste-system, in observing its rights perfectly in temporal and celestial affairs. However, the Hindus are not proud of this system. They feel shy of discussing this issue on international human platform. In the political field the Brahmins play caste-cards but strictly object when the caste factor is being used by the populous low-caste people. Whatever a Hindu may say, the Caste stratification is a reality, a hard reality in the society. "Caste is a vital aspect of Indian reality, even though the State officially denies its existence and refuses to record caste based data in the census", held the recent editorial of a daily newspaper.[15] The microscopic Brahmin caste forms the class of masters. The remaining society acts as the work-force with different and specific charges subservient to the Brahmins. Caste is a gold-chain for the microscopic minority and iron corns for the majority working class.

The upper sections of the working masses are grouped in a broader category of caste called *Sudra* that is servants of the society. They are responsible for performing domestic and other related work.

Some other very large groups engaged in menial work and placed at further lower and lowest scale of society are the Untouchables. They are also known as *Panchamas*. The people at the bottom who according to the spiritual injunctions of the Hindu pantheon are treated as untouchables and non-human beings cause pollution to castes placed in upper strata. Their physical contact, touch and even sight pollute. They have the power even to pollute gods and goddesses. As such, even colonial British rule in 1808 declared 15 groups including untouchable, incapable of entering the temple of Jagannath at Puri. They are 'divine-slaves' and do not belong to any individual master. They were created by the Hindu gods to bear the burden of the upper strata and to hold its level up on their shoulders by paying their all-out services without expectation of any return or remuneration or ambition. These divine-slaves '*Nripasus*' or 'two-footed animals' as described in the hymns of the Rig Veda, '*Dwipada Chatuspada Shang No Bhava Dwipade Shang Chatuspade*'[16] seem to have been treated eventually as untouchables. Untouchability, which flows from the spiritual flux of the Hindu philosophy of hatred towards even manual work and workers, and out of 'caste system', is the worst form of exploitation and oppression.

Caste system de-humanizes a man. This process of de-humanisation through a well organised system started about three thousand years ago in the cities of Harappa, Mohenjodaro, Daimabad, Lothal and Dholavira on the banks and plains of the river Sindhu. The first-foreign intruders, the Aryan-vandals had invaded the Assura-empire on the banks of the Indus River and destroyed their opulent cities. They also carried war against the prevailing indigenous religious culture and economic-structure. The highly civilised country since proto-historic period was dotted with innumerable urban centers and opulent metropolises. Some of these metropolises had developed ports and docks along with other effective paraphernalia for navigation to carryout thalassic commerce up to the far-land of Phoenicia, Sidon, Tire, Bybol on the eastern bank of Mediterranean seas and Babylon. These ancient pre-Vedic Indian cities according to the evidences of the Vedic literature belonged to the potentates called '*Raja*' or '*Samrat*' (King and Emperor) of Indian *Assura* race. The people of Assura race travelled throughout the ages all over India in the form of different clans. They preserved with them their cultural traits. The presence of the Assura people has been traced even today. A good number of people belonging to the Assura race have been referred to even in the authentic modern literature.[17] They are found also to have been continually ruling the kingdoms in the North Eastern regions from the city of ancient '*Pragyotispur*' of Assam since time immemorial till recent past.[18] The current Census Reports also enumerated people belonging to Assura race in the provinces of Bihar,

Orissa, Bengal and Assam. In the Siliguri-Jalpaiguri regions of West Bengal, the tea-garden workers who belong to the Assura race still maintain anti-Aryan cultural heritage. The descendants of the Assura race of Indus Valley are still found to have been living in the villages of Sahebganj area of Bengal-Bihar border in *Jungle Mahals* and maintaining their ancient *Shramana-culture* and traits of Buddhism in the modern society of the Santhals.[19] Many of the civilisations of ancient world in the Middle East Asia like 'Katal Hyuk' in Turky's Anatolia province, 'Assyrian' of Nineveh and Assur cities, 'Sumerian' of Sumer, Akkad and Babylonian and 'Persian Assurs appear to have belonged to the Assura race only. Highly advanced urban civilisation and pre-Vedic or pre-Aryan ancient Indian Assyrian society had left no sign of caste.

The warmonger Aryan clans were controlled and led by their chief. The victor Aryans established the maiden colony on the Earth in *Bharatvarsa.* The vanquished natives of the country, the Assuras finally became 'divine slaves' or Sudras and the victor Aryan, '*Devatas*' that is 'divine masters' became the Brahmins. '*Daiba vai Brahmana, Assurya Sudras*'[20] In the circumstances, during the course of consolidation and assimilation of the vanquished autochthons by the victor *Aryas* the four social strata they developed. According to the Vedas caste thus became a product of a divine covenant of permanent settlement.[21]

The nomadic and pre-civilised Aryans henceforth had put the vehicle of civilisation on back-gear. They force-imposed rural or village way of life by replacing much advanced and developed contemporary urban civilisation. Instead of enjoying or appropriating wealth and the material aspects of civilisation that was conquerred, the Aryans destroyed the metropolises. Instead of pushing it forward for enhancing human personality, material prosperity and skills they dehumanised the homo-sapien species to untouchable creatures. The self-developing human-society with its stagnant caste economic structure reduced to a never changing destiny. The 'Curse of Caste' developed at this stage in course of the consolidation of the Aryan colony in India. They divided their slaves into two distinct categories i.e. '*Dasas*' and '*Nripasus*'. 'Nripasus' were addressed in the Vedic hymns as 'two-footed animals'. In the later age they seem to have become untouchables. Material, intellectual and spiritual aspects of human beings advance at parallel pace. During pre-Vedic period the native Indians had their spiritual philosophy and religious belief as advanced as their material development. They were the followers of *Shramana* culture and Buddhism as their faith. The Vedic hymns and literature and the archaeological objects from the Indus valley abound with illustrations to vindicate the existence of the faith propagated by the 'Former Buddhas' in ancient cities of India. Aryan '*Devatas*' are found to have been engaged in ceaseless battles to annihilate indigenous people of '*Anyabrata*' and '*Yogis*' or '*jyotis*' who did not bow before the

Vedic rituals or adopt the '*Yagna*' culture, a culture of animal sacrifice.

Undisputed traces of evidences have been available to understand that the autochthons of India of pre-Aryan age were highly literate. Innumerable seals from the ruins of the cities of Harappa, Mohenjodaro, and Dholavira etc. display the existence and intensive use of scripts by the pre-Aryan Indians. Yet no obvious record in regard to the actual condition of the natives of ancient India and their struggle for survival are available in their own description. All their records are found to have been destroyed completely during the dark-age of Vedic regime from 1500 B.C to 600 B.C. Vedic Aryans were illiterate. No archaeological evidence in regard to their script and knowledge or method and mode of recording in those millennia is available. It has been accepted by the historians that the Vedic *Devatas* did not know the art of recording.

Impact of the Pre-Aryan Urban-Class-Society: In the historic period, India is found to have remained a class-society. With the resurrection of the pre-Vedic indigenous tradition of the *Purva-Buddhas*, the Buddhism and *Shraman* culture in the 6th century B.C. and with the advent of *Tathagata* '*Sakya-pungaba*' Lord Gautam Buddha, the sunshine of letters and scripts, education and culture of vibrant intellectuality once again tormented human mind and society in India. This opened up the windows of freethinking, based on the philosophy of liberty, fraternity, love and knowledge in all directions. It pronounced the victory of human-power. It released the floodgates of liberty of the subdued and oppressed by breaking off the lock gates of the closed-class society created by the Vedic or Aryan Brahmins.

It ushered the dawn of liberty and light of knowledge after the end of the dark-age of the Vedic period from 1500 to 600 B.C. The Prince of Kapilavastu got enlightenment in 528 B.C. The Buddha declared war against sufferings caused by exploitation, "There is no greater suffering than hunger, as hunger creates havoc, destroys human bodies, well-being, peace and joy." He thus resolved to eradicate sufferings of poverty, the '*Dukkha*', uprooting it by its roots. Once the prince Siddhartha reached in the farm house of his father, King Suddhodhan with friends and on observing the fatigue condition of the labouring creatures exclaimed, ".... can it be right that one man should exploit another? How can it be right that the labourer should toil and the master should live on the fruits of his labour?"[22] Aswaghosh, in his Sanskrit drama named Buddhacharit, (the earliest available biography of Lord Buddha) has also vividly described the basic contention, 'Pigment of the bodies of the peasants have got rotten by the erosion of wind, sun and dust; the bulls have got exhausted with the burden of ploughing and tilling. He expressed deep disgust on seeing this exploitation'. Here standing in the field, the prince of Sakyas declared the essence of his future faith, "The world is full of miseries...".

"Krisata Purusangscha Bikshamana Pavanarkangsurajobivinnavarnan, Bahanaklamaviklabangscha dhuryan Paramarya Paramang Kripang Chakara."[23]

In the battle against exploitation and poverty, miseries and sufferings Lord Buddh's strongest measure was to abolish the right to private property, especially and strictly for the monks or *Bhikkus*. He banned the right to private property of any types within the *Viharas* and monasteries. Viharas were tens and thousands in number. The Emperor and many of the potentates in the country were Buddhists. The Commander-in Chief of the Royal army, all army generals, Ministers, Counsels, Governors in bureaucracy; big Bankers and *Sresthis* all were the followers of the Buddha. Consequently, the doctrine of no private property for the Bhikkus had its definite impact on the economic policy and pattern of the country. The Buddhist Emperor Asoka the great engraved his immortal instructions in the rock and pillar Edicts in this regard for his councillors and governors, "Excellent is small expense with small accumulation." The Council also will inculcate (the same) on the officials in the Accounts Department with regard both to the principle and the text (of the order)."[24]

Buddha declared that the essence of his *Dhamma* was "*Majjhim Patipada*" the middle course. Neither too much of privileges or property nor too little of it is to be the way of economic life for any individual, and that is the means to reach to the target of equality and happiness for the immense majority; to minimize the tension between the masters and servants. Buddha declared that 'gift of '*Dhamma*' was the best gift' "*Sabdanang Dhammadanang Ginati Sabbang Rasang Dhammaraso Ginati.*"[25] The Buddhist Emperor Asoka instructed on '*Dhammadanang*' too, "Here does it consist in proper treatment of slaves and servants, in harkening to father and mother, in giving to friends, comrades, relatives . . .". In advanced and developed society, it is natural that there will exist the working classes and servants along with the privileged classes of people. But he desired to ensure that there must not prevail a reign of terror of exploitation.

A respectful distance and co-operation of fraternal bond of universal humanity must have prevailed amongst different strata of classes. The Emperor appointed '*Dhamma Mahammattwas*' to preach religion and spirituality. Preaching and performing spiritual rituals no more remained a hereditary prerogative of the Brahmins. Earning out of religious performances became open to all. These factors demolished the roots of Caste system. The triumph and revival of Buddhism over the Vedic social system ushered the reign of the immense majority. The autochthons became the ruling class and were placed on the platform of dignity and importance in the post-Vedic Buddhist period. Indian society regained new energy and life. In the accounts of Megasthenes, therefore, the seven divisions of social strata never mentioned any caste hierarchy. The period that followed Gautam Buddha's time therefore, witnessed many civil wars and people's upraise proclaiming the superiority of command of the subjects, the voice of the people.

During this glorious period, under the influence of Buddhist philosophy of dignity of work, love and equality Indian society expanded in all directions. It entered in the international arena. Universal brotherhood and religio-cultural bond, international trade, university education and international politics saw its birth during this period in India. The artisans (Sudras of the Hindu society) and the merchants of our country dominated world trade-market with favourable balance of trade. The big '*sresthis*' and artisans, peasants and youth being dignified and encouraged by the principle of humanity and equal-rights to every aspect of life maximised productivity in those days. Their contribution in commerce and the scope of their joining in the military in large number (it was no more monopoly of the minority Kshatriya) not only established large empire and kingdoms for the first time in Indian history but also crossed the international borders. The Roman Councils are found to have vehemently objected trade with India as it drained 550 million 'Cesterii' (Roman gold coin) every year[26] from the exchequer of Roman Government to import scent, spices, medicine, precious stones, cosmetics, muslin and calico. The trade guilds heavily influenced the contemporary political decisions and cultural trends. Educations became universal and accessible for all. Question of debarring the Sudras was redundant as there remained hardly any Sudra. Resultantly high rate of literacy is understood to have prevailed in those days, hence everyone could go through the road-side edicts of the Emperor Asoka. The level and standard of higher education became remarkable. Universities like Nalanda, Vallavi, and Odandapuri dotted the country.

But the Brahmanical Hindus, the protagonists of divine-slavery once again defeated the Indian kingdoms of golden era glittering with all out prosperity. The Brahmanical forces invited foreign invaders to aggress the country and defeat the native ruling classes.[27] 'By the first part of the first millennium, India was still linked to world trade, but it was Arabs and other merchants who controlled this. Indians who had once traversed the highest reaches of the Himalayas and braved the seas of the world in trade and missionary enterprises became an ingrown people priding themselves on the purity of their insularity.'[28]

Little expenditure and little accumulation of wealth by individual in a state of unbridled production and free and fair distribution system has been the essence of that economic structure. The Brahmanism on the other hand, represents the divine-capitalists, spiritual-exploiters and the theocratic-ruling class. Endless struggle was sure to follow between these two groups.

The Hindus—Their Society: The Indian Hindu society was a non-entity in the ancient and historic period till the end of AD 9th century. The Vedic literature did not teach us the word Hindu. The religion of the Aryan stock has been called Brahminism all along till the Islamic rule started in India by the Pathan and Arabians. In the edicts XIII of Emperor Asoka the great who ruled the largest territory of the sub-continent, there has been a mention of the contemporary five religious groups, Buddhist, Ajibiks, Jains, Nirgranthis, and Brahmin. The terms 'Hindu' and Hinduism had come to our notice only after the Muslim conquest of India starting from AD 712 with the defeat of Dahir the Brahmin King of Deval. He was defeated in the hands of a punitive force sent by Khalifa, under the young general Muhammad Bin Kasim. The word Hindu is not traceable in any Sanskrit or Pali literature composed before this period. In Persian language, Hindu means, black, heathen, slave, cow-thieves etc. This derogatory and contemptuous term seems to have been given by the victors for the vanquished Indians irrespective of the faith. "That is why the Hindu cannot be defined in clear terms. Such as, "The Hindus". The term is itself indefinable and paradoxical, too complex to comprehend and too diverse to define. Since Hinduism is primordial religion, it is an evolved phenomenon where over the ages, the religion, and the people who practice it, have transformed simultaneously. Hinduism did not have any fixed structures like Ten Commandments or the Quran. Therefore, the tenets of the Hinduism have changed over the ages, and interestingly enough, it is only Hinduism which has the concept of Yuga dharma..."[29] In 1930, in a lengthy article, titled '*Banglar Bouddha Samaj* : Hindu O Bouddha' Achariya Haraprosad Shastri had in a very articulated way tried to define 'The Hindus'. Those who believe that without a Brahmin worshiping of a *Devata* or receiving of religious discourse is not possible are Hindus. Hindus believe in Caste divisions and believe that once born in a caste there is no escape or way to ascend to higher status; those who believe in gods but do not want to elevate them into the position of a god are Hindus."[30] He has categorically stated, "The Muhammadans called the Indians, Brahmanists and Buddhists alike, Hindus or Indians. The Brahmins were not slow to take advantage of this and to make it appear that the Buddhists did not exist. All the intellectual followers of Buddhism were either massacred or compelled to fly away from the country. The Brahmins found themselves masters of the situation in the Indian or Hindu community. Muhammadans either by force or by persuasion converted a large number of the Buddhists into Islam.... Before Muhammadan conquest, Bengal was divided between the two communities of Brahmanists, and Buddhists, and after that the entire population was divided into the two great classes of Hindus and Muhammadans...... After the Muhammadan conquest Brahmanic ideals were super-imposed on the Buddhist ideals".[31]

A school of scholars had interpreted that the nomenclature, 'Hindu' was given by the Persians as they could not pronounce '*Sha'*. They pronounced '*Sha'* as '*Ha'*. As such, they corrupted the name of Sindhu or Indus River and as a result they called the people beyond the eastern part of Sindhu that is Indus river as Hindu. This is a simplified interpretation. Actually the people of Iran, Persia, Saudi Arabia, Sudan, etc. do pronounce, 'Shah' perfectly. The 'Badshah' of Iran, Saddam-Husain is pronounced Saddam correctly. None pronounce him as Haddam; Shaha as Haha; Sudan as

Hudan. They did not change the name of the river Sindhu as Hindu river. This was not a corrupt or distorted from of any word. The word in its original form is available in the vocabulary of Persi literature. Even races or clans like, Jats and Gujars are treated and called as distinct and different caste.

The Hindu scholars fail to define the essence of the 'Hindu-Indian' society. It had been described with acute phenomenal accuracy by Karl Marx. In his letter on July 22, 1853 while concluding his observations on India he had recorded, "A country not only divided between Mahammadam and Hindoo, but between tribe and tribe, between caste and caste; a society whose frame work was based on a sort of equilibrium, resulting from a general repulsion and constitutional exclusiveness."[32] What a paradoxical situations he has rightly noted. 'Exclusiveness' and 'repulsion' are two strong forces that divide, never unite. But in case of Indian society, according to Marx, a sort of 'constitutional exclusiveness' and general attitude of repulsion between its components generated the equilibrium of social bondage. Incredible though, there can be no better manifestation of Indian society in words. Where do the factors of exclusion and repulsion in social intercourse lay? Such potentially divisive, anti-brotherhood and strongly anti-national pivot is not observed in the Muslim or Tribal society of India. And this 'equilibrium' is not a result of any sort of an associative attitude, this is rather strongest dissociative force. It is not a fraternal bond that emerged out of affection or an associative attitude. Nothing but a grave state of barbaric tyranny clamped through physical and metaphysical atrocities and oppression that compelled the helpless servile natives to remain in a flock in the same society. This 'Engine of Oppression' is called Hinduism, the other side of that coin is called caste. The essence of Hinduism thus, remains Casteism a common element throughout India.

The system of caste or the process of de-humanisation eventually rendered Hindustan a state of semi-civilised society of composite-culture and composite society of human and sub-human groups of different species. Karl Marx had got the opportunity to further analyze, "We must not forget that this undignified, stagnate, and vegetative life that this passive sort of existence evoked on the other part, in the contradistinction, wild aimless, unbounded forces of destruction and rendered murder itself a religious rite in Hindostan. We must not forget that these little communities were contaminated by distinctions of caste and by slavery, that they subjugated man to external circumstances, that they transformed a self-developing social state into a never changing natural destiny, and thus brought about a brutalizing worship of nature, exhibiting its degradation in the fact that man, the sovereign of nature, fell down on his knees in adoration of Hanuman, the monkey, and Sabala, the cow."[33] And the British, "dissolved these small semi-barbarian, semi-civilised communities and thus produced the greatest, and to speak the truth, the only social revolution ever hard in Asia." Sir

Winston Churchill, the hero of the Second World War, distinguished Statesman and the then Prime Minister of England, on the basis of his personal experiance opined in 1942, "Indians are a beastly people with a beastly religion."[34] Aplication of the term 'beasts' for humanbeing, however, is not the original work of Churchil, Sage Manu had used it in his Smriti sloke 10/30 during AD 1st century.

Genesis and Mechanism of Caste-system

In the annals of world history, this unique social or economic structure called caste is not found in any other human society in the same or in similar form at any stage of time. The Pali-cum-Sanskrit word 'Jat' 'Jati' or 'Varna' is expressed in English term, Caste. The word 'caste' is not of Indian origin. It is derived from Portuguese 'Casta', which means 'breed', 'race', or class. The word commonly used amongst the Hindus themselves is '*jat*' or '*jati*' which means 'birth' or descent" has been affirmed by the scholars.[35] According to Swami Vivekananda, 'caste is the most wonderful thing that India has contributed to the civilisation of the world'.

The castes denote and define social strata or class hierarchy without any social mobility. It is a closed class society. No class struggle that can change the profession and social strata is allowed. Even in the age of e-servicing; e-mailing; e-tendering and the impact of colonial economy and globalisation, professional mobility, caste does not fade out. With the changed profession too, the caste clings to the individual. It is connected with birth of a '*jatak*'. Karl Marx had defined it perfectly, ". . . the hereditary divisions of labour, upon which rest the Indian castes, those decisive impediment of Indian progress and Indian power."[36] This clearly indicates that caste system is an economic institution rather than a mere social institution. It is social institution based on the basic structure i.e. economic-structure of the society. Gandhiji is understood to have known this truth as he has observed, "To destroy caste system and adopt Western European social system means that the Hindus must give up the principle of hereditary occupation which is the soul of caste system." He also explained, "The object of Varna system is to prevent competition and class struggles and class wars. I believe Varna system because it fixes the duties and occupations of persons. Varna means determination of a man's occupations before he is born. In the *Varna* system, no man has any liberty to choose his occupation. His occupation is determined for him by heredity system."[37]

What Gandhiji wrote during the decades of 1920's was actually taught decades ago by the Hindu Prophet Swami Vivekananda. Swamiji was a strong upholder of ancient caste stratification for the modern Indian society. He had the blue-print of it to be implemented in modern India. He advocated, "I do not propose any leveling of castes. Caste is a very good thing. Caste is a plan we want to follow . . . Indian caste is better than the caste that prevails in Europe and America . . . Caste should not go . . . It is sheer nonsense to desire the abolition of castes."[38] Vivekananda too explained frankly, "Make caste; priesthood is hereditary. Rigid, high-power, it has a great side, and that side is (that) it really rejects competition. It is that which has made the nation alive..."[39] The Hindu nationalists tried to make India a nation without creating the feeling of nationality amongst its subjects. With a view to defeating the democratic challenges of people, Gandhiji, like Vivekananda, wanted to implement the scheme of caste that kept the servile-classes fragmented and that 'rejects competition' and plugged the avenues of liberty for those who were victims of the caste-system.

That is why Casteism was made to have had its genesis in God and spirituality. This made caste system a natural phenomenon and a subject beyond objection, question or correction. Greek philosopher Aristotle tried to become the Lord Krishna of Athens. He endeavored to create an anti-democratic social-structure in the democratic political structure of Athens. He gave a caste-like social structure in his treaty. He divided human beings in four groups. Groups were composed of different elements such as gold-soul, silver-soul, brass-soul and the iron-souls. These four groups were divided, like Indian castes, distinctly in four social strata and as a natural phenomenon. The ruling class was composed of gold-souls which is available in less quantum. The aristocracy was composed of Silver-souls. The middle class was composed of brass-souls, while numerically large working class had their souls made out of iron. Like iron they were plentiful. He suggested that if this theory can be propagated for some generations, then people would believe it and accept it unopposed. The immense majority composed of iron will never challenge the kings and the rulers of gold-souls, silver and brass souls so on and so forth. Here the Greek philosopher committed a mistake by pronouncing the existence of gold-soul, silver-soul, brass-soul and of iron-souls with different vote-value himself as a political thinker. He committed an error of judgment by ignoring the existence of the third-party, the creator God. It was the function of God to create such souls, and as such, Lord Krishna in India has been made to assume God-hood. In Greece, a political thinker, an agent of the beneficiaries created the social structure of human beings. In India, it was God who became the political thinker and created castes the component of social strata. A man, when he is a Hindu, can challenge neither God nor the Brahman a '*Bhu-devata*', a god on Earth.

The Rig Veda holds the picture of a class society in a crystal clear manner when the hymns describe, "One who possesses one fourth of assets praises the other who possesses double. One who possesses two-fourth stands behind the owner of wealth of three-forth. And the owner of the whole wealth sits above all. Such is the classification of backward and forward position. Owners of less wealth praise the owner of more wealth. Our both hands are alike in form but their strength differs. Two cows from the same mother do not produce same quantum of milk. Even two brothers are not same valiant. Two from the same family are not similar in the act of charity."[40] These hymns are believed to have recorded the condition of pre-Aryan and pre-Vedic class-society of India that was replaced by the caste or Vedic closed-class inhuman and artificially stratified society.

The earliest references to caste system are available in the 10th Mandal of Purusa Sukta of the Rig Veda. The hymns while describing the process of creation of the entire subjects of the animates and inanimate by the *Virat-Purusa* narrates,

ब्राह्मणोहस्य मुखमसीद्वाहु राजन्यः कृतः।
उरू तदस्य यद्वैश्य पद्वभ्यं शुद्र अजायतः।।
चन्द्रमा मनसो जातश्चक्षोः सुर्या अजायतः।
मुखाहिन्द्रश्चग्रिश्च प्राणाद्वायुरजायतः।। 10/90/12-13

That horses and animals with rows of teeth were born, there were born the cows, goats and buffaloes.[41] His mouth became the Brahmin, from arms the Rajnya, from thighs the Vaisyas and the legs became the Sudras. There came moon from His mind, Sun from His eyes, Indra and Agni from His mouth, air from his life. From the naval came the sky, heaven from his brain, soil from two feet, from ears were created all the directions and the earth.[42]

In the Sukla and Krishne Jujur-Vedas, that followed Rig-Veda immediately after, described in details the entire phenomenon like duties and rights of each of the caste groups and characteristics of castes in details.[43] Therefore, it would not be prudent to support the view that in the early stage of the Vedic-society castes or Varna strata were three and not four in number. The hymns mentioning names of the Brahamins, Kshatriyas, Vaisas and Dasas are available in the entire Vedic literature. It is interesting to note here that the Hindus scrupulously believe this creation process of four fold caste as sacred, scientific and real. Devoutly they observe caste but never accept other hymns immediately before and after as scientific.

The Hindus never agree to the contents of the other hymns of the same Sukta which say that Sun was originated from the eyes of God, Moon was originated from the mind of God, Air was created by God from his life and the Heaven from His brain. This position further testify that the entire verdict was an outcome of ignorance and unwise contemplation by artificial means with the motive of exclusion of some and inclusion of the others.

It is in the Bhagavat Gita where Lord Sri Krishna declared, "*Chaaturvarnang Maya Sristang Guna Karma Bibhagasa.*

चातुर्वर्ण्य मया सृष्टं गुणकर्मविभागशः।
तस्य कर्तारमपि मां विद्धयकर्तारमव्ययम्।। 4/13

ब्राह्मणक्षत्रियविशां शूद्राणां च परन्तप।
कर्माणि प्रविभक्तपानि स्वभावप्रभवैगुणैः।। 18/41

श्रेयान्स्वधर्मो विगुणः परधर्मात्स्वनुष्ठितात्।
स्वभावनियतं कर्म कुर्वन्नाप्नोति किल्बिषम्।। 18/47

These four fold division of human beings were created by Lord Sri Krishna and He seems to have used the term '*Varna*' for the first time. Here the word '*Varna*' does not denote colour. It denotes species.

Lord Sri Krishna, the god-incarnate of the Hindus, not only created the universe but also constructed the whole fabrics of the human society. This is called Chatur Varnashram Dharma. Not only the social strata but he also defined the profession of each group permanently as a natural, '*Swadhamma*' phenomenon in the concluding chapter of Gita. Wisdom and lordship was the monopoly of the Brahmins. Warfare was the basic duty of the *Ksahtriyas*. Commerce and management of agriculture was the responsibility of the *Vaisyas*. The *Sudras* were to give all required services. This was their sole right and responsibility of life. And there was no question of 'Merit'. 'For performing the duty ordained by his own nature man does not incur sin. Though devoid of merit one should stick to one's own duty and would not encroach to others duty where one may have merit. Any encroachment will cause sin. To destroy the sinners who caused caste contamination or breached caste-laws i.e. '*swadharma*' (naturally ordained-duty) and protect the followers of '*swadharma*' and to kill those disturbers of *dharma* (*Papis*) the Lord god will repeatedly take incarnation.

Despite all odds the crafty Brahmins established their scheme and operated the engine of oppression on the plea of divine sanction. Politics and political power operate the instrumentalities in the direction that there does not occur any '*Varna-shankara*' (caste-contamination by marriage etc.) or '*karma-shankara*' (professional-mobility).'Arthashastra' written by Kautilya or Vishnugupta claimed to be the only secular treaty in ancient period too instructed same guidelines in the '*Traiye*' lessons that the prime duty of the Kings was to maintain the purity of *Varna Dharma*. In the 2nd Chapter of Arthashastra four *Varnas* are described. In the 3rd Chapter, the author after describing the rights and duties of the four *varnas* gave his verdict, "When *Varnasaram Dharmas* are observed it opens up the way for infinite merits for attaining '*Swarga*' the heaven. When the *Varna* rules are violated the whole society would go to dogs. Therefore, the duty of a King is to maintain *Varna-Dharma* scrupulously." The Indian society as a result of these scriptural dictates of mandatory nature remained a static, without social mobility, without any class-struggle and hence bereft of history of the society. It has no brother-hood, notion of equal status, equal and common rights to the means of production.

Caste annihilates the spirit of universal competition, contest and conflict for capturing ownership of or establishing common rights on the same means of production, which results in growth of excellence in merit and skill. The meritless society, however, very quietly solved the problems in regard to public administration to minimize the social-tension amongst the haves and have-nots; the exploiters and the victims. It is a disintegrated and graded-society based on the philosophy of hatred and spiritual superstition and horror. It has dehumanised the human species. The caste or V*arna* being an economic structure, the labour, which is one of the four basic means of production being without merit, efficiency or skill of production has seriously damaged productivity, hindered nation building and process to growth of civilisation. In it the ignorant remain ever ignorant and the poor in perpetual poverty. In the circumstances, Karl Marx, appears to have very rightly assessed, "...the hereditary division of labour, upon which rest the Indian castes, those decisive impediments to Indian progress and Indian power." The force of economy and the state of economy with its structural base where it reached during the pre-Vedic period of Mohenjodaro-Harappa cities of Assura civilisation, would have reached to a limitless height of modern days even two millennia ago, had it not got paralysed due to the advent of the stagnant caste-economic structure.

The entire vanquished groups of the native Indians, especially who refused to surrender and accept Aryan supremacy and their religion were clubbed together by victors and were called 'Shudra'. This theocratic-society was born out of the oldest 'colonial constitution' called the Vedas. The autochthons such as Kols, Vills, Mundas, Sabars, Santhals, the Murmus, the Sorens, the Baskes and Chakmas etc. who have still maintained their separate existence since time immemorial[44] remained afar and out-side the pale of the Brahmanical culture of servitude. These autochthon races are found to have no caste or caste-like elements in their social or economic structure.

One of the branches of the Vedic literature named, *Taitareya Brahman* very clearly pointed out that the Sudras are no new group of people in India. The native Assuras have been called as 'Sudras' in later period. "*Daiba Vhai Brahmana, Assurya Sudra:.*" The *Devatas* became Brahmans and the Assuras were called as Sudras. In pre-Aryan advanced civilisation of opulent urban cities the Assuras were the ruling class; from amongst them emerged the Kings and the Emperors of the country. They followed Shramana culture of Buddhism. The Parsis who follow Zoroaster, worship the Wise-Assura or the *Ahur Mazda*. The Ahur-Mazda is the sovereign God who stands against the corrupt 'Devatas' like Indra, Mitra etc. Their temples are called the '*Ageari*' the place for the worship of '*Aag*' (*Aag Ki Aagar*) the abode of fire. Their *gathas* in the Avesta scripture are full of Indian 'Pali' words. They wear some white thread-band called *Sudri* around their shoulder during the religious performances. The word *Sudra* seems to have come from there. The ethnic groups in the Middle-East who have been the worshippers of 'Wise-Assura' or '*Ahur-Mazda*' seem to have migrated, being persecuted at the time of Aryan aggression in the Indus region, from the main land of India.[45] The Aryan Brahman *Devatas*, apart from the servants, *Dasas* and *Dasis* maintained many two footed animals.

Outside the Vedic culture, there developed a story of caste like division in the tribal society. Kolas are one of the autochthons of the ancient groups in the Eastern India. They are said to have been created by two gods called *Ote Boram* and *Singbonga*, "they created one boy and one girl and kept them in a solitary place so that they procreate and multiply. But they did not. They were then given fermented rice. In course of time, they had twelve sons and twelve daughters. These children gradually created all races. The races and castes were created in accordance with their food intake. Those who took ox-meat became Kolas. The buffalo-meat eaters became 'Bhumiya'. Those who ate only vegetables created the Brahmins. Those who lived on fish and goat became Sudra. Those who depended on pork meat became Santhals. Etc. There became thus thirty six races or castes."[46] The story seems to be a mixed one. It gives a new angle to artificial nature of creation of Caste system.

At a much later period, during the Puranic age or precisely during the post-Gautama Buddha period this caste system was propagated in the name of Lord Krishna. Krishna (black pigment) was a patriot-hero of Indian origin who lived during Indus valley war period. The light-footed Krishna along with his large army of ten thousand strength, opposed the Aryan war-lord Indra in defense of his country on the bank of Ansumati river.[47] The Indian patriot-hero was eventually killed. The Hero's name seems to have been used while implementing the anti-native-Indian caste system on Indians. In Gita, the personified God-hood Lord Krishna took the odd responsibility of creating socio-economic strata on the basis of the philosophy of hatred and discrimination. 'Four *Varnas* have been created by Me on the basis of (non-commensurable) qualities and active tendencies. '*Chaatur Varnang Maya Sristang Guna Karma Bibhagasa.*'[48]

Here also we find that Varna or caste was not created on the basis of pigment of body. And *Varnas* contained the elements of different species. In the last chapter (XVIII) He also defined distinct occupation for each particular Varna. Gita even asked to perform one's caste duty only, even if it was not possible to perform well. And one must refrain from doing job that has not been assigned to his caste even if one could do it excellently.[49] There was no question of merit or quality maintenance. Profession was to be decided by the caste rule only. Different species holds no common right on same means of production. The potency or probability of generation of any class-struggle or caste-war was thus blotted out of exploitative social-tension. Observance of this divine-rule has been prescribed as '*Swadharma*' and a cause for prosperity. For avoiding caste contamination due to war, as the question was raised by Arjun before the beginning of the battle of the Kurukshetra, Lord Krishna did not even hesitate to prescribe '*Sati*'.[50]

Caste structure is not a super structure in Indian society. Besides, Caste essentially being the social, political and religious it became the basic structure of the society, a unique economic structure. It is neither Feudalism nor Capitalism. It is not Socialism as well. It is Casteism, an artificial economic structure without class mobility. The paraphernalia like *Sati*[51] or burning the young widows who may cause caste contamination, in the husband's funeral pyre, untouchability, child marriage and many other institutions support and protect the structure.

The other supportive institutions are the permanent widow-hood, strict endogamy by way of banning inter-caste marriage, inter-caste-dine, inter-caste-mixing and imposition of untouchablity. Creation of Chinese Walls of regional barriers and strong parochial sentiment by encouraging innumerable vernacular languages helped prevent '*Karma-Shankara*' to a great extent and eventually the growth of nationhood. This condition completely killed associative attitude of human beings that create society, country and a nation. Even gods and goddesses, faith and philosophy in the society are found to have been fragmented with conflicting and contradicting rules and regulations. By pampering regional languages and dialects people were prevented from coming closer on the basis of obvious understanding by exchanging mutual feelings and emotions and form a mono-cultural society instead of a society of composite-culture. It is like a bunch of grapes; each one is separate but held in one bid.

Indian society, as a consequence, remained an antic-society[52] throughout the pre-British period. In the latter period, particularly from the beginning of the British rule in India, since the 'Rule of Law' prevailed, since universal education in the army of the British East India Company was introduced even for the untouchables and since the process of social democratisation was initiated by the British bureaucrats-cum-politicians, the Indian society came superficially under the purview of social mobility. But fundamentally or in essence Indian society has no history, at least no known history even today. The society fundamentally remains caste-society and without mobility even in the third millennium.

The All-Bengal Namasudra Association submitted memorandum to the statutory Commission called, Simon Commission in January 1929. In its supplementary they described Indian society, "You will be pleased to find that in that letter (in 1917) of ours, we have tried to give you an idea of the position of the community in so far as its social, educational and political aspects are concerned. It may not be out of place, we venture to think, that we should try and give true indication of the caste system that obtains in this country and how the said fact determines not only the social and educational conditions of the people, but their political conditions as well. It is no doubt difficult for one living in this country to realize truly the situation that is created by the caste. It is therefore, still more difficult for one who has had no opportunity of living in this country and of coming into direct contact with the facts and circumstances created by it. We desire, therefore, to reaffirm the view, which is the result of the past experience, which a man is born with his caste and dies with his caste in India.... "The caste system stigmatised these classes as untouchables as water touched by these classes of people is not drunk by the so called higher castes. Their presence in a room is said to pollute water and cooked food. They are not allowed to enter the public temples ... though these suppressed classes are classes and reckoned as Hindus they are denied all rights as Hindus as are really treated as people out side the pale of Hinduism."[53] These Chandals who formed around double the Brahmin population of Bengal, thus, simply are found to have allowed the KABAB[54] to use them for the benefits of the Brahmanical classes. Mukunda Behari Mullick, the gem of the Chandals deposed his statement in the Simon Commission as oral evidence, "I myself had the experience in my boyhood that we had to wait out side 'class room' where water was kept till a caste Hindu friend came and put water in our hands."

"We have known and seen of many instances up to now where the simple fact that a man is born in a particular caste has not only debarred him from having his true and just share in various branches of the State administration, but also debarred him from little self-realisation through education, for which there has been any obstacle in any part of the civilised world..... We desire, therefore to assert once again the simple fact that the term 'Hindu' does not connote any homogenous race. It is difficult to indicate any reason for this difference in situation, but the fact is that it does exist......" Mr. M. C, Mitra, in "A study in ideals' says:- "Caste is another form of the institutions which by rigidity and tyranny plays a considerable part in retaining and hindering India's advancements." Sir T. Madhava Rao said, "The longer one observes and thinks, the more does one feel that there is no community in the face of the earth that suffers less from political evils and more from self-inflicted, self-accepted or self-created and, therefore, avoidable evils than the Hindus."[55]

The economic portrait of Indian society that has been founded on the economic structure of hereditary division of occupation is like a dead-body lying under the slabs of ice-blocks for centuries. It will withstand and sustain natural degradation process, but would not rot and crumble down, however, it will remain lifeless. The unique socio-economic structure will remain immobile, never to advance it is a state of ever lasting tranquility. In the words of *Pandit* J.L. Nehru, "A rational spirit of enquiry so evident in earlier times, which might well have led to the further growth of science, is replaced by irrationalism and a grand ideology of the past. Indian life becomes a sluggish stream, living in the past, moving slowly through the accumulation of dead centuries. The heavy burden of the past crushes it and a kind of coma seizes it."[56]

References

1. *India Today*, May 24, 2010 Issue p. 25.
2. The Rig Veda, 1/142/9; 3/4/8.
3. The Constitution of India, Article -1.
4. M.O. Mathai, Reminescences of Nehru Age, p. 23.
5. Priya Sehgal, Divide and Rule, India Today, May 24, 2010 issue p. 25.
6. N.K. Verma and Arun Pathak, IAS, Echoes of Indus Valley.
7. *The Times of India*, New Delhi, Thursday, May 6, 2010.
8. *Sunday Times of India*, New Delhi, May 1, 2011, p. 20.
9. Romila Thapar, A History of India, p. 115.
10. Karl Marx, In his letter on India in 1853.
11. Shramana Culture is maintained by the Buddhist-Jain religious Schools of Pre-Vedic Period. The Tradition of 23 Tirthankaras of the Jainas and 28 'Former Buddhas' (Purba Buddha) may be referred to in this regard. The dignity of labour has been the essence of the Shramana Culture. Labour has been a matter of below dignity in the Brahmana culture.
12. Dr Ambedkar W and S, Vol. 3 (Fall of Buddhism).
13. Kautilya, Arthashastra.
14. Marx and Engels, Selectes Works, Vol. 1, p. 493.
15. The Telegraph, dated 6 March, 2010.
16. Rig Veda, 10/85/44; 10/97/20; 10/165/1; 4/27; 3/62/1 etc.
17. Sanjiv Chandra Chattopadhaya, Palamou.
18. Refer to any Census Report on Assam and Bngal and Detail Report on Assuras in Majherdabri, Alipurduar, 120 km from Jalpaiguri, West Bengal in the Times Of India, (Kolkata) dated, September 7, 2009.
19. Arun Pathak IAS, and N.K. Verma, Echoes of Indus Valley, Appendix-C, p. 33.
20. Jajur Veda (Krishna) 1/7/3 and Taitereya Brahmana, ½,6-7.
21. Refer to Rig Veda and the Jajur Vedas for gradual and elaborate development of caste role; S.K. Biswas, Autochthons of India and the Aryan Invasion, p. 200-210.
22. Dr Ambedkar, Buddha and his Dhamma, p. 10.
23. Aswaghosh, Buddha Charit, 5th Canto, 5/6.
24. Inscription of Emperor, Asoka the Great.
25. *Ibid.*
26. Romila Thapar, Ancient History of India.
27. Swami Dharma Teertha, The History of Hindu Imperialism (Published in 1941) pp. 114-123.

28. Gail Ombet, Article.
29. Introduction, The Hindus Encyclopaedia of Hinduism, Editor, Subodh Kapoor, Published February 2000.
30. Haraprosad Shastri, Beesai : Buddha Dharma, p. 170.
31. Nagendranath Vasu, The Modern Buddhism and its Followers in Orissa, (Pub. in 1911) pp. 14, 23 and 24.
32. Karl Marx and Engels, Selected Works, Vol. 1, p. 494.
33. *Ibid*, pp. 492-93.
34. Richard Toye Henry Holt, Churchill's Empire: The World That Made Him..., Sunday Times of India, October 3, 2010, p. 10.
35. The Hindus Encyclopedia of Hinduism, Editor, Subodh Kapoor, Published February 2000, p. 4.
36. Karl Marx and Engels, Selected Works, Vol. 1, p. 497.
37. Gandhiji, Navajivan (Gujrati) journal
38. Works of Swami Vivekananda, Vol. 5, pp. 214-15.
39. Works of Swami Vivekananda, Vol. 5, p. 515.
40. Rig Veda 10/11/8-9.
41. Rig Ved, 10/90/10.
42. Rig Ved, 10/90/13-14.
43. Sukla Jajurveda 30/ 1-22 Mantra 177 ; 31/1-5 etc.
44. Arun Pathak, IAS, the Former Chief Secretary, Bihar; N.K. Verma, Echoes of Indus Valley.
45. S.K. Biswas, Autochthons of India and the Aryan Invassion.
46. Walter G. Grifith, Kole Tribes of Central India, p. 5.
47. Rig Veda.
48. Gita, 4/13.
49. Gita, 18/ 41-44.
50. Gita, 1/31-41.
51. Srimad Bhagavat Maha Puran, 11/31/19-20.
52. M.N. Roy, Historic Role of Islam in India, p. 6.
53. A.K. Biswas, The Namasudras of Bengal, Appendix-II.
54. The Dalit intellectuals call the Kayasta-Brahmin-Baidyas (The so-called Bhadroloks that mentlemen). In short form as KABAB.
55. A.K. Biswas, The Namasudras of Bengal, p. 72.
56. J.L. Nehru, Discovery of India, p. 54.

2

The Chandals of the East

Standing in the fire-circle of socio-political turmoil created by the untouchables of Eastern Bengal on the soil of British-India, during the end of the 19th century, a terrified Hindu and a hardcore protagonist of caste-system Swami Vivekananda advised the Hindus to tackle the terrible danger that has cropped up out of the teachings of the Westerners. 'They have now tought us that those stupid, ignorant, low-caste millions of India, clad only in loin-cloths, are non-Aryans. They are therefore, no more our kith and kin.' He with a view to damage controlling measure suggested, "Forget not that the lower-classes, the ignorent, the poor, the illiterate, the cobbler (*Moechis)'* the sweepers (Bhangis) are thy flesh and blood, thy brothers. Thou brave one, be bold, take courage, be proud that thou art an Indian, and proudly proclaim, "I am an Indian, every Indian is my brother." Say, "The ignorant Indian, the poor and destitute Indian, the Brahmin Indian, the Pariah (Chandal) Indian is my brother." Thou, too, clad with but a rag round thy loins proudly proclaim at the top of the voice "The Indian is my brothers" . . . *Methors* and *Mochis*, *Chamars* and *Chandals* are my brothers!!!. . . "[1] Vivekananda visualised the Hindu catastrophe in the end of the 19th century, which was to come as a result of the self-assertive democratic movement by the Chandals and other untouchables in the Eastern India. They declared themselves as a nation, separate from the Hindus, Muslims or Christians and had got a nomenclature 'Depressed Classes'.

Vivekananda, therefore, traced the Chandals as the saviors of the Hinduism! Why he directed the supercilious and notoriously orthodox Hindus to extend their feeling of brotherhood towards even the Untouchables? How the pure Aryan blood flowing the blue-veins of the Brahmins could be same as that of the An-Arya Chandal! Why the most neglected and despicable Chandals were to be called brothers? He narrated, "The ideal at one end is the Brahmin and the ideal at the other end is the Chandal" and suggested, "and the whole work is to raise the Chandala up to the Brahmin"[2] However, he declared, "I do not propose any leveling of castes. Caste is a very good thing. Caste is a plan we want to follow. . . . It is sheer nonsense to desire the abolition of castes."[3] What was the specialty and strength in the *Chandals* that he even got ready to be a heretic by planning caste contamination; by leveling Brahmin and a Chandal? It is found that even before the advent of Mahaprobhu Chaitanya, in eastern India, during last decade of 14th Century, the Cobbler-sage, Sant Shiromoni Guru Roi-Das of the Punjab-Varanasi region advised his people to 'Refrain from worshipping the inert and meritless Brahmins and to worship the worthy and meritorious Chandals'

गुरु रैदास ने कहा।

रैदास न ब्राहमन पूजियें, जउ होयें गुनहीन।।
पूजे चरन चण्डाल के, जउ होउ गुन परवीन।।

Mahatma Gandhi started close friendship with the Chandelias (Chandals) or Bhangis of Delhi-Punjab region in the 1930's. Why then Gandhiji and Pandit Nehru gave this community the new identity as Valmiki community? Why even in the 3rd millennium the most powerful and popular Brahamin leader of Bengal Ms Mamata Banerjee had to touch the feet of '*Bara-Ma*', (Great-grand-daughter-in-law of Guruchand) the icon of Matuas?[4] Why Manu to Mamata via Chaitanya *Mahaprabhu,* Vivekananda and Gandhi bow before the untouchable *Chandals*? How the *Chandals* became a threat to the Hindu despots to the extent that they were to be wooed as brothers!!! Who are these *Chandals*? In the Census reports, the Chandal population has, however, been wiped out under cover of some other proper noun or by not enumerating them. Though, the population of ancient Assura race along with many other pre-historic races have been enumerated in the Census Operation 2011.

The races called 'Chandal' and 'Chamar' are found to have been mentioned in the earliest literature not only in India but also in the annals of the world history, be it the Buddhist Pali or Vedic literature. Despite their earliest existence in the most parts of the land, surprisingly they have never been shown as a distinct autochthon group especially in the literature created in later Puranic period. A conscious and continuous endeavour, though unsuccessful, on the contrary is noted to have been active, throughout the ages to assimilate this particular autochthon group of ethnic people in the Aryan population. Simultaneously, the Chandals, however, are found to have continued as an object of contempt by the Brahmanical system. Most rationally, the race is found to be too self-conscious to surrender. They put constant challenges to the Aryan ruling classes. Eventually, the Chandals are found to have been recognised by the European scholars to be one of the races that emerged out of mixture of native-Indians.

In the scheme of '*Chatur Varna Dharma*' or caste-system the scope of inter mixture of castes has totally been banned by spiritual taboos. No exogamy or inter-caste marriage was allowed. Endogamy was the only prescribed system. Inter-caste marriage, however, does not annihilate caste. It, on the contrary, increases the number of castes or *Shankarvarnas*. Yet, any sort of caste contamination due to inter-caste marriage is strictly denied, lest it destroy the basic structure of the society by creating inter-occupational mobility. It causes greatest sin, which even damages the glory of the ancestors in the haven of the sinner, "Strisu Dustasu Barsneya Jayate Varnasankara; Shankaro Narakayba Kulaghnang Kulasya Cha. Patanti Pitaro Hesyang Luptapindodakakriya"

"स्वीषु दुष्टासु वार्ष्णेय जायते वर्णसडःकरः।।41।।"[5]

सङ्करो नरकायैव कुलघ्नानां कुलस्य च।

पतन्ति पितरो ह्येषां लुप्तपिण्डोदाकक्रियां।। 1/41-42

Caste contamination destroys the society. Therefore, the entity of the Chandals does not come in the *Chatur Varna* scheme. The native Chandal race seems to have been hijacked as '*Shankar varna*' in the lowest rung of the Hindu society as the despised creatures at a latter period. With a view to facilitating this scheme, some of the religious scriptures are found to have allowed provisions for *Varna*-'*Shankara*'. These creatures called Chandals have been accommodated as one of the tributary to the Hindu masses in ancient as well as in modern time. Manu Smriti a Sanskrit product of AD 1st century by a Brahmin named Bhrigu holds, '*Yathaiba Sudro Brahmanyanh Bajhyang Jantung Prasuyate. Tatha Bajhyatarang Bajhyachaturvarnayang Prasuyate.*'[6]

यथैव शुद्रो व्राह्मण्यं वाहयं जन्तुं प्रसुयते।

तथा वाहयतरं वाहयश्चातुर्वर्ण्ये प्रसुयते।

'As the creatures called Chandals, reproduced by a *Sudra* father and a Brahmani are inferior; the inferior creatures' progeny out of the three higher Varnas are further inferior.

The Jain scripture, '*Acharanga Nirukta*' (Gatha-12/27) claimed to be given by Bhadra Bahu, the Guru of Chandragupta Maurya, the first empire builder and the founder of the Mauryan dynasty in the mid 4th century B.C. held the same as Manusmriti, that the Chandals were the descendents of the *Sudra* father and the Brahmin mother. "With the mixture of four *Varnas* there arose 16 *Varnas*. Prodhan Kashatriya came out of Brahmin male and Kshatriya female; Prodhan Vaisys were born out of Kshatriya male and Vaisya female. Prodhan Sudras or Sankara Sudras were born out of Vaisya male and *Sudra* female. Thus were born the seven Varnas. There came another nine such as Ambastha, Ugra, Nisad, Ayogab, Magad, Suta, Khattwa Vaideha and out of the union of the *Sudra* male and Brahmin female were born the Chandals."

In earlier Buddhist or PaIi literature of 6th century B.C. or even before, the Chandals have, however, been described as an independent and distinct ethnic group of the land. They have been staunch Buddhist in faith and strongly challanged the supremacy of Brahmins and their claim of divinity. In the Jataka and in many other Buddhist literatures they are found to have subdued the supercilious Brahmins and kept them as their stand-by. The Orhat Matanga was served by Brahmins. Therefore, the question of their being crossbreed of different human species like the Brahmins (female) and the Sudras (male) does not arise.

Obvious and an unambiguous mention of the ethnic group called '*Chandal'* is found in the Chapter 30 of the Sukla Yajur Veda. The members of the Hindu Sect who worship the Sun as the Supreme Lord and creator of the universe have derived their fundamental '*mantra*' i.e. "*Tat Sabuturvarenya vargo Devasya Dhimohi ....*" from this chapter. As has already been stated in the previous chapter, that the hymns of this chapter of Sukla Yajur Veda allot specific profession/ occupation or attach each caste group with different sets of means of production. Brahmins have been attached with Brahma, Kshatriyas with Kshatra, Vaisyas with Marut, Sudras with service, Thieves with Tama, impotents (worthless-duffers) with sins, Magadhas with Atikrusta etc.' (30/5/10) In the process the Chandals have been attached with wind or void ....., "*Vayabe Chandalamantariksham Vanshanartinang....*वायवे चन्डालमन्तरिखसाय वंशनर्तिनं"[7] Suta with dance, Natas with song (30/6-7/10) Fishermen with lakes, (*Saravyo Dhaivara*) Kirat with den, Kaivarta with *Avara* (*Mavaraya Kaivarta*) Swarnakara with Varnang (30/16-17/10) Charmakar with *Sadhya* or Ritu (30/15/10)

From sociological standpoint these hymns are found to be exceedingly significant. These Indian autochthons (mentioned separately and apart from the Brahman, Kshatriya, Vaisya and Sudra) the *Kiratas, Shabaras, Nisadas* and *Magadhis*, the *Karmakaras,* and *Swarnakaras*, the Fishermen, *Kaivartas, Chamars* and *Chandals* definitely came not from the Aryan stock. Besides, they have been shown very carefully along with their distinct occupation. The *Chandals*, thus are found to be very ancient and Pre-Vedic autochthons of the country. These socio-economic rather occupational groups are different and distinct with their profession.

The Chandals in the hymns have, interestingly not been mentioned either as Untouchables or as a mixed race or '*Varna-Sankara*'. During this early period when Castes or Varnas were yet to be rigidly rooted in the society, the question of their having sprung out of racial admixture of the Brahmins and Shudras was completely redundant. Their connection with void or *Sunya* '*Vayabe*' tends to relate them with the Buddhist heritage who follow '*Sunnya Vad*'.

Manu, at a period much later to the Pali Buddhist literature, further declared, "Brahmano Kshatriyo Vaisyastryo Varna Dwijataya. Chaturtha Aka Jatistu Sudro, Nasti Tu Panchama" 'Brahmana, Kshatriya and Vaisya these three Varnas are Dwijas. Sudras are not Dwija. There is no fifth Varna, all others are Shankara-Varnas Dev.'[8]

ब्राह्मण: क्षत्रियो वैश्यस्त्रयो वर्णा द्विजातप्त:।

चतुर्थ प्रकजातिस्तु शुद्रो नास्ति तु पचम:।। 10/4

There is no problem that all Varnas other than the four Varnas are Shankar Varnas. But here the social position of Chandals is peculiar even as one of the Shankar-Varnas. They are claimed to have been the progeny of the Sudras and Brahmins. Both belonged to the *Chatur-Varna* system. None of the Varnas was supposed to be non-Aryan. Besides, another source holds that the maternal side of the Chandals, belongs to the top holy-cow-group of Aryan stock, the Brahmin. On that ground at least the Chandals should not have been an out-caste or untouchables. According to the chart of Manu , '*Sankara-Varnas*' some who are the product of Kshatriya and *Sudra* or Vaisya and *Sudra* (both lower to the Brahmani in socio-spiritual status) like '*Karan*' (*kayastha*), Kshatta, *Ayogab* etc. are found to have been placed in the 'touchable' group. The product of the top and the bottom was expected a better deal and higher placement than that has been granted to the product of the middle and the bottom. "*Sudradayagaba Kshatta Chandalaschadhamo Nrinam; Vaisyarajanyabiprasu Jayante Varnashankara*" 10/12 Both the shankara-varnas 'Ayogaba' and 'Khatta' are placed on the higher ladder than the Chandala. Even 'Margaba' or 'Dasha' who are called Kaivartas socially enjoy higher status than the Chandalas. "Nisado Margavang Sute Dashang Naukarmajivinam; Kaivartamiti Yang Prahuraryavartanivasina.' 10/34 Whereas, in violation to the arithmetical calculation the Chandals, according to the Law-givers (also in the Parasar and Narad Smriti) are declared as lowest of untouchables who received unimaginably raw and contemptuous deal from the entire society. The reasons of such cruel treatments seem to be hidden in the treasure of socio-historic turmoil.

As the word, Chandal is familiar in ancient Pali and Sanskrit literature, so also it has been referred to in other language and literature. References to the term abound in the medieval Bengali, Hindi and in many other literature in our country. The stories of Chandal and Chandali are available all over India. The ethnic identity of Chandal is understood to have definite derivetory connection with the ancient mother goddess Chandi. Chandi is a non-Aryan and pre-Aryan entity. The temple of ancient goddess Chandi is situated on north of Chandigarh on the way to Jammu-Kashmir or Simla. In the Doda District of J&K near Ramvan and PatniTop area on the way to Srinagar there occurs big annual festivals of Chandi Devi in her ancient temples. There is a famous village called Chandic, seven km. away from the Poonch Town. Ancient Chandi Devi temple is very famous in the village. The Howrah-Chandelia Express railway train travels to the destination of Chandelia

Terminal in Tribal Jharkhand. The word relates to Chandal. Chandelias are in Delhi region and they belong to the untouchable Bhangi castes.

However, there are controversies and differences of opinion in regard to their original home-land and racial genesis. The ancient Chandals are easily found in the 3rd millennium too. It would not be out of context to mention that the name of the mother of one of my young friend working in the Delhi University (*Bhangi* or Valmiki by caste) is '*Chandali*'. Many individuals as well as ethnic groups, today in the Northern India, use the word to identify them. Around three millions of *Bhangis* in Delhi and many others in the Punjab, Hariyana and UP claim that they belong to the Chandeli race. The existence of the term denotes an ancient and sharply distinct group of indigenous people. Their pan-Indian presence is found in modern time too. In his book, 'The Untouchables Who Were They' Dr Ambedkar had mentioned the names of all the Scheduled Castes in India as prepared by the Census Commissioner in 1931. In the vast list, the 'Chandals' have been mentioned in the Madras province[9] only. The community called Chandal is conspicuously missing in all other provinces. Even in the eastern region like Assam, Bengal, Orissa or Bihar. Practically, the Chandals of the east have under gone the serious drill of assimilation by the Hindus. They have been enumerated in different names like Namasudra, Pods etc. Similar process of wiping out their racial identity seems to have been in operation in all the provinces all along. In the first Census the Chandals were enumerated as 16, 20,545 in Bengal. In Bihar Chamars, Dusads and Domes were the major untouchable caste. Even in Bihar Chandals were 4,564 and in Assam they were 23;241 souls. In Assam Koch-Rajbansis were the major Untouchables. In 1981 Census, the Chandals were enumerated 184; 175; 90; and 37 in the provinces of Andhra, Karnataka, Kerala and Madras respectively. They were enumerated in different new names as in Bengal. Consequently, from 1911 Census Operation no Chandal was found in Bengal. The entire race has lost its original or traditional ethnic name under the artificially created Hindu name, Nama-Sudra.

In British India, their numerical strength augmented remarkably. In 1911; 1921 and 1931 the Namasudras (earlier Chandals) were enumerated 19,13,343; 20,28000 and 20,94,000 souls respectively almost with no decennial increase.

Though available in the Pali literature, the word 'Chandal' is not found in the Asokan inscriptions (from the debris of vandalism and destruction only a few of the Pillar and Rock Edicts so far have been discovered). The Emperor himself has, however, been referred to as a Chandal, the Chandasok, during 3rd century B.C. The ninth book of the Khudaka Nikaya of Suttapitaka is distinctly famous as the 'Therigatha'. This is the most ancient female literature in the annals of world literature. This is the compilation of poems written by about five dozens of Theries (the enlightened Nuns or Bhikksunis). All of them were contemporaries to Gautama Buddha. Theri Sumedha in her

Chattalisanipato Samatto had praised the Chandalas as the conquerors of desire, 'Khahinati Khu Tang Kama Chata Sunakhang Ba Chandala'. (509) Number of the Sanskrit literature have narrated many Chandal characters. Banabhatta, the poet of A.D. 5th 6th century, depicted the *Chandal* and *Chandali* in a highly placed and esteemed position in his book 'Kadambari'.

The community called *Chandals* has been mentioned by Alberuni who was brought to Delhi by Sultan Mahmud as a prisoner in his famous book, '*Bharat Tattwa*'. It was written in AD 1030. In the 9th Chapter of his book, called '*Varna* Classes and the Lower Order of the Society' he had described that below the four *Varnas* or caste strata there had been the working class. Their professions are their *varnas*. The people of four *Varnas* do not mix with them. Apart from these group, there remains people called 'Handi' 'Dome' 'Chandals' and 'Bhagats'. These groups do not form any social strata. They are treated untouchables and regarded as the beast of burden as well as beast of prey outside human social-structure. Cattle and animals are domestic pets of the Hindus and form part of human society but the untochables do not form any social strata as they are not permitted to live in the society. They are disqualified from the common rights to the means of production of the society. Commonly it is believed that they are the offspring of a Brahmin mother and a *Sudra* father.[10]

The Brahmin saint, Chaitanya Mahaprabhu, (family name Nimai Chand Mishra) of early 16th century (expired in AD 1534) had to tackle many Chandals during his period. Those were the days when there prevailed social tension due to the process of conversion of the untouchables and Sudras to Islam for equality and brotherhood in contrast to the crude and heartless spiritual persecution by the holy-Hindus. To save the situation, Chaitanya took special concern to woo the Chandal community. He even tried to lure them back by offering a position superior to 'Twice born' the Brahmins (*Dwija*) had they accepted his sect, '*Chandalohopi Dwija Srestha Haribhakti Parayana*'. However, there are many twice-born castes besides Brahmin. Many Chandals got trapped in the net. But history abounds with illustrations that the Chandal race or nation maintained their exclusive identity till the end of the 19th century. Even as Vaishnavs they retained their racial name Chandal and continued to be treated as untouchables. The British authorities, however, indulged with a new tern 'Namo-Sudra' as substitute of 'Chandal' from the beginning of the last quarter of the 19th century. Eventually, with the advent of the democratic era, the new name Namo-Sudra has been officially imposed. It helped hijack and Hinduize the Chandals.

As per documents, both the terms, 'Chandal' and '*Nava Sudra*' (means 'New Sudra' not Nama-sudra) are found to have been in prevalence during 17th century in the Jungle Mahal of Orissa. They seem to be the ancient people of Buddhist faith. One of the areas of the Mahal of 'Garjat' is called 'Bodh' means Buddha. The influence of Buddhism still continues in the area in some form or other especially amongst the untouchable Dom community. It is also a historical fact that the temple of Lord Jagannath at Puri was a temple of Lord Buddha in pre-Islamic period. It was forcibly converted to Hindu temple. The local people in the 'Bodh' locality never accepted Hinduism and preferred to follow Buddhist tenets of spirituality in the form of different sect in different names. In the Garjat mahal there prevailed, a religious sect called 'Mohima Dharma'. They worshipped a deity called '*Alekh*' or *Sunya Purush*'. They did not believe caste. And the adherents were regarded by the Hindus as low caste. The chief guru of this religion was Vimbhoi or Bhimsen Bhoi Arakshitdas. Bhimbhoi once made an expedition to recapture the Buddha-temple of Puri now called Jagannath temple. However, he had retreated after he was badly beaten up. In the literature of 'Koli-Bhagabat' and 'Beshmoti Malika' detail descriptions of the sect are available. It is interesting to note that in the book it has been instructed to accept alms or '*Bhiksa*' from the '*Naba Sudras*' but alms are not to be accepted from the nine '*Jati*' namely, *Teli, Tantri, Bhat, Kera, Rajak, Kularak, Brahma, Kshatri*, and *Chandal*.[11] The Naba Sudras and Chandals appear to be different communities of people here in the poem. In the circumstances, it is not clear as to why and since when the two proper nouns amalgamated? What were the common phenomena between the two?

The Chandals have been identified as 'Namasudras' officially since 1901 and in 1911 Census. But the new Sudras or Namasudras are a regional caste or Varna of the Hindus. They are natives exclusively, of Bengal. Moreover, this is a caste created by the Census Office rather than by the Divinity, however, with the same objectives.

The word '*Namo*' or '*Nama*' is found to have got a mention in the Bengali literature composed during the 12th — 13th century, after the Turkish conquest of Bengal. In the section called '*Atha Baitarani*' (the river as the hurdle for salvation) of '*Sunya Puran*' written by Ramai Pandit[12] it is written that '*Namo Sab Paralo Pandit Charijan; Pandite Daxina Dila Rajata Kanchan*'. 'Four 'Pundits' or Buddhist scholars coached all the 'Namos' who gave the Pundits silver and gold as fees.' The situation reveals that all the Namos were qualified for education. Besides, they were not poor but exceedingly rich to offer education-fees in gold and silver. It appears that the 'Namos' in the context, belonged to affluent class and they were definitely neither untouchables nor debarred of education right.

It is important to note that '*Sunya Puran*' too is a Buddhist literature in disguise. It describes the stories of worship and glorious merit of 'Dhamma Thakur' who spreads the philosophy of '*Sunya*' i.e. non-entity and '*Nibban*' of Buddha. Shankaracharya in his treaty '*Tarkapad*' satired these '*Sunyavidis*' i.e. the Buddhists by saying that there was no point or scope of debate with those who held that everything dilutes into void or nothingness. Ramai Pandit and his 'Dharma Thakur' were popularly accepted by the people from the locality called *Radha* in the Mayurbhanj district of Orissa up to the vast regions of Eastern Bengal. When the Hindu (Vaishnava) religious cult of "*Pravritti Marg* did incalculable mischief to the society the '*Nivritti-marg'* system became a no less potent factor in moulding and regulating thoughts of society, as is evidenced by a critical study of the *Sunya Puran* and *Dharma Mangala* literature and several other Oriya manuscripts, recently brought to light from some of the backward villages of Mayurvanja. The devotees "aimed at and taught others to aim at, the attainment of *Bambha Nibbana* which really refers to Buddhistic idea of salvation."[13] Ramai Pandit was followed by even Achyutananda Dasa who wtote '*Sunya Samhita'*. In its Oriya manuscript he asked the people, "Thus I say, take refuge in Buddha, in *Mata Aadishakti* i.e. the primordial energy (*Dharma*) and in the *Sangha*."[14]

It is further interesting from sociological and historic perspective to note that the '*Namos'* in the Ramai Pandit's Sunya Puran were rich and wealthy that the '*Namos'* of Sunya Puran-period and contemporary society were equally literate and learned. There were many 'Pandits' or teachers readily available to coach them. The *Namos* are found to have performed spiritual rituals comfortably. Though 'Puran' means old, the Sunya Puran was not a Hindu scripture. These *Namos* of Sunya Puran were therefore, not Hindu-Sudras or semi-Hinduised untouchables or the root of Namasudras. Nimai Chand Pandit[15] (*Pandit* is not a Brahmin scholar or *Achariya, Guru.* They were originally Buddhist monks and scholars; the word has been hijacked by the Brahmins at a later period) a school teacher of Kalna School in Bardwan District of West Bengal claims to have descended from the family of Ramai Pandit. He, however, at present writes his community name as Namasudra.

These ancient Buddhist-Chandals who used to chant 'Namo Buddhaya", '*Namo Tassya Bhagabato Arhatyo...*" etc. turned to be 'Namos' or 'Naba Sudras' of Sunya Puran and '*Mohima Dhamma'* of Jangal-Mahal of Orissa. They tried to recapture the ancient Buddhist shrine of Jagannath. These former Buddhists of eastern region eventually are likely to have been referred to as Namasudras by the British Government Order (1808) to debar them from the entry in the Puri temple. Chandals of Eastern Bengal (who were equally Buddhists in faith) may have got their nomenclature 'Namasudra' from this source at a later stage. Why did the Census Commissioner not use the term in 1872 especially when the British used the word 'Namasudra' in the Office Order of 1808 on temple of Jagannath, Puri? Whatever might have been the reason for confusion and controversy behind the derogatory, abusive or prestigious word, Chandal it is a historical fact that a very large section of Indians all over the country, especially in the Eastern India maintained their identity as Chandals in the society as well as in the literature throughout the ages. And literature is the reflection and mirror of the society.

Schools of Thoughts on 'The Chandal'

From the preceding short discussion, it can be well said that the British Census authority, while conducting their maiden Census of India in 1872, on the basis of rational and realistic facts adopted the word 'Chandal' to enumerate a nation of autochthon group. This group in eastern India, are found to be exceedingly courageous, self-respectful and skilled in all trades. The British scholars are found to have committed no mistake, being dispassionately sincere to the target of their duty to identify the genesis of these tribes. The first Census Commissioner in 1872 recorded very significant though apparently incorrect fact in regard to the Chandals. "The Chandals or Charals aggregate upwards of a million and a half. This was the great sweeper caste to which were doubtless consigned the great bulk of the aboriginal tribes who embraced Hinduism. They are most numerous in the Eastern districts of Jessore, Furreedpur, Bukargang, Dacca, Mymansingh and Sylhet." The English bureaucrat definitely did not witness the Chandals of Eastern Bengal to sweep streets. They did not belong to any Hindu caste. The community was treated as untouchables or out-caste, outside the pale of 'Chaturvarnashram Dharma'. Yet the great agrarian people have been described as 'sweeper-caste'. This expression of the learned authority appears to have emerged out of his vast experience with the Bhangis, Chandelia, Mang, Dusads, who originally belonged to the Chandal race and were forced into sweeping profession after erasing their Chandal identity. These communities and the tribal people were enumerated as the Hindus under the heading 'Religious Groups' such as the Hindus, the Muslims, the Christians, the Sikhs and Anglo-Indians only.

Neither the Buddhists nor the Chandals, better to record that no caste or ethnic groups of native Indians were identified separately. Even though each autochthon or aboriginal ethnic group in India maintained independent and separate religious identity within their own space of social and cultural activities their religious identity was not recognised by the Census Department. All were officially recorded to be the members of the Hindu society. In this connection we may recall what Dr Ambedkar opined during 1946 in his book 'Who are the Sudras': "The Brahmins believe in the two nation theory. He claims to be the representative of the Aryan race and he regards the rest of the Hindus as descendants of the non-Aryans."[16] Despite this reality of the social-condition the untouchables on record, remained semi-Hinduised. A section of the educated untouchables of the British period wanted or made to raise demands to get rid of the appellation 'Chandal'. This little literate and ill-informed individuals were made to seriously consider that the 'stigma' of untouchability was due to the nomenclature. Unwisely they tried to wipe out this stigmatisation by adopting a new name for the community and by getting enslaved in the Hindu-fold as Namo-Sudra or new-Sudra.[17] At the same time people's democratic struggle started by claiming their nationhood separate from other creeds. Eventually they succeeded in their attempt in 1911.

Semi-Hinduised ethnic group a Distinct Race: A school of social thinkers and anthropologists opines that the Chandals have been one of the ethnic groups or races of native Indians. Sir Herbert H Risley, ICS, and the Census Commissioner of 1901, authored the book, 'The Tribes and Castes of Bengal'. It was published in 1891. In it, he ventured to define the Chandals, "The derivation of the name Chandal is uncertain, and it is a plausible conjecture that it may have been, like Sudras, the tribal name of one of the aboriginal races whom the Aryans found in possession of the soil." He in the Annex of Census Report of 1901, which was printed as a book later on, further held, "Of the localised groups a large number are admittedly tribes. The Bhil, Gond, Koli, and Santal come within this category and are still outside the Hindu social system. The Doms, Dosads, Gujars, Jaths, Kaibartas, Namasudras (Chandals) Pods, Nayars, Pallis, Paraiyanas (Pariahs), and Rajbansi-Koch represent tribes which have been transformed into castes at a comparatively recent date and retain some traces of the tribal stage of development."[18] This view is the result of a prolonged and scientific analysis conducted by the efficient and exceedingly huge machinery under the very sincere and dispassionate bureaucrats of steel frame ICS in British Government.

In the British period the Chandals are found to have largely concentrated in the eastern part of India, particularly in Bengal, Assam and Tripura. In other parts of India the Chandals, with a view to avoiding lethal persecutions, seem to have got assimilated in Hindu body under some other nomenclature. Consequently the Chandals are also regarded very rightly as one of the autochthon races of Bengal by many European and Indian scholars.[19] Their language is modern Bengali which originates from Charya >Chandali >Pali-Prakrit.

Aryan-Hindus: Sudras or Brahmins: There is another group with strong conviction that the 'Chandals' had originated out of foreign Aryan stock and belonged to no less than the highest strata of tyrannical Brahmin family. This view is the product of the subdued Indian-minds mingled with inferiority and superiority caste-complex. This was arrived on the basis of the research and data prepared by the Census authority. Many newly educated people of the erstwhile Chandal family hold such views perhaps to elevate their social position and to make them acceptable to the urban-Brahmanical or creamy-layer-elite set-up. Even the British authorities are found to have accepted the importance of a social group only when they were recommended as respectable one by the Brahmin scholars or the Brahmin called '*Judge Pundit*' who used to sit beside an European Judge whenever an Indian was tried in the court.[20] The thinkers of this school argue that the Chandals were Brahmins, because they follow social customs called '*Shradh*' similar to and followed by the Brahmins. They also refer to some dubious references in regard to their origin from certain unimportant Sanskrit literature etc that tend to declare them as Brahmin origin. These suit their purpose.

They claim that Chandals' (Namasudras) *Gotra* (ancestral lineage) name is Kashyap. And Kashyap was the father of Namas, a Hindu sage. Therefore, the Chandals were Brahmins. They also depend on the cephalic index given by Risley by distorting and contradicting him. These views, however, are found to have got no historical foundation behind their claim. Kashyap was rather one of the very famous 'Old or Former-Buddhas' who lived long before Siddhartha Gautama and attained enlightenment.[21] The Chandal race who were former Buddhists naturally carried 'Buddha-Kashyap's' name in their '*gotra*' tradition till modern time.

It is claimed that the Namasudras (former Chandals) perform '*Sradh*' or '*Sruddhi*' purification on the 10th day from the death of their relatives similar to that the Brahmins do. In reality, the Chandals as well as the Namasudras according to the scriptural injunction are found to have born impure and forever remain a source of pollution. The Brahmins and the Chandals stand just on diametrically opposite platform. The '*Shradh*' ceremony, of which this school of thinkers refer to, indeed, is found to have been a non-Vedic and non-Aryan-subject. Good Brahmins (Vedic) give little or no respect to such ceremonies. Therefore, the Brahmins of low castes who had native origin might have taken their own ritual of *Shradh* along as one of the Brahmin's ritual. Not only cephalic index of the Chandals, but their pigmentation also is similar to the majority of the Brahmins of Bengal and Kerala. But this is no proof of the status of a race or caste.

Some scholars of this school argue that Namasudras or the Chandals were the descendants of Namas Muni, son of Kasyap Muni who was a Brahmin. Yogis, Joyotis and the sages of the pre-Aryan India who belonged to the Shraman culture were called *Muni*. Interestingly, in no major Hindu scripture Namas Muni is traceable. The protagonists of such theory have ignored to note that the common noun 'Namasudra' is available only in the 19th century onwards and not from old-time Namas Muni.[22]

Besides, Caste or *Jat* is the product of God. The essence of caste is that it was the will of the Supreme Creator. Caste is not just a dynasty. Genesis of Caste cannot be traced to any other source like a *Muni* or a Sage or a demi-god. While 'Namasudra is purely a phenomenon of East and W. Bengal only. Was their fore-fathers, Namas or Kashyap a non-Aryan Eastern subject totally disassociated with the main land of Hinduism? Chandal, however, is a pan-Indian phenomenon.

A mixed people: Hinduised or Enslaved: The third and cautious group of scholars had taken the middle course and gave a clear verdict that the Chandals were a mixed race of *Dravid* and Nordic that is Indian and Aryan origin. The scholars have taken the stand on the basis of ancient Shastras like Jain 'Achar Sanhita' and Hindu Manusmriti which hold that Chandals were born out of the illegitimate union of a Brahmin mother and a Sudra father. Therefore, Bankim Chandra Chatterjee argued that at least from the stand point of mother's lineage the Chandals, i.e. the Namasudras were Aryans. But the question is why from maternal side only? Are not the Sudras an integral part of the Aryan Four Varna system?

Regal origin from Chandellas of Central India: Some are inclined, in this regard, to settle the dispute of race or nation having a similar name of a royal clan of Central-Western India, better known as Bundelakhand. They are the Chandelas who ruled over a vast territory in southern Rajasthan and Bundelakhand area. Some even tried to say, on the basis of simple pivot of phonetically two similar proper nouns, that the word 'Chandal' has been generated as a corrupt dialectical form out of these 'Chandella' Rulers. This speculation, however, remained unfounded both from the angle of historical as well as philological perspective till palpable cultural and archaeological evidences corroborated or substantiated it. Due to rampant damages and willful distortion of the history of culture and civilisation of the autochthons, in particular the Chandals many vital clues had so far been ignored. Above all, in Indian academic circle, there has been a reign of notion that whatever belonged to native India and created by the pre-Vedic non-Aryan aborigine were base and without aesthetic value. Besides, whatever was connected with the Vedas and contributed by the intruder Aryan people were of grandeur value, fine and important. Dr D. P. Chattopadhay had termed this notion as an 'Aryan-centric sentiment'.[23] This attitude too prevented historical truth in this regard to come to light.

After the death of the last central Indian Buddhist monarch, the king of Thaneswar and Kanouj (Raja Harshavardhan) in A.D. 642 there emerged many newly Hinduised clans of Rajput families. They had entered India from abroad and were reckoned as the members belonging to the 'Solar' and 'Lunar' races of the Hindus. The 'Chandel' or 'Chendella' according to the Official Historians had their dynastic genesis out of one of these clans. This theory appears to be misnomer, misleading and contrary to actual present-day situation as the descendents of this race all around the area of Bundellakhand are known as Chandelia and treated as Untouchables. They are also known by a new name Bhangi and very recently since 1930s as Valmikis. Their profession is known to be sweeping. The Chandals of Eastern Bengal have officially been called as Namasudras since 1911 Census.

No mention of these ruling families is available before the A.D. 7th Century even in the western region of the river Yamuna or anywhere else. There has been no mention also of the Jat, the Gujjar and the Rajput during this period in the pages of history. In the absence of recorded documents of the region and the local clans, it was easier for the English spoken historians of colonial-period to recreate history that suits purpose for writing history. Ramesh Chandra Mazumder has described the Chandellas, "The power of the Chandellas was shattered by Qutab-ud-din Aibok in AD 1202. Like the contemporary dynasties of Gujarat and Malwa, the Chandellas showed their interest in the work of reconstruction of Building of temples at Khajuraho and the encouragement of poets like Krishna Mishra who adorned the court of Kirtivarman. The political condition of Northern India had changed considerably since the days of Sultan Mahmud. Though a part of Bihar was in the possession of the Buddhist Palas, Bengal had passed under the control of the Hindu dynasty of the Senas. Bundelkhand remained under the rule of the Chandellas, but the Pratihars in Kanauj were displaced by the Gahadevas. Delhi and Ajmer were under the Chauhans. Some of the Chandella kings ruled over Malwa and Rajputana during medieval period........."[24] "After the break-up of the Pratihara Empire a number of dynasties rose to power in Central and Western India. One of them, known as Chandella or Chandratreya, held sway over country now called Bundelkhand.

The Hindu historians found traces and genesis of the Chandellas to the sage Chandratreya who was born of the Moon or 'Chand' i.e. the first five letters of the word Chandal. The Chandravansi or Lunar family appears to have connection with the Chandalas rather than with Varna or Vedic Virat-Purusa. This factor too reveals that the Chandellas were away from the Vedic Varna or Caste which sprang out of the *Virat-Purusa* or God. Their social status was equal to that of Chahamanas. The bards mention them as one of the thirty-six Rajput clans. The dynasty was founded by Nanuka in the 1st quarter of the Ninth century A.D. Epigraphic records connect the early kings of the family with Kharjuravahaka, the modern village of Khajuroho, in old Chhatrapur State, Bundelkhand..... Khajuraho, which lies between Deogarh and Kalinjar, was obviously under the supremacy of the Pratihara kings, and the early rulers of the Chandella dynasty may therefore, be regarded as vassals of the Pratiharas of Kanouj,"[25] Ms Romila Thapar has described, "The Chandella kings are Chandravansi (Lunar) lineage and are Kshatriya in status and, in spite of obscure origins and having acquired the status, continued to marry into the local Gonds."[26] Gond Tribes were too rulers of the Gondwana Hill region, near to the Nagpur city till the British period.

Some even have not hesitated to push their pen in casual manner to distort the history of Chandals who remained insignificant throughout the ages in main stream or Official-history on the basis of obscure stories.[27] Nowhere in any Bengali major literature during 12th to 17th Century mention has been made in regard to the Chandella connection. Nor the Chandellas of Bundelakhand left any record of their Bengal connection. Manu, however, mentions the Chandals long before the Chandellas of Khajuraho came into existence as a ruling clan in India. Chandals of Manusmriti are clans or ethnic group of ancient India. The Chandellas are a royal dynasty; their ethnic identity is narrated by the Official historians in distortions. The ancient Chandal Race does not belong to the Aryan Nordic stock. Chandals have a pan-Indian phenomenon. They too had established many royal dynasties in the main stream Magadhan regions even prior to the Christian era. Indeed, they were the empire builders in or around Rajgriha-Pataliputra regions.

The Chandellas are found to have been active for a short span of period within a limited geographic area of Central Indian Bundelakhand. Despite being in existence in recent past and over a large part of Indian Territory as dominant ruling dynasty, they failed to maintain records to tell that they had their ethnic relation in Eastern India or to say that they had once advanced to the eastern part of India. No document of importance and authenticity where the Chandals hold some references to their activities indicates any Chandella connection. However, it is a greater truth that the Brahminic ruling class as the spiritual sanctions, destroyed all records kept by the well versed autochthons of India and her ruling families .

When the genesis of the Chandals of East is tried to be linked or located amongst the Chandella kings or dynasty of the Western or Central India of medieval period then the thinkers appear to have ignored to examine some fundamental social phenomenon like cultural proximity and commonness of tongue. The language of the Chandals of East and the Chandellas of Central India is in no way similar. It does not belong to the same or similar school of language. The ancient language of the Chandals of East is found to have its link with Austric group[28] which was used by the Assura race of Assyrian or Sumerian civilisation of ancient Middle-East whereas the language of the Chandellas (Malvi, Rajasthani, Gujarati) are claimed to be of Central-Aryan language family. Traces of Khajuraho School of Art and culture are also not traceable in Bengal.

The Chandals as untouchables are innumerable in their active presence in the eastern India today, but it is interesting to note that the remarkably robust Chandellas are almost a non-entity in the Western or in the Central India as a vibrant community. They are now treated as one of the untouchable community under different names in the Brahmin-British Census. The powerful Chandellas a powerful regal dynasty of an important and vast region copletely vanished into the blue with the fall of rulers like many other dynasties. But the Chandellas in Bhangi name have been a race powerful and numerous enough to sustain and survive through all odds and state sponsored oppression.

The conspicuous simile between these two common nouns Chandal and Chandella, however, cannot so plainly be ignored without adequate examination. One is to consider the aspect that both these groups of people belonged to the same spiritual school, Buddhism. We find the prominent traces of Matanga temple constructed by the Chandellas in the Khajuraho region. The untouchable Bhangi or Valmiki community is found to be tending pigs and maintain piggery all over India. Pigs are their social identity. And it is noteworthy and interesting to mention that just in front of the Matanga temple there is a large sculpture of a pig. The locals worship it. The existence of Matanga Temple in the region obviously indicates that the Chandellas of Bundelakhand in Central India were the followers of Lord Buddha and Buddhism. There can be no other angel in it. Their deity was Chandal Matanga. Matanga was a Chandal and a powerful Buddhist sage. It is on record in the ancient Pali literature that King Possendi of Kanshi-Kosala, the disciple of Lord Gautama Buddha was a son of a Matangi, the Chandal girl. It is realistic and possible that the ancient Chandal families of the Bundelakhand region, in a favourable situation, re-captured their patrimony and became rulers once again. Colonial historians, better to say the Official historians hijacked them as the Hindu rulers. Similar was the modus operandi by which the family of Sudra Chatrapati Shivaji was hijacked and their original ethnic name was confused. Gradually they were alienated from their own Chandal society. Their family name was changed slightly in the records so that in future, all remain confused and the race got disconnected with its traditional origin. The autochthon Chandals who are found to be very peace-loving but excitingly brave and of marshal-character having a history of ruling dynasties like King Prasanjit, Emperor Asoka and Palas of Bengal (all Buddhists) are definitely compatible with the war monger western Chandellas of Western India.

Vallal Sen the Genesis: Some thinkers did not hesitate even to hold that the genesis of the Chandals rest with the royal injunctions issued by the Hindu Raja of Bengal named Vallal Sen who uprooted the Buddhist Pala dynasty from Bengal in 11th century. According to the tradition, 'Buddhist-Brahmins' did not attend the jamboree hosted by the king to celebrate his marriage with a beautiful girl from washer-man community. Being insulted with this conduct of certain section of his subjects the arrogance of authority came upon those who dared not attend the royal dinner and outcaste them as Chandals, untouchables.[29] Vallal Sen is also known to have introduced a social institution called '*Kulin*' (elite) strata in the social hierarchy. According to this claim, the 'Chandals' comes to be a demographic factor of Bengal only. But this is not a fact. The Chandal ethnicity is a pan-Indian factor.

The '*Mulniwasi*' Chandals are understood to have even gone under a conspiratory move of intellectual dishonesty of the official historians who resorted to make them foreign intruders, like the Aryan-Brahmins. They are up to making them migrants from the banks of the river Nile of Egypt. The mastery of the Chandals in every trade as boat-men, as fisher-men, as Chandsi-physicians, as exceedingly industrious peasantry, as strenuous amphibians, as intelligent traders, as fearless brave-heart martial art soldiers, as the freedom monger individualists, as peace-loving social beings has led the social thinkers and historians relate them to the glorious Egyptian civilisation. They are left only to be recognised for their own and independent pride and gracious importance as natives of the country.

Who are the Chandals?

In central and northern India, the Chandals were recognised as Bhangi (Broken) though many families of the Bhangis retained their family name 'Chandellia' derived from the ancient ethnic identity. In Bihar region, they are known as Dusads. The differences of opinion held by the modern scholars, however, failed to resolve the dispute on the ethnic question and of the genesis of the Chandals. The official historians love as well as need to maintain confusion over history of the country. Suppressing or distorting history is the cultural heritage of Brahmanic teachings. Who were the Chandals and what were their links with the Namasudras of the 20th century? Why have the Hindus kept these teeming millions of robust and potentially meritorious people of agrarian background under contemptuous situation? Why on the other hand have these people loved to embrace even Islam and Christianity instead of surrendering to the Brahmanical tyranny? As Buddhists, they were definitely people of letters. Still there exists literature called '*Charya Pads*' written by them. The treasure of their literature have been destroyed by the intruder Aryan groups during Islamic attack. In the absence of available records written especially by the Chandals on the Chandals, it remains as a very curious phenomenon still to find their roots and history.

The Chandal race or the people called Chandals in our discussion are found to have actually been a very powerful element in the formation of Indian society throughout the ages. They existed even long prior to the age of Manu or Acharanga Sutta period. Their active and influential presence is observed both in ancient Pali and in Vedic-Sanskrit literature of later age. They are observed to have been standing erect before the existence of the Brahmins. The Chandals have been following the faith propounded by the Buddhas of very old lineage as the people of Naga race were. The romantic episode of Bhante '*Dhammagarika*' Ananda, the chief disciple of Lord Gautama Buddha and the untouchable Chandal girl named 'Prakriti' or Matanga Darika is very popular. This Chandal girl who was admitted to the Bhikshuni Sangh by Gautama Buddha himself attained '*Arhatta*' in course of time. The Naga chiefs went to pay homage to the new born Siddhartha with the belief that '*Tathagata*' Buddha had appeared on the earth.[30] The stories of Guhak Chandal of Ramayana and of Raja Harishchandra who lived as a Chandal have become the subject of children's literature today. It is observed that in Baal Kanda of Ramayana (58/9) Trishanku of Solar dynasty became a Chandal. It is mentioned:-

"*Chandaligarbho Sambhuto Viswamitra Maha Muni.*"

Yudhisthir, the eldest son of Pandu, has been instructed in the Mahabharata, 'Bho Yudhistir! Brahmana is not one's caste, clan or profession, but one Chandal who is of good profession and of etiquette also is a Brahmin:-

"Nakulena Na Jatya Ba Kriyati Brahmaner Bhaveth'
Chandalohpi Hibrittena Brahmana Sa Yudhisthara."

These references out of the ocean of such old-schools of language and literature vividly tend to prove the existence of the Chandals all over India with their un-ignorable importance in social interactions since time immemorial.

The ethnic group called Chandal, on the basis of their presence in the ancient literature, appears to be one of the strong non-Aryan autochthon groups who had nothing to do with Brahman or Hinduism. They formed no sub-caste of either Sudra or Brahman. They belonged to a pure tribal group, race, or a nation.

Sir Herbert Risley, the Census Commissioner has categorically pointed out, "Considerations of space preclude me from attempting an exclusive enumeration of the castes which may plausibly be described as tribes absorbed in Hinduism, but I may mention as illustrious of the transformation that has taken place, the Ahir, Dom and Dosad of United Province and Bihar, the Gujar, Jat, Meo and Rajputana of Rajsthan and the Punjab; the Koli, Mahar and Maratta of Bombay; the Bagdi, Barui, Chandal (Namasudra) Kaibarta, Pod and Rajbansi-Koch of Bengal and in Madras the Mali, Nayar, Vellala and Paraiyan or Fariah of whom the last retain traditions of a time when they possessed an independent organisation of their own and had not been relegated to a low place in the Hindu social system."[31]

This nation called Chandal numerically was very vast. Many of the turbulent Kings, Buddhist in faith, of India, at least of the northern India belonged to this Chandal nation. Evidences from history reveal that Kosalan King, Pasendi or Prosenjit who became an ardent follower of Gautam Buddha and who was the maternal uncle of the king Ajatsatru of Magadh was born in Chandal Jati. Genealogy of many of the ruling families has been given in the 'Lalit Vistar' where King Prasenjit or *Pasendi* has been described as a descendant of '*Matanga Jati*' that is Chandal.[32] Here the word '*Jati*' however, does not mean Caste or *Varna*. He was born of a Chandalini. The word '*Jati*' is available in Pali literature where it means a 'race' 'tribe' or 'clan'.

In the dialogue between King Bimbisar and Siddhartha Gautam, narrated in the Pabbajya Sutta of Sutta Nipat, we observe that the prince belonged to the Sakya Jati or family. Siddhartha Gotam who after renunciation of family had reached at the city-gate of Rajgir, being asked by the king Bimbisar disclosed his identity:

"Adichha Nama Gottena, Sakia Nama Jatia,
Tamha Kula Pabbogitomhi Raja Na Kame Abhipalayang."

'O King! I was born in the small Janapad called Kosal on the foot hills of the Himalayas in the *Sakya Jati* and in the Aditya *Gotra.....*" Sakya was no caste; it represented a family name or a name of a clan. The Sakyas definitely did not belong to any of the *Varnas* or castes that the Hindus were divided into. They belonged according to the experts, to the Indo-Mongoloid race. In the Buddhist Pali literature the Sakyas are claimed to be of Kshatriya race. The governing and marshal clans and tribes are called Kshatriyas[33] They do not necessarily belong to the 2nd *Varna* of the *Chatur-varnas* of the Hindu society. Mahabharat too holds similar stand in its slokas:

"Mekala, Dravira Lata, PoundraKonashirasthatha'
Soundika Darda Darbaschoura Shabara Barbaba.
Kirtata Yabanaschaiba Tanda Kshatriya Jataya'
Vrish ılatwamanuprapta Brahmanammaryanat."[34] (10/44-45)

Alon·, with the foreign races like Pallavas, Saks, Huns, Chin, Dard, Mlechha etc. the aboriginal Indian tribes like Paundra, Shabar, Shanak, Dravida, Lata were also been described as Kshatriyas. Many Hinduised tribes have also been shown in such lists.

These Puranic expressions are found to be in consonance with the narration of the modern historians. "Foreign conquest is nothing new in Indian history. But the Muslim conquest affords a striking contrast to other foreign conquests in past. The pre-Muhammadan foreigners like the Greeks, Scythians and Huns never became a distinct factor in Indian politics. After their settlement in India they had to succumb to the assimilative power of Hinduism and sooner or later became merged in the general body of Hindu population."[35] Thus, during these periods the Puranic-Kshatriyas appeared in the literature from amongst these assimilated foreign-blood. They were not Hindus or Vedic-Aryans.

Chandals – Buddhist Literature: In the Buddhist Jataka stories, the Chandals are found to have been imminent and powerful religious leaders. Some of them have been of the high status as *'Arhat'* Shramanas and *Gurus*. One of these Shramanas of repute was Matanga. In the following *gathas* of 'Basalsutta' the stories regarding their power and acceptability are traced:

"Tadamina Pi Janatha Yatha Medang Nidasmanang,
Chandaloputto Sopako Matanga eti Vishmuto.
So Yasang Panamang Patto Matanga Yang Sudullavang,
Aagachhung Tasmupatthang Khaoa Brahmana Bahu."

'Let me illustrate, a Chandal who eats the meat of dogs had a son of high repute called Matanga. That Matanga was exceedingly superior and he earned outstanding merits. A band of Kshatriyas and Brahmans kept themselves stand-by for his services.'

Pali language is the mother of Sanskrit and many other modern Indian languages of North and South.[36] The other name of this language is Prakrit. This was the natural tongue or lingua franca of the subjects of ancient India.

This is why Pali is found to be so similar to Bengali, Hindi and Sanskrit. The mentions and availability of the common noun 'Chandal' in this pre-Sanskrit ancient Indian language prove the existence of this race in very early period.

The aboriginal language of the Indian autochthons was basically of Pali-Prakrit-Kol-Chandali family. The National Professor and linguist, Achariya Suniti Kumar Chattopadhaya. have certified this. "The Aryans came to India with their Vedic language and terribly powerful clannish force. A part of them remained in Persia. But the country was not void, there settled the highly civilised Das or Dravir Jat, may be a bit less developed a race than these called Kol race also lived in the country, they lived all over the territory"...... Before them none of the native groups of Bengal seem to have spoken Aryan language. There lived varieties of Kols and Dravid races in the country. They had everything like their own and separate language, religion, culture, civilisation and way of life with distinct rituals."[37] In the circumstances we may safely infer that when the land was thickly populated with Kols and Chandals and they were highly civilised, the language of the land was bound to be 'Kol-Chandali'.

One very interesting reference can be considered for reaching to the correct conclusion in this regard. Still today, in the grammar of modern Bengali language, the mixture of dialectical form and official pattern or flow of composition of a sentence is not considered correct. It comes under the fallacy called '*Guruchandali Dos*'. Using mixed words from the *Guru* (Sanskrit) and *Chandali* (local-language) is not permitted. Such a proposition would have been redundant had there been no use of *chandali* language. That is the pure (*Guru*/Sanskritised Bengali) form of diction in the sentence had got mixed with *Chandali* language.

In the very ancient tradition of Pali literature the word 'Chandal' has been referred to on several occasions in various contexts as a race, 'Chandal village' 'Chandal Shraman' 'Chandal Guru' 'Chandal Language' 'Chandal King' so on and so forth. These references tend to prove that the Chandals belonged to a powerful ancient race or a nation who had distinct religion, culture and civilisation. Even in the literature of proto-historic period, the Rig Veda we trace the existence of the Chandals. There are mentions of 'Chamar' race as well. One European scholar has opined that the Chamars were the progeny of the union of Chandal and Mallah.[38] Ancestors precede the descendents.

In Pali literature, we find a word, '*Vrishal*' which in Sanskrit literature has been explained as 'Sudra'. This does not appear to be correct. The abusive word is applied to an individual, not a group or a social stratum. The Matanga race in Jataka and other Buddhist literature was also a distinct nation with its separate clan identity; many of the Shramanas of repute are found to be of Chandal-origin. A Chandal named Matanga, a *Shramana*, according to the "Matanga Jatak" compelled a powerful *Shresthi* (Banker) to give his daughter Dristi Mangala by name in marriage to him against her wish as she considered the Chandal monk low. She insulted the monk by calling him Chandal and by washing her eyes and face because of its getting polluted by the sight of the Chandal-monk. Matanga subdued the supercilious Brahmin named Jatimantak along with sixteen thousand Brahmins with his power of penance. The tale of Matanga seems to be of a period when the Aryan Brahmins had already made dent in the society with their culture of hatred and conflict started between the two diametrically opposite faith, Shramana and Brahmana culture.

In the 'Aamra Jatak' (Mango Jatak) a story of a spiritually powerful Chandal who had the miraculous power of spell to produce delicious ripe mangos instantly in the tree in any season has been narrated. One Brahmin after he had served the Chandal and his wife with utmost penance and loyalty succeeded to become his disciple and learnt the spells. The Brahmin, due to his imbibed malicious character, used the spell for commercial purpose. But having been asked by the King, he did not disclose the fact that his guru was a Chandal. Consequently, he lost his wisdom. The 'Swetaketu Jataka' narrates the story of a Chandal boy who defeated the Brahmin student Swetaketu in a quiz contest. The 'Chittasambhuta Jatak' (498) story is very significant due to its rare mentioning of the 'Chandal language'. The story of 'Sevak Jatak' (309) is very interesting for its beautiful story on love and respect to wife and women. The Chandal youth, in the story is found to have finally got appointed as the Police Commissioner of the city by the King. According to the story the Chandal youth is described to be 'Sariputta' of Nalanda who became very close and famous disciple of Gautam Buddha in his next birth. Gautam Buddha himself is found to have had taken birth in the Chandal village in one of the Boddhisattwa life'.

In the latter period also, we find that amidst the tens of thousands of names of monarchs that crowd the columns of history, the name of the greatest monarch comes to be Asoka the Great of Magadhan Empire of 261 BC. The Buddhist monarch too belonged to the Chandal family. That is why he is called '*Chandasok'*. This word might have been used for derogation but it also indicates his clan's name. Cruelty and killings, destruction and damages are pre conditions of big victories in wars. For such acts no other ruler in the world has been abused by name. Neither Parasuram, Arjuna nor Lord Krishna has been called 'Chanda-Parasuram' 'Chandarjun', 'Chanda Krishna' for instigating Arjun to kill 18 Akshouni soldiers along with his all near relations. Right from the King Prasenjit of Magadha in 6th century B.C. to the archaeological relics of the palace of the Chandal King of Bhawal in the Dacca district of Bengal in the A.D. 17th-18th century the saga of the Chandal race shines with glory.

Maiden Effort to Hinduize the Chandals

It has already been observed that the mortal conflicts between the Brahmins and the Chandals remained unsettled till modern era. The Chandal nation have been hideously averse to the Aryan culture that remained protagonist of hatred philosophy of castes. The Brahmins too retaliated with their characteristic ferocity of cultural hatred and servitude. Being inspired with the philosophy of Liberty, Equality and Fraternity; culture of universal love, knowledge and rationality of the social interactions of Buddhism, the society was shaped in consonance with the no-caste cultural structure. The later Mauryas did not discriminate on caste basis and ignored the Brahmin's imbibed and inherent spiritual attitude of caste bias and inhuman policy of graded hatred. Consequently it becamme a serious blunder when they appointed a Brahmin named Pusyamitra to the post of Commander in Chief of the Mauryan army. Due to this '*Sarvajan*' attitude, the Buddhist-Maurya rulers had to pay a heavy and never ending price of damage and destruction to the human civilisation and culture not only of India but also of the whole World.

Pushya Mitra, the Brahmin Commander-in-Chief of the Mauryan army slew the king at the guard of honour and established Sunga dynasty. During his time Manu Smriti was codified. Manu on behalf of Bhrigu Brahmin, went against the directives of Lord Krishna in the Gita and sanctified the cause of greatest sin, the caste-contamination by permitting '*Varna-shankar*' in the law-book. The Divinity itself will incarnate on the Earth repeatedly to save the world. With a view to avoiding the danger of skewed male female ratio of the Kshatriyas after calamity and casualties of war, Lord even suggested burning young widows (*Sati*) on the funeral pyre of their husbands.[39] Gita declared that Lord had created only four Varnas and Varna-Shankar was impossible and would create catastrophe. With the fall of Mauryan dynasty, there came the tyrannical rule of Brahmins in the AD 1st century. They wiped out and completely vandalised Buddha and the Buddhism with an uncompromising and illustrious cruelty. They showed senseless neglect towards the faith that enshrined the liberty and prosperity of immense majority, the Bahujan of the society. They annihilated the universal education system, schools, colleges and Universities along with the Buddhist shrines, Bihars and Monasteries. The Hindu army massacred the Monks and adherents of the Faith.

Nevertheless, Manu codes sanctify the caste-contamination or *Varna-sankara*. He enumerated a long list of *Shankar-Varnas* that came out of inter-Varna consummation instead asking to annihilate the Shankar-Varnas. He seems to have got motivated to Hinduise or hijack these numerically vast, culturally consolidated strong race called Chandal into the body of the Aryan Hindu fold.[40] What cannot be ended must be mended. This was the period of transformation of Buddhist Bharat into Brahmin Bharat. On the one hand, merciless mass killing of Buddhist monks, Bhiksus and Bhiksunis and destruction of their monasteries and literature continued; on the other hand identity of the lay Buddhists was wiped out by including them in Brahmanic fold i.e. caste system. It was not prudent from the part of the Brahmin rulers to let these teeming millions remain as the Buddhists.

Aryanisation of the autochthon Buddhists was attempted through the path or process of casteisation. Caste is the essential and basic identity of an individual in the Brahmanical social order. This is a unique feature of Hindu faith. Besides, a low caste man individually or collectively accept the supremacy of the Brahmins. The process of Sudraisation is a process of enslavement. With a view to enslaving Manu declared the Chandals as the progeny out of Brahmin mother and Sudra father. At the same time all Varna-shankar castes were not declared untouchables.

Yet Manu had utterly failed to achieve his goals of annihilating Chandal's exclusive identity or in wiping out the common noun. We find the existence of Chandals in independent capacity even in the British Raj. They have even been challenging the superiority of the Brahmins throughout history. The greatest challenge had come from Harichand and Guruchand who within one century won their laurel of victory. They in this regard have also procured certificate from the competent authority. C.J. O'Donnel, ICS and the Census Commissioner during 1891 enumeration had recorded his assessment on the Chandals, "Tall and large limbed Chandals were the active and successful enemy of the Aryan invaders."[41] He had also recorded, "The Buddhist sovereigns of the Chandals, known as the Pala dynasty" ruled in Dacca.[42] The relics of the royal palace of the Chandal Raja of Bhawal, Dacca are available even today. The population of the Chandals has been enumerated in large number since the first Census operation during 1871 and 1872. In Bengal, they were enumerated 50 per cent more than the Brahmin population. Chandals were 16,20,545 and the Brahmins were 11,00,149 only. The nation, under the undisputed leader, Guruchand announced their independent identity by claiming a separate community named Matua during the last quarter of the 19th century. He is however, found to have officially accepted, to get rid of hostile circumstances, a new name 'Namasudra' in 1911 for his community which has been traditionally called Chandal. The efforts of the contemporary ruling classes to thrust upon the Chandals, a new name, as per documental records, started at least from 1880.

That this process of hijacking attributed to Manu was artificial and unfounded in history. The Manu Smriti was composed during AD 1st Century. But as has already been discussed, the existence of the Chandal race has been in the proto-historic period, in pre-Aryan India and in the Vedic scriptures. During AD 1st century, Bengal seems to have been left untouched by Nordic race and Aryan culture. There was neither Brahmin nor Sudras in eastern-dark of Bengal. Therefore, in Bengal there was no question of mixture of blood of Brahmins and the Sudras and consequently of no Chandal. In 1883, Rhisi Bankim Chandra Chattopadhay in his article 'Arya and An-Arya' had conclusively recorded, "The three castes Brahman, Kshatriya and Vaisyas are of Aryan stock. They only wear sacred threads (*Upavit*). Sudras are not Aryans. When we find that Kshatriyas never came to Bengal, a few Vaisyas had entered Bengal for commercial activities and Brahmins were also very rare in the 11th century Bengal then it can comfortably be said that nine hundred years ago Bengal was not a land of the Aryans; it was a land of the non-Aryans and relation with the Aryans and Bengal was similar to that of between the Englishmen and India today. That is, before AD 8th century Bengal was a land of *Anariyas* and without a single Brahmin. Had any Brahmin come in Bengal in isolation it would not come under enumeration." Before the 8th century there was no Brahmin society in Bengal."[43] The amazing is the statement from '*Sahitya Samrat*', the creator of the 'Bande Mataram' mantra on this controversial issue. It is decisive. Why and how the Chandals (had they been progeny of Brahmin and Sudra) have been enumerated in so larger number visa-vis the Brahmins during Census operations in Bengal?

There was no Brahmin girl in Bengal before AD 8th century to mother a chandal. However, other records testify the existence of Chandal habitats abundantly in Bengal. The specimen of the oldest Bengali-Oriya literature, the Buddhist gathas called '*Charyapadas*' were uncovered from the Royal Nepal Library by Pandit Haraprosad Shastri in the beginning of the 20th century in 1907. In the small number of couplets of available Charyapadas several references to Chandals and Doms have been traced. It has also been noted that Chandals held honourable position in the *Charyapad* literature. This literature is said to have been composed before AD 9th to 10th century by the literate as well as talented Chandal and Dom poets. It illustrates:

(1) "Kanhe Gai To KamaChandali" (Chandali is a means of penance) "Dombi Ta Aagali Nahi Chhinali."

(2) "Kamala Kulish Majhe Bhai Ma Mitali Samata Jotrna Jalia Chandali." (Chandali lit light of equality)

(3) "Aaji Bhusuk Bangali Bhaili Nia Gharani Chandali Leli." (Chandali is a high spiritual-status)

(4) "Ak So Padma, Chausatti Pakhuri, Tahe Chari Nachatahi *Dombi* Bapuri"

The language is obscure, as it was just born out of Prakrit. Let us have an illustration of Charya Giti. It was composed by Siddhacharya Bhusuk.

"Baj-nawa Pari Panua-Khale Bahiu
Adaya dangale des Luriu
Aaji Bhusuku Bangali Bhaili
Nia Gharani Chandale Leli"

Srikumar Bandhyopadhya has translated the same couplets in different terms and language from Sukumar Sen.[44] "Siddhaachariya Bhusukpad after accepting 'Chandali' as his wife, that is after attaining the knowledge of universality of the creation achieved the highest position (Bengali) in the domain of penance. The author transmitted this glorifying condition."[45]

These couplets discovered by Mahamahopadhaya Pundit Haraprosad Shastri were called as *Charyapadas*, Charyacharyavinischai or Ascharyacharyachai. These are the only specimen of the available earliest Bengali-Oria-literature created by the sons of the soil. In these poems the secret process of spiritual penance in way of Tantric-yoga of the Buddhist sect called *'Sahajjan'* seems to have been described. "The poets of *Chariyapads* have tried to transform the negative aspects of Buddhistic *'Nirvan'* into a positive phenomenon of natural-joy. They rejected the inclination of the Mahajani scholars towards Sanskrit language. Further, they expressed and manifested creativity in Bengali literature for the first time by adopting the traditional language of the common people as its medium for execution. These *Achariyas* of 'naturopathy' (*Sahajachariyas*) remain ever salute-able to the readers of Bengali literature for this work."[46] Acording to Shastri, "the sahajan had three different ways of salvation, the Avadhut-marg; the *Chandali-marg*; and the *Dombi-marg*.... The Chandali lives apart but she has a community to mix with. She therefore not so strong a representative of duality as Avaduti, but she is not yet absolutely one. But *Dombi* lives far away from the inhabited locality and has no society. Therefore to a *Sahajiya* to go to Dombi means to be absolutely undual."[47] From sociological standpoint these observations come to be very significant as both the communities called *Chandals* and *Doms* are found to have played their great role in formation of socio-cultural vibrant life in Bengal-Bihar-Orissa regions by their presence in several millions. These ancient races called the *Chandal* and *Doms* have been Buddhists no doubt. And they possessed high esteem and special social status. Shastri further records, "How Buddhism fared under Brahmanic sway is best evidenced by a study of the Buddhist community in Nepal. To the Brahmin the Buddhists are *'An-achariya'*. ....In Nepal too the Buddhist priests are subject to a greater share of the Brahmin's ire than their lay followers."[48] "The study of Buddhism in Nepal under Hindu supremacy showed that the *'Anachariya'* (untouchables) classes, at least some of them, were the remnants of the Buddhist population. *Sahajiyas* in Bengal has always been regarded as a recent development of Vaishnavism, but the study of ancient manuscripts in Nepal showed that there were *Sahajiyas* also even in the Pala period, and that they were strongly imbued with later Buddhist ideas. The Vaishnava *Sahajiyas* are really a continuation of the old Buddhist *Sahajiyas*."[49]

The language school of *'charyapad'*, at present is claimed to be the original language also of the modern Oriya. The poets were Luipad, Kukkripad,

Sabaripad, Dombipad etc. All these populous ethnic-groups are living in Orissa in big number. They are treated either as Tribes or as untouchable Scheduled castes. Of the Scheduled Caste population the Doms are most numerous; they form around 30 per cent of the untouchables in Orissa. Their profession is mainly boating, fishing, beating drums and playing other musical instruments. They possess the Buddhist cultural heritage (Mohima-dharma) on their background. They very rationally claim that 'Dombipad' one of the '*Dohakar*' of Charya literature was their man. The spiritual-literature was the product of the highly literate Dom community.[50] In the *dohas* also there has been mention of '*Dombi*' (a female Dom) with same importance as the '*Chandali*' (a female Chandal) has been referred to. Some very prominent Bengali linguists have also agreed to the point that '*Charya*' has been the origin of modern Oriya language. The controversy is meaningless and motivated. Let us not forget that before 1911, Orissa was Bengal and Bengal included the area where Doms are found to be predominant. Doms are also in Bengal. Chandals are everywhere. Even in Andhra and other Southern language the word 'Chandal' is used profusely. The word 'Chandal' is at present synonymous to the word 'Dalit' in South India though any particular community called Chandal is not enumerated in the Census in those regions. People refer to whole of the untouchable community (composed of different castes) as 'Chandal'.[51]

The process of enslavement was not a historic process and hence it was left with full of errors. On the basis of statistics only, the historian in Ramesh Chandra Dutta, the 2nd Indian ICS, found heaps of mistakes in the scheme of Varna-shankara propounded by Manu. He opined:

"Manu has it that they (Chandals) are the issues of Brahman women who yielded themselves to the embraces of Sudras. As the number of Brahman in South-Eastern Bengal was never very large in olden times, and does not even in the present day come to even a quarter of a million in the five districts named above, it is difficult to account for the presence of a million Chandals in those districts on Manu's theory. Shall we suppose that fair-skinned Brahmin Desdemona's habitually bestowed their hands on swarthy Sudra swains? Shall we suppose that beauteous but fair Brahman girls were seduced from their parents – by the hundred thousand – by gay Sudra Lotharios intent on creating a new caste? And shall we further suppose that the children begotten of such thrived and multiplied in marshes and fishing villages, amidst toil and privation, more than true-born Brahman children basking in the sun-shine of royal favour and priestly privileges? We have only to state such suppositions to show their utter absurdity; and with this supposition, Manu's theory of mixed caste is brushed aside to the region of myth and nursery tales!"[52]

The historian Ramesh Chandra Dutta, ICS belonged to a low grade of Kayasth, (Sudra) caste. His comment in the book, which was published in

1908, is of great significance. The Chandals had not yet got their new nomenclature Namasudra officially. They along with their Muslim compatriots and comrades were engaged in an uncompromising battle against the Hindu minority who opposed administrative division of Bengal in 1905. They were, in modern age, yet to be Hinduised. No scholar before him could dare operate his pen in so articulated manner in criticizing Manu so mercilessly. Having been terribly frustrated and horrified by the offing prospects of Untouchable-Muslim movements in the democratic India under the leadership of the Chandals and with the execution of administrative-partition of Bengal in 1905, the Hindus accelerated the calculative move to woo and include the brilliant race of the Chandals in the fold of Hinduism. In a later period, Dr Ambedkar on the basis of same numerology commented that the theory of 'mixed' caste in regard to the origin or genesis of Chandals was completely false. In his words, "So vast is the Chandal population that even if every Brahman female was a mistress of a Sudra it could not account for the vast number of Chandals in the country."[53]

There is enough truth in the logic in the above propositions. However, challenging the validity of Manu's theory simply on the basis of population will bear some fallacious factors too as disproportionately heavy number of the Chandals vis-a-vis to the Brahmins may have had many reasons in support of Manu's doctrine. The Brahmin couples were the only source to increase the number of the Brahmins. However, the tribe called Chandals multiplied by its own progeny as well as by the illicit way (Brahmini and Sudra; and Brahmani and Chandal) which must not have been one time affair. There were also some other feeders for augmenting the count of Chandals i.e. many Brahmins directly became Chandal.

In view of the above, the question arises from different angles, as to why Manu the Hindu Law giver had violated the fundamental principle of Hindu socio-spiritual doctrine of society and accommodated these dubious schemes of 'Shankara Varnas'. What made Manu to sanctify the aspects, which went against 'Manuism'.

In the Gita (part of the Mahabharata) Lord Krishna repeatedly reminded Arjun that there was no greater sin than Varna-shankar. Consequently, the Pandava hero refused to fight the battle of Kurukshetra. He appealed to Lord Krishna, "*Strisu Dustasu Barseniyo Jayate Varnashankar. Shankaro Narokaiba Kulaghnang Kulasya Cha. Patanti Pitaro Hyesang Luptapindodkkria*"[54] 'Hei Lord! Due to destruction of the clan's male-folk, the women get corrupt. Resultantly sinful caste contamination arises. In case of caste contamination the killers of caste-men and his ancestors all go to hell.' Despite such a clear picture available what was his compulsion that Manu gave approval in the dangerous scheme of caste-contamination.

Manu stated that Brahmins will leave the land where a Sudra is a King or the country is predominantly inhabited with the Sudra, Chandal or Buddhist, '*Pasandis*'.[55]

In such circumstances what happened to the Brahman society? Had it got paralytic-attack that they failed to arrest the advancing march of their daughters and girls lured by their libido affairs? Did the rulers of the land forgot to fulfill their commitment to the society and Dharma as prescribed even by the so-called secular treaty Arthashastra? Ramachandra killed Shambuk easily for nothing in the name of protecting Brahmin. It is a fact that there was no Hindu ruler to protect the Brahmin Dharma? Why the members of the *trivarna*, the Kshartiya, Vaisya and the Brahmin jointly failed to tackle the heroines of Brahmin caste going to the Sudra youth? What was their connecting point; were they students of same co-education-school or college? All these questions remained un-answered from historical point of view.

Therefore, we find the historian in R.C. Dutta to give the Chandals of Bengal a glowing tribute and honourable position of a race, "Let us next turn to the Chandals of Bengal. They too form a solid body of people numbering a million and a half, and inhabiting mostly the southeastern district of Bengal, Bakergunj, Faridpur and Dacca, Jessore and Khulna. They are patient and hardworking, and unrivalled in boating and fishing; and landlords like to have them as tenants for bringing waste and marshy lands under cultivation. Nevertheless, the Chandals are a soft, timid and submissive race, and bear without a complaint many wrongs from the sturdier Mussulmans of East Bengal. There is a marked family likeness, both physical and mental, among the Chandals, which shows them to be one distinct race."[56]

It has already been shown that since the beginning, all the Census Commissioners held the view that the Chandals were a tribe. In 1872, the Census Commissioner Mr. H. Beverly held, "The Chandals or '*Charals*' aggregate upwards of a million and a half. They seem to be hardy people, semi amphibians almost in their habit, and capable of enduring considerable expose and fatigue.. ... At some remote time they may have been a people of some importance. In the Ramayana the powerful prince of Oudh is represented as courting the alliance of a Chandal Chief Guhaka."[57] Startling tribute of merits of different dimensions of human traits of character and physique has been showered on the Chandal race by the serious thinkers like British Bureaucrats. Amazing past of enormous magnitude of the Chandal nation has been noted.

Hinduisation (Enslavement) in the Modern Time

Necessity is the mother of all creation and inventions. The Brahmins had faced the challenge of supremacy of Buddhism and the Buddhists in ancient period. In the medieval period, they faced a threat of Islamisation of the Indian natives who were ill treated by the Hindu spirituality. They tackled these threats by Hinduizing the common people. A critical necessity for Hinduizing the untouchable population and the Chandals once again became more serious during the second half of the 18th century. The combine strength of the Chandals and the Muslims or the possibility of these autochthons peasantry and producing class termed as 'Depressed classes' by the British administration, coming together on the same platform due to the growing process of democratisation of society and polity with new policies of the British since 1980, became an absolute threat to the Hindu spiritually and the governing class. The British experienced dangerous political developments out of American Revolution or War of Independence (during 1775-83) and in Europe due to the emergences of nationalism, socialism and series of civil wars and revolts triggered off by the poor peasants of France in 1789. At this stage, therefore, they had started contemplating the scheme to maintain control over their colonial market and economy through a subservient agent-government run by a group of people who would be Indians in body and blood but British in soul and spirit. The British who held the tradition of 'Queen's Democracy' decided even to transfer power to the hands of these elite-creamy-layer-Indians groomed and trained by them for Democratic Parliament, the members of which would act as the secretariat of the modern bourgeois.

Democracy needed representation of all groups of the country in the legislature. They started building paraphernalia and entire superstructure of a gigantic system with international net working. One of the parts was information and data analysis. This was initiated through Census Operation. And for the first time census in India was conducted in 1871-72. A democratic setup needs a government, a participatory government of the people. In larger structure, it must be represented by all sections of the people of a country. In local bodies it must be a participatory 'Village *panchyat*' which must involve each and all the adult citizens in the governance of the country. At the apex it is representative of the people who rule the country. It is the politics of number.

Drive behind Hinduisation: The British bureaucrats in 1885 gave the Indian National Congress to the 'Creamy-layer-elites' of India. The Muslims had established their own political party called Muslim League around two decades later in 1906. Hindu Maha Sabha was established in the same year. Guruchand Thakur too started agitation along with the Muslims for the Untouchable's political rights for participating in the governance of the country. A perfect and healthy democratic structure (in political sphere) as in Europe could have developed in India gradually. A strong and healthy nation could have developed in course of time in India. But the British, Brahman and Bania combine (B+B+B) did not allow such thing to come up. The poisonous seeds of separatism and anti-national divisive elements were planted in the name and form of (Hindu) nationalism in the pre-feudal body polity of India.

As a natural corollary, manipulation took its reign in the Census operation and enumeration from the beginning, despite the impartial sincerity of a band of Imperial British bureaucrats. In the beginning, the enumeration in Census Report showed it's counting under the following columns, Hindus, Muslims, Sikhs, Christians and Anglo-Indians under the head "Population by Religion". But for the first time on 1st October 1906 'the nobles, jagirdars, taluqdars, lawyers, zaminders, merchants and others representing a large body of the Mahomadan subjects of His Majesty' under the leadership of Aaga Khan submitted to the then Viceroy Lord Minto at Simla an 'Address' for securing adequate representation of the Muslim Community. The address reads: "The Mohammedans of India number, according to the census taken in the year 1901 over sixty-two millions or between one-fifth and one-fourth of dominions, and if a reduction be made for the uncivilised portions of the community enumerated under the heads of animist and other minor religions, as well as for those classes who are ordinarily classified as Hindus but properly speaking are not Hindus at all, the proportion of Mohammedans to the Hindu Majority becomes much larger. We therefore, desire to submit that under any system of representation extended or limited a community in itself more numerous than the entire population of any first class European power except Russia may justly lay claim to adequate recognition as an important factor in the State." The Untouchables of Bengal from Orakandi too in the same year sent their representation to the governor of Assam Bengal Government that they were in no way Hindu, they were completely a different community and they demanded 'special political privileges' similar to the Muslim community.

In pursuance of this address and demands of the Untouchables of Bengal, E. A. Gait, ICS, the (1911) Census Commissioner enumerated the erstwhile so-called Hindu population in three heads i.e. the untouchables (semi-Hinduised tribes); the animists/ tribal (non-Hinduissed tribes) and the Hindus. As a result the proportion of population of the Muslims surely increased but more important factor in Indian democratic movement that emerged out of this Census Report was that the Untouchables became officially a distinct factor in demanding their share in the governance of the instrumentalities of the State. But the problems of stupendous and difficult task of deciding as to who were and who were not Untouchable was magically solved by the experienced and learned bureaucrat. On the basis of the following 10 points criteria the Untouchable communities were recognised and their population was counted, segregating them from the fold of the Hindus, for the first time in the Census of 1911:

(i) Those who decline the supremacy of the Brahmins

(ii) Those who do not take Mantra or *Diksa* from a Brahman or a Hindu Guru

(iii) Those who do not accept the authority of the Vedas

(iv) Do not worship the Hindu gods and goddesses

(v) The people in whose house good Brahmins do not attend as a priest

(vi) Those who had no Brahmin priest
(vii) Those who were denied entry in a Hindu temple
(viii) Those who create pollution with their sight or touch
(ix) Those who bury their dead
(x) Those who do not believe cows as sacred and who eat beef.

All these traits of socio-cultural phenomenon that were covered in the above mentioned ten points were not merely theoretical or speculative phenomenon. The Census Commissioner collected these social phenomena out of the alive social and palpable political movements and agitations created by the Untouchables of Bengal in the contemporary period. Similar socio-economic and political agitations existed in several other states like Trivankur, Punjab, Madras, Andhra of contemporary India. These traits were also available easily in the vibrant social and cultural tradition of interactions in the contemporary period. Even children in rural Bengal used to chant the rhyme, "*Kalir Bamun Dhora Sanp, Je Na Mare Tari Pap*" (The Brahmins of modern period are non-venomous snakes. One who does not kill it commits sins) during their play.[58] The untouchables were regarded by the British Government as Depressed Class and the year 1911 thus became the turning point of Indian history.

Indeed, this census enumeration was one of the tangible and success results of the ceaseless struggles by the combine forces of the Muslims and the Untouchables of Bengal for liberation from the Brahmanical thralldom. Only within next two decades, they became the third major group to aspire share for political power in the governance of the country in the London Round Table Conference.

The untouchable population in major provinces in 1911 was found[59] as follows: Assam 0.3 million 5.0 per cent Bengal 9.9 million 22 per cent; Bombay 0.6 million 3.08 per cent; Central Prov. 3.7 million 30.83 per cent; Madras 6.3 million 15.83 per cent; Punjab 1.7 million 8.72 per cent; U.P. 10.1 million 21.49 per cent; Bihar and Orissa 32.4 million 28.70; all India 18.94 per cent.

For the last four decennial censuses, the Hindus never objected on the modality of enumeration. Now when the untouchables were identified as a separate group the Hindus opposed the move. They got seriously cautious and conscious about the possible future impact of this block of people in the democratic frame. Long after, Dr Ambedkar analysed the issue of numerical position of the Untouchables in the following terms: "This operation came soon after the address given by Muslim community to Lord Minto in 1906 in which they asked for a separate and adequate representation for the Muslim community. The Hindu smelt a rat in it. The Census Commissioner observed,

"Incidentally, the enquiry generated a certain amount of heat, because unfortunately it happened to be made at a time when the rival claims of

Hindus and Mohammedans to representation on the Legislative Councils were being debated and some of the former feared that it would lead to the exclusion of certain classes from the category of Hindus and would thus unfavourably on their political importance......".[60]

That day when the demands were raised to count the Untouchables and Tribals under separate heads none perhaps could have had remotely imagined that they were going to give birth to a strong 'Third Front' of untouchable-power in Indian Democracy. None could have visualised that the ongoing movements of the Chandal peasantry of East Bengal under the leadership of Guruchand Thakur would soon turn into a political wild-fire throughout the Indian territory and eventually the ancient nation of single geographic mass would be vivisected into three different and hostile sovereign countries. And the strongest philosophical theses supporting vivisection of the country would be delivered in 1940 in Thoughts on Pakistan, the leviathan by the untouchable leader in Dr Ambedkar.

Modality of Hinduisation of the Untouchables: With a view to countering the move of the Muslims to reduce the Hindu-population in Indian Census report, the Brahmins immediately made the anesthetic-devise to Hinduize and absorb and assimilate the vast chunk of the Untouchables or the 'Depressed Classes' in the Hindu camp. The bloodless and painless device to retain the subdued and disdained nation and races as Hindu was the process of changing their clan-name with a caste-name of Hindu label. So after being *Nama-'Sudra'* officially they became an integral part of the Hindus even though they appeared in the census reports under the column "Religion" separate from the Hindus.

The Chandals of turbulent and of independent nature after becoming Namo-Sudras lost their fighting-spirit against injustice, inhumanity and oppression of Hinduism. The law is, 'Hatred begets hatred'. Nevertheless, Sudras never can rebel against their Sudrahood. They remain within. Opposite and equal reaction of an action is available only when they mutually act from outside. In course of time, these non-Hindu and non-Aryan ethnic groups got semi-Hinduised once again. Already they were forcefully merged in Hindu political-population by giving Separate Electorate to the Muslims in the Government of India Councils Act 1909. Muslims were isolated in the political arina. As Nama-Sudra (of lowest grade) the former Chandals, now were placed on the lowest rung of the social hierarchy. Thus, they were unconsciously made to accept the political-suzerainty of the Brahmins. Panchanan Sarkar, a talented Rajbansi (Koch) became the first Untouchable Graduate in 1893. The Rajbansis were anointed as *'Rajbansi-Kshatriya'* by a band of Brahmins who came from Kashi through a prolonged and expensive Vedic-Yadna that was conducted on the bank of River Karotoa in 1912. They were given holy thread of the Brahmin and a new surname, Varma.

Thakur Panchanan Barman (Sarkar) now preached that 'it was the duty of the Kshatriyas to shed their blood to protect the interest of the Brahmins.' The Pods of south Bengal were declared as 'Poundro-Kshatriya'. The outstandingly marshal race called the 'Dusads' were also brought in this process of Hinduisation when we find them appealing to the Government to change their community's name as 'Dusad Kshatriya'. This process continued on national level.

Indeed, a small section of the Brahmin-British elite are found to have managed to inspire a few newly educated Chandals to launch a stir called "Status (caste) Elevation Struggle" and put demands and prayers for changing the original ethnic name Chandal by a new Hinduised nomenclature. In Sylhet it was an educated *Moktar* in the Court who made an appeal in 1881 to this effect. Promptly positive steps were taken by the lower level Officer. In reality, their status in the social hierarchy altered in no way by this self-insulting movement of the semi-literate-untouchables. The Hindus treated them in no different way. All the members of these ethnic groups remained pure Untouchables and were treated as untouchables by the Hindus. The drama was staged in such cunning way that the process of Hinduisation through casteisation was done notionally in official records. Neither the Muslims had anything to object nor did the untouchables have any grievances.

On the other hand the social consolidation that started growing amongst all the untouchables of Bengal since 1880's, and which was a requisite pre-condition to fight for regaining their lost rights through the democratic process was seriously fractured. The oneness amongst the victims of Brahmanical caste system like Chandal-Pods, Koch-Rajbansi and Chandal-Namasudras were fragmented with the walls of speculative walls of superiority and inferiority. All remained untouchables. However, the first two from North Bengal and South Bengal were declared Kshatriya with notional weight-age while Namasudras were placed on lower pedestal. The fanciful poison of superiority or inferiority slowly damaged the whole process of a united liberation movement of the downtrodden. Instead of creating the bridges of brotherhood amongst the downtrodden or producer depressed classes they built up strong Chinese-walls of division on the basis of virulent psychology of baseless inferiority and superiority of Hindu castes. Eventually the consolidation of the political liberation movement of the working and exploited untouchables under the banner of parliamentary democracy got gradually shattered to doom. The oppressed people got socially and politically disintegrated. They also got alienated from their natural ally, the Muslims in political arena.

Enslavement by the Creamy-layer Hindu and British Elite

On the pretext of an insignificant appeal from one individual, an Assistant Commissioner in the District is found to have very obviously instructed lower employees, "The Namasudras must always be written and not *Change* or *Chandal* for all persons of the said caste. Deputy Commissioner has ordered that anyone who does not write Namasudra shall be removed from employment." Mr. W. C. Macpherson, the Assistant Commissioner of Sylhet (Assam) in the Eastern Bengal, is understood to have simply resorted to implement the order of the District Commissioner vide the Notice dated 9.9.1882. This order was issued soon after the Census of 1881 in a district where Chandals were predominant. He had recorded punitive measures too for the defaulter employees. However, it was a fact that even in the succeeding decennial Census reports of 1891 and 1901, the community have not been enumerated plainly as Namasudras by the mush higher Competent authority. The Census Commissioners of 1881and 1901 as well as the author of 'Tribes and Castes of Bengal' H.H. Risley carefully mentioned these ethnic groups as race not caste. Why then either the Deputy Commissioner or his subordinate Mr. Macpherson in direct violation of the much superior Officer, the Census Commissioner issued such sensitive and important order that pertained to the entire Bengal or the Eastern region of India and on a matter, which came under the jurisdiction and competency of the Census Commissioner? On record, other than an appeal from a *Moktar*, named Khusiram, there is no reference to any popular agitation or demands in the district in contemporary period from amongst the Chandals in this regard. It is also not on records as to whether Mr. Macpherson was show caused for such peculiar act of breach of discipline and insubordination.

In this context, we come across another bureaucratic correspondence from Mr. F. B. Peacock, the Commissioner of the Presidency Division. He had written vide his letter dated 18th July 1881, to the Secretary (General Dept.) Bengal Government, "The improvement in the condition of the Chandals who are the chief agriculturists in Narail subdivision has led them to aspire to a superior status in Hindu caste system. They now call themselves Namasudra and profess Vaishnav".[61] The letter discloses two obvious aspects firstly, that the original name of the community was Chandal and that the acquired 'improved condition' in the society; and secondly that such dignified status they sought to have within the Hindu caste system. There was no resentment or aversion for their being treated as subhuman and untouchables by the Hindus. That is why they are found to have called themselves as Namasudra and Vaishnav. There is no hint of any type of agitation on such demands.

Those who were Chandals in 1872 and in 1881 Census became Chandals or Namasudra in 1891 and Namasudra /Chandal in 1901. The same people were recorded as Namasudras in the 1911 Census. It took four decades for evolution of Chandals into Namasudra. Caste was created by God and it is not in any way, a product out of evolution. In this process of gradual change we do not find any universal, steady and confident strength behind the demands for change of community name either from the Chandal community or from the Ruling classes or from the Brahmins. It is on record that from Orakandi, the head Quarter of Matua socio-religious movement in Faridpur district of Bengal, one memorial dated April 1901 was submitted to His Excellency the Lieutenant Governor of Bengal. The memorial was drafted in beautiful words and in an exceedingly articulated language. It is not known which experienced hands were behind the drafting. Though contradictory to the Matua faith, at the outset the memorial claimed, "That the Nama-Sudras follow the tenets of Hindu religion and perform marriage, shradh and other ceremonies according to Hindu….. That the Nama-Sudras are chiefly agriculturists, although many of them are Zamindars, Talukdars Traders….. That the humble memorialists answer the Puranic caste *Kudar* and have been certified by many distinguished Brahmin Pundits of Bengal to be identified by the caste…. So as to draw a clear line of separation between Nama-Sudra and Chandals and that their caste may in future be designated as Nama-Sudra or *Kudar* but not as Chandals." Once again another memorial is found to have sent to the Lieutenant Governor of Bengal from Gopalgunge, Faridpur in the month August, 1901. The draft is almost a copy of the earlier one barring a few minor changes. It prays to designate their caste "as Nama-Sudra, and not as Chandal."

But six years later, 'the representatives of the Namasudra community of the Eastern Bengal and Assam' submitted a 'humble appeal to the Government' through the Lieutenant Governor of Eastern Bengal and Assam. In this appeal in the newly created province the approach was diametrically opposite and firm in its approach. In the new politico-administrative circumstances their confidence and clarity on the subject became sharper and to the point. In para 5 of the draft it held, "We beg to add that, though our religious rites and their observances, and social customs are similar to those of the high caste Brahmins, we have not the slightest connection with any of the Hindu communities. We are not allowed to join them in their social and religious ceremonies. They have been continuously looking down upon us with contempt and malice; have kept us under subjection and total ignorance. It is absolutely absurd to anticipate that they would, in future, mix with us in social and religious performances. Thus we desire to be recognised by the Government as entirely a different community having separate claim to political privileges like Mohamedans."[62] Along with the demand for getting the political privilege of 'Separate Electorate' to burst the core of the problems of the Chandals, the appeal demanded to be recognised in the Census enumeration as Brahmin, "as the Namasudra Brahmin." Along with this appeal they furnished '*VYAVASTHA*' or certificate given by Mahamohopahhaya Rashmohan Sarbabhoum and countersigned by other forty *Pundit* Brahmins of Bengal. None, however, was from elite Kolkata or its surrounding regions.

What prompted the big-boss Brahmins, the policemen of the temporal and celestial world of the Hindus, the dreaded persecutors of humanity to come down to shower the lowest of the low, the 'Orphans of the World' named Chandals with meritorious virtues of the holy Brahmins? The answer appears to be in the chronology and demographic factor of Bengal politics. In the newly created province Eastern Bengal and Assam the untouchables were around 28 per cent and the Muslims formed another 68 per cent of the total population. Hindus became an abject minority. Besides, by the time, the Muslims launched their political party, Muslim League. (In the undivided Bengal Hindus were only 18 per cent, Muslims 55 per cent and Untouchables 24.7 per cent) In such circumstances, the Brahmins made their desperate attempts to include the Chandals in their fold at any cost. Necessity knows no law. Brahmins came in lot from Kashi to declare Koch-Rajbansis as *Kshatriya* at this precarious point of time, neither before nor after.

However, the traits of a martial race (*Kshatriya*) are found to be amazing degree and in full brim in the Chandal or Namasudra community. They very easily parallel to the Santhals and the Sikhs of Western India in courage and martial-skill. Even their girls are equally skillful beside their male folk in the battle fields. They are the '*Dhalis*' (those who held *Dhal* i.e. shield; shield-bearers) of Bengal. They are out-standing in hitting the target even throwing their spheres and javelins of around 2 feet length called '*Kuras*' simultaneously with their legs and hands. During those days not only intellectuals, historians, sociologists and anthropologists but the Sanyasis too came down to certify the non-Sudra traits of character of the untouchables. Swami Pranabananda, the founder of the Bharat Sevasram Sangha certified, "Amongst the scheduled castes of Eastern Bengal the Namasudras are most powerful and uprising.... Out of them only the '*Kshatriya-Shakti*', martial-power of the Kshatriya will emerge and will glorify the entire Hindu-nation once again."[63] It is interesting to note that neither the Chandals claimed nor the Brahmins ever resorted to certify the children of 'Namas Muni' who are found, in the story, to have most of the time the rulers in different kingdoms as Kshatriyas the rulers of the country. In that case it would have fulfilled (and would have been in consonance with) the political wish of Guruchand who dreamt to make his people '*Taja*' and '*Raja*'. It would have also added a tremendous lustre of consolidation between the Koch-Rajbansi of North-Bengal and the Poundras of south-Bengal with the Namasudras, all as Kshatriyas. However, it would have proved the biggest bolt from blue for the creamy-layer elite-castes.

The Brahmanical society conspired and added fuel to the fire to change nomenclature in the pretext of elevating social status in the higher strata of caste-pyramid without struggle and without enhancing merit. Now, the Office of the Census Commissioner assumed the status of God-hood and created castes or Varnas anew. Many of the ethnic groups who would be numerically meaningful in the democratic ballot-box became mad to submit their representations to the Commissioner of the Census. The appeals which were submitted to the Census Office from different communities for changing their old name in 1911 weighed around 60 KGs.[64] The Kayasths, Pods, Koch-Rajbansis, Mahesyas etc wanted to be *Kshatriya*; Vaidyas, Namasudras, Hanri etc wanted the status of a *Brahmin*; Kapalis, Basaks, Suvarnabaniks, Sahas etc wanted to be *Vaisya* and the Sudras were abundant. It is good that there arose waves of sudden impulse of craze for social mobility by defying the spiritual injunctions. This was attempted not through the process of constant struggle but with the blessings of the Brahmin Bhudevatas. The social mobility is the result of a constant class struggle. Therefore, instead of gaining desired boon the working class people, composed of *Kisan-Kamar-Chamar-Chandal-Mali-Malla-Majhi-Lohar-Sonar-Dhobi-Nai*-fishermen-boat-men or the wealth producer masses got permanently divided into several hostile and warring camps with hatred towards each other and claimed superiority over each other. This is the natural concomitant of caste system. It divides and does not unite. The Untouchables of Bengal started splitting into water-tight factions of castes of higher and lower grade and inferior status and selfish-interest to be engaged in internecine quarrel. The neighbours became enemy and the heavenly Brahmins became the friend-philosopher, leader and Gurus to liberate in this world and in the next. As faithful Hindu, they were groomed to be anti-Muslim, anti-Christian and anti-Sikh. Consequently, the favourable circumstances for the growth of Indian Nationalism rather 'Bharatiya jatiyata' through belongingness of all Depressed and servile classes irrespective of Dalits, Hindus, Muslims and tribals in the coming period got heavy hindrance and jolt.

That the change of name of a caste failed to change the heart of a Brahmin or the divine dictate of the Hindu scriptures is evident in the history of society. The motto of issuing the covenant of caste-system was to make the divine-slaves permanent. The caste is to perpetuate. It cannot be changed by simply changing its label. The 'All Bengal Namasudra Association' expressed their grievances and demanded democratic rights in a memorandum to the Simon Commission in 1929. The memorandum holds, "The caste system stigmatised these classes as untouchables as water touched by these classes of people is not drunk by the so called higher castes. Their presence in a room is said to pollute water and cooked food. They are not allowed to enter the public temples.... Though these suppressed classes are classed and reckoned as Hindus they are denied all rights as Hindus and are really treated as people outside the pale of Hinduism." These Chandals, thus, simply are found to have allowed the 'KABAB' to use them for the benefits of the Brahmanical classes. Mukunda Behari Mullick, the gem of the Chandals deposed his statement in the Simon Commission as oral evidence, "I myself had the experience in my boy hood. We have to wait outside (class room) where water is kept till a caste-Hindu friend comes and puts water in our hands." The proceedings of Bengal Legislative Assembly in 1938 reveal a strange fact in its support. Not just an ordinary Namasudra, even the police constables of British Calcutta police force, belonging to the Namasudra caste caused pollution for other constables in the same hostel or Police-barrack. When the allegation was raised by Jogendra Nath Mandal, in the House, the then Home Minister Sir Khaja Nizamuddin made an inquiry. The fact was established. And as a remedy[65] the Principal of the Calcutta Sanskrit College gave the verdict that, "In case there was sky above (top-floor) and the rooms were of bricked walls then there occurs no pollution." In the circumstances, it is obvious that it was a process of enslavement rather than the move of status elevation by changing mere the traditional community name.

It is, however, amazing to note that the Gurus of all the '*Varnas*', the creators of all these Sanskrit scriptures and lord of the spirituality and temporal world came down individually and in groups to don the Chandals as Brahmins during these days. Nobody ventured to question, why? Why the foxes adopted the welfare scheme for the hens? On the one hand, they taught Hindus to practice caste and untouchability scrupulously. On the other hand they certified that the race who "From time immemorial (the Chandals) have been despised by the upper class Hindu and a Brahman thought himself defiled by even treading the shadow cast by the body of a Chandal"[66] were none but Bhudevata and holy Brahmins. Even Guruchand seems to have ignored to catch its impact. He too did not object to accept such an insulting term like '*Namate*' or Namasudra for the great race.

It was obvious that a common noun was not the essence of caste, caste hatred or of caste discrimination. The genesis of caste was religion, spirituality or God. The motive of caste, the operative organ of the Hindu-engine of oppression was to exploit people facing minimum or no resistance by keeping the ignorant in perpetual ignorance and the weak in permanent weakness. Therefore, by changing the nomenclature a Hindu cannot avoid impact of caste. The Chandals too did not get any elevation in any respect. They were simply brought under the system of coercive exploitation and slavery supported by the hate philosophy. It is noteworthy that the galaxy of Brahmins with excellent scholarship and recognition had gladly issued one after another certificate, as has already been mentioned, to the untouchable Chandal community for further use:- "The caste called Namasudra is Brahman by origin being descended from the great Brahmin, Kashyapa and not "Chandal". 'Bipratulyaschouchabhagitwang Manutwachandalatwa Pratipadcrura Karmadi Tatha Kesanchit Pakkannidina Sraddhakartritwwasbarnaccha…..' They were so blind-folded in issuing the certificates that contradictions in it were over looked. 'Caste called Namasudra were not Namasudras they were Brahmins and they were not Chandals. The

Brahmins did not get hindrances in collecting all supporting documents in the holy scriptures in favour of the Chandals. The principle of democracy, 'One man one vote and one man one value' haunted and prompted the Brahmins of those days to behave as catalysts in the process. The certificates were signed by the team composed of Shiroratnopadhik Sri Shishir Kumar Sharmanam, Vidyabhusanopadhik Sri Mohimchandra Sharmanam, Tarkapanchanopadhik Sri Visweswar Sharmanam, Vidyaratnopadhik Dwarikanath Sharmanam, Nayratnopadhik Sri Umakanta Sharmanam, Tarkoratnopadhik Janakinath Sharmanam, Tarkoratnopadhik Sri Shashibhusan Sharmanam, Vedantaratnopadhik Sri Krishna Das Sharmanam, Nayabhusanopadhik Sri Shambhu Charan Sharmanam and such more big Sharmanams. These scholar Pundits belonged to and represented different districts of Bengal like Kotalipara, Dalairdanga, Nayakandi, Pangsa, Kumarkhali, Narail, Chandsi, Shantipur, Kalgaria, Barakair, Binnafair, Mathurabhangar, Aalishakanda, Deuli, Kustia, Hatail and Samudnagar. It is surprising that in the long list of these 40 Sharmanams there was none from Calcutta zone like Ganguly, Sanyal, Mookerjee, Banerjee, Chatterjee etc who belonged to 'Kulin' Brahmins. In 1901, the Chandals of Orakandi, Dacca, Faridpur, Bakharganj, Jessore, Khulna, Pabna etc submitted a memorandum requesting to change their name as Namasudra. Along with the appeal these certificates were annexed. These Brahmin Pandits and scholars are famous to have got the capacity for doing anything and everything by taking bribes.[67]

Other intellectuals were also engaged in researching to reach to a truth to this end. Achariys Suniti Kumar Chatterjee drew out attention towards the issue in 1921, "A new discipline called Anthropology tends to say that from the stand points of physical structure-formation, similarities and closeness what are observed between the Brahmins and the low-caste Kayasth, Navasakha, Namasudra are not found between the Bengali Brahmins and the pure Kanoujiya-Brahmins of Aryavarta. This is a matter of concern."[68] And in the end of the 40's decade of 20th century Bengal, Dr Nihar Ranjan Roy in his famous book, 'Bangalir Itihas', categorically recorded, "The anthropological findings on the Namasudras are very curious. From the stand point of physical features their relation with the elite-Brahmins of Northern India is closer than the relation of the Bengali Brahmins and Kayasths and Vaisyas with the Brahmins of UP. But the Namasudras belong to the lowest stratum of the present day Hindu society. We know them as Chandal or '*Charal*'. There is no consistency found in this social position and the findings of the anthropological studies."[69] After partition of India, however, such attempts to anoint the social position of the Chandal/ Namasudras have gone into oblivion.

One of the distinguished Namasudra intellectuals from Bangaladesh has mentioned some incidents, which had some historic relevance behind the changing of nomenclature in his book.[70] This incident may be taken as one of the pinpointing factor for the name of the community as Namasudra. It is found that the Namasudras endeavored to gain the highest social status from the British authority as Brahmin Aryans which was ratified by the Brahmins, the trusted agents of the British. For this purpose they managed to have scriptural support, whatever might have been its value as a holy shastra. It was the Sanskrit 'Shakti Sangam Tantra'. Nadiar Chand Sarkar the father of the author of the book was one of the members of the team which was sent to collect the book. The incident was:

"In 1882 Khulna district was created by taking Satkhira, Bagerhat and Khulna Sadar subdivisions. Earlier, the subdivisions were with Jessore. The concerned Commissioner of Presidency Division (an English man) was stationed at Calcutta. He used to travel from Calcutta to Khulna occasionally to look after the developmental works like establishment of offices, courts, and road construction etc for the new District. The scheme of construction of road from Khulna to Satkhira via Daulatpur was taken up in those days. The work of pilling up of mud to construct the road too started. The Rangpur area adjacent to Daulatpur on the stretch of the road was an expanse of low-land, marshy and jungle. Consequently, the progress of work of construction of the road halted at the point of Rangpur. In such condition a wealthy and philanthropic Namasudra zamindar named Jivan Joddar at his own expense cleared the jungle, filled the low swampy lands with earth and completed the proposed road in 1887. (This portion of the road is known today as Jivan babu's road) On receiving the news of the completion of the road by this manner, the Commissioner had invited Jivan Babu to greet him with thanks. He also requested to take refund of the expenses for the government work. But Jivan Babu declined to receive money. As a result being exceedingly glad the Commissioner nominated Jivan Babu as a Hon'able member of the 'Development Committee' set up to supervise the developmental activities for the district. Being invited by the Commissioner, Jivan Babu attended the Meeting. But those were the days of the caste-Hindus. The Committee was composed of only the Brahmins, Kayasth and Vaidyas. Namas / Chandals were considered low in those days. Therefore, it became irritating for others to have a '*namo*' member to take part in the meeting as one of them equal.

In the next meeting when Jivan Babu appeared, all tendered a mass petition before the Commissioner. It was alleged that Jivan Babu was a Namasudra, a Chandal and without any religion. They did not have any rituals of purification, any priests, any washer-man a barber to serve them. They did not follow any system or even any specific profession. It was not possible to sit with him on equal status. It was below dignity. Quick redressal was sought. Jivan Babu's view points on the allegations were called for by the Commissioner. Jivan Babu requested for six month's time to file his reply..........

The social turmoil might have had slowed down in front of the sympathetic and already satisfied British administrator with the story of 'Saktisangam Tantra'.[71] Nobody had ever seen the book. Such cock and bull stories are available abundantly in the store of Sanskrit literature. There is no historic perspective in the story and it is to be easily believed by the credulous people like Indian masses.

The Shakti Sangam Tantra has, however, been referred to by the celebrati author Mahamahopadhyay Haraprosad Shastry who had in the introduction to the book titled 'The Modern Buddhism and its followers in Orissa' written in 1911, "The Cakti-Sangam tantra, a later work, declares that the object of that Tantra is to rout out Buddhism and establish Brahmanism."[72] As a result whatever has been written in the Tantra which was not dispassionate on discussing the main subject, 'Tantra', it is to be carefully studied. Brahmanisation, Hinduisation or enslavement has been the target of the book and the Chandals got trapped into it. In this Shakti Sangam Tantra, it is interesting to observe that the mention of the Pods or the Poundra Kshatriya had also been made. There is a proverb that 'Pods were originally the half-brothers of the Chandals'. Bankim Chandra Chatterjee too mentioned that the Pods were Chandals in his story Ramdhan Pod.[73] Such is the overwhelming impact of the Chandal race in Bengal's social interactions and culture that none of the modern literates of Bengal including Rabindra Nath Tagore or Swami Vivekananda failed to make good mentions of the Chandals or their ancient traditional stories. The dance-drama called 'Chandalika' reveals not only their remote ancestry in pre-Gautama-Buddha era but also their strong and unique position.

How a state which had been condemned by the Aryan scriptures as a non-Aryan and fallen state, away from Arya-varna could ever been flooded with Brahmin population? Therefore, it would be a high misnomer to say that the Chandals were ever Brahmins. The protagonists of the Chandal's Brahmin theory blindly overlooked all such negative-factors that the Namasudras had no permission to enter Hindu-temples, schools, houses of good Hindus, learn Sanskrit, get a government job. These were the prerogatives of the Brahmins.

They banked only on the ten-day' '*sradh*' ceremony. They over looked the fundamental principle in the existing pattern of relation between a Brahmin and a Sudra. With the rise of Sudra Shambuk comes there the immature death of the Brahmin boy and with the beheading of Sudra Shambuk the dead Brahmin regains his life. The moral of the story of the epic Ramayana is classic to understand the situation. How can the tribe of great Harichand, the deliverer of the downtrodden belong to such a heartless marauder Brahmin race. Brahmins are foreign Aryan intruders in our country. It is they who vandalised Indian Assura civilisation on the banks of Indus Rivers; they colonised their settlements in *Aryavarta*. As a result the classified

Sanskrit literature is bereft of a word like 'Patriotism', '*Desprem*', '*Deshbhakti*', motherland and fatherland. They are not the sons of this soil. But the modern day Namasudras are the autochthons of the country. Harichand was born to fulfill the dreams and mission of Lord Buddha in a Chandal family. While the Brahmins destroyed, eliminated Buddhists and Buddhism from India. How can the tribe of Hari-Guruchand be Brahmin?

During the period when Bengal was inundated with the waves of 'name-changing struggle' in 1910-11, the ethnic and occupational groups like Kayasth, Mahisya, Rajbansi, Pod-Poundra, Handi etc. wanted themselves to be enumerated as Kshatriya. Total population of Kshatriyas in non-Vedic Bengal then comes to be about 35 per cent and Brahmins to 55 per cent of the total population. In such circumstances the Sudras and Vaisyas are reduced to microscopic minority.

The traits of character of the Namasudras or of the Chandals are diametrically opposite to the imbibed virtues and active tendencies of the Arya-Brahmins. The Chandals or the Namasudras belong to the most diligent working class, they are the producers of wealth and proud to uphold the dignity of labour. They on the contrary enjoy difficult and hard manual work. They are most humane with heart-full virtues of love, compassion and creativity. They are benevolent in nature. They feel proud and lucky to earn their own bread by the sweat of their brow. They are independent in their individualistic character. They are the most challenging, adventurous and pragmatic in their approach in life style. Their society is empowered and glittered with luster of high-status of their women. In contrast to the traits of characteristics of the Chandals/ Namasudras, the Brahmins are the embodiment of fossils of most orthodox tradition. They are unscientific and superstitious. The Brahmins are supercilious disproportionately. They are matchlessly avaricious, greedy and liars. The Brahmins are a caste who live on others' income. As a religious and spiritual right they beg alms and they have taught through their scriptures to others to offer them alms as a meritorious and spiritual duty. Alms-giving to a Brahmin is meritorious per-excellence. They are the parasites of the society. They hate labour and consider productive activities a matter below dignity. They exploit surplus of others. They are heartless cruel creatures[74] and do not even have any feelings for the women folk. At the death of their son-in-law, father, brother-in-law they burn down their daughter, mother and sister respectively alive in the funeral pyre. The Brahmins are bereft of any creative quality. How can such contrasting groups belong to the same stock!

The Chandals were characteristically charming race having skill of amphibian and the imbibed virtues of love, fraternity, equality, truthfulness, vigour and valour, humane, philanthropic, extremely hard-working, diligent and sincere; they are worshippers of freedom, profound freedom. Standing on the principle of dignity of labour, the exceedingly skilled Chandals/

Namasudras stands just diametrically opposite to the Brahmins who are cheats and economic parasites of the society who believe in the philosophy of hatred and gave birth to the first traitors of the country in *'Bhakta Prahlad'* and *Bajrangbali Hanuman*. How can the brave-hearts scrupulous race like Chandal/Namasudra would like to be of the Brahmin origin? The Census Commissioner Mr. L.S.S. O'Meli, ICS had made a comparative study to understand the criminality and its impact amongst Indian castes. He has concluded: "The number of Muslim and Hindu convicts in Bengal is almost exactly proportionate to their strength in the population.... The largest numbers of Hindu criminals are Kayasthas and Brahmins." Why to enroll the Chandals (Namasuds) in the gang of the criminals? The world cannot forget the horrors of '*Sati*', a system of burning of women alive in husband's pyre, the '*Kulin*', a prestigious system of polygamy, permanent widow-hood, system of child-marriage, the institution of untouchibility that were the business of the Brahmins. Why and how the brave-hearts, nothing-daunting warrior-race like Chandal-Namosudra, be identified as tricky and treacherous Brahmins? Who would like to identify themselves with such a Brahmin group who gave birth to and have been proudly up-holding such thousands of barbaric institutions even in the age of electronic media? Brahmins remain afar and above all others. They are distinct and different from others around them.

References

1. Swami Vivekananda, (Narendra Nath Dutta) Swadesh Mantra, Vol. 4, pp. 479-80; Translated from Bengali.
2. Complete Works of Swami Vivekananda, Vol. 3, p. 295.
3. *Ibid*, Vol. 5, p. 214.
4. Mamata Banerjee, the Union Railway Minister after an odious long 80 Km travel by the Jessore road through rural bumpy Bengal paid a visit to *Bara Ma* at Thakurnagar village, North 24 Parganas, the present day Headquarter of the Namasudra (Chandal) *Matuas* during their three-day '*Baruni*' festival in the mid-March 2010. She touched the feet of the holy-lady of the Untouchables for her blessings. Another Brahmin leader Comrade Subash Chakraborty (CPM) too went to Thakurnagar to get her blessings. Photos in the daily news papers like Ananda Bazar etc of next day may be referred to.
5. Gita, 1/41-43.
6. Manu, 10/30.
7. Sukla Yajur Veda, 30/20/10 *Kanda* 22, Mantra 177.
8. Manu Smriti, 10/3-4.
9. Published in 1948, p. 14.
10. Albaruni, Bharattattwa, Chapter-IX, p. 77.
11. Prof. Mahamahopadhaya Haraprosad Shastri, 'Orissar Jangle' or 'In the Jungles of Orissa' written in 1916, Bisak : Bouddha Dharma p. 86.
12. Published by Bangiya Sahitya Parisad in 1909.
13. Nagendranath Vasu, Modern Buddhism and its Followers in Orissa, (pub in

1911; reprint 1986 by Gian Publishing House, Delhi) p. 9.
14. Nagendranath Vasu,Modern Buddhism and its Followers in Orissa, (pub in 1911; reprint 1986 by Gian Publishing House, Delhi) p. 145.
15. Courtesy, Prof. Sunil Kumar Roy, (Chemistry) Kalna Collage, teacher of Nimai Chand Pandit.
16. Dr Ambedkar, Vol. 7; p. 80.
17. N. B. Roy, A People in distress, p. 89 onwards.
18. Sir Herbert H Risley, ICS, The people of India, pub. 1915, Second Ed. 1969; p. 126.
19. Satish Mitra, Jessore Khulnar Itihas, pp. 179-80.
20. Shib Nath Shastri, Ramtanu Lahiri O Samakalin Banga Samaj, p. 74.
21. Dhammapada, Buddha Bagga, 14/182.
22. Asokan Inscription, 'Sav Munis Paja Mama'; Rig Veda, '*Munis*' aborigines of Bharat, attacked and subdued by the 'Aryas' and in contemporary rural dialect, '*Munis*', the labouring or producing class.
23. Dr Devi Prosad Chattopadhay, Bharatiya Darsan, Introduction.
24. Dr R.C. Dutta, Dr Kalikinkar and Dr Roychowdhuri, Advanced History of India, p. 186.
25. The History And Culture of The Indian People' The Age of Imperial Kanouj, Bharatiya Vidya Bhavan, Vol. IV, p. 83.
26. Romila Thaopar, Cultural Past (Society in Ancient India) p. 335.
27. Nimai Sadhan Basu, History of Chandal.
28. Suniti Kumar Chattopadhaya, Bharater Bhasa O Bhasa Samasya, pp. 7-9 and 17.
29. Mahakabi Mahananda Halder, Guruchand Charit.
30. Asgwaghosh, Buddha Charit, 1st Canto.
31. Sir Herbert Risley, People in India, (2nd edition) p. 760.
32. Dhamma Nanda Kosambi, Bhagwan Buddha.
33. Jyotirao Phooley, Slavery, Introduction.
34. Mahendra Nath Karan, Poundra Kashatriya Kulatilak, p. 78.
35. Prof. L. Mukherjee, Indian History (Medieval period), Introduction, p. 3.
36. Dr Md. Sahidullah.
37. Prof. Suniti Kumar Chattopadhaya, Bharater Bhasa O Bhasa Samasya, p. 10 and Bangla Bhasa Twttwer Bhumiks, p. 22 and 31.
38. Geoge W. Briggs, The Chamars, pub. 1920, p. 15.
39. Bhagwat Puran, Chapter-XI.
40. Manu Smriti, 3/21.
41. Census Report 1891, Vol. III, pp. 255-257/ (p. 42).
42. Dr A.K. Biswas, The Namasudras of Bengal, Preface.
43. Bankim, Bivid Prabandha [(Bangiya Sahitya Partsad), pp. 315-340; Rachanavali, Vol. 2nd, Aryakaran, p. 311-12].
44. Prof. Sukumar Sen, Bangla Sahityer Katha, pp. 4-6.
45. Prof. Srikumar Bandhyopadhay, Bangla Sahityer Vikaser Dhara, p. 33.
46. Dr Asha Das, Bangla Sahitye Bouddha Dharma O Sanskriti, p. 1.

47. Nagendra Nath Vasu, The Modern Buddhism and its Followers in Orissa, (Pub. in 1911) p. 10.
48. *Ibid.,* p. 19.
49. *Ibid.,* p. 27.
50. Basudev Sunani, Dalit Sanskrutir Itihas (in Oriya).
51. Courtesy Prof. Dr Kancha Ilaiha, the celebrity author of Why I am not a Hindu
52. R.C. Dutta, Civilisation in the Buddhist Age, 320 B.C to AD 5009, Pub. 1908) pp. 175-76
53. Dr B.R. Ambedkar, R and S, Vol. 14, p. 225.
54. Gita, 1/ 40-41.
55. Manu, 4/61.
56. R.C. Dutta, ICS, *ibid.*
57. Report on the Census of Bengal 1872.
58. Swapan Kumar Biswas, Bharatiya Samaj Unnayan Dhara ; Dr Ambedkar, p. 315.
59. Dr B.R. Ambedkar, W and S, Vol. 5, p. 364.
60. Dr B.R. Ambedkar, The Untouchables, Who were they? (October 1948; Amrit Book Co.) p. 73.
61. Letter No 87; Administrative Report, Presidency division 1880-81.
62. GanaMukti, April-September 2006 (Namasudrader Utsa sandhan sankhya) p. 221: Dacca, Bangladesh.
63. Bharat Sebashram Sangh, Edited Letters, pp. 270-71.
64. Smt. Shipra Biswas, Annesan, Appendix.
65. Jagadish Mandal, Mahapran Jogendra Nath Mandal.
66. W.W. Hunter.
67. Kali Prasanna Singha, 'Hutumpanchar Naxa' p. 59 (Pub. 1796).
68. Suniti Kumar Chattopadhaya, Bharater Bhasa O Bhasa Samasya, pp. 10-12.
69. Dr Nihar Ranjan Roy, Bangalir Itihas, Vol. 1, p. 36.
70. Gour Priyo Sarkar, Jati Tattwa Sangraha, pp. 26-29.
71. Swapan Kr. Biswas, Hari-Guruchand Banglar Chandal O Bharater Bahujan, pp. 55-60.
72. Nagendra Nath Vasu, The Modern Buddhism and its Followers in Orissa, (pub. in 1911) p. 11.
73. Bankim Chandra Chattopadhaya, Ramdhan Pod, Banga Darshan, 1288, Bhadra Month.
74. Gita 2/1-2 Lord Krishna advised Arjuna that Compassion etc. were of the 'An-Aryas' Compassion is non-Aryan character.

3

Hari-Guruchand: Matua Religion and Philosophy

The quenchless flux of self-conscious human zeal for independence and to attain, enjoy and clinch the lamp of liberty of the Chandal race pervades the eternity of historical periods. The struggle for liberty marks its evidential influence in modern stream of life as well. Their cravings for boundless liberty arose out of the eternal philosophy of 'love' and 'knowledge', 'fraternity', 'equality' and 'freedom' that were preached by the tradition of ancient Indian Shramana culture. Flames of that free and national identity resurrected amongst the Chandals of Bengal in the name of Harichand. Hinduism that prevailed upon the society in the contemporary rural Bengal very precariously subdued the non-Muslim population of lower strata. People of this strata were called Sudras, Untouchables and 'Bunos' or 'Banabasi Tribes'. They have been treated as sub-human and non-human creatures, as beast of pray disqualified to fulfill any of the human aspirations.

In the circumstances, Harichand courageously rose to cure all ills and had sought remedies. He gave birth to a new religion in the midst of the Muslim-Hindu society that turned to be completely wretched and wrecked due to the cancer of castes. The corns of caste-system debarred the lowest stratum of the society from enjoying political rights that the British and Europe opened up for all citizens of a country. He, therefore preached a new religion which imbibed the spiritual ideals of love, knowledge, equality and dignity of labour. His quest for spiritualism was not just to get a happy life after death. He was not to get just the blessings of the gods and goddesses. His faith preached to expand one's life in all directions towards all pursuits of a man on earth. He sought to improve and advance the temporal as well as celestial life-standard. Within a short span of period, his dream and precepts are found to have yielded illustrious and tangible success in all expected directions. Consequently, a century later, Mahakabi Mahananda Haldar is found to have assessed the position, 'Whatever has been achieved by the downtrodden Scheduled castes, these are the fruits of Harichand Thakur's movements.....'

"Tapasili Jati Madhye Ja-kichu Hoyeche,
Harichand Kalpa Brikhe Sakali Phaleche."[1]

Harichand played the pivotal role of the pioneer in ushering a new era in Indian society by transforming the unresistive, passive and outcaste or excluded section of the immense majority lowest stratum that is, the producing classes of the society into a dynamically proactive, democratically demanding, respectfully responsive and sharply reactive one. He infused the blood and vigour of self-respect in the sleeping minds and vegetative life of poor people in agrarian sector. They became participative in every aspects of life. He exorcised the spectre of 'divine-contentment' in their minds and made them throb with the hunger for boundless discontentment and human aspirations. He had revolted against the contemporary belief, practices and socio-religious traditions; opposed all economic and administrative arrogance and atrocities caused by the all powerful Hindu Zamindars and European agents upon the servile classes. He struggled to replace and fill up the vacuum by creating bridges of brotherhood amongst the varieties of groups of Sudra and Untouchable artisans and peasantry who remained busy in internecine quarrel. He was the first one who dreamt of the concept of forming a 'Bharatiya' nation the 'Bahujan Samaj'.

No Reform: Total Transformation of System

Harichand arrogated to himself the status and power of being a Prophet, rather a God with little or no temporal paraphernalia at his command. As a prophet he preached a new faith or '*Mat*' called "*Matua*" in Eastern Bengal. It swept away millions with him during his lifetime. This was indeed the declaration of self-identity of the untouchables and Sudras in eastern India.

Around fourteen hundred years ago, standing on the fire-circle of parched sand of the Arabian Desert one camel-driver declared himself as a Prophet. Prophet Muhammad. The soul sent by God, the Allah. The world obeyed the hero of Mecca as a Prophet. Even half a millennium prior to the Prophet, in the village of Bethlehem of Nazareth in Jerusalem, Jesus the son of a maiden Marry and a carpenter named Joseph declared himself as the son of God. Humankind accepted him. Some five hundred years before Christ there was born a baby, a boy in standing position in the Lumbini Garden of Kapila Vastu in Nepal *terrain,* on the full moon day of Baisakh in 563 BC. He attained enlightenment or '*Bodhi*' and was called the Buddha. The boy soon after his birth is claimed to have declared, "I am born to rescue the people in distress and to bring welfare for the suffering world." Similarly, in the bosom of Bengal was born Harichand, the lord '*Bhagwan*' in the Falguni Purnima in AD1812. Tens of millions of people follow him; teeming millions worship him. He preached that the life is the ocean of love and the waves of wisdom. The untouchable artisans and peasant-disciples of Harichand under the leadership of Guruchand Thakur also entered with illustrious and tangible triumph in the social and political arena in the last quarter of 19th and first quarter of 20th Century Bengal.

In this context, we may not forget that it was not easy and simple for Harichand to assume the role of '*Thakur*' or to become God as it was simple and easy for Muhammad and Jesus Christ to become *Paigambar* and Prophet. There remains fundamental and un-crossable gulf between these two situations. Siddharth Gautam, Jesus Christ and Hazrat Muhammad were the free and respected members of the society, they were human beings; not debarred or disqualified for attainment of spiritual excellence and highest celestial position.

The dictum of divinity of Hinduism, and consequently the official society, however, did not accept Harichand as a human being. He was born in an agricultural family, treated as untouchable by the Brahmins and debarred from entering into a Hindu temple or spirituality. What to talk of celestial subjects he was denied access even for temporal and mundane matters. Education and learning, the gate-way into spirituality even were shut for him. He was forced to remain a bundle or irrevocable source of pollution. Narendra Nath Dutta of Shimla, Kolkata, a junior contemporary of Guruchand Thakur had abandoned his name given by his parents and adopted the new nomenclature Swami Vivekananda as suggested by the Maharaja of Kshetri, Rajasthan, was not eligible to adopt the course of spirituality. Yet he became a *Sanyasi*, a '*Dandi*' and presented religious discourses. Consequently, the then judge of the Supreme Court, Kolkata Sir Gurudas Bandhopadhya declined to preside over the felicitation function that was arranged at the Town Hall, Kolkata after Vivekananda had returned from the World Parliament of Religion at Chicago in 1893. The Hon' able judge declared, "Had there been a Hindu Raja in the country, Vivekananda would have got hanged."[2] Once, soon after the death of Ramakrishna in AD 1884, when Swamiji entered inside the temple of Kali at Dakshineswar the entire premises of the temple was washed off with the water of the Ganges to purify it.[3] How could, in such circumstances, an untouchable peasant, poor and illiterate Harichand be a god? Yet, Thakur Harichand was accepted by the vast size of the Chandal community as God. He gave his disciples the single '*Mantra*', "Haribbol", chant his name 'Hari' and get rid of all sufferings. Entire society woke up and accepted the spell.

The resolute in Harichand, his strong determination to liberate the Chandals from the thralldom of the Brahmin's tyranny as a natural corollary made him to decide to break the shackles of 'divine slavery' and to bring them out of the Hindu fold. He had mustered courage and denounced Hinduism during 1835. He asked his people to deny and to refuse the authority of the God, demy-gods and Hindu goddesses like Sri Rama, Krishna,

Vishnu, Hanuman, Laxmi, Saraswati, Ganesh, Durga, Kali and Shiva who deserted them in the blinding darkness of disdain and contempt. He directed not to worship the idols of gods. He himself assumed the status of God and gave his own name as the '*Mantra*', "Haribbol". Not only Harichand, there were born a dozen of such elevated souls amongst the untouchables in contemporary Bengal to denounce Brahmanical magic-spells in the name of spirituality. They challenged superiority of the Hindus and commanded the masses towards the new path of salvation. These rebellious personalities were known as '*Pagal*', '*Sadhu*' a man superior in conduct and capacity bestowed with spirituality. Famous amongst them were 'Khejur talar Pagol', Nanda Pagal, Kshyapa Pagal, Kesav Pagal. Inspired with the supernatural performances of these philosopher leaders the untouchable Chandal society became audacious to enter into the arena of battle against the elite social-order. They demanded equal right to freedom and began struggles to govern themselves as free citizens of a democratic country.

With the 'Midas-touch' that Harichand gave, within moments, the iron-souls of the society were transformed into precious gold-souls. The Guru Harichand was not a guru like a Brahmin. He was not simply preacher or an advocate of a faith, which had been given by other authority. He was the author of the faith, which he preached. Matuaism did not introduce initiation or '*Diksha*'. The Brahmin gurus adopted the modality of initiation by pronouncing some secret spells (Seed-words) in the ears of the disciples. He objected the validity and denied any need for the classified mantra or '*Diksa*'.

"Diksa Nai, Karibe Na Tirtha Paryatan,
Mukti Spriha Sunya, Nahi Sadhan Bhajan."[4]

'There is no need of Baptism or receiving '*Diksa*' or undertaking pilgrimage. Be truthful. 'Truthfulness' is the matchless spot of pilgrimage'.

He was even conscious to condemn the process of initiation by secret mantras as useless and an act of cheating. 'Gurus initiate by pouring Mantras putting his mouth in the ears of the disciples. However, all but Harinam Mantra are cheating. This Harinam *mantra* is boundless, pure and tranquil, it is not secret. What is the necessity of secrecy? Can one deny the day-light by bolting the doors?'

He openly distributed his magical proper-noun 'Hari' for his disciples to chant as panacea. 'His disciples did not bother to know or care for any god or goddess of Hinduism, Islam or Christianity. They maintained no portrait or idol of any god but were devoted to Harichand only.'

"Nahi Chene Kono Devi, Ghat, Pat Kimba Chabi,
Jane Mane Prane Sudhu Harichande...."

The luminous aura of the transparent, tranquil and clear 'Haribbol' *mantra* definitely placed the untouchable Chandal nation on the solid rocks of spiritual domain. With the advent of Harichand the untouchables of

Bengal had no more a reason to consider the issue of conversion to Islam or Christianity. They were blessed with their powerful religion. He rejected the authority of the Vedic scriptures and rituals, denounced caste or *Varnashram Dharma* and blatantly attacked idol worship, Hindu pilgrimage and visiting holy places for merits. He claimed that the Chandals and all the untouchables of Bengal were not Hindus. Harichand was a child of the French revolution of 1789 which was led by the peasantry of the country and gave birth to National Democracy. The essence of his claim within a span of half a century matured to the political demand for special or separate representation in the Legislature for the untouchables as separate nation. The nation was soon recognised by the British as Depressed Class.

Harichand's heart bled for the suffering-people. As a natural corollary, he became convincingly anti-Brahmin as the fundamental element behind all these sufferings were the Brahmins. His conviction towards the cause of humanity and liberty was manifested in the form of deep apathy, distrust and hatred for the Hindus and Hinduism. He was comfortably ready to eat food from the plate of dogs but was unwilling to tolerate the caste division and its associated customs of purity and impurity, '*suddhachar*'. He was an ardent adherent of 'suddhi' that is cleanliness and purity of body and mind. However, his concept of purity was rooted purely in his own system. He was independent and self-conscious.

Harichand had no Guru (Brahmin or otherwise), got training from no Brahmin. Indeed, no untouchable Chandal was, as the caste law, entitled to have any Brahmin as a Guru. Once one Dasarath Biswas (a Chandal) who had full faith in Brahmins and Hindu religion had come to discuss the philosophy of purity and the strength of '*Mantras*'. The Guru declared, 'I do not believe in Tantra, Mantra and Purity (*Suddhi*), why have you come to me. You are a man who observes the rules of purity, perform rituals of purity thrice a day and also in the evening. But I do not have sense of purity. I cannot maintain timings of bathing, worshipping and '*Sandhya*' rituals. I eat, as a holy meal, if I get it from the plate, the left out eaten by dogs. Look, I do not believe in the Vedic dictum and do not observe purity' :-

"Tantre Mantre Sauchachre Na Hai Biswas,
Kenore Aasili Bacha Aamar Nikate."[5]

Harichand was more than a Guru; he gave a new faith a religion, a path of salvation. He performed many miracles. The Buddhist Shranmanas advised that it was not mandatory for the faithful to go for pilgrimage. The pleasure of salvation is situated near, there is no need to travel far to go to the holy places in Lanka now known as Ceylon. "*Niare Bohi, Ma Jahure Lanko.*" Similarly, Harichand restrained his followers repeatedly from traveling to the holy-places as there was no merit in pilgrimage. "*Diksha Vrithaa, Kara Vritha Tirtha Paryatan. Mukti Vritha, Kiba Karo Sadhan Bhajan.*" He even declared that penance and practice of rituals were useless.

His religion did not emerge out of the Hindu religion. 'Matua' religion was not a sect of Hinduism. Guruchand did not know ABC of Sanskrit language, the divine and communal language of the Hindus. Only the Brahmins were, according to the scripture, eligible to learn and use Sanskrit language. Manu had prescribed inhuman corporal punishment for a Sudra if he hears Sanskrit. The Hindu gods and goddesses are said to be non responsive to the prayers in any language other than Sanskrit. In a sharp contrast to it, the entire spiritual instructions and gospels given by Harichand were in the local rather indigenous 'Chandali' language.

In the circumstances, the question of Hindu connection or as to whether Matua faith was an offshoot or branch of Hinduism should not rationally have arisen. It is a historical fact that the Holy Bible is divided in two parts, 'The Old' and the 'New Testament'. The Holy Qur'an is inseparably connected with the Holy Bible. Yet it has created three different religions of the World. The faith of Matuaism is not at all connected with Brahmanism and is diametrically opposite in its origin, essence, tenets and practice. The faith called Matuism was born out of modern democratic and national circumstances. Still the untouchable adherents are questioned as to whether they follow Hinduism or a distinct Matua faith. The reason is that the Brahmins or the Aryan-social-psychology never allows its components in servitude to go away from the concentration camp of Hinduism.

Hari-Guruchand became the spiritual Guru of the untouchables simply by ignoring Hindus and declaring their sovereign right to religion and spirituality. There came therefore no question of conversion. They appealed and prayed for redresses of all problems direct to the Divinity. Consequently, they stood up robustly on their independent vertebra to demand adequate share also in all worldly desirable things with equal dignity and right with any other citizen of the country. Standing on the platform of self-conscious identity the Matuas in course of time, in the appropriate circumstances, even did not hesitate to demand equal share in the governance of the country and adequate representation in the instrumentalities of the Democrat State as a nation.

Harichand's movement or religion was fundamentally limited to the preaching amongst local people and it was a '*Lokayat*' *Dharma* or a local sect of Hindu religion. Matuaism, is 'Lokayat' if it means 'a faith of the people', a faith spread amongst or accepted by the people in general. Each religion was born at a particular place. It cannot be called local on that ground. His movement was neither limited to local people nor for mere attainment of speculative or spiritual solace. It does not ask the adherents to move towards the unseen destination of *Swarga*. It did not produce only the '*Sadhus*', '*Sants*', 'Holy-men', Saints, '*Matua-Rhittiks*' with flowing beard and long haired mendicants and philosophers. He did not create irresponsible members of society apathetic towards worldly affairs. Harichand's revolt essentially yielded fruits that eventually became the harbinger of the process of social democracy and people's democracy. The light of renaissance that he ignited in the untouchable Chandal people of eastern Bengal paved the path of national feeling amongst Indians in general. He became the rising sun of the Indian 'dalit-bahujan' movement of future India.

Harichand Thakur was much ahead of his time. The age in which Harichand courageously revolted against the ills of the contemporary society was unaware of the democratic movement that had already completed its course in Europe and America. The Indians, as subjects of the British colony, had just started experiencing the rule of law imported from English Parliament, but no Indian could yet dream of demanding democratic rights; to be one's own ruler. The concept of individualism and the issue of self-respect was an unknown factor in the servile society. Religious sentiment remained the only bonding force for the formation of a community or a nation. All reformers in our country in the contemporary period rallied around the platform of religion. Indian polity essentially is a theocratic and Hinduism directly interferes in political matter. Sudras and untouchables are debarred of political rights by scriptural dictum.

Harichand was born as the deliverer, as the savior, the '*Massiah*' of the 'Dalit-bahujan Samaj'. After his demise in 1878, his son Guruchand assumed 'avatar', the dream-cum-true of his father's mission. Harichand had incarnated in the body of his son and fulfilled his mission of liberating the untouchables and servile 'Dalit-bahujan Samaj'. Guruchand Thakur like his father gave a clarion call to the servile classes of people to strive for becoming rulers themselves in their own country by joining political movements of democratisation. These political ambition and activities do not seem to be contrary to the ideals of spirituality. Indeed, the battle of liberty is a spiritual fact.

Hari-Guruchand very sagaciously indulged in politics of modern India along with the British authorities. On the Harichand like '*Kalpa-Briksha*' no Temples, no Mandirs, no Math or Monastery appear to have come up. A tree is known by its fruits. What were the fruits that were produced on the grand-tree called Hari-Guruchand? Answer has been given in a dispassionate discloser of history in analytical manner :-

"Aain Sabhai Sav Jaai Pratinidhi,
Tarai Sristikare Dese Jata Bidhi.
Aain Sabhai Aaj Jara Shaktishali,
Tar Mule Guruchand Agatir Gati."[6]

'The people's representatives who go in the Legislature enact the laws of the land. Those who are found to be very powerful were low and week before. The Namasudras are in a leading position in the Cabinet; Namasudras lead the communities who are known as Scheduled Castes. Guruchand, the resort of the shelter-less is the root of this. And without education the advancement and progress of the Scheduled castes was not possible.' Promotha Ranjan Thakur, the celebrity grandson of Guruchand Thakur in his autobiography had described the tenets of Matua religion. P.R. Thakur was a London return barrister and a Member of Parliament. "He (Harichand) realised that men could easily understand and develop spiritual side (*Swattick/* metaphysics) through creative activism (*Rajasik/* physics) or material development. His religion was primarily based on material realisation (*Rajasik*) or development. With that target in mind, he preached a religion not of monks but of ideal family members. Family life is not without social and political activism. The ideal family duties cannot be performed without actively participating in Politics.... The persons or the nation which remain detached from politics cannot perform Family-religion."[7] This is an absolute truth in a democratic society and country.

Harichand, right from his childhood had to fight his Hindu adversaries. The Hindu imperialist forces razed the houses and villages of the poor Chandals. Like most of the families around, the family of Yasavanta was also a Vaishnav family. Sri Krishna was their Lord God. Like Prophet Muhammod, Harichand too had to revolt against and purify his family first. And for that he had to suffer punishment from his father and relatives. Undaunted was the boy Harichand to declare the truth:-

"....Duranta Asanta Putre Pita Dei Danda,
Kende Bale Harichand, Bairagira Bhanda." (HL, p. 51)

'Whenever the Vaishnavs visited the family, all the members of the extended family assembled to worship them. Four of the elder brothers of Harichand served them at the command of their father but Harichand became a problem. What to talk about touching feet, he even refused to fold his hands. Torture and beating failed to yield any result. Father punished the prodigal son. Still the tearful Harichand declared Vaishnavas were corrupt' Matua faith as a result caused maximum damage to the Vaishnav Sect in Bengal.

Five pillars on which stood the edifice of Hinduism or Sanatana Brahmanism are (i) Vedic or Sanskrit mantras to please or control gods and goddesses (ii) Indispensible prerogative of the Brahmins as *Gurus* in spiritual and social system (iii) No religious performance without Brahmins (iv) Varnashram Dharma or Caste system and (v) Non participation of the women in any temporal or celestial affair. The *Matua* faith stands erect without any of these fundamental characters and in opposition to all these factors.

A strong and well knit organisation grew on the pivot of the faith preached by Harichand Thakur. The followers were called '*Matua Sampradai*', the Matua Community. Institution is called '*Matua Maha Sangha*'. In Hari Lilamrita, the biography of Harichand written long ago and published in 1917, the author Tarak Gosnai had written:-

"Prem Anurage Sab Bhakta Jutila,

Matua Bolia Dese Ghosana Hoila."[8]

'With devotion and love assembled all the devotees who were introduced as *Matua*' in the country'. With the declaration of exclusive identity of the 'Matua' religion separate from all other prevalent faiths it was categorically assessed that prevailing Hindu sects were corrupt. 'Where will you find a Brahmin, where is a Vaishnav? All are avaricious, selfish and cheats. Self-less Matuas only are devoted to the praising of the Lord. They will be famous as a Distinct religious Faith':

"Kothai Brahman Dekho, Kothai Vaishnav?

Swarthabase Arthalovi Jata Bhanda Sab."

The 2nd edition of the biography of Guruchand was published in 1942. In publisher's appeal, Mahakabi Mahananda Halder clarified, Sri Sri Hari Thakur was known as Harichand. His followers and people who were emotionally sawed by his love and charm became famous as '*Matua*' means mad in love 'Mast'. This position has also been corroborated by Devendra Nath Thakur in his book, "Before entering the discussion, it is to be clarified that Matua religion is not Hinduism. Though it was born amidst the Hindus it is neither a Hindu religion nor a branch or sect of Hinduism. It completely is a separate and independent religion like Buddhism and Sikhism." Dr Nittaya Nanda Halder has also affirmed that though it was difficult to accept the poison easily but, "It (Matua Religion) is purely a distinct religion as the faiths like Islam, Christianity, Hinduism, Bouddhism, Sikhism are distinct and different from each other." He has also gone deeper to analyze, "To day at the end of life, on the basis of historical developments and perspective I have realised the fact that the Namasudras have lost their vigour and talents as well as their separate national identity and the power to challenge and to prove to be equal to the situation has been lost due to their entry in the refuge of Hinduism. The heroes of the fighting race have turned to be the lambs. With a view to re-energizing and transforming these lambs back into the original form of cubs of lion Harichand preached Matua religion". It is therefore, contradictory to identify Matuas as Namasudras. Sudras are inseparable part and lowest stratum of Hindu caste system and society. In that case, it will not be possible for the untouchables to come out of the fireplace of the 'concentration camp' of Brahmanism. Therefore, he prescribed, "The days are no more to get shivered to know that Matua religion is anti-Vedic. No more are those days to be frightened with the proposition that with the advent and spread of Matua faith Hinduism will go to docks."[9]

Philosophy and Practice of Matua Faith

The strength of the faith, preached by Harichand emerged out of the simplicity in its approach and the philosophy. In a sentence, we can say the philosophy of Matuaism is the spirit of eternal Liberty associated with Love,

Knowledge, Action, Equality and Fraternity. Standing in the Sakya Gana Parisad, the young prince Siddhartha two and a half millennia ago proclaimed the essence of Dhamma. "Dhamma as I understand it, consists in recognizing that enmity does not disappear by enmity, it can be concurred by love alone'[10] and this is the eternal religion. "*Eso Dhamma Sannantano*".[11] Love is God; Love is spirituality and the essence of life, happiness and religion. Truth is God. Truth is wisdom. Life and action is God. God is Truth, the all Knowledge. God is ever active. Liberty is God. God only is the sovereign and attainment of that state is salvation. Freedom or manumition from slavery is salvation.[12] The first universal-king, Emperor Asoka the Great did spread the message of conquest with love, the catalyst of universal fraternity, not of conquest with sword, and thus turned to be the greatest of the monarchs of the World.

Matua religion and its philosophy is the manifestation of the synthesised form of these above mentioned phenomena. It is the path to explore and to attain love-wisdom-liberty by means of optimum utilisation of active tendencies of one's working force. One is to remain active in day-to-day work while praising the Lord was his dictum. "*Hate Kam Mukhe Nam*". As it denounced the sanctity and validity of castes so also it rejected the Hindu concept of four *Ashramas* or stages in a religious or pious life. This religion strictly banned the idea of renunciation of family life. *Grihasthasram* that is family-stage was mandetory for the practice of religion. One is to practice religion and remain pious staying in the family.

Love is Religion: Love is the highest degree of associative attitude. Love unites. Love is the starting point of family and of clan, society, nation and country. Love generates fellow feeling and fraternal bondage, which further play the role of catalyst to share problems and difficulties of life. Love leads to concentrate on singularity. It expands the singular into many and cares for plurality. It inspires one to share bread with another. Love never reacts in a hostile or coercive manner. A lover never resort to subdue or exploit others whom he loves. It ignites the light of liberty and acts as the essence of communism, the doctrine of equality and liberty. Fraternity is nothing but the manifestation of Love. Without fraternity, equality fails to manifest. Love is the essence of Nationalism. Absolute freedom demolishes the state of equality. Hinduism, as a protagonist of slavery, on the other hand is based on the philosophy of hatred. Castes, therefore, divide and weaken the humanity. Caste is travesty of democracy. It is anti-social and anti-national. According to Hinduism, all other than Brahmins are impure and objects of contempt and hatred. The intensity of hatred differs in degree as per the difference in castes but not in kind. No Hindu can love other Hindu irrespective of caste. No member of a particular caste is equal to the members of other castes. Hindu society is composed on the basis of constitutional exclusiveness amongst all its members or social groups. The universal phenomenon of hatred in Hinduism differs in degree only from caste to caste.

The essence of Matua religion, on the other hand, is Love, which consolidated the fragmented Chandals and other untouchable communities across Bengal. It raises the feeling of nationality amongst all.

Harichand's teachings did not push any one out from the space of courtyard of fraternity as unapproachable, as base, useless or dirty. Waves of ocean of love inundated all, the rich and poor, men and women, all in the society. It melted the hearts of the suffering masses to hug and embrace each other without considering difference of sex with emotional touch of spirituality. Harichand opened the floodgates of the religion of fraternity, religion of humanity, the religion of liberty. It was essentially the religion of all Love.

"Meye Purusete Basi Ak Pate Khai,
Meyether Ento Khai Padadhula Lai,
Meyera Dhalia Pare Puruser gai." (lila, p. 142)

'The devotees shout the praise, "Haribbol". They have got carried away as mad with emotion, left pecuniary interests for the sake of love. Sitting together, male and female dine from the same and single plate. Food left out by the women is consumed by male members; dust from the feet of women is taken by male. Female embraces male.'

Matuas were taught to adopt a simple way of life as a religious measure. It was not only in consonance with the life style of the peasantry of Eastern Bengal; it was also in consonance with the 'Middle Path' or '*Majjhim Patipada'* which was given by Lord Buddha some two thousand five hundred years ago. A '*Matua*' maintained distinction of a separate and independent faith in various aspects. The Hindu Vaishnavas use tight garlands of '*Tulsi*' around their neck, the Shivaites use garlands of *Rudraksha*.. Matuas rejected flower, *Rudraksha* and *Tulsi* but prepared garlands for their use out of '*Achiya*', the hard and black shell of coconut which was easily and abundantly available.

Freedom is Religion. Freedom is joy. Subjugation is the greatest source of pain, killer of peace and hindrance of prosperity and pursuit of happiness. Harichand in his personal life stood firmly against unjust and illegal dealings of the powerful local Zamindars and their agents. He did not surrender. Instead, he had left his birth place and settled in adjacent village to maintain his free and independent entity with dignity and peace. Slavery is the greatest horror and acute hurdle for attaining a state of bliss. Servitude and helplessness before the tyranny and arrogance of authority cripples the inner self of an individual every moment. Bondage is the greatest misery; it is the biggest constraint on the way to happiness.

The battle of liberty is thus, nothing but spiritual. Indeed, manumission from slavery is 'Salvation' or 'Mukti'. All the Hindu gods and goddesses appear with lethal weapons in their hands. Lord Krishna incarnates to demolish and kill the majority of the people and protects the microscopic minority, the Brahmins. The god-fearing sentiment might have emerged out of the situation. God cannot be an object of fright or terror. Not 'God-fearing' but people need to be 'God-loving'. God, the supreme father saves and rescues his creation. The humble creatures remain at the mercy and compassion of the Lord. The God in the Holy Bible disclosed his identity. In reply to Moses the power declared, "I am the Lord your God who brought you out of Egypt out of the land of slavery."[13] Here is God who rescues. This is 'Salvation'. This is '*Nirvan*' a state of bliss.

The first man, Adam violated the command of the Lord God of Eden Garden. Lord God threatened Adam, "If you eat it (fruit from the tree of Knowledge) you will surely die." Still Adam had rebelled against the Lord God and risking his life and existence ate the fruit from the tree of Knowledge. He ate it, because he too wanted to be equally knowledgeable like the Lord God to be endowed with the capacity to understand his surroundings, good and bad, to realize what was beneficial and what was detrimental for him. Consequently, he discovered his self and that he was exploited by the Lord God, that he was completely naked. He was thus blessed to put his maiden steps in the realm of his own free-land where he was to earn his bread by the sweat of his brow and his consort was to beget her baby through labour pain. Adam no more remained dependent on the command of the Lord God.

Knowledge is Religion: Wisdom is God. Philosophy is the starting point of spirituality. To acquire '*Para Vidya*' that is knowledge of the other-world or celestial objects, mastery over '*Apara Vidya*', that is the temporal knowledge is essential for one's all round growth. Knowledge only can make one capable to have, to feel, to understand a touch, or realisation or vision of God. God is all wisdom. Knowledge of physics helps explain and understand metaphysics easily. These two are not contradictory. These two aspects are complimentary to each other. In some respect and in some degree these two are one and the same thing. The Lord God of Hinduism, however, left no stone unturned to transform the highly literate India of Emperor Asoka the Great into the land of illiteracy, where in spite of the spread of universal education system by the British East India Company and Government under the Crown, the largest number of world's illiterate still reside. Lord Krishna asked the knowledgeable or learned people (mainly Brahmins) not to inspire the working or labouring masses for education. Instead they must, as desired by the Lord, be pushed to the work-force.'[14] Manu banned transgression of caste laws by which the immense majority of the lower and lowest strata of the society including women were debarred or disqualified for the 3 R's.[15] This has been the surest method to maintain the servile people in perpetual servitude and blinding darkness of ignorence.

Guruchand demolished the rocky mountains of obstacles for getting the Chandals education. '*Anunnata Jati Majhe Shiksha Pracharite, Aggna Kare Harichand Tare (to Guruchand) Bidhimate*'. In a formal way, Harichand instructed his son Guruchand to spread education amongst the untouchables. He announced, "*Mor Pita Harichand Gache Bole More. Vidya Sikshs Dite Ghare Ghare*". 'My father had asked me to light the lamp of education in every house.' Without the weapon of knowledge, the corns of slavery cannot be removed. Slavery and ignorance are the two sides of the same coin. The gospels of Holy Bible disclose the fact that only when the caretaker of Eden Garden, Adam and his consort Eve had eaten the fruits from the tree of Knowledge they were manumitted. They became free and independent. Like Eve, Harichand baptised his son to the path of Liberty. The peasantries were asked to cultivate the fertile land of knowledge; the Chandals once again picked up pens along with the ploughs in their hands. Matua religion is a religion of learning and knowledge. The tapestry of blinding darkness of illiteracy was removed to usher the day-break of political life of the Depressed class.

'*Karma*', Work is Religion: Industriousness, that is, work is the '*Dharma*'. Holy Bible declares, 'No work, no food'. Hinduism, however, condemns and disdains labour. The working classes are contemptuously called Sudras, Untouchables. Brahmins never do manual or menial work. The peasantry, on the contrary, enjoys industriousness and maintains dignity of labour. Harichand refrained from doing Yoga practice sitting quite with closed eyes in a corner, in solitude for hours together for attaining peace of mind and salvation of souls. Matuas do not practice Yoga for religious purpose. Yoga not only taught to abstain from physical movements but its goal also was even to cease the function of mind and heart, conscience and rationality. '*Yogas Chittwavritti Nirodha*' that is what Patanjali advocated. Complete indifference towards the vibrant life and the natural rules for struggle for existence was suggested to be the means for happiness. Concentration to the inner-self and irresponsibility to the surroundings led the society to be apathetic towards others. Matuas do not practice '*aasan*' '*pranayam*' and '*dhyan*' or meditation; they jump and chant "*Haribbol*". Harichand did not see much merit in the system of yoga, which teaches people to withdraw from the active tendencies of human mind and body, which do not encourage productivity in the fields of creative labour. Yoga is the Pre-Aryan native Indian practice and philosophy of middle path of balanced life associated with ancient *Shramana Sanskriti* and Buddhism. The Hindus had corrupted it before they assimilated or hijacked the system. Yoga in modern world is found to have become the luxurious and fanciful past time for the elite and exploiter ruling classes in exercising their muscular and nervous system. For the toiling masses, such yoga practice was almost useless. He was very careful in instructing his disciples not to neglect the prosperity of the mundane aspects of family-life. The act of 'Praising the Lord' was to go along with the process of maintaining the rate of productivity high. "Hate Kam Mukhe Nam"[16]

Harichand had to desert his patrimony because of ill treatment and extortion of the local *Gomosta* of the *Zaminder*. He settled at Orakandi village. There, he experienced the pathetic plight of poverty and people's grappling with it in helpless conditions. He therefore, advised his disciples to be attentive consistently to the soundness of the family's pecuniary condition. Improve productivity was his motto. He taught the reality that in the material world, money was just one-step less than the position of God. Poverty is the cause of all miseries and servitude. His teaching was to remain always liberated, out of want, out of poverty and out of servitude. The best means to that end was nothing but hard labour. God blesses only the diligent one, with fortune of wealth. He had advocated and favoured the agro-based economic growth. He suggested many untouched sectors of wasteland to bring under furrow lands for the growth of agrarian economy. Hari Lilamrita narrates:

"Basia Basia Britha Gata halo Kal,
Aai Mora ak Din Chas kari Hal."

The Pali literature abounds with evidences that Prince Siddhartha along with the members of the Royal family and court members used to plough agricultural fields in annual '*Vapramangal*' festival. Agriculture was the main profession of the great Sakya clan. Agricultural income was the major source of government revenue during Harichand's time. Harichand belonged to the peasant family. He even as Guru, personally is found to have tilled lands to inspire his people to do the job with utmost pride, interest and sincerity. He also advised them to bring all wasteland which was supposed to be not yielding high under cultivation.

The days of white-collar jobs, for the educated masses was yet to come within the reach of Harichand. Even the elite and ruling classes Indians had a little share in it. He therefore, directed his people to explore excess and more income through trade and commerce so that the problem of seasonal unemployment was wiped out completely. Harichand himself started business to teach the proper way of doing it. "Nija Hate Byabasa Kare harichand."[17]

Matua Religion Stands without Caste System

The spiritual virtues and philosophy of 'Liberty' and 'Love' have taken tangible shape in the life style of the Matuas. The rituals and philosophy of 'Hatred' have been palpably manifested in the day-to-day practical life of the Hindu caste laws. The Matuas who were to set sail on the boat of love and equality do not have any room for and influence of Brahmanical Castes in their daily life. Concept of love and practice of caste were objects of two poles that rudely oppose each other. Harichand was born in a respectable Chandal family of rural Bengal, who were engaged in agricultural profession.

His advent was destined to free the '*Dalitbahujan*' immense majority Indian autochthons from Aryan-Brahmanic divine-slavery.

In the biography of Harichand, the purpose of his arrival on the earth has been recorded in unequivocal terms that '....to fulfill the targets of Lord Buddha Harichand arrived in the family of Yasavanta':-

"Buddher Kamana Taha Paripurna Janya,
Yasavanta Grihe Hari Haila Avatirna"[18]

After the elapse of two thousand and five hundred years of '*Maha Pari Nibban*' of *Tathagata* Lord Gautam Buddha what was the target, what was the relevance of Buddha's philosophy and mission that was to be completed by Harichand in modern era of British rule under the influence of capitalism? Why Harichand was born in the Eastern dark of ignorance, illiteracy, neglect, poverty and untouchability? They had narrated the fact that 'with the advent of the incarnate of Buddha, a time will come when level of the low and the suffering masses would be raised. And when Lord Buddha had strived, the Sudras got the '*Mantras*', and touch of spirituality':-

"Buddhadev Bahudin Tapasya Karila,
Tate Brahma, Pranabadi Sudrate Paila....."[19]

The Matuas were fully aware that the teaching of the Master, his philosophy and penance had rendered the slaves manumitted and placed them on the dream land of a plateau of social equality. Philosophy of Buddha was nothing but the grand message of Liberty. Lord Buddha, from his deathbed advised his disciple Ananda, "*Atma Deepa Bhava*" 'be your own light'. Ananda do not stay like a satellite as a moon dependent on the light of the Sun. Travel by your own light. Do not follow, simply because Buddha had said so. Only after assessing with your conscious reasoning you accept the truth in case it works for the welfare and happiness for the immense majority. Full and self-conscious independence is the philosophy of Lord Buddha. That is why he rejected the entity of any speculative God. Instead, in the place of God he accepted the existence of all pervading miseries, the "Duksha', 'Misery'. The existence of miseries and sufferings are experienced in all conditions and circumstances. He therefore, proposed to eliminate poverty and slavery of any kind as a definite path for happiness. Buddha agreed to the proposition that 'each individual is an end in him.'[20] Each one is equally important. No one is inferior to the other. All must therefore, be respected and duly honoured. No one as a class or as a sex is disqualified for attaining the '*Arhattwa*', the supreme spiritual position. No one was a Brahman or a Sudra in the Buddhist Sangha. Everyone a Bhikksu and a Bhikksuni, all were learned. No one was to coerce other. There existed in India, the most ancient women literature, '*Theri Gatha*' available side by side the '*Thero Gatha*' during Buddha's time.

With great esteem the disciples of Harichand have followeded the great history of struggle by the Buddha. Mahananda Halder records the salient features of Buddhism, as an embodiment of knowledge; non-violence; unity; nationalism and International approach.[21]

But the Brahman religion became its nemesis to conspire its down fall. The golden miner of Liberty and Equality failed to come up.[22]

Consequently, the advent of the incarnate of Buddha in Harichand was a *sine-qua-non*, a precondition to bring forth a state of society where there would prevail absolute freedom. People of this country though have failed miserably in this regard; slaves and indentured labours, who had gone abroad created a changed circumstance. There, in the land of no-Brahmans, they have successfully alleviated the problem of their slavery. The newspaper The 'Hindu' reports on February 2008, "Mauritius Prime Minister Navin Chandra Ramgoolam on Wednesday expressed his desire to import labour from Bihar. Dr Ramgoolam made his appeal in the press conference concluding his three day visit to Bihar saying, "We will rewrite the story in a different way. We don't have labour and we are now importing labour from other countries. We will welcome labour from Bihar." Dr Ramgoolam's grandfather Mohit Ramgoolam had gone to Mauritius as an indentured labour way back in 1871 and his son has liberated the country to become its first Prime Minister. Harichand also was struggling during 1870's. India, the Hindu country of eternal labours, continues to be a good source of labour supply for the world market.

Harichand came to fulfill the mission of Buddha in the British rural India. 'Openness is the ethics of Buddha, it does not recognise separatist feeling and does not create divisions. It brought the feelings of fraternity with the bond of love and tears of emotional attachment.' The God of compassion and Love once again came to render assistance to the native-society of Eklavyas with cut-off thumbs and severed tongues and Shambuks with cut off heads and to install them as the ruling class in their own country. With the thunder-rod of spiritual-power in hand, Harichand stood erect to cross swords with the terrorist, tyrant Hindus. He came to inspire the spirit of courage to colonial India to be free and independent.

Harichand was born in Safaladanga village amongst the Untouchables as an incarnation of this irresistible force of the Buddha. He gave to the *Sangha* and his disciples the 'Red Flags' to carry in their hands and directed to rebel and declare freedom. The top end of the pole with red-flag was fitted with the iron-heads of sphere. The Matuas used to beat '*Danka*' and '*Damama*' (War-Drums) along with '*Singa*' (Horn/Triumph) and 'Conch' as their musical instrument while chanting Guru Hari's name. Their '*Kirtan*' procession marched through the village. They used to pass paths by jumping vigorously with the rhythm of battle beating produced out of those high-sounding instruments. This also was added with encouraging sounds called '*Ulu*' produced by the participating women by articulately twisting their tongue. These fierce and extremely strenuous constant jumping force of the red-brigade really raised yell of war cry in the name of Harichand. It was the war for 'Annihilation of Castes' and for achieving total Freedom. Their ardent prayer was, "*Jadi Prabhu Punarai Hao Avatar, A Deshe Thakena Jeno Jatir Vichar*", 'O Lord! In case you incarnate, let castes be annihilated in this country'. The battle between the protagonists of caste-system and slavery and the antagonists of slavery was inevitable. The obvious battle line was drawn.

Essence of Sanatan Hindu Dharma is four Varnashram Dharma. Thakur Harichand began his journey of spirituality by denying its validity and defying its practice in the society for achieving the sunshine goal of liberty of the human society. According to Harichand, 'Men are best of all creatures; divisions of castes and purity and impurity are useless. One is respected due to his conduct not because of his birth. Matuas hold such views that they never talk of the caste system by birth.'... "*Manus Sabar Sresta Bhedaved Istanista; Karma Gune Man pai, Janma Gune Nai. Je Jan Matua Hai Sei Ai Katha Kai, Janmagata Jati Katha Tara Nahi Kai.*"[23] Guruchand stretched on it:-

"*Samajik Niti Sab Shono Bhaktagan,*
Jati-ved Pratha Nahi Manibe Kakhan,
'Jatived Kare Bale Balitechi Tai,
Janmagata Samajik Bhed Jaha Pai."[24]

Guruchand simply reiterated the definition suggested by Karl Marx in 1853 for caste system, '....the hereditarily division of Labour upon which rest the Indian castes' and condemned in the same language, 'is the decisive impediment of Indian power and progress.'[25] So he had asked his followers to decline to obey the command of Lord God Sri Krishna to practice caste or '*Chatur Varna*' created by Lord Krishna. Hinduism prescribed that '*Vanaprastha*' and '*Sanyas*'-*ashram* or the stage of 'Old age' and 'Ascetic stage' were to be adopted for the spiritual life. Guruchand had adopted a life of regal stature and started improving the mundane aspects of life for himself, for all of his disciples and the community. It was so vivid and startling that a section of Matuas even protested. He relished expensive attires and used to sit like a potentate on the raised armed chair with a ruling stick in hand as the Sikh Gurus used to sit on the throne in regal style and dress with swords on their waist. He taught that the children of God, the Supreme sovereign must not pose in a beggar's posture in any respect. He advised, "*Sattwa Raja Milanete Garhastha Jivan. Mor Pita Harichand Karilo Gathan*". My father Harichand asked to follow the family life as a place for and composed of both virtues of idealism and of actions. Matua religion thus stood diametrically opposite to the principles of Hinduism. He instructed his disciples that 'Along with the wife one is to perform responsibilities of family duties with indifference and virtues. One who remaining in family speaks the truth is matchlessly superior to a Sanyasi in the Ashrama:

"Karibe Grihastha Dharma Lae Nija Nari,
Grihe Theke Nayasi, Vanaprasthi Brahmachari."[26]

Matua religion is the religion of a democratic society. His new religion introduced a new path, a new philosophy of life which discarded the system of withdrawal of active life from family. "*Prashasta Grihasta Dharma Jive Siksha Dite; Harichand Avatirna Haila Abanite.*" 'The advent of Harichand was to teach people a perfect life of a social man.' The great sage fulfilled the target of Lord Buddha but refrained from making a single one a Bhikshu or Bhikshuni. In the modern democratic polity each of the citizen is a ruler; he is to take part in the governence of the country. How could he choose a life of An-nagarik? He asked to remain responsible member of the family and the society and to perform all duties. And, the family members only need a king and perform a role of a king. Monks are generally averse to enter the arena of political life. His *Rajasik Dharma* led his people to be the rulers in the modern democratic country. Without such religious tenets social democracy, consequently participatory democracy would have remained an utopian concept in India.

Empowerment of Women

Shakya Singha Siddhartha Gautam Buddha was not the pioneer of Buddhism. He was the 28th of the Buddhas' line and the last one. However, when he had preached the ancient Indian religion of *Shramana* culture and the religion of '*Purba*-Buddhas' his teachings were definitely not restricted to the teachings of the 'Former Buddhas'. He added and introduced many fundamentally original aspects that he inherited from the 'Buddhas of Old'. Similarly while fulfilling the mission and executing the philosophy of equality, fraternity and liberty of Lord Buddha, Harichand introduced many new and startlingly different aspects. Gautam prescribed strict and complete bachelor life for the Bhikkus and Bhikkunis of his Sanghs.

Harichand gave the opposite and created more responsible members for a family, society and for the State. He adhered to the truth and beauty of the natural process of life, a responsible and difficult family life for his Sangha. Matua Sangh of Harichand did not create the institutes like 'Bhukkus' and 'Bhikkunis'. These institutions instead of generating democratic aspiration to be the rulers of their own country lead to passive life. The contemporary social atmosphere was fraught with stink of the rotten moral value, the characterless and irresponsible use of women especially widows by *Sanyasis,* Vaishnava *Bairagis* and polygamous elite-Brahmins. This band contributed nothing for the society in its wealth production system but simply consumed the cream and exploited the civilisation like parasites. The degree of miseries of women during the entire medieval period, mainly under Muslim-Brahmin rule, of the country knew no bounds. Women were not allowed to move out of doors. Education was a strict taboo for them. Shameful and horror-institutions like *'Sati'* (widow-burning), *'Kulin'* (large scale polygamy), *'Rakhel'*(an institution of concubine), 'Whore-House', 'Permanent-widowhood', 'Child-marriage', *'Thagi'* (inter-state gang of dacoits operated on guerilla style being blessed by the Brahmins as well as the local rulers on share holding basis), 'Animal-sacrifice' etc. flourished as prestigious and practiced with pride.

Condition of women of the Chandal and other Untouchable Samaj, however, was considerably different from this wretchedly foul condition of the Brahmanical official society. Rammohan, never supported education which had no sanction of Hindu Shastras. Like Rammohan, Iswar Chandra Bandhopadhay (Vidyasagar) who was born in 1820 also supported the reform movement within the permissible jurisdictions of Hindu Shastras only. In 1851 Vidyasagar cited *slokes* from the Shastras in support of the 'Widow Re-marriage' bill brought by the British. Harichand, in the circumstances delivered in different terms. Monogamy (One lady) and controlled conjugal life in the family, he declared, is the best way of religion. If one fails to maintain purity of family life all his penance and pious work will be spoiled':-

"Ak Nari Brahmachari Palo Griha Dharma,
Griha Dharma Nasta Hole Nasta Sab Karma"[27]

Harichand's instructions frustrated the Vaishnavas who followed the teachings of Nemai Chand Mishra, (Chaitanya Mahaprobhu) who married twice and renounced the family life after deserting his aged mother Shachi and young 2nd wife Vishnupriya in distressing condition. Hindu scriptures declared that 'Women are the gate ways of *'Narak'* the hell'. Manu placed women in ever-lasting servitude and subordination to men. As a girl she was to be under her father, as young woman under her husband and in old-age under her son. As a consort of her husband she was to be burnt alive in the funeral pyre of her husband. Polygamy was an honorable practice in Hinduism. Lord God Krishna had a band of wives. "His sixteen hundred and odd wives could not shake His mind by their shafts of cupid and other charms, skilled in conveying the message of love dispatched by their eyebrows fascinating with the sentiment expressed by their suppressed smile and sidelong glances," describes Sreemad Bhagavat.[28] Polygamy (*Kulin*) combined with *Sati* system produced a horrible state of fallen humanity. Women carried no price on them; they were naturally not capable to read and even hear the Hymns of the Vedas. They were declared born impure. In the age of blinding darkness of 'Kulin Bengal', infested with the devotees of Lord God Krishna, introduction of monogamy as a religious practice was a terribly challenging job for Harichand. In this respect, he was much ahead of his time.

Apart from philosophy of love and purity, Harichand by his spiritual command sanctioned educational rights, equal status, and equal right to property for women. Monogamy was the only valid institution. He advised the followers strictly to adhere to the conduct, "*Para Nari Matritulya, Mithys Nahi Kabe. Para Dukkhe Dukkhi Sada Sachcharitra Rabe*" One is to regard others' woman as one's mother, and remain faithful to wife and one must not tell a lie. Be sensitive to understand suffering of others and be a man of character.

Harichand consigned women with equal right not only to religion but he also offered the same status in social and organisational fields. These rights were absolute. Women were not mere consort in her family maintenance work. Chandal women traditionally, like the Santhal tribe, enjoyed great freedom and equal status in the society. They were not an object of misuse and neglect. Adultery was almost nil amongst them. They participated along with their men-folk in agricultural work even in the production fields. The Chandal women held equal right to share of paternal property. It has been a historic fact that women only mothered agriculture. The Chandal women during 1860 and 1880 decades, like modern women of 21st century used to visit markets and marts for actual shopping purpose and even as sales-girls. Unlike Hindus, they never became victims of horrible *Sati* (burning alive on husband's pyre) practice and permanent widowhood. Widow re-marriage for the young girls and women were common amongst Chandals. Had the Chandal women simply been educated, they would have become object of envy of today's Mall-moving women folk of India. As *Matua* she once again enjoyed full and equal liberty in participating in religious rituals. Women devotees danced and beat drums and '*dankas*' side by side with their male-fellows.

Harichand like Lord Buddha did not create separate Nunnery or Bhikkuni Sangh, subordinate to Bhikku Sangh for women in Matua Sangh. All Matuas men and women remained in the family of same sangh. The idea of equality and concept of creating the abode of love on the Earth do not leave any room for unequal treatment with men and women. No sex discrimination in any respect was accepted in Matua faith. The Bharatiya Brahma Samaj was divided into two hostile sects. Keshav Chandra Sen led one. Devendra Nath Thakur expelled him simply because Kesavchandra allowed women to attend prayer in the same hall with the separate sitting arrangement in separate enclosures. There was no separate enclosure for women in the place of Matua religious gathering. In the enclosure of religious conglomeration, "All male and female, mingling together without any rhythm or rhyme chants Haribbol. No one was conscious of the differences of sexes when Kirtan proceeded":-

"Meye Madde Ak Sathe Misia Sakal'
Tal Nai Man Nai Bale Haribol.
Sankirtan Haiteche Kari Nai Hoos,
Veda Ved Gyan Nai Nari Ki Purus."[29]

Harichand foresaw the irresistible storm of democratic movement on the silver line on social and political horizon. He introduced the training programme in regard to organizing peoples gathering or mass-meetings amongst his disciples. And so much was the sincerity and his trust on the women power that he entrusted responsibility of organizing the maiden struggle on a widow Matua named Naiere. The poor widow had no resource but wanted to host a large gathering in a big and expensive function. Guru trained her:-

"Prabhu Bale, Naieri Matua sab Dak,
Janamer Mata Ak Kirti Kari Rakh."[30]

'Lord asked Naieri to summon all Matuas and organize them to create history. Around 20 mand rice will be consumed and you organize this and all other required staff'. The function was a grand success. Thus was started the activities of public gatherings with peoples support.

In the whirlwind of such a concept of equality the first Brahmin, Akshay Chakraborty came to be the disciple of Harichand. Abandoning sacred thread of nine virtues the Brahmin had taken the garland of coconut shell around his neck and did not care for his caste pride.

Conflict and Conquest

Nothing on the Earth can go up or ahead without facing resistance from within and outside or without facing opposition. Resistance is the proof of one's existence and separate entity. Even Lord Gautama could not preach his *Dhamma* of equality and fraternity, knowledge and liberty, the religion of universal love without facing resistance. At least thrice, attempts were made on his life. Lord Jesus Christ, the apostle of forgiveness was crucified. Prophet Muhammad was driven away from his family and country. Matuas too had to face bitter criticism and all out social attacks. It has been claimed that Harichand was born to fulfill the mission of Lord Buddha. However, he did not preach Buddhism. That was a time when the Sudras and the Untouchables of Bengal already had gone proselyte themselves to Christianity and Islam to breath in the just and human society. Missionary activities started in right earnest after the expiry of the first phase of Company's rule when propagating Christianity was banned in the British dominated areas. The new rulers being afraid of the Brahmins' non-cooperation in establishing their colonial rule in place of the Muslim rule in India, always supported Hindu customs and religious performances in the temples and other places. Rather they encouraged them by offering prayers and '*puja*' in Hindu Kali temples before setting to the battlefields. They even used to give gun-salutes to the goddess Kali of Kolkata after the victories were gained with the blessings by the Hindu pantheons.[31] The British enormously upheld the prestige of the Brahmin priests and granted official sanction in favour of the all temple rituals and the caste-system since their advent in the country. 'The co-operation between the Company's servants and the Brahmins was nowhere more hearty and intimate than in the management of the rich temples. Many causes contributed to this strange alliance between Christian people and the pagan priests'.[32] After establishing the unchallengeable supra-social status of the Brahmin the British withdrew their scheme of direct participation in the Hindu religious matters since 1840 by the order of Governor General Lord Auckland. By then the Brahmins regained their force and authority to execute their tyranny over the rest of the society independently.

In the early parts, only the Jesuit Fathers carried missionary activities in French colonies in India. However, as luck would have been, a year after the birth of Harichand in 1813 the Reforms Act lifted the ban on Christianity to preach their faith in India. It is true that the Aryan Brahmanism, Christianity and Islam all were foreign religions. However, there is a fundamental difference between Hinduism and other two foreign religions. The nomadic and savage Aryans lost their foreign roots as they came from no motherland. They, however, retained their distinct clanish entity and claimed to be of pure and superior identity by creating *'Aryavarta'* or civil-lines of their own. Side by side, they had declared the native people, their language, culture and religions as low, worthless, contemptuous, separate and useless. The Aryans lost their foreign roots because the barbaric nomads could have everything but motherland.

The vandal and barbarian race eventually had hijacked cultural and religious aspects of native Indians, assimilated and preached those as their own. The epicenter of Hinduism is therefore, found to be only in India and nowhere else. But the religious head quarters and roots of other two religions are in foreign lands. It is controlled from Vatican City and Mecca. Harichand found that it was not honorable but injurious for the Sudras and the Untouchables to remain within the concentration camp of Hinduism. They realised the truth of pains behind subordination of the Indians that was sure to come upon the servile people even after conversion to Islam or Christianity which had already come under heavy and ill influence of the Hindu Brahmins.

Mere right to religion and participation in the spiritual-rituals was meaningless for the Untouchables to gain total-freedom and democratic rights in the people's representative government. Even dogs and cats roam in the Hindu temples, gods and goddesses are associated with the animals like rats and cats. The Hindu devotees worship cows and monkeys. Karl Marx had recorded his conclusive verdict on Indian society. "Now, sickening as it must be to human feeling to witness those myriads of industrious patriarchal and inoffensive social organisations disorganised and dissolved into their units, thrown into a sea of woes, and their individual members losing at the same time their ancient form of civilisation, and their hereditary means of subsistence, we must not forget that these idyllic village communities, inoffensive though they may appear that always been the solid foundation of Oriental despotism, that they restrained the human mind within the smallest possible compass, making it the unresisting tool of superstition, enslaving it beneath traditional rules, depriving it of all grandeur and historical energies..... We must not forget that this undignified, stagnate and vegetative life, that this passive sort of existence evoked on the other part, in the contradistinction, wild, aimless, unbounded forces of destruction and rendered murder itself a religious rite in Hindustan. We must not forget that these little communities were contaminated by distinctions of castes and by slavery, that they subjugated man to external circumstances instead of elevating man to be the sovereign of circumstances, that they transformed a self developing social state into never changing natural destiny, and thus brought about a brutalizing worship of nature, exhibiting its degradation in the fact that man the sovereign of nature, fell down on his knees in adoration of Hanuman, the monkey and Sabula, the cow." At the same breath, Marx also did not forget to mention that being the unconscious tool of history the British "...produced the greatest, and to speak the truth, the only social revolution ever heard of in Asia'... 'having placed the spinner in Lancashire and the weaver in Bengal, or sweeping away both Hindo spinner and weaver, dissolved these small semi-barbarian, semi-civilised communities, by blowing up their economical basis."[33] Harichand was in the middle of his active life in the same year, 1853. In the circumstances, it is not gain said that by embracing the religion of the ruling race considerable advantage, economic and administrative would have come upon them as a reward for strengthening the foreign rulers. This phenomenal and superficial advantage was not the target of Harichand's mission. He wanted a self-conscious, independent stand and all out development of the liberated autochthons of India by way of self-government. He attempted to create an independent sovereign nation and to govern own country.

Harichand did not launch any temple entry movement to open the doors of the orthodox Hindu temples for the Sudras and the Untouchables. He never begged for the right to approach God. He did not go to any Brahmin, Mullah or a Christian-Father for getting baptised in spirituality. Instead of knocking at other's doors he had taken up arduous responsibility of leading his ignorant followers in correct path and directly gave the religious and spiritual right to his people. He taught the fundamental truth that to have access to the Supreme father one need not appeal through the commercially motivated and corrupt Brahmins. There was no need for any temple of God who is omnipresent. He rather refused to accept any Hindu god who helped impose and spread servitude.

The East India Company was indebted to the Untouchables for their joining the Company-army and winning battles of Palase in Bengal and Koregaon in Maharashtra in 1757 and 1818 respectively.

Harichand Thakur unlike his senior contemporary, Roybahadur Raja Rammohan Roy was not a mere family reformer or reformer of Hindu society or Hinduism. He did not attempt, unlike his junior contemporary Narayan Guru of Kerala and Dayananda Saraswati of Punjab who founded 'Arya Samaj' in 1875, to establish any reform movement. Harichand was not contented in social justice. He struggled for social transformation by annihilating castes and Hinduism. The audacity of Chandal Harichand was noted by the Brahmin society seriously. The Brahmins have been the most orthodox, heartless and supercilious creatures of the World. They never tolerate an iota of deviation from their prescribed social and spiritual rules and divine injunctions that were created to keep the immense majority in servitude. According to Hinduism the role of Harichand as a Guru and preacher of spirituality was highly heretic and an act of blasphemy. There arose therefore, an unavoidable and precarious tension in the social fabric. But the Brahmins were extremely helpless before the turbulent and marshal race called Chandal. Besides, more than half of the eastern Bengal was already Islamised. And these Muslims were primarily the converts from Chandal stock. They maintained social bonds. The image of the Brahmanical opposition shed its picture in the mirror of Matua literature:-

"... Ved Bidhi Nahi Mane Na Mane Brahman,
Nischai Korite Habe A Dale Shasan."[34]

'They have assumed godhood merely by chanting Hari, Hari; all the cheats have ganged up and they march on enmass. They do not show slightest regard or respect for the Vaishnavs and the Brahmins. Day and night, they chant 'Haribbol' and have become 'Gosain'. They do not believe in the Vedas and out rightly defy the Brahmans. This band has to be unpardonably chastised.'

In this communal tension and conflicts out of the spread of the new religion, the team of Harichand always gained an upper hand. 'In fact, the mischievous Brahamns, in order to teach a good lesson Hari Thakur and his disciples had organised a social boycott against them by instigating a section of the Chandals of Oakland and its surrounding villages. The boycott, however, failed after some time when the people realised their own mistake.'[35] Even some of the Brahmins became his disciples. It became a unique phenomenon that a Chandal not only became spiritual Guru of Brahmins but also propagated a new faith. Some Brahmins once came to verify supernatural power of Thakur Harichand. The visitors did not pay their respect to the Guru by touching his feet. The chelas of Harichand could not tolerate the insulting situation. They did not hesitate to show the superior position of their Guru and forced the visiting Brahmins to bow their heads to the feet of Harichand:-

"Thakur Dekhite Ale Pranamite Hai
...... Atek Balia Brahmaner Griba Dhari,
Mattwa Mateler Prai Bale Hari Hari.
Griba Dhari Chanp Mari Bhumite Felai,[36]

'On paying a visit, one touches feet of 'Thakur' the god-hood, did not you see that one Brahmin touched the feet of Harichand? Why do you hesitate so long, why you too do not touch the feet (Pranam) for blessing? With the same breath one (Matua) had held the neck of the Brahmin and pressed him down and chanted Hari Hari, with drunken force and asked the Brahmin to touch the feet. Being forcibly pressed, the Brahmin took his blessing. On seeing it Mangal shouted Hari Hari! Collecting dust of the Harichand's feet they puffed it on the head of the Brahmin'. Fired with the sense of self respect and enthusiasm of executing the philosophy of equality what the Chandal Matuas did was dangerously insulting and breach of code of conduct of Hindu society. The hymns of the Vedas and Manu Smriti declared capital punishment for such a conduct of a Sudra to a holy Brahmin. Manu prescribes, 'If any Sudra dares giving advice or preaching religious discourse to a Brahman then his tongue is to be severed and boiled oil is to be poured in his mouth and ears'.[37] However, the Brahmin Samaj of that day did not react to the incident. They were no match to the organised strength of the Matuas in the Districts. Who was to punish whom? Matuas traveled enmass with the red-triangular flag in hand. With the rhythm of war-drum, the Matuas advanced restlessly in volatile mood for revolution. Fearless were they. The Hindu society had to keep quite.

The Maiden Revolt of Red-flags

Harichand prepared the fertile ground for starting such democratic and people's movement to shake the plinth of the British Government at the grass-root level of the far-flung villages of Bengal. Marxist-red flag was quite unknown to Indians. The Matua triangular red flag created the history.

The first tangible manifestation of his teachings became known in the beginning of 1870. Describing the movement a modern social-historian comments, "The first organised endeavour at self-affirmation started in Faridpur-Bakharganj region in the late 1872, when in official documents they were still being referred to as Chandals. The movement had no political significance at that time and was only an effort made by them to raise themselves in social scale among the Hindus. The immediate occasion was the *sradh* or post-funeral ceremony of the father of a well-to-do Chandal headman of village Amgram in Bakharganj. Disregarding the established norms he invited his higher caste neighbours to attend the ceremony and dine in his house. The latter at the instigation of the Kayasthas, refused to accept the invitation and the reasons cited were as follows: that the women of this caste visited the market place without any sense of shame; that their degraded status was even acknowledged by the government; that in the jails only the Chandal inmates were employed as scavengers for removing filth. A meeting of all the Chandal headmen was therefore, organised immediately and following resolutions were adopted:

(1) women must not in future visit Haats (periodic rural marts) and Bazaars;
(2) service of no kind whatever be taken with the other castes; and
(3) food prepared by all other Hindu castes, other than Brahmins, was not to be eaten. Their demand for equal treatment in jails was also duly communicated to the government officials visiting the locality"[38]

These social decisions were not actually without great political significance and impact, as commented by the author in the preceding paragraph. Let us not forget that the decision was taken in an assembly by the heads of village *Panchyat* of many villages. As a result of Matua movement the Chandal villages got consolidated with democratic consciousness. The village cluster where Harichand was born was thus called '*Agarokhan Gram*' eleven villages. It was a confederation of eleven adjoining villages. The heads, called *Matubbar* of eleven villages sitting together used to take unimous decision of '*Agarokhan gram*'. Very famous and powerful was the consolidation of ninety six villeges '*Chiyanobboikhan Gram*' and of one hundred twenty one villeges '*Akso Akushkhan Gram*'. The decisions in such *Panchayat* meetings were very decisive in nature. No one was to challenge or disobey it. This virtually acted as catalyst for the growth of future democratisation process of India in the formation of its participatory and representative form of Parliamentary Government. Just a decade later in 1882, Lord Ripon disclosed his 'Declaration' to create Local Boards like *Tahasil* and *Taluks* to be headed by the elected representatives.

The decisions taken in the meeting of Amdanga village was circulated amongst the people in general at length all over the Districts by means of beating drums in the periodical '*Haats*' in different places in a routine manner. During those days that was the most powerful and effective method for mass communication. The decision of boycotting all domestic-job in the places of the caste-Hindus, indeed, transformed into the maiden 'Agrarian Trade Union Movement' in Indian history. The movement got complete success. The organizers were carefully skillful enough in protecting the interests of the daily-wage labour and the needy Chandal work force. With a view to arranging their daily supply a big crisis-fund, rather welfare-fund was created by collecting huge and liberal donations from all families worth of it. It was also declared by the Depressed Classes peasantry and artisans that the instructions so circulated had the blessings of the British Government. Therefore, stringent measure of punishment including 'social boycott' against one who violated the same would be taken.

Very quickly, the movement gained momentum and spread like wildfire to the entire part of Faridpur district. The Central Office for organizing it was set up at Gopalganj town. The District Magistrate of Faridpur dispatched the report on the impact of this powerful and long effective trade union movement to the Commissioner Dacca, in his letter dated 8th April 1873. It reads, "So complete was the Strike that the fields...... untilled, the houses not thatched, and not a Chandal in the service of the Hindu or Mahamadan, and not a Chandal woman was seen in any market. The situation was so volatile in Muksudpur and Gopalganj that extra police had to be mobilised from the Divisional Headquarters for maintaining peace and order."[39] The maiden agrarian strike in Indian history, interestingly, took place soon after the Paris Commune was crushed by the European powers in 1871.

During his life-time Harichand had the occasion to taste the fruits of success of his mission. He expired in 1878 after passing the baton in the able hands of Guruchand.

Counter Religions and Politics

As has already been mentioned, the efforts of the Untouchables to convert to other religions like Islam and Christianity was hindered by the Hindus as well as by the English in various manners. The process of desertion of Hinduism for other religion ceaselessly, however, continues to avoid Hindu-atrocities and servitude organised under caste-system in Hindu Concentration camp. According to an English educated *sanyasi,* Swami Dharma Teertha of Trivankur, "The Hindu system of religion is nothing more than a lever of which the Brahmans make use habitually for influencing the passions of a credulous people and turning them to their own advantage."…. "The caste, the temple and philosophy are the pillars which support the huge system of Brahman imperialism called Hinduism. Caste is the common law which defines the status, rights and responsibilities of the rulers and the ruled, the masters and the slaves corresponding to, but much more deadly than the enactments of European imperialists concerning their subject nations. The temple stands for the system of exploitation, which they call capitalism in modern language. Capitalism, however, is economic only, where as temple-craft is an intellectual, moral, emotional and economic exploitation of subject people."[40] In the circumstances, the Brahmins were successful in retaining their supercilious position simply by maintaining the divine slaves within the campus of Hinduism. The Brahmins would not allow them to go for conversion to any other organised religious institution.

The British colonial power too realised this paradoxical and atrocious socio-spiritual rather politico-economic frame no sooner than they interfered in the governance of the country. They too helped their Brahmin-stooges to retain all their subservient subjects in perpetual servitude. The colonial motivation of the British, eventually made them surrender to the 'Spiritual fascism' of the Hinduism, which helped even the democratic struggle to be kept within the networking of religious sentiments. Colonial interests of the trading corporation of British East India Company as well as the Hindu Aryans were best fortified in it.[41] A nation of religion called 'Hindu-nationalism' in India thus grew in course of time under the Union Jack. In

India, therefore, those who rule over the temples, the place of war and warship, rule over the modern politics of the nation in the name of democracy.

Brahmo Samaj

The Brahmins wanted to save their position. Being in distress, they too planned to democratize their engine of oppression. Many sects and groups of the Hindus came up to meet the challenges put up by the Matuaism and the resurrected Buddhism. Even the religions those were created by the sages of the Untouchables independently are found to have, in course of time in a calculated manner, been assimilated in the word Hinduism. Their Prophets and preachers have been hijacked along with their deities with form or formless. Role of Chaitnnya in Islamic period was re-enacted by Raja Rammohan Roy in the British period. Raja Rammohan Bandhopadhaya (Roy) initially was a follower of Islamic culture, language and Monotheism. However, with the increasing influence and power of the British East India Company after 1813 he leaned towards Christianity and English language and culture. 'Rammohan used to attend religious prayers regularly in the Christian Chapels with his fellows. One day, on their way home back from one such function Tarachand Chakraborty and Chandrasekhar Dev were in his 'Fitton'. Suddenly, Chandrasekhar Dev suggested, 'Dewanji! we attend the prayers of the foreigners. Cannot we arrange our own system of '*Upasana*', 'Praising the Lord'? Raja Rammohan in the next winter in 1828 established Brahmo Samaj….. Function of the Samaj started in the house of an Anglo-Indian, Kamal Basu. The premises was taken on rent. Every Saturday, in the evening there was conducted 'Brahmo-Upasana'. The process was like this, In the starting two Telegu Brahmins would recite the hymns of the Vedas. It was followed by the recitation from the Upanisad by Utsavananda Vidyavagish. Thereafter with the songs and sermons preached by Ramchandra Vidyavagish the function would have completed.'[42] Brahma-dharma, also called as 'Vedantic-True Religion', 'Vedanta Pratipadya Satyadharma' was Brahmanical in every respect. Indeed, there was nothing new in it. In the functions even Bengali Brahmins were not allowed to recite the hymns from the Vedas. Bengal, according to the scriptures remained outside the pale of Vedic culture hence the Brahmins of this non-Vedic land were disqualified for reciting Vedic hymns.

Despite this, the Hindus dramatised the Brahmos as anti-Hindu; dangerous for the orthodox and fanatic Hindus. Raja never supported anything, be it in the field of education, culture, language, dress, food-habit and even politics, which had no support of the Hindu scriptures. *Raibahadur* Raja Rammohan Roy, till his last breath at Bristol maintained his sacred thread around his neck. He never took food with anyone other than a Brahmin. He also took along with him a Brahmin cook, Ramgopal Banerjee to London. Still he was opposed vehemently for his family-reform activities like supporting the British Government in anti-Sati action, in spread of

English and Female education etc. This Brahmo Samaj in course of time primarily was active in anti-conversion propaganda amongst the untouchable-villages and opposed independent and democratic political move of the Untouchables.

With the demise of Raja Ram Mohan Roy the activities and influence of the Brahma Samaj diminished and declined. But it had its role to play in future. With the establishment and growth of Matua influence challenging the Vedic culture and social order the Brahma Samaj got revitalised. A pure and orthodox Hindu leader Devendra Nath Thakur joined Brahma Samaj on 7th of *Pous* in 1843, to shoulder the heavy burden to spread the activities of the Samaj. Upto this date the Brahmos believed the Vedic dictums as infallible. Matua Guru Harichand Thakur and his powerful Untouchable Samaj challenged such unfounded and irrational proposition. Akshay Kumar Dutta, the close associate of Devendra Nath Thakur son of Prince Dwarakanath Thakur, too insisted on changing the stand on the infallibility of the Vedas and that the Vedas were the scriptures delivered by the Divinity. After great resistance Devendranath eventually yielded to Dutta and in 1850 accepted the view that the Vedas were not infallible. The Brahmo Samaj got full zeal and force with the joining of Kesav Sen in 1859. He created new streams for giving more reformist turn which in reaction gave birth to vigorous Hindu-nationalism by Raj Narayan Basu and others.

With the completion of their phenomenal responsibility of Hinduisation of national politics by several other institutions, the Brahmo Samaj went into gradual withdrawal process and virtual extinction.

Arya Samaj

With a view to keeping the rebellious Sudras and the Untouchables in Hinduism and in the Hindu political forum there emerged in northwestern India another group called 'Arya Samaj'. Dayananda was born in 1824. In course of time, he became an outstanding Vedic scholar. Dayananda Saraswati an orthodox Brahmin from Gujarat eventually founded Arya Samaj in 1875 in the Punjab. The name of the Samaj denotes its motto and objectives. "One of the Arya Samaj's objectives was to prevent the conversion of the Hindus to other religions. This crusade became a contributory factor in the growth of communalism in India in the 20th century. While the Arya Samaj's reformist work rendered to unite people, its religious work tended, though perhaps unconsciously, to divide the growing national unity among Hindus, Muslims, Parsis, Sikhs and Christians."[43] Arya Samaj also vehemently acted upon holding those untouchables who called themselves not-Hindus, Ad-dhammis, Ad-dravids etc. Arya Samaj for all practical purposes thus nourished and watered the thorny sentiment of Hindu fundamentalism and the already grown up political concept of Hindu-nationalism in Bengal. "The most characteristic feature of the Arya Samaj is the emphasis it laid upon the work of *Suddhi*. This means the re-conversion of those Hindus, millions in number, who had once been willingly or forcibly converted into other religions like Islam or Christianity, but were now willing to come back to the fold of Hinduism. Orthodox Hinduism had always barred its doors against them; the Arya Samaj threw it wide open. As a matter of fact, this aspect of the Arya Samaj excited the greatest interest in it among the people outside its own ranks. It was strongly resented by the Muslims and was a source of almost chronic feud between the two. At the same time the *Suddhi* was looked upon by the Samaj as a potent instrument for affecting that religious, social, and political unity of India which came to be cherished as its great ideal by the Arya Samaj."[44] The constitution which was drawn up for the Arya Samaj on the occasion of its foundation in Bombay in 1875 laid down some of the fundamental doctrines and rules of conduct. Three of these may be noted:

1. The Samaj shall regard the Vedas alone as independently and absolutely authorities.....

Two years later (in 1877) this creed and constitution were replaced by Ten Principles. These Ten Principles appeared to have been consciously launched to be akin to the 'Ten Commandments' delivered by the God of Abraham in the Old Testament.'[45]

In view of the above, it becomes clear that the motive behind these social reformists was nothing but to establish Brahmanical or Hindu Raj with the transfer of power by the British. The teeming millions of untouchables and Sudras while have been suffering in their 'Concentration Camp' as inhuman beings from time immemorial, the Arya Samajis, instead of rescuing or releasing them from pathetic-bondage, on the basis of Vedic-dictum, showed their eagerness to rescue the converts through the funny 'Suddhi' Vedic-Yadna which had no locus-standi in the scriptures. Where should they place the re-converted untouchables? Will they be Brahmins? *Vaisyas*?

Theosophical Society

Even international politico-spiritual group came over to India during this period. Their role seems to have been to impress and to confuse the already ignorant, credulous, superstitious people to remain contented in the concentration camp of Hinduism. In 1880, standing beside the American Colonel H.M. Alcott, wife of a Russian General Madam Helena Patrovna Blavetskay embraced Buddhism. Madam Blavetskay, though had deserted her husband Major Blavetsky soon after their marriage, she retained her husband's family name throughout her life. She was the daughter of Russian Colonel Piter Hunn. Initially she became a Hippi. Amidst the atmosphere of all army personnel and with marshal mindset Madam Blavetsky and Colonel Alcot embraced Buddhism by pronouncing spells in Pali language before a huge gathering of the Buddhists in the open ground in the city of Galle, Srilanka. Soon after, having conquered the hearts of the enchainted Ceylonese people, they landed in India. With the assistance of an orthodox Tamil Brahmin T. Subbarao, they had procured a plot of vast area measuring 358 accores in Adyar, just on the bank of River Adyar flooded with backwater on the Madras seashore. In 1882, here, they founded the Indian Head Quarters of the International Spiritual Centre of Theosophical Society. Colonel Alcot also founded a very beautiful school of the society in the campus. For the first time the untouchable children of locality entered in the school run by the white race. Madam Blavetsky, along with Colonel Alcott established the centre of Theosophical Society in New York in 1875, the same year that, Arya Samaj came up in India.

The teenager Anagaric Dhamma Pal at his 18 only, came over to India to preach Buddhism in the land of Buddha. Initially 'Theosophical Society appeared to be a centre to preach the religion of Equality, Fraternity and Liberty, of Lord Sakya Muni. In the centre of the sprawling campus there stands a Buddha Temple. By the side of the pond beside the Buddha shrine there was planted a branch of 'Boe'-tree which was brought from its origin in Bodhgaya in 1950. Adjacent to the shrine the main temple Structure of Theosophical society exists. Under the roof of this temple representatives of all the World religions are sheltered.

Madam Blavatsky was a member of the School of World Magicians and a successful pass out from the Egyptian school of magic named 'Copt'. However, from her death bed in London in 1891, she instructed her followers and friends, in her Will, to recite from 'Light of Asia' and verses of the Gita on her death anniversary every year at Adyar. Blavetsky knew well that it was Lord Krishna who created *Chaturvarna-ashram-dharma.* Lord Krishna propagated the philosophy of hatred between man and man. She knew well that Lord Krishna was the cause of all miseries of the untouchables. Hinduisation of Adyre-center, though started during the time of Madam Blavetsky, its course was completed by Mrs. Annie Besant who became its president after Madam by making it a complete Hindu politico-religious organ with International link. As a result of her outstanding work in this target she got double crowns one from the Hindu orthodox Feudal-Lords and the other from the British Government. That is why we find Lord Hamilton, Secretary of State write to Lord Curzon ….. "to grant the request of Ms Besant as she had been very useful in Madras in combating the Congress leaders and denouncing the Western method of education as wholly unsuited into India, and endeavoring to establish a system of modern education associated with definite religious and moral training."[46] And Mrs. Besant declared, "It (India) only throbs with full response when the religious note has been struck which call out its sympathetic vibration." Thus, the Theosophical-cum-Buddhist-cum-Hindu spiritual-institute got itself transformed into a pure, orthodox, superstitious and caste-based Hindu organisation, a launching pad for Ms Besant to be the President of the Indian National Congress repeatedly. She also was the founder of the Benaras Hindu University.

Resurrection of Buddhism

Anagaric Dharmapal, a young Ceylonese Buddhist was present in the Galle's conversion ceremony of Madam Blavatsky on May 21, 1880. He was completely swayed by her charming personality, her powerfully sweet deliverance of discourses and devotion to Buddha. The young talent had instantly decided to renounce family life to preach Buddhism in the vast land of Buddha and became her devout disciple. "So no sooner than she proposed that it was the holy desire of Master Kutuhumi that Dharmapala must join her at Adyre as one of her disciples, Dharmapala with great eagerness availed himself of the opportunity so that he could establish direct contact with the competent brothers."[47] He had joined Theosophical Society in 1884 and came to Adyar along with two other monks. In 1885, the London Weekly, the Telegraph published article of Edwin Arnold, the author of the 'Song Celescial' and the 'Light of Asia'. The reality now stormed the domain of fantasy. It revealed the pathetic condition of deserted place of Bodhgaya where Siddhartha got enlightenment and became the Buddha. The entire temple was under the control of a Saiva Mohanta. Dharmapala visited the place in Janury 1891 and since then started a battle royal to liberate the Buddhist temple from the Hindus. In India soon he became the champion of Buddhism, the faith of fraternity, equality, liberty, knowledge and reasoning. The entire Hindus and the Parsis stood firmly against the crusade of liberating the faith and institutions of Buddha which Dharmapala started with undaunted courage in the land where there was not a single Buddhist to stand by him. He established 'The Mahabodhi Society' in Calcutta in the Templeton Colege Square. The struggle still continues. However, since the beginning the Buddhist movement was hijacked by the Brahmins, right from Neel Kamal Mookherjee to Shyamaprosad Mukherjee who became its president. One of the distinguished members of Arya Samaj Pandit Rahul Sankrityayan (Kedar Nath Pandey) a Brahmin of orthodox family from Ajamgar became the Buddhist philosopher of note and repute. Ravindra Nath Tagore showed much interest in Buddhism. However, with the mass conversion of Dr Ambedkar and his untouchable followers in millions on 14th October, 1956 the elite-Hindus lost interest in Buddhism. The resurrected Buddhism has been under clouds of Hinduism with the intervention of Hindu-billionaire Birla, Goenka and Modi. Buddha has been propagated as the 9th Avatar of the Hindu god Vishnu. Vipasana-Yoga, not the principle of equality, fraternity, liberty and middle path in economy has been made the essence of Buddhism and its practice. Hindus have become quite formidable. These forces eventually helped damage the growth of Indian nationalism and strengthen the political forces of Hindu Nationalism.

Ramakrishna Math

With the opening up and rising of the sun shine of democratic declaration of Lord Ripon, there arrived, during 1885, an Indian *Sanyasi*, graduate from

The Scottish Church College, Calcutta. He became famous as Swami Vivekananda. His family name was Narendra Nath Dutta and belonged to a *Sudra Kayastha* caste of Bengal. Vivekananda initially was a sincere member of the 'Gang of Hope' created by Keshab Chandra Sen for complete social reform. However, when Sen fell in trouble Vivekanand joined Hindu-nationalist group. The entire Kali temple, once was purified with the waters of the holy Ganges as Vivekananda (a Kayasth, Sudra) entered in the main precinct of the temple.[48] Census Commissioners and Calcutta High court too refused to accept that the Kayasthas were Kshatriyas. Vivekananda, however, up. held the Brahmanical-supremacy in political, social and economic fields, throughout his life. He was doggedly loyal to Hinduism that declared him and his class of people, slaves, and as a slave of the Brahmins enjoyed slavery comfortably. He was badly used by the Brahmins to damage the interests of the Sudras and the untouchables.

Vivekananda, after his return from America and England purchased 22 *bighas* of land in 1898 from Babu Bhagwat Narayan Singh, a man from Bihar on the western bank of river Hoogly at Belur. He purchased the plot in his own name after getting donation of Rs. 40000 from the American Buddhist woman Mrs. Henrieta Mullar. On this plot of land, he established the most influential Hindu Mission after the name of his Guru, Rama Krishan. This was a pioneer institution like ISCON. Swamiji institutionalised the Mission in a huge Mandir and framed many rules and conduct to be strictly adhered to. The number one of the rules of the Mission is, "Math/ Mission will not pay much attention on social reforms, because those social ills and customs are a type of disease of the social body. When that body will become O.K. and strong enough after getting nutrition of education etc. those diseases will disappear automatically. Therefore, instead of wasting time by disclosing those social evils, the Mission will take care of feeding the society to strengthen it."[49]

The founders of the Mission knew well that the principle of casteism and caste-structure, which has been termed by Karl Marx as the 'decisive impediment of Indian power and progress' has been created, maintained and imposed by the educated creamy-layer-elite and spiritually powerful section of society. They were the educated lot. This has been the fundamental source of all social diseases and weaknesses. The uneducated or illiterate Shudras in any way were not the creators of those oppressive and discriminatory social evils and customs. The Brahmins who invented all these social evils and inhuman customs and executed in the name of divinity were educated enough. How could disease be cured by the causing elements? Having been armed with modern education and knowledge of science why the oppressors will take a suicidal path and how without destroying the agent or engine of oppression? A Sudra *Sanyasi*, Vivekananda Swami in a calculated manner was used by the Brahmanical lobby for their own interest.

Vivekananda never wanted that the Sudras and the Untouchables ever get any type of freedom. He like any other staunch Hindu remained a casteist par-excellence. According to him, the most outstanding contribution of the Hindus towards the World civilisation was the Caste-system. He preached, "I do not propose any leveling of castes. Caste is a very good thing. Caste is a thing we want to follow….. Indian caste is better than the caste which prevails in Europe and America….. Castes should not go…. It is sheer nonsense to desire the abolition of castes."[50]

His reactionary mind always has been anti Depressed class people and he advised the caste Hindus to lure the low caste Muchis and Bhangis, the poor and wretched Tribal with lip-sympathies and sweet words that they were their blood-brothers. "Go to them in loin-cloth or else the British are teaching them that they are not Aryans and you people are Aryans.[51] He advised, in his article *Swadesh-mantra,* the Brahmanical people to penetrate among those people in loin-cloth to gain back their trust and declare with loud-voice that 'The ignorant Indians, the poor Indians, the Chandal Indians and the Muchis, Methats and Brahmin Indians are my blood-brothers'. The orthodox Vivekananda had opposed widow-remarriage. He gave arguments even in favour of burning widows alive as '*Sati*'. He advanced even one-step further to put hurdles on the forward march of the country's unfortunate untouchables and the animists/tribes who were shown a path of prosperity.

Narendra Nath Bhattachariya (M.N. Roy) made a bold assessment of Swami Vivekananda's role of spirituality as follows: "Religious nationalism of the orthodox as well as reformed school had begun to come into evidence in the province of Bengal since the first years of the twentieth century…. Like Bal Gangadhar Tilak, Dutta (Narendranath Dutta) was also a prophet of Hindu nationalism. He also was a firm believer in the cultural superiority of the Indian people, and held that on this cultural basis should be built the future Indian nation. But he was not a partisan of orthodoxy in religion; to social conservatism. He was avertable iconoclast. He had the courageous foresight, or perhaps instinct, which convinced him that if religion was to be saved, it must be given a modern grab; if the priest was still to hold his sway over the millions of Hindu believers, he must modify his old crude ways; if the intellectual aristocracy of the fortunate few was to retain its social predominance, spiritual knowledge must be democratised…… His nationalism was a spiritual nationalism…. His philosophy on which was subsequently built the orthodox nationalism of the de-classed young intellectuals, organised into secret societies advocating violence and terrorism for the overthrow of the rule….. This youthful rebels fanatically believing in the spiritual mission of their Motherland, embodied in themselves the clash of two forces; that of reaction inducing them to put their nationalism on a religious basis, to hoist the so-called 'aggressive-nationalism' which proposed to put up a determined resistance to the menaces of materialism in order to preserve the assumed superiority of their spiritual heritage.... In their religiousness and wild spiritual imperialism, they embodied the reactionary social forces. Their no less sincere and ardent desire, on the other hand to educate the people, to improve the latter's conditions, to revive the golden age unsullied by the vices of the existing system, were generated by the objectively revolutionary forces heralding a coming social struggle."[52]

The Official historians therefore, glorified these "counter-liberation movements" led by the creamy-layer-elite of microscopic minority to suppress the democratic upsurge of the immense majority as the 'Awakening of India' and Indian nationalism. "The nineteenth century, specially the latter half of it, saw the beginning of new stirring in the minds of Indian people..... In every sphere of life, they had to meet the challenges of a new culture, which forced them to revise their orthodox ideas and to make a revaluation of their old values. With the spread of English education new wine began to be poured into old-bottles."[53] Here the phrase, 'Indian people' meant the microscopic minority Brahmins and 'awakening' meant to wake up to arrest the process of liberation-march of the immense majority, the lowest stratum of the society whom they call touchable and untouchable Sudras. Hindu nationalism continued its forward march in opposition to what Hari-Guruchand and the Indian peasantry started half a century ago.

The 'awakening of India' was nothing but issuing of the prescription of the 'opium of religion' sugarcoated by the combined forces of modern-educated Hindus right from Raja Rammohan Roy-Dayananda Saraswati-Blavetski-Besant-Ramakrishna-Bankim-Vivek-Ravindranatn Tagore to Tilak-Gandhiji's 'Gita-Rashaya' against the sole-power of the Matua-faith. Matua-faith, which was propounded by Hari-Guruchand, stood diametrically opposite to the doctrine of hatred, inequality, caste, infallibility of the Vedic scriptures, rituals, superstition of inhuman mode of human interactions. It upheld the spirit of liberty, equality, fraternity, rational movement of democratic rights of the Indian autochthons (*Mulniwasis*).

Consequently, a century after, Dr B.R. Ambedkar, being ditched by the Hindus in every respect, in May 1936 disclosed, "Hinduism is not a religion, it is a slavery.....Thus Hindu religion is not the religion of our ancestors, but it was the worst type of slavery that was thrust upon them. Our ancestors had no means to fight this slavery and therefore they could not revolt. They were compelled to live in the religion..... " "The religion which teaches man to behave in an inhuman manner is not religion but infamy. The religion, which does not recognize a human being as a human being, is a curse. The religion in which the touch of animals is permitted but the touch of a human being pollutes is not a religion but the mockery of a religion. The religion, which precludes some classes from education forbids them to accumulate wealth and to bear arms, is not a religion but tyranny." He therefore questioned, "Why do you want to remain bound to a religion which does not even treat you as a human being? Why do you remain in a religion, which prohibits you from entering its temples? Why do you remain under the religion, which prohibits you from drawing water from public wells? Why do you remain in the religion, which bars you from decent occupations and job? Why do you remain in the religion which insults you at every step?"[54]

Since the beginning of the 20th century the Hindu-India is found to have given more stress on building and expanding macro-temples like Somnath, Vaishnudevi, Laxmi, places of pilgrimages and micro-level Sani-Mandirs on street corners instead of establishing schools, industries and health-centers. Consequently, today India has become a country of roadside temples, *maths* and ashrams. Apart from household temples, the spots of public-worship (temporary and permanent) have increased by thousand folds. Opium of religion has been prescribed by the ruling class to retain their soverignty over the immense majority. A census of temples will reveal that the temples are active to work as permanent political-unit in every block level. In Indian democracy, fundamentally a theocratic, those who control temples control Parliament. Despite this powerful and multi-dimensional counter religio-political attack of Hinduism and the Hindus the *Matua* faith advances its forward march.

References

1. Mahakabi Mahananda Halder, Guru Chand Charit, p. 145.
2. Shankari Prosad Basu, Vivekanand O Samakalin Bharat Varsa, Vol. 3, p. 155.
3. *Ibid.*
4. Tarak Gosain, Hari Lilamrita, p. 23.
5. *Ibid*, p. 138.
6. Mahakabi Mahananda Halder, Guru Chand Charit, p. 145.
7. P.R. Thakur, Atmacharit Ba Purwasmriti, (pub. In 1995) p. 118.
8. Tarak Gosain, Hari Lilamrita, p. 84.
9. Nityananda Halder, Jatirjanak Guruchand, pp. 138, 145.
10. Dr B.R. Ambedkar, Buddha and His Dhamma; and Dhamma Pad, 1/5.
11. Dhamma Pada 5/2.
12. The Bible, Exodus 20 : 2.
13. The Bible, Exodus, 20:2.
14. Gita.
15. Manu Smriti.
16. *Ibid*, p. 23.
17. *Ibid*, pp. 71 and 73
18. Mahakabi Mahananda Halder, Guru Chand Charit, p. 40.
19. *Ibid*, p. 39.
20. Dhammapad.
21. Mahakabi Mahananda Halder, Guru Chand Charit, p. 101.
22. *Ibid*, p. 111.

23. *Ibid*, p. 73.
24. *Ibid,* p. 570.
25. Marx and Engels, Selected Works.
26. Tarak Gosain, Hari Lilamrita, pp. 22-23.
27. *Ibid*, p. 14.
28. Srimad Bhagwad, 1061/4.
29. Tarak Gosain, Hari Lilamrita, pp. 161 and 145.
30. *Ibid*, p. 97.
31. Shivnath Shastri, Ramtanu Lahiri O Samakalin Banga Samaj, pp. 53-54.
32. Swami Dharma Teertha, History of Hindu imperialism, p. 159.
33. Letter written on June 10, 1853 by Marx and published in New-York Daily Tribune on 25th instant/Selected Works Vol. 1, pp. 492-493.
34. Mahakabi Mahananda Halder, Guru Chand Charit, p. 94.
35. Advocate Nirod Bihari Roy, A People in Distress, Vol. 1, p. 37.
36. Mahakabi Mahananda Halder, Guru Chand Charit, p. 94.
37. Manusmriti, 8/272.
38. Sekhar Bandyopadhyay, Caste, Protest Identity in Colonial India, p. 34.
39. *Ibid.*
40. Swami Dharma Teertha, History of Hindu Imperialism, p. 139, Edition 2003.
41. *Ibid,* p. 158.
42. Shivnath Sastri, Ramtanu Lahiri O Tatkalin Banga Samaj, p. 78.
43. Bipin Chandra, Modern India, (NCERT), p. 220.
44. Bhartiya VidyaBhawan,Vol. 10, The Heritage and Culture of Indian People, p. 111.
45. *Ibid*, p. 110.
46. Bhartiya Vidya Bhawan , Vol. 10, part-II.
47. Shankari Prasad Basu , Vivekanand O Samakalin Bharat Varsa.
48. *Ibid.*
49. *Ibid.*
50. Complete Works of Swami Vivekananda, Vol. 5, pp. 214-215.
51. Vivekananda, Swadesh Mantra.
52. M.N. Roy, India in Transition, pp. 190-92.
53. L. Mukherjee , History of India (Modern Period), p. 175.
54. Bhagwan Das, Thus Spake Ambedkar, Vol. 4, pp. 43 and 61-62.

4

Guruchand the Dream of His Father

Harichand courageously rose to dispel the blinding darkness of his society that was ushered by Brahmanical caste system. In the course, the greatest contribution of Harichand towards the *Mulniwasi* '*Bahujan Samaj*' is his son Guruchand. It is not possible in one life to demolish the concrete walls of caste-system built bit by bit through the ages by the priest-crafts with the direct sponsorship of the state machinery. Caste vanishes in the blue within moments as soon as one comes out of the Hindu fold. But coming out or pulling someone out of the Hindu circumstances is very difficult task. Harichand successfully passed his baton in the hands of the next generation. Had there been no Guruchand, the history of modern India would have been shaped different geographically and in its socio-political character. It is he who in pursuance of his father's dream impregnated the independent '*Bahujan-samaj*' movement to be created by the self conscious '*Bahujan-Samaj*' to protect the interests of the '*Mulniwasi-Bahujan-Samaj*'. Harichand had an incredible audacity of dream to transform the vanquished and servile class untouchable autochthons into the ruling-*samaj*.

Harichand passed away in 1878. Karl Marx survived him by half a decade more. Marx propagated the ideology that targeted to establish the rule of the lowest stratum and the immense majority of the society. Harichand taught his people the basic tenets of Marxian ideology even before the name of Marx had entered into Asiatic zone. Now there came Guruchand. The exceedingly excellent skill to maneuver public sentiment, political sagacity combined with quenchless flame of energy and a long life of 91 years of Guruchand was dedicated completely for fulfilling the mission of his father. His majestic appearance and dynamic personality inspired the brave-heart Chandal-army with missionary zeal to face all risks and adversities in the battles of liberty. They with the belief in the deep of their hearts to overcome all dangerous hurdles marched with the banner of *Matua* red-flag *Lal Nisan* for equality and Liberty. Within a few years, the matchlessly ambitious dream of Harichand came true.

The series of well-organised peasants' revolts, led by Chandal-Muslim combined forces, during the decade of 1840s and onwards already drew the attention of the British administration. All the waves of peasant movements or peasant revolutions right from the beginning of Titumir, Samser Gazi revolt, Midnapur Choar-Gharui revolt, Sandeep Peasant revolution, Bakharganj-Subandia peasant revolt, Garo revolt, Santhal Revolt (*Hool*) to Neel revolt and Narail, Mollahati-Sirajgang revolt of 1872-73, targeted to get mere social-justice, relief from atrocities and safeguard of right to live in peace. The rebels wanted to have guarantee for the comfortable pursuit of happiness in life, and to remain free from coercion, persecution and economic exploitation. Except Sidhu-Kanu, the heroes of Santhal Revolution of 1855, none of the peasant-leaders wanted to establish their own king. Therefore, it would be misnomer to term the 'Santhal-Hool' a revolt. Indeed, this was the first war of independence. Indians organised and sacrificed lives in the matchless battles with extreme courage and determination for setting Indians as the rulers of India. The rebels in other cases helped the ruling class and the ruling families to rectify the wrongs done on the subjects and left the potentates to rule over them. These peasant insurrections took place in the second half of the 19th century and continued up to 1880. These revolts had already shaken the Brahmanical social-order. The 'Paris-commune' established by the working-classes and their organisations was destroyed by a combine force of ruling families of entire Europe who came under a 'Holly alliance'. At these, the socialists in Europe, instead of being saddened celebrated the incident as the beginning of their victory. The echoing effect of the grim victory-celebration by the Socialist-cum-Communist revolutionaries of entire Europe soon after the fall and crushing of the Paris Commune in 1871 was immediately felt in India too. As a result, the British Government had taken many corrective measures.

The target of all previous movements of the servile classes was seeking mere relief through social-justice, deterrent or punitive measures from the ruling classes against the economic exploiters and offenders of socio-religious atrocities. Guruchand now turned his attention towards the goal of achieving all democratic rights, rights of the governed to govern the country. Finally, he worked out the blueprint for his struggle to make his '*Bahujan Samaj*' ruler of the country. Marx had assessed this situation, "..... but is there any revolutionary pary that ha generated agrarian revolution like those in Bengal....?"

Guruchand for the first time inaugurated the struggle for social transformation and wanted to make a king out of the *Bahujan Samaj.* This was the tenets and targets of the *Matua Garhasta* (Household) religion. This was possible in a democratic polity. He was lucky to have favourable situation created by Lord Ripon's declaration for democratisation. Guruchand could see his dreams come true in the prospect of future democratic form of Government. He dreamt to have the rule of the people, the rule of the immense majority. He dreamt a government of the people and by the people; a government dependent on the will of the people or the subjects of the country. He began a ceaseless struggle to have a government with proportional representation of every community in the instrumentalities of the State. The harbinger of his ideal-struggle reverberated in the schools he established in the untouchable-villages.

He gave a clarion call for 'Educate'! 'Agitate'! and 'Organize'! in 1880s. This turned into a reality due to his tireless and ever-awaken personal efforts within a decade. He was virtually an illiterate. He attended village '*Pathsala*' and '*Muktab*' to learn Urdu and Arabic. However, lack of proper schooling failed to damage his spirit to be equal to the loftiest situation and prevent him from leading a delegation to the Governor General of Bengal in 1905 or giving a regal appearance at Calcutta Palace to receive in1912 the 'Durbar Medal' for meritorious services that he rendered to his servile society for empowerment. In his epoch-making historic action, he rejected the appeals of Chitta Ranjan Das for joining anti-British *Swadeshi* movement. Guruchand asked his people to boycott the Congress meetings that were organised to facilitate Gandhiji against the interest of the people. As a result, Gandhiji's public meeting at Barishal was a complete flop in 1930.

Guruchand shouldered the burden of responsibility for giving a powerful lead of the leaderless society of the de-humanised creatures. It was a battle for regaining their lost political-rights and kingdom. The man of outstanding merit, physical stamina and courage did not hesitate to don himself with the crown of thorns to be the Commander-in-Chief of the army of gullible, ignorant, credulous and highly impulsive, peace-loving but courageous peasantry of Bengal. Guruchand was born in 1846 on the full-moon day of *Falgun* month. As an *Avatar* of his father Guruchand was a complete success in giving tangible shape to all the dreams he inherited. Guruchand not only successfully capitalised the devotion of the band of disciples of his father in organizing democratic movement (of both social and political) but he very quickly also expanded the number and influence of Matuas. *Matua Sangh* magnified into the *Matua Maha Sangh*.

Guruchand manifested his ability to penetrate into political arena and in marching ahead with tremendous speed to be equal to the situation that was created by the British for rapid democratisation of Indian polity during the last quarter of the 19th century. The British nation needed almost eight hundred years to march through several bloody civil wars to establish Parliamentary Democracy under the Crown, in England. Now they wanted to implement the democratic phenomenon within decades, in Indian anti-democratic society. The Hindu society has been fundamentally 'a menace to liberty, equality, fraternity and on that account it was incompatible with democracy'.[1] Politics remained the monopoly of the microscopic minority the

Brahmins and their subordinate Kshatriyas. They maintained a theocracy under the aegis of the foreign races like Shaks, Huns, Jaths, Gurjars, Pratihars, Pathans, Mughals, etc. The 'semi-civilised' and semi-barbaric'[2] society of India, for the first time was brought under the plough of civilisation, under democratic polity by the British East India Company Rule. Henceforth not the 'Rule of the Brahmins' but 'Rule of Law' became the system. People cannot rule a country without being educated on the functioning of the government or the process of governance.

The English merchants of East India Company, therefore, are found to have introduced English education amongst '*Bengalee Babus*' at a great expense with the target of placing them in the services of the Company with lucrative salaries as mere clerks or babus. At a later stage, the English rulers, under the British Crown, are also found to have inspired these *'Bengalee Babus'* to aspire and express their demands for self-rule. And the British eventually donated the political institutions called the Indian National Congress to these microscopic minority elite '*Babus*' of India so that the British could comfortably transfer or abdicate power[3] in the hands of their London Returned agents and stooges. Neither the British nor the Indian Babus felt it necessary to percolate all the benefits of gradual advancement down to the wealth-producing classes, the Sudras, Untouchables and Tribals. In such a hostile and apathetic situation, Hari-Guruchand quietly marched ahead to carve out an honourable and exceedingly effective position in political field and had played a brilliant dynamic role in democratisation of Indian society and polity as a whole.

The schools of modern democracy sprouted in England in the Gamut of 'Oath Salisbury' convened by King William in AD 1086. The rulers of this dynasty came from outside England. Therefore, with a view to ending the continuous threat from the native royal families and the feudal-lords they decided to take the peasantry in confidence by granting civil rights to the peasantry. The sibling of democracy in the form of the 'First Charter of English Liberation' the 'Magna Charta' signed in AD 1215 by King John was watered with blood and tears of a series of popular upsurges and civil wars in later period. The history of people's war for liberation is written with golden letters of blood and fire in every country in Europe. However, the British Democracy remained 'Queen's democracy' as it was created by the nobility step by step.

Therefore, the British vehemently opposed each of the democratic movements in Europe that started in France by the peasantry in 1789. The democratic movement in France and Europe neither was sponsored by the 'Kings' nor the rebel peasantry 'obeyed the Kings'. The rebel peasantry got victory by storming the fort of Bastille. The lowest rung of the society, the peasantry, raised the cry of democracy in Europe. The dreams of the peasantry expressed in the La Merciless,

"To arms citizens
From you battalions
March, march
Let impure blood
Water our furrows
What do they want this horde of slaves
Of traitors and conspiratorial kings?...."

This has been adopted as the national anthem of today France. Fired with the enthusiasm and spirit of American Revolution against colonial ruling class, the people of France rose to revolt. The conceptuality of Democracy in France brought a new phenomenon in the governance of a nation, that the government shall remain dependent on the governed. Not the aristocracy but the Peasantry begot nationalism in Europe; in the history of humankind. The servile class rose in revolt to chisel out their own fate and freedom. This fundamental departure made the imperialist Britain horrified in their colonial quest. Consequently, in their Empire, the British remained careful and cautious all along to regulate democratic movement, its growth and spread. Parliamentary democracy in India thus, in course of time, remained hereditary democracy. It has become a polity managed by the hereditary creamy-layer ruling castes of India in the name of immense majority servile class. The British preferred an oligarch, limited, or hereditary democracy which has turned to be a Brahmanic-Democracy within half a century of transfer of power in the hands of the Brahmins.

India never experienced any such civil wars for acquiring right to share or right to representation in the instrumentalities of the state to govern it by the people. Democratic structure and form of government in India is a gift of the English nation. The members of the ruling class or castes in the Indian theocratic-polity remained from the beginning vehemently opposed to such a transition of social conditions in favour of a structure of polity that may empower even the low-caste members of the immense majority with political and executive power.

In the circumstances, the peasantry and their untouchable leader Guruchand, emerged as an indispensable element in the process of democratisation of Indian society and Polity. Democracy remains meaningless without the participation of all sections of a country. Guruchand, however, had no connection with the civilised corners outside his world of village community that lived in wretched condition of marshy lands and jungles of Eastern and South Bengal. He enjoyed no sponsorship of any benevolent Brahmin, the Rajas, *Nawabs* and the British Raj. Besides, in Bengal, the touchable Sudras never raised any anti-Brahmin movement as in Madras and Bombay Presidency. As such Guruchand was not supported by any Sudra or 'Backward-movement' in his battle against the Brahmanical suzerainty or for establishing democratic realm and the rule of the immense *mulniwasi* majority.

There developed a very strong non-Brahmin movement and Political Party in Madras and Bombay Presidency during the early 1920s. The Backward-Sudras strongly supported and actively helped develop untouchable movement in the province in the following years. But in Bengal backward Sudras, numerically a minority, never challenged the Brahmin's supercilious claim of superiority. On the contrary, they became the tools, as *bhadroloks*, in the hands of the Brahmins to oppose teeth and nail the democratic move of the untouchables. Thus, Guruchand had to depend completely upon his grass-root-level organisation, his indomitable courage and quenchless thirst to get liberation from the clutches of the Hindus.

Spread of Education

Mass education is the *sine-qua-non* for the process of democratisation of a society and a country's polity. In 1881, Guruchand Thakur issued directives at the Dutta Danga conference where he flagged off the movement for establishing schools to spread the light of learning amongst the rural peasantry of Bengal. Schools are the institutions where social-animals called human beings are given formal lessons for socialisation. Schools are the temples of knowledge where eyes of a human being get energised and eye-lead opened. Hardly there is any difference between a blind man and an illiterate man. And a blind is debared of ascending the throne of governence even in democracy. There was no school in the vast areas where lived the Chandal peasantry and other Untouchable communities. The Hindu scriptures forced the untouchables and Sudras to remain blind by banning them education.

When the British won the Battle of Palase in 1757 schooling facility was restricted to the elite Muslims and Brahmins and it was confined to Urdu and Sanskrit scriptures only. Literacy rate was extremely low. Lord Gods in all theologies and in all the countries wanted that the caretakers of their Eden Gardens, Adams and Eves and their tribes must remain without schooling; they must not eat fruits from the tree of Knowledge. The Lord God of the Hindus, however, unlike Bibelical God showed no mercy. Ours is the country of no-literacy. Lord-god Sri Krishna had preached in Gita that he did not create Sudras with such virtues, qualities and active-tendencies that they could learn and get knowledge. According to Manu, all other than the four *varnas* were *shankara-varna*s and lower in order and in merit and they must not learn any lesson. They severed the heads of Shambuks and cut off thumbs of Ekalavyas. A dead man and a thumb less man cannot indulge with the pen. Crown Prince Dhritarastra of the Kurus was debarred of his throne as he was blind. That eventually led to the Kurukshetra battle in Mahabharata. Keeping the subjects illiterate means making them disqualified for becoming the ruling class in their own land. By divine sanctions, the Brahmins got monopoly over literacy as well as politics. All other caste-men were debarred of this fundamental right to literacy.

In our country too, as good luck would have blessed us, the children of Adam, the English foreign rulers had come, seen and conquered us without any difficulties by using people of our country against one another. They, the Anglo-Saxons as in England started the process of democratisation under the compulsion of historic situation, fulfilled their historic responsibility to bring India under the democratic purview. They allowed the untouchable commoners, for the first time to be recruited in the army, get into educational institutions and participate in politics along with their Indian ruling caste subjects. What started in England during AD 10th Century, the same process ironically was started by the English people in India in the 19th Century.

Condition of Education in General

With the expansion of territorial limit in India, the East India Company felt the need to have a good number of local people complete-loyal, absolutely devoted to the British rule to assist them in administering the vast country. Their civilians initially learnt Indian vernaculars, especially Bengali language by developing it in their own way. With a view to raising a band of English-knowing clerks to be harnessed in the Company's administration, from the affluent '*Bhadrolok*' citizens of Calcutta, under the instructions of Lord Wellesley, William Carry established the Fort William College in AD 1800 for educating the newly recruited English Civilians in the local languages and laws. For assisting in judicial matters the British maintained for a long time, one (*Judge-Pandit*) *Brahmin-Pandit* and a *Maulavi* with the District Judge. For understanding local language and spreading education in Bengali language he also engraved the 'Bengali' scripts for the first time, with the help of Panchanan Karmakar in the same year. The aim of their education policy was "...to form a class of people who may be interpreters between us (the British Masters) and the millions whom we govern, a class of persons Indian in blood and colour, but English in taste, in opinion, in morals and in intellect."[3] In 1817 Sir Haud East, the then Chief Justice of Calcutta Supreme Court and David Hair along with Roy Bahadur Raja Rammohan Roy established Hindu College in Calcutta. The college was open for the Brahmins only. Immediately after, 'School Book Society' came up to assist and supply English and Bengali books for the elite classes of Calcutta. For elementary education, during this period the British did almost nothing.

A Madrasa was established for the Muslims so that educated Maulavis could represent criminal cases in the British courts. Warren Hastings established the Madrasa-building in Calcutta by spending Rs. 60,000 from his pocket in 1781, without waiting for the approval of the Court of Directors of the Company. Next, one decade later in 1792, a Sanskrit College was established at Kashi by Jonathan Dankun. Only Brahmins were qualified to be admitted as students and teachers in this college. Method of teaching was as prescribed by Manu, the Draconian law giver of the Hindus. The doors of learning was completely closed for others. The Directors of the Court of the East India Company specifically mentioned in their order issued in 1813 in this regard. "That a sum of not less than one lakh of Rupees, in each year, shall be set apart, and applied to the revival and improvement of literature, and the encouragement of the *learned natives* of India and for the introduction and promotion of a knowledge of the sciences among the British territories of India." Thus, British Government's decision of spending Rupees one lakh every year was not only restricted to the spread of Persian, Arabic and Sanskrit but also to the Pundits or the Brahmins.[4]

In 1823, Raja Rammohan, therefore, protested such step of the 'Public Instruction Committee', in a letter to Lord Amherst, "If it had been intended to keep the British nation in ignorance of real knowledge, the Beconian philosophy would not have been allowed to displace the system of the school-men, which was the best calculated to perpetuate ignorance. In the same manner, the Sanskrit system of education would be the best calculated to keep this country in darkness, if such has been the policy of the British Legislature. But as the improvement of the native population is the object of the Government, it will consequently promote a more liberal and enlightened system of instruction, embracing Mathematics, Natural Philosophy, Chemistry, Anatomy, with other useful Sciences, which may be accomplished by employing a few gentlemen of talent and learning educated in Europe, and providing a College furnished with necessary books, instruments and other apparatus."[5] Raja is found to have never cared for the commoners who needed education, at the first instance, in vernacular. Even then, the orthodox section opposed spread of schools in English medium. They favoured learning of Sanskrit which Raja Rammohan (Bandhopadhay) Roy described as the best method to keep this country in darkness. In the post-independent India too Sanskrit learning has been made very popular by the government grace.

Eventually only when Lord Macaulay came over to India and was appointed as Secretary to the Governor General Lord William Bentinck, steps were taken in positive direction with force. On 2nd February, 1835 Macaulay declared in a statement, "To sum up what I have said: I think it clear that we are not fettered by any pledge expressed or implied; that we are free to employ our funds as we choose; that we ought to employ them to teaching what is best worth knowing; that English is better worth knowing than Sanskrit and Arabic; that natives are desirous to be taught English and are not desirous to be taught Sanskrit or Arabic; that neither of the language of law nor as language of religion, have the Sanskrit and Arabic any peculiar claim to our encouragement; that it is possible to make natives of this country thoroughly good English scholars; and that to this end our efforts aught to be directed." He with sufficient courage also recorded, "I have no knowledge of either Sanskrit or Arabic. But I have done what I could to form a correct estimate of their values. I have read translations of most celebrated Arabic and Sanskrit works. I have conversed both here and at home with men distinguished by their proficiency in Eastern tongues. I am quite ready to take the oriental learning at the valuation of the orientalists themselves. I have never found one among them, who could deny that a single shelf of a good European library was worth the whole native literature of India and Arabian." At this, even James Princep and Shakespeare, one of the orientalists of that period resigned from the Public Instruction Committee in protest. Still undaunted Macaulay was made the president of the Committee. The mission was considered as a correct and appropriate one. Karl Marx with the insight of his wisdom of a genius concluded his observations on India, "The free press, introduced for the first time into Asiatic society, and managed principally by the common offspring of Hindoo and Europeans, is a new and powerful agent of reconstruction...... From the Indian natives, reluctantly and sparingly educated at Calcutta, under English superintendence, a fresh class is springing up, endowed with the requirements for government and imbued with European science."[6]

However, as per their spiritual duty the elite-India the 'fresh-class' is found to have opposed and closed doors of educational institutions built up by the foreigners for the country people, the *Sudras* and the *ati-Sudras*. In his letter dated 21st November 1855, as the Principal of Sanskrit College, Pandit Iswar Chandra Vidyasagar Bandhopadhay is found to have written to the Director of the Public Instruction, G. Gardan Young Esq. not to allow low caste Sudras or backwards in college education. "With reference to the Memorial of Babu Shamacharan Sen forwarded for report under your endorsement No. 11289 dated 15 August last, I have the honor to remark that up to year 1851 the admission to the Sanskrit College, were confined to Hindoos of the Brahmin and *Baidya* caste only. When under order of the late council of Education the privilege of studying in the institution was extended to the *Kayasthas* the most respectable caste among the *Sudras*. In the year 1854 this privilege was further extended to all the respectable castes of Hindoos under further orders.

But these orders I regret cannot apply to the people of the caste to which the memorialists belong nor it would in my humble opinion be expedient at present to admit applicants of that class. It is true that some families of Sonar Bania of Calcutta are popular men but in the scale of caste, the class stands very low. Admission from that class will I am sure not only shock the prejudice of the orthodox Pundits of the Institution but materially injure to its popularity as well as respectability. Personally I have always been opposed to the exclusive system, will appear from my former reports to the late Council on the subject of admitting applicants of other castes than Brahmins and *Baidyas,* I would have been glad to admit the son of the memorialist. The greatest attitude that expediency would allow, has I believe already been given and I regret that. I cannot recommend any further extension under present circumstances."[7] 'In another letter to Sir John Peter Grant, the lieutenant Governor of Bengal on September 29, 1859, Pandit Iswar Chandra Vidyasagar (Bandhopadhay) wrote, "As the best, if not the only practicable means of promoting education in Bengal, the Government should, in my humble opinion, confine itself to the education of the higher classes on comprehensive scale." The Brahmins never forget to protect their caste interests. *Vidyasagar* is also known as '*Dayarsagar*' means sea of compassion and kindness. However, a Brahmin's compassion never raises beyond his own caste interests to touch the minimum level of a human being.

In such circumstances, in 1870, we find W.W. Hunter to disclose a heartrending truth of discriminatory attitude of the Brahmins for the Chandals, "Both Muhammedans and Chandals.... who form the whole native population of the district Faridpore is averse to education.... The Chandals are willing to accept education, if the Government provides it for them.... Out of total population of more than 156,000 of this curious race in Faridpore, less than 200 boys are to be found at school."[8] The Chandals were definitely longing for learning but could not practically dream to afford the luxury of schooling. Despite the fact that the Hindus prevented them from even approaching schools and their poverty standing in their way to school, yet they came up remarkably on the front line of the educated population within the next two decades.

In 1800, the new District of Bakharganj came into existence with a population of 9,26,723. In 1801, Doctor Hamilton during his Census operation found not even a single Primary school in the entire District.[9] This was but natural in a state of Brahmanical Caste-society. Even a few who were educated were half-literate. In 1811, Governor General Lord Minto disclosed a horribly negative picture of education in India. "It is a common remark that Science and Literature are in a progressive state of decay amongst the Natives of India. From every inquiry, which I have been enabled, to make on this interesting subject, that remarks appear to me but too well founded. The number of the learned is not only diminished, but the circle of learning even amongst those who still devote themselves to it, appears to be considerably contracted. The abstract sciences are abandoned, polite literature neglected, and no branch of learning cultivated but what is connected with the peculiar religious doctrines of the people."[10]

The English people knew well the mind and hearts of the elite Brahmins of India. Despite that, they expected that this English educated elite class would eventually educate their country people. This was the Lord Macaulay's 'Down Filtration Theory' of education. But Lord Mayo in 1872 countered it, "I dislike this filtration theory. In Bengal, we are educating in English a few hundred '*babus*' at great expense to the state. Many of them are well to pay for themselves, and have no other object in learning than to qualify for Government employ. In the meanwhile, we have done nothing towards extending knowledge to millions. That the '*babus*' will never do. The more education you give them, the more they will keep to themselves, and make their increased knowledge a means of tyranny." The comments became prophetical for the future India. "The ultimate effect of this latter system, it was urged, would 'filtrate' downwards. Its immediate result, however, was to arm the rich and powerful with new weapon – knowledge – and to leave the poor under their old weight of ignorance in their struggle of life", assessed Sir William Wilson Hunter, ICS. The '*Babus* will never do' it. Lord Krishna instructed, "*Na Buddhibhedang Janadeyajanang Karmasanginam....*", 'the educated class (Brahmins) must not lead the labouring class (Sudras) to the field of education'.[11] Command of God is scrupulously and precisely maintained even after independence.

Consequent to the continuance of this primitive socio-spiritual mind-set of the educated ruling class Brahmins, the Census Report of 1911 reveals a normal but shocking picture of 1.1 per cent total literacy in India. In 1921, the percentage increased to 8 per cent only. Literacy here means only the capacity to read and sign one's own name and nothing more. No David Hare, the watch-dealer came in rural Bengal to lure the talented children in wretched condition to take for free English education in his school.

Tradition Continues: Describing the situation one official historian in India comments, "All these three classes of Indian society the peasants, the artisans, the workers constituting the overwhelming majority of Indian population discovered that they had no political rights or powers, and virtually nothing was being done for intellectual or cultural improvement. Education did not percolate down to them. There were hardly any schools in villages and those a few existing schools were poorly run. The doors of higher education were barred to them in practice. Moreover, many of them belonged to the lower castes and had still to bear social and economic oppression by the upper castes."[12] When the '*Mulniwasi*' immense majority and the lowest stratum of Indian society were struggling for a piece of bread and for the right to elementary rather primary education the English people constructed expensive buildings in posh areas of capital Calcutta to locate institutions of higher-English education at their own cost. Even without tuition-fee, the children from wealthy families of Calcutta and other Metropolis were admitted into those institutions. Those wealthy and newly educated-people were freely given jobs in the British-Indian administration. They formed an exceedingly selfish creamy-layer-elite class. It took another seven decades for the educated oppressed to place demands for Government jobs by initiating pitch-struggles. They have never been welcomed in the Government job-market by the Brahmins who got it easily from the British and monopolised it.

The Brahmins virtually vied with each other to get maximum benefit from the English education. "But many celebrity Indians of colonial era unequivocally opposed mass education. Rabindra Nath Tagore too condemned the same class of people, and opposed education reaching the lower strata on the plea that "if every man were allowed to receive education, where would they get menial servants for performing their domestic chores?"..... This morbid attitude of the Hindus continues to be apathetic to national cause. We find a shocking disclosure by Ashok Mitra, ICS; the then Census Commissioner and a teacher in the Jawharlal Nehru University for some times, recalling his experience as first District Magistrate, Malda after partition. He writes, "On matter of primary education, a casual conversation with a member of CPI, in English Bazaar revealed a logic which I had not suspected. I collared this person and asked him why the CPI, now advantageously placed in opposition, was not insisting on rapid expansion of primary education. I asked him whether he would not agree that the difference between a literate person and an illiterate one was as great as between a man of normal vision and a man born blind. He nodded in agreement but did not answer. I collared him a third time within the next six weeks (the party having been banned, it was difficult to meet him), and asked the same. He looked slyly and said softly, "You see, Mr. Mitra, our leaders are loath to push this programme. They fear that if people get to be literate, they will not so implicitly listen to their leaders and exercise their own judgment instead."[13] The ruling class/caste of our country wants to keep the native and autochthons of the land in perpetual darkness of ignorance, in a state 'born blind'. The born blind subjects were to follow and serve the creamy-layer-elite blindly as a dumb-man and 'die-blind'.

Consequently, the Brahmins even opposed the foreign-colonial British to spread mass and universal education on the plea that the Hindu spirituality will be hurt. They never cared to understand that if 85 to 90 per cent of the total population remains without proper and adequate education, then the society remains weak. The country as a nation of 'Born-blind' continues to stay in a perpetual blinding darkness and abject servitude. A 'born-blind' nation cannot advance much in any respect. The largest number of illiterate (not educated) of to-day's world live in India.[14]

In the government run schools in constitutional India, the system of taking examination or testing the result of being educated or learning by way of 'pass' and 'fail' in the Examinations have been abolished up to class VIII. Schools have been converted to a mid-day-meal centre. Students need not take books to the schools. A food-plate and bowl have taken their place. Up to class VIII, students and teachers are busy in this noble cause in the Schools. They are sure to produce slaves and beggars in mind and physique. Slum-dogs must quietly perpetuate as slum-dogs in this country. A Raja Rammohan, from amongst them, who will lodge protest with reason and logic, data and statistics demanding, 'light more light' is yet to born.

Struggles Know no Bounds: It would be very difficult for us today simply to understand as to how much it was difficult and what sort of hindrances were to be overcome to get education by an untouchable child of illiterate peasant family. Extreme poverty, absolute inexperience, crudest form of spiritual-orthodoxy, opposition of social taboos, absence of guidance, non existence of any school within a radius of 10 to 15 km, no approach roads or communication in the areas, etc. were mentionable. The absurd hostile situation that the untouchable Chandals had to face even for primary education and for planning for spread of education amongst them during 1880's in colonial Hindu India knew no bounds. The situation that there was no teacher, nobody with sufficient education to show them the light of learning to their children did not prevent their leaders to establish school. The cravings for education in their hearts came out like amazing sparkles of luminous fire to light the blinding darkness all around. The indomitable sincerity of the Chandal leader, Guruchand issued his 'Three Commandments, what was completely unknown in India during those days, Educate! Agitate! Organize!,

"Vidyahin Samajer Kono Gati Nai,
Vidya Sekho, Vidya Sekho Balilen Tai.
Ghare Ghare *Andolon* Prayojan Holo
Sabha Karo, Sabha Karo Prabhuji Hankilo." (GC, p. 108)

Mahakabi Mahananda, here, even for the sake of poetic logic did not miss the sequence. 'An illiterate *Samaj* has no way to go; Educate! Educate! Instructed he. People must agitate for getting education and once educated they would push the stage to Organize and further Organize!" Education gives information and facts of reality in regard to self and surroundings and generates the sense of deprivation and feeling of being usurped by the exploiters. Agitation emerges out of this condition. Agitated victims feel the necessity to organize themselves against the powerful usurpers to gain back his lost privileges. "Aami Bali Vidyasunya Rabe Jei Jan, Namasudra Bali Tare Bolona Kakhan..." (GC, p. 108)

Guruchand did not inaugurate any temple of god in his lifetime but established hundreds of schools in different villages inhabited by the Untouchables and Sudras. A series of schools for the girls also came up in the region. Amongst the girls' school, the school of Taltala, Orakandi became very famous. To enter in the temples of power of democracy the sleeping nation of the Sudras and Untouchables needed the appropriate religion named Matua. 'Try to understand that without education everything is useless. If Namasudra nation longs to live, get educated even at the cost of lives.'

He could not get satisfied with a form of democracy and a government which will be of the illiterate people by the literate people and there by for the literate elite-people of the country. He targeted for establishing a total democracy or people's democracy. Therefore, he cautioned:

"Khao Ba Na Khao Tate Duikkha Nai
Chele Pile Shikha Dao Ai Aami Chai." (GCC, p. 144)

He was well aware of the pecuniary condition of the majority of his people. Therefore, his wonderful instructions included even poorest section within his scheme of universal literacy. 'Any one who believes me is asked not to spare an illiterate son in the family. Even if you fail to collect daily bread remain on fasting but educate your children.' Beg to give children education. Neither before him nor after his departure none struggled to spread education on so large scale. Universal education was his motto; each and every one of each and every village must be educated. None ever supported education movement from such grass-root level. He advocated for '*Sarbosiksha*' 'Education for All' scheme. He did not ask children to come to schools with the plates and bowls for mid-day-mill in their school bags and not with the books. He asked children to remain empty stomach, if need be; but one must go to school with bag full books to get educated.

The first primary school he established in the village Orakandi at his own residence in AD 1880, the year when the English nation brought their girl children in the ambit of compulsory education. Many students from his family and surrounding areas very happily, with much fanfare and enthusiasm enrolled in the school. But initial and teething problems were serious. The educated Caste Hindus from near by places due to religious sanctions refused to be a teacher in the school established by a Chandal for the Chandals. Guruchand became furious like a wounded tiger and took it a challenge with greater seriousness. He declared, 'The teachers from other castes consider Namasudras as fools and coach them only for earning money. If I get a teacher from our community we will appoint him a teacher.' Within a very short time an educated Namasudra, named Raghu Nath Sarkar had come to Orakandi to engrave his name in the pages of history. He was entrusted this historic responsibility of becoming the first teacher in this maiden school in a Chandal village.

Next year, in 1881, all the eminent personalities and leaders (village head man) called '*Matubbars*' of far flung areas and districts were invited on the occasion of the '*Sradh*' of the mother of Iswar Chandra Gain, a middle level Zamindar of Chandal/ Namasudra family of Dutta Danga. It became an inter-district gathering of galaxies of the Chandals of Bengal. Guruchand too was one of the special invitee. He in fact guided the meeting's arrangement from the beginning. Such gatherings were called as '*Kharecher Sabha*' because heavy expenditure (*Kharach*) was involved on such occasion for arranging community feast involving several quintal of rice. This was one of the cultural aspects of the Chandals of Bengal those days. Such functions acted as catalysts that cemented universal brotherhood in the community.

Guruchand took full advantage of this gathering to turn it into the First Chandal/Namasudra conference for using it as a platform for starting a socio-political rather democratic movement. In the meeting, Guruchand in his presidential address gave a clarion call to the community for launching 'spread education scheme' at the first instance. He asked people to establish schools in each village. This was the beginning and continued ceaselessly till Bengal was partitioned in 1947.

In 1906, the year when the 2nd and the 3rd political party namely Muslim League and Hindu Mahasabha were established, the remote land of Orakandi was honoured with the maiden touch of the ruling white people. With an invitation from the Guru, Australian missionary Dr C.S. Mead established his Mission at Orakandi for spreading Christianity and lit the torch of education. He established a Home for the widows and a Girls' school. One Miss Tuck used to manage the institutions. In 1908, Dr C.S. Mead established the English High School in Orakandi.

Masiahati Middle English School: It would be like a fairy tale to tell the history of founding schools by the Chandal/Namasudras who passed millennium in the blinding darkness of illiteracy in their villages. The absurdity of the dream and audacity of hope surpassed all barriers of odds before the stubborn determination of the slum-dogs. The villagers held schools for their children in the cow-sheds with poorly thatched roof and some times under the trees in the open. Early in the morning, the cows were taken away to the surrounding grazing fields. The emptied sheds would be cleaned by the women as a routine with mud rather liquid-paste prepared out of cow-dung, soil and water to wipe out all dust and germs. The local teachers 'Master *Mosai*' would use the Cowshed as classroom for the children of primary stage.

It was during 1916-17 when there was not available a single educated man in the '*Chhianabbuikhan Gram*' (confederation of 96 villages) amongst the Namasudras. Not even a single matriculate or trained untouchable was available to be a teacher. However, there arose the audacious dream to establish the Masiahati English High School in the village. During those days, the nearest Middle English School was available near the Nehalpur *Hat*. Maulavi Aakhejuddin Biswas established the school beneath a banyan tree in a room with tin-shed. Incidents of humiliation on the Namasudra students in the school by the Kayasth and Brahmin went on increasing. Consequently, one day while digging the pond of Sribatsa Kumar Biswas suggestion was made by Balai Krishna Mallick of Kultia village to start a Middle English School in their area. Decision to establish the school was taken in a small meeting in the house of Darsan Mallick of Kultia on 1st February 1918. Immediately classes started in his Kacharigarh. Eventually, after the school came up on the bank of Masiahati village-canal.

On the venue there was constructed a room of the length of 48 hands (72 feet) and breadth of 8 hands (12 feet) by erecting poles of *Neem* and *Jewli* tree donated by Sudharam Biswas of Dumurtala village. It was covered with the leaves of *Gol*. The Middle English School started in the room. The plot of land was given by Pulin Behari Roy.

Next year, in the beginning of 1919 the maiden annual meeting of the Chhiyanabbuikhan Gram as well as of the school committee took place. Almost all the *Matubbars* (Headmen) of the surrounding villages, including Jyogendra Nath Chakraborty, the priest of the Namasudras and an educationist attended the meet. In the meeting liberal collection was accepted from various doners for the developmental purposes of the School. Raicharan Mazumder of Poradanga village, Darshan Mallick and Mathura Mallick of Kultia, Kailash Chandra Dhar and the Palanquin carrier Navin Chandra Oria from Orissa donated Rs100, Rs50, Rs30, Rs52 and Rs1 respectively. The school started and gradually developed. During these days the *Brahmo Samaj* formed an association called, '*Bangla O Assam Anunnata Srenir Unnati Bidhayni Samiti*' an organ to uplift the down trodden of Bengal and Assam. They appeared in Masiahati and donated a total sum of Rs. 500.[15] In a later period Rasik Lal Biswas as a Secretary of the Bengal Legislative Assembly brought a grant of rupees six thousands for its buildings.

It did not take much time for the girls to come up from the surrounding villages to attend schools. No one wants to remain in the blinding condition of darkness. Bengal has been the last seat of Buddhism. Buddha was the first revolutionary to create nunnery, that is Bhikkuni-Sangha and to enroll girls in the *Sangha* with full rights to get knowledge. As such, his direct disciples created the maiden female literature of the world, '*Therigatha*' which reveals rare exposition of life and reality. In 'Kultia' of Masiahati in the cluster of 96 Villages, untouchable girls sprang to life as a result of their liberty struggle. The 'Kultia Girls High School' (1968) was started initially in a small hut of '*Do-chala*' in the month of May 1921 as Lower Primary School. It started with 27 girls as the student of 1st standard. In 1946 it was elevated to the Middle English Girls High School. Interestingly all the students of the school came from the Namasudra community. Ali Ahmed, the Commissioner Khulna Division in his letter dated 12th May 1962 (after partition) had described, 'I was very pleased to preside over the annual prize distribution ceremony of the Kultia Girl's Junior High School today. The School is housed in two '*Pacca* Buildings and a thatched house with *pacca* walls. There are 162 girls in the school of whom 152 belonged to the scheduled caste….. I was very much impressed to find the girls giving display of their recitation, music etc. in a smart fashion. They were well dressed and absolutely stage-free. The standard of the school is certainly above average. More grants are needed for the improvement of this school. I recommend to the District council that the grant of this school should be raised and so also the Government grant. I have given Rs. 500 from my discretionary fund for the purchase of furniture and equipment of the school."[16] These development efforts for raising the standard of women of the untouchables in the democratic frame started with the Guruchand-Mead initiative by starting Taltala Girls High School two decades back. "A day school and a Sunday school for girls were opened" in 1906 under the supervision of Miss Tuck, the associate of Rev. C.S. Mead. This mission of liberty, advance and elevation ended with the final blow of the Brahmins to shutter the socio-political consolidation and growth of more than twelve million untouchables of Bengal by vivisecting it in the name of Partition of India.

First Untouchable Graduate: "*Parte Hai Naile Pichie Parte hai: Larte hai Naile Golami Karte Hai*" 'You are to read and learn, else you remain backward: you are to fight or else you remain slave."[17] Removal of slavery was the motto of Guruchand. As a result of the education movement started by Guruchand, Shyam Lal Sarkar, the first graduate amongst the Namasudra community came out successfully in 1902. The waves of his education movement yielded excellent result all over Bengal. Panchanan Sarkar, a *Rajbansi* from North Bengal Victoria College got bachelor's degree with Sanskrit (Honours) in 1893. It was he who held the distinction of becoming the first Graduate from amongst the Untouchables in India. He got his MA and LLB degrees in 1897 and 1898 respectively. From South Bengal, Raicharan Lal Sardar, a Paundra became the 2nd untouchable graduate when he passed BA from the University of Calcutta in 1900. By the year 1911 there were 522 doctors and 192 teachers working amongst Namasudra. In 1931 there were 784 Namasudras in Gazetted and non-gazetted posts of government jobs. In 1911 literacy rate amongst the Namasudras was 1.1 per cent only. This increased to 6 per cent in 1931. Yet Guruchand was not happy with the performances and achievements.

While presiding over a 'Namasudra Conference' at Khulna in 1923 Guruchand expressed the desire to send his men for acquiring foreign degrees. "*Sagar Dingate Chai, Dekhi Setha Kiba Pai.*" 'We need to cross the seas and let us see what we can have from there.' In 1926 the first batch of scholars set sail for England via Bombay on their own expense. There was no Maharaja or *Nawab* to sponsor them. Three Namasudra Matuas, two grand sons of the Guru, Pramotha Ranjan and Bhagawati Thakur and Amulya Charan Das who was the nephew of Advocate Bhiswadev Das. P.R. Thakur became Bar-at-law from London. Bhagawati Das got his Doctoral Degree in 1929. Amulya Charan got degree of Mechanical Engineer from the University of Glasgow.

Surmounting all barricades put by both the Hindu gods and goddesses and their orthodox fanatic devotees, when the untouchables particularly Namasudra, Rajbansi and Poundra communities, on their own became a political force in Bengal it started getting assistance and special care and attention of the British government. The cunning Hindus had started paying visits in their remote villages crossing the muddy and dusty path on foot with great difficulties (as there were no roads or convenience) to express their sympathy and good will. They offered financial assistance to run their schools in good condition. It were the agents of the Brahma Samaj who knocked the doors first. They, while assisting in educational sphere had their secret agenda to make them loyal to the Hinduism and join in *Sarbajana* politics of Gandhian Congress.

The tangible result of the movement started by Guruchand is being reflected in a letter written by Dr Ambedkar to the Government of India for sanctioning a loan of six lakhs of rupees for setting up of a collage in Bombay. He furnished the report in 1930, reflecting the condition of education in India and it shows illustrious advanced condition of education amongst depressed classes in Bengal in comparison to other provinces. A portion of the report is quoted bellow:

Depressed Classes (Boys and Girls) 1930[18]

Province	*Primary stage*	*Middle*	*High*	*College*
Madras	224,873	2,647	...	47
Bombay	58,651	730	....	9
Bengal	310,398	8787	5996	1670
United Pro	88,383	1367	42	10
Punjab	14,284	914	110	nil
Bihar and Orissa	24,574	52	7	nil
Central Province	33,123	1022	59	16

Condition of female education in Bengal was considerably high in the report and this was the manifestation of challenging life of the martial races like Chandal/ Namasudra, Rajbansi and the Pods under the able leadership of Guruchand and some others under the British liberal protection. It was an incredibly difficult 'long-march' comparable with 'Maoist Read Guards' march, in so far as spiritual, social and state-sponsored resistance, the Namasudras had to face to reach to that destination. The Namasudras who alone numbered more than two million populations scrupulously proved them equal to the situation that was created by the generous patronage of the colonial Government for spread of primary education. "In March 1918, O'Malley, who was then in charge of education department, claimed credit for the education of 41,105 Namasudras (36,932 boys and 5173 girls) who were under instruction in Bengal Presidency during 1916-17. Of them 100 boys were reading in colleges, 1,489 boys were in the high school stage, 1,690 boys were in the middle school stage and 32,087 boys and 5,138 girls were in the primary school stage. The rest were reading in special and indigenous schools."[19] Observing this rapid advance, despite all hurdles, the creamy-layer-elite ruling class got alarmed.

Organise, Unite and Struggle

It has already been seen that the Dutta Danga Conference in the district of Khulna, as an unconscious tool of history, was turned to be the maiden platform for launching socio-political agitation for liberation. This platform eventually paved the path for expressing the demands of the voiceless for gaining adequate share in the governance of the country. The British Government under the Crown and Parliament of Great Britain intended to set Parliamentary Democracy in India. The British government consequently, … 'thought of the administrative and political value of ethnological enquiries…' 'in 1869, under Sir W. W. Hunter, ICS had commenced the statistical survey of India, the result of which embodied in the first edition of Imperial Gazetteer published in 1881-82. Census enumeration also started in 1868-69. Education Commission headed by Hunter was established during these days. All these high-powered administrative activities had set a target of transferring of power in the hands of British Indian elite-agents groomed by the British.

The elite India too was preparing to prove themselves equal to the situation. Prince Dwaraka Nath Tagore (grandfather of Ravindra Nath) who was the first business partner of the East India Company took a lead to focus their existence and expressed their desire to render the most loyal and valuable services to fulfill the targets of International Scheme of the English nation. He formed the 'The Bengal Landlord's Association' in the year 1842. In 1843, George Thomson established another organisation named, 'British India Society'. The new society indicated enough obviously to rectify and shift the terms of object of the platform from Bengal to 'British-India'. The strong force of unity got victory after the death of Tagore in 1846. On 31st October 1851 both the institutions merged into one, 'British India Association' under the President-ship of Raja Radha Kanta Dev of Sobhabazaar, Calcutta. A handful of Zamindar-families and extremely orthodox Hindus of Calcutta took the lead to shape the future India in a democratic structure.

In 1865-1866 Babu Raj Narayan Bose established, "*Jatiya-Gaurav-Sampadani Sabha*" to express exclusive Hindu domination through Hindu-nationalism in India after breaking from Kesab Chandra Sen's Brahma Samaj. Nearly a century after the French revolution, Bengalese for the first time talked about nationalism in India. However, it had smelt foul with communal odour of Hindu-nationalism. In the pamphlet that was circulated in its inaugural gathering, he expressed a desire and need to have, "A society for the promotion of national feeling among the educated natives of Bengal." And the educated Bengal under the leadership of Navagopal Mitra took up Bose's banner and responsibility to start with holding annual '*Hindu Mela*' as '*Jatia Mela*' that is 'Hindu Festival' as 'National Festival'. Ravindra Nath Tagore as a teen actively participated many of its annual gathering. The word 'Hindu' significantly transformed into a synonym 'Nationality' and became the genesis of the dangerous doctrine of 'Hindu nationalism' in latter period.

The days came closer to the formation of Indian National Congress, a full-scale political organ of the British groomed creamy-layer-elite of India. Immediately before, in 1875 an organ named 'Indian Association' was founded by Surendra Nath Banerjee who was dismissed from the ICS on the charges of inefficiency and dereliction of duty with a hefty monthly pension of Rs. 50. On the other hand Dada Bhai Naroji an Indian multi-billionaire Parsi representative of a few thousand population in the country, established 'British India Association' in London. All these outfits joined Congress soon after its birth.

Without having any touch or connection with all these developments in the country there held the most significant incident in the process of democratisation of Indian society and polity from its grass root level. The Dutta Danga Conference at Khulna in 1881 was attended by more than five thousand strong gathering of prominent personalities. Guruchand was greeted by people in the meeting with a standing ovation on behalf of the mute-India. At this stage, such organised gathering was possible only and only by the untouchable Chandals of Bengal who learnt to 'lift their heads, but refused to 'bow their heads in living and lowly homage at His pierced feet'.[20]

Guruchand brought the geographic boundary of the then Bengal within the purview of his organisation for the servile class people. Initially, though, he concentrated his efforts on the spots where concentration of the Namasudras was more. Then his lieutenants went all around with the mission of uniting all the untouchable communities like the Rajbansi of North Bengal and the Poundra of south Bengal. All equally were the victims of the Brahmanical social order. They united against the common enemy and struggled to restore democratic rights. As he focused his attention for expansion of organisational limit beyond geographic or administrative barriers he stressed on the fund-building scheme in the grass-root level of small units of village and union bodies. Well calculated and scientific was his approach in this regard. 'Unanimous decision was taken by sitting together that it is the unity which shall eradicate all germs of sufferings..... We belong to one nation and will form a human chain....'

A right man needs to be placed in right post. However, in the land of spiritual-discrimination and spiritual illiteracy, the matriculates and graduates from the Untouchable communities did not get welcome from the governing class. Their entry in services, as a result of 'Filtration' or percolation policy was on the contrary resisted by the newly settled gang of '*Bhadralok*' the 'Bengali *Babus*' who were created by the British Bureaucracy. The newly educated untouchable youths got satisfied with some jobs they could manage as teachers in the schools they themselves established in their localities. Doors for Government jobs for them were closed. Their efforts to struggle and enter in the government job were blocked by every possible means.

As such, there were no such Government instructions disqualifying or debarring the Untouchables for jobs. But they were denied to be recruited by the caste Hindus on some pretext or other. As a norm, they term them 'Not suitable'. The Brahmanical social order, as we see today in case of SC, ST and OBC and during the Mandal Commission's agitation, has been all-along, notoriously anti-people and anti-national for the obvious reasons. Soon after Raicharan Sardar's becoming a graduate, he approached some one Mr. Basu, a Kayasth who held a middle-level post of an officer in the Railways for assistance to manage an appropriate job in the Department of Railways. Sardar was harshly rebuffed and admonished for his audacious aspiration for securing a Government job despite being an untouchable Pod. In such circumstances, all like Panchanan Sarkar, Raicharan Sardar etc had to go for LLB degree. They had to remain contented by maintaining life with profession of pleaders on private practice only. The number of lawyers and doctors as a result was predominant amongst untouchables in those days.

Governance through Representation in Government Jobs

Within two decades henceforth, with the starting of the new century there emerged, in Bengal, a band of middle and highly educated youths with brilliant scores and result from amongst the Untouchables, Sudras and the Muslims. Guruchand took a bold and timely stand before the British authority with democratic demands for Legislation on adequate and fair share of representation for these educated destitute in the executive sector of Government. This lot composed of the traditionally neglected and the victims of Brahmanical discrimination continued to be discriminated in the British Raj too in their job-sector. The Brahmins even prevented the touchable Sudras and others from entering the British services from within and from outside the Government. The East India Company and British *Raj* inducted the Brahmins in English education with specific intention; consequently, they monopolised the job-sector within a short span of period. The queen of England had assumed the reign of India, soon after crushing of the '*Sepoy* Mutiny' in 1857. Soon after, the Queen as the Empress of India declared the Royal Titles Act of 1876. With the announcement of Allahabad Durbar declaration of the Queen by Lord Canning, the table of government jobs turned completely in favour of the Brahmins and it was officially closed for the Sudras, Untouchables and the Muslims. The Proclamation of 1st November, 1858 promised for the Crown Government, "....to abstain from all interference with the religious belief or worship" of the subjects and declared that all "of whatever race or creed, may be freely and impartially admitted to offices in our service, the duties of which they may be qualified by their education, ability and integrity duly to discharge." The declaration appeared to be very innocent, impartial and just but the rational verdict in the irrational social set up yielded unfair result. The Muslims, the Untouchables, Sudras and the Animists who formed 90 per cent of the total population and the lowest stratum of the society became the victims of such policy. The Muslims were marked to be the people of doubtful 'integrity' due to their earlier act of participation in the great-mutiny. The Untouchables and others, who were simpleton subjects of the British so long, were automatically eliminated from job-market as they were for centuries forced out of education, out of schools. They were treated unsuitable for government jobs due to lack of appropriate or adequate education. The share of jobs in the British Government henceforth continued to be a monopoly of the Brahmins and their close, favoured or blessed associates. With the assistance of the English, the Brahmins eventually became the real masters, the '*Bhudevatas*' of the Hindu society and British Government.

The First Untouchable to Meet a British Master, Sir Lancelot

It is evident that the Company had the urge to create a band of 'Bangalee babus' who would doggedly be loyal to the British rule in India and sincerely display a disloyal disposition to the cause of India. They wanted a band of people who will be Indian by birth but English in mind, who will perfectly dream in English, laugh in English, cry in English talk in English read English and serve the English. They found the best of its specimen in the Brahmins and some associated castes who felt it a matter of pride even to declare their ancestral relationship with Nordic blood of Europe. So, the British authority initiated all necessary actions for "educating in English a few hundred *Babus* at great expense to the state. Many of them are well able to pay for themselves, and have no other object in learning than to qualify for government employ"[21] and offered jobs of all types and ranks. But for the autochthons, who refused to feel proud to be of 'Nordic' blood or who were declared as Austric, Negrotic or Mongoloid etc. by the new branch of knowledge called anthropology, the Untouchables and Tribes it was a matter of opposite direction. W.W. Hunter confessed, 'In the mean while we have done nothing towards extending knowledge to the million'. They had to struggle through the protracted course of getting elementary education to higher education at their own expense after defeating all possible resistances from powerful corners. They had to struggle for getting government sympathy what to talk about jobs. Guruchand had accepted the reality created by his so-called countrymen of elite class and therefore, had no hesitation to fight out the solution. He appealed to the Government that the British authority following the principle of equal treatment and equal right to jobs and protection of laws might kindly provide Government Jobs to the members of the Untouchables:

"Aami Bali Raj Karya A Jatike Dao"

Samadristi Rakho Raja, A Niti Dekhao. (GCC, p. 213)

Sir Lancelot Hare, the then Governor of East Bengal and Assam Government visited Gopalganj Headquarter of Faridpur district town chiefly inhabited by the Namasudras during 1906. Guruchand had taken full advantage of the situation and in a personal delegation submitted a charter of demands. The draft of the 'Welcome address' was prepared by Dr C.S. Mead. The charter of demands chiefly focused on the job crisis due to machinations created by the Brahmins. "A Jatir Siksha Diksha Raj Karya Chai...." (GCC, p. 450)

'These people need education, vocational-training and Government jobs, we have never been against the British Rule in India. We are known to be loyal to the British Raj and knowing the facts of our claim the Government may please take action.' The appeal yielded good fruits.

Until then no Indian raised any demand for democratic rights to be a partner in the governance of the country. *Rao Bahadur* Raja Ram Mohan Roy, a *Dewan* in the Company's service on the contrary welcomed the British Raj as the providence of God. In the 'Appeal to King in Council' he declared, "Divine providence at last, in its abundant mercy, stirred up the English nation to break the yoke of those tyrants (Muslims) and to receive the oppressed Natives of Bengal under its protection." Para three of the appeal reads, "The great part of Hindustan having been for several centuries subject to Muhammadan Rule, the civil and religious rights of its original inhabitants were constantly trampled upon, and for the habitual oppression of the conquerors, a great body of these subjects in the Southern peninsula (*Dukhin*), afterwards called Marhattas and other body in western parts now styled Sikhs, were at last driven to revolt, and when the Musalman power became feeble, they ultimately succeeded in establishing their independence; but the initiatives of Bengal wanting vigour of body; and adverse to active exertion remaining during the whole period of the Muhammadan conquest, faithful to the existing Government, although their property was often plundered, their religion insulted and their blood wantonly shed."[22] The '*Bharat Pathik*' the first modern man of India, Raja preferred to take refuge under the providence of God not for freedom, not for liberty but for slavery under the British yoke. With a view to overthrowing the Indian Muslims whom he called tyrants, he did not give a call for the Hindu masses of the country to unite and push out the foreign invaders, be it Muslim tyrants or the British colonizers. Instead, he had ridiculed the health and strength of Bengalis and welcomed the stronger foreign masters to rule over them. Earlier, ironically he was a strong supporter of Islam and Muslim rule in India.

There ruled several Indian potentates too in the country. Amongst them, many were Sudras and Tribals. Chatrapati Sahu Maharaja of Kolhapur became king during the end of 19th century and ruled in early decades of 20th Century. Chatrapati Shivaji belonged to the Sudra caste. Therefore, he was coroneted only after being anointed as a Kshatriya.....

This divine curse eventually loomed large on the regained reign of Sahu Maharaja of Kolhapur. After the untouchable army of the East India Company stormed the Brahmin-Kshatri-Pathan army of the Peawas in the battle of Koregaon the devilish rule of tyrant Brahmins ended. As Sahu Maharaja belonged to the Sudra Chatrapati Shivaji's family, the Brahmin administrators of his own Estate did not carry out many of his major decisions. 'Important posts of Kolhapur administration were almost monopolised by Brahmins and even in 1894, 10 years after Shahu's coronation, 60 out of 71 bureaucrats were Brahmins.'[23] He decided to put an end to it and inspired backward Sudras to pursue education vigorously. For giving placement of the newly educated Backward young men he declared 50 per cent representation of the Backward classes in the job in the territory of his kingdom. On July 1902 he declared, "In all Offices, in which the proportion of officers of Backward classes is at present less than fifty percent, the next appointment shall be given to a member of that class."[24] As per the order, except the Brahman, Prabhu, Senavi, Persi and other advanced classes all were declared as Backward. Bal Gangadhar Tilak, the Chaitpawan Brahmin of Pune, a leader of the Congress declared battle against the order in his Journal. The untouchables of India were still sleeping in their slumber of ignorance being unorganised. The only exception was Bengal and Madras.

In Bengal, rather in India, none but Guruchand was there to demand representation for the Untouchables in Government offices and public jobs in proportion to 25 per cent of their population. The Muslims were also highly disappointed due to their extremely disproportionate low representation in Government jobs due to the Brahmins' monopolizing all posts and services. The Muslims of Bengal were also struggling for their representation in jobs in British administration proportionate to their population (55 per cent). Even from the platform of the Indian National Congress, since Sir Saiyad Ahmad Khan joined Congress politics, they were pressing for job representation. The Namasudra and the Muslim agitators of Bengal supported each other for the common cause since 1890's simultaneously. Guruchand started pleading his demands for representation in Government jobs right from the end of the 19th century. But the stubborn resistance from the Brahmins jeopardised all his efforts. The epicenter of the Brahmin lobby remained close to the European rulers in Calcutta. Most of the Zamindars and newly emerged Hindu bourgeois and educated lot sitting at the Headquarter easily influenced all decisions in Bengal Assembly and controlled it. As a result the Muslims and Untouchables in East Bengal longed to have their Headquarter shifted to Dacca where they had overwhelming majority.

Luckily, due to the exigencies of good administration, the British Government at this point of time proposed division of Eastern part of India in two separate and independent administrative units. Both the Muslim community and the untouchables under the leadership of Guruchand gave hearty and solid support to the proposal for the administrative division of Bengal. They indeed, for long time had been focusing on the plethora of manipulative power-play by the Brahmanical Hindus of Calcutta-surroundings in the detriment, disadvantage and non-development in the regions predominantly occupied by the indigenous Muslims and untouchables. Consequently, plenitude of disloyal display of irresponsibility continued towards the advance and prosperity of socio-economic and health-education of these groups in the region. The British wanted to redress the crises of all-out corruption and backwardness that arose out of the vast administrative jurisdiction of the state.

On the 4th July, 1905, Lord Curzon, the then Governor General of India announced the decision of Partition of Bengal in two provinces, Bengal and the Eastern Bengal and Assam. The Government of Eastern Bengal and Assam got its new capital at Dacca. Sir Bamfield Fouler became its first Lieutenant Governor. Being out of the clutches of the Hindu domination of creamy-layer-Calcutta-clique the untouchables of Chandal-Rajbansi communities got a sigh of relief along with their Muslim brethren. The Muslims of Bengal equally felt the joy of being manumitted from the combine exploitation and coercive measures of the Brahmin-Kayasth-Vaidya of Calcutta lobby, which misused and manipulated the paraphernalia of British administration.

In the new Assembly of Dacca, the demands for proportionate share in job-sector for the Untouchables and the Muslims who lagged behind with shortfall in representing in the job-field were forcefully reiterated. The Namasudras called a largely attended meeting at Orakandi on 2nd October 1906. The meeting was presided over by a Namasudra Zamindar, Brajendra Nath Mandal. The following resolutions were passed:

(1) that 'The meeting is greatly indebted to the Secretary of State for India for his declaring the partition of Bengal as a settled fact and admissible of no amendment';

(2) that this meeting prays most earnestly that the Hon'able Mr. Herr will bestow the same rights and privileges upon the Namasudras as have been done upon the Mohammedans, in as much as the Namasudras and the Mohammedans are predominating communities of Eastern Bengal, and the latter unlike the Hindus possess a good deal of sympathy for the Namasudras'; and

(3) that it is simply owing to the dislike and hatred of the Brahmins, the *Vaidyas,* and the Kayasthas that this vast Namasudra community has remained backward; this community has therefore, not the least sympathy with them and their agitation, and will henceforth work hand in hand with their Mohammedan brethren."[25]

The resolutions impregnated with political wisdom of the day are remarkably historic. It reflects the psychological anger and reaction of a vast community of Untouchbale i.e. Depressed Classes and expresses their determination to fight it out both socially and politically. They did not hesitate to declare that their relationship was better with the Muslims than their tormentors, the Hindu-Brahmins. They openly opposed the anti-Bengal-partition movement launched by the Hindus.

First Untouchable Who Enjoyed Job-Representation: Government accepted the demand of the 2nd resolution i.e. the demand for job representation on the basis of the principle, what was in terms of *Manyawar* Kasi Ram in later age, '*Jiski Jitni Sankhya Bhari, Uski Utni Sankhya Bhari*'. 'Let there be share of power and privileges in consonance with the proportion to the community strength in number.' Dr Ambedkar raised this demand of representation in Government jobs exclusively for the Hindu Scheduled Castes, in his Memorandum only in 1942 when he was the Hon'ble member of the Viceroy's Executive Council. He pleaded his demand on the basis that the provisions of Communal Award as the Poona Pact too recognised Depressed classes as a different community like Muslim and Sikh etc. Or else as Scheduled Castes i.e. Hindus the low castes lost all justifiability to demand for separate reservation in the job sector like other minorities. Their share they got as Hindus.

In the Memorandum, titled 'Grievances of the Scheduled Castes' submitted on 29th October 1942, as the Labour Member of the Viceroy's Executive Council he had placed the position on the data from the Census of 1941as below:

(i) Inadequate Representation in the Central Legislature

(ii) Inadequate Representation in the Central Executive

(iii) Inadequate Representation in the Public Services

No greater injustice has been done to the Scheduled Castes than in the matter of their employment in Public services.... Anyone who examines the communal composition of these services can have manner of doubt that the Scheduled Castes have been rigorously excluded from these (ICS and Central) Services.

The condition of the S. Castes is not only deplorable, but it is also intolerable".... Besides, the two remedies suggested namely (1) declaring them a minority (2) fixing their proportion in the annual vacancies, it will be necessary to sanction other remedies to the S. Castes for securing to their fair share in the services. They are (i) Raising the Age bar (ii) Reduction of the Exam. fee, and (iii) Appointment of a S, Caste Officer to see that the provisions made in the interests of the S. Castes in this behalf are carried by all Departments."[26]

It is obvious from the discussion that neither Sahu Maharaj in his Act of 1902, nor the Assan-Bengal Government in its act of 1907 and not even Dr Ambedkar in 1942, used the word 'reservation' in their approach papers. It was purely the democratic need and demand for the proportional representation. There was nothing else; neither reservation nor community preference, nor discriminatory justice. Representation is the right, fundamental democratic right and not any gift of charity from the powerful privileged minority groups.

Just half a decade after when Dr Ambedkar as the Chairman of the Drafting Committee placed the draft constitution bill to be passed on the 26th November 1949 by the Constituent Assembly he did not go even an inch beyond the reservation policy of Shahu Maharaj or of Guruchand Thakur. Constitutional reservation remained confined to the political and executive sectors only. The polity structure of the Parliamentary form of democratic government was composed of three wings such as the Legislature, Executive and Judiciary. In the Constitution, there is no provision for reservation in the post of judges. As a result, the judiciary remains absolutely Brahmanic managed by 70 to 75 families of India. There is no independent recruiting institution of Government to test the impartiality and suitability of the candidates being selected for the posts of judges. This sector has been left for the struggling Sudra masses of 3rd Millennium to settle.

The Aryan Brahmins are found to have transformed this land of 'gold-gees' into an eternal colony and a land of reservation. The other name of Caste system is nothing but 'Spiritual-Reservation'. All privileges and ownership of entire means of productions, including working-class population have been reserved (including temple jobs, education) for the Brahmins. The microscopic minority, in violation to the essence of democracy, kept 90 per cent of the socio-economic and above all political privileges reserved for them. Some security, administrative and law-and-order responsibilities were given to the Kshatriyas. A little share of economy production, maintenance and finance-management act was kept for the *Vaisyas*. All duty to serve the society was reserved for the Sudras and Untouchables. They were to get in return servitude and hatred. The British Government for the first time came down, by the providence of God, to repeal this spiritual-tyranny with the sure antidote of constitutional reservation. Constitutional reservation (not representation) along with the 'spiritual reservation policy' provided the deprived segment with the things and objects those were denied to them by the entire band of holy Hindu-gods and goddesses. It was nothing new essentially.

In the month of February 1907 there came the "Proportional Representation of Communities in Public Employment Act" of Assam Bengal Government. By availing himself of the benefit of the provisions of this representation Act, Shashi Bhusan Thakur, a Matriculate and worthy son of Guruchand was the first Indian Untouchable to secure a Government job in British India. He joined as a Sub-Registrar in the Jalpaiguri district in 1907. Next year in 1908 Kumud Behari Mullick, BA and Dr Tarini Bala were appointed as Deputy Magistrate in Hoogly district and Government Physician through the right to represent in executive sector. The process would have continued unabated and soon engulfed the entire nation had the Hindus not raised a clamor and violent protest. The Hindus got the deadliest kind of thunderbolt. It shocked and rocked up to the core of the Hindu thought-process. It threatened them from heaven to hell. They could tolerate anything but the breaking of the divine-chains of the tens of millions of suffering masses called Sudras and Untouchables. They were enjoying entire cake of power as a divine providence. How could they even mistakenly dream to part with that? How could they give share, that too to their 'divine-slaves' the Untouchables and to the *Mlechha* Muslims? Maybe men are born free. But in accordance with the holy prescriptions in the Hindu-*Shastras*, the 'Sudras' and the 'Untouchables' are not 'Born Free'. They were born in chains; born-slaves, the 'Divine-slaves'. How could they tolerate the fact of their 'Divine-slaves' managed to escape in this tricky way provided by the British nation and achieved freedom? They intensified the fury of their anti-partition agitation '*Swadeshi*' all over Bengal and outside from political platform, The Indian National Congress. The Hindus resorted to terrorism in the name of Lord Krishna's Gita.

The movement was not really an anti-partition movement. It was, in the name '*Swadeshi Andolon*', an anti-untouchable or anti-freedom movement created by the Brahmins of Bengal. Bengal *Swadeshi*-leaders are found to have, therefore, agreed cheerfully to get Bengal divided into Assam, Bihar, Orissa in 1911. But they did not allow East-Bengal (the land of *Chandals, Rajbansis* and *Pods* etc) to get a separate administrative identity. They were happy with a very small Bengal and interestingly with the Capital of India shifting from Calcutta to New Delhi. The enormous impact of shifting of India's capital from Calcutta to New Delhi in politics, economy, culture and developmental areas had virtually started to cripple Bengal bit by bit. And the process of slow-killing of Bengal continued unending and eternal.

The Hindus, under the leadership of Rashtra Guru Surendra Nath Banerjee had started and intensified the '*Swadeshi* Movement' with the call for boycotting the purchase of British goods so that the volume of Company's favourable balance of trade was adversely affected. They started non-cooperation with the British in many other forms to pressurize them to withdraw the action that proved to be detrimental to the interests of the Brahmins. Eventually, the British agreed to unite the administrative units of two Bengals on certain conditions. Despite immeasurable and permanent loss of Bengal's future development and prospects of prosperity, the Creamy-layer Hindus agreed to the proposals. The Brahmins only gained. But it was the utter defeat of Bengal as a whole and eastern sector of India in general. The Capital of India was shifted from Calcutta to New Delhi. Calcutta turned to be the hub of the eternal-refugees and slums. West Bengal became the most backward province in the post independent India. Bihar, Orissa and Assam were geographically separated. Bengal reduced to a much smaller state and proved to be vulnerable to have her great impact in future democratic movement of India and in the Parliament. Practically this unity move or *Swadeshi* was the beginning of the preparation for Bengal's political-partition as two sovereign States in future on the eve of the transfer of power in 1947. Partition or no partition of Bengal, the Namasudras and Untouchables of Bengal continued their march ahead by sailing against the odds and all-out counter forces.

The First Indian-Untouchable as a Legislator: There yielded the sweet fruit of the long-drawn incredible political movements that were fired with the hopes of arrogance of the untouchables. In 1917 when Lord Montague came to India to give the Government of India Act of 1919, Prof. Advocate Mukunda Behari Mullick, the undisputed leader of Depressed Classes of Eastern India in his strongly worded draft memorandum demanded for separate electorate (like Muslims) for the Untouchables. The British, badly engaged in the 1st World War could not grant that, as they owe much to the Indian ruling classes for huge donation of money and man power for war. However, he was crowned with the franchise right along with representation through election and nomination by the Act of 1919. Advocate Bhisma Dev Das, a Matua disciple was nominated as MLC of Bengal Legislature (the 1st in India) in 1921 with recommendation of Guruchand. One of the greatest contribution of Bishma Dev Das as the member of the Legislative Council of Bengal was pressing for implementation of the earlier job-representation policy of the Government in the floor of the House. The benefit of proportional representation of communities (not of castes) in government jobs what was given by the Assam Bengal Government in 1907 was obviously neglected and buried by the government of Bengal once it was reunited. With a view to fulfilling the dream of his Guru as well as the necessity of his people Bhisma Dev Das, MLC demanded 18 per cent reservation in Government jobs for the Untouchables of Bengal. One of his questions raised in the House reads as follows:

"157, Babu Bhisma Dev Das:

(a) Will the Hon'able Member in charge of the Appointment Department be pleased to state,

(b) On what basis the classification of the depressed or backward class was made in the selection of candidate and making appointment for the Bengal Civil Service and

(c) What proportion of candidate was selected from these classes and what proportion of appointment was given to them?

(d) Will the Hon'able Member be pleased to state whether the Government are considering the desirability of reserving at least 1/6 th or a fare proportion of the appointment in every department for the Depressed classes as enumerated in the Calcutta University Commission Report?"[27]

As a result of vigorous stress on spread-education programme of Guruchand by the year 1930 there came a band of educated and suitable candidates for different levels of posts in government jobs. However, they were neither adequately nor fairly given chances to come up with their proportional representation in the offices which were controlled primarily by the Brahmins. There representation in jobs in the district of Faridpur was 5.47 per cent; Bakharganj 1.83 per cent; Jessore 1.0 per cent; Khulna 1.26 per cent; whereas the percentage of their population in the districts were 23 per cent; 15 per cent; 22 per cent; and 35 per cent respectively. Those who held almost 66 per cent posts in job market represented the population of 13-14 per cent in these districts. The ceaseless democratic demands and stubborn struggle of the Namasudra community on behalf of the Depressed Classes in this regard with sensible arguments on the basis of data and facts yielded result. In 1930, September, the Government of India took a decision that in the areas one in each three posts of Government Departments will be filled by the candidates belonging to the Depressed classes. All the District authorities were instructed to implement the orders strictly. But compliance report never was near satisfactory. However, we may find in the order the universal approval of the job-reservation policy by the Government of India in 1930 itself. In the same year, the London Returned Barister Promotha Ranjan Thakur, the grandson of Guruchand, for the first time, demanded reservation in the Judiciary.

Nothing concrete came out of the assurances from the part of the Government in regard to the reservation policy and its implementation till the month of February 1934. Now, Amulya Dhan Roy and Sharat Chandra Bal two of the Namasudra members of the Bengal Legislative Assembly submitted a Notice for discussion on the subject demanding 25 per cent of the posts in the Government jobs to be reserved for the Scheduled Castes. By the time in pursuance of the Poona Pact of 1932 a new era of 'Chamcha Age' started. The era of 'safe-guard' for the helpless and hopeless untouchables began. The Depressed Classes people were given a new term as 'Scheduled Castes' in 1933 as the untouchable population once again were assimilated in the lowest rung of the Hindu society by the terms of the Poona Pact, the caste was attributed to each group and they were listed in the schedule officially. Still the audacity of hope and the arrogance of dream for equality haunted the 'Orphans of the World' in Bengal. The Notice given by Roy and Bal was admitted but it was not tabled for discussion. In 1935, a similar resolution brought by the Hon'able Member Mukunda Behari Mullick had the same fate; it was tabled but left un-discussed. "The Bengal Depressed Class Association" during this period "submitted a complaint to the Government….. and demanded reservation of at least 20 per cent of all positions in Public Services." The Untouchables of Bengal are found to have gone further ahead successfully in these fields of acquiring executive share in the governance of the country when we observe that in 1935 in a vast Namasudra Conference at Orakandi they placed a demand to the Government to establish a 'Special Commission' to recommend the candidates belonging to the Scheduled Castes. "A memorandum was therefore, issued in September 1936 with the stipulation that 15 per cent of all vacancies in the District of Dacca, Bakharganj, Faridpur, Jessore, Khulna, Birbhum, Burdwan, Murshidabad and 24 Parganas would henceforth be filled in with the members of the Scheduled castes. The policy of Job reservation for these sections of the Hindu society, which was started experimentally for two Districts was thus given nearly a general provincial extension. This was no doubt a remarkable victory for the campaign that had been launched and orchestrated mainly by the Namasudra leaders," so comments a scholar historian.[28] The undisputed leader of these counter-reservation movements to the spiritual reservation of the Brahmins was no doubt, Thakur Guruchand. It started in 1906 at Orakandi and ended at Orakandi in 1937, the year before the Grand Leader breathed his last.

References

1. Dr Ambedkar W and S, Vol. 8, p. 359.
2. Karl Marx and Engels, Selected Works, Vol. 1, p. 492.
3. L. Mukherjee, History of India (Modern) and Shiv Nath Shastri, Ramtanu Lahiri O Samakalin Banga Samaj, p. 48.
4. Shiv Nath Shastri, Ramtanu Lahiri O Samakalin Banga Samaj, p. 53.
5. BVB; and Shiv Nath Shastri, Ramtanu Lahiri, pp. 56/63.
6. Marx and Engles, Selected Works, Vol. 1, p. 495, letter, London, Friday, July 22, 1853.
7. Vidyasagar O Bangali Samaj, Vinoy Ghosh, p. 545.
8. A.K. Biswas, The Namasudras Of Bengal.
9. Shiv Nath Shastri, Ramtanu Lahir O Tatkalin Bango Samaj, p. 48.
10. *Ibid*, pp. 56/54.
11. Gita, 3/26.
12. Bipin Chandra, Modern India, NCERT, Pub. 1976.
13. A.K. Biswas.
14. *TOI*, dated, 27th August, 2008, Front page.
15. Upendra Nath Mullick, Mosiahati Vidyalay.
16. Upendra Nath Mullick, Kultiya Valika Vidyalay: Itikatha.
17. S.K. Biswas.
18. Dr B.R. Ambedkar, W and S, Vol. 17 (2), p. 423.
19. Sekhar Bandopadhaya, Caste Protest and Identity in Colonial India, Namasudras, p. 104.
20. *Ibid*. p. 31.
21. W.W. Hunter, ICS, Chairman, Education Commission, 1882.
22. BVB, The History and Culture of the Indian People, Part-II, Vol. X, pp. 12-13.
23. H. Kotani, Caste System, Untouchability and the Depressed, p. 183.

24. Dhananjoy Keer, Chatrapati Sahu Maharaj, p. 117.
25. H. Kotani, Caste System, Untouchability and Depressed (Pushed Towards Partition), p. 232.
26. Dr B.R. Ambedkar, W and S, Vol. 10.
27. N.B. Roy, A People in Distress, Vol. 2, pp. 147-148.
28. Shekhar Bandhyopadhay.

5

Sunrise of Bahujan-Politics in the Eastern Sky

The sun-shine-dawn of democracy from England and Europe, across the seven seas had started flooding the eastern dark of India soon after the battle of Palasse in 1757. In the battle of Palasse and in other military mobilisation for territorial conquests and expansions, the British East India Company defeated only the Muslim *Nawabs*, Hindu Kings, hereditary Chiefs and absolute *Thagi* and irresponsible dacoit-rulers.[1] Indians of contemporary period had no concept even of the rule by the people or of a democratic Government. The British did not topple any representative government in India. All earlier autocratic governments were conquered with the swords and maintained by the swords. The foreign phenomenon, such as 'rule of law', the Constitution, Parliament, Legislature and the process of enactment of laws and the Acts passed by the members of an institution called the Parliament was unknown and unheard of. The English from a land of democracy thus, had come to India to encroach or supersede the Brahmanical divine-laws at last by the divine providence.

During the past two millennia, India neither witnessed any Parliament nor had any set of laws framed by human beings. There had been no proper jurisprudence either. However, with the advent of the British Rule in India, the irresponsible days of the glorious (as has been claimed by the official historians) dynastic-rule of the autocratic, tyrant Hindu-potentates from successive families of divine-despots under the protective commands of the Brahmins disappeared. 'England has to fulfill a double mission in India; one destructive, the other regenerating, the annihilation of old Asiatic society, and the laying of the material foundations of Western society in Asia'. Consequently, the British Rule in India proceeded towards the path of democratisation. Towards the target of democratisation the British monarchy, in England, turned to be the 'new-monarchy', 'benevolent-monarchy' and finally to the 'constitutional monarchy', discussed Karl Marx. The history of England and of entire Europe therefore, is found to be the history of successive civil wars with the slogan of 'Liberty' and 'Nationalism'. This is the secret of the advancement of the people of Europe and other countries.

The ancient Indian 'divine-rulers' however, had no chance to behave democratic or benevolent as they were strictly, rather scrupulously dictated by the spiritual-scriptures which believed on the other side only divine-slaves. The 'Draconian' Manu-laws were caste-laws, which knew no words like people, discrimination, or individual freedom. Rather discrimination was the basis and objective of the Manu-laws. Members of no caste were born free; they were divine-slaves; born 'Sudras' or Ati-Sudras'. In practice, they were not treated human beings. These anti-human, anti-people, anti-national laws, in essence and practice, in a straight way are anti-democratic. Consequently, this barbaric and semi-civilised society has not witnessed even a single civil war. It remained, therefore, as a country without history, at least any known-history of her society. The history of India is only the tale of consecutive defeats and subjugation in the hands of the foreign invaders.

The Brahmins were not only the authors of the Holy Scriptures but they also were the sole guardians or interpreting agents of those spiritual constitutions. There were only divine-masters and divine-slaves. F. Barnier had reported this fact to his French Master, the Emperor that, 'There was no middle class in the Mughal India'. The socio-economic scene of present day too reflects the same picture of the super rich ruling-class rolling in wealth, wine, women and wanton festivities and the below poverty level, servile classes in distressing and destitute condition. There is no middle class in India. Mughal India was not actually of the Mughals. The Mughals only ruled the Hindu India. Hinduism is a menace to equality and fraternity, therefore, is not compatible to democracy.[2] The Muslim rulers virtually never ran Indian 'theocratic' government with the Islamic laws and democratic principles. Entire country was run, primarily with the verdict and instructions of the Brahmins.

In the circumstances, it is now a historical fact that the Untouchable races of India helped initiate the act of establishing the banner of democracy in this 'semi civilised' country of castes. Caste is synonym of corruption. As a result, the country is composed of the 'beastly people with their beastly religion', which has finally made a society of irrevocable 'graded inequality' in every respect. There was nothing sort of social democracy in the country. Concept of brother-hood amongst fellow human of the society was regenerated into a constitutional system of one-way downwards hatred. There was no inclusive or unifying force among different classes or groups in the society. A reign of exclusion prevailed upon every social condition.

The Untouchable heroes of India shed blood and gave their lives in the battle fields, from the mango-groves of Palasse in 1757 to the battle grounds of Koregaon on the bank of Vima river in Poone in 1818. "Many Britishers think that India was conquered by Clives, Hastings, Cootes. Nothing can be a greater mistake. India was conquered by an army of Indians and the Indians who formed the army were all untouchables."[3] Thus these two nations, British and Indian Depressed Classes, in combine brought down the curtain of corrupt Kingship rather, theocracy, in the country and raised the banner of democracy. The native army (*Sepoys*) composed of the Untouchable Dusads, Chandals, Pariahas and Mahars was raised and trained by the British drill-sergeants[4] during this period. The Untouchables thus became equal partner of the British in displaying the dawn of democracy in India. They together struggled against the all out resistances rendered by the Brahmins and their associate castes in establishing the Parliamentary democratic structure in the country.

It is generally misconceived that Indian elite castes welcomed democracy as those vociferous people were found to be the vanguard of Indian National Congress. Nothing can be untruth than this. Democracy or its concept is incompatible to Hinduism. Hence, "Ever since 1919 when Mr. Gandhi captured the Congress, congress men looked upon the boycott of Legislature as one of the sanctions for making the British Government concede the demand of *Swaraj*. Under this policy, every time there was an election in which the Congress decided not to take part, the Congress would not only refuse to put candidate on the Congress ticket but also would carry all propaganda against any Hindu proposing to stand for election as an independent candidate. One need not quarrel over the merits of such a policy. But what was the means adopted by the Congress to prevent Hindus standing on an independent ticket! The means adopted were to make the Legislature object of contempt. Accordingly, the Congress in various provinces started processions carrying placards saying, "Who will go in the Legislature?" Only barbers, cobblers, potters and sweepers." In the procession one man would utter the question as part of this slogan and the whole crowd would repeat as answer to the second part of the slogan."[5] Balgangadhar Tilak adopted the policy in all his public meetings even before. In such circumstances, the citizens belonging to the untouchable and castes of very lower order stood erect in favour of the democratisation process of Indian society and polity.

Democracy – The Gift of the English Rulers: Mercantile companies had come from Europe for trading in India. They, in course of time, established political dominance and control over our country. The East India Company, naturally after securing '*Dewani Sanad*' in 1774, started ruling India with mere commercial motive. They operated the instrumentalities of the state and handled Indian-politics, which had been in a muddled condition in such a manner that they could maximize their favourable balance of trade. 'The ruling classes of Great Britain have had, till now, but an accidental, transitory and exceptional interest in the progress of India. The aristocracy wanted to conquer it, the 'moneyocracy' to plunder it, and the 'millocracy' to under sell it. But the tables are turned now. The millocracy have discovered that the transformation of India into a reproductive country has become of vital importance to them."[6] It is a historical fact that the British who came to India with mercantile motive to exploit the colony-market eventually gave India a system of Democratic Parliament. They introduced their secular and social science literature in India when they became rulers of the Empire. The Untouchables struggled with them to establish democracy in the country because they had a hope to live like a human only in the democratic structure. It was the British who being driven by their vilest design of selfish interests looted the colony but simultaneously they brought social revolution without which the destiny of mankind could not be achieved for the first time in Indian stagnant society.[7]

Thus, for the first time the 'hereditary subjects' of India experienced that it was no more mandatory for only the persons of Royal dynasties to govern the country. Common subjects and their representatives in the Parliament administer and handle the instrumentalities of the State.

British Planned Freedom Movement for Transfer of Power: In the annals of Indian history, there is no documentary evidence that the Indian governing classes or castes at any stage of time dreamt or initiated freedom struggle against any foreign ruling dynasty or government. There has been all along the rule of the divine-monarchy with absolute power. The kingdom was held on the point of sword, foreign or native. The waves of American and French revolution in 1789, 1830, 1848 or in 1871 and the process of counter revolutions all over Europe failed to torment the minds of Indian peasantry or working class because there was no common platform. There was no middle class to agitate or use the lower order to protect their interests. Indians, are therefore, not found to have initiated freedom struggle even against the British colonial regime. The Government of Great Britain and the British nation opposed nationalist democratic movements in France with other European powers and cautiously had *suomoto* planned to transfer political power in the hands of the creamy-layer elite Indians and to rule the country through agents who had been groomed by the British. It was calculated to be less risky and fairly easy for the British to manage and exploit the colonial market through the natives without taking any responsibility or accountability of their malfunctioning or bad-rule. Democratic structure of government, especially the British model, is discovered to be the best safety valve to minimize the social tension between the rich and the poor. This is some sort of liberal or benevolent mode of exploitation in the name of the people.

It was, however, a well nigh impossible task for the British to start with democratic paraphernalia and schemes in a 'semi-civilised' 'semi-barbaric' country like India where 99 per cent of the population were illiterate and around 40 per cent have been treated as dehumanised creature. The Sudras and the Untouchables were forced by the Brahmins to remain illiterate for millenniums. Being hand to mouth and illiterate generation after generation the untouchables lost mental appetite and physical capacity to be in democratic politics and govern their own country.

The year 1880 when Guruchand set up the first school in his village coincided with the enactment by the British Parliament for compulsory education and voting right to the girls in England. It was historically significant of Lord Ripon becoming the Viceroy of India in the year. Lord Ripon unfurled his 'Declaration of 1882'. In it, he, for the first time, disclosed the plan to democratize the administration of base or rural level where representatives of people, as far as possible would be elected by the tax-payers. Lord Ripon, as has already been stated, appointed a Commission under William Wilson Hunter, ICS to enquire into the condition of education, resulting increase and improvement of the primary and secondary school which stood till now neglected by the State. Lord Ripon for the first time took steps for democratisation of Indian society and administration by involving the subjects of grass root level irrespective of caste or creed in the act of governance. In disclosing his 'Resolution of 1882, he proclaimed, "If the Boards are to be of any use for the purpose of training the natives to manage their own affairs, they must not be overshadowed by the constant presence of the *Burra Sahib* of the district."[8] This declaration may be called as the first milestone for social-democracy in India. These steps for training for social and political democracy became the life-line of parliamentary democracy.

As a follow up action, the British Bureaucrat A. O. Hume in a letter to the students (all creamy-layer-elite-Indians) of the University of Calcutta right in the starting of 1883, openly instigated and inspired to come forward to claim share in political power. "He asked for fifty men, good and true, men of unselfishness, moral courage, self-control and active benevolence.... To join as founders, the thing can be established and the further development will be comparatively easy."[9] His letter dated 1/3/1883 reads: "And if even the leaders of thought are all either such poor creatures, or so selfishly wedded to personal concern that they are not ready to strike a blow for their country's sake, then justly and rightly are they kept down and trampled on, for they deserve nothing better. Even nations secure precisely as good a government as it does merits.

If you, the picked men, the most highly educated of the nation cannot, scorning personal ease and selfish objects, make a resolute struggle to secure greater freedom for yourselves and your country a more impartial administration, as large share in the management of your own affairs, then we, your friends, are wrong and our adversaries right, then are Lord Rippon's noble aspirations for your good fruitless, then at present at any rate all hopes of progress are at an end and India truly neither desire nor deserve any better government than she enjoys. Only, if this be so, let us hear no more factions, peevish complaints that you are kept in leading strings and treat like children, for you will have proved yourselves such..... If you lack that public spirit, that highest form of all altruistic devotion that leads men to subordinate private ease to the public will that patriotism that has made Englishmen what they are, then rightly are these preferred to you, rightly and inevitably have they become your rulers. And rulers and task-masters they must continue, let the yoke gall your shoulders never so sorely, until you realize and stand prepared to act upon the eternal truth, that self sacrifice and unselfishness are the only unfailing guides to freedom and happiness."[10] Hume, the then Secretary to Agricural Department, reported on the restless peasantry of the country. He cautioned that the peasantry might break out into dangerous revolt any time as they had their back to the walls due to ill treatments and exploitation of the local Zamindars and *Mahajans*. In March 1885, once again he held another conference at Pune of Indian National Union where highly educated (London returned or groomed) elite Indians of urban background were invited. The circular of the meeting disclosed its intention and terms of references obviously. "The leading politicians, well acquainted with English language, from all parts of Bengal, Bombay and Madras Presidencies were invited to attend this conference whose objects were stated to be (1) to enable all the most earnest labourers in the cause of national progress to become personally known to each other; and (2) to discuss and decide upon the political operations to be undertaken during the ensuing year...... Lastly a hope was expressed that indirectly this Conference will form the germ of a native Parliament and, if properly conducted, will constitute, in a few years, an unanswerable reply to the assertion that India is still wholly unfit for any form of representative institutions."[11]

Congress the Creamy-layer Hindu Nationalists: Eventually the British royal planning yielded expected result. In October 1885, the political institution called Indian National Congress came into operation with the 'leading politicians well acquainted with English language'. Soon after his retirement, A. O. Hume, I.C.S established the Indian National Congress. Not just the ruling elite class joined it. The creamy-layer of the elite took its charge. Woomesh Chandra Banerjee, an Indian Christian (Brahmin) and a former clerk in the Company's service became the 1st President of Indian National Congress. In the initial years, many Europeans decorated the post of President of the Congress. One of the most influential of them was Ms. Anne Besant who became president of Congress twice. The Grand Old Man, Dadabahi Naroji, a representative of financial tycoons of the Parsis and Badruddin Tyabji, the Muslim leader became its 3rd and 4th President respectively. For the years, 1888 and 1889 two English men George Yule and William Wedderburn became Congress President. It became really a matter of confusion to know distinctly whether the Congress belonged to the Indians or to the English men. In such circumstances, entry of the rural elements especially of Indian untouchables and Sudras in this well-planned international and colonial imperialistic political arena, be it in democratic or oligarchic form, was a matter beyond even dream or concern.

In the beginning, it was only the Indian supra-social elites, who efficiently learnt to dream in English, laugh in English and cry in English, started forming powerful organisations to focus their politico-economic aspirations to their Lords in the Company service. Entire proceedings of the Congress was restricted to English language only. Prince Dwaraka Nath Tagore, the first Indian who elevated himself to be the business-partner of the East India Company, established the maiden organisation called, "Bengal Landlord's Association in 1842. Dwaraka Nath and his family had very close relation with the British queen. The forum paled into insignificance no sooner than Tagore had died in 1846. In 1843, George Thompson established another organisation named "British India Society". It did not take time for the Elite India to understand the direction for immediate erasing the word 'Bengal'. Consequently, on 31st October, 1851 the Rajas and *Zaminders* of Bengal established "British India Association" by merging the two earlier organisations. The composition of the first Executive body of the organisation will obviously disclose its aims, views and limitations. The body is given below:-

(1) Raja Radha Kanta Dev, President (2) Raja Kali Krishna Dev, Vice-President (3) Babu Devendra Nath Tagore, (s/o Prince Dwarakanath) Secretary with the following members (4) Babu Digambar Mitra, (5) Babu Payeri Chand Mitra, (6) Babu Sambhunath Pandit, (7) Babu Jagadananda Mukhopadhya, (8) Babu Joykrishna Mukhopadhaya, (9) Babu Prasanna Kumar Thakur, (10) Babu Ramnath Thakur, (11) Babu Harakumar Thakur, (12) Babu Satyasaran Ghosh, (13) Babu Ramgopal Ghosh, (14) Babu Krishnakishore Ghosh, (15) Babu Harimohan Sen, (16) Babu Umesh Chandra Dutta, and (17) Babu Ashutosh Dev.

In the mean time, there occurred the revolt of the *sepoys*, famous as the *Sepoy* Mutiny of 1857. Brahmins in the Company's army organised this mutiny. Brahmins were agitated because the British recruited untouchables from the beginning in large number in the army. Thus very speedily the lowest stratum of the society started transforming the socio-economic and educational status in the society. They were coming in close proximity of the ruling class also. However, when the mutiny lost its strength, the expected anti-national attitude of these *Zamindars* and *Rajas* individually and collectively was manifested excellently. They all assisted the British colonial rulers in suppressing the revolt of the Indian *sepoys*. During this period, the *zamindars* also were entangled in the peasant's exploitation and suppressing series of peasants' revolts in collaboration with the British *Kuthiyals*. Consequently, the King of England, as the Emperor of India had taken the reign of administration soon after the revolt was suppressed.

In 1875, another organisation called 'Indian Association' was founded at Kolkata by Surendra Nath Banerjee. Banerjee was dismissed from the ICS on the charges of dereliction of duty with a hefty monthly pension of Rs. 50/= per mensum.[12] A few years later when the Indian National Congress came in existence under the President-ship of Woomesh Chandra Banerjee, Surendra Nath Banerjee merged his Association officially with the Indian National Congress.

So long as Bal Gangadhar Tilak, the typical orthodox Brahmin from Pune, remained at the helm, the Congress remained an institution for gaining right to interfere in peripheral administration and conducting business exclusively for the Brahmins and the associated creamy-layer-ruling castes from the British Government. It demanded participation of the English-knowing Indians in the bureaucracy in a bigger number. Tilak even did not hesitate to declare, at a certain point of time that I do not want a *Swaraj* the 'self-rule' if it means the '*Swaraj*' of low caste people and Untouchables also. His dream of *Swaraj* was nothing but the sovereignty of the Brahmins. The Brahmins felt quite at home under the British Raj. Mohandas Karamchand Gandhi had returned to India from South Africa to join politics in January 1915. He led the Indian National Congress from 1919 though his arrival was planned at least since 1912.[13] With a view to introducing himself in the Indian political market, Gandhiji published his autobiography in Gujarati prematurely, long before he really contributed his services to the nation. Mahadev Desai published its English version in 1927.

Simultaneously, the bugle of Hindu-renaissance and establishment of the hereditary Brahmin-Democracy was blown by a band of intellectuals and literalists some under the garb of Hindu *Sanyasi* like Dayananda Saraswati, Vivekananda, Narayan Guru, Rishi Aurovindo Ghosh, Madam Blavatski, Anne Besant and some in the attire of Social reformers like Raibahadur Raja Rammohan Bandhopadhay, Iswar Chandra Vidyasagar and others as social-activists cum literalists like Roybahadur Vankim Chandra Chatterjee, Bala Gangadhar Tilak, Ravindra Nath Thakur, Sharat Chandra Chatterjee etc. Once again all were associated with direct politics in some open form as well as in clandestine manner.

Entry of Untouchables in Democratic Struggle: Sitting far from the warmth of these economic, social and political activities of high-power international significance and importance, the audacity of hope and irresistible drive of ambition was born in the heart of Guruchand. He had the arrogance of dream; an incredible urge to liberate his people in bondage of Hinduism by thousand folds. The dream was natural. Men are born free but the

Untouchables, Sudras and Tribes are in chains in every respect. The aspirations of freedom of both the groups, the oppressed and oppressors, ruled and the rulers, exploited and exploiters, the Brahmins and the Chandals, Hindus or non-Hindus now came to the dot for acquiring Democratic power, an optimum point of political liberty. Not being acquainted with the British move or not being invited to participate in the process of democratisation in any way, Guruchand seems to have been dragged into the central point of democratisation process of the country by the invisible forces of history. 'What touches all must be approved by all', is the plinth of democracy. It would be, in essence, a government by the governed and for the governed. In democracy, one's freedom ends where other's nose starts. Though illiterate and completely inexperienced, the traditional and ethnic courage of the Chandals carried undaunted Guruchand to the fields of relentless struggles. He, therefore, could easily touch the height and length, value and warmth of democratic life and functioning of the British Government in India with his tireless endeavor and active assertion.

The democratic aspirations of Guruchand was soon recognised first by the local authorities of the British Government and then by the power at the helm. He was quickly co-opted and given chances to play his important role as an active partner and equally important hero of the team which was set in motion to make a new nation in India as designed by the British rulers. Political participation of the untouchable masses was inevitably required for giving democracy a right shape. The alarm bell tolled in 1872 when the Chandal peasantry carried out the first ever successful, agrarian-general-strike in Faridpur District. It occurred just after the ruling classes of Europe had stormed the 'Parish Commune' established by Marxists. This maiden self-respect and democratic struggle by the peasantry of India to fulfill their socio-economic aspirations became significant because of its ceaseless follow up actions culminated in direct political movement.

By the providence of Lord Ripon's declaration of 1882, the elected representatives of the Chandal/ Namasudras and Muslim peasantry started participating in all the local bodies like Taluks, Tahasils, Union Boards etc wherever they were numerically predominant. They proved themselves very skilled and worthy in the field of education and the developmental activities. The poor peasantry proved themselves equal to the situation in administrating the local bodies. The quenchless appetite led the Namasudra leadership to place their cards finally for political birth.

We find Herbert Risley, ICS who depicted in his book, 'Tribes and Caste of Bengal' (published in 1891) "In the Pirojpur *thana* of Bakharganj the Chandals have recently started a movement to call themselves *Namas*, to wear shoes and not to taste rice from Kayasthas or Sudras….." This reveals that within a few years from the starting of the organised and conscious movement of the untouchables in the Dutta Danga Conference in 1881, they touched the entry point of the democratic movement. Soon the self-conscious, self-respect movement of Indian proletariat was pushed towards an independent political movement.

Target of their movement turned into a political one for social transformation with the definite goal of becoming free and rulers of the motherland. This was a struggle for total freedom; an uncompromising move to bring democracy, a form of government where the ruling classes would fail to capture power. Guruchand taught the Mantra, "*Kiba Vidya, Kiba Dhane, Kiba Shlipe Ki Vigyane Rashtraniti Kshetre Raj-kaje Sabkhane Thaka Chai. Rajbese Sajo Rajsaje*" 'Be it in the field of education or commerce; industry or science we need to enter in every sector, in the politics of the nation, in the government jobs. There is no other way. In regal attire, behave like a *Raja,*'a King.' He gave a clarion call to his emotionally '*kirtan-mast*' spiritualist *Matuas* to go ahead for politics as an indispensable part of spirituality and taught that a nation which has no organised entity has no strength. A race without a King is bereft of strength. '*Je Jatir Dal Nai He Jatir Bal Nai; Je Jatir Raja Nai He Jati Taja Nai*'. He preached, "Only the religion which has the King in its fold is alive.' .... "*Dharma Rajye Baas Kare Dharmasil Praja. Raja Yadi Hate Chao Dharo Raj Bhab. Bhab Anujaye Ase Bhaver Swavab. Dharma Kshetre, Karma Kshetre Bhav Hai Mul. Bhab Chara Dharma-karma Sakali Nirmul. Sakal Saktir Kendra Rajshakti Pai. Grihijane Uddharite Raj Shakti Chai.*" 'The religiously minded subjects can flourish only under the constitutional-rule. If one wants to be a King one is to get his regal aptitude. Temperament and ideals are the essence of Royal personality. The temper of a man is reflected in his actions, temporal or celestial. I find that the political power is the source of all power. Therefore, to rescue the family-holders we need political power.' The *Matuas* did not believe renunciation of family life. Their target was to improve conditions of family life in all respect. So he concluded: "*Raj sakti Bina Dekho Gristha Bachena, Saktibina Jiba Madhye Paran Nache Na*" .... "*Grihasthajaner Dukkha Nasibar Tare, Mama Pita Harichand Aasila Sansare. Gristha Janer Sresta; Raja Jini Hai. Raja Hole Sangsarir Sab Dukkha Jai.*" 'Be hold! without having political power the families get ruined as animates cannot move without the power of life. My father Harichand was born to eradicate the miseries of the family-members. The King is the greatest of the householders. When one becomes a King one's miseries wither away.' There was no ambiguity or hesitation in declaring his doctrine of religion for political battles.

Finally, he urged, 'I ask you to enter in the Legislature! Be nothing but the ruler in your own country and alleviate the miseries of the community'. "*Aami Bali Aain Sabhai Jao, Raja Hao. Dur Karo A Jatir Byatha.*"[14]

There was nobody to protest against these ruinous tortures and exploitation on the incredibly industrious and peace-loving peasants of the then Bengal, either in the British imperial government or in Indian society. That is why *Shahid* Bhagat Singh is found to have recorded with fire and blood on 3rd March 1931, the previous night to gallows, in his last wish, "The peasants have to liberate themselves not only from foreign yoke but also from landlords and capitalists" "....a handful of exploiters goes on exploiting the labour of the common people for their own ends. It matters little whether these exploiters are purely British capitalists or British and Indian in alliance, or even purely Indians."[15] It will be curious for the civilised world to learn that this food producer peasantry especially in Bengal are declared by the holy Hindu scriptures and Brahmins as untouchables of lowest grade in every respect even in the 'age of emailing'. They have been sustaining from time immemorial being surrounded by the ocean of enemies.

In such a suffocating situation of blinding darkness of illiteracy, superstition, poverty and spiritual-persecution the peasantry, the artisans, the land-less labours continued to offer an incredible fight for justice against their natural enemies. The political system of parliamentary democracy coming out of the Magna Carta of AD 1215 in England, the 'First Charter of English Liberty' paved the way for democratic rights for Indian commoners composed of the Untouchables, Tribes, Shudras and their proselyte Muslims to march ahead to regain freedom. They advanced through heavy odds and oppositions of all possible types launched by the 'first foreign intruders' of India.

Democratic-Hope in the New-Province

Lord Curzon, the ablest of the Governor Generals was sent out by England to succeed Lord Elgin and to govern India in 1899. His name goes down in the history of India as one who partitioned Bengal to govern and effectively administer too large a province like Bengal by two instead of one Lieutenant Governor. It was in AD 1905 on 16th of October when he created a new province called 'Eastern Bengal and Assam' and placed it under a Lieutenant Governor with its capital at Dacca.

The then province of Bengal was composed of Bihar, almost entire Chhota Nagpur, Orissa, West Bengal and Eastern Bengal and Assam of today. Virtually it was the whole of the eastern sector of India. On the east was the border of Burma and in the west her border touched United Province, Central Province and Madras. However, only the elite and orthodox Brahmins mainly of Calcutta and adjacent areas ruled it as the agents of the British. It was too large a province to manage administratively from Calcutta. Even it was not possible to satiate democratic aspirations of the newly emerged, politically conscious people of different groups suffering from diverse set of problems for their community development. The image of a representative government in a single Legislature at Calcutta was far from reality in the united Bengal. Besides, Calcutta was not capital of Bengal alone it was the capital of India.

People of Eastern Bengal suffered from non-development, neglect and discrimination as 90 per cent of the population were Untouchables and beef-eater-Muslim *mlechhas*. The Hindus used to call this part of the country as a land of '*Nere-Charal*' (Buddhists converted to Muslims '*Nere*' and Chandals) for which they had natural apathy to develop the part. The Hindus, who believed in graded purity and impurity of human beings, as a natural corollary considered people of this part impure and rightfully neglected them from the depth of their souls.

The Government of India, Home Department by its resolution No 2491 issued, "In December 1903 the Government of India in letters to several of the local Governments, announced their desire to consider the redistribution of certain of the territories of Eastern and North eastern provinces of India, notably Bengal and Assam. Their attention had been called to the matter by the constantly accumulating evidence of the excessive and intolerable burden imposed upon the Bengal Government by a charge too great for any one administration, and of the consequent deterioration in the standards of Government, notably in portions of Eastern Bengal." In pursuance the Simla proclamation of 1st September directed, "...that the said Province be called and known as the province of Eastern Bengal and Assam, and further to appoint the Honourable Mr. Joseph Bampfuled Fuller, CSICIE, of the Indian Civil Service, now Chief Commissioner of Assam to be the first Lieutenant-Governor of that Province. 3. .... The said Province of Eastern Bengal and Assam the districts of Dacca, Mymensingh, Faridpur, Bakharganj, Tiperra, Noakhali, Chittagong hill Tracts, Rajsahi, Dwinajpur, Jalpaiguri, Rangpur, Bogra, Pabna, and Maldah which now form the part of Bengal Division of the Presidency of Fort William shall cease to be ..... and included within the limits of the Lieutenant-Governorship of the province of the eastern Bengal and Assam."[16] By this declaration, Bengal was composed of Bihar, Chhota Nagpur, Orissa and Western part of Bengal.

This division of Bengal into two provinces for administrative exigencies benefited the Muslims and the Untouchables of Bengal. They became free to assert and execute their democratic rights and privileges by representing themselves in the Legislature and administration. In the new circumstances, they got, for the first time, chances to participate in the representative government freely sitting in Dacca without being dictated or oppressed by the creamy-layer-elite Hindus from Calcutta. They were in a position to chisel out their own fate. Despite their being majority in the vast Eastern part of the excessively large province, the unfortunate people were ruled by the decision taken and influenced by the Calcutta-lobby. There was almost no development amongst the people in the region without a single University, good college and schools.

Consequently, the newly emerged and politically conscious groups of the Untouchables and Muslims started demanding better deal in administrative sector for self-governance. The controversial and highly sensitive issue in regard to the administrative partition of Bengal in two parts, West and East had been going on in the house of Commons, London since long. The microscopic minority Hindu lobby (of 18 per cent) tried their level best to thwart the scheme from the beginning with their vociferous protests. But the statement of the Secretary of State in the House of Commons on the 4th of July 1905, made it clear that sanction had been given to long awaited decision for the partition of Bengal. Lord Curzon, the then Governor General declared, "Partition of Bengal as a settled fact and admissible no amendment."

As a natural corollary, the Hindus got seriously nervous and used the platform of Congress to launch a movement against the British government protesting the new arrangement and revocation of partition order. In early August, Congress in Calcutta called for boycott of British imported goods and pleaded for the use of *swadeshi* goods only. Therefore, the anti-partition movement of the elite Hindus was called Swadeshi movement.

The administrative exigencies were termed by the official and nationalist Hindu historians as an attempt to disintegrate Hindu-Muslim unity and national consolidation. A large group of Bengale leaders also argued contradictory to it that the Bengales would be reduced to minority in West Bengal. Actually, there was hardly any phenomenon, which could have been termed as 'unity' between two distinct communities like the Hindu and the Muslim. It has already been noted from the verdict of Raja Ram Mohan Roy, that the Hindu elite terribly disdained the Muslims, in particular those Muslims who were converts from low castes. The two communities exist on the diametrically opposite spiritual philosophy and hostile socio-cultural traits. There prevailed, however, a scheme of peaceful coexistence and mutual co-operation amongst the elites of all religious groups on the common agenda for perpetuating ruthless and indiscriminate rule of atrocities, hatred, exploitation on the teeming millions of the peasantry, artisans and members of other unorganised groups of producer classes or castes. The jewels and diamonds in the crowns of the Indian Muslim Emperors, Sultans and Nawabs, the Maratha Peswa, Sikh chiefs, Rajput Rajas and the British Queen Empress were nothing but the crystallised blood rolling down the tearful eyes of the artisans and peasants. There has been no middle class in the medieval or modern India. The exploiter and oppressor Hindus and the Muslims had some obvious superficial unity, however. This unity continues even today. This eventually turned into an uncompromising, irreversible and everlasting hostility.

From the outset of the *Swadeshi* movement, the Hindu leaders irrespective of their linguistic background are found to have utilised the image and power of Indian National Congress. Even the Marathi Brahmin leaders of Congress and other Parties very actively supported the anti-Bengal Partition movement. In the circumstances, it is not understood as to how the issue of linguistic minority or majority only of Bengale arose when the concept of a type of nationalism was playing its violent role? It is interesting to note that those who talked about the integrity of Bengali speaking people began their movement in foreign language. On 16th October, 1905, Ananda Mohan Bose inaugurated the agitation. "Here let me address a few words of the agitation, which has convulsed this province for the last two months in connection with the question of its partition and stirred to its innermost depths, the heart of every section of the communities from the highest to the lowest, from the rich zaminder in the town to the poorest in his humble cottage". Common people failed to follow the tongue. Hence, Ravindra Nath Tagore had to translate the speech. In such a situation, the Bengale and non-Bengale question was rather an anti-national phenomenon. What could have been the motive of the British to reduce the Bengali speaking people to minority in greater Bengal? Do the Brahmins rule by their number in the population?

The Indian National Congress was divided into moderate and extremists; nationalist and reformist groups on the question of social reform. The issues like untouchability, poverty alleviation and underdeveloped condition of the low caste Hindus were not acceptable for many. There emerged Social Reformist group in the Congress who wanted to take up reform moves with equal importance with political movement. They were severely criticised and brutally opposed. In 1905, the difference and hostile attitude between the two groups widened further in the Beneras Session. 'The differences between the parties came to head at the Surat session of the Congress in 1907 where a heated dispute ended in a free fight.' Balagangadhar Tilak, the *Chaitpawan* orthodox Brahmin of Maharashtra did not hesitate to declare from the rooftop, 'If Swaraj means to manumit the untouchables, the '*Telis*' and the '*Malis*' then such a Swaraj he does not want'. Congress and other Hindu body were forced, at this point of time, to consider these inconvenient issues due to rise of untouchable mass-movement mainly in Bengal, Punjab and Madras. Even the British authority refused to hand over more autonomy in the hands of the elite Indians who treat their compatriots in extremely inhuman and anti-democratic manner. How could the Hindus who had their spiritual society fragmented with water-tight compartments of castes talk about the Hindu-Muslim united society.

Clash–Elite-movement Vs Mass-movement: It is observed that the *Swadeshi* was an elite-movement raised by the creamy-layer microscopic-minority Hindus of Bengal. Whereas, the '*Mulniwasi*' natives started countering it with a pro-partition movement. As such, it was a mass-movement of the immense majority. *Zamindars* and educated Bengalee *babus* as a whole throughout the province appealed to the general people to boycott British merchandise including common items of daily use. The rich Hindus are found to have not so seriously implemented the scheme of boycott in their daily life. During the decade of *Swadeshi* movement, the import of Scotch whisky and such luxury items consumed exclusively by the elite and privileged classes of the Hindus augmented remarkably. Even common people in the beginning did not respond to their call. "By the end of 1906 the agitation began to lose much of its vitality, not merely because the masses did not respond to the solicitation of the agitators but because they were now resisting the pressure more sturdily than they were able to do at first. Interestingly, the Muslim League was born in Dacca as the child of this elitist Hindu Swadeshi movement.

'During these early years of the *Swadesi* movement, apart from some occasional attempt to mobilize the Hindu masses, the main attention of the leaders was focused on the problem of mobilizing the Muslims, who were by now more or less convinced that "the partition would be a boon to them and their special difficulties would receive greater attention from the new administration."[17] The common people, the peasantry of Bengal abstained from the *Swadesi* movement, as they were hardly concerned with it. The Untouchables and the Muslims not only not participate in the *Swadeshi* movement of the elite Hindus but they also vehemently opposed it. However, from national platform Gopal Krishna Gokhle is found to have claimed in his Presidential address in the Beneras session in 1905, "The tremendous upheaval of popular feeling which has taken place in Bengal in consequence of the 'Partition', will constitute a land-mark in the history of our national progress….. Bengal's heroic stand has astonished and gratified all India."[18] But these concepts of 'popular feelings' and 'heroic stand' were nothing but the expressions of words and of the stand taken by the "microscopic minority" as Congress was defined by Lord Duffrin. This euphoric expression was nothing but an expression that "represent nothing but the social anomaly of their own position.", as Lord Litton expressed for Congress, which 'was the handiwork of a few educated Indians 'Indians in blood and colour but English in taste and opinions.'[19]

The actual situation has, however, been revealed in the anxiety recorded by *Gurudev* Ravindra Nath Tagore. Tagore personally came down on the street of Calcutta to support the *Swadeshi* call with his unique method of convincing the mutually hostile Muslims and Hindus the utility and urgent need of unity and fraternity. The Hindu, however, did not forget to fan Hindu-chauvinism; the great Tagore inaugurated the '*Rakshabandhan Yatra*' with a pious dip in the Holy-Ganges with his band of followers and family members at *Jagannath Ghat*. He had entered the Nakhoda Masjid and tied friendship-band called *Rakhi* on the wrists of the Muslims of Calcutta. But the Muslims offered cold response to the nationalists' programme for opposing the British decision from the Hindu-Muslim united front. In such condition, Ravindra Nath Tagore in his article, in 1908, '*Sadupai*' (Appropriate means) described the relationship between the Bengalis of elite Calcutta or W. Bengal with other parts, "Beharis are neighbours of Bengal. Bengales have been interacting with the Biharis since long but any Bengale residing in Bihar will agree that there prevails no good relation between Biharis and Bengales. Educated Orias are eager to stand separate from the Bengales; same is the attitude of the Assamis. Therefore, all the people of the region of Assam, Bihar, Orissa, East Bengal and W. Bengal what we know as Bengal never accepted them as Bengales. Bengales too never accepted them as Bengale; on the contrary they have been treated as inferior and kept agonised." ..... "In this context we are not ready to confess that we arranged to suppress the wills and benefits of the low or depressed classes of the country. But the situation is a fact. .... We have never tried to draw them near, but we have only tried to exploit and use them for our benefit..... Without constructing the bridges of relationship we have demanded relationship from them." He has also recorded the act of defying *Swadeshi* call by Chandals and the Muslims, "Muslims have started using English-salt which was expensive. In many places the Namasudras are also reported to have done so." "The Namasudras are reported to have had ferociously joined with the Muslims against the Hindus in the riots. Should we not now consider as to why there came draught in the responsibility to show relationship?"[20]

In the beginning of the *Swadeshi* movement Tagore appealed to the *Bhadroloks* of Bengal in a *Vijaya Sanmilani*, "Friends, let us expand the horizon of our hearts to all corners of Bengal. Address the *Chasis,* peasants who have just returned to their dwelling after day long ploughing act, address those shepherd-boys who have just returned home after tending the fleets of cattle, address those who have assembled outside the temples, address those Muslims who have started calling *Namaj* facing towards the setting sun." He called to give attention towards those 'Bengalis' who stand outside 'We the Bengalis' and who are not integrated with 'We'.[21] Now, who were the members of the *Bhadralok Samaj*? Brahmins only were originally to compose the *Bhadra Samaj*. However, to strengthen the microscopic minority Brahmins during crisis period out of Chandal-Muslim democratic struggle, Ravindra Nath suggested in 1902 to include Vaidya, Kayasth, and Vaniks within the *Bhadra Samaj* to augment its numerical strength. "The *Bhadra Samaj* of our present day Society that is, Vaidya, Kayasth and Vanik castes in case the society refuse to accept them as 'Twice-born' *Dwija* then there is no hope of the rise of the *Brahmin Samaj*."[22] It is in the interest of the Brahmans in opposition to the Chandal/Namasudra-Pod-Koch-Rajbansi-Bagdi-Kaivarta in the democratic battle of ballots the other backward Sudras, in Bengal, were anointed in the *Bhadra-lok Samaj* that is respectable-society.

"Thus it is evident that 90 per cent of the producer classes of people remained afar and against the *Swadeshi* movement.[23] Indeed, there were two worlds; the world of the British groomed and sponsored creamy-layer-elite microscopic minority Indians. They were to defend their prerogative of privileges to remain exclusive ruling class. And the other was the world of the hapless, helpless 'orphans of the world', the 'divine-slaves' of the creamy-layer Hindus. Fired with the enthusiasm in democratic rights they were up to claim and establish their freedom in their own land to be its *defacto* ruling class. The first group was composed of the first foreign intruders of India the 'Indo-Aryans'. The second was composed of '*Mulniwasi*' autochthons. There has been nothing common between the two but a common dislike, conflict of interests, distrust and profuse hatred for each other. "All these three classes of Indian society the peasants, the artisans, the workers constituting the overwhelming majority of Indians, discovered that they had no political rights or power and that virtually nothing was being done for their intellectual or cultural improvement. Education did not percolate down to them. There were hardly any school in villages and the few that were there, were poorly run. The doors of higher education were rare to them in practice. Moreover, many of them belonged to the lower-castes and had still to bear social and economic oppression by the upper-castes."[24]

The target of Rabindranath Tagore's move (a Pirali Brahmin, an untouchable to enter Puri Temple) as of Swami Vivekananda was to make India a Hindu *Rastra*. While criticizing the book 'Dhammapad' of Buddhism Tagore recorded, "The Europeans through constant struggle and changes targeted to establish the State. But, Indians have tried to establish *Dharma* the religion through changes and struggle in the society. Only in these efforts there is unity in the ancient and modern India".[25] The same Ravindranath is found to have embraced the Muslims and established the '*Raksabandhan*' festival only to deceive the unfortunate unprivileged lots of the country.

Political Maneuvering of the Untouchables and the Muslims:

This *Swadeshi* movement was obviously retaliated by the Muslims and the Untouchables not just for political reasons. The social and human considerations played their pivotal role. The Muslims had started their own political forum both on national as well as in the State level. A Muslim deputation to the Viceroy, Lord Minto to promote the cause of the Muslim's political, economic and social aspirations was organised. It was led by H H the Aga Khan, of Dacca, the spiritual head of the *Khoja* community. In pursuance of the Muslim deputation, which received glowing encouragement from the Viceroy, Nawab Salimulla Khan of Dacca founded the Muslim League in Dacca in 1906. For the first time the Muslims came with their independent political party to rightfully hold the instrumentalities of the state where their population actually was more than 50 per cent and their untouchable ally with the population not below 24 per cent of the total souls.

The official historians condemned the British for this act, which according to them was done for promoting the loyalty of the Muslims to the British Government and for safeguarding their political and other schemes. The Hindus perhaps considered that the loyalty towards the British that they had been very scrupulously rendering or showing with utmost sincerity and devotion from beginning of the British Raj was their divine monopoly right. And the Muslims were not fit to encroach upon the same or similar conduct. The Untouchables and Muslims were spiritually debarred of that chance of becoming loyal to the Government run by the British.

Both the communities stood firmly by the decision of Bengal partition. It was not a support to the British; it was to support their own cause. Consequently, the Hindus, the '*Swadeshis*' failed to paralyze British administration and give a dent in the balance-sheet of their trade. Having failed in the Muslim front they were compelled to turn their attention to the untouchable masses of Bengal, the beast of burden and the beast of prey of the Hindus. But the situation was so precarious and the necessity was so acute that they begged and bargained for untouchables' help which they considered highly unbecoming and below dignity. Even orthodox Brahmin like Shyama Prosad Mookerjee and Hindu leader Ambika Charan Mazumdar made it a routine to pay brotherly visits in the houses of the Namasudra leaders. They had started taking regular meals with the untouchables and organised successive meetings only to deceive them finally.

But the untouchables, the blood brothers of the Muslims of Bengal changed the situation. They felt quite at home and comfortable with their Muslim neighbours and professional partners having same and similar sets of problems. Now when the question of protecting their common interest emerged out of the decision of partition of Bengal, both the neglected groups instantly came closer in the battle field against the common enemy. The untouchables for the first time in the millennium started taking free breathing and dreaming for education and freedom of profession under the British Raj in the new province.

First Dalit-Muslim Unity on Political Platform

'In 1906, on behalf of the Dacca 'Namasudra Hitakarini Sabha', Nagarbasi Mazumdar and Raghunath Sarkar met Sir Bampfylde Fuller, the Lieutenant Governor of the new province of East Bengal and Assam. They apprised him of the socio-economic condition of the Namasudra community and demanded political rights for the Depressed classes as those were granted to the Muslims.'[26] Soon after this, Shasibhusan Thakur the son of Guruchand had a meeting with Salimulla Khan, Nawab of Dacca. They decided to oppose the '*Swadeshi*' Hindu-nationalists and support the British jointly. The

Namasudras of Bakharganj district passed a resolution by declaring their war against antagonistic and discriminatory treatment of the Hindus. "Simply owing to the dislike and hatred of the Brahmins, the Vaidyas and the Kayasthas that this vast Namasudra community has remained backward; this community has therefore, the least sympathy with them and with their religion, and will henceforth work hand in hand with the Muhammadan brethren." The resolution is significant to reveal the exact and focal points of discontent that the untouchables got extremely fed up (i) with Hinduism (religion), (ii) with the Brahmins and their two allies, i.e. Baidyas and Kayasth and (iii) they felt quite at home with the Muslims and considered them as 'brethren'.

From Orakandi, the Headquarter of the Matuas the politically conscious community-leaders did not miss the rare opportunity to put on record and dispatch the formal congratulatory message expressing their gratitude to the Secretary of State 'for declaring the partition of Bengal as a settled fact and admissible of no amendment' on 2nd October 1906. These supports to the decision taken by the colonial government and opposition to the '*Swadesi*' movement launched by elite Hindus of the country were thus the outcome of conscious and calculated political strategy in self-defense against the extreme animosity of the Hindus and Hinduism. It was a perfect strategy. These had tremendous significance and impact in the formation of future government in the Bengal province and in the country especially because, the establishment of the second political party by the Muslims in 1906, Indian National Congress lost monopoly in political arena. The Muslims and the Untouchable peasantry would have gone together in the ballot boxes for Muslim League and against the minority Hindu votes of National Congress.

Another resolution of the contemporary time ratifies the condition, "..... the Hon'ble Mr. Hare will bestow the same rights and privileges upon the Namasudras as have been done upon the Mohammedans, in as much as the Namasudras and the Mohammedans are the predominating communities in Bengal'.[27] This was the manifestation of a realistic reaction of the untouchables to the inhumane torture of the Hindus through spiritual caste-system and their ardent desire to get freedom from it. The '*Swadeshis*' the minority *Bhadraloks* launched their independence struggle simultaneously against the colonial rule of the British as well as against the immense majority countrymen whom they regarded 'divine-slaves' to serve them. Similarly, the untouchables and low caste people also raised their banner of revolts against the tyranny of the Hindus. Therefore, they sided with the British. This saga of Dalit-Muslim united battle of 'Liberty' was also pen-pictured by the Namasudra poet, Raicharan Biswas in the accurate terms. This was published in the journal of the untouchables named, 'Jagaran' in 1908. A few of the lines are quoted below:

"Laye Bhai Namasudra Hoye Aaguan.
Alahi Bharasa Kari Jaga Musalman.
Bhratittwer Mamatai Akatai Bhai
Anurage Chala Dohe Aage Chute Jai." (Jagaran, 1908)

After partition, the Bengalee elite raised nationwide protest against the decision on various pretexts from Congress platform. The real cause remained un-spelt and hidden in their paradoxical logic. Eventually the much-cherished dream of these neglected '*Mulniwasi-nation'* came true in the form of the Act in February 1907, which promised representation of communities proportionate to their numerical strength in the public jobs or bureaucracy. The untouchables and the Muslims tasted first blood of the practical benefits of the partition of Bengal after enjoying facility of getting more jobs and asserting more political rights and sharing in various other economic and cultural fields. This on the other hand came as a bolt from the blue for the Caste-Hindu elite of India. They could foresee that the impact of such an Act would spread like wildfire all over and in course of time, not far ahead.

This shattering blow terrorised the national leaders with its future impact and pan-Indian implication. They got ready to do anything for stopping the process. Division like Punjab and Hariyana, Bihar and Jharkhand in independent India never became a problem. The administrative division of Bengal into West Bengal and East Bengal-Assam had its distinguished element of danger in pre-independent India.

***Swadeshi* Terrorists: Up against the *Dalitbahujan*:** In such situation, the '*Swadeshi*' terrorists resorted to terrorism on the unaware untouchables of rural Bengal. The Indian National Congress turned into a national platform of terrorism. Barin Ghosh, younger brother of Rishi Aurovindo Ghosh and a front rank leader of Anushilon Samiti, led a team to Shilong to assassin Sir Bampfuled Fuller, the 1st Lieutenant Governor of Eastern Bengal and Assam. Fuller escaped and went safely London back. Terrorism, in India, is the child of the Brahmanical Hindu nationalism. Under the leadership of a Barrister P. Mitra, the terrorist outfit called "Anusilan Samiti" was born. The members of the Anusilan Samiti terrorised people with firearms and country made bombs. They raised suicidal squad and collected huge funds by dacoity. There emerged many other such underground outfits in Calcutta and Bombay. The British government had to create Andaman Cellular jail to tackle these terrorists. The members were initiated to the institute by taking oath, keeping an open sword and a Gita in their hands. The 'Bhagavad Gita', was regarded by Kashmiri Pandit, Bajaj very rightly as a gospel of terrorism. War and worship is the essence of *dharma*. One of the basic rule of the 'Anusilan Samiti' was :- "No one who is a non-Hindu or who has any spite against Hinduism was to be admitted" in the Samiti as a member. In pursuance of this rule, all untouchables who had no reason to be proud to be a Hindu and definitely had had some quantum of spite against the faith were debarred of membership. As a non-Hindu, particularly the Muslims were excluded from taking part in the national movement as a member of the 'Anusilan Samiti'. The rule of the Samiti held:

'Exclusion of Muhammadans'

So far as can be foreseen, it is our firm belief that within a year to two the entire Muhammadan nation will become submissive to the Hindus. But if the Hindus then abandon their firmness and national glory, and sink so low as to court friendship with the Muhammadans they will be puffed up and no good but only evil will be brought about. The nation, which cannot preserve its national glory, national greatness and dignity, and national firmness and pride and on the contrary exhibits levity, baseness and waywardness, can never be respected by other nations. But in no circumstances would it be proper to show hostile feelings towards, to deal unjustly with Musalman as a nation."[28]

Many educated Hindus became heroes by offering supreme sacrifice, by giving their lives in the gallows and taking other's lives with bomb and bullets. Not only the Hindu terrorists were anti-Muslims but they also were cunning enough to keep it secret so that a vast section of the Muslims, Untouchables and low-castes could be befooled with their false-sympathy and friendship-show. They perfectly pretended to be secular and believer of no caste. With their false-secular image and progressive propaganda, they easily exploited a large section of both Muslims and Untouchables to establish their supremacy over the immense majority working classes. '*Bharat Pathik'* Roybahadur Raja Rammoham Roy, expressed this anti-Muslim attitude in the 'Appeal to the King of Council in 1823'. "Divine providence at last, in its abundant mercy, stirred up the English nation to break the yoke of those tyrants (Muslims) and to receive the oppressed Natives of Bengal under its protection". This continues even after the country has been vivisected in three sovereign countries.[29] Prominent leaders like Chitta Ranjan Das (Congress), Narendranath Bhattachariya (M.N. Roy) the founder of the Communist Party of India and many other eminent national leaders of those days were the primary members of the '*Anusilan Samiti*'.

The Matua and Chandal peasants were at loggerheads with the *Hinduttwa*. They are found to have openly defied and challenged the infallibility of the Vedas and authority of the Brahmins. The *Swadeshi* terrorists are reported to have not even spared their women to undergo heinous kind of atrocities. "In the district of Dacca, the Anusilan Samiti of Pulin Das recruited low caste-*lathials* (clubmen) and thus tried to win the sympathy of such elements in rural society. But mostly the poor Namasudras in the districts were subjected to intimidation and coercion when found buying foreign goods during Puja holidays. A particular flagrant incidence of this variety occurred at Sholla, where in late October 1907, a party of young men visited the quarter inhabited by the Namasudras in a boat and conducted a series of door-to-door searches with a view to seeing that no foreign goods were used. In one instance they are reported to have stripped a woman of the cloth she was wearing on the ground that it was foreign."[30] Even under the leadership of Bipin Behari Ganguly two other *Swadeshi* terrorists went to East Bengal, Pabna to bombard the solidarity of a peasant revolt by the combine forces of Namasudras and the Musalmans against the local *zaminders*. From Calcutta, they set out with three bombs named, '*Kalimayer Bomb'* the Bomb of goddess Kali.[31]

During these days of serious turmoil, the combine force of Namasudra-Musalman resisted the attack of the *Swadeshis*, the volunteer '*Goondas*' of the Indian National Congress and Anusilan Samiti. For committing offence of purchasing cheap mill-cloths, salt, matchbox etc the pauper Namasudra villagers were attacked by the wealthy Hindu terrorists. The brave heart of human race called Chandals retaliated with tremendous fury against these acts of savagery of the coward Hindus. According to the news of the journal 'Namasudra Surhid' the resolution of the meeting of April 1909 at 'Machkhali' village of Faridpur reveals, "In 1909, the Namasudra and Muslim peasants of Narail sub-Division of Jessore made common cause to protest against the low opinion in which they were held by the higher caste Hindus. With this objective, they combined for some months and decided not to work as menial servants in the houses of the latter, or eat food cooked by them. In Magura subdivision also, the Namasudras refused to serve in the houses of the caste-Hindus or cultivate their land." "The Namasudras of Faridpur and Barisal have virtually declared a boycott against the Brahmin, Kayastha and Baidyas, noted one of them with alarm. There were possibilities of their being united with all other lower classes and if this happened, he feared, the happiness and honour of the higher castes would all be wasted away."[32]

The Hindu leaders also tried to lure the untouchables by extending their liberal hearts and helping hands to the Chandal villages however, with specific condition that the Namasudras of the village must join the *Swadeshi* i.e. anti Bengal-partition movement. Chandra Bilash and Kunja Bilash Mukherjee the *Zamindar* of the Dhalgram village assured the Namasudras to help them in repairing their school house which was in a dilapidated condition only after they took '*swadeshi*' vow. Even the students of the School were compelled to take the oath in this regard. During these days the peasant community belonging to the low caste Mahesya and Poundras of vast regions of Midnapore, Khejuri and adjacent areas of Calcutta in the South 24 Parganas like Kestopur, Mohisabathan, Garia, Sonarpur, Canning, Kakdwip, Gosaba, Jainagar, Baruipur, Diamond Harbour and Shirikol supported and actively participated the '*swadeshi*' movement.

The talented Poundra youth, Mohendra Nath Karan, the celebrity author of 'Paundra Kshatriya Kula Tilak' even composed the ballad-book, 'Banga Laxmir Brata Katha' in 1909 to inspire the *Swadesi* heroes. The creamy-layer

Hindus used the weapon of Hinduisation to create confusion, crack and even animosity in superior and inferior status amongst the untouchables one being *Kshatriya* and another *Suddra.* It destroyed the solidarity in the rank of the servile peasantry classes of Untouchables. The move to alienate was effectively palpable as the Rajbangsi leaders refused to use their traditional name, '*Koch*' or '*Rajbangsi*'. They claimed to have descended from the *Varna-Kshatriyas* who fled for life from Karnataka region of Hayhala at Jalpesh in North Bengal when Parasu Ram, the 5th incarnate of Vishnu annihilated the Kashatriyas for three-seven times to take revenge of the killing of his father by the *Kshatriya* king Kartvirjarjun. They established various Rajbangsi Kshatriya Associations. Harikishore Adhikari had written a book on ethnic history of the community, 'Rajbangshi Kulapradip' in 1907 and claimed that they were Rajbansi Kshatriya. In 1908, they established Kshatriya Students' Hostel. Pods or Poundras also started claiming superior Hindu caste status as Paundra Kshatriya. Prasanna Barman was elected as the Vice-President of Bengal branch of Bharatiya Kshatriya Mahasabha. Their representatives even participated in the All India conferences at Alwar in Rajasthan in 1924 and at Indore in 1927 as representative of the Kshatriyas. The untouchable Koches or Rajbansis were recognised as untouchable Kshatriyas in the census of 1921. A section of their educated and well off members started feeling more comfortable and dignified in the company of the Brahmanical Hindus as subservient untouchables. They worshipped the KABAB elite (Kayasth-Baidya-Brahmin) but did not like a respectful situation of easiness with own communities of peasantry in rural Bengal.

Isolate Muslims as a Community: The new political situation that emerged out of democratisation of Indian polity. The demographic situation in eastern India, especially after 1905 proved to be precariously fatal for the 18.2 per cent minority Hindus including backward and a high percent of Tribal or 'Buno' people. The entire rural population, composed of peasantry, artisan and labournig classes were preparing to use their ballot-power on socio-political consolidation. Monopoly of a single party democracy ended. The ruling class, the British, Brahmin, Baniya combine (B+B+B) with a view to minimizing the threat, launched a series of schemes to isolate the Muslims from the numerically big and lowest stratum of the society composed of untouchables and tribes. One method of isolation was to spread mutual hatred and hostility between these groups on religious line. The surer and deadly mode was legal. The first constitutional reform Act, the Councils Act of India of 1909 was promulgated to foster the Indian self-governance scheme. It gave 'separate electorate' for the Muslim for the first time and for the Sikh community in the second constitutional Act, the Government of India Act 1919. This political isolation of the minority communities made a virtual and unavoidable joint electorate for the untouchables with the Hindus. Whether they liked it or not the Untouchables and Tribes had no option but to cast votes to the Hindus only. They lost their freedom to exercise their franchise. This political separation and its practice in the ballot-box on regular interval gradually created uncrossable and wide rift and eventually animosity in socio-cultural plain of the proletariat class. The Hindus who cried foul during '*Bangobhango*' for rifts between Hindu-Muslim unity only a year back uttered no word against such exclusion policy called 'separate electorate'.

Untouchable-Muslim Riots Created: The Brahmins never plotted against the Muslim rulers since the defeat of Dahir in 712 to overthrow or to oust them of the territorial boundaries. On the contrary, history abounds with illustrations that they had been in league with the Muslims, Pathans or Mughals to suppress the countrymen. The Brahmins are even alleged to have invited the Muslims to invade India. During the currency of the *Swadeshi* movement and its after-math to shatter the Dalit-Muslim unity in Bengal, flood-gates of big and small communal riots were released by the Brahmanical forces. Many incidents were noted where during riots the houses of the caste-Hindus were marked by the Hindu-Muslim rioters in the previous night. During riots, carefully those houses were spared. Casualties came in the camp of the Namasudras and the poor peasantry of Muslims only. The spectacular rioting skirmish took place in the name of Hindu-Muslim riot in eastern Bengal. Actually, these were limited between the Untouchable-Chandals and the Muslim converts out of them.

As a result, there were no riot between the Caste-Hindus and the Muslims in those days and no casualty of Brahmins, Vaidyas or Kayasth occurred. A historian of repute explained the situation, "In the nineteenth and the early twentieth century an articulate community-consciousness had developed both among the Bengali Muslims and the Namasudras. Two large compact bodies of people, both sensitive about the honour of their communities, were thus living side by side. Each considered themselves to be superior to the other and slightest offence to any member was regarded as an affront to the entire community which required immediate redress. As a result a series of riots broke out between the two communities, the first of it being in 1889 at Gazirhat, in the District of Khulna."[33] In most of the cases the cause of the riots was some petty issue. In one of the riot, the Muslim rioters marked the houses of the caste-Hindu on previous night so that even by mistake no Hindu was attacked. They were operating against the Namasudras. Nor any caste-Hindu interfered in these so called Hindu-Muslim riots to protect the lives of the Namasudras. 'Social consolidation between the Muslims and Namasudras nearly broke down due to the outbreak of a series of riots between the two communities at different places of eastern Bengal. And the nationalists, by supporting the cause of the Namasudras, tried to earn their sympathy."[34] This is the old Brahmanical trick of trade union movement. Many lives of Namasudras were lost in the January, May and June riots in the Jessore and Khulna districts.

"This particular feature distinguished this riot of May 1911 from the ordinary Hindu-Muslim riots and gave it a character of a Namasudra-Muslim riot *per se*. The members of various other Hindu castes, living in the area, being concerned about the safety of their houses, consulted the local Muslims and were instructed by the latter to put up flags to distinguish their houses. They had no fear from the local Muslims who knew their houses….. None of these houses, except only one of Brahmin, was attacked by rioters and that too was by mistake."[35] When the riot took place in Gopalpur the British Government wanted to impose '*Pituni* tax' by declaring the Namasudras as 'rioters'. Guruchand advised his people be educated and fight. Your action will not be condemned as rioting.[36] But when there broke out the 'Padmabila' (Faridpur) big riot, Guruchand Thakur himself led the Ṇamasudra army in the field with arms in his hands. The superior skill of Brave-heart Namasudra women-folk, with weapons in hand, too participated in these riots.

"*Bhai Nai Virgan! Karo Gie Ran,*
Nije Juddhe Asiben Sri Gurucharan."

'O the Brave-hearts go and fight in the battlefield, Guruchand himself will join the advance."[37]

First Untouchable to Addresses Annual Congress Session: In the situation, the Hindus left no stone unturned to create division amongst the Untouchables. The ill-informed and credulous untouchables of illiterate background strengthened the furious fists of the Brahmins without knowing that the same were raised actually to their detriment only and to knock them out. Even Nayeb Ananda Chandra Sadhak, the head of the famous Chandsi Namasudra family joined Congress. And in 1906, he got the rare opportunity to be one who amongst the untouchables of India addressed the annual session of Congress. The Indian national Congress invited the Chandsi Doctor Padmalochan Das to deliver his speech in the Congress session. All proceedings of the Congress during those days used to be carried out in English language only. But necessity knew no rule. To facilitate the Namasudra delegate who did not know English language special arrangement was made. Chandsi doctors unanimously selected '*Naieb Mosai*' as their representative. He spoke in Bengali vernacular from the Annual Session of Congress platform.

The political sagacity of Guruchand, however, did not fail to identify enemy. He very successfully thwarted all propaganda of the Hindu leaders that were trying to confuse the Namasudra/ Chandal community. He with his able guidance led his people in right direction to support the decision of the British government for partition of Bengal. Guruchand Thakur, on the contrary proved to be a strong catalyst in favour of the formation of an Untouchable-Muslim United Forum against *Swadeshi* and the Hindu nationalists. The untouchables who supported Congress Party were completely ignored and sidelined by the society. The educated and wealthy members of the Chandsi-Das family of Barishal, were the original founders of the 'Chandsi School of Medical Science'. This discipline has been the monopoly of the Namasudras. Still such a family of high reputation and esteem suffered great humiliation from the entire society as they supported Congress.

Guruchand took very strong attitude towards those who in some or other manner credulously inclined to the cause of the '*Swadwshis*' and expressed his disgust, "*Ki Bolibo Dukkher Katha, Buk Phete Jai; Satru Ki Bandhab Era Chene Nako Hai*". How do I express my pains, my people cannot recognize 'Friend' and 'Foe'. Burdened with the unprecedented responsibility of a leader, Guruchand took his stand at the centre of the battlefield surrounded with the ocean of Brahmin enemies. Identifying enemies is the first responsibility of the commander. He convinced his people, 'Do you understand why these people are moving amongst and around us with the slogan of patriotism? Why the people today pay visit to our doors, who in their good days simply hated us? These varieties of people are skilled enough to protect self-interests and they approach you for their interest only.' 'The zamindars exploit and torture us. Has any one of these ever protested against it? Touch me not, touch me not! shout the Brahmins and Kayasths. Has anyone ever broadened his heart?' 'All the people of oppressed castes in Bengal remained in abject poverty and distress. They do not have any share in the politics and in economics. Entire privileges have been monopolised by the caste-Hindus. They never had considered us as brethren as we were backward. They kept us like the slaves and hence they cannot even trust us'. His message travelled all over Bengal and put off the light in the lamps of the Swadeshis.

Finding all attempts unsuccessful, the *Rashtra Guru* finally had come down to appeal to the Chandal *Raja* Guruchand to participate in the *Swadeshi* movement. Resultantly Guruchand had to assume the role of the Achariya, the Principal to teach the philosophy of patriotism, "Desh Nahe Mati Sudhu, Desh Deshbasi." 'Country is not just a geographic land-mass; people of a land are the country indeed.' Simultaneously he supported and upheld the decision of the British government as beneficial for the country's prosperity and advancement. Thus the death-knell of the 'first-foreign intruders' and colonizers, the Aryan-Brahmins of India began to ring. The autochthons, he declared, were not even ready to trust the heartless-Brahmins any more. 'When in trouble they show sympathy and affection. And with disperse of clouds of trouble they forget all. The educated lots are expert in the art of flattery. The truth I speak may sound caustic.' In the circumstances, he explained the position of *Dalitbahujan samaj* vis-à-vis the caste-Hindus. Therefore, he gave a clarion call for the final showdown, "Swajati Sajite Hole Tarai Sajuk; Panchajanya Sankha Yadi Baje To Bajuk." 'If one needs to be a fake Patriot, let them take the disguise. If there comes a civil war let it come.'

Guruchand made his stand clear:

"Desh Seba 'Deshmata' Tara Jaha Bujhe
Sei Arthe Nahi Bujhe Dalit Samaj.....
Bhai Pai Kono Kaje Yogdan Dite."

'Dalit-society understands the meaning of 'patriotism' and connotation of 'Motherland' in a different way the elite understand. In the deep of the hearts of the Dalits reign the terror for the caste-Hindus. They never trust the Caste-Hindus to join hands with them to go ahead with any joint-scheme. So in the political matter they have different front.' The elite consider that the service to the ten percent is the service for the country, '*Daser Seba Daser Seba'*. The dalits consider the entire population in villages and cities.

Chitta Ranjan Das of Indian National Congress had invited Guruchand to join the *Swadeshi* 'Boycott' movement along with his community. In reply to the letter Guruchand explained his stand, "It is the Caste-Hindus who only use these expensive foreign (imported) goods. Therefore, such boycott movement must remain within that circle exclusively. Having no political right so long, the Namasudra nation maintains its entity in their motherland in helplessly suppressed and oppressed conditions. It would be proper to bring a reign of brotherhood and state of goodwill in the hearts of the caste-Hindus for the lower orders at the first instance. Otherwise the downtrodden people of Bengal will never agree to launch any *Swadeshi* movement jointly with the caste-Hindus." As they were neither associated nor involved with the governance of the country, the question of disassociating or non-cooperating with the government does not arise. In the circumstances, he welcomed the impartial and humane administration of the imperialist British Government instead of letting the tyrant-countrymen to enslave the helpless natives of Bengal.

'We all are wretchedly poor, there is nothing to eat in hut, everything has been mortgaged against debt. It is no matter for us whether our country stands united or divided. Let the benevolent King decide our fate.' The fighting spirit of the Chandal race still was intact; they were yet to be Hinduised officially by a new name, Namasudra. They therefore, won the battle. The '*Swadeshi*' boycott movement therefore, got stuck in the muddy paths in the rural Bengal.

In their battle for liberty, in their battle for "ethnic freedom"[38] the indomitable race generated their own mouth piece, their own journals to preach their philosophy of 'freedom-battle' to express their democratic aspirations. For this purpose they also raised units of 'People's Drama' '*Kabigan*' i.e. 'people's song'. In a large meeting in Jessore in 1908, it was resolved that each village will be the basic unit and 15 village units will compose one 'Union Committee'. This 'Union Committee' will function under the 'District Committee'. They will compulsorily hold annual conference to review the entire situation, political, social and economic. Fund will be raised from each household by collecting '*Musti Chaul*' a unit of rice in the fist on daily basis. This mandatory donation was collected by the volunteers. A member of the village committee will pay 1 'Ana', Union Committee member will pay 2 '*anas*' of contribution. Apart from this, a levy was collected @ 3 per cent of the total expenditure of each marriage or '*Sradh*' ceremony.

In this battle of liberty, the Hindus were discarded as enemy but the Muslims were accepted as friends, brethren and co-fighter. An accurate assessment of the political situation helped Guruchand to decide to work hand in hand with the Mohammedan brethren henceforth. The situation has been reflected in the long poem composed by a Namasudra poet Raicharan Biswas. The poem was on high demand in the large meetings of the period for recitation:

"'Namasudra Musalman anye kare Tulya Gyan,
Jal Mare Gharegele Dujane Saman.
Jagate Badshahi Jati Dhanya Musalman.
Laye Bhai Namasudra Hoye Aaguan.
Alahi Bharasa Kari Jaga Musalman.
Bhrittwer Mamatai Akatai Bhai
Anurage Chala Dohe Aage Chute Jai." (Jagaran, 1908)

'My dear Namasudra brothers! just think once, we quarrel uselessly with them who are our friend in need and a brother in distress. They mix with you frankly. The Hindus treat Namasudras and Musalmans alike. The Hindus' water gets spoiled/ polluted by the touch of both, the Muslims and the Namasudras. The Muslims are ruling nations in the World. O the Namasudra brothers let us march ahead taking them along. O the Muslim brothers! Wake up in the name of Allah. Fired with the sense of fellow-feeling of a brother with love let us proceed ahead......'

To tackle the situation, the rulling class shifted the capital of India complete quietly from Calcutta on the bank of River Hoogly to New Delhi on the bank of River Yamuna. In 1912, the Union Jack was lowered in the City of Howrah Bridge and was re-raised in the city of Lutyens, by the side of Qutab Minar, in New Delhi. The then Bengal of Alivardi Khan or the British East India Company was vivisected in four provinces, Bihar, Orissa, Bengal and Assam in the name of 'anti-*Bangabhanga*'. With a view to appeasing the agitated Muslims, Nawab of Dacca, Salimmulla was given a lollipop of assurances for establishing a new University in Dacca. However, due to opposition of Shyamaprasad Mookerjee and Calcutta based ruling classes it never came within the next decade. Only after the threat from

A. K. Fazlulhaq of a bloody-civil-war, the University started in Dacca at the site of Salimulla's palace. The untouchables were compensated with a gesture of honour only. Guruchand was given a *Durbar* medal. The beggars were not the choosers. In the name of 'anti-partition' Bengal suffered the effect of multi partition.

The audacious untouchables of Bengal were brought back under the control of Calcutta-elites. This began the fall of Bengal in every respect. During *Swadeshi* movement, Gopal Krishna Gokhle proudly declared, "What Bengal thinks today, rest of India thinks tomorrow." The situation started a complete reversal from 1911. Bengal has by now reduced to a useless tail of Indian economy, politics and culture.

Untouchables a Distinct Political Group – Change of Guard in 1911: Since its inception, in 1871-72, the decennial census enumerated the population by Religious Heads like Hindus, Muslims, Sikhs, Christians and Anglo-Indians. Various Untouchable groups and Tribes were counted in the column 'Hindus'. Thus, the Hindu population and their proportion vis-à-vis other minority groups or creeds got inflated. The Census of India 1911, for the first time, enumerated the Untouchables and Animists/Tribes of India as separate groups under Religious Heads. No more, were they shown as Hindus. From 1911 onwards, the untouchables were called officially as Depressed Classes as they belonged to no caste of the Hinduism. Thus, this was their maiden appearance as an independent political 'Third Front' beside Hindus and Muslims. They started demanding political share as per the proportion of their population.

The Hindus too did not remain far behind to counter the move made by the Muslims and the Untouchables. In the Census Report of 1911 itself, efforts were made to re-Hinduize these untouchable masses by casteizing them simply by changing or adding their community names with caste identity. This was a sure method for controlling damage caused due to the Muslim demands. However, the untouchables continued to be in separate group under population by religion. They continued to be termed as 'Depressed Classes'. The entity of the tribes remained unaltered in 1911. As the tribes posed no threat in the democratic front yet, the Hindus left them live peacefully. They were enumerated by the Census Commissioner as non-Hinduised tribes while the untouchables as the semi-Hinduised tribes. Before 1911, neither the Untouchables nor the Tribes had any different entity.

Besides, consequent to the shifting of the Indian capital to New Delhi, Calcutta and the Eastern India lost its all glow and future prospects of growth and importance in economic and political activities. It became the gateway to Gurgaon, Faridabad, Gaziabad, NOIDA to come up in future. The pendulum of Indian politics very quickly started shifting its swing to Western India. The limelight of Assembly House of Job Charnak's Calcutta was put off; the glow of the Calcutta port got dimmed; the throbbing activities of the

Howrah Railway station were dampened, silenced, traditional glory in corridors of the University of Calcutta gloomed and the importance of the cantilever bridge of Howrah got clouded. The city of Lutyen under the tower of Qutab got luminated with the sun-shine of new-hopes. George the Vth and Queen Mary landed in India in 1912 at the 'Gate Way of India' on the seashore of Bombay and not on the Calcutta Port beside the Fort William, which had been the 'Gate way of British Empire in India' since 1757. Rabindra Nath Tagore, the crown of Indian intellects in a giggling mood composed praising songs to welcome the Royal couple, '*Jana Gana Mana Adhi Nayaka Jaya He Jaya He*...'. Never after this, Bengal got a chance to contribute country's national anthems.

The year 1911, the Hallmark of modern Indian History paved the way for the London-return Indian leaders like Gandhi, Jinnah and Ambedkar to play their assisting role for the British to decide the future shape of India. The epicenter of Untouchable movement slowly shifted from the East to West; from grass-root movement to the sponsored elite-movement. From Bombay Presidency emerged the new leaders. The banner of the Indian National Congress and of the Hindus passed into the hands of Mohandas Karamchand Gandhi and Patel. The '*Bhagua*' flag of the Hindu Mahasabha of Shyama Prasad Mookerjee passed to Golwalkar to play its scrupulous role as RSS, Shiv Sena, Bajrang Dal. Muhammad Ali Jinnah son of Punja Gandh and son-in-law of a Parsi tycon represented Bombay presidency where Muslims formed less than 9 per cent of its population. Dr Ambedkar was sponsored from Bombay Presidency, where untouchable population was less than 8 per cent, as the only official leader of the untouchable-India. Even the communist leadership was abdicated in favour of S.A. Dange from the same Bombay province where the Hindu population was more than 80 per cent of the total souls. Bengal-leaders who pioneered all these movements went into oblivion. Some became forgotten past while the history of Untouchables' glorious movement became a forbidden subject. No historian, not even Dr Ambedkar recognised it in his big volumes. The proverb that 'What Bengal thinks today India would think tomorrow' became a phrase maintained in the folklore. Position of Subash Bose and Mukunda Behari Mullick, MN Roy and Surawardi etc became subordinate and assisting partner to the Bombay based London Returned National Leaders.

The Hindus quite happily accepted division of Bihar, Assam and Orissa from Bengal Province under the cover of the funny slogan of nationalism. Bengali scholars like Annada Shankar Roy, ICS as father of modern Oriya language helped build separate linguistic identity of the new born province. Similarly distinct twists were brought in language and culture of Assam and Bihar. This division separated the offing consolidation of billions of the Chandals-Chamars-Doms-Dusads and their proselyte Muslims in Bengal, Bihar and Orissa. Nevertheless, they did not accept the Muslim majority portion of Bengal to be separated as an independent administrative part. The policy of exclusion and inclusion was executed by the Hindu Nationalists very calculated and scrupulously to reach to their destination, establishing Hindu Raj. The great national Hindu leaders, official historians and sociologists of contemporary period and of later era overlooked all contradictions. Virtually everything but administrative separation of Eastern Bengal-Assam or the liberty of the Dalit-Muslims was acceptable to the Brahmanical forces of Bengal. And interestingly enough, West Bengal, Eastern Bengal and Assam was reunited in 1911 simply to be vivisected permanently into two sovereign countries namely India and East Pakistan/later as Bangladesh in 1947 by the same group of people who fought to unite it. The same target or motive played its obvious role in both the occasion in 1911 and in 1947. The Sudra, Tribe and untouchable masses, the 'Proletariat" must remain subservient. The proletariat must not get a chance to establish their rule.

Home Rule of British-Hindu Agents: Opposed by Untouchables

With the advance of the Bolshevik movement and the principles of state-socialism in Russia and on the eve of the fall of tyranny of Czar, the World order started thinking in a cautious manner. There came on the stage, at this juncture, the former 'Fabian Socialist' Madam Annie Besant to play her 2nd innings as the President of Indian National Congress. Outside Bengal and Eastern India, in Madras, Karnataka and Bombay province under banner of the 'Non-Brahman Political Party', 'Justice Party' also strong anti-Brahmin socio-political movement built up during these days. They captured power in the state. They even passed laws in favour of backward Sudras and the Untouchables. They revolted against the anti-democratic dominance of the Brahmins who captured all economic executive and political power. "Only 3.2 per cent of the population, Brahmins in the Madras Presidency held 55 per cent of deputy collectors and 72.6 per cent of district Munsiffs in 1912. Brahmins at times were also big landowners.... In the princely state of Mysore, a mainly urban Brahman community (3.8 per cent of the total population) held 65 per cent of gazetted posts in 1918."[39] However, the official historians with their jaundiced eyes assessed it, "CN Mudaliar, TN Nair and Tyagaraja Chetti on behalf of intermediate castes therefore felt jealous of Brahmin predominance in education, the services and politics."[40] Ms Besant, the lady from Ireland appeared at this crisis point to tackle the volatile situation created by different hostile groups of native Indians. In the month of October 1915, they declared 'Home Rule', the rule by the people of home. Tilak followed suit, launched Home Rule League in April 1916. The hidden agenda of Hinduizing Indian politics and nation-formation into a '*Hindu Rastra*' was thus carefully placed in the official-cover of an Irish-British sugar coated-envelop. In 1916, *Rashtar Guru* Surendra Narh Banerjee too established 'Home Rule League'. The entire educated, fabulously rich and former *Zamindars* of Calcutta and surrounding area in a body stood by the 'Home Rule League'. The sky of Bengal reverberated with the demands of the 'KABAB's (Kayasth-Brahmin-Baidya) for 'Home Rule'. The entire nation could apprehend, by seeing the faces of the agitators and the persons or sources behind as sponsors with funds and their remote-controlled politics that the agitation was nothing but an attempt to establish a Hindu Rastra in India. 'Muslim Hitaisi' a journal run by the Muslims wrote, "Time is not far when the 'Home Rule' will turn to be the "Hindu Rule". The Namasudra and many other untouchable leaders too got horrified with the prospect of the return of the 'Hindu Rule' under the cover of 'Home Rule' to thwart all their prospect of advancement in every respect. Guruchand-group naturally maintained safe distance with the 'Home Rule' movement. Prof. Sekhar Bandhopadhaya has very scrupulously narrated the situation, "The Namasudra response was also in the same tune. As the nationalists demanded self-Government, the educated members of this caste apprehended that if more privilege was transferred, it would only be monopolised by the more privileged upper castes." The Muslims, Untouchable and Sudra Backward leaders knew Tilak, Besant and Surendranath Banerjee gang very well. A stranded wife of a clergyman, a former member of Fabian Socialist group Mrs. Besant came to India in November 1893. She founded the Central Hindu College at Benaras in 1898. Annie Besant was a votary of Caste system and declared that in her previous birth, she was a Hindu and her name was *Anna Bai*. She took her birth in Europe only to know their weaknesses from within. She was to fight against the superiority of the Europeans and hence had come to India. She believed that in the water of the Ganges there was spiritual and magnetic power to cure many diseases. She almost forcefully had entered in the governing body of the 'Theosophical Society' at Adyar after the death of its founder, Madam Blavetsky and after assuming its highest post hijacked and transformed the institution into a camp of Hinduism. Mrs. Besant as an stounch and orthodox hindu entered in Indian politics directly in 1913. She was logically a terrible castist and hated the untouchable and Shudras.[41]

Untouchable Chandals Initiate Journalism: During the *Swadeshi* movement the nationalists inspired their comrades and supporters by publishing provoking articles and news in various English and vernacular papers. Guruchand realised the necessity of an organ for the peasantry of Bengal to carry on their struggle for regaining their lost political rights and emancipation. He became the first untouchable in India to enter into the arena of journalism with the launching of the monthly journal, "*Namasudra Shurid*" the friend of the Namasudras as a mouthpiece for expressing their political and executive demands. Its first editor was Aditya Chowdhury from Orakandi and the proprietor was Guruchand. It kicked the ball of literary activity by the untouchables in Bengal. "From the October 1907 issue of their Journal, '*Namasudra Shurid*' we learn that the delegation had met the

Lieutenant Governor Sir Lance Lot Hare, and expressed their hopes that the British Government in India might remain forever." The Poundra Kshatriya *Kula Tilak* Raicharan Sardar started editing a monthly journal in 1908 from Diamond Harbour with the title, "*Bratya Kshatriya Bandhav*". Mohendra Nath Karan was a regular contributor in the journal. In 1908, another journal started from Dacca by name, 'Namasudra Patrika'. Mukunda Behari Mullick started editing a Journal called '*Pataka*' from Kolkata. The opponent groups of Guruchand also started many rival journals, which were helped by the Caste-Hindus. Nevertheless, the '*Namasudra Shurid'* continued with flying colours. "In 1908 the circulation of Namasudra Patrika was 500, while that of '*Shurid*' was 550, in 1910 the year the nationalists take over, the circulation of Namasudra went down to 300 while that of '*Shurid*' to 450; but in 1911, the year of census while circulation of Namasudra remained at 300 that of '*Shurid*' shot up to 700."[42]

Volte-face of the Brahmanical Forces to Deceive Lord Montague: In 1917, Ms Annie Besant became the President of Indian National Congress for the 2nd term. The Indian National Congress which repeatedly and very resolutely declined earlier to indulge in any social reform scheme tangibly shifted its stand and in December 1917 at Calcutta, under the Presidentship of an Irish-Hindu lady of dubious mind-set had passed in its Annual Session the following resolutions:

"The Congress urges upon the people of India the necessity, justice and righteousness of removing all disabilities imposed by custom upon the Depressed Classes, the disabilities being of a most vexatious and oppressive character, subjecting those classes to considerable hardship and inconvenience."

The resolution was moved by G.A. Natesan from Madras. In his seconding speech Bhulabhai Desai from Bombay said, 'This disabilities under which some of our brethren suffer are a great blow to equality and brotherhood..... With what face will we approach the British democracy or any other power if we are unable to uplift our own brethren? They will say, 'what lies in your own power, the obliteration of the social degradation of a section of your own people..... And if you fail to do that, what justice, with what face, will you demand Self-Government?" All Congress members rose to support the resolution. Mr. Rama Iyer interestingly exceeded the limit even, and said:- "This..... Remember that a man, a social slave cannot be a politically free man. We all have come to see the vision of United India, not only politically united but united all along the line.... Therefore, let those of us, who are Brahmins, who belong to the higher castes, go to our villages and shutter the shackles of the low castes, people who are struggling against our own men the social bureaucrats of our own land."

There was rather a tough competition in proving eloquence and broad-heartedness on this sensitive issue. Without waiting for the generations gap what Besant wrote only in 1909, an untouchable and illiterate Chandal Bhagai Haldar, was exhibited on the Congress Platform in 1917 Session. Since Haldar did not know English, he was allowed to break the tradition to speak in Bengali. "But the symbolic gesture that was followed was perhaps more interesting, as Bhagai Halder, a Namasudra Congressite from Bakharganj, amidst great applause, as a representative of depressed classes attending the session and was allowed the privilege of formally supporting the resolution on self-government (Resolution No XII) along with the Congress stalwarts Bipin Pal, Tilak, CR. Das, Sarojini Naidu and Madan Mohan Malavya. Surendra Nath Banerjee himself moved the resolution and Jinnah seconded it. But the strategy ultimately did not bear fruit, as the depressed classes were no longer to be impressed by mere symbolic and gimmick-action and Haldar came to be caricature as a puppet in the hands of the self-seeking upper-caste politicians."[43] The 'Creamy-layer-elite Hindus did not stop here, launched several schemes from various platforms with the same object.

Bengal-Untouchables Faced Lord Montague: There were thus clouds and thundering roar in the political-sky of western India in the Untouchable sector but as usual, without a drop of rain in the social plains. These were conducted just to face the challenges of political aspirations of the Untouchables in the Eastern India, which was to be aggravated by Lord Montague, the then Secretary of State for India who made on August 20, 1917, the historic declaration in regard to the Indian constitutional restructuring in the House of Commons of Great Britain. He declared the "Policy of gradual development of self-governing institutions with a view to progressive realisation of responsible Government in India as an integral part of the British Empire."

The British power which had permitted the untouchable to enter the Durbar Hall of the Emperor for the first time in the annals of history of India in 1912 and opened up the doors of all round progress in life, deserved full support in the War from the untouchables. Guruchand with all humble gratitude firmly stood with the British. He helped in recruiting several thousand excellent soldiers for the British army, who heroically gave up their lives in the battlefields in the World War. "*Bivhinna Bibhage Tara Karilo Chakuri, Keha Keha Yudhhakshetre Prane Galo Mari.*" The blood-bath of the heroes did not go waste. For the first time the 'Bahujan Samaj' secured franchise right after the passing of the Constitutional Government of India Act 1919 : "Deser Ainsabha Bistrita Hailo

Bangadese 'Bahujan' Votadhikar Pelo." (GC, 284)

Immediately after his declaration, Mr. Montague came to India to review the effectiveness of the Government of India Act 1909 and to suggest further extension of constitutional involvement of the Indians. The English people at the same time condemned Indian ruling classes for their inhumane treatment towards a very big section of their own country, the Sudras-Untouchables and the Tribes in particular. To face this challenge the Manuwadi-nationalists took their positions. The Untouchables too tried their level best to be equal to the situation.

It was veterans of Bengal and some newly formed untouchable's organisations who virtually raised their voice to express their political crisis and necessities of the constitutional representations before Montague. "Among those institutions which represented the Untouchables was the Pancham Kalvi Abhibharti Sangh, a Madrass Presidency Untouchables Association. It deprecated any political change and appealed to Government to save them from the yoke of the Brahmins whose struggle for greater share in the administration of the Government they likened to the struggle of a cobra that seeks guardianship of a young frog. The Madras Adi-Dravida Jana Sangha, representing 60,00,000 aborigines made a vigorous protest against the caste Hindus who hated them as lepers and denied them any chance of betterment in their life."[44]

The anti-democratic caste-Hindus by force prevented different low caste communities from submitting their oral and written statements in connection with their viewpoints on the constitutional changes to be brought in the Government of India Act 1919. In 1917, Mukunda Behari Mullick MA, LLB, and a Barrister in the Calcutta High Court, being directed by Guruchand had drafted and sent the appeal to the Committee, narrating the socio-economic and educational status of the Namasudras and other Untouchable communities along with their political aspirations and necessity of constitutional provisions. "A strong representation was made before the Secretary of State for India, Mr. Montague on behalf of the Namasudras of Bengal. The main credit for this goes to Mr. Mukunda Behari Mullick who took a leading part in the matter including drafting of the representation itself."[45] The supplementary statement of the All Bengal Namasudra Association submitted to the Simon Commission in 1929 reveals the history of past struggle of the Namasudras in the process of constitutional making by referring to the incident of 1917. "We may be permitted to record our agreement in accepting generally the pronouncement made by the late Secretary of State for India in Council, on the 20th August, 1917, in connection with the Indian constitutional changes. The same was followed by a personal tour of his, along with H.E. Viceroy, with an object of seeing and studying for themselves the various aspects of the said constitutional questions, by receiving the views of different bodies of people in India. We do not desire to indicate in details how, through the intervention and ill-advice of several castes-ridden Indians, the millions of Indians were prevented from not only having had any opportunity to submit their points of view with regard to the said matter before the said enquiring Commission, but that they were also prevented from submitting, even in writing, their views about such a momentous issue effecting their interests in a very considerable degree."[46]

The attitude of the protagonists of the Home Rule in India was dangerously hostile. The Untouchable leaders of Bengal too proved equal to the situation. "On 3rd November 1917, in a meeting held at the 'Dalhousie Institute' 300 strong delegates representing teeming millions of Sudra, Untouchables and Muslims the undaunted leaders took 16 resolutions. By these, they reiterated their affirmation behind the British Raj in no uncertain terms. Side by side, they condemned the treacherous and false activities conducted by the caste-Hindus. The protest agitation was so intense and solidly organised that the Caste-Hindus virulently attacked in the nationalist paper, 'Bengalee', "Those Namasudras who are opposing Home Rule are either idiots or victims of the enemies of the country."[47] Who were the enemies and of whom? Who were the autochthons and who were 'the first foreign intruders' of the country?

The list in the charter of demands submitted to Mr. Montague by M.B. Mullick though was exhaustive, little they gained. Out of the Montague-Chelmsford report there was enacted the Government of India Act 1919 which extended the "Communal Electorates" first set up in the case of Muslims in 1909 to other groups like Sikhs, Europeans, Anglo-Indians and Indian Christians. The demand of the untouchables for separate electorate was declined. Adult franchise and nominated membership were given to them. In this context, the historian Sekhar Bandhyopadhay has recorded: "The Government of India Act of 1919 formally recognised their 'special needs' by providing for inclusion of a 'depressed class' representative among the nominated non-official members of the Bengal Legislative Council. The Government of Bengal agreed that one such member would be adequate, as it was difficult to find more suitable non-official candidate from amongst these people. Of all these groups, it was agreed that only the Namasudras had come to the forefront and submitted representation."[48] This maiden award after the elapsing of millennium was welcomed by the untouchables of India with their heads bowed with gratitude before the British authority.

In pursuance of the provisions of the Government of India Act 1919, Advocate Babu Bhisma Dev Das a *Matua* and a disciple of Guruchand was nominated as the Member of the Bengal Legislative Council in February 1921. He brought the proposal in the Council to constitute a High Level Committee to examine the aspects of the 'Bengal Tenancy Act', which required changes. He had also proposed amendments in the 'Bengal Local Self Government Act 1915', 'Bengal Village Self Government Act 1919'. He also urged to set up Committees to examine the necessities for rural Bengal. In the Act, there was a provision for five more elected members from amongst the untouchables.

Maiden Attempt for Political Party of Untouchables: By the time Hindus and Muslims of divergent interests and problems founded many political parties, which were a precondition in the democratic structure of polity,

Political will and aspiration of a nation manifests in the democratic parliament through a political party only. Depressed Classes, led predominantly by the Namasudra community, though came in existence as separate entity since 1911 (as a result of Census) but failed to establish their independent and own political party. During the early 1920's though there was no political movement by the untouchables in the Bombay Province, but there was very strong 'Backward-movement'. Their political party called 'Non-Brahmin Political Party' not only was active but also it held the reign of power in Madras and Bombay province.[49] The '*Bahujan* Concept', i.e. the rule of the majority prevailed amongst the Depressed Classes in politically matured Bengal. Guruchand gave great stress on the issue of unity amongst the oppressed and common victims of the Brahmin social order for gaining political reign. He declared 'Though I was born amongst the Namasudras but I belong not to the Namasudras alone. Teli, Mali, Kumbhakar, Kapali, Mahisya, Chamar and Kamar all come to me. There come the Pods, Tanti, Malakar and Musalman in big number. I belong to all, all of the '*Dalit*' community; all the '*Dalit*' and oppressed in the working classes and the suffering masses. They are my own people:-

"Namasudra Teli Mali Aar Kumbhakar
Kapali Mahisyadas Chamar Kamar....
Katai Musalman Thik Nahi Tar......
Dalita Pitijati jata aache sab.... Aisab....Aapanar Jan." (GCC, p. 144)

Next year, in 1918 the leaders of different untouchable communities and low castes assembled in a meeting at the same venue, 'Dalhousie Institute' to discuss the issue of formation of a political party of the '*Bahujan Samaj'*. The leaders from the Namasudra, Poundra, Rajbansi, Kapali and other oppressed communities in the meeting ratified the Reform Scheme while expressing doubt in the dubious activities of the Hindu leaders. "The diarchy of a handful of limited castes is to be ended and arrangement must be made to form a Government with the representatives from each of the 190 caste groups on prorate basis of their population." 'so that the oligarchy of a handful of limited castes' was prevented. Mukunda Behari Mullick resolved in the meeting, "The permanent installation of an oligarchy…. Which means a death blow to the responsible Government itself." Without hearting the Reform Scheme tabled by the British, efforts were made by the untouchable leader to protect their interests. The sunshine of political wisdom is found to have been reflected in the report, which was submitted to the Governor by Mukunda Behari Mullick on behalf of the Namasudra Association in December 1918. It reads, "The conference was thoroughly representative…since the publication of the report of the conference no dissentient note had been raised by any Namasudra or by the member of any other backward castes'….'If the present Reform Scheme was implemented at the bidding of a vociferous and small band of organised castes pretending to represent interest of the masses' it would 'weaken the impartial hand of the British administrators."[50]

In 1920, once again the untouchable Namasudras placed their demand for "Separate Representation" as the same was sanctioned for the Muslim community since 1909. They demanded one third of the total Non-Muslim-Seats of the Bengal Legislative Assembly to be reserved for the Untouchables as per their proportion in population.

The First Batch of Untouchables in the Legislature: In pursuance of the provisions of the Government of India Act 1919, general election was held in 1921. The vast population of the Namasudra community calculated to win at least four five seats for themselves and similar number of seats for other untouchable communities like Rajbangsi and Pods in the election. However, due to various reasons like hostile Hindu bureaucracy and lack of experiences only Nirod Behari Mullick, Younger brother of Mukunda Behari won the election from Barisal constituency. Guruchand had taken active part in this election. He himself toured different places for election campaign in favour of Nirod Behari. For the first time the untouchables of India were baptised in the fierce battle of ballots. 'The Lord Guruchand asked the people of the constituency to vote for Nirod Babu enmasse':

"Tathakar Bhaktagane Prabhu Daki Bale,
Nirod Babuke Vote dieo Ak Dale" (G.C. p. 285)

"But the Guru could hardly do anything for other constituencies where most of the Namasudras possibly did not have the voting right."[51] In 1921, despite such an anti-democratic situation, two Namasudras, Advocate Bhismadev Das (nominated) and Nirod Behari Mullick, (elected) along with four more elected untouchable members had demolished the 'Divine-walls' of theocratic rule of the Brahmins and entered in the Bengal Legislature. History was created. Other four members were Thakur Panchanan (Sarkar) Barman and Prasanna Chandra Raikat (both Rajbangsis), Hemchandra Naskar (Poundra) of Calcutta and Rasik Chandra Charmakar from Noakhali constituency. All but Charmakar of this team were highly educated and independent candidates.

Quenchless was the ambition of the Untouchables of Bengal. Never satiated Namasudras are found to have vigilantly struggled for more power, authorities and privileges in the democratic set up in accordance with the strength of their population. Before the Simon Commission in 1929, they placed on record, "We venture to state that the British Government, on whom we look not only as our protector, but also as the God-sent deliverers of our misery, thought it insignificant, while enacting the Government of India Act 1919, to take into consideration the claims and miseries of the Depressed Classes, and made no provision for the safeguard of these unfortunate people. How indecorous it is that in the Act only one representative was suggested of so many people, numbering about one third of the total population of the province, and that also is by nomination, while other classes who have been occupying all the seats of the Council by election, with as many as five more seats by nomination.

While employers have got the right of sending a large number of representatives, the labouring classes have got only two members by nomination. The land-holders, or Zamindars, have got a special favour of sending from special constituency five of their men, in addition to about 75 more from the general constituencies. Over and above these, many of their men come in by nomination. As for the Assembly, the depressed classes have got no right to send their men. Even the nominations are made from the classes who have already captured the Central Legislative bodies, and are friends of the high Officials or Ministers. Only for an excuse of the Statutory Royal Commission one gentleman from the Depressed Classes has been nominated to the Assembly this time. It is still more ludicrous that the members of the non-Depressed classes have been eligible to represent the Depressed Classes." Here started the real process of democratisation in an uncompromising and fearless manner.

M.K. Gandhi's Defeat in Bengal: Non-cooperation Movement

The boon of the Untouchable's gaining political power through the Government of India Act 1919, was simultaneously clouded with the advent of Mohandas Karamchand Gandhi, an orthodox Vaishnava Vania. He hailed from Sudamapuri, Porebandar, Gujrat of the then Bombay Presidency. Gandhijii's father Karamchand was Prime Minister of a ruling family in Gujrat.

Mohandas Karamchand Gandhi, grandson of Uttam Chand alies Ottaa Gandhi all of a sudden, without any previous record of leading any social or political movement in India or active association with the organisations in India ascended the throne of the Indian National Congress in 1919. 'On his return from South Africa in 1915, Gandhiji was honoured by the British Government with the title, '*Kaiser-I-Hind*', the emperor of India. The crown was bestowed on him for his excellent services for helping recruit soldiers in the Zulu and Boer War and for the Red Cross services.'[52] At this stage, Gandhiji was advised by Gopal Krishna Gokhle to understand Indian political situation by touring places like Champaran, Lucknow, Allahabad. In course, he settled some public disputes in favour of the local feudal lords. He was one of the London and South Africa returned British associates. Gandhiji was a non-graduate-Barrister from London.

Red-carpet welcome of Gandhiji's entry in Indian politics was, however, a long-awaited arranged festival for the Indian creamy-layer-elite. As Nirod C Chaudhuri had exposed, "On this point we had already arrived at a degree of certainty which amounted to cocksureness; to our thinking, there was only one thing to apply passive resistance; and only one thing to get done as a prerequisite transform the middle-class nationalist movement into a mass nationalist movement. Already, by 1915, the man who was to bring in the masses and conduct the passive resistance campaign had become identified to us as Mr. (not yet Mahatma) Gandhi. Although all the old leaders, and more especially Tilak, were still living and active, our eyes were fixed on Gandhi as the coming man."[53] M.K. Gandhi, while in South Africa till December 1914 was sincerely busy, as one Sergeant Major in recruiting soldiers for the British army who were badly engaged in First World War and campaigning anti-black operations in various forms there. "But although the jarring note came early enough into my mind, as early as 1913 to be precise, it was effected quickly because it was neither sustained nor sounded afresh by any reports besides those given to me by my nephew. Thus, my old notion of Mahatma Gandhi prevailed. In fact it was confirmed by the favourable account which my younger brother brought to me after hearing him at the time of the 1917 session of the Indian National Congress in Calcutta." This young nephew of Chowdhari 'who had been sent to Tagore's famous school at Santiniketan, had to be brought back because he was feeling more and more unhappy there. This boy told me that servants had been dispenses with in the hostels of that school at the instance, as he put it, of "Gandhi and his gang".[54] Gandhiji's actual and tangible advent in the Indian politics in 1919 was thus a pre-decided and pre-arranged state by the creamy layer ruling classes and the British. They created a charged atmosphere clandestinely amongst the newly established intellectual classes in the cities and metropolises. The east of Vivekanand-Ramakrishna was kept stand-by to see that the sun of liberty raises in the Western sky for more than half a decade before the incident took place.

Gandhiji started leading the 'Passive Resistance Movement', a policy that the Indian National Congress adopted since 1917 in the name, '*Satyagraha*'. This mode of *satyagraha* was also followed by a newly groomed leader, Dr Ambedkar to lead the Untouchables of India and Qaid-E-Azam Jinnah to lead the Muslims' point of view in future democratic India. They too were London Returned Barrister-politicians from Bombay Presidency.

Certainly, the non-cooperation movement created some disturbances all over India. But the rural agitators crossed its defined limit in Chauri Chaura in the Gorakhpur district, United Province. The infuriated mob in the name of '*Satyagraha*' set fire to the police station where 22 police-men (all Indians) were charred to death. These policemen had in possession, glorious records of serving local Zamindars and wealthy money lenders who were mercilessly atrocious on the local peasants and landless labourers who belonged to low caste groups. Gandhi rose to senses, called off the *Satyagraha* and declared his maiden resignation from active politics in 1922. He was, however, thrown behind bars by Lord Reading.

The Untouchables of India too proved equal to the situation. They defeated all efforts made by the leaders of Bengal Congress and paralysed

Gandhi and his non-cooperation movement. Guruchand refused to help and support Gandhiji. Tagore even refused to support Netaji Subash Bose when Gandhiji opposed him. Guruchand frustrated the plans of the Congress and Gandhi. He taught and advised his people:

"Rajniti Kshetre Tara Kabhu Nahi Chute,
Swadhinata Ki Padartha Bojhe Nako Mote,
Rajnitir Sange Jar Jogajog Nai'
Asahayoger Prasna Tar Kiba Bahi?" (GCC, p. 414)

'How can I describe the hopeless situation that the Hindus have even divided the gods. They have created Untouchables who are subjected to severe ill-treatment all over the country; they are regarded worse and inferior to animals. As they had no right to education, they failed to acquire adequate qualification with their little learning. They do not go for politics. They do not understand what it means by 'Freedom'. The very question of non-co-operation with the government is absolutely redundant for those who have no concern or connection with political matters.' The simple logic based on hard and tangible traditional facts of the social system that, where there was no attachment the question of detachment was completely redundant, out of nothing only nothing comes, convinced his people as well as Chittaranjan. Chittaranjan had no reply.

Despite this, Gandhiji asked the militant cadres of Congress to hold a mass meeting at Barishal where Congress claimed to have strong holds. The meeting, after great efforts and huge expense, turned into a grand flop. People did not turn up in the meeting. Gandhiji became furious at such a poor performance. The Barishal Congress Committee gave excuse that it was due to the apathy of the people in general of this part. Who were the people and what were their inspirations behind such audacious steps to stand united and to ignore the call of the would-be 'Father of India'? The research scholar Sekhar Bandhopadhay has recorded the answer, "This apathy was largely due to the non-participation of the Namasudra peasantry, who constituted a sizable section of the population in this part of Bengal."[55] There were many other untouchable communities who stood behind the call.

Gandhiji asked the Congress-leaders of Bengal to take all necessary steps to convince the Namasudra leader. Chittaranjan Das had written letter to Guruchand. In reply Guruchand advised, "The untouchable people being without political right so far was unable to help Government. In the circumstances it is all one to ask to co-operate or non-cooperate with the Government. Had the leaders instead of spending all their strength in such activities resorted to rescue the oppressed society, the possibility for getting '*Swaraj*' would have been quicker.[56] 'Please go to those fallen and Dalits with sincere hearts. Whatever strength is being spent for the movement would have yielded better dividend had it been spent for the Dalit-cause.

India is a country of villages; her soul is in the countryside. Leaving the cities, you go to villages. Bharat will rise if Village raises and the path of freedom will definitely be clear.'

"Ever since 1919 when Mr. Gandhi captured the Congress", the Congress adopted a modality to prevent the untouchables standing on an independent ticket "the means to make the legislatures objects of contempt. Accordingly the Congress in various provinces started processions carrying placards saying, "who will go in the Legislatures? Only barbers, cobblers, potters and sweepers." ...... Believing that respectable people would not be prepared to stand for election if they felt certain that they would have to sit with the barbers, potters, and sweepers etc. in the legislature, Congress actually went to the extent of putting up candidates from these despised communities on the Congress ticket and got them elected. A few illustrations of this outrageous conduct of the Congress may be mentioned. In the (1920?) 1921 election, the Congress elected a cobbler (Faguwa Rohidas) from Central Provinces Legislature. In 1930 election, they elected on the Central Provinces two cobblers, one milkman and one barber and in the Punjab one sweeper."[57] The Untouchables of Bengal, the pioneers of the Indian Untouchable or servile class movement, however, held the British scheme of democratisation high. Here too Congress succeeded in returning one illiterate cobbler in the Bengal Legislature in 1921 election by defeating Calcutta High Court Advocate and Professor of Pali language in the University of Calcutta, Mukunda Behari Mullick. In the constituency, untouchable cobblers were insignificant in number. In Assam too Congress adopted the same modality. The Brahmanical ruling classes denied the mandate that democracy was the rule of the majority. The Brahmanical leadership of Congress bargained with the British for a rule of the Legislators who represented 2.2 per cent of the population only. These people belonged to the exclusively privileged and powerful feudal section. They had no concern for the nation. They never had helped build national integrity. But the masses strived for a policy of the rule by the majority people of the country. We therefore, witnessed a spectacular sight, standing in the Legislative Council, the disciple of Guruchand roared : "I know the term nation in India is a misnomer..... responsible government cannot be established unless there has been an all round progress of all classes... If there is a desire in a certain quarter to establish a pre-mature self-government by any such... movement as that of non-cooperation the sooner the idea is vanished from Bengal and India is better."[58]

The Untouchables, already had entered in the Legislature. They were no more only in the streets and villages. Consequently, their roaring voice started reverberating in the walls of the Bengal Legislative Assembly. Their elected representative Nirod Behari Mullick on March 2, 1921, opposed the very basis of 'Non-Cooperation Movement' of Gandhiji, "A nation, like nature, abhors artificiality. By merely swinging, the pendulum from outside you cannot advance the hands of the clock permanently. And indeed the whole machinery might get wrong to the great detriment of the best interest of the country. If then there is a desire in a certain quarter to establish a pre-mature self-government by hoodwinking a certain class of England's politicians by any such movement as that of non-cooperation, the sooner the idea is banished from Bengal and from India the better. And on the other hand, it behooves those who are responsible for peace and tranquility and dispensation of even-handed justice to all classes to remove those weak spots on which flesh-flies of a handful of non-cooperators work." He further added, "In this connection I should like to submit that a real responsible government, capable of withstanding any storm cannot be established until and unless there has been an all-round progress of all classes."[59] In 1922, there held a large meeting of the Namasudras in Pirogepur, Barishal. The meeting was presided over by Rajani Kanta Das. The pamphlet, which was issued and widely distributed, was nothing but a challenge to Gandhiji's programme against untouchability. It declared, '*Bahujan's* battle was to achieve total-liberty; it will not stop just with eradication of untouchability.

With a view to establishing the rule of the '*Mulniwasi-Bahujan*' in their motherland after breaking the corns of chains of servile classes of native Indians through a self-conscious, independent movement of the '*Bahujan*' by the '*Bahujan*' and for the interest of the '*Bahujan*', Guruchand eventually convened a public-meeting in 1923 in Khulna. The target of the convention was to fix political strategy keeping in view the diverse interests of different warring factions of Indian and English bodies. The convention was named, "Nikhil Banga Namasudra Conference or Khulna Conference". "Teroshata Trish Sale Namasudra Jata Aache Bange, Khulna Jelai Ase Sanmelan kare Sese. Aso Sabe Baso Ak Sange. Ai Sanmelan Hate Namasudra Kon Pathe, Chalana Karibe Rajniti. Jaha Bale Dayamoy, Sabha Madhye Path Hai, Tate Sabe Janai Swikriti." The conference was presided over by Thakur Guruchand himself. Along with common subjects all the government officials and officers, businessmen, land-lords, lawyers, pleaders and political and social leaders, headmen of villages and elected MLAs and MLC all attended the conference. The presidential speech was red out by Nirod Bihari Mullick, MLA:

"Jati Dharma Jati Maan Jati Mor Bhagaban
Jati Chara Anya Chinta Nai."

'We do not know anything but welfare of the Nation, advancement of Nation is our religion, our self-respect and our God.'

The furious battle-cry of the depressed and oppressed for establishing Liberty and Equality in a state of Fraternity after capturing political power has been continuing since time immemorial in the name of Chandals in India. The tangible-tradition was manifested in the modern period, in the 'First battle of Independence', in the first attempt to establish the rule of self-government, the rule of the people by overthrowing the tyrannical oppression of a few, the Brahmins. The battle of liberty by the native Indians was initiated in 1757 under the banner of the British East India Company. The Company army was composed of 500 untouchable sepoys and 200 British officers. They brought the maiden victory for the British in India. It was also the beginning of the end of untouchables' silence of centuries. The untouchables of the then Bengal particularly the Dusads (now in Bihar) and some Chandals had sacrificed their lives and blood in the battle of Palasse and decisively defeated the Pathan-Brahmin army of Siraj-ud-daula. The natives as a result did not interfere in the matter. They had on the contrary reasons to rejoice. "That the inhabitants, who were spectators on that occasion, must have amounted to some hundreds of thousands, and if they had an inclination to have destroyed the Europeans they might have done it with sticks and stones", commented one English man.[60] Lord Clive personally went to Patna to recruit the untouchable Dusads in his army. With the light of wisdom, Karl Marx could visualize correctly its resultant impact when he recorded, "The native-army organised and trained by the British drill-sergeant, was the *sin-qua-non* of Indian self-emancipation, and of India ceasing to be the prey of the first foreign intruders".[61] The brave-heart untouchables got descent jobs of dignity in the governing class of British army. The doors of education were opened up for them in Army-schools. All that was denied to them as Hindus was regained by the untouchables of India now. Both the question and answer of the phrase used by K. Marx, (ceasing) getting rid of being prey to the 'first foreign intruders', too was latent in the same act. And it started paying its dividend in the form of untouchable Chandal, Hari-Guruchand.

Hindus started welfare activities in the remote villages of untouchables and Motuas. Many got misled. These welfare activities naturally were restricted to the areas where advanced untouchable communities resided predominantly. The '*Bagdis*', one of the untouchable communities of Bengal were numerically on third position. Congress volunteers and the *Brahma Samaj* activists and preachers never approached them with schooling and other benefits. They are found to be very backward even today. This attitude of the Brahmanical society reveals their motive of 'welfare scheme' of the period. '….the cruel cultural and economic systems that makes Indian society cruel, so vulgarly unequal.'[62] The untouchable leaders knew the situation, so the main stream movement of the untouchables still remained un-dented and undeterred.

References

1. W.W. Hunter, Annals of Rural Bengal, published in 1868.
2. Dr B.R. Ambedkar R. and S., Vol. 8, pp. 355-58.
3. *Ibid.,* Vol. 10, p. 496.
4. Marx and Engels, Selected Works, Vol. 1 (Moscow Punlication-1977), p. 495.

5. *Ibid.,* Vol. 9, p. 210.
6. Letter of Karl Marx, dated July, 22, 1853.
7. *Ibid.*
8. L. Mukherjee, History of India (Modern Period) p. 173.
9. Dr Pattabhi Sitaramaya, The History of Congress, Vol. 1, pp. 8-9.
10. Ibid, p. 11.
11. *Ibid*, p. 11-12.
12. Surendra Nath Banerjee, A Nation In Making.
13. Nirod C. Chowdhury, Autobiography of an Unknown Indian, p. 468.
14. Mahakabi Mahananda Halder, Guruchand Charit, p. 554.
15. *Ibid*, p. 283.
16. A Summary of the Changes in the Jurisdiction of Districts in Bengal, West Bengal District Gazetteers, pp. 144 and 148.
17. Sekhar Bandyopadhayay, Caste, Protest and Identity in Colonial India, Namasudras, p. 64.
18. L. Mukherjee, Indian Hisory (Modern Period) p. 208.
19. *Ibid*, p. 187.
20. Ravindra Rachanavali, Kalantar, Hindu-Musalman.
21. Ravindra Rachanavali, Vol. 13, p. 182, pub- W. Bengal Govt.
22. Rabindra Nath Tagore, Brahman, p. 133 in 1902.
23. Prof. Dulalkrishna Biswas, *Bangali Hindu Madhyavittwer Swarup*, p. 69.
24. Bipin Chand, MODERN INDIA, (NCERT).
25. Prof. Dulal Krishna Biswas, *ibid*, p. 81 and in Palikrit (Quarterly Bengali Journal).
26. Sekhar Bandyopadhayay, Caste, Protest and Identity in Colonial India, Namasudras, p. 64.
27. Sekhar Bandyopadhayay, Caste, Protest and Identity in Colonial India, Namasudras, p. 65.
28. Com. Muzaffar Ahmed, Aamar Jivan and Communist Party of India, pp. 432-33.
29. Bharatiya Vidya Bahavan, Cultural History of India.
30. Sekhar Bandyopadhayay, Caste, Protest and Identity in Colonial India, Namasudras, p. 68.
31. Suprakash Roy, *Bharatvarse Krisi Biplaver Itihas.*
32. Sekhar Bandyopadhayay, Caste, Protest and Identity in Colonial India, Namasudras, p. 81.
33. Sekhar Bandyopadhayay, Caste, Protest and Identity in Colonial India, Namasudras, p. 61.
34. Sekhar Bandyopadhayay, Caste, Protest and Identity in Colonial India, Namasudras, p. 86.
35. Sekhar Bandyopadhayay, Caste, Protest and Identity in Colonial India, Namasudras, pp. 87-90.
36. Mahakavi Mahananda Haldar, Guruchand Charit, p. 220.

37. Mahakavi Mahananda Haldar, Guruchand Charit, p. 449.
38. Sekhar Bandyopadhayay, Caste, Protest and Identity in Colonial India, Namasudras.
39. Sumit Sarkar, Modern India 1885-1947, p. 159.
40. *Ibid,* p. 159.
41. Dr Ambedkar W. and S., Vol. 9.
42. Sekhar Bandyopadhayay, Caste, Protest and Identity in Colonial India, Namasudras.
43. Sekhar Bandyopadhayay, Caste, Protest and Identity in Colonial India, Namasudras, p. 113.
44. Dhananjoy Keer, Ambedkar, Life and Mission.
45. N.B. Roy, A People in Distress, Vol. II, p. 167.
46. A.K. Biswas, The Namasudras of Bengal, pp. 61-62.
47. Sekhar Bandyopadhayay, Caste, Protest and Identity in Colonial India, Namasudras.
48. *Ibid*, p. 116.
49. Dr B.R. Ambedkar, Vol. 17(3) p. 298.
50. Sekhar Bandyopadhayay, Caste, Protest and Identity in Colonial India, Namasudras, p. 115.
51. Sekhar Bandyopadhayay, Caste, Protest and Identity in Colonial India, Namasudras.
52. S.K. Biswas, Gods, False-gods and the Untouchables, (Orion Books) p. 263.
53. Nirod C. Chowdhury, Autobiography of an Unknown Indian, p. 467.
54. *Ibid*, p. 468.
55. Dhananjoy Keer, Dr Ambedkar, Life and his Mission.
56. N.B. Roy, A people in Distress and Acharya Mahananda Halder, Guruchand Charit.
57. Dr Ambedkar W and S, vol. 9, p. 461.
58. Dr Ambedkar W and S, Vol. 9.
59. Com. Muzaffar Ahmed, My Life and Communist Party of India, p. 391.
60. Bharatiya Vidya Bhavan, The History and Culture of Indian People, Vol. X.
61. Karl Marx and Frederick Engels, Selected Works, Vol. 1, p. 495.
62. Arundhuti Roy, Azadi, India Today, September, 2008, p. 20.

6

Sunset of the Liberation Movement of the Untouchables Starts in the Western Sky

The Brahmins and their religion called Hinduism retained the masses of Indian autochthons or the *Mulniwasis* in a perpetual state of servitude. The Hindus treated these 80 per cent of the countrymen as sub-human or even non-human beings. The Hindu scriptures dehumanised and termed this immense majority section of the society as Sudras and Untouchables. They were forced to be 'divine slaves' the perpetual slaves of the Brahmins by a spiritual arrangement. From the temples, with the rod of spiritual sanctions the Hindus plan and control politics and the instrumentalities of the state. Several scriptural injunctions kicked out these people from political, economic, intellectual and spiritual arena. They were even sterilised to desire to fulfill these basic human aspirations. They were debarred of putting a bite on the fruit from the tree of knowledge. Thus, the divine-slaves fail to understand what was good or bad for them. Therefore, without revolting against the religion, or without destroying the corns of Hinduism, they had no chance, no political hope. When they are Hindus they remain the divine-slaves automatically.

With the advent of the British rule, with the fall of theocratic-kingship or monarchy, therefore, the struggle of the untouchables took the shape of social-justice movement by revolting against Hinduism. At the first instance, this revolt was manifested in a tangible shape of deserting Hinduism. The Untouchables and Sudras of Eastern India embraced Islam en-masse. Village after village of Eastern Bengal turned green. It was primarily not in quest of a new God or Allah. The autochthons were doggedly happy with their ancestral religion, gods and demigods. They worshipped Chatt or Shasti mata, Dharmathakur, Neel, Charak, Ghetu, Panchamma, Shitala Manasa,

Olabibi, Hachra, Banbibi, Alakh Niranjan etc. Their spiritual hunger was quenched with the woman's '*Brata-kathas*' and thirteen '*Palas* and *Parvans*' in twelve months. These people seem to have taken refuge under the shelter of Islam for getting manumitted from slavery. They tried to get rid of the coercive and discriminative treatments rather persecution of Hindu Concentration Camp. Hindu persecution pushed the producing-class, peace-loving peasantry of Bengal in the camp of Islam. Freedom, human rights, self-respect, dignity and security were the prime motive behind conversion to Islam.

The number of the proselyte Muslims increased in galloping speed in each decennial Census Report after 1872. According to the 1872 census report Hindus in Bengal were 1,81,00,438 and Muslim population was less than this, i.e., 1,76,09,135 souls. In 1931 the figures were 2,22,12,069 and 2,78,10,100 respectively. In 1941 Census the Hindus reduced to 1,76,80,054 while the Muslim population of undivided Bengal was enumerated 3,30,05,434 souls. According to F. Barnier's famous 'Travels Account' at the end of the rule of the Great Mughals in 1707, the Muslim population in India was less than one per cent. It started increasing only during British India.

As the Untouchables, village after village deserted Hinduism, the Muslim society and the former-ruling class gained considerable strength and confidence. With declined number, the Hindu society thus was weakened alarmingly in the democratic situation further advanced. In such circumstances, the humiliated and subdued autochthons gained a scope to stand up on their own feet. They declared their own spiritual entity. This religious revolt in the form of conversion soon entered into the second stage. In the second stage, the untouchables declared their own religion, completely separate from Hinduism, Islam and Christianity. They dared declare spiritual freedom; their souls no more were in bondage or mortgaged to the institutions other than their own. In Bengal particular, they refused to be identified as a Hindu. They called themselves *Matuas* since 1835. Another large section of the Chandals of Eastern Bengal declared their religion 'Satya-Dharma' completely different from Islam, Christinity and Hinduism since 1886. Untouchables of Madras and the Punjab followed suit. They too declared themselves not Hindus but *Ad-Dravid* and *Ad-Dhammi* respectively. "The Punjab *Ad Dharma Mandal* had petitioned the Punjab Government before census operations started in 1930, representing that the Depressed Classes should be permitted to return Ad Dharm as their religion at the time of census, as they were aborigines of India and the Hindus kept them at a respectable distance. They did not believe in the Hindu religion. The President of the Punjab *Ad Dharm Mandal* was informed that a clause was being provided in the Census Code requiring that persons returning their religion as *Ad Dharm* would be recorded as such. *Ad Dharm* literally means original or ancient religion". "Dispute over the *Ad Dharmi* agitation became so serious that several murders were committed".[1] In the vast plains of United Province where the strength of the Untouchables was more than 10 millions and around 26 per cent of the total population of the Province, the 'Adi-Dharma' movement was carried by Swami Achhutanand on the same line as in the Punjab since 1920. 'Ad Dravid' movement in the south was equally forceful. This self-conscious independent and courageous declaration of their distinct Faith naturally became the vertebra of their nation building in democratic frame. This became the powerful catalyst force for their social consolidation, which in course of time boosted political ambition in a favourable condition.

Now the untouchables entered in the third phase of their revolts. The third stage was manifested with the expression of fury of the patient peasantry. In many cases it took the shape of a crude form of aggressive revolt of the peasants both Muslims and the Untouchables of the eastern-dark of India against economic exploitation by the ruling class. Since 1835 onwards eastern India, rather Rural-Bengal witnessed series of serious peasant-revolts caused by different Tribal groups, the Untouchables and the proselyte Muslims. Karl Marx in his letter on India in early 1853 did not miss to pay glowing tribute to these exceptional revolutionary actions by the Bengal peasantry, 'Did any revolutionary party ever originate agrarian revolution like those in Bengal....?'[2] Other than the Santhal revolt of 1853, which was led by Sidhu and Kanhu none of these violent and well organised revolts was aimed to install their own rule by replacing the Hindu or British rulers. During the war of independence, the 40,000 Santhals who took active part in the war against British bullets and bayonets, cried out to make their own ruler. Target of all other peasant-revolts was to have social justice or economic justice only. These trains of bloody revolts are said to have even compelled the British bureaucrats to enact the corrective laws like Factory Act of 1881 and Bengal Tenancy Act of 1883 to suggest for establishment of democratic safety valves like Indian National Congress. The British authority noted all these steps of the underdogs of their colony with due care and caution.

Having impregnated with the hope of getting chances to govern in the democratic structure waves of militancy gradually ceased to be in operation. The declaration of Lord Ripon's democratic features and their implementation in the Local-Boards, *Taluks*, *Tahasils*, Sub-divisions had great and obvious impact. Thus the well organised militant-struggles of the peasantry of Eastern Bengal (untouchable Chandals/Namasudras' and Muslims together) in the form of 'agrarian-strikes' in 1872 and the spread-education movement of Guruchand since 1880 culminated into political and freedom movement of the servile class untouchable and the *Bahujan Samaj*. The trains of earlier militant struggles called 'peasant revolts' ceased their arms to be settled in the quite pages of forgotten history.

These democratic features gained fundamentally a new dimension in the struggles of the Untouchables. The leaders of the Untouchable peasantry secured the provisions for nominated members from amongst the Untouchables in the Legislature in the Government of India Act 1919. They secured franchise right. As a result, Advocate Bhiswadev Das, an Untouchable entered in the Bengal legislature in 1921. In 1922, D.D. Gholap and M.C. Raja became MLC in the Legislatures of Bombay Presidency and Madras province respectively.

This prolonged democratic movement produced, as has already been discussed in the earlier chapters, many excellent leaders from amongst the untouchables in Eastern India. Mukunda Behari Mullick and Thakur Panchanan Sarkar (Barman), Rasik Lal Biswas, Manindra Nath Mandal, Birat Chandra Mandal were some of the leaders with outstanding caliber. Mukunda Bihari Mullick, a graduate from the Presidency College, Calcutta passed MA with Pali language from the University of Calcutta in 1912. He was appointed as a lecturer in Pali Department of the University of Calcutta in 1914 by the Vice-Chancellor Sir Ashutosh Mookerjee to teach Buddhist literature. For this, Mr. Mookerjee was heavily criticised and condemned by the Hindu body as 'Chandals are being worshipped in the University of Calcutta'. In the same year, he became the first Indian Advocate from Untouchable communities in a High Court, namely the Calcutta High Court. He was a part-time lecturer in Law Collage, Calcutta University. He was also nominated as a Fellow of the Calcutta University Syndicate. All his five brothers, elder and younger passed BA, MA and LLB during those dark age of education and illiteracy.

Mukunda Behari Mullick, however, joined socio-political movement of the Untouchable Namasudras since his tender age even though a large part of his student life was spent in Calcutta. "Mr. Mukunda Behari Mullick had developed a knack for social service while he was still a student. He led a deputation (political) to the then Governor of Bengal immediately after passing MA Examination" in 1912. In his maiden speech in the Bengal Legislative Council on March 9, 1930 Mukunda Behari had said, "I myself had the proud privilege and high honour of leading several deputations before Lord Carmichael, Lord Ronsardshay, and Lord Litton and also before Sir Stanley Jackson. I must admit that we had very sympathetic and encouraging replies to all our deputations…"[3] He, in 1912, led a deputation to Lord Carmichael, the then Governor of Bengal along with eight other elderly Namasudra leaders. Guruchand led a delegation to Sir Lancelot Hare, the Governor of East Bengal and Assam in 1907, however, the written appeals for government job were crossed out by his guide and associate Dr C.S. Mead. But in 1912, for the first time, in the annals of Indian history an Untouchable youth personally pleaded to the Governor of Bengal,

Lord Carmichael in English language, on behalf of the entire servile and untouchable classes of India.

He is found to have been active as one of the leading member of the 'Bengal Namasudra Association' in 1912, at Calcutta as its President. Mohini Mohan Das was its Secretary. As Mohini Mohan had Congress background it did not gain ground. It was not accepted in the grass-root level. Mukunda Behari presided over the large Namasudra meeting held in Munsiganj of Dacca in 1915. Under his leadership there was born 'All Bengal Namasudra Conference' in the Dalhousie Institute, Calcutta next year in 1917. As the President of the Association Mukunda Behari personally led a deputation on 20th July in 1917, to Lord Ronaldshay, the Governor of Bengal, and demanded special favour for the Untouchables of Bengal, in particular the Namasudras for their progress by removing the road blocks created by the Hindu social order. During this period, Mukunda Behari along with Muslim national leaders stubbornly opposed the move of Anny-Besant and Surendra Nath Banerjee for 'Home Rule' which according to the non-Hindu block was a scheme of 'Hindu Rule' in disguise. In reply to the appeals of Mullick, the Governor of Bengal assured in his communication. "The Government desires to make no distinction between one caste and another;...... that is, the Government is prepared so far as patronage is concerned, to give equal opportunities to the members of all communities who proved themselves competent, and you may rest assured that Government will consider not only fairly, but also somatically, the claims of such members of your community as have proved themselves competent."[4]

In 1917 August, when Lord Montague came to review the Government of India Act of 1909 and to replace it by another Mr. Mullick was mature enough to interfere in the process of framing the Constitution of India. He submitted a written memorandum and demanded protection of 'Separate Elecorate' for the untouchables in the Government of India Act 1919. Apart from his historic role in the shaping of Government of India Act 1919 Mullick continued to lead his people from various forums.

Out of the above mentioned conference at Dalhousie Institute there emerged an Institution called 'Calcutta Namasudra Samiti'. The two Mullick brothers Mukunda and Nirod Behari Mullick (MLA) addressed the first conference of the 'All India Depressed Classes Association' on 5th of February 1922, in the venue of City College Hall, Calcutta. In those days the untouchables were officially accepted as neither caste nor Hindu. They belonged to the 'Depressed Classes'. The national conference of the Depressed Classes was called mainly by Manindra Nath Mandal, a prominent leader of the Poundra Kshatriyas. This National platform was founded by Manindra Nath Mandal long back in 1917 as a common platform of all the Untouchable communities of the country with pan-Indian vision of the

Depressed Classes. They had also a policy to go in consonance with the 'principles and policies' of the Muslim League. Mukunda Behari placed a glowing picture and a blue-print for a future all India Depressed classes' movement. Out of this conference was born an organ called, "*Bangia Janasangha*'. The Hindus got terrorised with its prospect and impact. Consequently, the Gandhian Congress with full fury fanned the germ of intra-community and inter-community rivalry amongst the Untouchable communities.

An Untouchable on the National Platform

During this period, another young and powerful untouchable leader from the Namasudra community emerged to encourage untouchables of other provinces of British India and to reverberate the demands for political rights of the untouchables from the said national platform. He was Birat Chandra Mandal. After passing BA from the Vidyasagar College, Calcutta in 1920 Birat Chandra joined active politics while studying Law in the University of Calcutta. While a B.A. student he stayed in the Ripon Hostel Calcutta. The atrocities of the Hindu students drove him out of the hostel. The spirited Birat Chandra instead of giving up, with his self-conscious independent drive rose to establish a hostel in Kolkata, the "Bani Mess" along with Mukunda Behari Mullick. M.N. Roy (Narendranath Bhattachariya) established Communist Party of India in October 1920. Birat Chandra, without being associated with the Communists started trade union movement and formed 'Kanchrapara Railway Workmen's Union' in 1925. While the vice-President of the Union, he was elected as President of '*Bangia Namasudra Samiti*' in 1926. Three terms he remained an elected Member of the Legislative Assembly. Twice he became MLC. He also served as the Deputy Chairman of the Education Committee. In the same year he attended the 5th National Conference of the 'All India Depressed Classes Association' at '*Sabji Mandi*', Delhi along with two others namely Bhiswadeb Das (former MLC) and Dhananjoy Roy. Birat Chandra Mandal was called the Gladstone of the Depressed Classes after he had presented his views in an eloquent speech. Next year Birat Chandra Mandal presided over the 6th National conference of the All India Depressed Classes Association in Madras at Victoria Hall. "The Organisation was accorded official recognition after a delegation headed by its secretary Bharat Chandra Sarkar met Sir Stanly Jackson….. The situation indicates that the Namasudra leaders had come to the forefront of the Bengal depressed-classes movement and had become the link between their provincial and national representative bodies…"[5] Birat Chandra Mandal represented Bengal Untouchables in its 9th Annual meeting at Simla on 13th July 1930. The Executives of the All India Depressed Classes Association "condemned this movement (Civil Disobedience called by the Congress against Simon Commission's Report) as an agitation 'started by extremist politicians in the country… to overthrow the British rule in India." He called upon the provincial associations to organize movements to fight it with all their strength. The meeting further expressed its pleasure at the announcement of the Round Table Conference, opposed the immediate granting of dominion status to India before the removal of the untouchability and demanded special electorate (Separate Electorate) to safe guard their political rights."[6]

The British authority plainly ignored such experienced and equipped leaders on the national platform while nominating the representatives of the untouchables in the Simon Commission or in the Round Table Conferences that followed the failure of the Simon Commission's report. In later life, after the Poona Pact, Birat Chandra instantly realised the sudden doom of the untouchable movement in India as well as in Bengal. Therefore, Birat Chandra led, the '*Nikhil Banga Krisak Praja Samiti*'. As the vice-President of the '*Krisak Praja Samiti*' he was elected as an MLA in the Bengal Legislative Assembly. In 1929 all Bengal Namasudra Conference was held under the presidentship of Birat Chandra Mandal. He also represented Bengal in 1930 in the national Executive of the All India Depressed Classes Association giving clear indication of forming a strong national political movement of the Untouchables by the Untouchables and for the Untouchables.

Out of his long organizing experiences and political sagacity, Birat Chandra Mandal could rightly realize the real necessity of the Untouchables in their movement to make them free and their own rulers in the polity-structure of Parliamentary Democracy. He too, like Mukunda Behari consistently supported and raised the demands for constitutional provisions for Separate Electorate for the Untouchables from various national as well as from Bengal platforms. He realised that in a state when all the minorities were excluded with separate electorate the untouchables without separate electorate were no more than disenfranchised votes in the Hindu vote-banks.

He understood the structural system of democratic-polity. In a democratic republic, the country belongs to the people in general and the people or the subjects rule or govern through the system of representation. He, like the British Prime Minister, J. Ramsay McDonald, also realised that the Untouchables needed "representation of their own choosing to speak on their behalf in the legislatures which will have a dominating influence over their future".[7] In the country where the society is constitutionally fragmented by water-tight castes, tribes and creeds which rests its existence on the basis of a kind of general repulsion and hatred of descending order between each of the social groups, political rights cannot be attained by the servile castes despite their forming the immense majority. The low-castes like the Sudras and the Untouchables because of their historic position, because of their being totally out of socialisation process, being weak and ignorant, illiterate and poor, subdued and exploited for millennium were completely unable to send 'representatives of their own choosing' to the Legislature through open election. The situation became further firm where their compatriots like Muslims were isolated from them by separate electorate. The method of joint electorate in such circumstances was nothing but a well calculated mode to force the helpless untouchables to cast their votes for the Hindus only. This disenfranchised traditional servile classes or the hereditary subject classes were reduced to the nominee of the ruling class in a nation that stands without nationalism. Therefore, the untouchables needed the protection of 'separate electorate' more than the same was required by the politically experienced minorities of India like the Muslims and Sikhs to make their franchise meaningful and effective. The provisions of Joint Electorate of the Poona Pact were transformed into the Government of India Act 1935. Accordingly, the first general election was held in 1937. Yet the untiring Birat Chandra did not give up hope. He tried to restore the provisions of Separate Electorate in Bengal even in its miniature form.

The Calcutta Corporation Administration Bill 1939 sought separate electorate for the minorities and the Scheduled Castes with seven seats reserved for them. The Minister for Autonomy, Nawab Habibulla Bahadur moved the Bill for discussion. On 27th February 1939, when discussion on the Bill started, Hon'able Birat Chandra Mandal, elected MLA from Faridpur argued in support of the Bill, "We had not any justice from the Europeans or the Congress or from anybody else, but we are going to get it from the Muhammadans who are regarded as the greatest enemies of the Hindus. I may call it the sense of justice of Islam, we are grateful to the Nawab Bahadur who is really trying to give something to the Scheduled Caste people. Just as arsenic is a great poison and is prescribed by doctors sometimes when the patient's condition is serious so also when the condition of Bengal politics is serious this communalism must be injected so that Bengal caste Hindus may learn a lesson. I claim 12 seats are given to the Scheduled Castes."

Jogendra Nath Mandal who had entered politics hardly two years back, with the support and backing of the caste-Hindus opposed the amendment Bill. Attacking the veteran untouchable leader of national repute, Birat Chandra, J.N. Mandal delivered, "Mr. Deputy Speaker, Sir, before I begin my speech I should like to say a few words in reply to the speech delivered by my friend Mr. Birat Chandra Mandal. He has prescribed poison for eradicating poisonous elements from a human constitution. But for the prescription of a poisonous drug an efficient doctor is required and this cannot be done by a quack. I hope, in these few words I have given the reply to my friend's speech.

Sir, rising to support the amendment for the circulation of the Calcutta Municipal Bill, I would like to remind the house at the outset that this is the first time that communal representation on the basis of separate electorate is going to be introduced in the formation of local bodies under the present autonomous Government. The system of separate electorate is not only against the fundamental principle of democracy but it stands also in the way of creation and development of a healthy atmosphere that is most congenial to the growth of national development".[8] By the time, Jogendra Nath Mandal is expected to have known the stand of Dr Ambedkar who had been fighting tooth and nails for re-gaining the provisions of 'Separate Electorate' from the British authority. Despite that, as a champion of Hindu nationalism and the defender of faith, Jogendra Nath maintained his pro-Hindu stand even after the partition of Bengal or India by way of opposing the scheme of 'Separate Electorate' for the minorities in the East Pakistan. The Muslim League wanted to grant the same for the untouchables there. The matter will be discussed later in appropriate place.

In the general election of 1924, both Nirod Behari and Bhisma Dev Das failed to make their re-entry in the Legislature. Charu Chandra Das was nominated in place of Advocate Bhismadev Das who had fought for gaining benefit for the Untouchable peasantry in the Council tirelessly by raising maximum number of questions some even highly embarrassing for the Government. Nirod Behari was defeated at the hands of a Namasudra Congress Candidate Dr Mohini Mohan Das (Chandsi) a close associate of Chitta Ranjan Das. Though Das won the election with support of the Caste Hindus he lost his credibility in his own community. The Namasudras boycotted him with strict method. 'Joining Congress during those days was regarded as a crime by the Depressed classes of people in Bengal. As a result, even being invited, Dr Mohini Mohan Das was not given an entry by the young volunteers in the pandal of the Namasudra Convention in Pirojpur.' However, this strong attitude damaged and divided the Namasudra movement considerably. This defeat at the behest of Congress strengthened the ground for demanding 'Separate Electorate' by the Untouchables of Bengal.[9]

Enter Dr Ambedkar in Indian Untouchable-Politics

At his crucially historic and socio-politically matured juncture, as has already been observed, the ruling class, be it Indo-Vedic-Aryan or the Nordic-British-Aryan, either united or separate, were not feeling comfortable to face the ambitious and stubborn, self-conscious and independent struggles, though peaceful and democratic, of the Bengal-Untouchables for total emancipation in the field of politics of a Republic. By the time, let us not forget, the fear of the communist revolution all over the world brought the rulers of the globe in a holy alliance to protect their system. Sahid Bhagat Singh had been quoted to have said that the Indian peasantry is to fight against both the exploiters foreign and Indian. The Chandal-Namasudras were determined to achieve their target.

The creamy-layer elite castes seriously need to shift their battleground in their own court and drag their untouchable opponents in the weak battle arena. They succeeded in their attempts. The opening of the Western front of the battle was a well calculated plan started long back when in Shantiniketan School, Rabindra Nath Tagore started pampering 'Gandhi and his Gang' since 1912.[10] Ravindra Nath Tagore is never known to have attended any programme of the Untouchables in Calcutta whereas he went to Bombay to actively participate the 'First All India Depressed Classes Conference' held by the Depressed Class Mission Society of Mr. Ganesh Chandravarkar on March 23 and 24, 1918. His Highness Maharaja Sayajirao Gaekowar presided over the conference.[11] None of the important untouchable leaders, however, attended the conference.

At this significant situation, one moderate and highly learned, bookworm Untouchable, Dr Bhimrao Ramji Ambedkar in the western-sky was projected as the untouchable leader. Ambedkar after completing his higher studies from the University of Columbia, USA and London School of Economics for a period of around eight years had come back to India to ascend the position in the national politics of India. The British authority made him to shoulder the precarious responsibility to plead for independent political share in the governance of the country for the untouchables of the entire country soon after. Ambedkar up to that period did not pay even a visit to the provinces other than Bombay.

In school, Bhim Rao's surname was recorded as Ambedkar. His father Ramji Sakpal superannuated as a Subedar Major, a Head Master in the Army School. Bhim (the noun was coined from the child's mother's name, Bhima) was born in the Cantonment of Military Headquarter of War better known as 'MHOW' just 21 km. away from Indore, Madhya Pradesh on 14th April 1891. In the school, a Brahmin teacher is said to have anointed Bhim Rao Sakpal with a Brahmin surname 'Ambedkar'. It is surprising as to how and why his well-placed and educated father allowed his son to be known not by their family name but by the identity of their persecutors and haters. He passed Matriculation in 1907 with 38 per cent marks.[12] A Brahmin, Krishnaji Kerluskar, sponsored Ambedkar from his boyhood. Kerluskar managed to get a high-sum (Rs. 25 per month) of scholarship for Ambedkar from Sayoji *Maharaj* of Baroda to study B.A. in Elphinstone College. Rishi Aurovindo Ghosh too served Baroda Estate for a long time. After his graduation, Kerluskar arranged to see that Ambedkar was further awarded a foreign scholarship for higher study in the Columbia University by the *Maharaj* Sayoji Gaikoar. Ambedkar secured M.A. and PhD in 1915 from the Columbia University, USA. He got further financial assistance from Sahu Maharaja of Kolhapur for doing his M.Sc, and DSc. in Economics from London School of Economics and Bar-at-Law from Gray's Inn.

Dr Ambedkar initially returned to India from America on 21st August 1917 when Lord Montague had arrived in India to review the Government of India Act 1909. During this period, he did not participate in any social activity barring attending some meetings with Sahu Maharaj in 1920. "Being fresh from foreign lands, Ambedkar was nobody in Indian Politics."[13] In 1920 Dr Ambedkar, however, was called upon by the British authority along with Shinde to give evidence before the Southborough Committee dealing with franchise question of the Government of India Act 1919.

On March 21, 1920, Dr Ambedkar was presiding over a meeting of the Untouchables at Mongaon in the Kolhapur Estate. Sahu Maharaja, in his speech made a prophetical discloser, "You have found your saviour in Ambedkar. I am confident that he will break your shackles. Not only that, a time will come when, so whispers my conscience, Ambedkar will shine as a front-ranked leader of all India fame and appeal."[14] Ambedkar here, started his maiden journal '*Muknayak*' with Rs. 20000 donated by Maharaja Sahu Chatrapati. He went back abroad.

Soon after his second return from London with all the exceptionally remarkable laurels of achievements in academic field in June 1923, Dr Ambedkar had got his *Sanad* and started the career of a Barrister in the Bombay High Court. Here he contested a case of defamation against two backward Sudra social activists of 'Non-Brahmin Political Party' named Jadhe and Javalkar for their circulating a pamphlet condemning Hinduism and Brahmins as the root cause of all evils and weakness of India. The Brahmins of Bombay took them to the court. Ambedkar won the case and gained popularity. For the first time he was found to have got involved in social activities in right earnest and got interested in organisational social activities to uplift the condition and interests of the Untouchables. He also started with small object to establish social organisation in various places. On July 20, 1924 under the title '*Bahiskrit Hitakarini Sabha*' he got the institution registered with the following objectives:

(i) To promote the spread of education amongst the Depressed Classes, open Hostels and other means necessary or desirable.

(ii) To promote the spread of culture among the Depressed Classes by opening libraries, social centers and study circles

(iii) To advance and improve the economic condition of the Depressed Classes by starting Industrial and agricultural schools.

(iv) To represent the grievances of the Depressed Classes.[15]

These objectives of the '*Sabha*' were far from political. The Bengal untouchables however, in 1890's established 'Namasudra Hitakarini Sabha' which activily struggled to oppose swadesi movement in 1906 and by 1921 it got into the national politics of Indian democracy. In Bombay, the Bahiskrit Hitakarini Sabha initiated agitation for mere social and civil-Rights.

It is interesting to note that the organisation was not purely of the Untouchables or by the Untouchables. 'The President of the Bahiskrit Hitakarini Sabha was a Brahmin, Sir Chimanlal Harilal Setalvad, LLD;[16] and its Vice-Presidents were Meyer Nissim, JP; Rustamji Jinwala, Solicitor; G.K. Nariman; Dr R.P. Paranjpye; Dr V.P. Chavan and B.G. Kher, Solicitor who fifteen years later became the first Prime Minister of the Bombay Province and gct Dr Ambedkar sent back in the Constituent Assembly as its member for the 2nd time. Dr Ambedkar became the Chairman of the Managing committee of the Sabha. Its Secretary was S.N. Shivatarkar and its Treasurer, N.T. Jadav.'[17] The cream of Bombay province came forward to grace the organisation of the Untouchables. The movement carried by this institution was thus a '*Sarvajan* Movement' under the lavish patronage, protective guidance and blessings of the creamy-layer people of the ruling class. Efforts were made to eradicate sufferings of the oppressed Indians with the blessings of the Brahmins who remained the cause of sufferings and destitution of the untouchables throughout millenniums.

This '*Bahiskrit Hitakarini Sabha*' was not a creation of Dr Ambedkar. The organisation is reported to have started by Pandurang Nand Bhatkar, a Mahar by caste in 1920. R. K. Kadam of Poona, also a Mahar, was its president. The annual subscription of the Sabha was being from *annas* four to one rupee.[18] Dr Ambedkar actually had taken over this grass-root-level organisation. He made it an opulent organisation of elite-movement in the name of the untouchables. The annual expenditure of the organisation in the year 1926 itself went to a fabulous figure amounting more than Rs. 30000. The source of such huge fund is not clear.[19]

Eventually, Dr Ambedkar joined the public movement of passive resistance in Gandhian model, which overwhelmed everything particularly in the region of Bombay Presidency. One youth leader named R.B. More was planning for Mahar[20] Talab agitation. He invited Dr Ambedkar who on March 1927, launched his maiden public agitation, '*Mahad Satyagraha*' for drinking water from the public well of sweet-water called '*Chaudar* Tank'. During March agitation, there was slogan shouting, "*Gandhiji Ki Jay*", "*Hara Hara Mahadev*". And in the agitation ground there was shown only the portrait of Gandhiji. This Civil Right agitation in Gandhian method even evoked violent reaction from the Hindus. At the second attempt on 25th December 1927, in his public address Ambedkar declared, "The conference is held to unfurl the banner of Equality and thus may be linked to the national assembly in France convened in 1789. Our conference aims at the same achievement in social, religious, civic and economic matters. We are avowedly out to smash the steel frame of Caste system..... We have all gathered here to establish the fact that we are also human beings and not for the mere purpose of using the water of one particular tank."[21] One of the Hindus who took part in the agitation, a Brahmin named G.N. Sahasrabuddhe conducted bonfire of Manusmriti, the scripture and the Holy Hindu Code in the evening on that X-mass-day. This act of bonfire of Manusmriti sent shock waves throughout Hindu society. Finally, in course of time the tank was opened only after the Court order.

It is clear from the circumstances and the speeches that in Maharashtra or in Bombay Presidency, the political movement of the untouchables was yet to start. During this period, Dr Ambedkar is found to have been engaged to anoint the social status of the untouchable Mahars as the Brahmins. 'Under the auspices of the '*Samaj Samata Sangh*', a society started with the object of promoting social equality, a ceremony for investing Mahars with the sacred thread was held at Damodar Thakersey Hall on March 22. Pandit Palayal Shastri performed the ceremony and about 500 Mahars were invested with the sacred thread. Dr B.R. Ambedkar, Dr M. B. Udgaosnkar, G. N. Sahasrabuddhe, D. V. Naik and Sitaram N. Shivtarkar were present on the occasion.'[22]

Advent of the Simon Commission: Its Failure

The bid to introduce the third constitutional reform by way of replacing the Government of India Act 1919 started in England. This process suddenly placed Dr Ambedkar under the limelight of Indian politics. Indeed his strong opposition along with other nationalist leaders and political parties foiled the laborious efforts of the Simon Commission to give India a new constitution. In the year 1927, Dr Ambedkar entered in the Bombay Legislative Council as a nominated Member of the British Government. Next year in 1928, in pursuance of the provisions of the Government of India Act of 1919, a Royal Commission was appointed to investigate the working of the existing Constitution i.e. the Government of India Act 1919, under the Chairmanship of Sir John Simon. A section of the Indian leaders, in particular Indian National Congress boycotted it on the pretext of inadequate representation of Indians in the Commission.

Bombay based leaders of the Untouchables, particularly of the Mahar community are found to have proceeded with close proximity to the nationalist Brahmin groups or Congress to settle communal issues in the Simon Commission. 'Eighteen Depressed Class Associations gave evidence before the Commission and placed their memorandum before it. Sixteen of them pleaded for Separate Electorate for the Depressed Classes. On October 23, 1928, the Simon Commission, the Central Committee and the Bombay Provincial Committee examined Dr Ambedkar in Poona. On behalf of the *Bahishkrit Hitakarini Sabha* Dr Ambedkar submitted a memorandum to the Simon Commission demanding Joint Electorate with the reservation of seats for the Depressed Classes.' Dr Ambedkar fundamentally differed with the Committee on the issue of separate electorate and refused to sign the report.

In his statement submitted separately on 17th May 1929, Dr Ambedkar even vehemently opposed the principle of prevailing practice of 'Separate Electorate' for India Muslims and Sikhs since 1909 and 1919 respectively. He not only tried to damage the source of 'benefit' what the Muslims and the Sikhs had been getting for the past two decades but also challenged the prudence and credibility of the British administrators and policy makers. "He observed, "It does not seem to be sufficiently known that India is not the only country where the Mohammedans are in a minority. There are other countries in which they occupy the same position. In Albania, the Mohammedans form a very large community. In Bulgaria, Greece and Rumania they form a minority and in Yugoslavia and Russia they form a large majority. Have the Mohammedan communities there insisted upon the necessity of separate communal electorates? As all students of political history are aware, the Mohammedans in these countries have managed without the benefit of Separate Electorates : nay, they have managed without definite ratio of representation assured to them. The Mohammedan case in India, therefore, overshoots the mark in my opinion and fails to carry conviction."….. "Although I am for securing special representation for certain classes, I am against their representation through Separate Electorates. Territorial Electorates and Separate Electorates are the two extremes, which must be avoided in any scheme of representation that may be devised for the introduction of democratic form of Government in this undemocratic country. The golden mean is the system of joint electorates with reserved seats. Less than that would be insufficient, more than that would defeat the ends of good Government."[23]

The statement of Dr Ambedkar on 8th May 1929 in the Simon Commission, in regard to 'joint electorate' and reserved seats sounded as the prompted version of the Hindu fanatical leaders. Had the views of Dr Ambedkar been accepted by the Simon Commission and the British Government, Gandhiji would not have required to play his unpleasant role in the 2nd Round Table Conference and thereafter. Dr Ambedkar, differing fundamentally with the Commission, during these days, instead of being the representative of his own people, the 'untouchable orphans of the world' became the tallest of the Hindu-nationalists. However, this was the strong viewpoint of many other Mahar leaders of the day. Many prominent Mahar leaders vehemently opposed and virulently attacked Dr Ambedkar when he in later days pleaded for 'Separate electorate' in the Round table Conference in 1930.[24] He declared, "For I am of the opinion that the most vital need of the day is to create among the mass of the people the sense of a common nationality." But, the Untouchable leaders of the other provinces did not see eye to eye with Dr Ambedkar. They had their caste or community interest to protect at the first and foremost. They refused to play the '*Sarvajan*' card.

In this context, it would not be out of place to mention that Dr Ambedkar in the starting point of his public life was not against the Brahmins to the extent what he is found to have become later on. Consequently, during the *Choudar* Tank *Satyagraha* Dr Ambedkar is found to have strongly opposed the suggestion of the Backward-leaders of 'Non-Brahmin Political Party', Dinkarrao Javalkar and Kesavrao Jedhe. They offered their full support to the untouchable's Mahar Talab Satyagraha on condition that "all the Brahmins should be weeded out from it".[25] Ambedkar held that their view that 'all the Brahmins were the enemies of the untouchables was erroneous.' During these days even Bal Gangadhar's son Sridharpanth (Sridhar Balbant Tilak) became friend and associate of Ambedkar in promoting social reforms on the line of social-justice. Indeed, Dr Ambedkar remained surrounded with illustrious Brahmins of Bombay in those days as has been found in the executive committee of the Bahiskrit Hitakarini Sabha. The Brahmins who helped Ambedkar were highly ill-treated by their holy-samaj; Sridhar Tilak unable to tolerate family ostracism eventually committed suicide in 1928.

Biblical Moses, son of a Jew of servile class was brought up by the Egyptian King Pharaoh and was lifted by the Lord God and he eventually had successfully liberated his people from tyrannical exploitation of the Pharaoh. Moses successfully placed them in their 'promised land'. Like Moses of the Old Testament, Dr Ambedkar was brought up by the Maharajas and lifted by the British authority. He, however, failed to liberate his people from the concentration camp of the Brahmanical tyranny. The Brahmins lifted the Sudras (representing 4 per cent of the population excluding Backward) like Narendra Nath Dutta (Vivekanand), Arobindo Ghosh, Chitta Ranjan Das, Aswni Dutta, Subhas Bose etc as their protectors to retain their over-lordship and supremacy in Bengal. Consequently, the backward Sudras remained subservient to the Brahmins and laboured to crush the untouchable leaders (representing 25 per cent population) and their movement in Bengal. In south India, in the Bombay province the backward Sudras declared war cry against the unquestionable divine and supercilious superiority of the Brahmins and posed serious threat by even launching a political party with a challenging nomenclature like, 'Non-Brahmin Political Party'. To tackle this problem the Brahmanical social order, in Bombay Province, are found to have lifted the untouchable leaders (representing 8 per cent population) to use them as the tool to protect their suzerainty. Eventually they crushed the cause of the untouchables too on national, rather pan-Indian platform.

Before the Simon Commission, the Madras Central Adi-Dravida Mahajan Sabha demanded nomination for the Depressed Classes. Interestingly enough, the Bombay Provincial Non-Brahmin Party (primarily led by Backward Castes/ Sudras) in its memorandum before the Simon Commission, recommended Separate Electorate and reserved seats for the Depressed Classes. The

Muslim League reiterated its demands for separation of Sindh, creation of a new province in the N.W.F. and Separate Electorate for the Muslims. The Sikhs reiterated their demands for continuation of Separate Electorate.

In the circumstances the untouchable-leaders of Bengal, who had been working on national platform and well experienced with political struggles and heroes of many battles of liberations at least for last half a century crossed swords in the Simon Commission for Separate Electorate. The British authority purged and kept these untouchable leaders of Bengal who represented 11.2 million untouchables of Bengal alone away from the Central committee or any other membership of the Simon Commission. They were, however, called to give their evidence before it. On January 21st 1929, Mukunda Behari Mullick appeared before the Simon Commission as the sole representative of the All Bengal Namasudra Association and the Bengal Depressed Classes Association to give evidence. They initially had submitted protracted written Memorandum to the Commission along with its supplementary from All Bengal Namasudra Association and a Memorandum from the Bengal Depressed Classes Association in 1929 separately. While deposing oral evidence before the Simon Commission, Mukunda Behari strongly pleaded that the Untouchables of Bengal were a distinct community, different from the Hindus as the Sikhs and Muslims were. Therefore, he demanded that they must be protected with the benefit of 'Separate Electorate' from the ruthless tyranny of the Hindus. The untouchables must be given democratic rights and liberty. He also pleaded for lowering the qualifications for universal adult franchise along with abolition of prevalent practice of nominated membership as those members remain grateful and subservient to the British authority who nominates.

Before the Simon Commission, Mukunda Behari deposed, 'The caste system stigmatised these classes of people as untouchables as water touched by these classes of people is not drunk by the so called higher classes. If a Depressed class man enters a room where there is water and food cooked by a high class Hindu, that water will at once become polluted. With regard to public temple, the Depressed class people are not allowed to enter into it. A case of this kind has happened recently, and the case went up to the court.' The question No. 8 was 'On page 96 of the memorandum from the Bengal Depressed Classes Association you say that the population of the Depressed classes in Bengal is eleven and a half million?- 'That is so; it will be more now. We have taken figure from the Government Census Report.', Answered he. Question No. 9. 'That forms about 58 percent of the Hindu population of Bengal? 'That is so', was the answer.

The Chairman of the Commission asked him, 'Now you say you would like to have Separate Electorates for the Depressed Classes?' 'Yes Sir', replied Mr. Mullick. Will you explain to us why? Quipped the Chairman "We see the position that we have been driven out after exercising our vote in the joint electorate with the High Caste Hindus, and but for that condition, perhaps there would have been no necessity for us to come before this Commission and put forward our grievances which we have been feeling from time immemorial. It is for that reason that we ask for a Separate Electorate, so that we might be entitled to return our own representatives, our true representatives to the Council from where we know all these may be remedied", explained Mullick.

Rao Bahadur M.C. Rajah, a member from Madras Presidency inquired, "What happened in the 1921 election? Am I right when I say that because you were in a Joint Electorate, the caste people, who predominated in a great numbers put up an ordinary illiterate cobbler to split your community, and he was returned to the council?"

"Yes, although there were many qualified candidates, these people put up an illiterate cobbler to put us to disgrace', narrated Mr. Mullick.

In reply to Lord Burham's question that "You would rather, I imagine, have a system of representation by nomination than a franchise restricted as the general franchise is now for your own castes?"

Mullick reiterated, 'We should go in for a separate electorate rather than ask for nomination." He once again confirmed to Mr. Hartshorn, 'We would not go in for nomination at all.... We expect to have seats (reserved in the Council) according to the proportion of our population.'

In answer to Sir Hari Singh Gaur's query he reaffirmed, 'Yes, that is what we have stated, "British Rule to Home Rule for India" is preferred."[26]

It was no more a barrister from Bengal, in 1928 (from June to August) Pandit Motilal Nehru drafted the *Swaraj* Constitution to be submitted in the Simon Commission. On the question of the Depressed or the Untouchable communities the Nehru report said: "In our suggestions for the constitution we have not made any special provision for the representation of the Depressed Classes in the legislatures. This could only be done by way of special elections or by nomination."[27]

The Chairman of the Commission had very carefully examined all depositions and representations before he finalised it. "At long last the report of the Simon Commission came out in May 1930. The Commission disapproved the demands and aim of Indian (Hindu) nationalism and its forces. (Including Dr Ambedkar's) It recommended continuation of Separate Electorate in Indian elections for want of any agreed pact among the Indian political parties. It was the opinion of the Commission that the Nehru report was not an agreed solution."[28]

Despite very strong opposition given by Dr Ambedkar, Congress Party, the Brahmins and Hindu nationalist forces the long drawn dream (since 1907) and a just struggle for 'Separate Electorate' for the untouchables of India finally came true in the report of the Simon commission. Consequently, a jubilant Birat Chandra Mandal greeted the report from the national conference of All India Depressed Classes Assiciation at Simla in the month of July. Mukunda Behari Mullick, at the provincial level, simultaneously 'wholeheartedly greeted the Report of the Simon Commission and condemned the proposal of joint electorate as 'positively harmful'.[29] Dr Ambedkar on the other hand had continued to organize several meetings in Bombay and opposed the report and the principle of 'separate electorate' and its execution.[30] At this juncture, all London returned Hindu nationalist forces and leaders, irrespective of their parties came to a holy alliance to press the authority of London not to accept the recommendations of the Commission. The British arranged for a review meeting.

Round Table Conference: Its Failure

On receiving the report of Simon Commission, His Majesty's Government announced that Indian representatives would assemble for a discussion before the Constitution is settled. However, when the question of getting nomination or selection/election of representatives from amongst the untouchables for protecting their political interests came, the British authority fluted all democratic values. A 'true patriot' and a 'nationalist' a supporter of '*Sarvojan*' policy, Dr Ambedkar gained tremendous mileage over everybody. He also got preference and blessings from the *Brahmins, Rajas, and Maharajas* and of the ruling classes of the country and abroad. He appeared to have been the most harmless (even as an anti-Communist) representative with moderate and Hindu-reformist attitude, especially in comparison to the veteran and drastically anti-Brahmin leaders of Bengal. The Indian ruling classes (including British) seems to have got relief in gaining a chance to side-line fire-brand Namasudra/ Chandal leaders of the grass-root-level. Dr Ambedkar, during those days represented only the Bombay-based oppressed-elite.

Dr Ambedkar's scheme of Joint Electorate for the Untouchables with reserved seats was rejected by Simon Commission. Ambedkar and his caste men Mahads of Maharashtra in public meetings condemned Simon Commission's recommendation for separate electorate. Even on 8th August 1930 there occurred the 1st Session of 'The All India Depressed Classes' Congress' at Nagpur under the president-ship of Dr B.R. Ambedkar to pass several political resolutions. Of them some were as follows:- "1. ...this Congress disassociates with the idea of independence by Indian National Congress as it was disastrous and detrimental to the interests of India... 2. In the matter of the immediate realisation of the goal of Dominion Status, this Congress has no objection.... 3.While believing in the efficacy of separate electorates this Congress is prepared to accept the principle of joint electorate and reserved seats for the representation of the Depressed Classes provided it is accompanied by the system of adult suffrage."[31] Dr Ambedkar represented only 17 lakh untouchables of Bombay province. Maximum number untouchable population hailed from Bengal and eastern India. It was followed by Bihar and Orissa and UP. Central Province contained 30 per cent of its total population with the Untouchables. The untouchable's democratic movement started in Bengal half a century back. The untouchables of Bengal were most educated and politically conscious. Despite all these, Viceroy of England invited Dr Ambedkar on 6th September 1930 to attend the Round Table Conference (RTC). He was invited to discuss and settle the issues with terms of reference of 'Separate Electorate' what he opposed vehemently till he received the invitation. During pre-RTC, Dr Ambedkar was completely against Separate Electorate. 'He wanted joint electorate but with some conditions. ... But now (in the 1st RTC) Doctor wants Separate Electorates.'[32]

From the standpoint of fairness of jurisprudence, Dr Ambedkar was the most unsuitable person (as a representative of the Untouchables) to be in the RTC to plead for the terms of reference, 'Separate Electorate' as he was fundamentally opposed to the idea of separate electorate. However, in the Round table Conference, as one of the two representatives of the Depressed Classes Dr Ambedkar showed his great eloquence and scholastic understanding of Indian society vis-a-vis to the Untouchables. Congress boycotted the round Table Conference. Dr Ambedkar too did not raise the nationalist 'sarvajan card' now. His ardent feelings, in contrast to his earlier stand in the Simon Commission, for the suffering people of the Untouchable communities came out like the volcanic eruption of lava with belching smoke and fire in his maiden speech at the 'Plenary Session' on 20th November 1930. He began, "Mr. Chairman,..... It is a point of view of 4,30,00000 people, or one fifth of the total population of British India. The Depressed Classes form a group by themselves which is distinct and separate from Muhammadans and, although they are included in the Hindus, they in no sense form an integral part of that community. Not only have they a separate existence, but they have also assigned to them a status which is invidiously distinct from the status occupied by any other community in India..... What is worse is that this enforced servility and bar to human intercourse, due to their untouchability, involves, not merely the possibility of discrimination in public life, but actually works out as a positive denial of all equality of opportunity and the denial of those most elementary civic rights on which all human existence depends.

It is this that the bureaucratic form of Government in India should be replaced by a Government which will be a Government of the people by the people and for the people..... The Depressed Classes welcomed the British as their deliverers from the age old tyranny and oppression by the orthodox Hindus. They fought their battles against the Hindus, the Mussalmans and the Sikhs and won for them this great empire of India. The British on their side assumed the role of the trustees for the Depressed Classes...... When we compare our present position with that one which it was our lot to bear in Indian society of the pre-British days, we find that, instead of marching on, we are only marking time. Before the British we were in loathsome condition due to untouchability. Has the British Government done anything to remove it? Before the British we could not enter the temple. Can we enter now? Before the British we were denied entry in the Police Force. Does the British Government admit us in the force? Before the British we were not allowed to serve in the Military......

.....The depressed classes find that the British Government in India suffers from two very serious limitations. There is first of all an internal limitation which arises from the character, motives and interests of those who are in power. It is not because that they cannot help us in these things but because it is against their character, motives and interests to do so. The second consideration that limits its authority is the mortal fear it has of external resistance..... it is afraid that its intervention to amend the existing code of social and economic life, will give rise to resistance..... This role the British Government will never be able to play. It is only a Government which is of the people, for the people and by the people that will make this possible.

The Muhammadans refuse to recognize their separate existence, because they fear that their privileges may be curtailed by admission of a rival. Depressed by the Government, suppressed by the Hindu and disregarded by the Muslim, we are left in a most intolerable position of utter helplessness."[33]

In the 2nd sitting of the Minorities Committee on 31st December 1930 Dr Ambedkar left no stone unturned to make his distinct stand in it. "My first submission to this Committee, then, is that it should realize that although to use an illustration, the minorities are all in the same boat, yet the most important fact to remember is that they are not all in the same class in the same boat. Some are travelling in 'A' Class, some are travelling in 'B' Class and some in 'C' Class and so on. I have not the slightest doubt in my mind that the Depressed Classes, though they are a minority and are to the extent in the same boat as other minorities, are not even in 'C' or 'D' Class but are actually in the hold."[34] Finally, in the memorandum, he submitted a detail demand. As one of the conditions, in No. IV, he placed, "(1) Right to adequate representation in the Legislatures of the country, provincial and central. (2) right to elect their own representatives, (a) by adult suffrage, and

(b) by separate electorates for the first ten years and there after joint electorates and reserved seats, it being understood that joint electorates shall not be forced upon the Depressed Classes against their will unless such joint electorates are accompanied by adult suffrage."[35]

The Round Table Conference created a sub-Committee to decide the questions of all minorities in combine. Dr Ambedkar's initial batting for the cause of 'Separate Electorate' for the Untouchables was outstanding and remarkable. He proved his selection by the British authority in the RTC to be the most worthy. Eventually, however, Dr Ambedkar did not maintain the fury and distinct position of the Untouchables as a community. What Dr Ambedkar did in the 1st RTC in regard to the separate electorate for the untouchables, where the 'Congress representatives abstained from' by seeing eye to the eye with the other members of the 'Minority Community, according to an eminent Buddhist monk and biographer of Ambedkar appeared to have been simply an act of convenience not of conviction.[36]

Further, no body raised a question in regard to the proper and adequate representation in the RTC from the vast population of Untouchables at this appropriate stage. Nobody even noted or demanded for elected representatives from amongst the untouchables in the RTC. The authorities or the ruling classes of Great Britain who boast of parliamentary democracy robbed the untouchables of their democratic rights to choose or to elect proportionate and true representative for a 'class which deserved to be given special political rights in order to protect itself against the tyranny of the majority under the *Swaraj* constitution'.[37] They were not allowed to elect or nominate their representatives who had the will and natural inclination to argue in favour of the terms of reference placed before the Round Table Conference. Instead of inviting one who had past-history of fighting for the cause, the ruling class invited one who gave a stubborn fight against it.

Having been deprived of his rightful place in the Round Table Conference, Mukunda Behari Mullick, the unchallenged leader of at least 11.5 million untouchables of eastern India (Bengal alone) was consoled with a thing that he objected just in the previous year. The British nominated him as a Member in the Bengal Legislative Council in 1930. The beggars were not the choosers. Mullick accepted the offer.

On 12th of November 1930, His Majesty King George V, formally inaugurated the Indian Round Table Conference in London. No leader from Bengal, who had been struggling for at least past four decades for separate electorate with exceptional political sagacity and with uncompromising spirit for the servile classes was invited in the RTC. Only two untouchable delegates were nominated by the British, Dr B.R. Ambedkar from Bombay Presidency and Dewan Bahadur Srinivasan from Madras Presidency.

Leadership focus was completely shifted from East to the West by the arbitrary will of the ruling classes. It was neither democratic nor realistic. It did not reflect the choice of the Indian Untouchables. Bengal leaders found themselves stranded in the evidence Hall of the Simon Commission just as deposers. Rao Bahadur M.C. Raja, BA, MLC (1922) (from Madras) came to Calcutta as a member of the Central Committee of the Simon Commission to take deposition of the untouchable leader like Mukunda Behari Mullicks of Bengal. The veteran leader from Madras province, Raobahadur M.C. Raja who earned his glowing fame as a staunch fighter against the ideal of Hindu Nationalism and an absolute supporter of Separate Electorate too fell from the grace of the colonial Masters. He got no room in the Round Table Conference.

With the advent of Dr Ambedkar straight on the national platform from Bombay region, the Untouchable-movement seems to have been alienated from the new-found friends in the Muslim-community as a result of Ambedkar's anti 'Separate Electorate' stand in the Simon Commission. The separate electorate was a calculated mode to exclude the Muslims and the Sikhs politically from the Untouchable voters especially in the Punjab and Bengal in pre-poll alliance. Now it started expanding its pangs of antagonism towards the untouchables in social plain too. The Muslims and the Sikhs were made to consider that the 'separate electorate' beneficial for them has been opposed by the untouchable leader Ambedkar. The Untouchables' movement got alienated from the non-Brahmin Backward classes' movements in Madras and in Bombay provinces as a result of Ambedkar's decline to 'weed out' the Brahmins from the *Mahar Satyagraha*, as was proposed by the militant non-Brahmin Party youth leaders. Ambedkar never spoke in favour of the Tribes of India who formed not less than 10 per cent of the total population. It became alienated from the strong-holds of *Dalit-bahujan* movements especially in the Punjab and Bengal. Finally, it became a movement that got oriented around the pivot of oppressed-elites in western and in south India. It failed to become a movement from the grass-root level as it was in Bengal. Ambedkar's movement started from the branches of the tree and within a few years, it transformed into a tale, edited by the Congress Party politics.

Dr Ambedkar was yet to involve or associate him with the on-going untouchable-movement at the national level. He by the time did not get any opportunity to visit any of the states of north India like Bengal, Bihar, UP, Orissa, Assam or the Punjab where the untouchable movement started and where the major chunk of the untouchables resided. He, however, maintained very close relation with the top brass of the rulers of British India. And it was the British who adopted and declared him as the sole representative of Indian untouchables in the constitution making process.

Indeed, Dr Ambedkar's approach from the socio-political and demographic stand point that prevailed in the Bombay Province was considerably pragmatic. The table of Relative strength of caste Hindu voters and scheduled caste voters in the 15 constituencies in which seats were reserved for Scheduled Castes in Bombay Province (by the Poona Pact) during election of 1937 reveals, 'how the scheduled caste, voters were vastly outnumbered by the Caste Hindu voters and how impossible it is for the scheduled caste voters to win the reserved seats in the joint electorate by dint of their voting strength, even if every one of the SC voters were to come to poll.'[37A] The total number of untouchable population whom he represented in the province was less than 8 per cent or 18 lakhs only. Out of these 1.8 million population Mahars were simply 34 per cent. Mangs and Chamars, two other untouchable communities in Bombay Province were not treated well by the Mahars and they remained divided in different political camps. In general and traditionally, these two communities supported Congress. The Muslim population was about 9 per cent or 19 lakhs only. The Hindus composed 82 per cent of the Province's population. With this poor strength of population, the fractured society of the untouchables could do a little or nothing independently, under the scheme of separate electorate in the Bombay province. As per separate electorate, they were to get only 12 or 14 seats reserved (according to the proportion of their population) in the legislature of 175 seats. In such circumstances, pragmatic mind of Ambedkar had no option but to prefer for Joint electorate with the Hindus as a Hindu. This was the stand of most of the Mahars, Mangs and Chamars. They were dependent on the immense majority Hindus. However, such pragmatism from the national stand point of the Untouchable's freedom movement was seriously harmfull. In Bombay too there prevailed a bright prospect for the Untouchabls to forge social and political alliance with the powerful Non-Brahmin shudras who in the Simon Commission demanded separate electorate.

Yet, standing in the midst of all the Minority groups in the Round Table Conference Dr Ambedkar, as the representative of the Untouchables, submitted his view points before the Minorities Committee. These were "....(2) Right to elect their own men as their representatives, (a) by adult suffrage, and (b) by separate electorates for the first ten years and thereafter by joint electorates and reserved seats, it being understood that joint electorates shall not be forced upon the Depressed Classes against their will..." The Minorities Committee was to examine the view points of each of the minority groups at the first instance.

The Minorities Committee in course of time after considering the view points and political demands of all the minority groups resolved, "(5) claims were therefore advanced by various Committees that arrangement should be made for Communal representation and for fixed proportions of seats. It was also urged that the number of seats reserved for a minority community should in no case be less than its proportion in the population. The methods by which this could be secured were mainly three: (i) nomination, (ii) electorate (iii) separate electorate." These resolution though a bolt from the blue for the Hindus it was placed before the Round Table Conference and was passed unanimously before the RTC was closed. The golden dream of the Hindus to create a Hindu India was shattered as their 'divine Slaves' were green signaled for political-freedom as a distinctly separate community as Sikh, Islam or Christianity.

When once again the recommendation of the Simon Commission for Separate Electorate for the Untouchables was virtually ratified by the London Round Table Conference, the Hindu Nationalists rose to the task to be equal to the situation and made the decision of the RTC also a failure. They managed to hold another round table conference famous as the 2nd Round Table Conference.

The decision in regard to the communal question in the Round Table Conference was also not acceptable by the same power-lobby of the Hindus. They were determined not to free the 'divine slave' of Hinduism for the cause of democracy. Despite their resistance through civil disobedience movement the British authority had to go in a democratic way to accept the recommendation that came out of their method. The third constitutional Act was to be passed. In the circumstances, Congress and all other forces made a truce with the British authority by withdrawing 'Civil Disobedience Movement' and assured to attend the extended round Table Conference. The British Government arranged the 2nd Round Table Conference. The issue of Separate Electorate was discussed afresh.

The Second Round Table Conference: Its Failure

It is interesting to note here that when initially Dr Ambedkar struggled for 'Joint Electorate' for the Scheduled castes with some reserved seats in the Simon Commission there was no uproar or protest. But when in the 1st and 2nd Round Table Conferences Dr Ambedkar raised a stubborn support for the 'Separate Electorate' along with the untouchables of other provinces and minority groups, there arose storming brouhaha in Bombay presidency. Different groups of Mahars in large number under several leaders like Gavai, Baloo and M.C. Raja organised large public meetings at different places. They condemned Dr Ambedkar and his new stand for 'Separate Electorate'. They preferred to remain with the Hindus and as the Hindus' Divine-slaves demanded joint electorate. With the support of the Indian ruling castes and the Congress these leaders even created 'All India Depressed Classes Association' of which Gavai was the General Secretary to oppose Dr Ambedkar's move and the 'Communal Award' declared by the British

Government granting separate electorate and double votes for the Untouchables. This protest cry continued until Dr Ambedkar signed the Poona Pact by disregarding all other minorities who had initially drafted the 'Award' and the Untouchable organisations of all other provinces.

With a view to opposing this anti-Untouchable move, the Untouchables of Nagpur raised an organisation called All India Depressed Classes Congress. They held a huge meeting in the month of May 7, 1932 at Kamptee, a few kilometers away from Nagpur city. Despite the place was the strong hold of the Hindoos and of Dr Moonje their leader, more than 15000 Untouchables actively participated to support Dr Ambedkar. 'In order to have a complete picture of the situation, it may be recalled here that immediately after the announcement of Raja-Moonge Pact (for Joint Electorate as part of the Hindus) in one of his letter to Gavai of All India Depressed Classes Association, Dr Ambedkar had, under great provocation given him a threat of "breach between us and war amongst ourselves" if the organisation advocated the system of joint electorates and reserved seats.'[38] In the Kamptee Congress, the Untouchables condemned Raja Moonje Pact. 'Hardas LN, the Chairman emphasizing the need for unity among the Depressed Classes, remarked: with separate electorate we will swim or sink." Dr Ambedkar spoke, "It is very necessary that the political reins should come in the hands of the Untouchables."[39] Alas! eventually Dr Ambedkar left his stand and went with Gandhiji within a few months.

Dr Ambedkar Declines the Call to Surrender

The Indian National Congress boycotted the First Round Table Conference. Muhammad Ali Jinnah, H.H. the Aga Khan, Fazlul Huq and Dr Ambedkar along with Raobahadur M. Srinivasan arrived in London to represent the Muslims and the Untouchables respectively. Soon Srinivasan went into oblivion due to withdrawal of official focus. Muslims and Sikhs demanded continuation of 'Separate Electorate'. They supported the same prescription for the Untouchables. It has already been discussed that Aga Khan Brothers and other Muslim leaders had pleaded during the 1st decade of the 20th century that the animists and the Untouchables were not Hindus. The 1st RTC thus had given recognition to the most vulnerable and weak section of Indians, the untouchables as distinct and separate from the Hindus along with the Muslims and Sikhs with political rights.

Soon after, while in India, Dr Ambedkar was politely and tactfully summoned by Mahatma Gandhi at his residence Manibhuban at the Malaber Hill, Bombay. "Dr Mr. Ambedkar, I would come to see you tonight at 8 p.m. if you can spare that time. I would gladly come over to your place if it is inconvenient for you to come." Yours Sincerely M. K. Gandhi, Bombay, 6-8-31"[40] On 14th of August, instead, Dr Ambedkar went to see Gandhiji at Manibhuban.

In the mean time, however, on March 5, 1931, at Delhi, after a day of protracted negotiation, Gandhiji made a pact with the Viceroy Lord Irwin for abandoning Civil Disobedience Movement, which was started fundamentally against holding of the First Round Table Conference, promising to attend the 2nd Round Table Conference. The purpose of calling Ambedkar seems to have been to take his consent to surrender the baton in Gandhiji's hand. At Monibhuban, Gandhiji tried to hijack and assimilate Dr Ambedkar's leadership. He proposed, "I am against the political separation of the Untouchables from the Hindus. That would be absolutely suicidal."[41] Dr Ambedkar had thanked Gandhi for this frank opinion and left the hall with disgust. Though Dr Ambedkar initiated the discussion with the salutation, '*Mahatmaji*' he failed to maintain the same at the end of the dialogue.

Though the Congress boycotted the First Round Table Conference, in a meeting at Madras, Jawaharlal Nehru clarified that 'Congress men had never banned the delegates to the Round Table Conference as traitors. What they had said was that they were not people's representatives.' On 7th September 1931 when the 2nd session of RTC started Gandhiji in his maiden speech claimed that he was the sole representative of the Indian National Congress which was the body of the women, Princely Estates, Landlords, Depressed Classes and other people of the country and hence the sole representative of the Indian nation. On the next day, he especially attacked the untouchable leaders that 'the Round Table Conference delegates were not the chosen ones of the nation, but chosen ones of the British Government.' Eventually it was Gandhiji who raised objection against this undemocratic method of pick and choose. On October 8, 1931, Dr Ambedkar clarified his position in this regard. "What disturbs me, after hearing Gandhi, is that instead of confining himself to his proposition, namely, that Minorities, Committee should be adjourned sine die, he started casting reflections upon the representatives of different communities who are sitting around this table. He said that delegates were the nominees of the Government, and that they did not represent the views of their respective communities for whom they stood. We cannot deny the allegation that we are nominees of the Government, but, speaking of myself, I have not the slightest doubt that even if Depressed Classes of India were given the chance of electing their representatives to this Conference, I would, all the same, find place here." Even Netaji Subash Bose raised the issue and condemned the delegates. However, no Subhas was there to criticize initially the non-representative character of untouchable members due to elimination of pioneers like Guruchand, Mukunda Behari Mullick or Birat Chandra Mandal. And when the challenge really came, it was found that Dr Ambedkar miserably failed to get him elected in the Constituent Assembly from his home turf. Without the organisational strength of the untouchables of Bengal and sacrifice of their candidature. Ambedkar was unable to return in the Constituent Assembly. He was a Congress nominee in his second term in the Constituent Assembly. His own people were unable to elect him.

In the Second RT Conference in 1931 Dr Ambedkar assessed, "unfortunately, the Congress chose Mr. Gandhi as its representative. A worse person could not have been chosen to guide India's destiny. As a unifying force, he was a failure.... From the point of view of knowledge, Mr. Gandhi proved himself to be a very ill-equipped person."[42] Dr Ambedkar with his articulated ferocity waged a war against the enigmatic Hindu leader Gandhiji on the Communal question. Dr Ambedkar remained ever-alert to foil all the tricks, mischief and intrigue that Gandhiji tried to resort in collusion with the representatives of Muslims or the Sikhs for whom the 'Separate Electorate' was never disputed. "Mr. Gandhi was making his plans to bypass the Untouchables and to close the communal problem by bringing about a settlement between three parties, the Hindus, the Muslims and the Sikhs. He had been carrying on negotiation privately with the Muslims before the Minorities Committee met, but evidently they had not been concluded".

When Gandhiji tried to jeopardize the entire proceeding of the conference, the Prime Minister concluded, "I appeal to the Delegates here today Delegates representing all communities Do not stand in our way; because that is what is happening." Muslims on the contrary came to rescue the entire matter including the Untouchables. On 13th November 1931, His Highness Aga Khan rose to submit the 'Minority's pact'. He declared, "Mr. Prime Minister, on behalf of the Muhammadans, Depressed classes, the Anglo-Indians, the Europeans and a considerable section of the Indian Christian groups, I present the document...." The Hindus and Congress got isolated on the question of Separate Electorate. Gandhi became furious. He attacked everybody and finally declared, "I was the only person to resist this thing and I would resist it with my life."[43]

Gandhiji opposing the proposal of political right or liberty of the untouchables from the bondage of Hindus by way of 'Separate electorate' declared, "I would not sell the vital interest of the Untouchables even for the sake of winning the freedom of India... "I will not bargain away their rights for the kingdom of the whole world..... I do not mind Untouchables, if they so desire being converted to Islam or Christianity, I should tolerate that, but I cannot possibly tolerate what is stored for Hinduism if there are two divisions set forth in the villages."[44] Gandhiji seems to have ignored the village situation where the untouchables were not allowed to live in the villages; in case allowed they were forced to live secluded and as bonded labour. Co-existence of the untouchables and the Hindus in a village was a Utopian concept. They were never acceptable even as domestic creatures by the Hindus, therefore; the question of unity with the untouchables on equal or democratic footing was redundant. In the Hindu nation that stands without nationality the untouchables have only exclusive position of servitude. The untouchables live in the 'ghettos'. Thus, the claims of Gandhi were quite baseless. The act of Gandhiji's giving recognition to Separate Electorate for the Muslims and the Sikhs and to refuse it to the Untouchables who needed the same acutely in the circumstances came to the whole world as a surprise. With the command over language and various social-subjects of law and jurisprudence, the articulated ferocity of Dr Ambedkar had proved Gandhiji a dwarf and he won the battle-royal.

In the circumstances, when the Indian communities failed to come to agreed terms the British authority was forced to take decision as they were running short of time for transferring power in the hands of the Indian representatives. In London, on 4th August 1932, the 'Communal Award' consisting of only 23 Para was issued. At the outset, in the Para 1 it recorded the fact. "In the statement made by the Prime Minister on 1st December last on behalf of His Majesty's Government at the close of the 2nd session of the Round Table Conference, which was immediately afterwards endorsed by both Houses of Parliament, it was made plain that if the communities in India were unable to reach a settlement acceptable to all parties on the communal question which the Conference had failed to solve, His Majesty's Government were determined that India's constitutional advance should not on that account be frustrated, and that they would remove this obstacle by devising and applying themselves a provisional scheme." Para 2 further made a mention, "On the 19th March last His Majesty's Government, having been informed that the continued failure of the communities to reach agreement was blocking the progress of the plan for the framing of a new constitution, stated that they were engaged upon a careful reexamination of the difficult and controversial questions which arise. They are now satisfied that without a decision of at least some aspects of the problem connected with the position of minorities under the new constitution, no further progress can be made with the framing of the constitution, Para 6 of the Award gave Muslims and Sikhs voting right on communal basis. "Election to the seats allotted to the Muhammadan, European and Sikh constituencies will be by voters voting in separate electorates covering between them the whole area of the Province." Untouchables were given special right as general. Para 7 held, "All qualified electors, who are not voters either in a Muhammadan, Sikh, Indian Christian, Anglo-Indian or European constituency, will be entitled to vote in a general constituency." For Bengal, special mention was made by recognizing the numerical strength of the Untouchables of Bengal in Para 9 of the Award. "In Bengal it seems possible that in some general constituencies a majority of the voters will belong to the Depressed Classes. Accordingly, pending further investigation, no number has been fixed for the members to be returned from the special depressed class constituencies in that Province. It is intended to secure that the Depressed Classes should obtain not less than 10 seats in the Bengal Legislator."

On 17th August, 1932 the British Prime Minister declared the 'Communal Award' in which the right to Separate Electorate with double voting right were sanctioned for the Untouchables. The Award declared that the Electoral College for the candidates contesting against the reserved seats for the Scheduled Castes would be composed of the Untouchable voters only. Besides, the untouchable voters (as the member of the Hindu community) will be voting for the Hindu candidates contesting from the general seats. Thus, it was no more a communal award as it was for the Muslims. The Untouchables not only became free from the control of the Brahmins in election but they also became masters of the Brahmins who remained dependent on the votes of the Untouchables. The Muslims, Sikhs, Indian Christians also retained their separate electorate. In the circumstances, the electoral college of the Hindus was to be composed of the Brahmin, Kshatryas, Vaisyas and the Backward Sudras only. As a result, in most of the major provinces they reduced to minority. Therefore, there was no way for the creamy-layer ruling class but to oppose and nullify the Award for the Untouchables.

Gandhiji, on the basis of the proceedings, the solidarity of the minorities on communal question and observing the mood of the 2nd Round Table Conference apprehended his defeat. However, the Hindus were surely to repeal anything to come on their way. Instead of wasting time, therefore, Gandhiji did not cease his tirade after the 2nd RTC. He initiated another innings of battle after coming back from the London RTC. 'Mr. Gandhi on March 1932 addressed from Yarvada-jail, Poone a letter to Sir Samuel Hoare, the then Secretary of State for India' to oppose the claims of the Untouchables. He wrote, "Dear Sir Samuel, You will perhaps recollect that at the end of my speech at the Round Table Conference when the Minority's claim was presented I had said that I should resist with my life the grant of separate electorates to the Depressed Classes. This was not said in the heat of the moment nor by way of rhetoric. It was meant to be a serious statement...... I am not against their representation in the legislatures. I should favour every one of their adults, male and female, being registered as voters irrespective of education or property qualification, even though franchise test may be stricter for others..... So far as Hinduism is concerned, separate electorates would simply vivisect and disrupt it.... For me the question of these classes is predominantly moral and religious. The political aspect, important though it is, dwindles into insignificance compared to the moral and religious issue."[45]

Gandhiji the Hindu leader, a staunch follower of Gita, knew well that even in democracy the reign or the rule and leadership of the entire nation will be in the hands of the Brahmins only if the Untouchables remain as the integral part of the Hinduism. As Hindus, they are instantly to accept the '*Varna-Srestha*' Brahmins as their natural rulers. Being instructed by their spiritual Gurus, they will use their franchise right in behalf of the Hindu leaders only. In the ongoing practice of joint electorate, after officially being re-Hinduised, as Scheduled Castes, even with their voting rights the Untouchables will remain completely disenfranchised.

Gandhiji was ready to become profusely generous to the Untouchables provided they (one fourth of the population of the country) remained subservient for eternity as 'Divine Slaves' in the Concentration Camp of the Hinduism. Caste does not unite, it divides. Hatred is not an associative attitude, it disassociates. Gandhiji knew it exceedingly well. Yet he sang the song of unity to deceive all. The Hindu-society or the caste-society, as has already been discussed, a constitutionally fragmented, spiritually graded, structurally separated and culturally decomposed society bonded only with the glue of tyrannical atrocities. Indeed, Gandhiji, attempted to keep it united as such by using threats of fasting-tyranny.

Gandhiji obviously wanted to keep this band of poor and illiterate untouchables simply to augment the number of Hindu-ballots in Parliamentary democracy. Therefore, he wanted to impress upon the British Government that the untouchables and human beings were for the religion, religion called Hinduism was not for the Untouchables or for men. Nevertheless, it is difficult to comprehend as to why even a single member of the 'Orphans of the World' loved so much to be proud to be an untouchable Hindu? Gandhiji in course of the proceedings of the Round Table Conference gave a clear option that he would not mind in case the Untouchables convert to Islam or Christianity. Still the Untouchables under the leadership of Ambedkar preferred to remain under the scourge of hatred of Hinduism.

'After giving this threat, Mr. Gandhi slept over the matter thinking that a repetition of his threat to fast into death was sufficient to paralyze the British Government and prevent them from accepting the claim of the Untouchables for special representation,' recorded Dr Ambedkar. The Award of 17th August 1932 is found to have been the 'First Charter of Indian Liberty' the Magna Carta of Indian Dalits. They were free to elect and send their real representatives. This double-edged sword of Separate-electorate crowned the Indian untouchables with the laurel of total-freedom.

M.K. Gandhi without loss of time on 18th instant wrote to the Prime Minister J. Ramsay MacDonald reiterating his threat in clear terms and condition in further details. However, Gandhiji addressed the colonial Master as "Dear Friend".[46] He recorded, ".. ....I have to resist your decision with my life. The only way I can do so is by declaring a perpetual fast unto death from food of any kind save water with or without salt. This fast will cease if during its progress the British Government, of its own motion or under pressure of public opinion, revise their decision and withdraw their scheme of communal electorates for the Depressed Classes, whose representatives should be elected by the general electorate under the common franchise, no matter how wide it is.

The proposal of fast will come into operation in the ordinary course from the noon of 20th September next....."

But the British P.M. remained unfased. From 10, Downing Street, the PM wrote back on September 8th, 1932 rejecting Gandhi's appeal in his lengthy letter with speaking detail. Not only the PM rejected Gandhi but he also had condemned him in strong words with the serious allegation that Gandhi was an anti-Untouchables. In the words of MacDonald, "Dear Mr. Gandhi,"[47]...."As I understand your attitude, you propose to adopt the extreme course of striving yourself to death not in order to secure that the Depressed Classes should have joint electorate with other Hindus, because that is already provided, but solely to prevent the Depressed Classes, who admittedly suffer from terrible disabilities today, from being able to secure a limited number of representatives of their own choosing to speak on their behalf in the Legislatures which will have dominating influence over their future.

In the light of these very fair and cautious proposals, I am quite unable to understand the reason of the decision you have taken, and can only think you have made it under a misapprehension of the actual facts.

In response to a very general request from Indians after they had failed to produce a settlement themselves the Government much against its will, under took to give a decision on the minority's question. They have now given it, and they cannot be expected to alter it except on the condition they have stated. I am afraid, therefore, that my answer to you must be that the Government's decision stands and that only agreement of the communities themselves can substitute other electoral arrangements for those the Government have devised in a sincere Endeavour to weigh the conflicting claims on their just merits."

Gandhiji once again from the Yervada Central Prison, on 9th September wrote back to the British Primer reiterating his stand, "...In establishment of separate electorate at all for the Depressed Classes I sense the injection of poison that is calculated to destroy Hinduism and do no good whatever to the Depressed classes."

Gandhi seems to have reiterated the moral of the Ramayana story of Killing of Sambuk, the native Indian great sage. With the rise of the Sudras, a Brahmin-boy died prematurely and with the chopping off the head of Sudra-Sambuk the dead body instantly got his life back. An example of reciprocal correlation between the servile castes and the Brahmins had been illustrated in the spiritual epic called Ramayana. With the rise or freedom of the untouchables, as Gandhiji considered, Hinduism is poisoned to death and by keeping them in perpetual servitude Hinduism shines to life. What is the secret or causal connection behind Gandhi's proposition that with the departure of these wretched untouchable and worthless creatures from the Hindu-court, instead of getting it cleaned up (being free from the unclean people who have been the source of all pollution) Hinduism will die of a slow death? Even if it is true, that due to the presence of wretched untouchable creatures Hinduism shines with the warmth of purity and holiness, why should the Untouchables bear the burden of keeping the Hinduism alive at the cost of their detriment and freedom?

Gandhi and his National Congress obviously made religion and politics a single whole. The Congress decisively shook off the secular-plank and political purity and bravely stood firm for Hinduism. This was anti-National and anti-democratic; not only anti-human or anti-untouchables of India. They wiped out the Karachi decision of 1931 Congress session that it regarded strict neutrality in matters of religions. Gandhiji and Congress in this regard defeated the *Hindu Mahasabha* resolutions quietly.

Census Department: Operation Eliminate Untouchables

In the democratic forum, number was to play the most vital and decisive role to fix and determine as to who will govern the instrumentalities of the Republican state. It was the majority to rule. Therefore, the voice of the Bengal's untouchables became unmanageably louder due to their numerical strength. The Hindu prophet Swami Vivekananda realised this phenomenon long back and wanted to augment Hindu population by re-converting the proselyte Muslims and Christians to Hindu fold. This was a cumbersome process started by the 'Arya Samaj' of Swami Dayananda Saraswati as fixing of caste status of the reconverts posed a serious and derogatory situation. "Certainly", said the Swami, "they can and ought to be taken." He sat gravely for a moment, thinking, and then revealed. "Besides, he said, "We shall otherwise decrease the number. When the Muhamedan first came, we are said I think on the authority,.... to have been 600 million Hindus. Now we are about 200 millions. And then every man going out of the Hindu pale is not only a man less, but an enemy the more."[48]

The creamy-layer elite ruling-class, therefore, seems to have started a calculated move to eliminate the untouchables through official machinery called Census Operation. The Census Department was used by the Hindu bureaucrats as the agent of the Hindu god to create and recreate caste, creed, class, tribes and its size for their benefit by manipulating the demography.

All possible means were adopted to reduce untouchable population of Bengal, Bihar and Orissa; the Punjab, Central Province and UP. One researcher comments on the issue, "That they (Namasudras) are more prolific than many other people has been clearly proved by the fact that their growth rate (Decennial) during 1872-1921 was higher than the average growth rate obtaining in the country during the same period. Following this pattern, we may reasonably infer that the growth rate of the Namasudras during the period 1921-1931 also was slightly higher than the average growth rate obtaining in the country as a whole. We have already seen that the average rate of growth of Indian population during the period 1921-31 was 11 per cent only. For the Namasudras we can reasonably fix this rate a little higher at 12 per cent. Calculating increase in the population of the Namasudras at this rate we arrive at the figure 22,71,360 which was roughly the Namasudra population in Bengal in 1931. The Census figure falls short of this figure by 1,77,360. It appears that the population of the Namasudras of Bengal was manipulated to this extent in the Census of 1931."[49] In the contemporary period of Bengal's history there occurred no incident that the Namasudras were divested or their women got sterile. The author also records, "Mr. J. Dutta Gupta, Superintendent of Census Operation, West Bengal and Sikkim, 1961 in his Census of India 1961, Vol. XVI, Part V A (2) writes, It was for the first time in 1931 that a definite return of 'nil' was accepted for caste as distinct from the individuals who on account of ignorance or accident failed to state any caste at all. These returns of 'caste nil' totaled 18, 83, 464 for India, 98 percent of which came from Bengal."[50] The number of the untouchables 'is urged to be taken with due caution for the simple reason that the census enumerators, who by and large, were drafted from the *bhadralok* class prejudices and predilections. It is historically correct to assert that their scruples did not permit them, in the given socio-cultural ambience, to visit the Chandal quarters for the sake of correct enumeration and report.'[51] One without experience of caste cruelty may refuse to accept such a point valid. Let us not forget that the Nobel laureate poet Tagore had even confessed, "*Gechi Ami Oparar Pranganer Dhare; Bhitare Prabesh Kari Se Shakti Chilona Akebare*… I had gone up to the vicinity of that locality. But I had no capacity to enter inside…."[52] With a view to avoiding obvious proximity of the untouchables, without entering inside the locality, the enumerators completed Census operation.

Even in the Census Report of 2001 such people who fail to call their exact caste name are shown separately under a new term 'Generic', not as SC or ST (Scheduled Castes and Scheduled Tribe). Their number goes beyond 1.8 millions. In reality, most of them belong to the SC and ST group. Absence of proper education, lack of social and political consciousness, fear for atrocities and ostracism make the untouchables avoid to disclose their caste status. Apart from this, the Census 2001 eliminates the population of the SC/ST, through a peculiar official method. A modality has been developed in the Census Office since 1971 Census that no migrant citizen whose caste is not recognised in the list of the SCs and STs maintained by the respective states is to be recognised or enumerated as SC or ST. Consequently, there is no ST enumerated, even though thousands of STs have been working in Delhi region. So also, SCs from other provinces working in Delhi are not enumerated as SC. During 2001 Census, the Census Commissioner, Jayanta Kumar Banchia is learnt to have paid a visit to the *Rashtrapati Bhavan* to enumerate the family of the Rashrtapati, Dr K.R. Narayan. The President of India is said to have claimed for himself to be enumerated as a member of the SC community, a '*Paravan*' by caste in Kerala. But, the 1st citizen of India too was not counted as a member of SC as the Paravan caste does not figure in the Delhi State list. He has been shown as a general. In the enumeration of 2001, a high figure of 27.2 per cent of the total population is recorded as migrant citizens. And almost 90 per cent of this migrant working-force belongs to the SC and ST. These huge populations have been eliminated from the surface of India in the official records in so far as their caste status is concerned. As one Muslim citizen is enumerated as a Muslim wherever he resides, similarly while counting the national figure of the SCs and STs they should have been counted as such. They do not cease to be SC or ST according to the Hindu religion and society. In each decade, their growth rate thus declines, and as such, they become an endangered species to be protected with special care. In the representative form of Parliamentary democracy, thus they are not allowed to claim their prorate based privileges.

Dr Ambedkar discussed this issue of erroneous census operation, as post-mortem operation, in his book. He did not take appropriate action to redress the problem on time. "To the question what is the population of the untouchables the replies received were enough to stagger anybody. Witness after witness came forward to say that the untouchables in his province were infinitesimally small. There were not wanting witnesses who said that there were no untouchables at all! It was a most extraordinary sight to see Hindu witness perjuring themselves regardless of truth by denying the existence of untouchables or by reducing their number to a negligible figure. The members of the Provincial Franchise Committee were also a party to this plan. It is strange to say that some of the Hindu members of the Lothian Committee were in the game. This move of denying the very existence of the untouchables or reducing their number almost nil was particularly rampant in certain provinces. How the Hindus were prepared to the economies truth, even to a vanishing point, will be evident from the following figures. In the United Provinces, the Census commissioner in 1931 had estimated the total population of the Untouchables at 12.6 millions, the Provincial Government at 6.8 millions but the Provincial Franchisee Committee at .6 millions only!! In Bengal, the census gave the figures of 10.3 million; Provincial Government fixed it as 11.2 millions but the Provincial Franchise Committee at .07 millions!"[53] Ambedkar, however, did not raise any objection on the issue or demand the right to proportional representation of the Bengali leaders in the Legislature or for the allotment of seats against the correct number of Bengal Untouchables.

Not only Dr Ambedkar but many other leaders of the contemporary period also recorded this manipulation of Census figure on Government deeds as and when it appeared inconvenient only for own interest and as such yielded no tangible result. In the 'Report Of Muslim Members' dated 28th July 1947, Justice A.S.M. Akram and Justice S.A. Rahaman recorded, "The population figures for any unit of division can only be taken from the census report of 1941. All the parties have cast doubt on the accuracy of the census figures, but there is no alternative to the acceptance of those figures as a working basis in the present case."[54]

All sectors and groups seem to have been in a holy alliance to defeat the growing strength of Untouchables in the eastern sector by all possible means. It eventually paralysed, disenfranchised or eliminated Untouchables of Bengal on the national platform. The Untouchables of Bengal, Bihar and Orissa failed to demand their due share in democratic forum and cast their votes to elect their representatives. Even the history of the democratic movement by the Untouchable leaders of these days in the eastern sector of India and thereby on national platform have totally been suppressed by all official documents and records so far available.

Indeed, this confusion and manipulation in the figure of the Untouchables, Muslims, Tribals etc in the Official Census had started since long. Muslims in the state of J&K even did not allow census operation during 1991 since the Muslims felt that they have been eliminated with the pens of the Census Enumerators. The militants are reported to have raised their voice to express that, like the police and military bullets, the pens of the Census Department eliminate Muslims by not counting them or by not showing them in the official record. They have always been shown in reduced number. Therefore, what Roy has taken as the base figure of 1921 Census, might have itself been a manipulated one.

The process of eliminating the Untouchables of Bengal continued for the second round of the battle that is for disenfranchising them by way of partition of Bengal. The table **'D'** reveals that according to the 1941 enumeration the untouchables' number was reduced further by more than thirty five (35) lakhs and their total population came down to only 73,78,970 souls and 12.6 per cent of the total population. Table **'C'** reveals that the Untouchables of Bengal according to the 1931 Census formed 24.7 per cent of the total population of the province. Their number exceeds 1 Crore and 18 lakhs or 11.8 millions. In 1929, Mukunda Behari Mullick as a mere Deposer, demanded in the Simon Commission that representation of untouchables was to be 25 per cent of the total seats in the Bengal Legislative Council on the basis of population 11.5 million enumerated in 1921 Census. The Census Operation in every decade eliminated the untouchable and Sudra population of Bengal in millions by statistical manipulation.

A comparative study of the decennial Census Reports reveals further interesting issues and questions. According to the 1911 report, population of the untouchables in different provinces were as follows: 63 Lakhs (15.83 per cent) in Madras, 6 Lakhs (3.08 per cent) in Bombay Province, 99 Lakhs (22 per cent) in Bengal, (Chandal/Namasudra population in Bengal alone was 19,08,718 souls i.e. three times more than the total untouchable population of Bombay Presidency) 1,01 Lakhs (21.49 per cent) in UP, 17 lakhs (8.72 per cent) in the Punjab, 93 Lakhs (28.70 per cent) in Bihar and Orissa, 37 Lakhs (30.83 per cent) in the Central Province and 3 Lakhs in Assam. With a total population of 41.9 millions, the untouchables formed 18.94 per cent of the national population.[55] There has been a jumping rise in the untouchable population only in Bombay Province. In 1931, it has been reflected as 8 per cent and the population crossed 17 lakhs. It was a big jump, from 6 to 17 lakhs. In 1941 it became 8.9 per cent and population was 18,55,148 souls.

But during these two decades the untouchable population not only had not increased but it had also declined in alarming proportion in some of the provinces. In 1931 Census Report 13.4 per cent were enumerated as untouchables in the Punjab but in 1941, they were enumerated 12, 48, 635 or only 4.4 per cent of the total souls. Same and similar has been the fate with Bengal. In Bengal in 1911, they were 99,00000 souls or 22 per cent. In 1931, their number increase marginally to form 24.7 per cent but in 1941, they surprisingly came down to 12.6 per cent.[56] This obvious manipulation was probably done with a conscious motive to make and justify proportional representation in the Poona Pact in earlier decade after the enumeration of 1931 Census. The growth rate of the Chandal or Namasudras who pioneered the democratic political movement of the Indian Untouchables are note worthy, in 1872, 1881, 1891, 1901, 1911, 1921, 1931 and in 1941 they were enumerated as 16,48,349; 15,76,076; 1768,219; 18,48,483; 19,08,718; 20,28,000; 20,94000; and 22,50,760 souls for the respective years. In comparison to the growth of untouchable population of Bombay province there has been no or negligible growth in Namasudra population during this crucial period of democratic battles in Bengal.

Bihar and Orissa where the number of tribes was large never got a clear demographic picture after 1911 census. In 1921 the population of untouchable in the province came down to 80,00000 from 93,00000 souls.[57] In the next decade, this was further reduced arbitrarily. Consequently, in the Poona Pact great injustice was done on the untouchables of the province. During the Poona Pact the Untouchables in Bihar was taken only 14.5 per cent of the total population. It was 15 per cent less than the 28.70 per cent enumerated in 1911 census operation. Consequently, Bihar got only 15 reserved seats instead of 44 seats out of the total 152 Assembly seats. Even with 14.5 per cent population their share would have been 22 seats in the Legislature. There was no leader from the Eastern India to protect their political interests.

In UP the case was almost similar in 1911, the untouchables were 21.49 per cent. In 1931, during Poona Pact they were 26.4 per cent but in 1941 they formed 16.4 per cent only. U.P. too got inadequate seats i.e. 20 in the Legislature instead of 41 as per proportion of the untouchable population by the Poona Pact. In other States too their population remained normal except in the Central Province where their number and percentage fluctuated abnormally.

The Muslim population in Bengal in 1931 was 54.9 per cent and it rather reduced in 1941 to 54.7 per cent or total 3,30,00434 only leaving the Hindus 18.3 per cent of the total population of Bengal. In the corresponding period in the Punjab Muslim population was enumerated 56.5 per cent and 57.1 per cent only with 1,62,17,242 population leaving the Hindus as 15.1 per cent of the total population. From the data, it is revealed that nearly half of the total Muslim population of India lived in Bengal alone. A mammoth size of untouchable population combined with them formed a formidable force of agrarian poor in the eastern India.

At the crisis point, Dr Ambedkar did not raise these issues for redress. However, at a later stage he recorded, "The Untouchables and the Christians, who are also interested in their numbers, have no hand in the cooking of the Census, for the simple reason that they have no place in the administrative services of the country which deal with the operations of the Census. On the other hand, the Untouchables are the people who are quartered, cooked and served by the Hindus, Muslims and the Sikhs at every Decennial Census. This has happened particularly in the last Census of 1940. The Untouchables of certain parts of the Punjab were subjected to systematic tyranny and oppression by the Sikhs. The object was to compel them to declare in the census returns that they are Sikhs even though they are not. This reduced the number of the Untouchables and swelled the number of Sikhs."[58] Dr Ambedkar never in his volumes of Works and Speeches is found to have discussed the incidents, struggles and problems of Bengal-Untouchables. When Dr Ambedkar became politically paralysed during 1945 and onwards he regained the lease of life by returning elected from Bengal to the Constituent Assembly in 1946.

Bengal untouchable-leaders were kept outside the room to discuss and object this malpractice in the Census Operation conducted at their detriment. No other leaders are found to have raised storm on such a serious issue in the share distribution in the instrumentalities of the state of the budding democratic Republican country. In some cases the helpless leader of Bengal recorded his dissent in the minute yielding no result.[59] In 1941 Census the total untouchable population of Bombay presidency, despite heavy growth rate, has been recorded as 18,55,148 only. While more than 3.5 millions of Bengal untouchables (just double the Bombay population) were simply wiped out of the surface of India to deprive them of their due and prorate-basis share in the leadership and politico-economic power. The 1941 Census Operation is found to have been the preparatory document for the partition of India on communal line. Dr Ambedkar had prepared a table by showing the variation in population by Communities, 1931 to 1941.[60]

Table 'E'

	1931	*1941*	*Increase*
Hindus	189,654,370	206,117,326	+26,462,956
Scheduled Castes	49,540,770	48,793,180	–747,590
Muslims	77,677,545	92,058,096	+14,381,551
Sikhs	4,335,771	5,691,447	+1,355,676
Christians	6,296,763	6,316,119	+19,786
Parsis	109,752	114,890	+ 5138

The data in the table reveals a horrible picture of conspiracy through government machinery. All communities small or large in numerical strength got fair chances to grow in size. Even the Parsees of one lakh strength who faces the acute threat of extinction due to ethno-cultural reasons, increased in number. The most prolific tribes called untouchables or scheduled castes received a blow of spectacular decline in number. And the victims of this 'operation elimination untouchables' became deadly for Bengal and the Punjab.

Dr Ambedkar discussed the issue, "Why did the Hindus suddenly turn to reduce the population of the Untouchables from millions to fractions? The figure 50 millions had stood on the record from 1911. It had not been questioned by any one. How is it that in 1932 the Hindus made so determined an effort without any regard to the means to challenge the accuracy of this figure?

The answer is simple, up to 1932 the Untouchables had no political importance..... Up to 1932 the political question was one of division of seats in the Legislature between Hindus and Musalmans only and as there was no question of the seats that came to the lot of the Hindus being partitioned between the Touchables and the Untouchables and as the whole share went to the Touchables they did not care to inquire what the population of the Untouchables was...."[61] The cunning ruling classes (B+B+B) in this game carefully did not touch the Bombay province and Madras. "The problem of Depressed Classes is not so acute in Bihar as their grievances in Bombay or South India." The issue of political share proportion to the population strength of the Untouchables in the polity of parliamentary democracy was definitely the pivotal motive for manipulating demography. However, the apple of discord emerged not from 1932, it prevailed since 1906-7 (launching of Muslim League and enactment of Proportional Representation of Communities in Public Jobs Act) in practical shape. Since 1932, (Poona Pact) the Untouchables simply started their loosing battles in which Dr Ambedkar was the opining-batsman.

Untouchables and the Poona Pact

Still at this stage, when the Hindu leaders were engaged in communicating with the Colonial masters in all possible means, Congress and Gandhi did not consider the Untouchables worth approaching for any type of solution or compromise.

It is surprising that at this critical situation, the Untouchables of India and their leaders are found to have been idle. They spent precious time without preparing strategy to counter the threat that was posed by the enigmatic Hindu leader Gandhi against their battle for liberty. Gandhi was repeatedly defeated at the hands of the Untouchables of Bengal. Now the leaders from the vast lands of eastern sector were sidelined by the combine forces of Western front of Europe and India. The British, Jinnah and Gandhi (the representatives of Christians, Muslims, Parse and Hindus) all gave importance and official recognition only to Dr Ambedkar. Leaders of Bengal behaved helpless and subservient to Dr Ambedkar because of official stand. Dr Ambedkar too failed to take firm stand to prove to be equal to the situation to retain the laurel of the Round Table Conferences. He is reported to have been rather puzzled and terrified with the whispering message of massacre of Untouchables in the villages. There were even some threat letters for his life. Once he declared, "I tell you I shall not deter from my pious duty, and betray the just and legitimate interests of my people even if you hang me on the nearest lamp-post in the street."[62]

This shows that he was aware of the position that withdrawal of the award for 'Separate Electorates' would be a betrayal to the Untouchable nation. Despite this, he agreed to go for Poona Pact. From nowhere in India, there came a single Gandhi from amongst the teeming millions of Untouchables to resist a train of Gandhis in the Hindus or the Congress camp 'with their lives' and to save their liberty which came in the terms of 'Communal Awards'. At least one untouchable leader, unsuccessfully, however, threw a challenge at Gandhi. Mangoo Ram from the Punjab province, the land of '*Panchpiyere*' braved to go for fast unto death after the national '*Satyagrahi*', an apostle of peace and non-violence started playing the violin of violence. Mangoo Ram threatened with the counter-fast-unto death and declared, "Gandhi! if you are prepared to die for your Hindus, then I am prepared to die for these Untouchables."[63] Mangoo Ram's fast continued even after Gandhi had ceased. But this yielded no result due to combine neglect of the ruling authorities. The remnant of the Punjab movement by the time had been divided by Valmiki-move created by Gandhi-Nehru team. A new community called Valmiki was created out of the Chandelias or Bhangi community. Therefore, Mangoo Ram's fast unto death continued for several days but finally failed. Decision of Ambedkar prevailed and was ratified by the creamy layer ruling-classes. Definitely going for fast unto death was not the monopoly right of Gandhi alone.

The 'Banner of Liberty' Surrendered: Dr Ambedkar, on the contrary, is found to have agreed to conditionally withdraw the 'Communal Award' in so far as the Untouchables were concerned without bothering to consult the other members of the Minority Committee who maneuvered the draft in the 2nd RTC. He become a member of the Committee to save the precious life of Gandhi and 'prepared the charter of demands' as the condition to give up the Communal Award. Ambedkar went back to his original stand of 'joint electorate' with reserved seats as desired by Gandhi and the Hindu leaders. The Committee was composed of Tej Bahadur Sapru, Dr M. R. Jaikar, Pandit Madan Mohan Malaviya, Mathuradas Wasanji and Dr Ambedkar.[64] It was operated from the Birla House. Dr Ambedkar finally, had put up the Charter of Demands before the Committee at 10 p.m. on 20th September in 1932 in Birla Bhawan. The fast was reported to have started at 12 O'clock on the same day. The text of the same is as follows:

"The Charter of demands made on the eve of Mahatma Gandhi's fast".[65]

Part One: Representation in the Legislature

(A) The Depressed Classes shall have the following number of seats in the provincial Legislatures:

	Demanded	*Strength*	*Award*
Madras ……	30 out of	215	18
Bombay ……	16 out of	200	10
Bengal ……	50 out of	250	10
Punjab ……	10 out of	175	9
U.P. ……	40 out of	228	12
Bihar and Orissa …	20 out of	175	7
C.P. and Berar ……	20 out of	112	10
Assam ……	11 out of	108	4

In the 'Charter of Demands', in lieu of the 'Communal Award or Separate

Electorate' Dr Ambedkar in consonance with his original stand in the Simon Commission wanted more reserved seats for the Scheduled castes as follows;- Madras -30; Bombay (including Sindh)-16; Bengal-50; the Punjab-10; UP-40; Bihar-Orissa-20; Assam-11 and the Central Province-20. This demand was made on the basis of democratic principle of representation in consonance with percentage of untouchable population in the respective Provinces. This increase was demanded in lieu of the reserved seats sanctioned in the 'Communal Award' in these provinces which was as follows:- 8; 10; 10; 9; 12; 9; 8; and 10 respectively. Two seats were further added totaling to 78. This reservation was restricted in eight Provinces only.

Populatiuon	*Data of % of SC population in 4 deccanial census*				*Total Population 1941*
	1911 (%)	*1921 (%)*	*1931 (%)*	*1941 (%)*	
Madras	15.83	21.30	15.40	16.40	80,68,492
Bombay	3.08	8.20	8.70	8.90	18,55,148
Bengal	22.00	24.40	24.70	12.60	73,78,970
United Prov.	21.49		26.40	21.30	1,17,17,158
Punjab	8.72	10.50	13.50	4.40	12,48,635
Bihar-Orissa	28.70	26.00	14.50	13.80	43,40,379
Central Prov.	30.83	25.00	23.70	18.10	30,51,413
Assam	5.00		13.40	13.40	6,76,291
Orissa	*	*	*	14.20	12,38,171
Total	18.94				3,95,74,657

It has already been discussed that population of many provinces in Eastern India was highly manipulated in 1921 and 131 Census. The demand of reserved seats in the Charter is found to be considerably justified in so far as (manipulated) population ratio was concerned in the provinces except the Punjab, Bengal, Bihar-Orissa and United Province. The percentage of population, as per the previous Census Report (as taken during Poona Pact) in the provinces were as follows: Madras 15.4 per cent, Bombay 8 per cent, Bengal 24.7 per cent, Punjab 13.5 per cent, U.P. 26.4 per cent, Bihar and Orissa 14.5 per cent, CP and Berar 23.7 per cent, and Assam 13.4 per cent.[66] It is interesting to note that in compromise with Gandhi the Charter demanded much less seats for Bengal, the Punjab, Bihar-Orissa and UP. This was further reduced while finalizing the Poona Pact to an extent to be termed as *sabotage* towards democratic principle of representation in these provinces.

It is further interesting that Dr Ambedkar, was well aware of the political situation of these states. Earlier he advocated more seats at least for the Punjab state soon after the announcement of the Award, "I see no justification for this enormity. What has, however, shocked me most is the denial of the right to representation to the Depressed Classes of the Punjab….. I have no hesitation in saying that comparatively speaking their social condition is really worse than that of their fellows in other Provinces of Northern India. Their case for special representation was the strongest."[67] But when his turn came he demanded only 10 seats in the Charter of Demands in place of 9 in Communal Award. Finally, he gave only 8 seats for the Punjab in the Poona Pact. According to the proportion of population, they deserved 22 out of 175 seats. Dr Ambedkar never raised the issue of Bengal, Bihar, Orissa and UP in this regard.

Table C: Reserved Seats for the Scheduled Castes in the Assemblies

Names of Province	*Total seats in legislature*	*Percent of Depressed population in 1931*	*Seats according to their population % in 1931*	*Seats actually settled in Poona Pact*
U.P.	228	26.4	51	20
Madras	215	15.4	31	30
Bengal	250	24.7	62	30
C.P.	112	23.7	23	20
Bombay	175	8	14	15
Bihar	152*	14.5	21*	15
Punjab	175	13.5	22	8
Assam	108	13.4	13	7
Orissa	60	*		6*
Total	1475	*Bihar + Orissa		*15+6*=21

Thus, the Poona Pact is exposed to be fraught with all fraudulent targets to deprive the right of proportional representation of the Depressed Classes, in particular of Bengal, Bihar, Orissa, UP and the Punjab in the Legislatures.

In Bengal, Caste Hindus were only 18.3 per cent and Muslims were 54.9 per cent. In UP Caste-Hindus were 58.1 per cent and the Muslims were only 14.8 per cent. In the Punjab Caste-Hindus were 15.1 per cent and the Muslims were 56.5 per cent. In the circumstances, the Depressed Classes people both in the Punjab and Bengal were more than 50 per cent in strength. As such, 20 seats for UP untouchables were made to be barely justifiable. However, only 8 seats in the Punjab and 30 seats in Bengal in the Poona Pact were drastically on low side and breach of trust against the people of these provinces. Besides, the untouchable leaders of Bengal were not consulted before the settlement. Dr Ambedkar arbitrarily decided it in consultation with the Brahman leaders of Bengal.[68] The arbitrarily manipulated figure of Depressed Classes in the province of Bihar and Orissa as finally accepted by the team is highly on lower side in comparison to the 1911 or 1921 census report. The Poona Pact made a big cut on the accepted number too while fixing number of seats in the Legislature. The whole of the Eastern India and the Punjab province came under the clouds of Hindu conspiracy.

The untouchable leaders are found to have instead of identifying and targeting their enemy, instead of standing on the national platform started an internecine struggle for parochial and selfish interests (more seats for Bombay) and easily became prey to the Brahmanical ruling castes. Allegation against Rao Bahadur Raja, by Dr Ambedkar himself seems to be unfounded as he is recorded to have had arranged series of large and forceful meetings in Madras in favour of the representation of Dr Ambedkar as the Untouchable leader in the RTC, when it was challenged by Gandhi in the 2nd RTC in 1932.

Save Gandhi: Save the Hinduism

Gandhiji from Yeravda Central Prison started the final innings of his Marathon 'Fast unto Death' on time on 20th of the September for keeping the Untouchables as Hindu slaves. Hindus as well as Persies along with many others started nationwide brouhaha for the endangered life of M.K. Gandhi. Even prayers were arranged in the Mosques in different important places of the country for 'Allah' to save the invaluable life of Gandhiji. The audacity of dream of the *Mulniwasi* of *Bharatvarsa* to be the *defacto* rulers and the ruling class got shuttered forever. Their struggle to be the rulers or '*Raja*' in their own country in the Parliamentary Democracy fell at the feet of simple method of 'passive resistance' of non-violent fast unto death. With a view to saving a single great life of Mahatma Gandhi Dr Ambedkar eventually agreed to sacrifice the liberty and lives of the teeming millions of *Mulniwasi* servile class people who bit by bit erected one irresistible movement against their Sudra-hood to manumit themselves from eternal slavery of Hinduism.

As a member of the Committee, Dr Ambedkar met Gandhiji more than once in the Jail during the fateful days to save his life. "Later in the evening (on 22nd September) Dr Ambedkar, accompanied by Jayakar, Birla, Chunilal Mehata and Raja Gopalachari, went to meet Gandhi in the Jail….. Gandhij was weak. He lay in his bed. The talk began. Sapru narrated to Gandhi the whole story. Malaviya put the Hindu point of view. Then in a soft, slow flow, Dr Ambedkar began. He said in a low voice: "*Mahatmaji*, you have been very unfair to us." "It is always my lot to appear to be unfair," replied Gandhi, "I cannot help it". The interview was protracted and Dr Ambedkar did most of the taking, while Gandhi lay weak and still in his bed. "I want my compensation" Dr Ambedkar urged repeatedly. "I am with you in most of the things you say," Assured Gandhi, "But you say you are interested in my life." Dr Ambedkar: "Yes, *Mahatmaji*, I am. And if you devote yourself entirely to the welfare of the Depressed classes you would then become our hero."[69] Not only the Communal Award, Dr Ambedkar is found to have been ready even to surrender his leadership and make Gandhi the hero of the Untouchable nation.

Devdas Gandhi son of Gandhi, came on Friday 23rd September, with tearful eyes, approached to Dr Ambedkar with the request to save the precious life of his father. Dr Ambedkar, like many others considered Gandhi as the 'Greatest enemy of the Untouchables' but eventually came down to save the life of the Greatest enemy called Gandhi and left the destitute of eternity, the Untouchables to lark in the blinding darkness, at the mercy of the despotic tyrants who were up to enslave the emerging untouchables.

On Saturday, the historic day of 24th September, 1932, in the compound of the Yeravda Prison, under a shady tree, Babasaheb Dr B.R. Ambedkar, the new *Messiah* of the Untouchables of India signed the pact; the death sentence of the 'Orphans of the World' called 'Poona Pact'. This was an act of recurrence of the blunder committed by the Sudra-hero of Puranic period. Akalavya was the most skillful archer of the epic, Mahabharata. Dronacharya, the Brahmin Guru of the Kurus and Pandavas refused to train Akalavya in archery because of his low origin. But in course of time Drona deceived the self-made archer Akalavya and accepted nothing but his thumbs as the tuition fees of a Guru. Dr Ambedkar gave off his thumb-like 'Separate Electorate' to Gandhiji, the archenemy of the Sudras and the Untouchables. He continued his tirade against Gandhiji during post-Poona Pact era as the exceedingly efficient but thumb less archer.

The following 23 personalities signed the pact on 24th September: Madan Mohan Malavya; Tej Bahadur Sapru; M.R. Jaikar; B.R. Ambedkar; Srinivasan; M.C. Raja; C.V. Mehata; C. Rajagopalachari; Rajendra Prasad; G.D. Birla; Rameswar Das Birla; B.S. Kamat; G.K. Deodhar; A.V. Thakkar; R.R. Bakhale; P.G. Solanki; P. Baloo; Govinda Malviya; Devdas Gandhi; Biswas; P.N. Rajbhoj; G.A. Gavai and Shankarlal Bankar.[70] It is not certain whether the signature 'Biswas' in the pact was of Rasik Lal Biswas' or not. In any way it is evident that he was shy to put his signature on the historic pact of surrender. He kept his name under cover. The banner of liberty, the red-flag of revolution which was raised by Guruchand in 1880's and was carried high throughout his life by sacrificing lives through the blood-bath of 'Untouchable-Muslim-riots' the new phenomena in the annals of Indian history called Hindu-Muslim riots starting from 1890 was surrendered on the feet of Gandhi whom Guruchand never cared even as an equal contestant.

With the end of the 'epic-fast' of less than four days, the Ramayana epic was recreated, 'With the death of the Shambuk, the prematurely dead Brahmin youth instantly resurrected'. The banner so surrendered was to never rise again. Gandhiji became, at once, the real *Mahatma* of Gurudev Rabindra Nath Tagore by saving his heaven-born children, the Brahmins from sure distress. *Mahatma* Gandhi took liquid and solid food with divine contentment.

The Poona Pact is a very small document composed of only 9 clauses or Para, a written document of one and a half page only. The provision of the Poona Pact holds, "(1) There shall be seats reserved for the Depressed Classes out of the general electorate seats in the Provincial Legislatures as follows: Madras 30; Bombay with Sindh 15; Punjab 8; Bihar and Orissa 18; Central Provinces 20; Assam 7; Bengal 30; United Provinces 20; Total 148.[71] These figures are based on the total strength of the Provincial Councils, announced in the Prime Minister's decision" (3 added for Bihar and Orissa later on) The remarkable cut has been made in the seats of Bengal by reducing it from 50 to 30 only. (2) Election to these seats shall be by joint electorates subject, however, to the following procedure:..."

Immediately the contents of the Poona Pact was cabled to the British Cabinet, Wire to the Viceroy on 24th of September. "At 2 p.m. the leaders held a meeting at the Indian Merchant's Chamber Hal." Dr Ambedkar disclosed his heart while he rose to declare amidst cheers, "I had to make a choice between two difficult alternatives. There was the life of the greatest man in India to be saved. There was also for me the problem to try and safeguard the interests of community which I was in my humble way trying to do at the Round Table Conference according to my light. I am happy to be able to say that it has become possible through the co-operation of all of us to find a solution so as to save the life of the *Mahatma*...."[72] The fate of the posterities of the untouchables were too mortgaged instantly. A single *Mahatma* was saved at the cost of ruination of the immense majority servile classes of the lowest stratum of the day and of those to come down the ages. The flag of Liberty once surrendered never was to be raised again. He virtually entered in untouchable-movement for liberty in 1927 and made an exit within a period of five years only i.e. in 1932. After Poona Pact, the movement of the Untouchables-Sudras-Tribals and minorities reduced to an endless struggle of seeking safe-guards and favour of mercy for the 'reservation' in some specific types of unimportant jobs for a temporary period. It initiated a train of selfish-movements to save and safe-guard personal interest of the 'Oppressed elites'.

Waves of protests raised in the Punjab and Bengal. Dr Ambedkar did not bother to take note or advantage of those objections against the Poona Pact to nullify it.

There was no body to protect the interest of the untouchables of

Bengal who were the pioneer of the untouchable-movement since 1880. Ambedkar further said to the British PM that although the "Poona Pact did not satisfy Bengal Depressed Class leaders who wanted 50 instead 30 seats in Bengal, he had forced the terms down their throats. The Depressed Classes in Bombay, Bihar, the Punjab, UP and Orissa too were not satisfied with the terms of the Pact, he concluded."[73] The golden dream of more than eleven million untouchables of Bengal shuttered into doom of the national platform. 'Outside Faridpur the Pabna Depressed Classes Association, also headed by a Namasudra leader called Madhusudan Sarkar, held a meeting on 20th September the day Gandhi started his historic fast. The meeting unanimously resolved that 'the depressed class people pray for and demand a separate electorate instead of joint electorate with the caste-Hindus', for they believed that 'no welfare can be done to them by the caste-Hindus'. The meeting also resolved that the depressed classes were not to be bound up by any resolutions passed or rules framed by the Provincial Hindu Sabha' which was an organisation of the caste-Hindus. Instead of co-operating with such people, they would rather 'like to live in a segregated condition as from time immemorial'.[74]

It were the untouchables of Bengal who in union with the Muslims of Bengal gave the untouchables of India a separate identity, emerged as a distinct ethnic and political group or a separate community to be recognised in the democratic-structure and in the governance with their proper representation in the instrumentalities of the State in the Census Report of 1911. The *Mahad* leader Dr Ambedkar, according to Dhananjoy Keer, pushed adverse terms of slavery of Poona Pact through the unwilling throats of the Untouchable leaders of Bengal.

Thus, we find that the leaders of Bengal from various Organisations vehemently protested the Poona Pact. The Depressed Classes Association of Faridpur protested, "The Communal Award was 'a political advantage unprecedented and unparallel in the constitutional history of India but Poona Pact is Dr Ambedkar's political blunder". The Depressed Classes Association and the Bengal Namasudra Association jointly passed a resolution in their meeting on 26th September 1932, 'The alleged settlement does not at all solve the problem so far as Bengal is concerned, and the Depressed classes of Bengal at least are not bound by it." 'Dr Ambedkar' the two Associations noted, 'with extreme regret' 'had assumed the role of a dictator' and practically gave away the real cause of the Depressed Classes' without even consulting the All India Depressed Classes Federation. The representatives of this classes who had gathered at Poona, it was also noted, had practically no experience of any election' and could therefore, be very easily 'hood-winked' by a body of clever, caste-ridden Hindus'.[75] Consequently, as the Census Department, so the Hindu leaders made the

Namasudras and the Rajbansis, the two more articulated groups amongst the depressed classes, targets of their lowly and mortal attacks. 'To ensure the withdrawal of the White Paper, Sir Nagendra Nath Sarkar, the Advocate General of Bengal, circulated in London a series of pamphlets amongst the members of the British Parliament and Joint Select Committee, complaining, 'If the proposals contained in the White Paper stand, it will mean nothing to the depressed classes, but the Council will be swamped by the well organised and advanced Namasudras and Rajbansis, who have no claim whatsoever to come under the depressed classes.'[76] The caste Hindus for protecting their microscopic minority interest went to the extent to officially declare that the *Chandals* etc were none of the untouchables. This was the stand of the Hindu nationalists, whom Dr Ambedkar gave humorous company during the period.

Even the Bengal Legislative Council opposed Poona Pact. "Just then The Bengal Legislative Council passed a resolution asking for the annulment of the Poona Pact." Unbelievable though, it is found on record that in a statement issued to the Times of India, (it was not Gandhiji but) Ambedkar resented the attitude of the Bengal Hindu leaders. He pointed out that the Bengali caste Hindu leaders had taken a very prominent part in negotiating with him on the terms of the Poona Pact at Parel and at the office of the Indian Merchant's Chamber, and hence their story that they were not parties to the agreement was false. He then revealed to the public how the British Primer had referred to him a telegram from Sri N.N. Sarcar, who said that the Bengal Hindus were unrepresented at the Poona Pact. Ambedkar had replied to the British Primer in these words, "My submission is that, assuming that the Bengal Hindus were not represented at the Poona settlement, it cannot for that reason alone make it inapplicable to Bengal. Paragraph 4 of the Communal decision of His Majesty's Government was for the whole of British India."[77]

In post-Poona Pact period, Gandhiji is found to have abdicated his authority to speak not only on behalf of the Untouchables but also for the Hindus. He left it to Dr Ambedkar to speak and decide on the role of the caste-Hindus too. For settling, the fate of the Untouchables of entire India Dr Ambedkar got the sole-dealing agency from the British government. In this act, he is found to have made regular and repeated negotiation and dialogue with the Caste-Hindus of Bengal. It is perturbing however, to note that Ambedkar never consulted any leader from Bengal-untouchables while deciding the settlement at their detriment and doom. It is revealed that with a view to defending the scope of all-India jurisdiction of the Poona Pact against the decision of Bengal legislature, Dr Ambedkar took shelter under Para 4 of the earlier Communal Award which was fundamentally rejected by the Poona Pact. Para 4 of the Communal Award even does not support the stand taken by Dr Ambedkar. Para 4 holds, "....If, therefore, before a new

Government of India Act has passed into law, they are satisfied that the communities who are concerned are mutually agreed upon a practicable alternative scheme, either in respect of any one or more of the Governors' Provinces or in respect of the whole of the British India, they will be prepared to recommend to Parliament that the alternative should be submitted for the provisions now outlined."[78]

Dr Bhadant Anand Kausalyan, the revered Buddhist monk and close associate of Dr Ambedkar had written in this regard, assessing the mind of Dr Ambedkar on the Poona Pact in his book published in early 1980, "After all, at one time Dr Ambedkar himself was vehemently opposed to separate representation. At his heart were the interest of the Depressed classes alone; separate electorates were only a means towards it and not an issue of principle. It was decided accordingly that the Depressed classes were to receive 71 seats."[79]

In 1932, before the Hindus and their leader Gandhiji, the main problem was to allot proportional reserved seats of the provincial and central Legislature for the untouchable Depressed Classes. The number of seats calculated on the basis of census report of 1911, 1921 or even of 1931 became fabulous. The Hindus could in no way agree to that. Therefore, Gandhiji had to continue his fast even after Ambedkar had agreed to his proposal for withdrawal of the Communal Award for the untouchables by submitting his demands of charter on 20th September 1932. The 1931 Census was already over. As such, the agreement was not on the basis of proportion of untouchable population. It was much less. As the damage controlling measure in 1941, the Census Department enumerated[80] the population of the Depressed Classes, now as Scheduled Castes, in tangible manipulation, only to make it arithmetically proportional to the seats for the Scheduled Castes in the Poona Pact.

Drifting Towards Congress

In 1928, in the Simon Commission Dr Ambedkar is found to have advocated for 'Joint Electorate with reserved seats for the Untouchables' a parallel line of action that was contemplated by Moti Lal Nehru in 1928 without prescribing any special method for the Untouchables. The untouchables had been voting to the Hindu candidates since the elections of 1921 onwards on the basis of joint-electorate only. Once again, a similar scheme was adopted by Gandhiji during the Poona Pact episode in 1932. Practically, there was no point of demanding 'joint-electorate' by Dr Ambedkar as it was redundant in view of the 'separate-electorate' already granted to the Muslims, Sikhs, Christians. As a natural corollary, the Untouchables being legally separated from other communities or being debarred of casting votes for either the Muslim or Sikh candidate were irrevocably tagged with the Hindus politically and to form 'Joint Electorate' with the Hindus only. They had no choice but to vote for the Hindus. This move of Dr Ambedkar was simply to counter the demands for separate electorate by sixteen other prominent and veteran untouchable leaders of different provinces. This act also countered his own viewpoints, which he expressed before the Southborough Committee in 1920. Even the Backward Sudras of Non Brahman Party (particularly in Bombay and South) who enjoyed separate electorate on economic and educational ground[81] supported the untouchables' demand.

Finally, the movement of the Untouchables that was led by Dr Ambedkar through the method of '*Satyagraha*' (starting from the Mahar Talab *Satyagraha* in 1927 to Pune *Satyagraha* in 1946) is found to have drifted to the proximity of the Congress movement. The result of the first general election in 1937 under the provisions of the Government of India Act 1935 reveals that the total Untouchable vote cast in Bengal was much more (despite the manipulated strength) than the combined figure of Madras, Bombay and the Punjab. The untouchables of all the provinces but Bengal and the Punjab strengthened the Congress Party. The table 'A' below may be referred to:

Table A: The Data Reveals the Voting Pattern of Untouchables, Polled in the General Election 1937[82]

Province	*In Favour of Congress*	*Against Congress*	*Total Untouchable Votes cast*	*Percentage of Congress votes*
UP	52,609	79,571	132,180	40
Madras	126,152	195,464	321,616	39
Bengal	59,646	624,797	684,443	9
CP	19,507	115,354	134,861	14
Bombay	12,971	158,076	171,047	8
Bihar	8,654	22,187	30,841	28
Punjab	Nil	69,126	69,126	0
Assam	5,320	22,437	27,757	19
Orissa	5,878	8,707	14,585	40
Total	290,737	1,295,719	1,586,456	

Total polled-votes of Scheduled Castes in Bengal alone was 6,84,443. This reveals a very startling political awareness of the Untouchables in Bengal. The exceedingly poor response came from the Bihar-Orissa and UP where untouchable population was huge. (In 1911 census the UP untouchables were enumerated more than 10 million and in Bengal it was below a billion. Bihar was almost touching Bengal) While the total polled votes in Madras+Bombay+Punjab including Assam+Bihar and Orissa was 6,34,972 only (3,21,616 + 1,71,047 +69,126 + 30841 + 14585 + 27757 respectively). This strength in UP was 1,32,180 and in Central provinces was 1,34,861 only.[83] The political awareness was damaged drastically in Bihar and Orissa after being separated from Bengal from 1911. Turnout was very little. Even the combined votes of Madras, Punjab, Bombay, and C.P. could just touch the total number of untouchable votes of Bengal. The total polled votes in Bengal were four times of the total polled votes that of Bombay. However, the total strength of untouchables in Bengal was six times more than total untouchable population of Bombay Presidency. Yet Bengal was not allowed to lead the movement. It was more than double the polled votes that of Madras. More strikingly, in Bengal untouchables were more than 58 per cent of the total Hindu or non-Muslim population in the state. Entire Punjab and Bengal, despite Puna Pact remained anti-Congress while the rest of Indian provinces tilted towards Congress Party. Bombay untouchables went over to 'Sarbajan plank' in the name of 'Indipendent Labour Party' which contested election in colaboration with socialists also. No Bengali untouchable leader, therefore, was allowed to enter in the slaughterhouse where their number along with their democratic right to participatory governance was butchered.

Table B

Province	*Assembly and Congress Strength in 1937 election*		*Seats as per Awards*	*Demands of Charter 20/9/32*	*Seats for U/T in Poona Pact*	*Congress gained back*	*Percentage of Congress Strength*
UP	228	135	12	40	20	16	59.2
Madras	215	159	18	30	30	26	74.0
Bengal	250	60	10	50	30	6	24.0
CP	112	70	10	20	20	7	62.5
Bombay	175	85	10	16	15	4	48.6
Bihar	152	95	7*	20*	15	11	62.5
Punjab	175	18	9	10	8	Nil	10.3
Assam	108	35	4	11	7	4	32.4
Orissa	60	36	*	*	6	4	60.0
Total	1475	692	80	197	151	78	46.9

Table '**B**' above also reveals a startling fact that out of total 250 seats in the Bengal Legislative Assembly the strength of Congress after election of 1937 was 60 (including 6 reserved seats out of 30) that is 24 per cent only. (In this election Krishak Proja Party under the leadership of Surawardi had a secret pact of seat adjustment with the Congress and did not contest against each other gained 59 seats. The Muslim League contested alone and won 60 seats) In Bombay (even after shedding 15 seats to the ILP of Dr Ambedkar) the Congress won 85 out of total 175 seats that is 48.6 per cent and in Madras Congress won 159 out of total 215 seats that is 74 per cent. In UP out of total 228 seats the Congress got around 59.2 per cent or 134 seats, including 16 out of 20 reserved seats. In Bihar too Congress captured 62.5 per cent seats including 11 out of 15 reserved seats. In the Punjab and Sindh out of 235 seats Congress, however, lost miserably and secured only 26 seats that is 10.3 per cent only.[84]

In Madras, Congress party captured 26 seats out of reserved 30 seats. The untouchables could retain only 4 seats. On the other side owing to the spectacular thumping support of the untouchables for the Indian National Congress, the 'Non-Brahmin Political Party' or Justice Party movement or the 'Backward class' movement' led by Thanthai Periyar got excluded or isolated from the servile-class movement and faced a serious setback. The startling fact in this regard is that in the Punjab out of polled 69,126 votes of the untouchables, the Congress secured not even a single vote and hence no seat. All the eight reserved seats were captured by the Ad-Dharm Mandal.

It comes to be a startling fact that the ruling class, foreign and Indian, British+Brahmin+Baniya (B+B+B), in a calculative manner nominated untouchable members from the provinces where their number was very low. The leaders dependent on the Hindu vote-support were sponsored as nominated representatives to decide political-fate of the Untouchables in the Simon Commission and in the Round Table Conference.

Soon after the successful election of 1937, Ambedkar was found to be completely paralysed in the political arena along with his Independent Labour Party in Bombay presidency. The nationalist Dr Ambedkar, with his cherished ideal-mode of Joint Electorate for a 'good government', never could win in any election after 1937. Despite his all nationalist views and actions, his surrender to Gandhiji in favour of '*Sarvajan*' interest by putting his signature on the Poona Pact, the nationalist forces led by the creamy-layer elite never accepted Ambedkar's leadership. He was trapped only to helplessly help his persecutors. Congress with 48.6 per cent seats in the Bombay Legislature could not form Government alone. The Hindus formed government by winning Muslim League MLAs. With his 15 MLAs in Bombay Legislature Ambedkar was not called to join the Ministry. In Bengal, however, the Muslim League formed Government by taking two of the 24 elected MLAs from untouchable community. Dr Ambedkar failed politically to become a national leader during his time. He remained a leader of the Mahar caste only. Even his rational call for conversion to get rid of the Hindu concentration camp was responded by his caste men, the Mahars only. In his extreme political distress, he is found to have knocked the doors of Bengal untouchables. With a view to getting his entry in the Constituent Assembly in 1946, he had to completely depend on their organisational strength and indomitable conviction to the untouchable cause. Had he not drastically reduced the prorate based reserved seats numbering 60-62 to 30 in the Poona Pact for Bengal, Dr Ambedkar and the untouchable leaders could have got much comfortable and better position to elect a stronger team in the Constituent Assembly, during 1945-46.

The Untouchables : Post-Poona Pact[85]

In pursuance of this agreement known as Poona Pact, there came the new Constitution, the Government of India Act 1935. From 1909 up to 1932 the untouchables or the 'Depressed Class' people were virtually forced to accept 'Joint Electorate' with the Hindus. They had no option but to vote for the Hindus only because the Muslim community for the first time in 1909 was isolated from them politically by the separate electorate. The Poona Pact of 1932 made the distinct departure from it by making the 'Depressed Class' part of the Hindus. Officially, they now got new nomenclature, 'Scheduled Castes'. They ceased to be called as 'Class', the Depressed Class. Unity of a class tattered into thousands of Hindu castes and sub-castes. They no more got seats in the Legislature as independent community share. They were allotted some seats in the Legislature from the share that the Hindus got as earmarked for General. With the arrival of the Poona Pact the minority Hindu group (not more than 24 per cent) became the majority group. The Muslims reduced to minority. Attitude of Congress towards Muslim League changed. This accelerated the process of partition of two provinces having Muslim majority.

They naturally lost their claim for representation in the Public jobs according to the proportion of their population, which they held from 1907. Now, on 4th July, in 1934 Government of India passes Office Order No. F. 14/17-B/33 and declared, "The intention of Caste Hindus in this respect was formally stated in the Poona Agreement of 1932 and His Majesty's Government in accepting that agreement took due note of this point. In the state of general education in these classes the Government of India consider that no useful purpose will be served by reserving for them a definite percentage of vacancies out of the number available for Hindus as a whole, but they hope to ensure that duly qualified candidates from the Depressed Classes are not deprived of fair opportunities of appointment merely because they cannot succeed in open competition."[90] Politically they continued to pursue the system of joint electorate and casting vote for the Hindus only.

Dr Ambedkar, within so short span of active socio-political life (from 1927 to 1932) became too busy, too close and intimate with the top-strata of politics to give attention or to spare time to form a political party of the Untouchables by the Untouchables and for the Untouchables. Initially during the period from 1924 to 1930, he was a strong votary of joint electorate. With the Poona Pact, he on the contrary merged the Untouchable and the Tribal population in the body of the Hind. They got Hindu name, Scheduled Castes. Hindus only have caste; they do not form any class. In the new circumstances, Dr Ambedkar had no reason to launch for the Untouchables a political party separate from the Hindu Political Party. All Hindu political parties belonged to them and they belonged to those parties. Besides, the strength of the Untouchables in Bombay province being merely 7-8 per cent had little chances to get success with an independent political party of the Untouchables by the Untouchables and for the Untouchables. Despite this, Ambedkar hurriedly formed a local Independent Labour Party in 1936 in the Bombay presidency. He did not contemplate for a national party.

In no other provinces, the untouchables erected any political party of their own. Perhaps national approach amongst the untouchable leaders prevailed less. They nourished parochial interests of each province more. This benefited the nationalists of creamy-layer-elite ruling classes. In Bengal and the Punjab, however, situation was completely different. When the general election was declared in pursuance of the Act of 1935, Untouchables of Bengal and the Punjab got ready to oppose Congress and other political parties. The leaders of Bengal were preparing to form a political party of their own since 1928. In the new situation created by the Joint Electorate the Bengal leaders were shocked to realize that there was no more necessity for a separate political party exclusively for the untouchables. The untouchable leaders rather started vying each other to join Congress. In the land of Punjab the Ad-Dharm Mahamandal under its banner contested and won all the 8 seats reserved for the untouchables.

The election result of 1937 revealed a serious and poor future for the untouchable politics. Untouchables' independent candidates in Bihar also lost to the untouchable-candidates nominated by the Congress Party in large number. 'Although under the Poona Pact it gave 151 seats to the Untouchables it took back 78 and thereby made a handsome profit on its political transaction', assessed Dr Ambedkar himself.[86]

The marching of this profit making by the Congress and other Hindu political parties continued, until within two decades, all of the disks of the vertebra of the Untouchable movement were dislocated and their leaders became paralysed. Independent Labour Party lost its credibility. Never again, it won a single seat in any election. Even Dr Ambedkar was defeated at the hands of insignificantly petty candidate of 4th standard who was set by the Indian National Congress. He never got success in any election from Bombay, Maharashtra and Madras. Being frustrated absolutely, when irrevocable damage had already been done to the democratic and constitutional movement for freedom of the untouchables Dr Ambedkar had started belching out venom in post-Poona pact era. In 1945 he recorded, "The Poona Pact has completely disenfranchised the Scheduled Castes in as much as candidates whom they rejected in the Primary election, which is the true index of their will have been returned in the final election by the votes of the caste-Hindus.' "The Poona Pact is thus fraught with mischief. It was accepted because of the coercive fast of Mr. Gandhi and because of assurance given at the time that the Hindus will not interfere in the election of Scheduled Castes."[87]

In post-Poona Pact years, Ambedkar paid repeated visits to London and got involved with supra-social level politics. Whatever correspondences he sent from different Hotel addresses, in London during this period was not at all encouraging for the untouchables of India in general. Different sections of the untouchable communities started disassociating with his movement of compromise with Gandhian movements (Kalaram *Satyagraha* in 1930, *Poona Satyagraha* of 1946). The Chamars of Maharashtra "accused Ambedkar of partiality for the Mahars..... the Chamars said that Ambedkar's organisation was dominated by the Mahars."[88] Such allegations had great significance and impact on the Untouchables' liberation movement all over India. Ambedkar took the responsibility of resolving national crisis of Indian untouchables but failed to rise beyond a Mahar leader. Even many of his Mahar lieutenants like B.R. More had left him soon after the Poona Pact was signed. He joined Communist movement of India. It was obviously understood by everybody, "The main point urged by the Hindu community now is that the circumstances in which the Poona Pact was evolved presumed without doubt that the Depressed Classes would remain as part of the Hindu community. Mr. Gandhi's fast, which was solely responsible for the Pact, was undertaken in order to prevent the dismemberment of the Hindu community, which it was feared would result from the allotment of a separate electorate to the Depressed Classes."[89] It was a natural concomitant that after Poona Pact the Depressed Classes would lose their universal class status and be regarded as Castes, Scheduled or no scheduled. Poona Pact, virtually, became the Magna Carta of Hindu Raj.

Yet, after coming back from London on January 8, 1934, he once again re-iterated his stand in favour of the Poona Pact forcefully against the Bengal's Caste-Hindus who demanded nullification of Poona Pact. 'The Joint Committee would not grant their request. It was a shame and disgrace to the Hindus if they were not in a position to respect their words', he admonished. Even Gurudev Ravindra Nath Tagore supported the cause of Bengal Hindus. "When Sir N.N. Sarkar produced a wire from Tagore supporting the cause of the Bengal Hindis, the Assistant Secretary of State for India simply quoted the Secretary of State."[90]

Instead of organizing, the untouchables on the national level to fight and win their political battles Dr Ambedkar went back to his legal pursuit and accepted a part-time professorship in the Government Law Collage in Bombay from June 1934. Soon after when he was dragged in politics once again, he faced the political betrayal of the Brahmanism and Brahman-social order. Assessing the ground reality of the contemporary politics of Indian nation his biographer D. Keer had very rightly recorded, "Ambedkar, the maker and defender of the Poona Pact, up to this moment little dreamt that he would one day be its worst enemy."[91]

References

1. Dr Ambedkar W and S, Vol. 17 (1) p. 248-9.
2. New-York Daily Tribune, August 8, 1853; Selected Works, Vol. 1, p. 498, Marx, letter.
3. N.B. Roy, A People In Distress, Vol. I, pp. 166 and 170.
4. Sekhar.Bandyopadhyay, Caste Protest and Identity in Colonial India The Namasudras, p. 110.
5. Sekhar Bandyopadhyay, Caste Protest and Identity in Colonial India The Namasudras, p. 143.
6. Sekhar Bandyopadhyay, Caste Protest and Identity in Colonial India The Namasudras, p. 153.
7. Dr Ambedkar W and S, Vol. 9, pp. 85-86.
8. Jagadish Chandra Mandal, Mahapran Jogendranath, p. 54.
9. Sakhar Bandyopadhyay, Caste Protest and Identity in Colonial India The Namasudras, p. 141.
10. Nirod C. Chowdhury, Autobiography of an Unknown India, p. 486.
11. Dhananjoy Keer, Life and Mission. of Dr B.R. Ambedkar, p. 36.
12. *Ibid,* p. 19.
13. *Ibid*, p. 33.
14. Dhananjoy Keer, Life and Mission of Dr Ambedkar, and Sahu Maharaja, p. 42.
15. *Ibid,* p. 55 and B.R. Ambedkar W and S, Vol. 17 (2) pp. 395-405.
16. *Ibid*, p. 55 and B.R. Ambedkar W and S, Vol. 17 (2) p. 395.
17. Source Material on Dr Ambedkar, (Government of Maharashtra) p. 2.
18. *Ibid*, pp. 8-9.
19. Source Material on Babasaheb Ambedkar, pp. 15-17.
20. Refer to the Speech of Dr Anand Teltumde, the grand-son-in-law of Dr Ambedkar in the Town Hall of Lahore on 17th April 2009 to observe Ambedkar Day in Pakistan.
21. Source material on Dr B.R. Ambedkar, p. 33 Bombay Secret Abstruct of 7th April 1928.

22. Refer to the Source Material on Dr Ambedkar.
23. Writing and Speeches of Dr B.R. Ambedkar, Vol. 17 part-I, pp. 65-71.
24. W and S of Ambedkar Vol. 17 (3), pp. 76-79.
25. Dhananjoy Keer, Life and Mission of Dr Ambedkar, p. 89.
26. A.K. Biswas, The Namasudras of Bengal, Annex-iv, pp. 77-98.
27. W and S of Ambedkar, Vol. 17(1) p. 64.
28. W and S of Ambedkar, Vol. 17 (1) p. 71 and Dhananjoy Keer, p. 139.
29. Sakhar Bandyopadhyay, Caste Protest and Identity in Colonial India The Namasudras, p. 153.
30. Reference in the Source Material on Dr Ambedkar.
31. Source Material on Dr B.R. Ambedkar, p. 40.
32. Ibid, p. 58
33. Proceedings of the sub-committee No iii (Minorities), Government of India Central Publication Branch, Calcutta, 1931, pp. 73-80.
34. D.C. Ahir, Dr Ambedkar at the Round Table Conference, p. 26.
35. Wand S of B.R. Ambedkar, Vol. 9, p. 47.
36. Bhante Ananda Kausallayan, Had there been No Ambedkar, p. 51.
37. *Ibid*, p. 85

37a. *Ibid*, Vol 17(2), p. 186; Reserved Constituencies were 1. Bombay City North, 2. Bombay City Parel. 3. Kaira District, 4. Surat District, 5. Thane South, 6. Ahmednagar South, 7. East Khandesh, 8. Nasik West, 9. Poona West, 10. Satara North, 11. Solapur North-East, 12. Belgaum North-East, 13. Bijapur North, 14. Kolaba, 15. Ratnagiriu North. In these seats total of SC voters, respectively were : 34,266; 28,520; 7,318; 4,765; 4,667; 7,382; 10,109; 12,698; 13,979; 11,152; 9,713; 18,303; 8,993; 5,001; and 3,329 where as caste Hindu voters were : 1,67,002; 1,52,991; 1,39,266; 85,670; 67,749; 75,607; 91,377; 99,271; 77,389; 94,200; 64,583; 79,422; 60,485; 1,02,637; and 33,002, only.

38. W and S of Ambedkar, Vol. 17 (3) p. 78.
39. *Ibid,* p. 79.
40. Ibid, Vol. 17 (1) p. 51.
41. Dhananjoy Keer, Life and Mission of Dr Ambedkar.
42. W and S of Dr Ambedkar, Vol. 9, p. 55.
43. *Ibid,* pp. 68-69.
44. *Ibid*, pp. 68-69.
45. *Ibid,* pp. 78.
46. *Ibid,* pp. 82-83.
47. *Ibid,* p. 83.
48. Complete Works of Swami Vivekananda, Vol. 5, p. 233.
49. N.B. Roy, A People in Distress, pp. 7-8.
50. *Ibid*, p. 9.
51. Dr A.K. Biswas, Namasudras of Bengal, p. viii, Introduction.
52. R.N. Tagore, "*Oikatan*".

53. W and S of Dr Ambedkar, Vol. 9, p. 76.
54. A Summary of the Changes in the Jurisdiction of Districts in Bengal, West Bengal District Gazetteers, Govt. of West Bengal, p. 201.
55. W and S of Dr Ambedkar, Vol. 5, p. 232.
56. *Ibid,* Vol. 1.
57. *Ibid,* Vol. 5, p. 240.
58. W and S of Dr Ambedkar, Vol. 9, p. 399.
59. *Ibid,* Vol. 5, p. 240.
60. *Ibid,* Vol. 1, p. 449.
61. *Ibid,* Vol. 5, p. 241.
62. W and S of Dr Ambedkar, Vol. 17 (1), p. 152.
63. Dr Suresh Mane, Socio Cultural Revolts, pp. 159-169.
64. W and S of Dr Ambedkar, Vol. 17 (1) pp. 153, 153.
65. *Ibid,* p. 154.
66. *Ibid,* pp. 97-98.
67. Source material on Dr B.R. Ambedkar, p. 83.
68. Dhananjoy Keer, B.R. Ambedkar Life and His Mission, p. 236.
69. W and S of Dr Ambedkar, Vol. 17(2), p. 250.
70. *Ibid,* Vol. 17 (1) p. 159.
71. *Ibid,* p. 168.
72. W and S of Dr Ambedkar, Vol. 17 (1) p. 166.
73. *Ibid,* Vol. 17 (1) p. 170.
74. D. Keer, Life and Mission of Dr Ambedkar, p. 236.
75. Sekhar Bandyopadhaya, Caste, Protest and Identy in Colonial India The Namasudras, p. 157.
76. *Ibid,* p. 158.
77. *Ibid,* p. 159.
78. Dhananjoy Keer, Life and Mission of Dr Ambedkar, pp. 235-236.
79. Dr B.R. Ambedkar, Thoughts on Pakistan, (Appendix-xi) (Pub. 1940) p. 367.
80. Dr B.A. Kausalyan, Had There Been no Ambedkar, p. 51.
81. W and S of Dr Ambedkar, Vol. 1, p. 448.
82. *Ibid,* Vol. 5, p. 243.
83. W and S of Dr Ambedkar, Vol. 9, p. 156.
84. W and S of Dr Ambedkar, Vol. 9, p. 147.
85. W and S of Dr Ambedkar, Vol. 9, p. 65 and Dhananjoy Keer, p. 177.
86. Dr B.R. Ambedkar, Thoughts on Pakistan, p. 376; Pakistan or partition of India, (Pub. 1942) p. 469.
87. W and S of Dr Ambedkar, Vol. 9, pp. 94-95.
88. *Ibid.*
89. Dhannanjoy Keer, Life and Mission of Dr Ambedkar, p. 242.
90. Dr Ambedkar W and S Vol. 17 (1), p. 245.
91. Dhannanjoy Keer, Life and Mission of Dr Ambedkar, p. 241.

7

The Triumph of the Champion Chamchas

Thakur Guruchand repeatedly cautioned his people during 1918 to 1921 when he refused to help Congress and Gandhi in their Non-cooperation movement, that the caste-Hindu oppressors have started knocking the doors of the untouchables and appealing them with brotherly gestures only to exploit their support and services. They were not trustworthy. They were not genuinely sympathetic to their distressing condition. That once their political target is achieved, the untouchables would be abandoned like the musical instruments and flower-garlands are swept away soon after completion of a ceremony. Guruchand never trusted the Hindu leaders and declined to join hands with them. He believed the principle of self-respect and taught his people to stand on self-help. 'Swa + Raj' i.e. the rule of self in a Republic was his target.

Two decades later in 1942 and 1945, the same feelings were expressed in articulated language by Dr Ambedkar. "To end this long and sad story, (the story of Poona Pact) the Congress sucked the juice out of the Poona Pact and threw the rind in the face of the Untouchables"[1] Dr Ambedkar in course of long time association and sincere services to the Brahminical system realised that he had been ditched by the caste-Hindus in political deals. And expressed to Mr. Baverali Nikolas, during 1942-43, the same what Guruchand taught his follower during '*Swadeshi* movement' in 1905-10 and during Gandhiji's passive-resistance movement called *Satyagraha* and non-cooperation movement in 1920, "The key note of my policy is that we are not a sub-continent of the Hindus but a separate element in the national life.' "Gandhi says to us 'Trust us Trust the caste-Hindus!' I reply 'We will not trust you, for you are our hereditary enemies.'[2]

He had further clarified in a plea to the foreigners in 1946, "The true answer is that a revolutionist is not the kind of man who becomes a Pope and that the man who becomes a Pope has no wish to be a revolutionist...". Therefore, he commanded, "Only those who belong to the servile class can be trusted to protect the interest of that class." Alas! It came too late, however, to get any effect out of it. Had Dr Ambedkar maintained this realistic attitude with the backward class leaders on the eve of the *Mahad Talab Satyagraha* and in the Simon Commission in 1928-29 and even after the declaration of the Separate Electorate on 17th August 1932 he would not have faced the situation to appeal to the foreigners, "Let not tyrants have freedom to enslave."[3] Had he not irritated the Muslim community with his actions and speeches in the Simon Commission the untouchable-Muslim unity that strengthened the untouchable-liberation movement in the Eastern India during last five decades to success would have had no such friendless and isolated situation to face.[4]

Trust or no trust, a dead patient never responds to medicine or nectar. Standing on the podium of the mammoth meeting of the Dalitbahujan in 1930, in the Sadar Town of Khulna in his presidential address Guruchand declared, "It is very urgent to accelerate the process of struggle of liberty of the low-castes. In no way the independent entity of the Untouchables can be established until they acquire proper share of political power through a series of Constitutional Amendment Acts." In this meeting, the educated, service-holder and political leaders of the different untouchable communities actively participated. Guruchand suggested that the best way of gaining political power could be materialised through a political party of the Untouchables, established, managed and led by the Untouchables. Nevertheless, the dreams of Guruchand went in oblivion because of *sabotage* by the Poona-Pact.

The provisions of the Poona Pact, the 'Magna Carta of Hindu Raj' made the subservient and dependent politics for the Untouchables. The Act separated the Untouchable communities from the rest of the non-Hindu communities and included them in the electoral college of the Hindus who were their hereditary enemy. Now the Depressed Classes being Hinduised once again were officially designated as 'Scheduled Castes'. Except in the Punjab and in Bengal the Untouchables exclusively were not in a position to win even a single seat under the scheme of joint-electorate. The untouchables in other states found them dependent on the Hindus as Hindus. As such, the political Party of the Untouchables never came into existence even in the main land where there was untouchable-upsurge.

Freedom Struggle Versus Struggle for Safeguards: Owing to the Poona Pact, there clamped, in the horizon of the political firmament, an era of the '*Chamchas*'. The Poona Pact, which sanctioned reserved seats along with joint electorate with the Hindus, killed the spirit of self-conscious independent untouchable-movement to emancipate themselves from the yoke of the 'first foreign intruders' of India. They, once again, were debarred constitutionally by the British Parliament to exchange political support with all communities but their tormentors, the Hindus. Therefore, there remained no special ground for them to have separate political party in the situation where vast Muslim and Sikh population were isolated politically from them by awarding Separate Electorate for the minorities. After the great debacle and political blunder in the Poona Pact, the untouchable leaders had nothing to do in political front independently. The Hindus established exclusive right over these votes and the 148 reserved seats. Non-Hindu citizens had no right to make even a comment over the issue of Scheduled Caste or the Tribes. This would have regarded as trespassing. Whatever they were to do politically, they were left with no option but to do with the help and sponsorship of their natural enemy, the Caste-Hindus led by the creamy-layer ruling class. The Indian proletariat or the working classes, the peasantry and artisans became fragmented and weak; the tendency of internecine quarrel of the working class was fanned instead of getting their solidarity consolidated to establish democratic polity on the basis of the principle of social-democracy. This eventually distanced the untouchables socially too from the Muslims, Sikhs and Christians. This helped grow Hindu (Untouchable) Muslim riots in India. Resultantly, the Untouchables rapidly became worthless political nominee of the Hindus in the reserved constituencies. The Hindu political bosses sponsored only their yes-men, the *Bhakta Prahlad, Bhakta Hanuman* and *Bhakta Vibhisan*. The *Chamcha* age began.

In the circumstances, the democratic movement for attaining liberty and freedom of the servile class turned to be a movement of securing safeguards for mere survival. They began their struggle for survival as marginalised citizens of the country. They remained at the mercy of the governing castes in every respect. They sought guarantee for safeguard in the constitutional Articles. In this respect too, they depended on the mercy of the caste-Hindu people who were the *defacto* guardian to interpret and execute the constitutional provisions. These provisions were simply to guard only a limited number of basic interests of human rights, civil and political safe, for a short and specific period. The Parliament in India, a country without the middle class, belongs to the hereditary and creamy-layer ruling families. The laws were left to the interpretery force of the judicial activism, exclusively under a few hundred families. The educated and thinking section of the untouchables remained ceaselessly disturbed and constantly engaged in officially created hazards. Low-profile Welfare Associations of the Untouchables constantly endeavoured to set right the wrongs done on them in this sector. Blessings! Blessings and Blessings of the 'Snakes' were the only hope and shelter for the 'Frogs' for survival.

The creamy-layer hereditary ruling-caste politicians, educationists, industrialists, theocrats, students, professionals, judiciary, bureaucracy, knowledge-councils and various Commissions all in a holy alliance continued to minimize, nullify and wipe out the issue of democratic right to 'representation' of the billions of Untouchables, Tribes and other Backward-caste Sudras in the Executive and Legislature under the term 'reservation' as 'positive discrimination' and 'affirmative justice'. On some pretext or other, these combine forces denied to implement the reservation policy. On the other hand, the thinking section of the untouchables launched organised struggle for implementing the constitutional provisions and statutory safeguards against social injustice and economic offences committed by the matchlessly powerful group of bureaucrats. The bureaucracy and Judiciary, which were maintained from the Government exchequer to implement the constitutional provisions to safe-guard the servile, weaker and backward sections continued to flout and betray them in a calculated and organised manner. They instead offered ceaseless state-sponsored atrocities on them. The responsible Government servants shamelessly behaved anti-national, anti-people and anti-constitution in this regard.

In the given condition, the political parties established and managed by the Brahmins sheltered only those untouchable leaders who served with extreme and undoubted *Bhakta Prahlad*-loyalty to retain Brahmanical sovereignty. In such circumstances, Dr Ambedkar had to declare, "We are as staunchly nationalist as any of the Congress. But we do not want the British to quit India till our rights are safeguarded. If they do, our fate will be more terrible than the fate of any of the oppressed people of Europe.'[5] Untouchable votes, ignorant of the democratic principles and mechanism; modality and functioning of its administration became loot-able, purchase-able, driven-able and mislead able. There was all-out bureaucratic bias against the untouchables and the Sudras, therefore none was there to protect them from the unbridled antagonistic forces of 'Mandirs-money-mafia-media' and state sponsored rules and statutes along with Police force. In such vulnerable condition, having no alternate the Congress people became their role model of a nationalist. However, Guruchand refused to acknowledge the Congress leaders as nationalists as all of them were concerned only with the interests of the urban elites. He, while refusing to join non-cooperation movement asked them to go to the villages where the people of India reside. Guruchand defined nationality and the country '*Desh*' as the people of the land who overwhelmingly are in the rural sides i.e. the country was there only. The country is not just a land mass.[6]

In Bengal, however, the percentage of the Untouchables was not only very high but concentration and socio-political consolidation in some of the districts was also strong to defeat the minority caste-Hindu candidates in many seats in election. A reign of strong apathy and antipathy for Hindus and their political party prevailed amongst the Bengal untouchables. Backward Sudras were numerically negligible. Besides, very large Muslim community was there to play the vital role as their social protectors and a neutral force in political battle. Muslim voters in a calculated mode therefore, were excluded by the legislation of the 'Separate Electorate' from the rest especially from the untouchables. Consequently, without the support of the untouchable votes Hindus faced difficulties to win election. Such a position did not exist anywhere, other than in the Punjab in United States of India. Before the combined force of money-mafia-media of the educated and religious Hindu Gurus, the Untouchables and the Sudras, the just awaken '*Bahujan Samaj*' with its immense majority of 85 to 90 per cent of the population took a miserable stand.

***'Chamcha'* Age Starts**: There was obviously created an era of the *Chamchas* in such a socio-economic and politico-religious situation in particular, under the ever-expanding capitalistic structure. The '*Chamcha-age*' attributed administrative and financial power on the traditional ruling castes besides, installing them at the helm of political affair. The representatives of the vast Untouchable and Tribal population started joining Government services including Indian Administrative Services rather in Indian Civil Services and Indian Political Services (under different *Manuwadi* political parties) against the reserved seats. Instead of launching their own political parties for self-conscious independent democratic movement to become the *defacto* rulers or the ruling class they vied with each other to join political services for other provincial or national parties for remuneration and certain privileges.

The class of people that controls religion reigns over the nation. The Brahmin caste holds divine prerogative over spirituality. They never share their authority with others over religious sector. "Religious nationalism of the orthodox as well as of the reformists had begun to come into existence in the province of Bengal since the first years of the twentieth century. Although its political philosophers and leaders were found subsequently in the persons of Aurobindo Ghosh and Bipin Chandra Paul respectively, its fundamental ideology was conceived by a young intellectual of petty bourgeois origin. He was Narendra Nath Dutta, subsequently known as Swami Vivekananda the *sanyasi* name he adopted.... This youthful band of rebels fanatically believing in the spiritual mission of their Motherland, embodied in themselves the clash of two forces; that of Reaction inducing them to put their nationalism on a religious basis, to host the banner of so called 'aggressive nationalism' which proposes to put up a determined resistance to the menaces of materialism in order to preserve the assumed superiority of the spiritual heritage; and that of revolution, driving them to political nihilism, together with tendencies towards religious or utopian socialism without, however, any appreciation of the laws of social progress. In their religiousness and wild spiritual imperialism, they embodied the reactionaries social forces."[7] With the advent of Poona Pact, in democracy, thus theocratic forces gained the fresh lease to retain their suzerainty in a stronger and absolute manner. *Matuas, Ad-Dhrmis, Ad-Dravids,* Sikhs, Buddhists and Jains, *Ad-Hindus,* Tribes whatever they may say they were hijacked as the Hindus politically.

The Untouchable communities hereafter had to pass decades with the safeguard and survival-scheme in their pockets. The oppressed-elites, i.e. the Untouchable-Leaders of all levels, after seeking assurances for justices and relief from the hereditary ruling class cease back home by leaving the rulers to rule over them. They become the objects for co-option and corruption. Those who refuse to be their *Chamchas* get ignored and neglected; thrown out of all prominence or importance in the mainstream of the official society. No recognition is given to them. Those who help or uphold the cause of the commoners or the depressed communities incur profuse wrath of the hereditary-ruling class. The educated, employed and thinking section of the oppressed-society, therefore, gradually are compelled to get completely alienated from the rural Depressed classes society in which they were born. They remained contented with their meager earnings in metropolises and urban centers being constantly harassed in all possible manners. The benefit of their being enlightened never reached in their dark-villages to relieve them of depression. They form organisations and welfare associations only when and where the hostile executives refused to execute the job-reservation scheme in various ways. In course of time, they gradually forgot and lost the urge for liberty and freedom. Consequently, in India 'Parliamentary Democracy' paved the avenue for establishing a government of 'the hereditary subject class by the hereditary ruling class.' It is thus, truly said, "Parliamentary Democracy is a form of Government in which the function of the people has come to be to vote for their masters and leave them to rule."[8]

At long last, at least two decades after the death of Dr Ambedkar, there appeared an exceptionally brilliant and the greatest social-thinker and political organizer amongst the untouchables, *Manyawar* Kansi Ram. He was a Chamar, a Ramdasi Sikh from the Punjab. He released his book, '*Chamcha* Age' in 1982, in a public meeting named, '*Poona Pact Dhikkar Diwas*' on 24th September, in a public ground at Poona. The book was "Released on 24th September, 1982 on the occasion of 50th anniversary of the Poona Pact". While dealing with the subject the author quoted Dr Ambedkar, "The Joint Electorate is from the stand point of the Hindus to use a familiar phrase a 'rotten borough' in which the Hindus get the right to nominate an untouchable to set nominally as a representative of the untouchables but really as the tool of the Hindus." In pursuance of this condition, he had further proceeded with correct exposition, "These tools, agents and stooges of the High caste Hindus have been increasing in numbers and varieties with the passage of time. The political exigencies of the post-independence period gave a big boost to these tools, agents and stooges. After the sad demise of Babasaheb Dr B.R. Ambedkar in 1956, the process accelerated so much that today these tools, agents and stooges of the High caste Hindus are found in abundance, not only in political field but also in every field of human activity and relationship. Initially these tools, agents and stooges were visible to Dr Ambedkar and to the discerning eyes. Later, they were to be detected by the intelligentia. But today, these tools, agents and stooges are so much a common factor of daily life, that they can easily be detected by the common man in the public. The common man has his own terminology. In his terminology a tool, an agent or a stooge is termed as '*Chamcha*.'[9] Depicting the situation Dr Ambedkar in the post-Poona Pact era, a decade after in 1942 wrote, "What a mentality for a Governing class! What a brazenfacedness for a governing class to use the servile class for such an ignominious purpose and yet claim to be fighting for their freedom. What a tragedy for the servile class to take pride in its own disgrace and join in it voluntarily!"[10] The pathetic cry of Dr Ambedkar expressed in a book to make the foreigners to understand the helplessness of the people of India in general and future of democracy in India touched the deaf ears of his countrymen.

When the Chamcha-Age Starts: Khanshi Ram, the greatest social thinker and organizer of India searched, 'When the '*Chamcha* Age' started?' Manyawar Kanshi Ram himself had stated in answer, "On 24th September, 1932, Poona Pact was forced on the Depressed Classes. With this, there started the *Chamcha* Age. When Hindus were forced to concede a little bit of power, they took to second lane of defense. They saw to it that they must not lose control over it. This was secured by it..... Whether the depressed classes liked it or not, they were pushed into the *Chamcha* Age by the Poona Pact, on 24th September,1932. This *Chamcha* age will be 50 years old on September 24, 1982 when DS-4 denounces Poona Pact at Poona itself."[11] He had also recorded the answer, as to how long the *Chamcha* Age will last. "The high-caste Hindus who are ruling India today had felt the necessity of creating the *Chamchas* only when there was danger to them of the real and genuine leadership of the Depressed Classes. Today, when there is no genuine and real leadership of the oppressed and exploited communities, the *Chamchas* are lying low and they are not much in demand. At any rate, there is no pampering of the *Chamchas* as in the past. But with the emergence of real and genuine leadership through the All India Backwards Minoritiy Communities Employees Federation (BAMCEF) and DS-4 the *Chamchas* may again assume importance. Such a situation will last as long as the struggle between the oppressor and the oppressed lasts." Dr Ambedkar too however, visualised the age of the Stooges or Chamchas to be followed because of the joint electorate and the Poona Pact. He had written, "The Joint Electorate is from the point of the Hindus to use a familiar phrase a 'rotten borough' in which the Hindus get the right to nominate all untouchable to set nominally as a representative of the untouchables but really as a tool of the Hindus." This word tool in Indian term is *Chamcha*. Therefore, his famous biographer recorded, "Ambedkar, the maker and defender of the Poona Pact, up to this moment little dreamt that he would one day be its worst enemy."[12]

Effects of *Chamcha* Age: The greatest damage that the *Chamcha*-Age inflicted upon the untouchable communities is on their voting-pattern; by the virtual disenfranchisement of it. They were no more in a position to select or elect their own representative by casting votes. They got the franchise right but that was to be used or exercised according to the planning and desire of their antagonists. Their franchise rights were hijacked. They lost all chances forever to emancipate them from their 'divine-slavery' as they reentered as part and parcel of the Hindu body. The freedom movement of the Depressed Class that was pioneered by Hari-Guruchand and carried forward by Mukunda Behari, Manindra Chandra Mandal, Virat Chandra Mandasl and Mangoo Ram was reduced to mere 'social-justice movement'; and they were to pray or beg justice from the hereditary Hindu 'Me Lords' as Scheduled Castes. It reduced to a mere safeguard movement. Though belated and post-mortem exercise, Dr Ambedkar raised the issue, protesting the British policy in his letter to Mr. A.V. Alexander, Member Cabinet Mission on 14th May 1946, "How are the Untouchables protesting to maintain their freedom? Only if their representatives in the Legislatures do not owe their election to the votes of the majority. This is the basis of their demand for separate electorates. No safeguards are going to be of any value to the Untouchables unless the Untouchables get a separate electorate. Separate electorate is the crux of the matter...... Realizing that there is no escape from giving the Untouchables some safeguards, the Congress wants to find out some way by which it can make them of no effect. It is in the system of joint electorate that the Congress sees an instrument of making the safeguards of no effect. That is why the Congress is insisting upon Joint Electorate. For joint electorate means giving the untouchables office without power. What the Untouchables want is office with powers. This, they can only get through separate electorate."[13] In 1928, before the Simon Commission Dr Ambedkar, a novice in Untouchable politics, very convincingly refused to understand this truth of the Joint Electorate with reserved seats despite the fact that 16 other veteran leaders from different state Associations of the Untouchable including Bengal strongly demanded separate electorate before the Simon Commission.

In the same letter to Mr. Alexander, Ambedkar mentioned about three (*Chamcha*) Harijan Members of the Congress Party who gave representation before the Cabinet Mission for joint electorate by claiming "We the people of England". Posterity of India had seen the fate of both Dr Ambedkar and J.N. Mandal. The Bahujan Samaj has also witnessed the life and death of Manyawar Kansi Ram. Resultantly, alienation of the newly emerged elites of the servile classes started, out of this so-called movement. The educated and thinking section of the 'oppressed elite's movement concern was only to save and guard their own superficial and ad-hoc interest merely.

The freedom movement of Hari-Guruchand which was initially supported by the British Government as an unconscious response of the history, or due to the impact of the Republican democratic revolution started by the peasantry of France and followed by European nations. Guruchand's protracted movement gave birth to a large section of educated, skilled and conscious population out of their almost void-life of nothingness. Their economic and political aspirations in the reign of the 'Rule of laws' and in the Parliamentary democratic frame created for themselves a distinctly powerful position in the society. There arose a self-conscious group with self-respect and independent aptitude. There came up an elite section in their society. The elites and intellectuals of the oppressed-society formed the harbingers of the freedom struggle of the servile classes. The '*Chamcha* Age' destroyed this vanguard of the *Dalit,* the new name of the oppressed or downtrodden society. Kanshi Ram described the situation, "The *Sudras* and *Ati-Sudras* had been oppressed, exploited and trampled upon for centuries. After getting recognition and some rights, the Scheduled Castes and Scheduled Tribes got education in large numbers. Today the number of these educated people was absorbed in public services is more than 20 lacs. Some of the educated and semi-educated were adopted by various political parties to have access to the SC/ST vote banks. This is the emergence of the elite amongst the 'Oppressed Indians.'

Keeping the nature of these elite in mind, I term it as the 'Oppressed Elites'. These elite are not absorbed either by the 'Ruling Elite' or the elite in the oppression. By both these varieties it (O.E) is used in the shape of *Chamcha*. The political part of these oppressed elites is simply known as the *Chamchas* and the bureaucratic part of it is termed as the *Chamchas* of *Chamchas*."[14] These oppressed elite are product of the scheme of 'Protective discrimination', which resulted out of the Poona Pact. These elite, therefore, tend to concentrate more on those items of Protective Discrimination to protect their own elitist interests. They never dare even to dream or support any freedom struggle lest they lose the favour from the ruling castes. A vested interest of protective discrimination has developed and the struggle for the annihilation of castes or to establish the rule of the immense majority, of the servile class, the lowest stratum has been degenerated into a culture of begging for more and more concessions. And naturally these sections of the society have become asocial if not anti-social, totally irresponsible, noncommittal and non-accountable to their own helpless servile society. They seldom get a chance to go back to their rural centers to develop their conditions. They have been alienated from the servile society; they even hesitate and refuse to give their identity as a member of low caste in the urban centers where they are dragged by the force of economy as *'Babus'* from amongst slum-dogs. Thus the democratic freedom struggle of the teeming millions of the SC, ST, OBC and Proselytes of them have become very difficult.

The Poona Pact thus not only alienated the oppressed elite from their society but it also made them completely apathetic towards the miserable plight of their society in which they were born and the villages or rural sectors they came from to live in comforts of the slums and low-middle class areas of the cities and metropolises. The Poona Pact also (i) destroyed and discouraged independent, self-conscious movement of the oppressed and exploited (ii) made the society leaderless (iii) killed the spirit of revolt (iv) made the Democracy meaningless and (v) sanctioned a lease to the Caste System to perpetuate the country *('Bharat'* and not 'India') as poor and backward. In the independent India the *'Bahujan Samaj'* remained in the state of servitude[15] *'Bharat'* continues to be in the below poverty level and miserable condition in the shining 'India'.[16]

Dr Ambedkar never was able to win election after his first victory in the 1937 election with obvious support of votes from the caste-Hindus. Even Kanshi Ram failed to get elected after his first two victories in election. Both these leaders were made to expire as members of the *Rajya Sabha.* He after getting repeated defeat in several places and elections and being themselves unsuccessful in election realised the real meaning of joint electorate. Ambedkar expressed, "Things will be much worse under the system of joint-electorates and reserved seats which will hereafter become operative under the terms of the Poona Pact. This is no more speculation. The last election (1946) has conclusively proved that the Scheduled Castes can be completely disenfranchised". In July 1946 he even expressed to repeal the Poona Pact. "The Poona Pact which prevented true representatives of the Scheduled Castes from being returned to Legislature must go. It had resulted in disenfranchising 60000000 (60 millions) Untouchables. Even according to the international laws no treaty was final or sacrosanct. As the Poona Pact had now become injurious to their cause, the Scheduled Castes were entitled to fight for its revision."[17]

Collapse of Untouchable and Non-Brahman Party: As the effect of the Poona Pact the untouchables had lay prostrate and politically paralysed as tools in the hands of the Hindu ruling-castes to be used against any minority cause. They became cadres, banner-bearer and vote-banks of the recognised political parties established by the Brahmins, funded by the Brahmins, organised by the Brahmins and led by the Brahmins. The torrential typhoon of politics that emerged out of the Poona Pact swept away all resistive walls built up laboriously by the Untouchables against the hereditary creamy-layer ruling classes in the Punjab, Madras and Bombay provinces. The considerably advanced and matured untouchable-movement and organisational solidarity of the uncompromising lowest stratum in Bengal was affected worst by the slash of this quake. The situation also destroyed righteous, independent political movement of the Backward Sudras under the banner of 'Non-Brahmin Political Party' and Justice Party. The untouchable vote-support was easily exercised against the Backward-Sudras whenever required. This resulted into the decisive doom of all prospects of assertion for emancipation of Indian proletariat or Depressed-classes through the democratic path i.e. on numerical strength, at the first step.

The Backward Sudras had no separate entity politically like the untouchables. They were enumerated as Hindus only. They were the lowest or the servile class of the caste hierarchy. Yet in Madras and Bombay provinces these Backward Sudras rose in revolt against the superciliousness, discriminatory and atrocious attitude of the Brahmins who monopolised almost all privileges, executive and legislative posts in the British Government. It would be very pertinent to quote from Mr. Masao Naito's exposition on the situation of the 'non-Brahmin Movement' in Maharashtra and Madras region. "One of the most conspicuous aspects in the modern history of Maharashtra and Tamil Nadu was the non-Brahman, particularly anti-Brahman, movement which incorporated not only religious, social and economic sphere but also the various forms of political agitation for power....".[18] "In the late 1920s when the non-Brahmin movement was gathering momentum, two young radicals, K. Jedhe and B. Jawalkar, entered the arena. In line with the young generations of Marathas they led active movement against the Brahmans ascendancy, and at the same time they took part in movement led by Ambedkar demanding the opening of public places and institutions to Untouchables. But most of the Maratha activists who took the place of the political leaders of Maharashtra, mainly Brahmans, in the process of the Gandhi-led national liberation struggled drifted away from the movement to fight against untouchability. It may safely be said that in 1932, when Keshavrao Jedhe formally joined the Indian National Congress, the Maratha-dominated non-Brahmin movement in Maharashtra was finally alienated from the anti-untouchability cause."[19] The remarks are obvious and historically very significant.

The fundamental reason of the shift of this non-Brahmin political aspirations from self-dependant, self-conscious independent movements to the selfish and subservient nationalist co-opt-movement in Madras and Maharashtra seems to be lying in the abject surrender of the untouchables' freedom movement to the nationalist Congress movement in Poona Pact 1932. In the post-Poona Pact era, there was no chance of winning the battle of liberty or capturing power-politics by the backward-class Sudras under the banner and from the platform of the 'Non-Brahmin Political Party'. The combine strength of the untouchables and the Brahmanical ruling classes (Brahmin-Baniya) in the non reserved constituencies, especially when the

Muslims got isolated politically due to 'separate electorate' was formidable in Indian tricky politics. Besides, it was not prudent for the non-Brahmins Backward Castes to continue tirade against the Brahmins when the wretched untouchables too surrendered and had started taking advantages in political field by joining hand with the Brahmin *Shatagrahis*. When the untouchables ran after the blessings of the Brahmin-high commands for social justice, the political party called Justice Party (created by non-Brahmins in Madras) no more remained dependable for getting justice. On the contrary, the Backward Sudras are found to have started causing all atrocities against the Untouchables in the villages and saluting the Brahmins or the Baniya-Kshatrias.

Thus, the historic cessation of anti-Brahman political march by the backward-Sudras of Bombay-Madras, right in the initial stage of formation of democratic polity and society in India, left the microscopic minority and anti-democratic hereditary ruling class to perpetuate their hereditary rule in the name of the hereditary subject classes under the banner of Common Wealth of Parliamentary Democracy. Had there been no Poona Pact, the threat to oust the Brahmins from their hereditary theocratic throne given by the backward Sudras of the South would have inspired and united the backward Sudras of East and North India to culminate the Peoples Democracy in India soon after. The Untouchables would have been their first ally in the process.

Bombay and Madras: Thus the Poona Pact not only killed the freedom movement of the untouchables but it also killed the prospects of '*Bahujan*-servile class movement'. The backward-Sudra leaders of the powerful Non-Brahmin Political party wanted to prove themselves equal to the situation, created due to joining of the Untouchables in the Hindu or the Congress Camp in Poona Pact not by challenging Brahmanical Manuwadi crder but by surrendering to them. They advanced to join Congress, Hindu Mahasabha or the Communist Party of India with equal speed to capture privileges even before the untouchable leaders. Overwhelming reign of *Chamcha*-Age started. Consequently, in a later period Dr Ambedkar dreamt to rebuild the 'Non-Brahman Political Party'. On 17th January 1943, while in Bombay he declared, "...that true democracy in India could be safe only in the hands of the Non-Brahman Party....he regretted that the Non-Brahmin Party which was in power in the Madras and Bombay Provinces had now disintegrated owing to various reasons..... It was pity that many members of the Non-Brahmin Party had left it and joined the Congress, but they were regretting their mistake. It was necessary not only for the members of the particular communities but also in the interest of democracy in India that the Non-Brahmin Party should rebuild itself and become a power."[20]

In most of the provinces except Bengal and the Punjab neither the concentration nor the numerical strength of the untouchables was very comfortable. They lacked socio-political ally like Muslims, Sikhs and Christians (except in the Punjab and Bengal) at a point of crisis. In Maharashtra, the non-Brahmin backwards initially were the allies and friends of the Untouchables. The struggles of Mahatma Phooley and Sahu Maharaja was not restricted to backwards only, they included untouchable's education, job and political problems too in their agenda. The Bombay Legislative Council too gained a nominated representative from the Untouchable community. D.D. Gholap was the first untouchable to be in the Bombay Legislative Council as their representative in 1922. As a legislator, he strongly fought to protect their interests. Amongst the backward Sudras, S.K. Bole, one of the most upright humanitarian, as an Hon'able member fought in the Legislative Council courageously fought for the justice for the Untouchables. On August 4, 1923, moving a resolution in the Legislative Council he said, 'that the untouchability was a great stigma on the good name of India and added: "We resent the segregation polity of the South African Colonies and therefore, we must set our house in order. It is in our interest and in the interest of the country that the Depressed Classes should be given better treatment."[21] The conflict between the Sudras and the Brahmins for social and democratic status reached at its zenith in the region during those days. Out of this turmoil situation, Dr Ambedkar even gained and secured his position as a lawyer. The belligerent low caste Sudra youths condemned Brahmins in a published pamphlet that the Brahmins had ruined India. The Brahmins of Poone knocked the doors of Judiciary to suppress the voices of the Backwards' anti-Brahmin tirade. Non-Brahmin leaders K.B. Bagde, Keshavrao Jedhe and Dinkarrao Javalkar were implicated in the lawsuit. Dr Ambedkar took up the case, with eloquence ferocity he defended the case. In October 1926 he won the case in favour of the non-Brahmin backward Sudras.[22] The Brahmins, out of this resounding victory, realised the quick, catastrophic collapse of the Brahmanical citadel in case the Untouchable joined hands with the non-Brahmin Sudra leaders in Bombay province too. In the entire region of eastern India and in the Punjab the situation was already precariously volatile for the Brahmins even without the interference of the backward Sudras for the cause of untouchables.

Consequently, with a view to solving this perennial problem of Brahmanism, Gandhiji and his National Congress even nodded to a proposal of the Muslim leaders in Bombay, engaged in the Gandhi-sponsored 'Khilafat' movement to convert 50 per cent of around 17 lakhs (total) untouchables of Bombay province to Islam and to leave the remnant 50 per cent for the Hindus to consume.[23]

Phooley is declared to have been the Guru, teacher/leader of Dr Ambedkar. Consequently, Dr Ambedkar, from the beginning of his public life seems to have not in favour of 'Separate Electorate'. It proved to have had two edges for him. By the demand of 'Separate Electorate' he would have alienated from his Guru and backward non-Brahmin Sudra friends. In Bombay province, they were their mutual hope and strength because the untouchables alone were microscopic minority. By not demanding 'Separate Electorate', he on the other hand alienated himself from the mainstream untouchable movements, which had started and had been going on in Bengal and the Punjab. However, this was beneficial for the Brahmins. Besides, he was not ready to abandon or even avoid his Brahmin friends who assisted him from his childhood and gave him the surname, 'Ambedkar'. He could not forget the assistance, guidance and help by Krishnaji Kerluskar, a Marathi Brahmin. Ambedkar no doubt suffered the dilemma in accepting the term *'Shatyagrah'* the Gandhian slogans and he adopted it as plank of his movement till last.

Besides, Dr Ambedkar's pro-Brahmin attitude initially gave a lethal blow to the formation and growth of backward-untouchable *Bahujan* movement. Four great leaders of the Sudras (touchable and untouchable) Guruchand, Sahu Maharaj, Periyar Ramaswami Naikkar and Dr Ambedkar were contemporary. Still EVR Naikkar and Dr Ambedkar did not launch any concrete or planned movement. None of them ever tried to meet Guruchand. Once, however, Jinnah, Periyar and Ambedkar shared the same dais of the 25th annual session of the Muslim League in 1945 at Madras. Periyar was the most dedicated anti-Brahmin leader. The millionaire EVR Periyar promised to weed out Brahmanism from its roots. He suggested for conversion to Islam, as Islam according to him was the only panacea for the cancerous disease of Hindu caste-system. EVR Periyar was of the opinion that there was no good Brahmin to support even the just cause of the Sudras. He declared that the Dravidians with their distinct and indigenous language, culture and ethnicity were not Hindus or Aryans who were of Nordic foreign origin. He asked his people to kill a Brahmin first if they face a Brahmin and a snake in the street; as the Brahmin was more dangerous than a snake. EVR stood erect against the Indian National Congress and Gandhi on this issue. Dr Ambedkar was a contrast to such a situation in the beginning. When Dr Ambedkar declared his maiden public demonstration of Mahad *Satyagraha,* the non-Brahmin leaders Javalkar and Jedhe tendered their whole-hearted support to the move on condition that the Brahmin should be 'weeded out' from the body of the organizers. But Ambedkar refused by telling, 'the view that all Brahmins were the enemies of the Untouchables was erroneous'.[24] Dr Ambedkar took along with him the celebrity son of the most orthodox Brahmin *Lokmanya* Tilak, named Sidharpant in the *Satyagraha*. The backwards yet stood behind Ambedkar during the *Mahad Satyagraha*. Those who without being united were most helpless failed miserably to forge a united front as the 'Non-Brahmin Political Party'. In those days, Dr Ambedkar instead of standing by them threw cold-water to the 'non-Brahmin Political Party'. The anti-unity situation culminated into the collapse of non-Brahman movement. Finality with the signing of the Poona Pact thus pushed everybody to the *'Chamcha Age',* the age of the stooges of the Brahminism.

The second largest untouchable community in Maharashtra after Mahar and Mang was the *Chambhars*. One of their prominent leaders Pandurang Nathuram Rajbhoj, 'after graduating from New Marathi School at the age of 18, had gone to Pune and joined the *Asprusyata Nivarak Mandal* (Untouchability Abolition Society, founded in 1917) headed by Sripad Mahadev Mate. It was the *Mahad Talab Satyagraha* in 1927 that gave Rajbhoj a complete turnabout. He had joined the *Mahad Talab* agitation launched by Dr Ambedkar and seriously got injured when the Hindus suddenly attacked them. He had to remain in a dispensary for 15 days because of serious injury inflicted on him by a farmer who opposed the *Satyagraha*. In 1928, he started the '*Dalit Bandhu*' (Friends of Untouchables), his first newspaper. But this spirited leader in Rajbhoj too in 1932 started showing more interest in Gandhi and his mission and finally in 1933 joined the 'Sabarmati Ashram' of Gandhi in Ahmedabad. "After this, in March 1935, Rajbhoj founded the *Bahratiya Dalit Seva Sangh* (All-India Untouchables Service League) at Kanpur in North India with other *Harijan* leaders like Rasik Lal Biswas (from Bengal) and Jagjivan Ram, a leader of *Chamars* of Bihar….."[25] There was virtually an exodus of the Dalit-leaders from the untouchable camp to the Congress camp. Dr Ambedkar defined Congress as the first Brahmanical Party, soon after the precarious and devastating landslide of the Poona-Pact. There arose rather a stiff competition as to who could have proved as one of the best and greatest *Chamcha*, the most obedient and loyal servant of the Hindu system and of the Brahmanical political parties, be it Congress, Communist or Hindu Mahasabha. Enrollment of the Harijan leaders in the party was made by the discretionary choice of the political bosses who as a norm preferred to choose the worst and most incompetent of the untouchable lot.

The British authority nominated M.C. Raja as an MLC in the Madras Legislature in 1922 just after Bhisya Dev Das in Bengal in 1921. Raja, an untouchable pariah was strongly anti-Hindu and a forceful supporter of 'Separate Electorate'. Indeed, he was the product as well as the propagator of Adi-Dravida movement which declared themselves completely different from the foreign Aryan-Brahmin stock. They claimed their ethnic, cultural and linguistic origin in the soil and wanted to liberate them from the British yoke as well as from Brahmin thralldom. And in this goal the British rule was regarded by the untouchable pariahs as their saviour and friend. Mr A.R. Cox, ICS Collector of Madras, while presenting the *sanad* and Badge of Rao Bahadur to Mr M.C. Raja MLC, on the 15th December 1922 at the Durbar held in the Pachiappa's hall, said, "You are such a well known public man that it is almost unnecessary for me to say much about you. No doubt you have received this title because of work you have done for and in esteem in which you are rightly held by the members of your important community of the Ad-Dravidians..... You have represented your community in deputations to the Right Hon'able the Secretary of State and to His Excellency the Viceroy. You are the first Adi-Dravida to enter the Legislative Council and you have the interests of the depressed and poor always at heart.... I understand that your grandfather was an Indian Mutiny Veteran."[26] It was he, who while taking the deposition of Bengal leader, Mukunda Behari helped make it more pointed for the demands of 'Separate Electorate'. He organised several meetings and sent cables supporting the leadership of Dr Ambedkar in the RTC when Gandhi challenged his nomination. But after the Poona Pact, he too surrendered to the Congress group and became exceedingly vocal in support of Hinduism and Joint Electorate. He became so passionately anti-Ambedkarite that in countering Ambedkar's tirade against Hindus during 1935 M.C. Raja declared, "I was born a Hindu and I will die as a Hindu." Little is known about the leader, M Srinivasan from down south, who was the co-representative of Indian Untouchables in the Round Table Conference initially. He was co-opted by the Gandhian Congress movement soon after.

The non-Brahmin leaders formed Justice Party. It formed government in Madras. "With the powers vested in the hands of the Justice Party Government, the right to make use of all roads by all castes was brought into practice. The Justice Party Government brought in a legislation, even in those days permitting the so-called low caste people to make use of water from the wells, which had all along been exclusively reserved only for the Brahmins.

These are all things, which took place before the days of Gandhiji. It is absurd and fraudulent to say that it is only Gandhi, who did all these things. Not only this. The justice Party people were the first people to pave the way for all castes to enter the Panchyat, Municipalities, Taluk Boards, District Boards and Legislative bodies even before the coming of Gandhi. They nominated the representatives of the so-called low caste people (the Untouchables) called as "Pariahs" to enter the Legislatures on par with the so-called High caste Brahmins. Chakilis, Pallars, were members of the Legislatures. I want you all to clearly understand this truth."[27] The situation that was created by the backward Sudras in democratisation of Indian polity and society was narrated vividly by Periyar the Great, contemporary Sudra leader. But it was altered diametrically with the advent of Gandhi-Ambedkar-Jinnah of Bombay in political arena.

The post-Justice Party politics in Madras as well as on national plane was spear headed by M. K. Gandhi. Periyar discloses on Gandhi, "As a matter of fact Gandhi's plans were different. He was not for allowing all the Sudras and the Untouchables to bale out water from wells and tanks along with high caste Brahmins. He was not for permitting Untouchables to enter the temples along with the high caste people. Originally, he only insisted on the continuance of certain rights exclusively for the highest caste. He upheld the Manu code. He was for separate temples, Wells, tanks and dwellings for the Highest caste Brahmins and the low-caste Sudras. That was the original plan of Gandhi, I know it. Let anyone deny. Today, false propaganda is carried on about Gandhi."[28] Gandhij's laurel, the Poona Pact as a natural corollary destroyed political dreams of the Untouchables, Sudras and the autochthon Tribes along with the Democracy. Champion Chamchas only glitter in the Indian democracy of hereditary ruling families.

Kerala: In those days, there existed no state called Kerala in the down south of India. On the southern tip, it was a princely state called Travancore. It (Malabar) came under British yoke for the first time in 1792. However, there prevailed crudest form of hate-philosophy and reign of Brahmanical purity since the advent of Islamic rule. Buddhists were tortured out of the scene and that gave birth to the extreme Hindu fundamentalist thinker like Adi Shankara. His militant and terrorist organisations and also the advent of the Namboodri Brahmanism not only rigidified caste but also introduced the most heinous form of inhuman torture on humanity by means of observing a social system that declared more than 20 per cent of people the lowest stratum of human society as even unapproachable. These untouchables and unapproachable two-footed animals '*Nripasus*' were engaged in all agricultural production units without any right to anything. They were debarred to tread and use main public roads and market places.

History, however, woke up in the south-west tip to fulfill its destiny by joining the anti-caste and anti-untouchability movement going on in the eastern sector of India. No outside factors or incidents influenced or ignited this anti-untouchability movement down south. Its history, therefore, remained exclusively confined to the state. The nationwide problem of untouchability, caste atrocity and hatred never got coordinated as a national problem. Saga of Kerala movement by the untouchable hero remained isolated; it failed to influence other states. Similar movements of other provinces never showed solidarity with them.

A boy called 'Ayyankali was born to Ayyar and Mala on 28 August 1863, in Venganoor, a small village 13 km north of Thiruvananthapuram'. Without being influenced and without having any information in regard to the untouchables' freedom struggle in Bengal that started in 1872 (first agricultural strike in Bengal) under the leadership of Hari-Guruchand, Ayyankali as a perfect tool in the hands of history raised the banner of same rebellion against Brahmanism and sought freedom for the pursuit of honourable human life.

His caste 'Pulayar' was un-approachable by the surrounding Hindu castes. His father earned five acres of land from his benevolent '*Janmi*', the landlord. Ayyankali was brought up to be a robust and exceedingly energetic young boy of exceptional physical strength and equally erect personality with self-respect. His courage and self-respect, his protest against the caste-Hindus and Brahmanical social order, his single-handed attacks on the Nairs against their atrocious and exploitative measures on his caste-men made him instantly a hero and leader of all the Pulayar youths. He trained them with martial arts and formed a formidable band of social-soldiers. He virtually declared war against the caste-Hindus and against their inhuman attitude and social activities. Several times, consequently with street-fights between the rebellious boys of Ayyankali and Nairs and Menons the region was engulfed and a situation of civil-war on caste line prevailed. "During the early phase of his career, his policy was to physically attack the caste-Hindu oppressors. It was a form of natural and raw protest because his caste-people were suffering from the brutalities of the caste-Hindus, particularly the Nairs. His tendency to challenge social oppression as well as external pressure from the people of his caste and their miserable living conditions might have greatly influenced him in opposing the upper-caste feudal lords. Therefore, the social activism of Ayyankali can be considered as a spontaneous revolt of the oppressed."[29] He did not believe in any kind of passive resistance. He refused to keep quiet and fall in line with the Hindu scriptural dictum of caste. He decided to win the problems by way of direct attack and war on the enemy.

In 1907, in his mid forties, Ayyankali established an organisation called '*Sadhujana Paripalana Sangam*' (SJPS) with all the untouchable castes to raise their organised demands. Ayyankali was planning to convert his entire community to Islam. However, the Hindu Swami Sadananda and Narayan Guru influenced them so that conversion move was arrested. They eventually succeeded to keep the untouchable 'divine slaves' as subservient to the Hindu society along with the huge percentage of Muslim and Christian population in the land. In 1904 for the first time in Kerala Ayyankali had attempted to start an independent school for the untouchables, as they were not allowed admission in the Schools maintained by the Hindus with public money. In 1910, P. Rajagopalachari, the *Diwan* of Travancore and Mitchell the Director of education department considered Ayyankali's petition favourably. In the Government-schools when the untouchable students entered the caste-Hindu students walked out.

"Even after large scale incidence of violence, the caste Hindus remained firm in their decision not to admit untouchable children into their schools. In order to make them relent, Ayyankali formulated a new strategy of agitation to challenge the upper caste feudal lords of Travancore. He and his associates organised the first ever strike of agricultural labour in 1912.'

'Unable to bear the 'insubordination', the landlords had tried to enlist a few turncoats to work in the fields, but Ayyankali's army of young men had not let that happen. The food grain stock dwindled and starvation faced the workers who began to waver. At this point of episode, Ayyankali provided the twist in the tale. He made a patch with the fishermen community of Vizhinjom, they agreed to take one person from each *Dalit* family in each fishing boat and give a share of the day's catch till the strike was over. The tyrannical landlords knew their impending doom, so they set free to untouchable habitations. In a typical eye-for-an-eye style, Ayyankali's men set fire to the landlord's homes.'

The untouchables of Kerala in those days were forced to wear a thick garleng of cord around their neck so that they could be identified by the Hindus from afar. Ayyankali asked his people to put off that garland of mark of slavery. Many left it immediately. However, many dared not. They told that the Hindus would beat them had it been removed. Then Ayyankali ordered his stout comrades to beat their own brethren who would be found in slave-untouchable garland. The boys arranged regular duty on the crossroads and would give street beating to any and every community man wearing the thread. They used to collect kilos of threads at the end of the day from each spots. Eventually the untouchables were thus forced to shake off the symbols of tyranny of the Hindu over-lordship on the body of the untouchables.

"When Ayyankali obtained permission from the Department of Education to start a school at Venganoor, he started to hunt (1913-14) for a teacher. No *dalit* was educated enough to take up the job of a teacher, and no progressive caste-Hindu wanted to risk his life in joining the schools of the Untouchables. Finally, Parameswaran Pillai of Kaithamukku in the capital joined as a teacher. The incensed caste-Hindus destroyed the school on the first day itself. The next day it was built back. The teacher could go to his home only with the support of his body guards. This school was destroyed at least five times by the frenzied caste-Hindus."[30] Ayyankali faced the same situation what Guruchand faced in the marshy lands of the Eastern Bengal when all the educated caste Hindus refused to be a teacher in his school four decades back. Condition in Kerala was worse because of their lesser number in comparison to Bengal. No Hindu dared set the schools on fire in Bengal as was done in case of Travankore. In retaliation, Ayyankali is reported to have set the Hindu's school on fire. And this only brought some relief for the untouchables.

Ayyankali's ceaseless struggle through the mass movement for democratic emancipation, as a natural corollary, also developed political aspirations amongst the untouchables of Kerala. Ayyankali and his people began to demand for getting share in the governance of the country as the British started replacing royal arrangements with democratic structure. Ayyankali was nominated in 1911 as a member of the *Srimoolam Praja Sabha.* He delivered his maiden speech in the *Praja Sabha* in 1912. By now the ruling classes adopted their scheme of passive resistance and destroying the untouchable movement by any means. They penetrated in the body politics of the Untouchables in different forms. The mental integrity and social consolidation amongst different castes of the untouchables that Ayyankali fostered needed to be destroyed at the first instance. The Hindus started weakening this phenomenon by disturbing their internal unity of castes by giving nomination in the *Srimoolam Proja Sabha* from respective caste groups simultaneously by instigating internecine quarrel. This culminated in the post Poona Pact era into a complete surrender to the Congress politics. Their main target reduced to a mere safeguard movement on social-justice line as it was on the national platform. Consequently, the Brahmins of Kerala under the banner of Congress-Communists gradually assimilated Ayyankali, his name and his mission of freedom totally.

The Punjab: The history of the Punjab during last one thousand years has been spectacularly distinct with valorous and crisscross warfare between both Indian rulers and Indian chiefs and between the ruling groups of the locality with the foreign invaders. It has been the history of successive defeats of the local tribes and rulers in the hands of the aggressors. The marching and counter-marching of army, ravages of soldiers and marshal or military mobilisations continually dismantled all long term social or cultural set up in the regions and failed to give birth to caste hierarchy and a fragmented society with a regular system. Majority of the population deserted Brahmanism and embraced Islam since 8th century. A large section also took refuge under a new faith Sikhism preached by Guru Nanakdevji. The region of the Punjab therefore, emerged as the weak place of caste divisions. Despite these hard facts Brahmins did not spare the land to pollute with the vulture-culture of casteism. We may not forget that the Brahmin Peswa rulers captured Delhi. In the 3rd battle of Panipath the Maratha (Peswa) army was defeated by Ahmad Saha Durani in 1761 to reinstall the titular Mughal Emperor Saha Alam who recognised the anchor-sheet of British Rule in India by sanctioning *Dewani* of Bengal Bihar and Orissa to the East India Company in 1765. Caste factor and caste-consciousness amongst the minority Hindus started emerging in the region only after the end of the 18th-19th century. The gangrene of caste eventually weakened its vitals within decades and finally vivisected the regions into parts. Sikhism was born in the region. Guru Nanak Devji tried to save the race by composing his Guru Granthsahib by taking most of the tenets of Buddhism in it. He preached for women empowerment and against caste-difference and caste-hatred along with opposing slavery.

There arose very powerful rebel in Kabir who raised 'Kabirpanthis' out of the oppressed Indians. Ravi Das or Ruidas became famous as a *'Sant'*. The son of a *'Chamar'* or a cobbler-family who have been treated by the Brahmanical Hindu as untouchable was accepted as a Guru, the spiritual and social leader or teacher by his community. This was a challenge and a direct threat to the Brahmanism. According to Brahmanical scripture, only a Brahmin can become a *Guru* as per their divine covenant. Ravi Dasji denounced Caste system and the hate philosophy. He refused to accept the Brahmin's claim of purity and consequential impurity of others. He declared, '*Man Changa To Kahtoti Me Ganga'* a man of clean-mind is pure as the water of the Ganges. In British India the untouchables like 'Ravidasis' and 'Kabirpanthis' along with 'Sikhs' worked together in the lower-strata of the society against the Brahmanical social order. With the beginning of the 20th century the Punjab Suba was dotted with innumerable '*Deras*' the camps or centers of their own and independent organisations and institutions under the leadership of different *Gurus*. During A.D. 1900 to 1905 the most powerful 'Dera' of '*Sachkhand Ballan*' the centre of truthful people, founded by Pippal Das who came from Ravidasi community was established.

The Hindus too started mischief of diverting their target by accepting the untouchables like Ravidas, Kabir Das etc as Hindu saints of *Bhakti* movement and as the *Avatars* of Hinduism by violating their doctrine of castes and against their spiritual philosophy that the Untouchables can never have even human status.

There came up movements in the Punjab for gaining democratic or parliamentary representation for untouchable in the early 1920 under active initiation of Sant Ram. They started rallying around the democratic structure for equal rights. It came as a reaction to the '*suddhi*' movement started by the Arya Samajis. With a view to arresting the contemporary process of exodus of the Untouchables and the Sudras in the Islamic fold, Arya Samaj was founded by a Hindu orthodox Brahmin sage. Arya Samaj was simply to exploit the volatile situation created by the democratic aspirations of the struggling untouchables against general hatred and caste oppression in the Hindu society. The sage, Maharisi Dayanda Saraswati and his team started hijacking and assimilating the thinking section of the untouchables by preaching that the Sudras and untouchables, the eternal source of pollution can be purified and taken even as the Brahmin Hindus. Attempts were started to win back even the converted Muslims through Vedic re-conversion ceremony. They actually purified many of the untouchable vanguards to pure and top caste Hindus. Nevertheless, this movement definitely could not open doors for all as it did not attempt any system correction. The philosophy of hatred and discriminatory actions all over India continued to pervade in a clandestine form as it was running as a latent force amongst the Arya-Samajists.

In 1922, Sant Ram established '*Jat Pat Todrak Mandal'* an institution to annihilate Caste-system in Lahore. However, the Untouchables of the province started the real and liberation movement of the Untouchables called '*Ad-dhammi'* movement, by declaring war against Hindu atrocities. They declared that the Hindus were foreigners and claimed for themselves as a distinct ethnic and religious group. A strong and uncompromising movement of the Untouchables began in early 1925 under the leadership of Mangooram, a Chamar by caste. Mangooram was born in 1886 in the Hosiarpur district in the Punjab. He got associated with the militant and nationalist 'Gaddar movement' in 1913 while he was in California. After passing Matriculation, he went there for earning his bread in 1909. While smuggling arms for his revolutionary-party to India via Java or New Caledona, he was caught along with four others by the British Police in Japan. The Jap-government imprisoned them for one year. But the British decided to hang them. However, before execution they were rescued by the Germans. Mangoo Ram then reached Singapore where two British spies Bhag Singh and Bela Sing caught and handed over him to the British authority. The British ordered to put him before the firing squad. Again, the Germans whisked Mangoo Ram away and placed on a ship for Manila. While he was in Rangoon in a fugitive condition, he read in the 'Manila Times' that Mangoo Ram had been tried and executed by the British police.

Thus, he got a new lease of free life in another man and decided to come home back. After a long gap, he returned to his native village in 1925 via Sri Lanka and Madras. In course of his long ordeal of journey through rural India he experienced the plight of untouchability. Standing in the fire-circle of inhuman cruelty of hatred, atrocities, exploitation and discrimination on the untouchables in India, Mangooram being fired with the enthusiasm of his past life with militant freedom-fighters rose to revolt against the Brahmanical system. He discovered the notorious enemy of the humanity in the Brahmins and their hate and purge philosophy. He resolved to rescue the victims of the system. Soon after reaching India Mangoo Ram informed about the pathetic plight of untouchables of the country. He immediately wrote back to his leaders in the Gaddar Party that he resigns from the party as he had discovered and identified the real enemy of Liberty. "He declared publicly, the freedom of untouchables is more important to him than of his nation. He emphasised that the untouchables have three layers of slavery and on the top of that was the slavery of Hindus; slavery of British and slavery of local state kings."[31] On the basis of the historical evidences he had claimed his ethnic, linguistic and cultural origin in India. As a member of the autochthons, he declared war against the foreign intruders, the Aryan Brahmins and *Arya Samaj*. In addition, he unfurled the banner of liberty for the 'Oppressed India'. .He established *Ad-dhammi* organisation in 1926.

The manifesto of the '*Ad-dhammi*' published in 1926 recorded, "We are the original people of this country, and our religion is '*Ad-Dharam*'. The Hindu Qaum (community) came from outside and enslaved us. When the original sound from the conch was sounded, all the brothers came together, the *Chamar, Chuhra, Sainsi, Bhanjre, Bhil* and all the untouchables to make their problems known. Brothers, there are seventy million of us listed as

Hindus; but we must separate ourselves and set ourselves free. We trusted the Hindus, but they turned out to be traitors. Brother, the time has come: wake up; government is listening to our cries. Centuries have passed, but we were asleep, brothers. Look at the lines that Manu had written, but he is a murderer. There was a time when we ruled India, brother, and the land used to be ours. The Hindus came from Iran and destroyed our *qaum*. They became the owners, and then called us foreigners, disinheriting seventy million people. They turned us into nomads. They destroyed our history, brothers. The Hindus rewrote our history. There is hope from god (*Bhagwan*) and help from the king. Send members to the Councils and start the *qaum* anew, brothers. Come together to form a better life"[32&33] Mark Juergensmeyer, Religious Rebels in the Punjab, pp. 269-288.

Their claim for religious identity was registered in 1930 by the Census Department. "Before and during the consensus of 1931, the Hindi-Sikhs jointly took action against the untouchables as they were registering themselves as Ad-Dharmis. They were trapped in their houses with thorny branches placed in their doors. They could not take water from wells and could not buy goods from shops. Their women and young daughters were raped on the roads and insulted. The houses of untouchables were burnt and looted. In cases like two men in Firozpur were burnt alive and a girl was killed in Lyallpur by upper castes. They were uprooted from their village in Kangra and Hamirpur. The Sikh volunteers were guarding the dirty pounds so that untouchables would not get water. Finally, 418,789 people registered themselves as Ad-Dharmis in Census 1931 including two Jains, twenty Brahmins, 5000 Arya Samajis, 350000 Sikhs, 2000 Christians. Due to the great efforts of Mangoo Ram, in 1931 Census, the Untouchable population in the state augmented to 13.5 per cent from earlier enumerated 10 per cent or a little less in 1911. In the Poona Pact, however, Dr Ambedkar secured only 8 reserved seats instead of at least 22 seats on prorate basis as it was done in case of Bombay and Madras Provinces.

The fight of Ad-Dharm for identity was proved and Lothian Committee came to India. After hearing the views of Ad-Dharma the Lothian Committee declared a Communal Award. This was the second win of the movement for their human rights. Though Poona Pact was done between Gandhi and Ambedkar but Ad Dharma Mandal was not satisfied because their identity was finished due to this pact. However, Ad Dharm won seven reserved seats of MLA in Punjab in 1937. Ad Dharm won four seats in next election in 1946 and Mangu Ram got elected from Hosiarpur."[33] The untouchable who won the remaining 8th reserved seat joined Ad Dharm soon after. The unique and exceptionally illustrious was the finding that out of 69,126 polled and valid votes, not even a single ballot went in the box of the Indian National Congress. Under the towering personality and sagacious political leadership of Mangoo Ram, the entire community in the Punjab stood behind Mangoo Ram like a solid rock in 1937 election. Congress failed miserably.

The Ad-Dharmis also issued the journal to express their democratic rights in the free country of their own in 1926 with their own resources; initially it was in Punjabi language. The journal called *'Adi-Danka'* the war-drum of the autochthons of India started appearing in the Urdu language too from 1930. They raised funds from the grass-root levels, as it was the self-conscious independent movement of the *bahujan* of India in the Western sector. The largest financial and philosophical contribution, however, came from Seth Krishna Das, a millionaire leather merchant from the Chamar community in Calcutta. Krishna Das supplied all information regarding the democratic movement of the Chandals of Bengal to the leaders of the Punjab. The history was waiting for Bengal-Punjab movement to come together that never came to reality because of the Poona Pact.

The powerful conviction, intense longing for manumission from the slavery of the Hindu Concentration camp and clarity for the target or enemy identification of the Ad Dharmis can be traced in their memorandum dated 12/ 10/ 1029 to his Excellency, Sir Geoffrey Fitzhervey, the Governor General of the Punjab. It reads, ... "Owing to the predominance of the Muslims there is less untouchability in this province, as compared with other provinces but as regards political condition we are not a bit better than the worst untouchables of other provinces, but we are in the worst condition from the political point of view. Not even a single member of our community has ever been nominated to the local legislative or to any local body although in other provinces such nominations, have been made by the Government to the extent of seats ranging between 1 to 11 in Local legislative. The present system of electorate cannot be of any use to us because the high class Hindus steeped with caste prejudices. Therefore, the only method open to us should be separate electorate where in our political social and even moral salvation lie.

Our position can be briefly described as follows:

1. That our community consists of about three million in Punjab, and about seventy million in whole of India.
2. That comparatively speaking we are the most backward people in the Punjab as because education, public service, social position etc.
3. That we do not believe in the Hindu religion nor do we hold it in high esteem, therefore, we do not wish to call ourselves Hindus but we the all untouchables of different classes being the ancient population of India wish to be called 'Ad- Dharmis'. And in the coming Census we should write Ad Dharmis'.
4. We do not desire to keep any close social or political contact with the high caste Hindus, who think that they are polluted by our mere touch or even by casting of our shadow on them, though they endeavour to count us with them so that they may enjoy greater right at our expense. So these aspects of our position can be remedied by our following petty demands.

Our Demands

(i) Necessary arrangement for better education of Ad Dharmis (untouchables) boys and girls and national scholarship should be separately given to them and introduction of free primary education.

(ii) Separate representations, in all public body and Legislature selected by the communities of our mandal."[34]

As a natural corollary, during the Round Table Conference in London in 1930-32, Mangoo Ram vehemently opposed the move of 'joint electorate' by M.K. Gandhi. With all his organisational force, he supported Dr B.R. Ambedkar for his struggle for 'Separate Electorate' for the Untouchables, the Muslims and for the Sikhs. His '*Ad-Dhammi Mandal*' played a historic role for the untouchables of the Punjab to be enumerated in the Census as Scheduled Castes. Their cry was, "Leave the bickering behind, and tie your turban red; We do not have to record any '*qoum*' or caste other than our own; So *Ad-Dhammi* be strong.

The *Ad-dhammi* movement obviously identified the enemy and friends. They, independently took similar path as Bengal started half a century ago, and declared that the British rule in India and the British were their friend and deliverer. The *Ad-dhamma* report of 1926-31 reveals, "As long as India's weak minorities, especially the *Ad-dhammis* and the Muhammadans are not given full representation, and there is no guarantee of their treatment, there should be no change in the Central Government.... India should not be given independence until the untouchables are free and equal. Otherwise, it would be a disgrace to the British rule." '....that is why we want to do away with untouchability and the whole system of castes.'

In 1929, the leaders of the *Ad-dhammis* moved the resolution before the British Government, "We are not Hindus, and we strongly request the government not to list us in the Census as Hindus. Our faith is not Hindu, but *Ad-dhamma*. We are not part of Hinduism, and Hindus are not part of us."[35]

At this juncture, the Congress, Gandhi and J.L. Nehru launched the '*Valmiki*'-card to Hinduize these rebels, patriotic and freedom-monger untouchables. Stories were spread that these '*Bhangis*' were *Valmikis*. They were later on treated as Valmiki caste even though there is no mention of such a caste either in Gita, Manusmriti or any other Hindu scripture ancient or modern. The name was actually derived from the sage called Valmiki, the author of Ramayana. Therefore, the Hindus should not call them anything other than the Hindus. They were the followers of Rama. In 1927, at Firozepur movement was sponsored under the banner of '*Valmiki Ad-Dhamma Mahasabha*' only to counter the '*Addhammi*' movement led by Mangoo Ram. Soon this Valmiki phenomena, being fanned by huge funds from the Hindus, engulfed the entire untouchable movement in the Punjab. Despite all these the intensity, conviction and sincerity of the untouchable movement was so strong that despite the 'Poona Pact' in the election of 1937, not a single vote out of 69,126 polled valid-votes in the Punjab *Suba* went in favour of the Congress. *Dalit*-Muslim combine force was equally strong and effective in the Punjab.

However, the Poona Pact ate away the vitals of the freedom struggle of the Untouchables and their separate identity in political ambition. It pushed them in the Concentration Camp of Hinduism once again. The movement for freedom was surrendered to the safeguard movement to protect their survival instinct. In protest to Gandhi, Mangoo Ram too started 'fast unto death' for retaining the 'Communal Award'. Mangoo Ram's 28 days long fast against Gandhi's 4 days fast unto death against the Separate Electorate in the form of Communal Award in 1932 drew little attention of the British authority. Dr Ambedkar even supported the untouchable candidate who contested against Mangoo Ram in 1946 election. Despite this, Mangoo Ram won the election. He lived till April 22, 1980 (age 94) and eventually joined Indian National Congress and remained contended even by being a Congress Legislator for a brief period.

Bengal

The volatile and distrusting situation that emerged out of the Poona Pact became beyond the capacity of the octogenarian Guruchand to tackle even within Bengal. The avaricious Brahmins were just waiting for Guruchand to expire. London Return barrister Pramotha Ranjan Thakur, the grandson of Guru soon after his arrival in India opposed, in 1932, Dr Ambedkar's move-forward for surrendering the Communal Award. He opposed Mukunda Behari Mullick too and went independently even to his grandfather to start separate Scheduled Caste organisation. He separated Matua Mahasangh with its Headquarter at Khulna. He as a leader of a newly formed organisation, the 'All Bengal Depressed Class Association' 'held a special general meeting on 22nd September 1932, i.e. two days after the commencement of the fatal-fast by *Mahatma*. The meeting participated by members of various castes like Namasudra, Kapali, Chamar, Malo, Kaibarta etc unanimously resolved to 'support and approve of the Communal Award', implicitly, even at the risk of Mahatma's life.' However, no sooner than the Poona Pact was signed, the London Returned Barrister took little time to realize the line of the British government, and supported it.

He drifted towards the mainstream political line. In 1936 Rasik Lal Biswas, said to be one of the signatories in the Poona Pact with Dr Ambedkar joined Congress' *Harijan*-band-wagon to work under the leadership of Babu Jagjivan Ram. Next year in early 1937, the young Jogendra Nath Mandal soon after becoming a pleader, entered in the Bengal Legislative Assembly. He won from North-Bakharganj general seat by defeating Saral Dutta, the nephew of '*Swadeshi* movement-fame' Aswini Kumar Dutta with the support of the Caste-Hindu votes. Jogendra Nath already was influenced by the

Congress-tradition in consonance with the line of *'Satyagraha'*, the term coined by M.K. Gandhi for the British scheme of 'Passive Resistance Movement' through his association with Bhagai Halder and Sarat Chandra Bose, elder brother Subas Chandra Bose. Demonstration was clear to emit its message to declare the method as to how the untouchables were to survive in the new political situation. In 1938, being asked by Gandhiji, Upendra Nath Verman, the Rajbansi leader of north-Bengal, Hemchandra Naskar, the Poundra leader of Calcutta and many others joined the Indian National Congress with great fanfare. Pramatha Ranjan Thakur grand-son of Guruchand Thakur, suddenly made a volte-face and led the exodus to the Indian National Congress in 1937.

The scholar has assessed the situation very correctly, "With the death of Guruchand in March 1937, the major influence that had kept the Namasudra movement away from Congress politics was removed. Then the Calcutta Scheduled Caste League, formed later that year, emerged as a new and a vital link between the Congress and the Namasudra leaders. Among the later those who were associated with the new organisation including such prominent personalities as P.R. Thakur, Rasiklal Biswas, Janeswar Mandal and Jogendra Nath Mandal who later became its president in 1940. The occasion that can be regarded as a turning point in the direction towards a new political alliance was the meeting held at Albert Hall in Calcutta on 13 March 1938 to commemorate the 1st anniversary of Guruchand's death. It was presided over by J.C. Gupta, the Chief Whip of the Congress Legislative Party in Bengal and was addressed by fourteen other prominent leaders of the province, including the Congress president Subash Chandra Bose. Netaji in his speech paid glowing tributes to Guruchand and described him as 'a super man' who had 'regenerated the Hindus of Bengal by infusing new life into them'. He had 'elevated the status of the Scheduled Castes who have been able to fall in line with the caste-Hindus in social and political life."[36] The Chandal movement is found to have been completely hijacked by the Hindu *'Shatyagrah'* through a bloodless coup.

From national level, Dr Ambedkar was yet to raise the demands for representation in the service sector. However, the Act to represent communities in Government jobs existed in Bengal. Consequently, in the Bengal Legislature vehement demands for increasing the scope of the existing provisions and strict implementation of the representation rule disturbed the proceedings of the Legislature repeatedly. Guruchand's demand for representation in government jobs was a means to the end for gaining 'Equal opportunity' and equal share in political and economic field by ending the Brahmanical monopoly. But now, in the post-Constitutional and in the Sovereign Republic of India, the term representation had got a new name 'Reservation'. To secure a reserved seat either in political or in executive office by defeating other untouchable candidates has became the end of everything now.

Guruchand demanded '*Raj*' (Rule). Guruchand asked, "*Aami Bali Aain Sabhai Jao, Raja Hao; Durkaor a Jatir Bayatha.*" 'I ask you to enter in the Legislature to become the Ruler and save the communities in distress'.[37] However, after Poona Pact leaders of the untouchables instead demanded '*Kaj*' jobs or service in political sector as well as in executive sector. They joined IPS, the Indian Political Service run and managed by the hereditary ruling castes. They forgot to join Indian politics. Thus in Indian Republic the ideals of democracy remained a far cry. Poona Pact turned the 'Means' shown by Guruchand to be the 'End' now. Skillful leaders who could bargain the alms from the ruling classes were on great demand.

Guruchand became sad. Though he enjoyed the achievement of installing his disciple, Mukunda Bihari Mullick as the Minister in Council of Bengal Government yet he lamented, "I could do nothing by taking birth amongst these castes. The dust and rust that accumulated for fourteen generations got not removed. Nothing could have been gained for them. These people understand nothing. I failed to make them understood." His movement was, however, not confined to the eastern boundaries of Hoogly river in Bengal. The fruits of Guruchand movements, as discussed earlier, landed on the national platform at New Delhi, Sabji Mandi to city of Madras. He himself defeated the National-International leader Gandhi on many fronts. He had been fighting successfully against the strength of the political parties, national and state-level yet he failed to give the untouchables their own political parties in his life time. Besides, as his revolt was uncompromising it was finally rejected by the British Rule.

With the death of Guruchand, the 'Sun of Dalit-bahujan-Liberty' was set. Guruchand failed to incarnate one who was to carry his banner of mission further. No one came forward to fill the blank to be the C-in-C. Poona Pact completely sterilised the Untouchables of India by laying prostrate as Hindu-Untouchable (SCs). No more the marshy-lands of rural Bengal remained the epicenter and venue of Namasudra conferences. The elite Albert Hall (Coffee House) of Central Calcutta, just opposite the Presidency College and beside the University of Calcutta and Elgin Road became the venue of prime activities of the untouchables. No more Orakandi, no more the small towns and cities of Khulna, Jessore, Bakharjang were chosen as the meeting places. Namasudra meetings started taking place in Calcutta, Midnapore, Hawrah and Hoogly where presence of Namasudras was negligible.

On 28th May 1939 we find the 'Bengal Namasudra Conference' being held in a venue at Tamluk town of Midnapore district where Namasudra was totally a non entity. The meeting was held inside the campus of the Hindu Kali Temple where the entry of the untouchables was completely a taboo and banned as usual. In the warmth of the sudden expanded hearts of Hindus the meeting was presided over by none other than P.R. Thakur, the celebrity grandson of Thakur Guruchand. In his presidential speech he advised the members of the Scheduled Castes, "...not to blame or abuse the Caste Hindus for their condition. Rather they should concentrate improving their educational status imitating the Hindus." On analyzing such speeches one of the scholars had evaluated, "This amounted to a complete and unambiguous reversal of Guruchand's political stand. The political alienation of the Grandfather, in other words, now gave way to the integrationist ideology of the Grandson."[38]

The long aspired and awaited Brahman-Untouchable '*Sarbajan*' scheme was immediately welcomed with tremendous fanfare and grand celebration with the 'Conference' of 'All Bengal Scheduled castes Workers' Conference' held on the very next day on the same venue of the 'Kali Temple'. The meeting was now presided over by the national famed Namasudra leader, Rasik Lal Biswas. In the conference among other prominent speakers were local Congress leader Satish Chandra Chakraborty and Ajoy Kumar Mukherjee (later on became Chief Minister of W. Bengal). All of them gave stress on the point that the Scheduled Castes must come up above all narrow casteist and small religio-political move. They advised the untouchables to join Indian National Congress to strengthen the struggle for freedom. It was very interesting and significant to note that the stage was decorated with two big flapping-flags on two sides of the seat of the president of the conference. On the one side there was a red and on the other the tri-colour Congress flag. This red flag definitely was not the flag of the Matua faith. It was definitely the disloyal display of the march towards a wrong and direction-lost destination of the movement of the Untouchables. Guruchand, after the promulgation of the Government of India Act 1935 directed, "*Aain Sabhai Jao, Aami Bali Raja Hao; Dur Karo A Jatir Baytha.*" 'Enter in the Legislature, I wish you to be the Ruler (*Raja*) and wipe out the sufferings of the downtrodden.' Nobody was in a position to pursue Guru's command. All vied with each other to install the Brahmanical representatives on the throne with their support. They ran after gaining only personal benefit, as *Chamchas,* out of the safeguard provisions for political and job reservation. Thralls enjoy thrills of thralldom. It took time and great sacrifices for the Untouchables to reach to the height but the catastrophe came quietly within five years of Dr Ambedkar's advent in politics. It was never to be built up again.

Sincere Fighters became Victims – Champion *Chamchas* got Rewarded: Once in a state of consciousness, the forward march of the liberty-seekers never stops. A man-eater repeats encounters. In the history of freedom movements of Indian autochthons too, the same phenomenon worked. Despite there was an irrevocable landslide in the body-politic of the depressed classes to join ruling class parties like Indian National Congress, Communist Party of India, *Hindu Mahasabha* etc innumerable splinter groups amongst them tried against all odds to hold the banner of struggle for total liberty high. When the leaders from poor, servile class miserably failed to sustain against the organised opposition of various political parties like Congress, the CPI, *Hindu Mahasabha* etc. they planned for no political party for themselves. These political institutions were founded, raised and maintained by the Brahmins of eminence such as W.C. Banergee, Surendra Nath Banerjee, Pt. J.L. Nehru, Bal Gangadhar Tilak, Narendra Nath Bhattacharya, S.A. Dange, E.M.S. Nambudripad, Shyama Prosad Mookerjee, Golwalkar etc and their associates of financial tycoons like Ambanis, Birlas, Tatas etc. Whatever these political parties and their leaders planned, it was to strengthen the social roots of their political movements and economic interests of the colonial frame within Common Wealth.

Dr Ambedkar in 1931-32 expressed, "Silver Bullets were freely used for creating division in the ranks of the oppressed classes. There have also been a few clashes ending in violence." And the tradition of this corrupt political culture continued. "Unwanted, undeserving favourable propaganda for the stooges is a regular feature of the *Chamcha*-age. 'Silver-Bullets' of 1930-32 have been replaced by 'Paper-Bullets' at present. The massive use or abuse of 'Paper-Bullets' is having a deadly effect on the movement of the oppressed, so much so, it is as bad as killed."[39] Indeed, the use of 'Gold-Bullets', 'Silver-Bullets' and 'Paper-Bullets' seems to have started playing its inevitable role since 1911 in the political arena of India if not from 1905.

After the success of the Bolshevik revolution, the Communists accelerated their move to spread its influence through the Communist International. In 1920, 17th October Communist Party of India was established by Narendra Nath Bhattachariya, the fugitive in Taskand in pseudo name, M.N. Roy. According to Karl Marx, "Communism is the doctrine of the conditions for the emancipation of the proletariat… the immense majority and the lowest stratum of the society…. Who have for the most part been poor." "The proletariats are the free labourer who once were expropriated from their land-holdings"[40] 'The goal of the Communists was to establish the rule of the proletariat, the rule of the immense majority and the lowest stratum of the society'. By its implementation, the economic structure called socialism, which place the entire means of production of the country under the ownership of the state communism attempted to minimize exploitation. This structure eliminates right to private property, thereby profit motive of the individual capitalists, and consequently maximize the productivity of the society.

The producer-classes became rulers as the ruling classes failed to capture power of the instrumentalities of the state in 1917 for the first time in the USSR. All other historical movements of the servile classes during previous centuries were the movements for the minorities and ended in protecting the interests of the minority ruling class. Those movements were primarily safeguard movements, movements for social justice. No sooner than some soothing ointments were achieved through the furious movements created by the servile classes for social justice, the ruling classes showed a little bit of sympathy towards the discriminatory atrocities and exploitation. The movements had been ceased in favour of the rulers, with little or no change of the rulers. Communist revolution, in Russia, however, was a total departure from the past. For the first time the fall of despotic Czar paved the way for establishment of the rule of the proletariat, the immense majority (*Bahujan-samaj*) and the lowest stratum of the society. The spirit of the self-conscious and independent movement of the producing classes of India, the Untouchables, Sudras, Animists/Tribals and proselyte minorities is found to have been attempted to be arrested and controlled by the imperialistic British by the Montague-Chelmsford Constitutional reforms in the form of Government of India Act 1919. The process continued in collaboration with the ruling castes of India in British India. As a result, after the Poona Pact the sincere fighters for liberty got victimised and the '*Chamchas*' and their champions got rewarded.

References

1. B.R. Ambedkar W and *S*, What Congress and Gandhi had Done to the Untouchables, (published-1945) Vol. 9, p. 102.
2. *Ibid*, Vol. 17 (1), p. 350.
3. *Ibid*, Vol. 9, pp. 480-481 and 439.
4. Refer to Dr Anand Teltumde, Myths and Facts Ambedkar on Muslims, published by Vak Publication, Mumbai, 2003: Ambedkar was against the Muslims; Ambedkar Muslims Traitors etc.
5. Dr B.R. Ambedkar W and S, (Verdict on India, p. 41) Vol. 17(1) p. 350.
6. Mahakabi Mahananda Halder, Guruchand Charit, pp. 412-15.
7. Narendra Nath Bhattachariya (M. N. Roy), India in Transition, p. 192.
8. Dr B.R. Ambedkar, W and S, Vol. 10, p. 37.
9. Manyawar Kanshi Ram, The Chamcha Age, p. 84.
10. Dr B.R. Ambedkar W and S, Vol. 9, p. 464.
11. Manyawar Kanshi Ram, The Chamcha Age, p. 89.
12. Dhananjoy Keer, B.R. Amberkar, Life and His Mission, p. 246.
13. Dr B.R. Ambedkar, W and S, Vol. 10, pp. 494-496.
14. *Ibid.*
15. Kanshi Ram, *Ajad Bharat Mein Bahujan samaj Gulam Kewn.*
16. J.L. Nehru, Discovery of India.
17. Ambedkar, R and S, Vol. 17 (II) p. 241.
18. H. Kotani (Edited) Caste System, Untouchability and the Depressed, p. 174.
19. H. Kotani (Edited) Caste system, Untouchability and the Depressed, p. 170.
20. Dr B.R. Ambedkar W and S, Vol. 17 (3) p. 298.
21. Dhananjao Keer, B.R. Ambedkar, Life and his Mission, p. 53.
22. *Ibid,* pp. 63-64.
23. *Ibid,* pp. 52-53.

24. Dhananjoy Keer, Dr B.R. Ambedkar, Life and His Mission, p. 89.
25. Caste system, Untouchability and the Depressed, Edited by H. Kotani, p. 20.
26. M.C. Raja, The Oppressed Hindus, p. 20, Pub. 1925.
27. Collected Works of Periyar, pub. By Periyar Self-Respect Propaganda, Institution, Vepery, pp. 137- 39; Courtecy, Dalit Voice, November, 1, 15, 2010.
28. *Ibid.*
29. M. Nisar and Meena Kandasamy, Ayyankali A Dalit Leader of Organic Protest, p. 69.
30. *Ibid*, p. 87.
31. Balbir Madhopuri, Gadari Baba Manguram, (Book in Punjabi) Introduction, p. 4.
32. Mark Juergensmeyer, Religious Rebels in the Punjab, pp. 269-288.
33. Balbir Madhopuri, Gadari Baba Manguram, (Book in Punjabi) Introduction, p. 5.
34. *Ibid,* pp. 64-65.
35. *Ibid,* p. 74; and Courtesy–Dr Suresh Mane, Glimpses of Socio-cultural Revolts, p. 163.
36. Sekhar Bandopadhaya, Caste, Protest and Identity in Colonial India, Namasudras, p. 180.
37. Mahakabi Mahananda Haldar, Guruchand Charit, p. 554.
38. *Ibid*, Sekhar Bandopadhaya, Caste, Protest and Identity in colonial India, Namasudras.
39. Manyawar Kanshi Ram, The Chamcha Age, p. 107.
40. Marx and Engels, Selected Works (Pub. 1977) Vol. 1, p. 81.

8

Ambedkar: Revolts, Compromises and Revolts Finally

Democracy, be it participatory or representative is fundamentally based on the principle of universal adult franchise. It helps all subjects of a Republican country to take part in the governance of the land. All adult citizens must get their right and freedom to cast their votes without any hindrance to elect their representatives in the legislature from amongst them, irrespective of caste or creed. In democracy, in its polity structure, a political party plays the very vital role. It is the institution, precondition to express the view points and the socio-political and economic aspirations of a particular, section, community or group of the subjects of a country. Representatives of people are elected from various political parties in the Parliament through prescribed mechanism.

Census of 1911, consciously gave the untouchables a recognition as an exclusive ethnic group or a nation completely separate from the Hindus, Muslims, Sikhs and Christians. They acquired after a protracted and ceaseless struggle for the past two decades, an identity as the non-Hindu nation or 'Depressed Classes' besides the Muslims, Hindus, Sikhs and Christians. In 1911, their tribe were enumerated 18.7 per cent of the total population of the then India. As such, they claimed their exclusive political share in the Legislature and Executive posts proportionate to their strength of population, side by side the Hindu nationalists and the Muslims. But as discussed earlier, the separate electorate since 1909 and Poona Pact finally compelled billions of untouchable population to cast their votes jointly for Indian National Congress or the Hindu nationalist party during general elections. Consequently, Indian democracy became a type by itself. It is a Democracy of the microscopic minority, the hereditary ruling classes in the name of the immense majority, the hereditary subject classes. It may be called Brahmanic democracy.

The vast autochthon population was swayed away by the torrential flood of the foreign Aryan religion and its culture to gear up establishing all targets of Hindu Nationalism. During Pre-Poona Pact era, all over India, the Indian autochthons are found to have declared their religious identity as the *Matuas*, *Satyadharmis, Ad-Dharmis, Ad-Dravar, Adi-Dharam* (in UP) *Kabirpanthis* etc. They on record, claimed that they were not Hindus or the Aryans. The poor *Matuas*, *Addharmis, Ad-Dravids* and many such non-Hindu 'Depressed Class' communities without their knowledge and their consent too became Hindus once again. Thus, they lost their distinct ethno-cultural identity after being assimilated[1] into the Hindu cultural stream of governing classes i.e. the Brahmin Baniya combine.[2]

The political identity of the Hindus and the Muslims and their demand for share in the Legislature and Executive rooted in their religions called Hinduism and Islam and the religious nationalism. The untouchables failed to retain independent political identity and national pride as they failed to stick to their own non-Hindu identity and religions called Matuaism, Ad-Hinduism, Satyadharma, Ad-Dravir or Ad-Dharmis in the Punjab. Dr Ambedkar realised at a later stage, that Gandhiji, the 'greatest man of India'[3] was 'fraught with mischief'.[4] The society being fundamentally theocratic, the class conflict had turned to be the mortal conflict of two main religions, Brahmanism and Buddhism.[5]

Hindu religious sentiment has been injected as the essence in Indian political mind or Hindu nationalism.[6] From temples the Brahmins control both Caste system and Parliamentary politics. The forces or the group that control the affairs of the temples or spirituality in India, manoeuver the instrumentalities of the state, controls Parliament. Spirituality and religion are the prerogative of the Brahmins alone. Consequently, the Poona-Pact, as it turned the minority Hindu group (34 per cent) into a majority group in India, ushered the rule of the Brahmins in the Indian Parliamentary Democracy. Dr Ambedkar is found to have recognised the irrevocable factor of caste-bias[7] of the Hindus in post Poona-pact era. With complete distrust and conviction, he recorded his view in his magnum opus called 'What Congress and Gandhi had Done to the Untouchables', "Only those who belong to the servile class can be trusted to protect the interest of that class".[8] He gave a call even not to trust the Caste Hindus.

Revolt Called Conversion: Once officially Hindu or a caste (scheduled or simple). it was difficult for the Untouchables to regain their independent identity without going through the process of conversion. Consequently, during post-Poona Pact period Dr Ambedkar revolted, campaigned against Hinduism and asked the Untouchables to desert Hinduism and embrace any faith where human dignity would be available after conversion. The masses of the country, especially the autochthons were disqualified to perform the orthodox spirituality. The native masses were not allowed to perform their religious rituals, worship. The masses of the country especially the autochthons *Sikhs*, the *Ad-Dhammis*, the *Ad-Dravids,* the *Matuas* the *Kabirpanthis, Ad-Andhris,* different tribal creeds were not allowed to learn or even pronounce Hindu spiritual-language, Sanskrit, worship the deities lest it is polluted with their presence.[9] In pre-Poona Pact era the Untouchables, therefore, simply could declare the factual position that they were neither Hindis, nor the Hindus have any relation with them. They were *Matuas* or *Addhammis* etc. Guruchand or Mangooram, therefore, never required using the term, **conversion while declaring their religious identity**. The Hinduised Untouchables in post Poona Pact era needed to get through the process of conversion to be recognised as non-Hindu.

Before the pact what was assured to Dr Ambedkar did not flow to him therefore, a decade after the Poona Pact, Dr Ambedkar retaliated, "... the Congress sucked the juice out of the Poona Pact and threw the rind in the face of the Unouchables."[10] "Poona Pact was fraught with mischief. It was accepted because of coercive fast of Mr. Gandhi and because of the assurance given at the time that the Hindus will not interfere in the election of the Scheduled Castes".[11] In such circumstances, Ambedkar began his tirade against Hinduism that Hari-Guruchand initiated while starting the Untouchable's liberation movement with declaring their own independent *Matua* religion in 1835 onwards. Ambedkar continued it until he finally deserted Hinduism and embraced Buddhism on 14th October 1956.

Dr Ambedkar, being surrounded and influenced by a band of influential Brahmins, and being a member of a very small untouchable community named Mahar in Bombay Presidency could not go, as a natural corollary, against Hinduism or Brahmins. He was not an iconoclast as he was found to be in the post-Poona Pact era. He is found to have embossed '*Jai Bhavani*" at the top of his letter-head pad[12] until 1927. He even sponsored his support to Brahmanize the Mahars by putting sacred thread of the Brahmins on the body of untouchables. But his ambitious projects with the Hindu nationalists had failed to yield much for him and he turned to be an anti-Hindu. Instead of attacking on political front Ambedkar is therefore, found to have sharpened his attack on religion. Eventually he died as a *Bodhisattwa* as his followers claimed. In addition, many have assessed that his name will go down to the history as one who brought Buddha back to his own country.

In 1929, Ambedkar advised the untouchables of Jalgaon of Maharashtra to embrace any other religion that would regard them as Human beings, gave them an opportunity to rise in the world and enabled them to act, eat, walk and live like men. Consequently, twelve untouchables had embraced Islam. At the appropriate moment, when Gandhiji in the 2nd RTC offered the untouchables to go for Islam or Christianity Dr Ambedkar did not accept the offer of golden handshake. In those days, he preferred to save Gandhi and

Hinduism than rescuing the Hindu 'Divine Slaves' by converting them to Islam. He arranged for another *Satyagraha*; Kalaram Temple *Satyagraha* to see whether they could ennoble Hinduism simply by securing entry of a few dozens of untouchables in the Hindu temples. What a cruel joke. The marriage of convenience and the politics of opportunism never yield any benefit for the week partner.

Dr Ambedkar was invited in the beginning of December 1935, at Lahore to preside over the annual conference with the target to ameliorate the untouchable lots from their distressing condition by the 'Jat Pat Todak Mandal'. In his Presidential speech (which remained undelivered due to controversy), Dr Ambedkar suggested that annihilation of Castes was a *sine-qua-non* to free the Untouchables from thralldom and the only way to annihilate caste was to convert to any other religion. "Caste is the natural outcome of certain religious beliefs which have the sanction of *Shastras*, which are believed to contain the command of divinely inspired sages.... Caste has a divine basis. You must therefore, destroy the sacredness and divinity with which Caste has become invested. In the last analysis, this means you must destroy the authority of the *Shastras* and the Vedas..... Some may not understand what I mean by destruction of Religion...' "This means a complete change in the fundamental notions of life. It means complete change in out look and in attitude towards men and things. It means conversion; but if you do not like the word, I will say, it means new life. But new life cannot enter a body that is dead. New life can enter only in a new body."[13] His tirade against Hindu religion or Caste system and his tireless quest for a new religion could have won the laurel of political freedom too had he taken the stand in the Simon Commission, in the Round Table Conferences and on the eve of putting his signature on the Poona Pact. His revolt was a postmortem pendulum attack to shake and re-shake the calcified orthodox-Hindu mind in so far as the issue of power share in a democratic manner was concerned.

At this point of time, he had no alternative but to blow the horn of threat so that Gandhi and his team Hindus come to terms. In the conference well attended by about 10,000 untouchables, at Yeola, near Nasik on October 13, 1935 he declared, "I solemnly assure you that I will not die as a Hindu." He gave a clarion call for the untouchables to leave Hinduism, which was nothing but slavery for them. Come out of the slavery. "If you want to achieve power, change your religion. If you want equality, change your religion. If you want your independence, change your religion.' He, however, cautioned that, "I advise you to sever your connection with Hinduism and embrace any other religion. But in doing so be careful in choosing the new faith and see that Equality of treatment, Status, and Opportunities will be guaranteed to you unreservedly." He explained in details, "....Thus Hindu religion is the religion of our ancestors, but it was the worst type of slavery that was thrust upon them. Our ancestors had no means to fight this slavery and therefore, they could not revolt. They were compelled to live in that religion. Nobody can force this type of slavery upon the present generation. We have all sorts of freedom and can free from the clutches of Hinduism..." He further questioned, "Why do you remain in the religion which insults you at every step? The religion which teaches man to behave with man in an inhumane manner is not religion but infamy. The religion which does not recognize a human being as human being is a curse.... The religion which compels the ignorant to remain ignorant and the poor to remain poor does not deserve to be called a religion."[14]

'Ambedkar's address rocked all circles, political parties and social institutions to the bottom.... A stream of letters and telegrams flowed in Ambedkar's residence in Bombay from all quarters of Hindustan and other parts of the world. Christian and Muslim leaders began to move..... Another appealing offer came from the Secretary of the Mohabodhi Society, Benaras..... Yet a strange appeal came from a brother community of the Sikhs.... The Congress President Dr Rajendra Prasad deplored the Yeola resolution...he said it was unfortunate that anything should be done to make the work of the reformers more difficult.... Hindu missionary leader Masurkar said that the exodus would not stop at that and it would be the death of Hindus in the long run"[15]

'A Sindhi Hindu wrote a letter in blood and threatened Dr Ambedkar with death if he renounced Hinduism.' The Sindhi Hindu perhaps thought that Dr Ambedkar would come down with the death threat as he earlier signed Poona Pact because he herd whisper of massacre to the Untouchables. It has been seen the 'conversion' call was not a new phenomenon in the history of the liberation movement of the Untouchables. It failed to spread universal appeal to all untouchable communities in all the provinces. It rather raised fresh confusions. In an another meeting on conversion on January 12-13th 1936, Prof. N. Shivraj said, 'The only way to get rid of untouchability is that the Depressed Classes should leave Hindu religion, not necessarily by conversion to another religion but possibly by starting a new religion or by reviving the ancient one practiced among the *Adi-Dravidians* already existing long before the Aryans brought to India Hinduism with its various customs." Dr Ambedkar ignored at the most appropriate time, during the 2nd Round Table Conference, and he never took up this fundamental measure for emancipation of the Untouchable even when Gandhiji offered the untouchables to go for enrolling themselves in the fold of Islam, Christianity, Matuaism, Ad-Dhammism etc. Dr Ambedkar used it as a threat for gaining political mileage without proper preparation to proselyte on national level. Whatever might have had happened this threat of conversion did not materialize before two decades elapsed. Consequently, a few only took up the call of conversion as a matter of concern. Babu Jagjivan Ram, in an interview before the Cabinet Mission in 1946, too mentioned especially that he and his people were not with Ambedkar in this conversion question. "The difference between the Scheduled Castes Federation (led by Ambedkar) and the Depressed Classes' League was that, where the Federation held the Scheduled castes were not Hindus but a religious minority of their own, the League held that the Scheduled castes masses considered themselves Hindus and that they had sacrificed much for the cause of Hinduism."[16] The glaring and paradoxical contrast, however, crawled out of the most significant scheme of Partition of India into two separate sovereign countries in her Eastern and Western sectors. Babu Jagajivan Ram of Depressed Classes League vehemently opposed partition of the nation but Dr Ambedkar passionately favoured and pleaded for the vivisection of the 'living entity'.

Conversion to Islam became in-fructuous : According to the UNESCO, E.V. Periyar Ramaswami Naikkar, was "The prophet of the new age, the Socrates of the South East Asia, Father of the social reform movement; arch enemy of ignorance, superstition, meaningless custom and base manners." He was the most powerful leader of anti-Brahmin and anti-Hindu movement in the south-India. In an unambiguous term, he explained that Islam was the panacea for a cancerous disease like caste. In the preparatory period, in undivided India, whenever the question of conversion of the Untouchables arose, Dr Ambedkar also at several instances referred to Islam as a safe refuge for the Untouchables. At a certain stage of his struggle, he was perhaps seriously considering the idea to embrace Islam. He analysed, "The first question is to the faith that the Depressed Classes are likely to embrace? Obviously the most advantageous to them. There are three faiths from among which the Depressed Classes can choose. (i) Islam (ii) Christianity and (iii) Sikhism. Comparing these three, Islam seems to give the Depressed Classes all that they need."[17] Even in 1946, when the rumours spread that Dr Ambedkar along with his people was going to embrace Islam, the entire creamy-layer Hindu society got scared. Ambedkar, however, remained ambiguous while clarifying the position before the press.

The demographic position in vast land of Bengal, the Punjab and NWF was already spiritually as well as politically precarious for the Hindus. A new and even a little wave of conversion to Islam would have brought inundation of exodus to make the position further vulnerable for the Hindus. The question of conversion to Islam after the partition of India on Hindu-Muslim line became completely redundant. Thus, the growing necessity and consciousness amongst the Untouchables for conversion eventually remained not as an effective but a mere threat phenomena. It played the role of one of the catalysts that pushed the country towards its vivisection within a decade. Here Ambedkar's call for conversion and simultaneously his strong advocacy for partition of India in his book Thoughts on Pakistan in 1940 were very confusing and conflicting. Hindus were thus too interested to resist the proposal for the partition of India. However, organised conversion by Dr Ambedkar remained unfulfilled for two more decades.

On the basis of distinct religious faith and culture there emerged new nationalism in opposition to the Hindu nationalism amongst these 'Depressed Classes' in the Eastern India almost a century back. Dr Ambedkar, however, is found to have started the quest for own faith, the basic and primary phenomenon for liberty at an advanced and secondary stage, long after his political movement started on national platform. He was born as a Hindu, re-Hinduised the untouchables by the Poona Pact and then struggled to gain political mileage by declaring that he would not die as a Hindu.

By seeking a new religion or going back to or reviving the ancient Indian religion that was prevailing since the pre-Vedic or Pre-Aryan period such as '*Ad-Dhamma*' or '*Adi-Dravida*' or Buddhism, it was rather a very remote possibility to capture political power, as the numerical strength of the new converts remained limited to the population of the Untouchables. Therefore, Dr Ambedkar's judgment in favour of conversion to Islam on the basis of the analysis between three religions in India such as Islam, Christianity and Sikhism seems to be correct. It is not gainsaid that Dr Ambedkar was aware of the situation. He disclosed, "We are fully conscious of the fact that go any where we will, we would have to fight for our welfare if we took to Christianity, Islam or Sikhism. It is foolish to suppose that in the event of our conversion to Islam everybody from amongst us would be a *Nawab* or would become a Pope if we went over to Christianity."

Ambedkar's tirade during this phase, even in the fashion of threat, against the Hindus, against the Congress, against the capitalistic system and even against the imperialist British power perturbed and rocked the entire oppressors. The attack was on the essence of the tyranny and structure of exploitation. They got unnerved and as a natural corollary tried to appease the agitated leader-intellect. And, the advantage was en-cashed by Dr Ambedkar in the full broom.

In the general election of 1937 Dr Ambedkar received tremendous support from the Hindus of Bombay Presidency in many respect. His regional political party, 'Independent Labour Party' formed just six months before the election, had no chance to have even a single seat without the vote support of the Hindus. However, his party won 15 seats.

Shocking surprise was that at this juncture, none else but Dr Ambedkar became a great Hindu. In 1940, within 8 months of Md. Ali Jinnah's Lahore Declaration for two sovereign countries by dividing India in Western and Eastern part Dr Ambedkar produced his great thesis, 'Thoughts On Pakistan'. Being a man, rather Untouchable from Bombay he was least concerned with the question of partition of India or creation of Pakistan and Hindustan by dividing Bengal and the Punjab for the prospect, peace and everlasting happiness of the Hindus. As a Hindu fundamentalist it is he who became the first Indian to propound the philosophy of Hindu-Muslim nationalism or two-nation theory. He aggressively started advocating for the creation of Pakistan for the Muslim nation and that would be the best for security, peace and prosperity of the Hindu nation. His doctrine, however, preached that the Muslims of Bengal and the Punjab only were 'Tyrants' for the Hindu nation, hence disqualified to remain in Hindustan. They were to form a Muslim nation in Western and East Pakistan. The Muslims of Bombay or Bihar, UP or Central Province, Madras or Trivancore, even the Muslims of West Bengal were neither 'tyrants' nor disqualified to stay within the Hindu-nation or Hindustan. In the name of partition of India, Jinnah and Ambedkar stressed to vivisect Bengal and the Punjab. During this period, in 1946, he also authored another book, 'Who Were the Sudras'. In it he strongly advocated that the Aryans were autochthons of India, they never invaded India and the Sudras were Aryans. Both these thesis went up to oppose the non-Aryan or 'Mulnivasi' and non-Hindu movement led by various contemporary untouchable leaders in the Punjab, UP, Bihar, Bengal, Madras and Kerala.

Dr Ambedkar did his best to use his reputation as the most learned Untouchable leader with outstanding intellectual ability to pursue the Bengalee and Panjabi Hindus to execute the doctrine of Hindu-Muslim two nations for dividing the ancient nation. In the book he argued, "There are two alternatives for the Hindus of the Punjab and Bengal and they may be asked to face them fairly and squarely. The Muslims in the Punjab number 1,33,32,460 and the Hindus with the Sikhs and the rest, number 1,13,92,732. This means that the Muslim majority in the Punjab is only a majority of 8 per cent. Given these facts, which is better: To retain the unity of the Punjab and allow the Muslim majority of 54 per cent to rule the Hindu minority of 46 per cent or to redraw the boundaries, to allow the Muslims and the Hindus to be under separate national states, and thus rescue the whole body of Hindus from the terrors of the Muslim rule?

The Muslims in Bengal number 2,74, 97,624 and the Hindis number 2,15,70,407. The difference is only of 59,27217. This means that the Muslim majority in Bengal is only a majority of 12 per cent. Given these facts which is better: To oppose the creation of National Muslim State out of Eastern Bengal and Sylhet by refusing to redraw the boundaries and allow the Muslim majority of only 12 per cent to rule the Hindu minority of 44 per cent; or to consent to redraw the boundaries, to have the Muslims and Hindus placed under separate National States, and thus rescue the 44 per cent of the Hindus from the horrors of the Muslim rule?

Let the Hindus of Bengal and the Punjab consider which alternative they should prefer. It seems to me that moment has come when the high caste Hindus of Bengal and the Punjab should be told that if they oppose to resist Pakistan, because it cuts off a field for gainful employment, they are committing to the greatest blunder. They may cheat the lower orders of the Hindus in the name of nationalism, but they cannot cheat the Muslim majorities in the Muslim Provinces and keep their monopoly of place and power. The resolution of the Hindus, if their cry against Pakistan can be regarded as such to live under the Muslim majority and oppose self-determination may be a very courageous thing. But it would not be a very wise thing if the Hindus believe that they will be able to maintain their place and power by fooling the Muslims. It is not possible to fool all people all the times. If the Hindus choose to live under a Muslim majority the chances are that they may lose all. On the other hand, if the Hindus of Bengal and the Punjab agree to separate, true, they will not get more, but they will certainly not lose all."[18]

It is exceedingly significant to note that during the period when Dr Ambedkar has been preparing this thesis, two of the representatives, Mukunda Behari Mullick and Prasanna Chandra Raikat, of more than a billion Untouchables, for the first time in the annals of Indian history were functioning as Cabinet Ministers of Bengal, the most important province of the British India. They were not at all under 'horror' or 'terror' of the majority Muslims in the state. Rather, to be true to the fact, they for the first time breathed freely being liberated from the spiritual tyranny of the minority Hindus. Besides, the past history of Bengal or of the Punjab does not, substantiate any horrific terror on the Sudra, Untouchable and Tribal Population. Contrary is the history rather. It reveals that peasantry of Bengal and other parts of India remained a prey of horrific persecution by the Hindu philosophy and practice of hatred in innumerable folds. The thesis of Dr Ambedkar simply arranged to kick out the Scheduled castes of Bengal out of power and install the Brahmins on the levers of the instrumentalities of the State. In this context, it is also perplexing to digest as to why even after the above situation explained by Dr Ambedkar, frankly and with all intellectual honesty, Md. Jinnah went for Pakistan leaving the Indian minority Muslims behind, under the perpetual horror and terror of the immense majority Hindus for the eternity to come. Why did he help establish Hindu Raj at the detriment of the vast Muslim population to stay in India?

The Brahmin biographer Dr Dhananjoy Keer has recorded his assessment on the book, 'Thoughts on Pakistan' in the following terms: "The year 1940 was coming to an end when Ambedkar's Magnum opus, Thoughts on Pakistan, was published. Written at a psychological moment, it fell like a bomb-shell on the heated atmosphere of the day. India's man of great learning, great constitutional pundit and politician of varied experience gave out his reflection on the political problem of India. The reference of the book was the division of India into Hindustan and Pakistan for the prosperity, peace and salvation of the Hindus to whom the book was mainly addressed.

That the Muslims, the book argues, are a nation must be accepted without cavil. It advises the Hindus to have no fear for want of a nationally, a frontier in the event of the birth of Pakistan because geographical condition are not decisive in modern world and modern technique. As the resources of Hindustan are far greater than those of Pakistan, the creation of Pakistan will not leave Hindustan in a weakened condition. It also impresses upon the Hindus that it is better to have Muslims whose loyalty to India is always doubtful, without and against, rather than within and against. A safe army rid of the Muslims preponderance is better than a safe border.

The book is not without its antidote to the poison of Pakistan. It prescribes a sovereign remedy for securing peace and homogeneity by arranging for a total exchange of population, Hindus from Pakistan, and Muslims from Hindustan, as did Turkey, Greece and Bulgaria to solve their internecine war.

But unlike M.N. Roy's Historical Role of Islam, this historic book castigate the anti-reformist tendency of the Muslims. It observes that the dominating influence with the Muslims is not democracy. The predominant interest of Muslim is religion, their politics being essentially clerical. The Muslims are opposed to social reforms, and are an unprogressive people all over the world. To the Muslims, the book states, Islam is a world religion, suitable for all people for all time and for all condition. The brotherhood of Islam is not the universal brotherhood of man. It is the brotherhood of Muslims for Muslims only. For non-Muslims there is nothing but contempt and enmity. The Muslims have allegiance to a nation which is ruled by a Muslim: a land not ruled by a Muslim is his enemy land. The book, therefore, concludes that Islam can never allow a true Muslim to adopt India as his mother land and regard a Hindu as his kiths and kin. The spirit of aggression is a Muslim natural endowment. He takes advantage of the weakness of the Hindus and follows gang-starism.

Some penetrating and caustic paragraph describing the regressive dent on the Muslim mind, however, were deleted, it is said, at the instance of Ambedkar's close admirers. Otherwise the author of Thoughts on Pakistan would have experienced what H.G. Wells experienced at the hands of Muslims in London!

With the cool intelligence of a doctor he viewed and examined the malady of India. A book by a vigorous man is unlikely to be dispassionate. The subject was dealt with candour, competence, knowledge, courage and excellence. Thoughts on Pakistan is a masterpiece in which learning and thinking are blended and displayed at their highest order. It is entrancing in its magic, intriguing in its construction, terse in its style, and provocative in its manner. It is a model in scientific propagation!

Ambedkar favoured the vivisection of one living entity. Burk committed a glaring miscalculation by throwing aspersion and making an onslaught upon the French Revolution in his reflections on the revolution in France. Similarly future historians may think about Ambedkar's Thoughts on Pakistan!"

At a later stage of political development especially after the partition of India in 1947, Dr Ambedkar is found to have heavily criticised the Islam, Christianity and Sikhism. He as a logical or rational concomitant picked up the cause of Buddhism what he hardly and seriously advised before 1947."

*** "That the communal antagonism exists nobody can deny. The question however is, is the antagonism such that there is no will to live together in one country and under one constitution? Surely that will to live together was not absent till 1937. During formation of the provisions of the Government of India Act 1935 both the Hindus and the Muslims accepted the view that they must live together under one constitution and in one country and participated in the discussion that preached and passes the Act."[19]

Dr Ambedkar, at this juncture, while propagating for conversion took a volta-face. So passionately he became a prophet of Hinduism and Hindu national cause that he forgot to record a dispassionate history. Even when he wanted to compromise with Jinnah and planned for the united India to maintain, he still ignored the elements and formative germs of Hindu Nationalism created long back by the Bengalee activists during 1866. Even prior to that Raja Rammohan Roy (Bandhopadhaya) sought 'divine providence' in English Rule to rescue the Hindus from Muslim tyranny. In 1866, Rajnarayan Basu created 'A society for the promotion of national feeling amongst the educated natives of society of Bengal'. This was soon transformed into Hindu-Mela, Jatiya Mela by Nava Gopal Mitra. Gospel of Hindu nationalism was preached by Bankim Chandra Chatterjee, the composer of 'Vande Mataram'. Vivekananda became the prophet to preach for aggressive Hindu Nationalism. Barister P. Mitra established the Hindu 'Terrorist outfit' called 'Anushilan Samiti' for establishing Hindu Rastra on the philosophy of Hindu nationalism. The Brahmins of Bombay Presidency actively joined it during the last decade of the 19th century. Bala Gangadhara Tilak establishe 'Goraksha Samiti', started Ganesh Puja and 'Shivaji Utsav' in the last decade of the 19th century and long before the birth of Muslim League, the 2nd political party in India. Yet Dr Ambedkar condemned Muslims, "Have the Muslims thought of this method of avoiding Hindu Raj. Have they considered how easy it is to avoid it? Have they considered how futile and harmful the present policy of the Muslim League is? The Muslims are howling against the Hindu Maha Sabha and its slogan of Hindudom and Hindu raj. But who is responsible for this? Hindu Maha Sabha and Hindu raj are the inseparable nemesis which the Muslims have brought upon themselves by having a Muslim League. It is action and counter-action."[20]

Regional Political Party to Face Election of 1937

Independent Labour Party was formed to contest election of 1937. With the providence of the Hindu voters the ILP won 15 seats of which 2 were general.

The election took place on February 17, 1937. Dr Ambedkar was overwhelmed with joy with the result. On this election, Dr Ambedkar's comments are very interesting. "Far from supporting the Congress version the results of the Election show: (1) that out of 151, the Congress got only 73 seats; (2) that the majority of the 73 seats won by the Congress were won with the help of the Hindu votes; and they do not therefore, in any way represent the Scheduled castes; and (4) that of 151 seats those won by the Congress with the majority of votes of the Scheduled castes were only 38. As to Independent Labour Party it was started in 1937 just a few months before the elections. It functioned only in the Bombay Provinces. The Independent Labour Party far from being a failure obtained an astonishing degree of success. Out of the 15 seats assigned to the Scheduled Castes in Bombay Presidency, it captured 13 and in addition, it won two general seats. I am therefore, glad that at long last I have succeeded in completing the work which proves beyond the shadow of doubt that the story that the Congress captured all the seats reserved for the Scheduled Castes and that the Independent labour Party was a failure."[21]

The animosity between Scheduled Castes and castes grew bitter to bitterest in course of time. In Bombay presidency, Congress failed to get majority with 48.2 per cent seats of its Legislature of total strength of 175 seats. This was mainly due to the Hindu support to ILP. Despite his 100 per cent success (with 15 elected MLAs) in Bombay Presidency, the hero of the Poona Pact was forgotten. Dr Ambedkar got no chance to become a Minister. The Hindus discarded the untouchable MLAs. The Indian National Congress preferred to form Government with the help of Muslim League members.

Here after, in a big gathering of nearly twenty thousand Railway workers who belonged to the Untouchable communities at Manmad, on 12th and 13th February 1938, as an MLA Dr Ambedkar taught, "There are two enemies of the working classes in the country and they were Brahmanism and Capitalism. I do not mean the power, privileges and interests of the Brahmins as a community. That is not the sense in which I am using the word. By Brahmanism I mean the negation of the spirit of liberty, equality and fraternity....So omniscient is Brahmanism that it even affects the field of economic opportunities." Though he tried to save the Brahmins by not declaring them as an enemy class, finally he defined them as a class against the interest of the working classes. Within sixty years of independence, it has further come to notice that since historical periods Brahmins and Brahmanism stand both as the fascist force as well as the capitalist part of a dictatorial monolithic-tyranny. In 1942 February 26, in a statement he strongly said, "The Congress choose to forget that Hinduism is a political ideology of the same character as the Fascist and or Nazi ideology and is thoroughly anti-democratic."[22] Initially, however, he was not so rustic to define political character of Hinduism in antagonistic tone. Dr Ambedkar is found to have addressed, at Monibhavan and in the Yarvada Jail during 1931-32, Gandhiji as *Mahatma*. But in August 1938, in an interview for a Marathi weekly he rebelled to describe the 'Holy' man as 'Owely', 'Woely' man. He described the conduct of Gandhi at the RTC as an act of treachery and said, 'If a man with God's name on his tongue and a sword under his arm-pit deserve the appellation of a Mahatmma, then Mohan Das Karamchasnd Gandhi was a *Mahatma*.'[23]

He addressed in his last meeting of the year, 1938 in December to the maiden Depressed Classes Conference at Aurangabad District of Hydrabad. It was the first ever attempt of the untouchables of Hydrabad. In such a gathering, it was revealed that there in the region until recently the medieval tactics was applied by the Brahmins to oppress, suppress and exploit the untouchables in collaboration of the Muslims and flouted their attempts to take water from public tanks and to enter Hindu temples. The untouchables in the region were yet to organize struggles for democratic rights in the convergence of their own country. They had organised for the civil, social, educational and religious rights. Dr Ambedkar led them for organizing Self-respect Movement.

The First Untouchable Cabinet Minister comes from Bengal

In the Punjab, Muslim League easily formed government. The picture in Bengal, however, was completely different. Twenty-four Scheduled Caste candidates out of thirty reserved seats, who fought as independent candidate, won election in Bengal. Leaders from the untouchable Namasudra community only won 13 seats. One out of these thirteen was from General constituency. The young lawyer Jogendra Nath Mandal, though with low margin, won the Pirogepur general-seat by defeating Saral Dutta, the nephew of Aswni Kumar Dutta of *Swadeshi* fame. The Hindu-Congress even compromised with a section of Muslim leaders but could gain only sixty seats (including six reserved seats) out of 250 seats in the Bengal Legislative Assembly. Remaining seats were bagged mainly by Muslim League and the Krishak Proja Party.

In Bengal and Bombay thus started the unique system of coalition government from the beginning of the process of democratisation in the country. Muslim League formed the government in alliance with Krishak Proja Party supported by the independent Scheduled Caste Members who formed a block in the Legislature. The Prime Minister Fazlul Haq (a member of Krisak Proja Party) in its Lucknow session, however, joined the League in October 1937. This coalition government opened up 'Royal Avenue' for the untouchables to become the ministers despite their small and inadequate strength in the Assembly. This coalition or post poll alliance between the untouchables and Muslims was not possible in pre-poll period because of the provisions of separate electorate in the Poona Pact. Such alliance was desirable and beneficial for the democracy as well as for the freedom struggle of the Depressed Classes irrespective of caste and creed. However, this went against the interest of the hereditary ruling class. Prasanna Dev Raikat from North Bengal Rajbansi community and Mukunda Behari Mullick were two untouchables inducted in the cabinet as important Ministers. The Muslim political groups did not approach the Hindu block having more than 60 seats.

Mukunda Behari Mullick was the first Untouchable in India to become Minister and remain in the post for a long time till the Haque ministry was dissolved on 1st December 1941, only to be reconstituted within three days with Shyama Prasad Mookerjee as a Minister. This was known as Shyama-Haqu Cabinet. The new ministry dropped the two existing untouchable Ministers and inducted only one in their place. The Prime Minister Kher in Central Province too appointed a well qualified Untouchable member named Agni Bhoj as a Minister within a few weeks after Mukunda Behari's becoming a Minister. But Dr Kher had to drop the Untouchable from his Cabinet due to strong admonition from Gandhiji. Gandhiji's objection was that an Unouchanle's entry in the Ministry will augment their ambition.[24] But the father of the Hindu nation failed to show his arrogance in case of Bengal. The only solution of this everlasting political problem was to permanently disenfranchise the Untouchables by dividing Bengal as demanded by the cousin of Mohandas Karamchand Gandhi, Md. Jinnah, the son of Punja Gandhi, grand son of Otta Gandhi and son-in-law of a Parsi tycoon. This was forcefully advocated by Dr Ambedkar, the Untouchable in 1940. The Hindus pushed the country towards partition.

In all the States except the Punjab and Bengal the National Congress succeeded in capturing the wheel of the Government. Inportance of Ambedkar diminished no sooner than the Hindus became majority group. In Bombay Province, in the Central Province, and in Madras the storm of conversion move, simultaneously raised by Dr Ambedkar was therefore geared up. It added fuel to the ongoing process. Bengal and the Punjab were most vulnerable. With a view to appeasing the Untouchable leaders of Bengal, the Congress Committee, in the month of July 1938, sent their untouchable members PR Thakur and Radhanath Das, the Deputy whip of the Congress Legislative Party on a tour to see, personally, the action taken on temple entry move in the Congress ruled states. They had paid visit to Orissa, Madras, Mysore, Bombay, Central Province, Delhi, UP and Bihar within a span of only three weeks and came back on 28th July to give a report, "We are pleased to see".[25] The non-stop excursion travel was coupled with generous hospitality. And it was not known whether the deputed members were pleased more with the condition of temple entry movement or with the hospitality.

On 16th March 1938, one year after the demise of Guruchand, twenty out of twenty four Legislators (Untouchable) assembled at the residence of Sarat Chandra Bose, the elder brother of Subash Chandra Bose, at Elgin Road and decided to co-operate with the Congress party and withdraw their support from the coalition government so that two untouchable Ministers are ousted. They formed a new Legislative Party, known as the Independent Scheduled Caste Party with Jogendra Nath Mandal as its Secretary. Two days after when P.R. Thakur and Jogendra Nath Mandal expressed their doubt on the genuinely of good-will gesture of caste-Hindus, Gandhiji advised them to join Congress, as it was the only party that stood for all communities and classes. But the landslide that was initiated after the Poona Pact did not stop with such hurdles of doubts and dilemma.

In Bengal, the Huqe Ministry was cleanly a non-Brahmin and non-Hindu Ministry. It was headed by a Muslim (Muslim *Nawab* or Emperor was no new phenomenon in India) Prime Minister, but there was no Brahmin. Besides, the tormenting uniqueness of fact was that, in the annals of Indian history, two Untouchables became Hon'able Ministers. This was too objectionable and heretic act to be tolerated by the Hindu nationalists. Consequently, they hatched a conspiracy. The Rig Vedic policy of breaking bones by knocking them together was re-used. On the third day after the submission of the earlier mentioned tour report by P.R. Thakur and another untouchable Congress leaders, Rashik Lal Biswas circulated a secret pamphlet among the members of the Assembly. The circular held:

"Those who are in touch with the political situation in Bengal know very well that a great opportunity has come to the Scheduled castes. If their MLAs can unite and manage affairs tactfully and properly, they can hold the balance of power..... and decide the fate of Bengal......

The Congress Party of Bengal is willing to setup a Ministry entirely of Muslims and Scheduled castes in Bengal, in the same manner as it has been done in Sind..... Many of the MLAs belonging to the Scheduled Castes know that responsible Congress leaders have already assured them in this matter.....

If at least 25 MLAs of the Scheduled Castes now join the opposition they can easily remove the present Ministry and in the new Cabinet they can easily get 5 Ministers .... If our Scheduled Caste MLA friends lose this opportunity it may not come to the community again. It is for this advantage of holding the balance for the Scheduled Castes. I think the whole Scheduled Caste Community should now realize the gravity of the situation and give a mandate to their representatives in the Assembly to available of this opportunity as early as possible."[26]

What an unfortunate situation advanced that the untouchable leaders so easily trusted to became a prey of their age-old natural enemy, the creamy-layer-ruling caste, the Hindu nationalists. Instead of helping and strengthening each other, the Honourable untouchable legislators, as the tools in the hands of the Brahmanical social order, joined the conspiracy to pull the untouchable Ministers who after millions of dreadful dark-nights of deprivation just ascended the thrown of their own motherland down. They were lured with a false dream for gaining five birth of Ministership with the blessings of the Brahmins provided the existing two were pulled down! They were not demanding three more in addition to the existing two.

In the month of March, on 26th at Sraddhananda Park, Kolkata the new alliance of Scheduled Caste MLAs were given a welcome. Subash Cnandra Bose the then President of Congress declared, "Scheduled Caste people and the caste Hindus, all belong to one community, there being no distinction whatsoever….The whole nation was a depressed nation, Brahmins and Kayastas being no exception to that…. With the attainment of freedom all these inequalities would automatically disappear." The sense of this oneness and of one distressed nation soon after is found to have manifested in effectively pulling down and kicking out the Scheduled Caste Ministers from their position.

The Haque Ministry got eclipsed due to the presence of two Ministers namely Prasanna Dev Raikat and Mukunda Behari Mullick from the Untouchable communities. In a most calculated manner, the Hindu nationalists operated their agents, the untouchable leaders to move ten 'No-confidence-Motions'. They moved it, one after another against three Ministers namely Mukunda Behari Mullick, Prasanna Dev Raikat and Satish Chandra Nandi (Backward Sudra). Muslims and the Brahmins were the traditional rulers. The 'Divine-slaves' could not digest their men as rulers. The slaves, better, enjoy slavery! They feel comfortable to be in servitude. Thralls enjoy the thrills of thralldom. The no-confidence motions are moved against the Government and not against any individual Minister. But in the instant bid these were moved not against the Government. The untouchable members moved no-confidence motion against the untouchable Ministers.

On 8th August 1938, the independent Namasudra MLA Dhananjoy Roy from Dacca moved first to place on the table a no-confidence motion against Satish Nandi. On 10th of August Namasudra MLA P.R. Thakur moved no-confidence against Mukunda Behari Mullick alleging nepotism and his failure to implement reservation policy in the government services, in his own department. Even before the expiry of four months in the office such charges were moved. Jogendra Nath Mandal supported this move. Then Jogendra Nath Mandal brought no-confidence motion against the Rajbansi Minister Prasanna Dev Raikat. The history records it as follows, "No-Confidence Motion : Mr. Jogendra Nath Mandal:- Sir, I beg to ask for leave to make the following motion in the current session of the Bengal Legislative Assembly:

"That this Assembly expresses its want of confidence in the Hon'ble

Prasanna Deb Raikat, Minister of Forest and Excise." May I have your consent to do so?

Mr. Speaker:- Leave has been asked for with my consent by Mr. J.N. Mandal for moving a motion of no-Confidence in the Hon'able Prasanna Deb Raikat, Minister for Forest and Excise. Those members who are in favour of leave being granted will please rise in their seats (more than 82 members having risen in their seats). Leave is granted for this motion being moved. I will fix the date later on."[27]

Consequently, the Muslims got frustrated with the short-sighted and self-destructive attitude of the Namasudra and untouchable leaders of petty mind. On the national platform Dr Ambedkar too launched Bengal and the Punjab partition move for the prosperity of the Hindu nation. Such separatist and stooge-masters were proved to be their own enemy. A final rift cracked in the unity of the untouchable communities to retain nationhood. Weakened they, by this internecine apolitical fight on the floor of politics, also severely devalued their weight in the eyes of all others. Still the untouchables of Bengal and the Punjab remained a potential threat. Their policy and prospect of post-election coalition or alliance with the Muslim MLAs made the Muslim community an unmanageable force for the Hindus. Thoughts on Pakistan virtually threatened the Muslims to be purged from Indian body politic had they continued honeymooning with the untouchables in politics. The Muslims as a result are found to have taken appropriate steps to save and guard their own political interests. They started corresponding with the British authority to form an alternative government, which could continue full terms without trouble. The secret telegram reveals that, "For two years or more Haque had been in a secret consultation with Sarat Bose and certain (Hindu) *Mahasaba* leaders for alternative Government."[28] Sarat Bose is understood to have maintained both the Muslim and Untouchable sides with him to be maneuvered by the Hindus. It was nothing but a natural concomitant of Brahmanical policy to keep the Untouchable as their 'divine-slaves'. British Government was not interested in such chaotic position as it was engaged badly in the World War II. The British were considerably dependent on supply of money and men by the Indian wealthy ruling section. However, consequent to the war-situation the untouchables Ministers got the lease of life despite these no-confidence motions.

In December 1941, Fazlul Haque dissolved his ministry only to form it again with Shyama Prasad Mookerjee and without any Minister from amongst the leg-puller and quarrelsome Namasudras. The only Scheduled Castes Minister was Upendra Nath Verma (Rajbanshi). Those who dreamt of five ministerial births had to remain contented without a single Minister. They silently ate the pie. Thralls enjoyed their thralldom. Shyama-Huq ministry now faced no trouble, no no-confidence motion. The Hindu press welcomed the new ministry. However, the 'Muslims felt 'to have been let down by the

Governor' and developed great indignation at the treachery of Mr. Fazlul Haque'. Now, on the contrary Namasudra-Muslim riots broke out in several places of rural Bengal. Instead of being aggrieved with Mookerjee, the untouchables in the villages became fans of Hindus and played the heroic role of the defenders of Hinduism in the milieu of Untouchable-Muslim riots during this period. These riots were the preparatory spade-work for the coming partition of Bengal on 'exclusion policy' planned finally by the same Hindu nationalists who once during 1905 to 1911 talked about 'inclusion policy' and fiercely launched a nation wide anti-partition rather *Swadeshi* movement with the same and sole target to establish Hindu Raj.

The scholar historian has commented on it rightly, "The local Muslim leaders alleged that the ill-feeling had been instigated by Hindu Mahasabha Organisations working in the area since the last Khulna riot of 1941..... Mookerjee arrived at Bagerhat in the morning of 2nd June (1941) and on being told that the meeting had been banned, proceeded on a launch towards Mollahat where the riot had just stopped two days ago. At Mollahat steamer station a large crowd greeted him with such overtly communal slogans as "*Hindu Sakti Ki Jai*" the victory of the Hindu-power.[29] Besides, publication of Dr Ambedkar's book 'Thoughts of Pakistan' added fuel to the fire. The Untouchables lost their new-found ally in their blood-brothers, the Muslim communities in rural Bengal in their democratic battles of power politics. They had no chance to know anything about the scheme of partition hatched by the Brahmanical social order to disenfranchise them permanently in near future. As a result, when time came the untouchable leaders were neither supported by the Hindus in Congress nor by the Muslims in League. They alone fought in the blinding darkness only to loose the battle to maintain integrity of their motherland.

Jogendra Nath was assessed adequately, 'Mandal's selfless behaviour was esteemed highly by the Bose brothers of the Congress. Up to 1940 Mandal kept in touch with the Congress and was in the camp of the opposition parties.....Subhas Chandra Bose's influence on him was obvious when he stated that he would make every effort to build an undivided Hindu society.... In the Calcutta Corporation election in April 1940, Mandal who was not an official member of Congress Party, ran as candidate for the reserved seat in Ward 3 on recommendation of the Congress and was returned on account of the effective backing given him by the Bose Brothers'.[30] He is found to have enjoyed extraordinary privileges of holding two offices (MLA and Councilor of Calcutta Corporation) simultaneously as an associate of the Ruling Classes in the Congress and the subdued Untouchables in the opposition. With the departure of Subash Bose from the Congress as well as from the country, Mandal became helpless leader. However, at this juncture he got another alley in Ambedkar on national platform despite the release of his scheme of creating East Pakistan out of Bengal.

During the following period, Dr Ambedkar gradually became very aggressive. Soon after the publication of his controversial book, 'Thoughts on Pakistan' on March 29, 1941, Cripps Proposal was published. It declared, "His Majesty's Government, therefore, make the following Declaration: (a) Immediately upon cessation of hostility steps shall be taken to set up in India , in manner described hereafter an elected body charged with the task of framing a new Constitution for India." It was clear that the Constituent Assembly was coming soon. "The new body shall be in number about 1/10th of the number of the electoral college." Consequent to this declaration Dr Ambedkar is found to have taken several steps. Immediately, as a result, Dr Ambedkar reprinted his book, 'Thoughts on Pakistan' by adding a new chapter where he now also propagated, "No partition, but abolition of Muslim League and the formation of a mixed party of Hindus and Muslims' as 'the only effective way of burying the ghost of Hindu Raj."[31] These Hindus were 'the lower order of the Hindu society'. He also took initiative to create a national political party of the Scheduled Castes (All India Scheduled Caste Federation) form the 'electoral college' and face the coming election to enter in the Constituent Assembly.

The Shyama-Huqe Ministry remained in power in coalition with the Forward Block (27 MLAs) and Mahasabha (11 MLAs) till March 1943. When it failed, the Scheduled Caste MLAs once again got united to play their game in the coalition politics and claimed to the Muslim League their demands (i) Three Scheduled Caste Ministers with three Secretaries (ii) Rs. five lakhs for spread of education for the Scheduled Castes (iii) Appointment of S/C candidates in all departments. Nazimuddin accepted these demands. Out of thirteen Ministers three were Hindus i.e. Tulshi Charan Goswamy, Tarak Nath Mukherjee and Barodakanta Pain and three were untouchables such as Jogendra Nath Mandal, Prem Hari Barman and Pulin Behari Mullick, the brother of Mukunda Behari. This Nazimuddin Ministry collapsed on 28th March 1945 and was placed under Governor's rule. And the process of next election started in the winter of 1945-46.

Before this, Dr Ambedkar visited Calcutta on official tour as the Labour Member of the Viceroy's Executive Counsel. Two groups of Untouchable leaders met him at the Howrah station. One group, associated with the INC, was composed of J.N. Mandal, P.H. Barman, R.L. Biswas, Kshetra Mohan Singh and Roybahadur Amulya Charan Das. The other group led by Mukunda Behari Mullick, the veteran leader and a follower of Guruchand's ideology of uncompromising struggle for freedom from Brahmanical thralldom. Birat Chandra Mandal and Amulyadhan Roy and others were with him. Dr Ambedkar took the side of Mandal's group who were with the Congress camp. Practically the senior Mullick was insulted.

The creamy-layer Hindu Brahmins in the circumstances had come down from their Calcutta-culture, entered in the rural marshy-areas and started knocking on the doors of the thatched-huts of the poor untouchable-peasantry. They successfully confused the untouchable movement further. Being Hinduised, as a result of the Poona Pact, their sharp attack on the Hindu-politics became considerably weakened. On the other hand, after losing the Depressed Class status the caste factor came in front. The Scheduled castes easily became the victims of inter-caste conflicts with interest of different caste leadership. The impact of all these factors in the 2nd election in the post Poona Pact era proved to be fatal for the Untouchable liberation movement in Bengal too. Dr Ambedkar though failed to attend the provincial conference of All India Scheduled Castes Federation in April visited Calcutta earlier in the first week of January 1945 to impress the untouchable leaders of Mandal fraction 'that the Congress after Gandhi's death would be blown to pieces. He stressed the importance of the Scheduled Castes Federation and added that it would be an eternal party in the country from the political and moral point of view.'[32] For the first time the Scheduled Caste Federation founded at Nagpur by Dr Ambedkar contested election in Bengal in 1946.

Dr Ambedkar was appointed as the Hon'able member of the Viceroy's Executive Council as its Labour Member or Labour Minister in the year 1942. M.N. Roy who founded the Communist Party on 20th October 1920 in Taskand initiated demands for the formation of a Constituent Assembly composed of elected and eminent Indian members from all walks of life to frame the Constitution of Free India. He was the Secretary of the Indian Labour Federation and had been working as one of the British highly paid secret Spy.[33] "After completion of six years sentence in jail, Roy was released on 20th November, 1936. Immediately after, he issued a public appeal asking the people to join the Indian National Congress in millions."[34] He had became a devout follower of Gandhiji and Congress and expected that he would become the member of the Viceroy's Executive Council that year. Finally, however, Dr Ambedkar was inducted. The process of creating a Constituent Assembly composed of the representatives elected by the members of the provincial Legislature went on speedily. Dr Ambedkar scented problem as it was impossible for him to get elected from Bombay province because of very low percentage of untouchables who were further fragmented by internecine quarrel.

He perhaps gradually got panicky by realizing the fact that in Bombay Presidency the strength of his untouchable rather Scheduled caste supporters were numerically too fable to return candidates and him in the Constituent Assembly. Therefore, he fell on the democratic system of the British Government.

In the valedictory address in the All India Trade Union Workers' Study camp held in Delhi from 8th to the 17th September 1943 under the auspices of the Indian Federation of Labour Dr Ambedkar heavily criticised the Parliamentary form of Government and its election process of which the

British nation has been traditionally proud of. He expressed, "It was felt that this was the last word in the frame work of the government. It was believed to bring about the millennium in which every human being will have the right to liberty, property and pursuit of happiness. There is no country in which the urgency of considering this question is greater than it is in India. India is negotiating to have Parliamentary Democracy. There is a great need of some one with sufficient courage to tell Indians, "Beware of Parliamentary Democracy, it is not the best product, as it appeared to be."[35] 'Parliamentary Democracy, notwithstanding the paraphernalia of a popular government, is in reality a government of a **hereditary subject class** by a **hereditary ruling class**. It is this vicious organisation of political life, which has made Parliamentary Democracy a dismal failure."[36] Parliamentary Democracy took no notice of economic inequalities and did not care to examine the result of freedom of contract on the parties to the contract, should they happen to be unequal.'[37] On January 1st 1943, in the broadcast he explained, "Parliamentary Democracy is a form of Government in which the function of the people has come to be to vote for their masters and leave them to rule. Such a scheme of Government, in the opinion of Labour is a travesty of Government of the people by the people and for the people...."[38] He is, however, found to have developed the idea of getting a government other than representative of the people in India. On 4th January 1938 he declared, "I am no believer in Democracy as an ideal to be pursued in all circumstances and in all claims; and having regard to the present-day conditions in India, Democracy is a most unsuitable system of Government. At any rate, for some time India needs the strong hand of an enlightened autocrat."[39]

In pursuance of the statement by Mr. Clement Attlee in the House of Commons, on 19th, February 1946, the Cabinet Mission, headed by Lord Patric Lawrance arrived in India on 23, March 1946. It came to finalize the political modality of the future Constitution etc. The Cabinet Mission did not feel it necessary even to invite the representative of the Untouchables now in the meet to express their viewpoints as they lost their independent identity as Depressed Class by the Poona Pact. "After a most careful consideration of the various methods by witch these points might be corrected, the fairest and most practicable plan would be (a) to allot to each province a total number of Castes proportional to its population, roughly in the ratio of one to a million, as the nearest substitute for representation by adult suffrage; (b) to divide this provincial allocation of seats between the main communities in each Province in proportion to their population; (c) to provide that the representatives allocated to each community in a Province should be elected by members of that community in its Legislative assembly. For these purposes it was sufficient to recognize only three main communities in India general, Muslim and Sikhs."[40]

In this policy, teeming millions of Untouchables who formed not less than 20 per cent of country's population and who participated for the last

60 long years or at least from 1911 as a third large political entity as Depressed Class were totally ignored. The Tribal people of around 10 per cent were brutally denied. They were ignored as they became Hindus, in the Poona Pact, now 'General' in the Cabinet Mission. A table of representation of the three communities was drawn as follows:

Table of Representation[41]

Section - A

Province	*General*	*Muslim*	*Total*
Madras	45	4 (8%)	49
Bombay	19 (91%)	2 (9%)	21
United Province	47	8 (14.5%)	55
Bihar	31	5 (14%)	36
Central Province	16	1 (6%)	17
Orissa	9	0	9
Total	167	20	187

Section - B

Province	*General*	*Muslim*	*Sikh*	*Total*
Punjab	8 (28.5%)	16 (57%)	4 (14.5%)	28
NWF	0	3 (100%)	0	3
Sind	1 (25%)	3 (75%)	0	4
Total	9 (26%)	22 (63%)	4 (11%)	35

Section - C

Provonce	*General*	*Muslim*	*Total*
Bengal	27 (45%)	33 (55%)	60
Assam	7	3 (30%)	10
Total	34	36	70

The number of the Untouchable races and nations was several billions; they formed one fifth of the country's population. They were present in each province in a very large number. They got recognition for demanding their political share as an element separate from the Hindus, Sikhs and Muslims since 1911. However, at the final stage, these vast autochthons became redundant in the process of power-share. It has been considered that their political wellbeing would be well taken care of by the Hindu big brothers.

However, the Sikhs who are found in one province only and who composed less than 1 per cent of total population (Census of 1941 enumerated less than 6 million or 56 lakhs 91 thousand 676 souls only) were given distinction and weight as they held separate religious entity. Not only they got right to representation, they also gained 14.5 per cent and 11 per cent in the province and in the 'B' region. The section 'B' and 'C' further show some kind of nightmarish situation for the Hindus who remained overwhelmingly minority in five large provinces. Its impact on the national politics was definitely detrimental for maintaining the Hindu-Rastra. This acted as the catalyst force for partition of India. The necessity for disenfranchisement of these undesirable elements in ballot boxes became acute to acuter.

At this stage, having lost all fair avenue Dr Ambedkar banked on the British authority for their charity on the basis of his personal strength and wisdom. On 3rd May 1946, Dr Ambedkar as a member of Viceroy's Executive Council wrote to Lord Wavell, the Governor General demanding (1) Separate Electorate (2) proper representation in the Central Executive, and (3) undertaking from parties to accept certain general principles in regard to safeguarding the interests of the Scheduled Castes in the future Constitution. On 14th May in another long letter to Mr. Hon'able A,V. Alexander, Member Cabinet Mission Dr Ambedkar had argued, "No safeguards are going to be any value to the Untouchables unless the Untouchables get a separate electorate. Separate Electorate is the crux of the matter..... There will be no wonder if you know what game the Congress is playing. It is a very deep game. Realizing that there is no escape from giving the Untouchables some safeguards, the Congress wants to find out some way by which it can make them of no effect. It is the system of joint electorate that the Congress sees an instrument of making the safeguards of no effect. That is why the Congress is insisting upon joint electorates. For joint electorates means giving the Untouchables office without power. This they can only get through separate electorates and this is why are insisting upon it." He eventually being teeth-less, helpless and friendless appealed to morality, "...the British have a moral responsibility towards the Scheduled Castes. ...It is a pity how few British are aware of it and fewer are prepared to discharge it. British Rule in India owes its very existence to the help rendered by the Untouchables. Many British think that India was conquered by the Clives, Hestings, Coots and so on. Nothing can be greater mistake. India was conquered by an army of Indians and the Indians who formed the army were all untouchables. British Rule in India would have been impossible if the Untouchables had not helped the British to conquer India.... You have come here to announce that the British are abdicating. It cannot be wrong for an Untouchable to ask, "...to whom are you leaving this legacy of authority and power? To the protagonist of Brahmanism, which means to the tyrants and oppressors of the Untouchables....."[42] On 7th June 1945 once again he wrote to Lord Wavell, "I feel it, therefore, my bounded and sacred duty to oppose the proposal by every means at my command. The proposal means death-knell to the Untouchables and will have the effect of liquidating their efforts over the 50 years for their emancipation." Dr Ambedkar perhaps for got his own saying, "Liberty is not a gift from the usurpers. It is to be gained by struggle and self-sacrifice." His efforts through appeals yielded nothing, as he could not build up people's struggle on national scale. Even the entire Untouchable population of Bombay province (less than 8 per cent of total souls were not united) was not in a position to yield any effective result. The British Government in the long-run decided not to give any representation of the Untouchables in the instrumentalities of the State. This appears to be the culminated manifestation of the British's scheme of 'Separate Electorate' for the Muslims and the Sikh to tag the untouchable population with their 'Divine Hindu-Boss'. In the interim Government, five seats were kept for the Muslims and remaining nine were given to the Hindus under the leadership of Pandit Jawhar Lal Nehru. Nothing was left in the Democratic India for the struggling Untouchables and Tribes of India who formed not less than 30 per cent of the total population.

Formation of Electoral College for the Constituent Assembly

The election of 1946 on national scale was exceedingly important because the elected members were to form the Electoral College in respective provinces for electing the members of the Constituent Assembly, which will eventually frame and finalize the Constitution of free India. The Bengalee Scheduled Castes failed to place their leadership or leaders on national platform. They even failed to remain united in their own province and on a single platform in any remarkable form. In 1946 election out of total 30 reserved seats in Bengal, Congress won 26 seats. Scheduled Caste Federation under the leadership of Jogendra Nath Mandal contested seven including one general seat. Jogendra Nath Mandal who had contested 3 seats won only one reserved seat. 'Kshatriya Samiti' of Rajbansis won only one seat out of five they contested. Mukunda Behari Mullick, P.R. Thakur and Prasannadev Raikat won as independent candidates. The later two also joined Congress subsequently. Thus, the result was a complete reversal to the 1937 result. Bengal untouchables fell on their knees and in the line to Madras, Bombay and other provinces to rally round the Congress. In the Punjab too the Ad Dharm Mandal won only four out of eight reserved seats.

In Bombay province Dr Ambedkar faced a complete debacle in the most important election of the provincial Legislature in 1946. All the three candidates of All India Scheduled Caste Federation were miserably defeated to the Congress candidates. The Provincial Legislatures were composed of total members of 1587. These seats were distributed amongst different communal groups as follows: Hindus 778, Muslims 517, Scheduled Castes (Untouchables) 151, Sikhs 36, Indian Christians 21, Anglo Indians 12, Europeans 46 and Tribals 24. All over India the Scheduled Caste Federation, the would be 'eternal' political party of Indian untouchables, fielded total 28 candidates. Their provincial distribution was as follows: in the Punjab 3, Bombay Province 3, Madras 10, Central Province 4, Uttar Pradesh 2, Bengal 6. All but Jogendra Nath Mandal in Bengal faced complete rout. Dr Ambedkar was unable to field even more than 30 per cent of the reserved seats in this crucial election. Even though All India Scheduled Caste Federation was raised in 1942 (Constitution of the party was made public on 7th September 1942). However, in 1937 election he is found to have fielded more than 100 per cent reserved seats on behalf of the Independent Labour Party, which was established six months before the commencement of the election. Thus the situation became hopelessly volatile for even Ambedkar. His party contested only 3 seats (in another statement this number is found to be 5 seats)[43] while to enter in the Constituent Assembly one required minimum 5 votes of any provincial Legislators. Congress leader the iron man of India, Sardar Vallav Bhai Patel declared, 'All doors have been closed for Dr Ambedkar to enter in the Constituent Assembly'. At this stage, Dr Ambedkar thundered once again, "Things will be much worse under the system of joint electorates and reserved seats which will hereafter become operative under the terms of Poona Pact. This is no more speculation. The last election (1946) has conclusively proved that the Scheduled Castes can be completely disenfranchised in a Joint Electorate."[44]

Finding no chance in Bombay, Dr Ambedkar approached untouchable leaders of Bengal and eventually could return from the Bengal Legislative Assembly[45] with maximum votes (six) to the Constituent Assembly. Bengalee untouchable leaders including both Mukunda Behari Mullick and Mandal sacrificed their own interests and leadership to elect Dr Ambedkar. Bengal remained, as a consequence, in a vulnerable position to protect their social as well as geo-political integrity when the question of partition of Bengal into East Pakistan came. Now Dr Ambedkar realised the importance of Separate Electorates for the Untouchables, the issue that had been raised by Guruchand and his disciple, Mukunda Behari right from 1907. Having been elected in the Constituent Assembly from Bengal, Dr Ambedkar went to London for discussing the British leaders for future course of action. On his return from London to Bombay in an interview to the international journal 'Globe' on 20th November 1946 he once again posed his bold stand and came back to the fundamental issue of liberty, "All that the Scheduled Castes want are political safeguards, over which there can hardly be any dispute." He concluded, "The principle demand of the Scheduled Castes is that they must have Separate Electorate, all other political safeguards that might be granted to them are useless."[46]

Transfer of Power with Partition of India

The British groomed the Brahmins so laboriously step by step for a century to be their agents to protect and work for their colonial market in India and south East Asia. Now their calculated move was going to fail haplessly. It came in the fore that the Hindus cannot have absolute over-lordship in the undivided India. It became clear that the 3 to 4 per cent Brahmin population would not be able to maneuver the growing democratic aspirations of the immense majority and hostile servile classes composed of Untouchables, Sudras and the Tribes. The powerful Muslim community was not very dependable as to play the role of perpetual slave. On the contrary, in Bengal, Kerala, Maharashtra, Madras and in the Punjab it became clear enough in several elections during the first forty years of the 20th century that there grew an active and effective trend of forming democratic alliance between the servile class Muslims and so-called Hindu low-castes in abject servitude even under the bold banner 'Non-Brahmin Political Party'. Dr Ambedkar thus recorded in his thesis in 1942, 'Pakistan or Partition of India', "If Hindu Raj does become a fact, it will, no doubt, be the greatest calamity for this country. No matter what the Hindus say, Hinduism is a menace to liberty, equality, and fraternity. On that account it is incompatible with democracy….. Not partition, but the abolition of the Muslim League and the formation of a mixed party of Hindus and Muslims is the only effective way of burying the ghost of Hindu Raj….. There are many lower orders in the Hindu society whose economic, political and social needs are the same as those of the majority of the Muslims and they would be far more ready to make a common cause with the Muslims for achieving common ends than they would with the high caste of Hindus who have denied and deprived them of ordinary human rights for centuries."[47] But the scheme of Hindu Nationalists got implimented by the ruling class.

Consequently, on fine morning of August 1947 Indians found their motherland vivisected potentially in three sovereign countries. Both Muslim nationalists and Hindu nationalists became happy. There was jubilation in Pakistans and in India. All nationalists celebrated the occasion. Only the refugees have been unhappy. Since it was a policy-division there was no question of becoming refugee. Yet the low caste people who were displaced from East-Bengal were declared refugee. The refugees were in distress; they were the victims of Hindu nationalism and sufferers.

The British, in the wake of European socialistic democracy, had been actuated with their selfish colonial aspirations only to perpetuate their control over colonial market in India through their Indian agents. Taking a point from the Roman policy, "Divide Et. Imperia" and from the more effective and prevalent Indian Caste System, they decided simply to add fuel to disintegrate the country and weaken the rising national power of the servile class. As an irony, in this conspiracy, the Creamy-layer-Elite-India (Hindu and Muslim both) in course of time joined hands. The British simply fulfilled a condition what the Hindus had demanded. *Mahatma Gandhi* certified the innocence of the British. On 2nd June, 1947, after the evening prayer Gandhi cleared: "The British Government is not responsible for the division of India. The Viceroy has no responsibility for this. Rather the truth is that the Viceroy has so many objections as much the Congress has for partition of India. But if we the Hindu and the Muslims cannot accept any other condition, what can the Viceroy do?"[48]

The major Muslim leaders too wanted to rule over the whole of India as Indians. In the manifesto of the 'Hindu-Muslim Relation', *Khwaja Hassan Namaji,* therefore, declared in 1928 in clear terms.

"*Musalamans* are separate from Hindus; they can not unite with the Hindus. After bloody wars the *Musalmans* conquered India, and the English took India from them. The *Musalmans* are one united nation and they alone will be masters of India. They will never give up their individuality. They have ruled India for hundreds of years and hence they have a prescriptive right over the country. The Hindus are a minor community in the world. They are never free from internecine quarrels; they believe in Gandhi and worship cow, they are polluted by taking other people's water. What capacity have they for ruling over men? The *Musalmans* did rule and the *Musalmans* will rule."[49]

Despite all political conspiracy, schemes and target of Jinnah, Ambedkar and Gandhi during 1940 and 1941, later on, Jinnah even launched a serious dialogue for forming a political party in collaboration with Dr Ambedkar and Periyar E.V. Ramaswamy Naickar. The 25th Annual session of the Muslim League in 1945, held in Madras was attended by Jinnah, Dr Ambedkar and Periyar Ramaswami Naikkar. The process started long back, "Plans for the anti-Congress front are being vigorously canvassed by Mr. E.V. Ramaswami Naicker, leader of the 'Justice Party' in Madras, who has been in Bombay for the last five days'........... Mr. Naicker had lengthy talks with Mr. M.A. Jinnah and Dr Ambedkar in the course of which he is understood to have narrated to them, with the help of an interpreter the alleged act of oppression against the non-Brahmins. He is also understood to have explained that there was not a minority question in Madras. The non-Bramins who formed about 97 per cent of the population were being subjected to the tyranny of the smalls Brahmin minority which was completely controlling the Congress policy in the Province. Since the Muslim League and the Depressed Classes were also fighting against the same organisation, he suggested that they should make common cause.'[50]

But the Hindus under the leadership of Shyama Prosad Mookerjee and Pandit Jwahar Lal Nehru led Indian creamy-layer ruling castes to take Jinnah and some powerful ruling class Muslims in their scheme for partition of India. The philosophic base which had a ready been drawn in the book 'Thoughts on Pakistan' by Dr Ambedkar had contributed more than required support for the two Nations theory and separate countries. He even attempted to rob off the political rights of representation of the aboriginal tribes by saying that they are devoid of political sense. On this issue being challenged by Thakeray he defended, "I have never claimed to be a universal leader of suffering humanity. The problem of the Untouchables is quite enough for my slender strength...." Yet, in his *magnum opus*, 'Thoughts on Pakistan' published in 1940 with articulated ferocity advocated partition of India.'[51]

He even before the actual birth of a 'Pakistan' and a 'Hindustan' that had created argued, "What is the unity the Hindu sees between Pakistan and Hindustan? If it is geographical unity, then that is no unity.... If it is administrative unity, that again is no unity. The instance of Burma is in point. Arakand and Tenasserim were annexed in 1852. Upper Burma was annexed in 1886. The administrative unity between India and Burma was forged in 1862. For over 110 years that administrative unity continued to exist. In 1937, the knot that tied the two together cut asunder and nobody shed a tear over it..... Judged in the light of this considerations, the unity between Pakistan and Hindustan is a myth. Indeed, there is more spiritual unity between Hindustan and Burma than there is between Pakistan and Hindustan. And if the Hindus did not object to the severance of Burma from India, it is difficult to understand how the Hindus can object to the severance of an area like Pakistan, which to repeat, is politically detachable from, socially hostile and spiritually alien to the rest of India."[52] He even prepared the map of Hindustan and Pakistan by colouring Hindustan with saffron and Pakistan with green.[53]

Neither Jinnah nor Dr Ambedkar, being from Bombay Presidency, unaffected by partition, was not in a position to realize or even visualize the effect of their perilous partition scheme. Owing to the scheme, "On the midnight of the 15th of August, 1947, India won her independence from the British Rule, but two provinces, Punjab and Bengal paid very dearly for it. Their partition was attended by large scale bloodshed, loss of home and hearth by millions and uprooting of whole populations. The scale of movement of population that followed the partition is without any parallel in world history. The suffering of the effected people knew no bounds and their trauma has been too deep a wound ever to be healed. In both the independent States of India and Pakistan these people still bear a stigma and many of them, with their past blighted and future blotted out, are yet to find a heaven for a settled life. Not only the normal rhythm of their lives has been broken forever but their very soul has been sered and singed."[54] The teeming millions of Muslims who remained in India instantly became servile subordinate of the Hindu masters in Hindustan. No escape. Alas! The politicians never consider any other factor but selfish victory. Gangadhar Adhikari, the famous Marxist philosopher leader of Bengal upheld the theoretical justification for partition as was done by Dr Ambedkar with Marxist approach.

Dr Ambedkar seemed to be a rebel and anti-Hindu, however, from the beginning neither he nor his All India Scheduled Caste Federation supported the Ad Dharm movement of Mangoo Ram in the Punjab or of Acchutanand of United Province. All India Scheduled Caste Federation even set candidate against Mangoo Ram in 1946 election. Mangoo Ram won the 1946 election. "The major issue of differences between Ad Dharm and Dr Ambedkar was the division of India. Dr Ambedkar wanted that Ad Dharm should vote in favour of Muslim League for Pakistan and join the new country. Ad Dharm rejected this proposal and Dr Ambedkar expressed his anger. Ad Dharm was not agreed with the theory of Ambedkar that Aryans are the native of this land."[55]

When the issue and situation got matured, the entire institution called the Indian National Congress came down to support such a precarious decision. Nehru and Gandhi are found to have forced the All India Congress Committee to pass the resolution by a landslide margin of 157:15. Some scholars did not, however, hesitate even to say that Nehru and Gandhi used all their might and influence in the All India Congress Committee to pass the resolution of Partition of India in its special meet, immediately after.[56] Indeed, the Hindu-nationalists vivisected the country to establish a Hindu Raj.

Undemocratic Mode for Partition of an Ancient Country

To ensure the successful execution of the scheme of amputate the country and cure, even an undemocratic modality was resorted to by the ruling classes. In his book, "Transfer of Power", V.P. Menon the personal Secretary to the then Union Home Minister *Sardar* Vallav Bhai Patel, described the process as to how the decision for the partition of India was implemented. He has narrated how the Hindus voted in fovour of Partition and the Muslims opposed it. The Hindu, Muslim and Sikh leaders conveniently saw eye to eye because political power was to be transferred in their hands in a divided India where the portion of share that belonged to the teeming millions of the Untouchables and tribes would pass in their hands. The British authority set about for a smooth sailing. His Majesty's Government issued the policy of statement to this effect for the "Provincial Legislative Assembly of Bengal and the Punjab" on 3rd June 1947 as follows:

"The Provincial Legislative Assemblies of Bengal and the Punjab (Excluding the European members) will, therefore, each be asked to meet in two parts, one representing the Muslim majority districts and the other the rest of the province..... the members of the two parts of each Legislative Assembly sitting separately will be empower to vote whether or not the province be partitioned. If a simple majority or either part decides in favour of partition, division will take place and arrangements will be made accordingly."

The legislators of the Muslim majority area and the legislators from the remaining non-Muslim majority area (Hindu-Sikh-Christian-Buddhist-Persis-Tribals) were to take decision by vote separately. Each of these two groups was to take the decision on simple majority vote in favour or against the "Yes Partition" move. It was also pre-decided that 'yes-partition' vote from either of the two groups would suffice for Partition; it would be final and effective. Thus it was obvious that the thrust of the policy regarding national integration was in favour of Partition of India. Because in any case, "No-Partition" decision needed two votes to win, whereas "Yes-Partition" decision needed only one vote.

A decision for keeping the nation as is where is, that is for No-partition move required simple majority approval from both the groups. But in case of "Yes Partition" single majority decision from either the Hindu (non-Muslim minority) or Muslim was sufficient. Besides, the Hindus were given extra weightage by denying the separate entity to any other ethnic or religious groups like Scheduled Caste; Tribes; Sikhs, Christians etc. All were combined and clubbed together to form one group against the Muslims.

The self-styled nationalists never considered to take referendum of the entire nation before splitting the country. They did not even pay any regard to the majority people of other provinces. Not even any special majority, like two-third majority was required for deciding such vital issue like vivisection of a nation. The first part of the process was democratic i.e. 'majority votes' but the later was on the basis of contract. Aggregate vote of the two groups was not taken into account for assessing majority or minority. What an act of treason that the representatives, elected on the limited franchise of only 11 Districts of Bengal were empowered to decide the fate of our country and of the nation permanently. All others, the entire country including Dr Ambedkar (the author of Thoughts on Pakistan) or his Bombay province quietly abdicated. During 1905 to 1911 the Maharashtra Brahmins preferred gallows for preventing even administrative partition of Bengal.

In this conspiratorial cruel game, rest of Indian nationalists happily abdicated their authority for deciding the fate of their Motherland. People of UP, MP, AP, Tamilnadu, Bihar, Orissa, Delhi, Rajasthan, Gujrat, Maharashtra etc. are found to have not shown concern in this high drama. A handful of Indian citizens belong to two of the provinces of India. i.e. Bengal and the Punjab were made the sole arbiters to decide the most important and permanent issue like partition of the country. How only the Punjab and Bengal got the status of Indian nation? Was Bengal for the Bengalees only? Do not the rest of Indians pay taxes for national question? Do Bengal and the Punjab only pay the taxes for the defense of our country's border in the East and in the West? Why the rest of Indian provinces very happily abdicated their most important and fundamental rights?

Soon after partition, before any protest had aroused, the nation was swept away by a well calculated and timely triggered turmoil of torrential typhoon of Communal riots. All hell was let loose. In that blinding darkness, both Hindus and Muslims lost every thing. The Untouchables were made the beasts of prey. The frenzy of fundamentalism of both Hindus and *Musalmans* knew no bounds. The nation was dased.

Creamy-layer Minority Hindu Bengalese voted for vivisection of the Nation:

The voting took place on the 20th June, 1947. The result of this historic vote, so far as Bengal was concerned revealed a shocking fact that it were the Bengalee Hindus who over-whelmingly favoured Partition of India. While the Legislators who represented the Muslim majority area, in a massive manner voted against it.

Very prominent and powerful nationalists of the then India took part in this decision-making. Mr. A. Leonard Gordon has given a detailed description of it. "Then the members divided into two groups and the *Maharaja* of *Bardwan (Sir Udai Chand Mahatab)* Presided over the meetings of members from the non-Muslim majority areas. There were eleven districts like, Bardwan, Birbhum, Bankura, Medinipur, Hoogly, Hawrah, Calcutta, 24 Parganas, Khuln, Jalpaiguri and Darjeeling. They voted for partition 58 to 21. On this vote Jyoti Basu and Ratanlal Brahman from Darjeeling (two Communists) joined the other Hindu members and voted for Partition. The meeting of the members from Muslim majority areas was presided over by Nurul Amin. The delegates voted against Partition by 106 to 35. Four scheduled caste members (Haranchandra Burman, D.N. Baruri, Bholanath Biswas and Gayanath Biswas) voted with Muslim majority, and Fazlul Haq did not appear to vote. Thus, the Congress-Hindu Maha-Sabha-Commnuist alliance successfully maneuvered to keep West Bengal as a Hindu Majority Province within India. Given the limited choice before them, the Hindu Bengalis voted to split Bengal and remain part of a larger polity. Even Sarat Bose's brother Satish Bose and Kiran Shankar Roy voted for Pakistan."[57]

The Communist legislators of the then Bengal jubilantly supported with their votes the proposal of Pakistan, which was raised in the 1940, Lahore Session: "Pakistan is just a progressive and national proposal." They also vehemently opposed the Quit India Movement of Congress in 1942.

Along with all other Scheduled caste Legislators of Bengal Jogendra Nath Mandal also voted against partition. He had resigned from the Cabinet and in his resignation letter disclosed. "I was opposed to the Partition of Bengal. In launching a campaign in this regard I had to face not only tremendous resistance from all quarters but also unspeakable abuse, insult and dishonour....."[58] It was almost natural. He really opposed partition move. At the same time he doggedly supported the cause of Hinduism and toured all Bengal with Shyamaprosad with slogan, "Hindu sakti Ki Jai" during the preceding years.

The country's integrity was split finally through an undemocratic mode and method. There was no question of majority or minority voting pattern. The essence of democracy, 'decision of the majority' 'the decision of *Bahujan*' was ruthlessly trampled upon in this infamous historic step on the question of the fate of a nation's existence. The maxim of the Charter of Human Liberty that, "What touches all must be approved by all" was just set aside, as it posed a threat to the interests of the motivated Hindu groups.

When decision was to be taken by either of the two parties it was enough to have the opinion of the team which was in favour of partition. The "Yes-Partition" decision could have easily been imposed on the other group without seeking their verdict, as per the terms and conditions of the policy. Only in the case of a no-partition decision by the first group, the question for vote by second group came. On the face of the "Yes-Partition" vote of the either group the "No-Partition Vote" of the other group was just meaningless.

Majority Muslim Bengalese and Untouchables Voted Against Partition

Yet the drama was played. The Muslims are found to have overwhelmingly voted in favour of "No Partition". The Untouchable leaders too voted against partition move. In these historic circumstances, it became very odd and difficult for the Hindus to blame the Muslims outright for the destruction of the integrity of our motherland in any respect. With the completion of this puppet show, though the wholesomeness of our motherland shattered, the history of black sheep and treason remained alive. Under the trap of these theatricals, they simply wanted to obfuscate the reality and crudeness of an arbitrary decision of the British Government to fulfill and satisfy the selfish, sectarian and anti-national desire of the Hindus and the Elite-Muslims. This way they simply tried to 'democratize' an undemocratic act of colossal magnitude.

Those who shout a slogan, "*Bande Mataram*" vivisected their motherland so unscrupulously. The Hindus gave the Muslims a separate country out of their ancient motherland. The Communists of top rank behaved as a Hindu first and a Communist last. Those who shout slogan, "Workers of the World Unite" divided the proletariats of their own country. Why? The wolves may have many points to justify their ignominious deed, they may have many defenses upon their sleeves, they know the art of corrupting and how to give a veneer of respectability to their shameful acts.

Motive Behind Partition

The necessity for splitting up of the country resulted out of the rise of a new factor, the factor of untouchables' liberty movement or caste struggle that had Republican dream from American War of Independence in 1780 to 1789 and the French Revolution of 1789 and posed to be an irresistable phenomenon in democratic structure. This stood as the greatest roadblock for establishing Hindu Raj by the Hindu Nationalists, right from Raybahadur, Raja Ram Mohan Roy, Raybahadur Bankimchandra Chatterjee, Devendra Nath Thakur, Swami Vivekananda, Tilak and others.

It was extremely necessary to break the potential prospect of unity amongst the peasantry and the producers of India, the proselyte i.e. the Muslims, the untouchables the Tribes and the backwards. Such a unity would have ruined the prospects of the Brahmins. The situation has been revealed in the panic stricken speech in the Congress Legislature Party, on 27th December 1939 at Bombay, of *Sardar* Patel, "We cannot forget how Sir Samuel Hoare set the Muslims against the Hindus when the unity conference was held at Allahabad. The British statesmen in order to win the sympathy of the world, now go on repeating that they are willing to give freedom to India. The 'Day of Deliverance' was evidently calculated to make the world and particularly the British public believe that India was not united and that the Hindus and Muslims were against each other. But when several sections of Muslims were found to oppose the 'Day of Deliverance', the proposed anti-Hindu demonstrations were converted into a Jinnah-Ambedkar-Byramji protest against the Congress Ministers and the Congress High Command...."[59]

These phenomenon were noted very seriously even in the writings of Hedgewar. The latent political cause of the establishment of RSS on *Vijaya Dasami* in 1925 was this very fear psychosis; it was not to oppose the British colonial rule.[60] He wrote: "As a result of the non-cooperation movement of *Gandhiji*, the vigour in our country was receding and various evil forces were raising their heads out of this struggle...... The fight between Brahmins and non-Brahmins had started occurring openly..... Being fed with the milk of non-cooperation, the grown up Muslim-snakes are instigating riots."[61] It is clear that Muslim-snakes have become dangerous for the believer of the doctrine of *Hindutva* because they are fighting along with the low-caste Hindus against exploiters and subjugators."

In his book, 'Who is a Hindu?' V.D. Savarkar, in 1923, gave the definition, "A person who considers *Bharatvarsa*, stretching from *Sindhu* to seas, as his holy fatherland and the birth place of his religion is a Hindu." On the basis of this notion, the followers of *Hindutva* wanted to establish "Hindu nation which obviously can be done by the Hindus only". Their target was to establish a *Hindu Rastra a Rama Rajya,* and not an independent united India.[62] According to the thesis, the Muslims, the Christians, the Persis were unfit to be the component of the nation as their religion was not born in this soil. They, with their bias, overlooked the fact that the Brahmanical Hindus too were debarred from becoming eligible for *Bharatiya* nationhood as the Aryan Brahmanism, their *mantras* and scriptures had foreign, Indo-Aryan origin.

At a matured stage, the Brahmanical society openly appeared in the arena with their scheme for disenfranchisement by driving out Muslims, the partners of the untouchables of the country. "Dr Shyama Prosad Mookerjee, The *Maha Sabha* Leader, addressing a meeting in New Delhi on Tuesday, the 22nd April 1947, emphasised that the principle of partition must be accepted with the least possible delay though its actual implementation might take time. He thanked such of those members of the interim Government and other leaders who had expressed their concern for Bengal's future and said:

"Today opinion is practically unanimous amongst Hindus, including Scheduled Castes, and other minorities in Bengal that both for end of communal strife and for self-development of the two major communities,

Bengal must be divided into two provinces, comprising the predominantly Hindu and Muslim areas respectively.

"Apart from all communal consideration, Bengal with more than sixty million, of her population may well be divided for administrative reasons in two homogeneous and self content provincial units. The separation must not be dependent on Pakistan. Even if Pakistan is not conceded and some form of a weak and loose centre as envisaged in the Cabinet Mission Scheme is accepted by the Muslim League, we shall demand the creation of a new province composed of the Hindu majority areas in Bengal."[63]

Dr Ambedkar kept on record a very significant phenomenon of this period to understand the historic incident. "Mr. Naicker used the anti-Hindi agitation in Madras to come into lime light and now that the Congress Ministry is out of power, he is trying to use the opportunity to resuscitate the Justice Party and 'smash the Congress." And in this task, he is trying to seek the help of Mr. M.A. Jinnah and Dr B.R. Ambedkar…. Since the Muslim League and the Depressed Class were also fighting against the same organisation, he suggested that they should make common clause."[64] To thwart the process immediately after, on January 11, 1947, The Indian National Congress from its Madrass unit published an 'Open Letter' captioned 'Dr Ambedkar's Personal Power, As Menace To Millions' and widely instructed all its "Dear Harijan M.L.As." The instruction was very plainly argued, "The Scheduled Caste Federation and the Muslim League constitute the spearhead of the men who disparage you. It is not necessary for me to tell you how these two parties have formed a united front. The basic object of this front is to discredit, through any and every means, the Indian National Congress, and expose the leaders of the Congress to ridicule.

You need hardly to know what tactics are employed by the Muslim League to discredit Congress. But you should feel concerned over the tactics employed by the Federation and its leadership. The Federation was brought into existence about three or four years back. Its creator is Dr B.R. Ambedkar who had earlier established the Independent Labour Party to fight his battle with the Congress. The ostensible object of the Party was to overthrow the Congress Raj and set up in its place the government of Peasants and Workers. But even after making full use of his organised campaign of slander, he could not succeed in overthrowing the Congress Raj or establish the Worker's Raj.

Man the positions with courage and determination to save your helpless people who are being misguided and maneuvered into a position of great danger. It is a duty you owe to yourself and your people. Driven by his ambition and hopelessness of his situation Dr Ambedkar is allying himself with a powerful political machine of the Muslim League.

This is a disaster for our people and you must avert it with all the moral and spiritual strength of which you, the authentic spokes men and guardians of millions of Harijans in the country, are capable. If you betray your people in this hour of decision through hesitation or in action, posterity will inherit the shame of this hour. Must I say more Jai Hind!"[65]

The Hindus all over India reacted promptly. On the 15th March, 1947, Shyama Prosad Mookerjee convened Bengalee intellectuals in a Conference. Dr Ramesh Chandra Mazumder, Dr Makhanlal Roychowdhuri the historians of repute and Dr Suniti Chatterjee, the philologist of nation fame were present amongst many other noteworthy personalities. It was declared, here that the *Bhadrolok* (Brahmins+Vaidyas+Kulin Kayasth) Bengalese could not live in the barbaric rule and culture of the Muslim tyrants. In Bengal, the Caste-Hindus i.e. the *Brahmin-Baidya-Kayasth* combines are called *Bhadrolok* means Gentlemen. On 14th April, at Tarakeswar of Hoogly District, in another Conference named, 'Bengal Partition Convention', Dr Shyama Prosad made it clear, "It is a question of life and death for us, the Bengali Hindu....... we want our Home land and we shall have it, let this be our motto. Now or never, let this be the slogan." In his personal diary too, Shyama Prosad Mookerjee has not forgotten to keep it in record, "Force must in the last analysis be met with force. An internal policy of non resistance to armed violence would eventually condemn any society to dissolution." This shows that the Brahmanical people were making themselves ready for a bloody show-down in a civil war. They were uncompromising with their programme for the Partition of India. Why to blame the poor Muslim minority? Why blame wretched untouchables or their hero Dr Ambedkar for any sort of anti-national activity? Were not the gods capable enough doing or undoing every thing? They had already, as discussed earlier, roped in the Untouchables both of east and west India in their scheme of partition of India on the side of the Hindus.

Soon after the infamous Calcutta holocaust of 1946, the united Front of the provincial leadership of Hindu *Mahasabha* and the Congress took up the scheme of collecting mass signatures from all the district in favour of partition of India and division of Bengal. They ensured to deliver all these appeals in the hand of the then All India Congress President, *Acharya* J.B. Kripalani. Dr Shyama Prosad Mookerjee and Dr Bidhan Chandra Roy were personally to supervise these grand affairs. The Central leadership of Congress, without any loss of time submitted these appeals to Lord Mountbatten and pleaded for the partition of India.[66] Leaders, eminent persons and different civic bodies including Bar Associations and intellectuals sent thousands of such appeals to Dr Rajendra Prasad, the then Chairman of the Constituent Assembly. More than ninety percent of these appeals were launched only by the Brahmins.[67] Most of the Indian industrialists expressed their views in favour of the partition of India, they supplied limitless funds to the political and other organisations who supported the idea. Ghanashyam Das Birla, in July 1942 told Mahadev Desai (a very close associate of Gandhiji) : "I will give my support in favour of Partition of India, because this division is not impractical and it will not go against the interest of the Hindus."[68]

Untouchable-Muslim Unity: An Obvious Threat

In pursuance of the result of the 1946 election, Bengal Provincial Government was formed with 8 Cabinet Ministers led by the Prime Minister Surawardi of Muslim League. They were:

(1) Hussain Sahib Surawardi (2) Khan Bahadur Muhammad Ali (3) Khan Bahadur Saiyaad Moyajemoddin Hussen (4) Moulavi Ahamed Hossain (5) Khan Bahadur Abdul Gaffar (6) Samsuddin Ahmed (7) Khan Bahadur Abdul Fazzal Muhammad Abdul Rahaman and (8) J.N. Mandal.

The swearing in ceremony took place on 24th April, 1946. There was virtually no Hindu in the Cabinet that ruled Bengal. The sole non-Muslim member in the Cabinet was an Untouchable. This was a shattering blow to the very roots of Hindu mindset, rather Brahmanical sense of divine supremacy as well as security.

Here again, it was not basically the Muslim hegemony that was not acceptable to the Hindu elite. Muslim rule in Bengal or in India was not a new phenomenon. The Hindus were happy under the yoke of Muslim rule for seven thousand years. Sharing of power with the Untouchable *Shudras* by the Muslims instead of sharing power with the Brahamanical Hindus became the new phenomenon. And this factor witnessed a complete drift of the Muslims from their attitude of medieval period. Besides, so far whatever elections had taken place after the advent of the Muslim League in 1906 all were conducted on the basis of separate electorate. But in the future free India, without any separate electorate this unity factor and its impact in elections overshadowed every rosy picture of the Hindu Nationalists.

The last Census Report of undivided India amply reveals the shocking fact. It is given in the table bellow:

(This demographic data, however, does not show the population of Bihar, a major state in Northern India nor the population of Scheduled Tribes and Sikhs).

		Hindus	*Muslims*	*Scheduled Castes*
1.	Assam	35,86,932	34,42,479	6,67,291
2.	Bengal	1,76,80,054	3,30,05,434	73,78,970
3.	Beluch	39,521	4,38,930	5,102
4.	Sindh	10,38,292	32,08,325	1,91,634
5.	NWFP	1,80,321	27,88,797	....
6.	Punjab	64,01,737	1,61,17,242	12,48,635
7.	Delhi	4,44,532	3,04,971	1,22,693
8.	U.P.(P)	3,4094,511	84,16,308	1,17,17,158
	Total	6,34,65,900	6,77,22,486	2,13,31,483

The census of 1941 (manipulated in favour of Hindu population by reducing Scheduled Caste population of the Punjab and Bengal in comparison to 1931 figure) reveals that several provinces like Assam, Bengal, that is the entire Eastern Region and Beluch, Singh, the N.W.F.P., the Punjab (including Haryana etc.), that is the entire North Western India including the capital Delhi, were overwhelmingly populated by the Muslims. The Muslims were in a position to create havoc in the ballot-box. Further, combined voting of Muslim and Scheduled Caste population would have completely sealed the fate of the Brahmanical people in the race of numbers in the Parliamentary form of Democracy. Demographic position of the then U.P. also was not much favourable. Besides, the Hindu governing class population was concentrated only in the cities and towns. Thousands of villages were packed with the Muslims and the low caste Hindus only.

It would also be wrong to conceive that the Muslim leaders did not know the magic of number-game in a democratic frame. It were, the Muslim leaders who rather prepared the situation in their favour long back in 1906 by submitting address to Lord Minto at Shimla.

The Hindus smelt a rat in it[69], justifiably. Yet the Bengal Muslims won the battle, despite the stubborn resistance of the Hindus, the untouchables were purged from the Hindu body. Had there been no partition of the country the Muslims would have surely controlled politics of Eastern and Western India. Why and for whose benefit Jinnah demanded partition? Why then, instead of utilizing this numerical power, the Muslims abdicated all opportunities when the appropriate moments came and went with Pakistan at the detriment of the Muslims too! What was the reason behind this? Was it not a conscious retreat of the Muslims for creation of a Hindu Raj for the Hindu nationalists?

Instead of becoming the ruler of the entire Bengal or of the entire Western Indian provinces and of India in course, what made, them to retreat to be the ruler of only East Bengal and a very small part of Western India? In these regions they alone could form Government with overwhelming majority of the Muslim population. In any case, the majority Muslims could have ruled these regions on their own strength and right. What did the Elite-Muslims gain then? What did they get by giving up India? Who became the beneficiaries in the post-partition era?

Constituent Assembly Begins: History Ups the Untouchables

After getting elected from Bengal as a member of the Constituent Assembly on 1st November 1946, Dr Ambedkar declared his project. "Personally, I feel that if Mr. Gandhi and the Congress give them (untouchables) 'political independence' there will be great unity, "cooperation and goodwill between the Hindus and the Untouchables.", but if Mr. Gandhi and the Congress seek to bring the untouchables under political dominance of the Hindus and to make them political slaves of the Hindus, the untouchables would rebel and would endeavor to seek their salvation by joining some other community."[70] This threat virtually was meaningless as we have already noted that by the provisions and preamble of the Poona Pact 1932 the Untouchables ceased to exist as a separate group or community as the Untouchable leader had already accepted dominance of the Hindus. Soon after being elected to the Constituent Assembly from Bengal, Dr Ambedkar went to London to discuss his strategy with the British. On return from London he also threatened on 20th November 1946, "The question to my mind is whether the Constituent Assembly would have any moral authority behind it if the Muslims absent themselves from the Constituent Assembly. If the Muslim decide to absent themselves, I don't know the Constituent Assembly could do anything if it met on the 9th or any other subsequent date." He also said, "All that Scheduled Castes want are political safeguards, over which there can hardly be any dispute. The principle demand of the Scheduled castes is that they must have 'Separate Electorates' the reason being that without Separate Electorates, all other political safeguards that might be granted to them are useless."... "The Muslim League, so far as I understand, has no objection to separate electorates for the Scheduled Castes. The only objecting party is the Congress which represents the Hindu points of view...."[71] In these circumstances, Dr Ambedkar joined the Assembly. "I would act in constitutional manner to further our cause. After all constitutional means are exhausted we shall then consider what other means we can adopt."[72] In course of time Dr Ambedkar, however, is found to have compromised with the Hindus and the Congress members in the Assembly. He never raised the issue of separate electorate In the Constituent Assembly.

On December 9, 1946 the Constituent Assembly was inaugurated in the Constitution Hall, New Delhi at 11 O' clock. However, only 207 out of total number of 296 invited members attend the meet. The Muslim League boycotted the function. The Assembly virtually belonged to the Congress as 90 per cent of the members belonged to the party. J.B. Kripalani proposed Sachidanand Sinha for the Chair. Dr Rajendra Prasad was made Chairman on the 11th of the month. On 13th December Pandit J.L. Nehru moved his eight point Resolution. This was discussed in detail and supported by Dr Rajendra Prasad, Purusottam Das Tandon and Nehru himself. But on 16th instant Dr M.R. Jaykar from Bombay released bolt from blue by moving amendment on the resolution of Panditji. Dr Jaykar was criticised by Congress members below the belt for showing sympathy to the Muslim cause. In this ugly situation when the Muslims had boycotted the Assembly and a section of the Hindus had moved amendment, importance of the voice of the Untouchables got maximised. The Hindus played their Untouchable-card. On the 17th morning, Dr Ambedkar was called by breaking the order of preference to speak his viewpoints. His maiden, long and conciliatory speech in the Constituent Assembly for solving the crisis and supporting the Congress attitude won the hearts of the opponent Congress members who never wanted him as a member of the Constituent Assembly.

Just after six months on 23rd July 1947 Bengal was partitioned and East Pakistan was created as a sovereign country. Dr Ambedkar consequently lost his membership in the Constituent Assembly. Now, Congress became exceedingly generous and Dr Rajendra Prosad, the president of the Assembly asked Mr. B.G. Kher the Prime Minister of Bombay Presidency to re-elect Dr Ambedkar before the next session of the Constituent Assembly sat on 14th July 1947. B.G. Kher was one of the Vice-President of the Bahiskrit Hitakarini Sabha of Dr Ambedkar in 1924. The 2nd term membership of Dr Ambedkar in the Constituent Assembly was as a Congress nominee.

Attempt to give Freedom to all Irrespective of Caste-creed-poor or Rich

Dr Ambedkar in consultation with Dr Moonge and other top Hindu leaders compromised and delayed the programme of 'conversion' and left the issue of separate electorate for the Untouchables in free India where none of the minority community was to get it. In the circumstances, Dr Ambedkar attempted to achieve a solution through constitutional means. The new scheme was horrifying for the ruling classes nationally and internationally for the colonial powers. Being totally failed to yield any result in his favour from the ruling families he adopted the Marxian means to seek his own position secured. He suggested to knock down both the class and caste system with a single shot. He proposed to bring forth total revolution and people's revolution on Marxian-Leninist line through constitutional or bloodless path. On 15th March 1947, (before partition of India) on behalf of the all India Scheduled Castes Federation he submitted a draft constitution for the future India to come. Instead of going for 'specific minority line' for salvation or political freedom he sought to achieve freedom for servile people universally. He sought to end servitudes by means of establishing 'Economic-Democracy' and 'Social-Democracy' both through the constitutional provisions. During this period he defined Democracy in its total form, "Democracy is a form of Government where the ruling class fails to capture power."

He attempted to bring through constitutional provisions the same liberty of the servile class that was achieved by Comrade Lenin and Red Army through the bloody Russian Revolution in 1917. In this draft called, 'The Constitution of the United States of India' he very strongly pleaded for 'State Socialism' as the political structure of free India. State Socialism was a scheme that targeted to establish socialism through a bloodless revolution by changing polity structure in the Constitution. As Fundamental Rights the provisions of the Constitution of United States of India declared, (1) "That all industries which are key industries or which may be declared as key industries…. (2) And which are not key industries …. Shall be owned by the state;...(3) That Insurance shall be monopoly of State... (4) That agriculture shall be State Industry... (9) Agricultural Industry shall be organised on the following basis.. (i) The State shall divide the land acquired into farms of standard size and let out the farms for cultivation to residents of the village as tenants... on following conditions: (a) The farm shall be cultivated as collective farm; (b) The farm shall be cultivate in accordance with rules and directions issued by the Governments; (c) The land shall be let out to villagers without distinctions of caste or creed and in such a manner that there will be no landlords no tenant and no land-less labourers....."

The social and economic programme of the Constitution was a) Abolition of Landlordism. All estates will be confiscated without any compensation.....(d) nationalisation of Public Utilities, Mines, Railways, Telegrams and inland-Water ways; (e) Modern industries will be developed with the aid and under supervision of the State; (g) No standing army will be maintained, but the entire people will be armed to defend the national freedom (i) people must have freedom, complete and unconditional; (ii) All caste and class privileges will be abolished. The country will be thoroughly democratised; (iii) The land belongs to the tillers."…. Dr Ambedkar advocated for a society where each individual will be an end in himself. In a complete 'social democracy' only political democracy can bloom. Therefore, he opposed private ownership of property. And under social-ownership of property or in socialism only industries can maximize its productivity. In a capitalistic society the crisis of over-production due to the profit motive of individual capitalists do not allow maximisation of productivity of the society. He therefore clarified, "...to put an obligation on state (society) to plan the economic life of the people on lines (State Socialism) which would lead to the highest point of productivity, without closing every avenue to private enterprise, and also provide for equitable distribution of wealth..... without the supply of capital by the state neither the land nor the industry can be made to yield better." He went to the deep of Indian economic situation and argued, "State Socialism is essential for the rapid Industrialisation in India, Private enterprises cannot do it and if it did it would produce those inequalities of wealth which private capitalism has produced in Europe and which should be a warning for Indians. Consolidation of holdings and Tenancy Legislation are worse than useless. They cannot bring about prosperity in agriculture. Neither consolidation nor tenancy Legislation can be of any help to the 60 millions of untouchables who are just landless labourers. Only collective farms on the lines set out in the 'State Socialism' can help them."[73]

He also elaborately justified as to why these economic structure was required to be specifically enshrined in the Articles of the Constitution. "Why not leave it to the Legislature to bring it into being by the ordinary process of law. The reason why it cannot be left to the ordinary Law is not difficult to understand. One essential condition for the success of a planned economy is that it must not be liable to suppression or abandonment. It must be permanent. The question is how this permanence can be secured. Obviously it cannot be secured under the form of Government called Parliamentary Democracy; under the system of Parliamentary Democracy, the policy of the Legislature and of the Executive is the policy of the majority for the time being. Under the system of Parliamentary Democracy the majority in one election may be in favour of State Socialism in Industry and in Agriculture. At the next election the majority may be against it. The anti-State Socialism majority will use its Law-making power to undoing the work of the pro-State Socialism majority and the pro-State Socialism majority will use its Law-making power to doing over again what has been undone by their opponents. Those who want the economic structure of society to be modeled on State Socialism must realize that they cannot leave the fulfillment of so fundamental a purpose to the exigencies of ordinary Law which simple majorities, whose political fortunes are never determined by rational causes – have a right to make or unmake. For these Political Democracy seems to be unsuited for the purpose."[74] Dr Ambedkar, however, is found to have compromised with the ruling class on this issue too by not insisting on execution of the scheme of 'State socialism' after partition of India when he was offered much privileged position in the Constituent Assembly, in the Nehru cabinet as Law Minister and in the Drafting Committee of the Constitution.

Dr Ambedkar Proceeds Towards the Final Revolt

This act of launching the scheme of 'State Socialism' through the constitution of the country was developed at a time when the peoples democracy in the USSR was shining in the mid-sky. By this, Dr Ambedkar might have played the role of a catalyst force for hastening the process of partition of India. Must there be the process of disenfranchisement of the Untouchables in the Eastern sector and in the Punjab immediately on permanent basis. The scheme of breaking the Dalit-Muslim unity in the political arena of Bengal on which the strength of Dr Ambedkar is found to have rested firmly was accelerated. 'Amputate and cure'. Ambedkar would have proved to be a serious threat had there been Untouchables and their leaders in Bengal behind him. With the elimination of the vast multitude of untouchables in Bengal from the electoral role of India and the departure of the Muslims, their political ally, Dr Ambedkar personally and the entire Untouchable's liberation movement instantly paralyzes. They became completely subservient to the Hindu power be it political or religious in the past-partition era.

On 23rd June 1947, with the decision for partition of India Dr Ambedkar lost his membership in the Constituent Assembly. Finally, the partition of India, philosophised by Dr Ambedkar now paralysed Ambedkar politically.

The movements of the untouchables for becoming the rulers were wiped out in the Eastern region. The pathetic condition that Dr Ambedkar faced, as a consequence, knew no bound. He dared not contesting any seat with the ticket of his party even if there were any vacant seat to re-enter in the Constituent Assembly. His people in the Bombay Presidency or in the Maharashtra region failed to give him any hope. He seems to have become a victim of his own deeds and policy. He became absolutely teeth-less after the Bengalee Untouchable leaders became foreigners and their organisations disintegrated. Bengal-movement for the Untouchables' Liberation was finished gradually to annihilation.

Dr Ambedkar Hijacked and Made a Hack before Final Revolt

Eventually it was Gandhi and his Congress with gesture of generosity came to rescue Dr Ambedkar. The hapless and helpless Ambedkar was hijacked openly. Congress got the teeth-less and support-less scholar gem Dr Ambedkar re-elected in the Constituent Assembly. He was officially to play the role of the representative of the Untouchable masses but with the direction of the creamy-layer '*Sarvajan Samaj*'. In his letter dated 30th June 1947, Dr Rajendra Prasad, the President of the Constituent Assembly instructed Mr. B. G. Kher, the P.M. of Bombay Presidency, "... I am anxious that he (Ambedkar) should attend the next session of the Constituent Assembly commencing from the 14th July and it is therefore, necessary that he should be elected immediately". Mr. G. B. Kher, the Prime Minister of Bombay was a long time friend of Dr Ambedkar. He was one of the five Vice-Presidents of 'Bahiskrit Hitakarini Sabha' which Ambedkar registered in Bombay in 1924. The Prime Minister Kher asked Mr. M.R. Jaikar to resign and in the vacated seat, Dr Ambedkar was elected without contest before the next session of the Constituent Assembly commenced. Though it was termed 'election' it is found to be more a nomination directed by Dr Rajendra Prasad than the reflection of the people's mandate or their representatives' will. Neither his party people, nor his untouchable community was required to be worried for his re-entry in the Constituent Assembly. Within a fortnight, election was over allowing him for the 2nd term. As a Congress nominee, he was made the first Law Minister in the divided and free India on 3rd August 1947 as the chair fall vacant due to the historic departure of his mentor J.N. Mandal to Pakistan as a foreign national. On August 30, 1947 he was elected by the Assembly as one of the seven members of the Drafting Committee. Next, the members of the Drafting Committee unanimously elected him as the Chairman of the Drafting Committee of the Constitution. He therefore, had to depend on the good will of the creamy-layer ruling castes or the Indian National Congress.

In a divided India, he had no alternative but to allow himself to be in his own words 'a Hack' in the drafting of the Constitution. The constitution that he gave is a capitalist-constitution and it provides a structure that goes in detriment to the interests of the servile classes. The scheme of 'State Socialism' became a far cry in the constitution now. It talked neither of 'Separate Electorate' nor of 'State Socialism'. He, on the contrary, appealed on 25th November 1949 in his final speech in the Constituent Assembly, "On the 26th January 1950, we are going to enter into a life of contradictions. In politics we will have equality and in social and economic life we will have inequality…. How long shall we continue to deny equality in our social and economic life? If we continue to deny it for long, we will do so only by putting our political democracy in peril. We must remove this contradiction at the earliest possible moment or else those who suffer from inequality will blow up the structure of political democracy which this Assembly has so laboriously built up."

His draft constitution having the scheme of 'State Socialism' was thrown in the holy waters of the Ganges. This draft constitution was never discussed afterwards. It is a forgotten thesis of today. The question of Separate Electorate was dumped in the waste-paper box. Conversion issue went in oblivion.

In the circumstances, the Bengal Untouchables, the earstwhile tarbulant Chandal race reduced to the position of 'Eternal Refugees'. They were not called as East Pakistan's Displaced Persons (EPDP). In the 3rd Millennium, they are significantly called 'Without' in UP, Bihar, Orissa and Maharashtra. That is, these people were without any proper position of a subject of a country or as human beings. They do not have citizenship right though such condition violates Human Rights of the UNO. The saga of their glorious movement to be the rulers in the Parliamentary Democracy lost in the stream of national amnesia. Dr Ambedkar and Babu Jagjivan Ram from Bihar became the face of Untouchable's social justice movement under the scheme of Constitutional safeguard. The 1952 Parliamentary election, first ever after the Constitution, was contested by Ambedkar From Bombay Constituency only to be defeated. This defeat is eloquent enough to expose the fraudulent impact of the Poona Pact or joint electorate along with baseless leadership of Dr Ambedkar.

Having got their scheme of weakening of the Untouchables' solidarity and breaking the backbone of their liberation movement in Bengal and in the Punjab decisively accomplished, Ambedkar is found to have been sidelined by the same Indian National Congress quietly. 'Use and throw' has been the principle of the Brahmanism in so far as the Sudras and the Untouchables were concerned. Their another modality is co-opt and corrupt the servile class leaders. Now, the Chief architect of the constitution and former Law Minister of India was crowned with the thorn of defeat by the same Congress. Dr Sahib again contested a by-election from Bhandara (SC) in May 1954 only to recur the defeat. Seeing this fate of Dr Ambedkare as the illustrious message, the helpless Untouchable Community as a whole fell on their knee to worship the Brahmins and their political parties in the respective provinces.

Now being abjectly helpless and being under the mercy of the Brahmins the *Mahar* Ambedkar discovered him surrounded with the ocean of enemies. He at the fag end of his life was pushed to start, with in right earnest, the final movement of discarding Brahmanism or the religion Hinduism. He picked up the struggle what Hari-Guruchand made a plank while starting their freedom movement in 1835. Dr Ambedkar revolted finally to embrace Buddhism on 14th October 1956 along with his half-a million loyal Mahars at Nagpur '*Dikshabhumi*'. He gave a clarion call that he will transform India into '*Probuddha Bharat*'. He had planned to hold a conversion move for one million people in the month of December that year. He, however, was not allowed to live long. Like the Buddhist Emperor Kaniska of AD 1st Century, he too was found dead in his bed early in the morning of 6th December 1956 at his residence 26, Alipur Road, Delhi. He was living with his Brahmin wife, Sabita Ambedkar there.

References

1. Achariya Suniti Kumar Chatterjee, Bharater Bhasa O Bhasa Samasya (pub. 1945) pp. 9-10.
2. Dr Ambedkar W and S, Vol. 9, p. 235.
3. Dr Ambedkar W and S, Vol. 17(1), p. 170.
4. *Ibid,* Vol. 1, p. 432.
5. Dr Ambedkar W and S, Vol. 3, p. 267.
6. M.N. Roy, India in Transition, pp. 189-91.
7. *Ibid,* Vol. 9, p. 480.
8. *Ibid,* Vol. 9, p. 981.
9. Prof. Kancha Iliyaha, Why I am not a Hindu.
10. Dr Ambedkar W and S, Vol. 9, p. 102.
11. *Ibid*, Vol. 1, Appendix- 3, p. 432.
12. *Ibid*, Vol. 17 (1) p. 221.
13. *Ibid*, Vol. 1, pp. 69-78; Annihilation Castes.
14. Bhagwan Das, Thus Spek Ambedkar, Vol. 4.
15. Dhananjoy Keer, Dr Ambedkar: Life and Mission, pp. 254-56 and 258.
16. Dr Ambedkar W and S, Vol. 17 (2), p. 505.
17. Bhagwan Das, Thus Spek Ambedkar, Vol. 4, p. 296.
18. Dr B.R. Ambedkar, Thoughts on Pakistan, p. 120.
19. Dhananjoy Keer, Life and Mission of Ambedkare, p. 348.
20. Dr Ambedkar, Vol. 8, p. 359.
21. *Ibid*, Vol. 9, p. iii, preface.
22. Dr Ambedkar W and S, Vol. 17 (1), p. 346.
23. Autobiography, (Marathi) NC Kelkar, p. 734.

24. Dr Ambedkar W and S, Vol. 9, p. 98 and 254.
25. Sekhar Bandopadhaya, Caste, Protest and Identity in Colonial India, Namasudras.
26. *Ibid*, p. 183.
27. Assembly Proceedings Vol. L III, No 1, p. 88.
28. *Ibid*.
29. *Ibid*, p. 221.
30. K. Kotani, Caste System, Untouchability and the Depressed, p. 244.
31. Dr Ambedkar, W and S, Vol. 8, p. 359.
32. Dhananjoy Keer, B.R. Ambedkar: Life and Mission, p. 368.
33. Dr Ambedkar W and S, Vol. 10, pp. 179-784.
34. M.N. Roy, The Historical Role of Islam, p. 3; Introduction of V.M. Tarkunde.
35. Dr Ambedkar W and S, Vol. 10, pp. 106-7 and 110.
36. *Ibid*, p. 109.
37. *Ibid*, p. 108.
38. *Ibid*, p. 37.
39. *Ibid*, Vol. 17 (3), p. 168.
40. Dr Ambedkar W and S, Vol. 17 (2) p. 501.
41. *Ibid*, p. 502.
42. *Ibid*, Vol. 10, pp. 489-499.
43. Dr Ambedkar W and S, Vol. 10, p. 536.
44. Manyawar Kanshi Ram, Chamcha Age, p. 109.
45. Dr Ambedkar W and S, Vol. 10, p. 527.
46. Dr Ambedkar W and S, Vol. 17 (1) p. 353.
47. *Ibid*, Vol. 8, pp. 358-59.
48. Editor, Nakul Mullick, Nilkantha, J.N. Mandal on Partition of India, 14th January 1996.
49. Dr Ambedkar, Pakistan or Partition of India, (Vol. 8), p. 359.
50. Source Material, Dr Ambedkar, pp. 208-11.
51. Dhananjoy Keer, Dr Ambedkar: Life and Mission, pp. 333-34.
52. Dr Ambedkar, Thoughts on Pakistan, p. 60.
53. *Ibid,* Appendix.
54. A Summery of the Changes in the Jurisdiction of Districts in Bengal, West Bengal District Gazetteers, p. 164.
55. Balbir Madhopuri, Gadari Baba Mangu Ram, (Punjabi, published in 2010), introduction, p. 5.
56. Dhananjoy Keer, Dr Ambedkar: Life and Mission, p. 395.
57. A.L. Gardon, India Partition: Process, Strategy and Mobolisation, (London University Press, 1993) pp. 310-312.
58. Shyamal Mandal, Mahapran Jogendra Nath, Letter dated 8. 10. 1950
59. Collected Works of Sardar Patel, Edited by P.N. Chopra, Vol. 8, pp. 194-97.
60. Atis Dasgupta, *BJPr Hinduttwer Rajnitir Kramavikash, Marxwabi Path,* August 1996 issue (Gana Shakti Printers).
61. *Ibid*.

62. *Ibid.*
63. The Hindustan Times, dated 23rd April 1947, Partition of Bengal.
64. Source Material on Babasaheb Ambedkar, pp. 210 and 330.
65. *Ibid,* p. 332 and S.K. Biswas, Hindu Raj, Today-Yesterday-Tomorrow, pp. 146-49.
66. Atish Dasgupta, *ibid.*
67. Indian national archive, (N. Delhi) Rajengra Prasad File.
68. Atish Das Gupta, *ibid.*
69. Dr Ambedkar, The Untouchables, (Published in October 1948) p. 73.
70. *Ibid*, p. 323
71. Dr Ambedkar W and S, Vol. 17 (1) pp. 352-53.
72. Source Material, Dr B.R. Ambedkar, p. 326.
73. Dr Ambedkar W and S, Vol. 1, pp. 396-97 and 408-12.
74. *Ibid*, p. 411.

9

Advent of New Era with Kanshiram Phenomenon

Dr Ambedkar's father was not known as Ambedkar, he was Ramji Sakpal. His grandfather was Maloji Sakpal. The surname, Ambedkar is used by the Brahmins. The surname instantly denotes the caste, Brahmin. It is like a surname 'Banerjee' or 'Chatterjee' in Bengal; 'Sharma', 'Mishra', 'Tiwari' or 'Chaturvedi' in the north, Aiyer or Ayengar and Namboodiri in south Indian belt. Neither his parents nor any other relative held the surname claimed to have been drawn from their original village Ambavade. The surname was recorded in the school registrar by a Brahmin school teacher having identical surname, without his guardian's objection. Bhimrao Ramji carried the surname and made it a world-fame. May be this emboldened the Benaras Hindu University pass-out, Koenrad Elst, a foreigner, a Belgian to author the famous book called 'Indigenous Indians, Agastha to Ambedkar' and conclude that both belonged to the Aryan Brahmin family. Ambedkar was a true Aryan.

Dr Ambedkar is found to have registered his maiden social institution, the 'Bahiskrit Hitakarani Sabha' for uplifting the Untouchables by decorating it with Brahmins and exclusively powerful friends in Bombay. It is a subject of Indian social thinkers to examine the situation as to why a band of Brahmins came down to uplift the untouchable society by holding hands of Ambedkar. What propelled the supercilious Brahmins to offer their funds and generous guidance for welfare and advance of the creatures, hated by them to the superlative degree during that period?

Dr Ambedkar made his maiden appearance in the public agitation in March 1927, at Mahad in 'Mahad Talab Satyagraha'[1] along with his Brahmin friends and supporters maintaining a portrait of Gandhiji on the dais. The agitation was closed on 25th December 1927, with bonfire of Manusmriti. 'His close associate, Sahasra Buddhe a Brahmin, burned the Holy Scripture. The next agitation was also carried under the Gandhian term, 'Kalaram temple *Satyagraha*'. He even ended the last laps of his struggles during British India in 1946, with *Satyagraha* agitations. "Followers of the Scheduled Castes Federation in the Bombay Province launched their 'non-violence *Satyagraha'* in Poona to protest against the "injustice done to them by the British Cabinet Proposal which is the result of Congress machinations".[2] Dr Ambedkar signed Poona Pact that made the Brahmins the master of Hindustan. He during 1940, in his famous book, 'Thoughts on Pakistan' also very forcefully advocated for the partition of India to make the country a Hindu Rashtra. When he re-married, he had chosen a Brahmin woman Sabita Kabir. Despite his all out cautious steps to remain with the '*Sarbajan Samaj*' under the protective umbrella of the Brahmin's blessings the '*Sarvajan Samaj*' never accepted or co-operated with Dr Ambedkar even to fulfill his personal end. The Hindus never treated the Colombia-London returned erudite scholar even as a human being. In Baroda Estate, as its Military Secretary, he failed to manage a rented dwelling place. At the instance of the orthodox-Hindus, the Parses drove him out of their Inn. Until his demise on 6th December 1956, the caste-Hindu society opposed and hated him at all steps except while getting their things done by him. His merits, virtues and excellent statesmanship have never been recognised by the Hindus. The Indian Hindu Universities or Institutions bestowed none of his academic degrees. The foreign Universities conferred all.

Dr Ambedkar, in his last and protracted speech in the Constituent Assembly on 25th November 1946, prophetically declared that when the Constitution of India would be operative on 26th January 1950, the Indians would enter into a life of contradictions. In politics they, irrespective of their castes or creed, are expected to have equality on the basis of one vote and one value but in social and economic life they would suffer inequality because of Constitutional provisions. He never raised his earlier stand that this structure was nothing more than a hereditary democracy. Mere principle of one vote and of one value in the anti-democratic and structurally fragmented Hindu society, however, was completely inadequate to ensure political equality. Dr Ambedkar, therefore, had to land in the same state of affairs with others to face manipulation in franchise operation by the political parties run and managed by the nexus of money-media-mafia and bureaucracy.

In pursuance of the provisions of the Constitution of India, the first general election took place in free India in January 1952. Dr Ambedkar, the chief architect of the Constitution, contested the election from his home state, Bombay City North (reserved) constituency. It has already been seen that the untouchable population alone was not numerically enough to win the election. There was alliance between the Scheduled Castes Federation and the Socialist Party. Despite the support of the socialists under the leadership of Asok Mehta and Jaiprakash Narayan the election was manipulated. Neither the Congress and Gandhi nor the remnant of the Hindu nationalists for whom Dr Ambedkar laboured so strenuously came to support the framer of the constitution of the nation. He failed miserably in his home-turf. The Congress nominee N.S. Kajrolkar secured 1,38,137 votes and defeated Ambedkar who secured 1,23,567 votes. "It was a colossal failure, and Ambedkar fell like a rocket."[3] The situation was such that eventually in the month of April 1952 Dr Ambedkar and Asok Mehta filed petition to the XI Court, Kurla, Bombay for revision of the election result, which was alleged to have been manipulated by the Communist leader Sripad Amrit Dange, the Respondent No 1 in the case.[4] On the basis of his personal experience during those active political battles the remark of Dr Ambedkar on Indian Communists or on the Party is very interesting and significant, "The Communist Party was originally in the hands of some Brahmin boys Dange and others. They have been trying to win over the Maratha community and the Scheduled Castes. But they have made no headway in Maharashtra. Why? Because they are mostly a bunch of Brahmin boys. The Russians made a great mistake to entrust the Communist movement in India to them. Either the Russians did not want Communism in India they wanted only drummer boys or they did not understand."[5] Once again in the last week of April 1954, Ambedkar filed his nomination to contest the reserved seat in a by-election to the House of People from Bhandara constituency. Ambedkar though bagged 1,32,483 votes, had to face a humiliating defeat by 8,381 votes to the 'Congress' Harijan' candidate of negligible stature. He could never enter the Parliament of India as one of its elected member.

Despite the heavy support of the socialist Hindus, the insufficient number of untouchable ballots repeatedly failed to crown their tallest leader with victory. Contrary to it, the numerical strength of the untouchables' ballots in Bengal was so much that whatever may happen the Chandals were in a position to elect numbers of their even ordinary leaders.

Jogendra Nath Mandal who virtually sent Dr Ambedkar in the Constituent Assembly as an elected member from Bengal became the first Law Minister of undivided India in the Nehru Cabinet in 1947. He also served as the first Law Minister of Pakistan with Muhammad Ali Jinnah. With the blessings of Jinnah, J.N. Mandal who represented the Untouchables of East Pakistan, inaugurated the Constituent Assembly of Pakistan. Still he had to suffer the same fate at the hands of the Hindus in India as he too belonged to the same stock of untouchable family. J.N. Mandal also was scrupulously loyal to Hindus and Hinduism, maintained close association with the Hindu Mahasabha activities during his early life. He won the first election in 1937 being supported by the caste-Hindus. He remained a close associate and blessed boy of Subhash Chandra Bose and his elder brother Sarat Bose. In his matured life, he served the causes of the Congress and caste-Hindus.[6] During the period from 1945 to the beginning of 1947 he vigorously campaigned for strengthening the '*Hindu Shakti*' under the leadership of Shyama Prosad

Mookerjee.[7] Dr Ambedkar, after the Poona Pact in 1932 revolted against Hinduism and continued his tirade against caste system till his last breath. However, J.N. Mandal never raised a banner of rebellion against Hinduism. He never uttered, "Though born as a Hindu I will not die as a Hindu." Living in the land of the Muslims and the *Matuas* he never liked to raise the issue of conversion. Sitting amidst his powerful Muslim friends, always he has been struggling to get adjusted in Hinduism as a Hindu. All along his life, he non-cooperated with, or even opposed Matua movement in each front.

While a sitting MLA from Faridpur he contested election in 1940 for the seat of a Corporate at Bartala (reserved) in the Calcutta Corporation with the blessings of Netaji Subash Chandra Bose as a Congress nominee. As part of the election campaign he distributed pamphlets. In the appeal to the local taxpayers and voters, he begged for votes on the grounds that, (i) he opposed other Scheduled Caste Ministers in the Haque Ministry by way of moving no-confidence Motion against them (ii) he opposed the move of granting 'Separate Electorate' in the Local body, that is, Calcutta Corporation and (iii) he helped establish united Hindu society.[8] Having been elected in 1939-40 election, he enjoyed both the positions of an MLA and a Corporate in the Calcutta Municipal Corporation simultaneously. He was privileged to get double salary and perks from both the Offices. He has been consequently very sincere and liberal to pay back to the Brahmin society and served their interest. Despite all these, the Hindus did not tolerate this great son of the nation in the Indian politics. The Hindus simply utilised his services against his own servile community without remuneration or recognition.

Even as Law Minister in Pakistan, sitting under the protective umbrella of the Prime Minister Jinnah he offended many Ministers and Muslim leaders by showing over-concern on the Hindu issues and Hinduism in the East Pakistan. He even neglected the political interest of the Untouchables or the minorities of East Pakistan and objected the proposal for granting 'separate electorate' for them by the Pakistan Government. He kept the untouchables within the Hindu fold as the same act was accomplished by Gandhiji in India in 1932. Eventually, soon after the demise of Jinnah, Mr. Mandal sensed trouble in Pakistan due to his proactive role as a Hindu and he had stealthily left Pakistan without tendering resignation from the Cabinet. After his arrival in India, as a fugitive leader, from Pakistan in 1950, he contested election for the first time in 1952. To contest his maiden election he did not choose a seat in rural Bengal where his people settled in large numbers as refugees. Instead, he fought the election from the reserved seat from Benepukur, Calcutta as an independent candidate. No political party gave him shelter and ticket to contest election. He, once again, depended on the support of the caste-Hindu friends of Calcutta. He perhaps expected return-good-will gift from the people in Kolkata whom he served well when he was in power. He organised a meeting on 23rd September 1951, in the Indian Association Hall with the caste-Hindus. They managed the entire election. He faced a pathetic defeat in this election. As a result, financially he became pauper. The caste-Hindu friends spent his purse freely. In independent India, he was vehemently opposed by the Congress leaders of Bengal to give him entry in the party despite the fact that the High Command in Delhi was inclined to take him back in the Congress.

Mandal, after realizing the mind of the caste-Hindus, contested the general election of 1957 from Bongon (reserved seat) where his caste men were numerically an overwhelming majority. The Congress Party now nominated Monindra Bhusan Biswas, once a disciple of J.N. Mandal against him. This time, Mukunda Behari Mullick and Charumihir Sarkar also contested from the same seat as independent candidates to ensure his defeat. As usual the veteran politician had to face a miserable defeat at the hands of Congress. Mandal experienced his third defeat in the general election in 1962, when he contested from two reserved seats Bagda (Bongon) and Hanskhali (Nadia). His fate of failure reiterated again in the general election of 1967 when he contested from Barasat constituency in coalition with CPI(M). The untouchable votes, were transferred to the CPI(M) consequently. But the Hindus did not vote for Jogendranath. The undaunted and tireless spirit of struggle for self-respect, liberty and political-freedom of the Chandal race got energised in the veins of the veteran and he contested the 1968 by election which came as a result of the fall of 'United Front' coalition government. This time he contested independently from three seats, Bagda, Gaighata and Bongon. Almost 70 per cent of the population of these constituencies was composed of untouchables and the Muslim population was dense. This time Mandal was not allowed to live long up to the date of election. On the bus-stop of Bongon when Mandal reached from Halencha village back in course of the election campaign he was offered a cup of tea by some unknown person and he had collapsed soon after taking tea on the road-side hut within a few minutes before the doctor came. J.N. Mandal never rebelled like Dr Ambedkar still he had to face the natural antagonism of the Hindu nationalists.

Mandal never followed the path of self conscious independent political movement by the Depressed class for the Depressed class that was created by Guruchand to liberate the Untouchables politically. He never endeavored to sit in the instrumentalities of the state independent of the Brahmanical control. He never followed the course of Mukunda Behari Mullick, Birat Chandra Mandal or Mangoo Ram of the Punjab. He never dreamt for separate electorate; never talked anti-Hindu nor ever threatened the Hindus with conversion move. He launched no scheme like 'State Socialism' to demolish the Chinese wall between the land-lords and landless labours as Dr Ambedkar did in March 1947. The Hindus and their natural Guru, the Brahmins despite all these yeomen services with absolute devotion never recognised and allowed the untouchable leader to be donned as the associate of the ruling class or even in the mainstream society. The low order of the Hindu society is excluded from power-zone by spiritual sanction. How the Hindu nationalists go blasphemous!

Though the Hindu leaders did not help Mandal in any way in his political struggle and goal, they issued written tribute as condolence message long after his death. In it they acknowledged his great service of keeping the untouchables within the fold of Hindus of East Pakistan which could become Bangladesh in course of time. Prof. Samar Guha, a former M.P. with the advent of Bangladesh summed up, "Today Bangladesh has got independence. For this, Jogendra Nath Mandal, though indirectly, had a great contribution. The leaders of Pakistan wanted to confirm the theory of 'Two Nations' of the Muslim League by imposing 'Separate Electorate' on the minority community of East Bengal. Had there been separate electorate for the minorities of the then East Bengal the (minorities) Untouchables would have been benefitted and they would have gained many seats in the Pakistani Parliament. But ignoring that superficial profits Jogendra Nath and me built up a formidable movement against the proposed 'separate electorate'. Had Jogen Babu supported the 'separate electorate' scheme it would have been impossible to thwart the conspiracy of 'Two Nation' theory. Government of Pakistan then proposed to give separate electorate exclusively for the untouchables. Jogen Babu refused to accept that too . . . . Thus in course of time there emerged Bengali nationalism. . . . Late Jogendra Nath's policy of 'Joint Electorate' thus played a great role in formation of Bengali nationalism and creation of Bangladesh."[9]

Babu Jagjivan Ram, the undisputed leader of the Chamars, the largest untouchable community distributed all over India served Congress and Gandhi ceaselessly with absolute devotion. All along he spoke the words that were prompted by the Hindu High commands. He never wanted to be his own boss. As a war-horse he helped Congress to win two-third majority in the Parliament. He never rebelled either against the Hindu religion or against the creamy-layer ruling class' political party. Still he was not spared by the Hindu nationalists and they had hit him below the belt. As a Central Minister he inaugurated the statue of Sampurnanand of Benaras Hindu University. The statue which got polluted with the touch of an Untouchable Cabinet Minister was purified by washing it with the waters of the Ganges soon after the Minister departed from the place. When the war-horse rose to fight his own battle to be a war-hero and the Prime Minister of India after establishing a separate political party, CFD in 1977, he had to remain contented by saying the classic tale, "*Is Kambakht Muluk Mein Ek Chamar Kabhi Pradhan Mantri Ban Nahi Sakta.*" 'In this wretched country a Chamar can never be a Prime Minister.'

The fate of other untouchable leaders who joined Congress-Communist party and nationalist movement, and who boastfully declared that the freedom movement of the untouchables on self-conscious, independent platform by the untouchables and for the untouchables, was a narrow casteist movement had faced equally deplorable fate, after partition, in the free India. Rasik Lal Biswas who was the first to abandon the line of Guruchand's movement and had joined Congress in 1936, who adored Brahmins and put his signature on the deed of the Poona Pact to save the precious life of Gandhiji faced a life like a beggar in the Mana Refugee Camp. No political party, no caste-Hindu friend came to rescue him. The 'Gladstone of India' Birat Chandra Mandal, who rose to the status of a national leader of the Depressed Classes and had been MLA for two terms went into oblivion to die a peaceful death as an ordinary teacher in the Kalikapur Middle High School in Sonarpur area near the Kalikapur railway station, South 24 Parganas.

Consequently, the microscopic minority thinking and educated section of the oppressed India who managed to get government jobs due to Constitutional 'reservation' policy, instead of 'representation' right, got completely alienated from the mainstream society in the rural areas. They led an isolated life in the cities and sub-urban centers to meet their personal interests. They formed numberless 'welfare associations' to safely guard their Constitutional rights in so far as service reservations were concerned. The Untouchables' struggle for freedom on the debris of the caste-annihilated society was abandoned. The concept for establishing the *'Raj'* of the Untouchables or their adequate representation in the levers of the instrumentalities of the state became a forgotten phrase. Instead of *'Raj'* (ruling rod) they doggedly fell after *'Kaj'* i.e. jobs in the Government to serve under harness. They forgot the battle lines drawn by Guruchand Thakur; no *Raja* no *Taja,* they ran after 'safeguard' policy under Brahmin *Raja.*

When the untouchables got bewildered and shuttered with their broken backbone after partition of India, when very rapidly the Republican Party lost its ground, charm and strength in Uttar Pradesh they over-depended upon the constitutional policy of reservation in political as well as in service matters. Protecting of personal interest became the main object and with that motto, the leaders vied with each other. Consequently they lost their independent political will and aspirations. And in the reserved seats it became almost impossible to get elected without the support and blessings of the Hindu governing classes under the scheme of joint electorate.

Advent of Kanshi Ram with New Political Lifeline

Two decades after the demise of Dr Ambedkar, and with the collapse of the independent and self-conscious democratic liberation movement of the Untouchables with partition of the Punjab and Bengal there was born in the womb of blinding darkness of despair, the greatest of the Indian social thinkers in the enigmatic personality of Kanshi Ram. He was not, however, a mere speculative thinker or a philosopher. He was rather the greatest fighter of liberty and a tireless organizer of freedom movements. He claimed that he was a natural alley of the weak and persecuted one. He was therefore, a practical and pragmatic thinker. He contemplated deeply; he meditated with concentration only on the issue he was to fight out next morning and next year. He meditated to discover the causes of the problems and hurdles on the path of freedom movement for those who were in bondage. Like the enlightened Lord Buddha, he meditated on the methodology that he was to execute to overcome his adversities and opponents. He knew the strength and weakness of his foes as well as of his friends.

He was an untouchable, a Mazubi Sikh (a convert from Chamar community) from Ropar in the Punjab. The tradition of self-conscious independent move of the Untouchables of Bengal to establish their own rulers in Parliamentary democracy, which was pioneered by Guruchand from 1882 and carried under excellent leadership of Mangoo Ram in the Punjab during the decades of 1920's and 30's, resurrected in Kansi Ram during 1970's. Once again he rose with the dream of determination to establish the Peasants' and Workers' Raj. He gave a unique slogun, "Vote hamara Raj hamara." The voters will be the Rulers. Otherwise, the minority ruling-class will repeatedly fail to rule.

The 'First Dalit International' held its seminar on 'Towards a Caste-less Society' on 10th and 11th October 1998 at Kuala Lumpur. From the international platform, Kanshi Ramji declared that he did not want to abolish or annihilate castes. Of course, he did not support the system of caste of which he and his forefathers had been victims for centuries. He told, 'No God has created castes.' It were the Brahmins who in the name of God created these six thousand castes and used the caste system to oppress and exploit the constitutionally fragmented immense majority and the lowest stratum of the society, the *Bahujan Samaj.* The Brahmins operated this system with scrupulous heartlessness to perpetuate their hegemony unchallenged. It was Madam Indira Gandhi, the last Brahmin who could play caste-cards in favour of the Brahmins. In post-Indira Gandhi era there has been no Brahmin who could play this Caste cards. Kanshi Ramji claimed that now it was the era of 'Kanshi Ram phenomenon' where castes of lower orders, the victims of the system would be forming *Bahujan Samaj.* All victims of the system will stand united against all the beneficiaries of the caste system. Victims of the system form the lowest stratum of the society; they are immense majority. The beneficiaries of the system create the apex strata of the society. They are a microscopic minority.

He further clarified, *Bahujan Sa*maj *Party* has already been created but the Bahujan Samaj is yet to come into existence by spreading '*Bhaichara*' i.e. brotherhood amongst the victimised castes. The microscopic society of the beneficiaries is united. Only sixty of the victim-castes have so far come together to form *Bahujan Samaj.* No sooner around six hundred out of six thousand castes will come closer to form the *Bahujan Samaj;* they will hold political sway of India independently. The prospect of unity, among the victims has become a nightmare for the ruling class. Therefore, till castes are there he was not interested to abolish it. He is interested in uniting the fractured immense majority society. He is up to use the caste phenomenon in a reverse way the Brahmins used, and facilitate his scheme to make the servile castes rulers of their own motherland. He has planned to consolidate the groups victimised by the caste system against the beneficiaries of the system. He resorted to consolidate the Bahujan-power and use it in the interests of the victims of the caste system. Now a days, in the ballot boxes of democracy as the caste-card is proving detrimental to the interests of the Brahmins the creamy-layer caste objects even the use of their scriptural sacred word caste in politics. This group forms an abject minority. But the Bahujan Samaj is determined to create stronger bondage through the scheme of '*Jati Todo, Samaj Jodo*' that is breaking the castes and integrate the *Bahujan Samaj.*

On 28 May 1996, on the floor of the Parliament Kanshi Ram delivered, 'Yesterday Atalji mentioned that everybody raised a discussion on Communism but none talked on Casteism, so I would like to discuss on 'Castes'. They mean to say that people of Bahujan Samaj remain and continue to be the prey of Casteism due to their Casteist approach. . . . But our aim is to '*Jati Todo Samaj Jodo*', integrate the society by destroying castes. It becomes mandatory to discuss Castes for those who are the victims and sufferers of Caste. We do not want to tolerate castes, we want to annihilate castes. Therefore, we consider it essential to discuss the disease of which we suffer from. By concealing the disease it won't be treated. We are to think over the disease deeply. We are to find out its appropriate treatment. We talk about Castes but for what? We want to annihilate Castes and we want to change . . . . Bring 'Change' social and economic condition in all sectors of life."[10] 'Change' complete change in every sphere of politics economic-structure, social and conceptual sphere became the motto of Kanshi Ram since 1982 onwards. 'Change' has been the indispensible target of Kanshi Ram phenomenon. He reached to this height and competency to say all these in the floor of Indian Parliament and from the international platform as a result of his protracted organised struggle and long drawn thinking process that he exercised on the chronic problem of the nation.

Creation of BAMCEF

Kanshi Ram, after completing B.Sc, started his service career in Dehradun. Later he joined Defence Research Wing at Poona. In 1964, he left his comfortable and secured government job for starting freedom movement of the Depressed classes by capturing political power. This decision was taken not sitting in the four walls of a drawing room for fanciful adventure. After winning a legal battle against the Government to save democratic rights of some suspended Scheduled Caste employees in the Department, he himself resigned from the harness. Initially he joined Republican Party in Poona. He did his level best to remain a very sincere and loyal worker in the party. But being disappointed with the working of the leaders he left the party. Kanshi Ram and some of his educated employee-friends at Poona decided to organize the 'educated employees on all India bases on firm footing' to accomplish something tangible in result through such organisation'. 'The idea of an organisation of the All India Backward (BA stand for SC, ST and OBC) and Minority Communities (MC for Muslim, Christian, Sikh) Employees Federation (EF for Employs Federation), Delhi was conceived on the 6th December, 1973. The organisation became famous as the All India BAMCEF. It was an all India institution in true sense. The objective was to organize the educated employees of these communities under a single banner to pay back to the society from where they emerged. It is obvious to note that the basic approach of the organisation was a fundamental departure from earlier movements of the Untouchables created from the Bombay based Western Sector. BAMCEF included all the oppressed. It was not confined only to the Untouchables or the Scheduled Castes. It became an organ or a mouthpiece of all the victims of the Brahmanism. The educated employees were the thinking part as well as somewhat economically established wing of the illiterate and below poverty-level population of the country. They were the only section capable, in many respects, to pay back to the oppressed and exploited society who live in 'distressing condition'. The BAMCEF made its maiden public appearance on the 6th December 1978 at the Boat Club, New Delhi. The employees of the organisation were mostly Government servants. Private sectors never indulge in reservation policy for the untouchables and Tribal people of the country. Cent percent of Private sector jobs are reserved for 10 per cent creamy-layer society.

Because of the inherent limitation of the members of the BAMCEF (being Government employees) who are controlled by the Service Conduct Rules, they could not indulge in any sort of political action or activities other than just casting their votes in favour of the ruling class. They were made paralytic by the ruling class through various such irrational laws and rules. Therefore, BAMCEF remained non-agitational and non-political in nature. They took the responsibility of educating the immense majority of their political rights, duties and inevitable role as subjects of the Republican Democratic country.

The BAMCEF remained secular too. The members will not practice any religious function or festival and refrain from criticizing or destroying any individual's religious action or institution. "However, freedom of religious belief in BAMCEF did not mean 'that they should be influenced by others through Brahmanism, the spirit of inequality. In fact this should be endeavour of all the members and functionaries of BAMCEF to uproot Brahmanism, the spirit of inequality." The manifesto of the BAMCEF (released on 14th October 1981, during 3rd National Convention at Chandigarh) further declared, "Once BAMCEF succeeds in acquiring the roots for the root-less society and helps further in strengthening the non-political roots of the society the political and agitational success becomes a natural corollary."

As the five thousand years' history of China written on the palm of the Chairman Mao Tse Tung helped him get success so also for Kanshi Ram in India. He went through the books on social science veraciously to understand the historical causes of the disease in the society he had to cure. The ethnic culture, the historic culture, the cultural history, the geographic and demographic culture of the people of his country in different regions, all he tried to know. Thus, Kanshi Ramji analysed the political significance of the Poona Pact and the impact of the 'Joint Electorate' on the Hindu society as a whole and on the Untouchable voters who were forced to remain ignorant, illiterate, poverty stricken, disintegrated and subservient to the traditionally powerful and 'divine ruling' class. He also assessed the impact of the ruling classes who were empowered with monopoly control over money, media, mafia and modern bureaucracy.

Before starting his own organisation, Kanshi Ram joined Republican Party of India in Bombay. While in Bombay and Pune, he worked with the RPI as a very sincere and loyal cadre with full devotion. He realised the organisational weakness and un-amendable mind set of the leaders with irreparable limitations of the Party. During this period, starting from 1964, with extreme and scrupulous attention, he red lots of books on Indian history, polity and in particular on the subject related to the pioneering Namasudra or Chandal movement in Eastern Bengal. He tried to follow the development and course of the Untouchables' freedom movement in British India. He was exceedingly impressed, as he expressed on several occasions, by the two books written by Dr Ambedkar. These books were 'The Annihilation of Castes' and a history book 'What Congress and Gandhi had done to the Untouchables'. He was also influenced by another book written by Gail Omvedt on Democratic movement of the Untouchables in Maharashtra. The Chandal movement organised and led by Guruchand in pre-Ambedkar period inspired him maximum. In the light of his deep meditation, he rightly understood that, if the untouchables moved alone, there was no way but to surrender at the feet of the ruling class in free India. The Untouchable people had no chance or means to adopt to make them free and liberated in the democratic structure of polity in the fragmented condition in thousand of castes.

Their educated masses as a result of personified reservation benefit have got alienated from the society and the untouchables became leaderless.

The immense majority of them were left in the rural darkness to be exploited economically, spiritually and emotionally by the Hindu agents. Their thinking and educated lot and the political leaders had became *Chamchas* of various denominations and different varieties of ruling lords and political parties. The Untouchables had entered, as Gandhiji planned, into the arena of Hindu Concentration Camp and had become 'divine slaves' the '*Gulam*' of the Brahmanical society and slave-culture.

After deep meditation, he realised that there was only one and simple solution to evade this state of servitude and break the chains of slavery. And that solution was available in committing suicide. The peasantry in different provinces of India had already taken up the course of suicide to escape the bondage of slavery. But Kanshi Ram was a man not to accept either slavery or the method of self-killing to escape the yoke of *Gulamgiri*. Therefore, he discovered the 2nd course, difficult and long method to fight out the slavery. He visualised the existence of two groups, hostile to each other and in two diametrically opposite camps in the Brahmanical Social system. One is the victims of the Brahmanical Social Order and the other is the beneficiaries of the Brahmanical Social Order. He found that the victims of the Caste system were not the Untouchables alone but there have been many more who also remained oppressed, exploited and disdained by the supercilious and orthodox, divine, ruling class named Brahmins. He therefore, decided to unite and educate the victims against their common enemy; train them to fight and win the battle.

He analysed, when the victims of the Hindu nationalism or the caste-system are united they form more than 85 per cent of the total population of India. Consequently, the beneficiaries of the system form the microscopic minority. In the Republican or in the Parliamentary Democracy, the Government should have been controlled by the governed. Democracy is the rule of the majority. However, in India its unique democracy in the name of the people allow the hereditary ruling families to rule. The Government is run by the governing class for the benefit of the microscopic minority hereditary ruling castes. Had the victims of the Hindu nationalism been on one platform, had there been no caste divisions which fragmented it in microscopic small units the hereditary subject class could successfully establish Parliamentary democracy in India.

The system called caste created by the Brahmins not only divided the society of the immense majority into thousands of small and weak societies but also made them hostile and disdainful towards each other. The system has beyond all doubt established the truth that it is Gold-chain for a few and Iron-corn for the oppressed immense majority. Each unit of castes was made to remain constitutionally excluded from the other. Therefore, Kanshi Ram explained, all the victims in small units must identify their common enemy at the first instance. They must unite against the common enemy to get back their lost strength. United they must fight and destroy the system that victimizes them. Kanshi Ram also foresaw that no sooner than the victim-units would initiate the event of formation of a '*Bahujan Samaj*' the minority beneficiaries of the system would rise in quicker speed with their powerful paraphernalia to defend and protect the system that exists and stands to benefit them. The beneficiaries of the system, the creamy-layer-elites (Brahmins and their associates) will push the victims in friction, fraction and in distressing troubles. The victims of the system if united are immense majority. They form the lowest stratum of the society. Therefore, this immense majority society must come up with careful and constant efforts as '*Bahujan Samaj*' to fight and destroy the system through a relentless self-conscious independent movement.

Affirmative Attitude: "Be prepare for insults and injuries" was Kanshi Ram's call for the struggling people through BAMCEF. 'Those who want to do good and serve their own oppressed and exploited society have been insulted and injured in many ways.' As a natural corollary, those who revolt or rise to change a system get opposed and attacked by the current system as well by the driving force of the system. Even many of the members of servile class refuse to understand the purpose of changers and social transformers. 'No change' is the essence of casteism as well as of feudalism. Therefore, despite being victims the low castes play the role of social policemen to execute the caste rules and rituals and oppose the antagonists and disbelievers of caste rules. The opium of religion continues to be the most effective and all pervading in India. They are licensed with the right to honour-killing. Mao Tse Tung in his 'Theory of Contradiction' explained that failure is the pillar of success. When one falls in the pit gets the wit. However, such contention in Indian context is not effective. When one of Indian servile class falls in the pit, one instead of struggling to come out of the pit, the poor, lucky fellow rather adjust there and live rest of the life into the pit, with divine-contentment. Kanshi Ramji termed these status-quoists as social police of the system. They play the role of the defenders of the faith of which they are victims. Therefore, he trained his cadres who shouldered the burden of the brand ambassadors of change to be ready to face intra-group as well as inter group injuries. Both the oppressors and the 'Bhakta-Vivison' or 'Bhakta-hanuman' of the oppressed-elite will injure the missionaries or social transformers. He instructed, 'Be prepare for insult and injuries'.

Kanshi Ram asked his team to be consciously ready to face hatred and torture of the antagonists both within and outside their society. He called this society as '*Bikau Samaj*' that is the section of the society which is ready to be sold out to work for the oppressors. He held that till the commoners' society would remain saleable, their leaders would go for sale. He instead wanted to create a 'pay-back society'. For recruiting cadres, the supra energetic leader moved through the entire country from Kargil to Kanya Kumari; from Kolkata to Kathiawad; from Nagaland to Nagarkoil. Not just in the towns and metropolises, he travelled through the villages from door to door. He paid visit to the real rural India where country reside. More than 50 per cent of the total number of Indian villages was covered by Kanshi Ram's personal visits. More than the Mao's Long March, Kanshi Ram travelled a large part of it by paddling bicycle individually or in rally. He was thus, in a real sense a national leader. No national leader in India has toured so much to know the nation, the country and her society. Millions of his followers had personal contact with him. Interestingly mention may be made in this context of one incident of meeting of two leaders. At around mid-night Gauri Amma, the veteran communist leader could spare time for Kanshi Ram at Kochi (Kerala) to meet. Kanshi Ram went to meet her on a pre-fixed appointment as Gauri Amma who belonged to the backward community and was thrown out of the Communist Party was contemplating to float a new party. At the outset Gauri Amma told to Kanshi Ram, 'I have sacrificed my whole life for the party; I married but did not get children for the party. I have kept nothing for my personal benefit. Now the party has done this to me.' Kansi Ram simply told in reply, 'I too have no child, I have not even married and moving all over India with the mission to free the servile classes. What have you done? You have never come out of your little Kerala state.' Almost all Indian leaders fall in this category of parochial leadership. They possessed only bookish knowledge of the geography, demography, social and economic conditions of India.

The fighters therefore, needed philosophical inspiration and regular training to endure in the battlefields. Untrained army cannot fight serious battles. He recruited the 'Salvation Army' from the fields, then prepared and trained them in innumerable cadre-camps held in different parts and corners of the country. They were mentally articulated and ready to face any atrocities and get injured by the lethal attacks from the oppressive ruling classes. Without proper education, one remains backward and vulnerable. Without battles, educated even remains slave. He educated his cadres to make them understand the necessity to fight, its target and the method and modality. He slowly injected missionary zeal in the hearts of his cadres and inspired them with historical knowledge and sure prospect of victory at last. Fired with the enthusiasm of missionary zeal to free the people in bondage, millions got ready, with sufficient courage and hope to pay back to their hopeless society. With this determination he decided, "Therefore, it is most essential to prepare an educated-band of well informed workers who should have a fair knowledge about mechanisms of this complex organisation and should have capacity to operate the organisation to deliver the goods.... The numerical strength of the cadre" must be not less than 5 per cent of the total strength of the members of the BAMCEF.

The political liberation movement in the Parliamentary Democracy is carried through the war of ballots, which was supposed to be without violence and weapons. It was not a battle of bullets but a democratic battle of ballots. The rod of governance of the nation or of the country is captured not in the battlefields of Kurukshetra, Panipat or Plassy. The Waterloo is decided in the Ballot Boxes. The oppressed people have immense majority franchise power to be the ruling class instantly in the polity of representative form of Parliamentary Democracy. By using their voting right, they could have driven the ruling classes off power easily. Democracy is a form of government where the ruling class fails to capture power. But it has not happened. On the contrary after sixty decades of independence Indian Democracy has tangibly been transformed into a hereditary democracy. More than two-thirds of Lok Sabha MPs under 40 years of age are hereditary.[11] This has happened because capturing power and remaining free and independent is a matter of constant fight. It needs sacrifice. In the annals of history without military preparation, no nation remains sovereign. Without supreme sacrifice, the nectar of freedom can never be tasted.

Kanshi Ram had a direct and realistic approach. During election campaign, he educated his followers not to see daydreams; be pragmatic to face the extreme adverse situation and fierce opposition by the powerful ruling castes. "*Main Apna Samaj Ko Gumraha Karneko Nehin Aya.*" I have not come to misguide my people with any useless rosy picture. Our candidate will not win the election now. Still we need to fight for the next steps. He said, 'Many of you argue that when we are not in a position to win the election why should we waste our votes casting it in favour of BSP? My suggestion is, when you have a low land, you are to waste some money to fill it up with soil before constructing house. If you refuse to waste some money now never you can build your house.' The beneficiaries of the system, powerful and influential, donned with cunning and cruel methods and weapons would definitely react to the oppressed that would revolt against the engine of oppression so laboriously they had prepared and maintain.

In most of the places, no political party exclusive of the Depressed Classes and by the Depressed Classes existed in free India, before 1984. The political party is an institution which expresses and executes the human aspirations of individuals and of the groups of the supporting subjects in the country and send their representative to rule and govern the nation which belonged to each of them. In the absence of such an institution vital and pre-requisite to be the ruler in a democratic country of the immense Bahujan Samaj, the ruling class remained problem free. Election was their friendly game. Where ever, the political party led by the oppressed and depressed tried to came up and contest elections, the Indian creamy-layer ruling classes (or the families with multi millions who comfortably survive on inheritance) however, regularly manipulate, loot and purchase ballots from the helpless, ignorant, impulsive, panicky and oppressed citizens. They with media-mafia-money power rig the elections by not allowing the low caste people approach the ballot-boxes. They resort to such undemocratic criminal means, as they do not have enough votes to win the elections. Kanshi Ram was a democrat. He declared that the 'Bahujan Samaj' needs not fear or rig elections as they have enough votes to win easily. The Indian ruling class or castes who have little or poor number of ballots or voting strength, resort to some or other form of rigging. They are afraid of the numerical strength and power of the oppressed. He simply asked and trained his people to protect their right as subjects of this Republican country to freely cast votes and to use the invaluable franchise right to elect their real representatives in the Legislature. He even gave a call to pick up even bullets to protect the ballots. He appealed donate one note (money) with one vote. Mere votes do not help; to transform votes into ballots a strong organisation is essential. To build up organisation money is indispensible. Such a call for sacrifice is mixed with the flavour of militancy. The target of Kanshi Ram's movement was not mere 'Social Justice' and 'safe-guard'. Kanshi Ram on the contrary, welcomed social injustice which was expected to demonstrate before his conscious army the immediate necessity to intensify democratic battle by the Bahujan Samaj independently. To keep the tempo up Kanshi Ram, like Karl marx in the Manifesto of the Communist Party, geared up the spirit of the Dalits during Etwa Election, 'Is Lari Me Marbhi Jaoge, Gulamihi Chor Jaoge.' 'If you die in this battle, you will lose nothing but your chains noly'. The wretched Dalits were going to lose 'Taj' or 'Takth'. As Netaji Subash Bose askede, "Give me blood I will give you freedom' so also Manyawar Kanshi Ram asked the Bahujan Samaj to protect their votes with blood. He advocated the policy of taking 'two eyes for one eye' as the manifestation of Dalit-power, not as a protagonist of violence.

Social Transformation was the target behind the motto of getting ready to be injured. He gave a clarion call to bring total and fundamental change by installing the oppressed as the governing class. It becomes a right to get back the desired result when got injured for the cause. One of the main targets of these cadre-camps was to raise the appetite and drive in the dead minds of the members of the Bahujan Samaj to become the rulers of their own motherland; to chisel out their own fortune as their own political-masters. He inspired the cadres to realize that the lowest stratum of the society, the immense majority Bahujan Samaj should have been the *defacto* rulers of the country because democracy is the rule of the majority. He gave the mantra, 'Vote *Hamara Raj Tumhara Nehi Chalega*' 'We are the voters so we are to rule'. After the lapse of a century Kanshi Ram echoed the voice of Guruchand, the race who do not have consolidation and party has no strength 'Dal nai to Bal nai'; a race who have no king is not alive 'Raja nai to Taja nai'. It was not a battle for '*Kaj*' (job) it was a war for '*Raj*' (Kingship).

Without active and positive participation with affirmative attitude to become the *defacto* rulers of the country it remains a dream. Without operating the instrumentalities of the State by the representatives of the immense majority there was no real democracy. It was like holding an office without portfolio. The Office can be held by establishing a Political Party and strengthening it to capture power. In India, because of her traditional spiritual-bondage and social structure, 'Parliamentary Democracy' is a form of Government in which the function of the people has come to be to vote for their masters and leave them to rule. Such scheme of government, in the opinion of Labour is a travesty of Government by the people'.[12] The subjects cast their vote repeatedly only to the Masters because the Masters only had created the instrument called Political Party to get votes of the subjects. People failed to launch a political party of their own to get their votes. Dr Ambedkar, once declared, "…it is felt that this (Parliamentary Democracy) was the last word in the framework of government…. India is negotiating to have Parliamentary Democracy. There is a great need of someone with sufficient courage to tell Indians, "Be aware of the Parliamentary Democracy, it is not the best product, as it appeared to be."[13] Therefore, with a view to turning hereditary democracy into a people's democracy, remedy has been prescribed by Kanshi Ram for the subdued immense majority and the lowest stratum of the society. He asked them to get assertive. Participatory government is democracy. He targeted to establish the democracy where the ruling class would fail to capture power. Bahujan Samaj will capture power through their own instrument a political party.

Government by the People: 'Vote *Hamara Raj Tumhara Nehin Chalega*'. 'Votes belong to us (90 per cent servile people) you (10 per cent oppressed rulers) have no *locus standi* to govern and you will fail to govern.' It cannot function well. Those who are majority must hold the instrumentalities of the State to operate or govern. This is the essence of democratic polity. He lost faith on Government of the people merely. In Parliamentary Democracy in India it is the hereditary ruling families (creamy-layer-elite) rule the country in the name of the people. They had launched dozens of political parties on various value system, from secular to fundamentalists; communists to capitalists to lure the voters. Their election machinery capture votes in various tricky forms sponsored by Government as well as by private propaganda power. Government of the people and by the ruling families is not dependent on the governed. It will not liberate immense majority of the lowest stratum from the thralldom of the minority ruling class. Government must be run and handled by the people to make it a government for the people. But in the traditional process of Parliamentary Democracy, especially in the anti-democratic Indian fragmented society, "has never been a government of the people or by the people and that is why it has never been a government for the people. Parliamentary Democracy, not withstanding the paraphernalia of a popular government is in reality a government of the hereditary subject-class by a hereditary ruling class."[14] When democracy is the rule of the subjects and the rule of the majority group then the group or sections of the society who form or represent the majority part of the society must hold the ruling rod. The immense majority must govern the country; their representatives must sit on the wheels of the instrumentalities of the State. Minority has no right to rule.

In the base or village level, however, it must be truly participatory governance not representative. 'Vote *Hamara, Raj Hamara'*, Those who possess majority of votes must Rule the nation. Kanshi Ram resorted to action to establish a Government by the people. 'It is our votes and it must have to be the rule (*Raj*) of ours; your rule will no more continue' he gave a clarion call to the nation. This call inspired to install a government of those who cast votes. It had a magic-spell. It is a state of 'Votes of Bahujan Samaj' resultantly the 'Rule of Bahujan Samaj'. Kanshi Ram rose to revolt to finish the system of divine-slavery. '*Arya Putra Hos Main Aao, Das Protha Ko Mat Baraho*'; The descendants of the Aryans come to senses you must stop the spree of spreading the reign of Slavery, cautioned he. '*Note Ka Raj Nahin, Vote Ka Raj*' Rule of ballots not of bullets (money) must prevail. And in this regard what Dr Ambedkar recorded in 1941 in his book 'What Congress and Gandhi had done to the Untouchables', "Only those who belongs to the servile class can be trusted to protect the interests of that class", comes to be the guiding target.

Kanshi Ram was very conscious about the fact that only a self-conscious independent movement of the Victims and by the Victims can evoke liberty of the Victims. Freedom cannot be achieved with the help of the usurpers. The powerful people if help the slaves to revolt and break corns it would invariably to resort to protect their interests at the cost they helped rather it would be investment of the ruling class for raising counter-revolution. Manyawar adviced, '*Sahara Ka Sath Esara Aa Hi Jata Hain*'. 'Without expectations helps do not come and directions come instantly from the financer or one who offers shelter' was one of the fundamental principle of *Manyawar* Kanshi Ram. Therefore, there must be independent political party of the servile class to express their aspirations directly and without any reservation. The political party must also advance on its own strength, remain self-conscious and independent in the fund raising aspect too. Kanshi Ram collected funds for organisation and party from its members and supporters for whom he fought. The national political parties are frequently alleged to have paid money to purchase votes. While Kanshi ram was the one who asked money with one vote from the electorates. He cautioned the ruling class that democracy must be a Raj of Votes and not a Raj of Notes.

He refused to address any meeting called by his supporters or cadres who failed to collect certain amount of fund for him. In many meetings he was weighed with coins and ornaments. The amount was handed over to him to build democratic movements. He said, '*Jiski Sath Dosti, Uska* Criticism *Bhi Nahin, Our Jiski Sath Dusmani Uski Sath Chalna Bhi Nahin'*. Friends should not be criticised and the enemy must not be trusted. The money from the treasures of the beneficiaries cannot manumit the Victims. So he begged, '*Ek Vote* and E*k* Note' give me one vote with one Rupee note '*Bahujan Ka* Vote, *Bahujan Ka Raj*'. Ballots of immense majority and rule of immense majority votes must prevail.

He knew that the immense majority 'Bahujan Samaj' has nothing to lose but their chains and they have entire Bharat to win. When Kanshi Ram was fighting the Etwa general constituency, election secret news came that the ruling class will resort to bullets to disrupt the election. He assured in public meetings, '*Is Larai Me Mar Vi Jaoge To Gulami Hi Chod Jaoge*' 'If you die in this battle of liberation, you will lose nothing but your chains of slavery.' Either way you are to gain liberty only; to come out of the land of slavery this was only way. Without ceaseless, self-conscious and independent movement through supreme sacrifice by the immense majority servile class, the Bahujan Samaj has no alternative. The immense majority never is allowed to perform as the head of the country to plan and lead they are forced to remain as tail. Kanshi Ram analysed that the political parties in the system are founded and managed by the ruling castes. Out of those political parties one which is backed by the servile classes by way of casting votes form the Government for a prescribed period.

Kanshi Ram realised the need tc form political a party exclusively of the *Bahujan Samaj* and by the *Bahujan Samaj*. Until and unless the servile Bahujan Samaj forms their political party it would become just a day-dream for them to reach near to the political power. The party high-power bosses formulate, regulate and control the entire affairs of the party and the subject bear the burden and follow blindly. Therefore, Kanshi Ram called, '*Bahujan Samaj' Pichlagu Banna chod Do'*. The immense majority society must avoid to be the followers and supporters of the minority ruling classes as their tails' '*Puch Lamba to Ho Sakta Hai Par Kabhi Takatbar Nehin Ho Sakta Hai*' The tail (*Puch*) can extend in length but it can never be strong', he advised and cautioned his cadres. The appendix can never be the main text. Tails never take or make decision. Therefore, Kanshi Ram asked the members of the Bahujan Samaj to abandon the path of supporting and voting the enemies in power and leave them to rule over them for five years. Instead, he asked them to build a political party of their own and by expressing their political dream capture power in the Parliamentary Democracy where citizens have been empowered with one vote of one value. Do not waste time, money and lives in the rented houses of the antagonists, build your own huts and shift immediately.

Bahujan Samaj Party a Un-precedented Great Leap

After a short time preparation of the cadre-based BAMCEF organisation composed of well educated and economically some extent sound employees and thinking section of the Untouchables, Sudras and their proselyte Muslims and Sikhs, Kanshi Ram launched an all India political Party called 'Bahujan Samaj Party' on 14th April 1984. He took all those who have been victimised by the Hindu Nationalism. This was a great and significant departure from the movement that was carried by Dr Ambedkar for two decades through his political party called 'Scheduled Caste Federation'. It was for the well being of the Scheduled Castes only. Tribes, Muslims, Sikhs or the Backward Sudras were not in the agenda. Besides, Ambedkar's was a movement merely for getting social justice from the hereditary rulers. Kanshi Ram transformed this movement of 15 per cent to the political movement of the 90 per cent immense majority of the lowest stratum of the society. It was a social transformation movement as well as a revolution to make the servile class the rulers of the country. Dr Ambedkar therefore, demanded 'separate settlement' for the Untouchables who remained in 'Ghettos'. But Kanshi Ram's target was to capture their motherland, the nation as 90 per cent of the country. Kanshi Ram was convinced that without the provisions of 'separate electorate' the untouchables who officially form around 16 per cent of the total population and different tribes (Scheduled) in India who form another around 8 per cent population cannot gain political freedom in Indian Parliamentary Democracy which is run by the powerful nexus of the Hindu-Media-Mafia and money.[15]

Kansi Ram found that all political safe-guards whether constitutional or extra-constitutional, for the servile population remain of no value, ineffective and meaningless.[16] He was completely convinced on the point also that the provisions of 'separate electorate', which the Untouchables failed to avail of due to the stiff opposition of the Hindus during the British Raj, cannot be made available now in the divided India where Hindu nationalists hold political-power. Therefore, the Untouchables along with the Indian Muslims became absolutely helpless to come out of their servitude especially in the 'Chamcha Age'. Even on 1st January, 1947 in a resolution the Scheduled Castes Federation declared, "Separate Electorates were the only way of guaranteeing real representation of the Scheduled Castes in the Legislatures without which all other safeguards were sure to be only paper safeguards."[17] Dr Ambedkar, perhaps desired to achieve the goal but surely failed to acquire the same even after becoming the Chairman of the 'Drafting Committee' of the Constitution of independent India. He was helpless and powerless because during those days he was a member in the Constituent Assembly as a Congress nominee from Bombay.

Besides, Kansi Ram further realised that in the democratic polity starting a political party is the precondition for gaining political power of any exclusive group. Therefore, a separate political party of the servile classes and by the servile classes of India who are the victims of the Hindu social system can play the same protective role that was expected from the provisions of the 'Separate Electorate' for the immense majority and the lowest stratum of the society. In independent India, a separate political party of the servile classes stands as the perfect substitute of the 'Separate Electorate' too.

And creation of such a political party was not only the sure avenue to liberate the subdued community but the sure way to establish democracy in India. "The Hon'ble Dr B.R. Ambedkar, Labour Member, Goverrnment of India' also expressed in Parel, Bombay on 12th Januarry 1943, "The democracy in India could be safe only in the hands of the Non-Brahaman Party.... He regretted that the Non-Brahman Party which was in power in the Madras and Bombay Provinces had now disintegrated owing to various reasons, and expressed the hope that, profiting by the mistakes of the past, it would shed the minor differences that existed among the various sections and rebuild itself into a united and strong force again."[18] Records, however, do not supply any follow up action by the great leader to transform the ideal into reality. After three decades, eventually Kanshi Ram formed a non-Brrahmin political party in the name, "Bahujan Samaj Party" to achieve the protective role of 'Separate Electorate' and establish real democracy in free-India.

He further clarified that the Bahujan Samaj is yet to exist. Only around 60 castes have so far joined hands against the Brahmanical hereditary ruling class to struggle. Bahujan Samaj will come into existence only when at least 600 caste would form an integrated society.

The servile class or castes and their proselyte sections, in India, comfortably form 90 per cent of the total population of the country. The BSP in any way was not a political party of the SCs and STs (new name of the Untouchables and tribes) only. Dr Ambedkar created All India Scheduled Caste Federation. During those days the Muslims and Sikhs (because of Separate Electorate) were debarred to vote for the Scheduled Caste candidates. Federation was then the party exclusively of the untouchables, by the untouchables and for the untouchables. During post-independent period, Ambedkar had the option to launch a party of the combine forces of untouchables, Tribes and the Backward Sudras. However, he never attempted to go on the line. On the contrary, till last he advocated to deprive the Tribes of their political share.

Within a decade in a very calculated method, and with a conscious target, Kanshi Ram elevated his political party into a national political party. BSP became the third national political party. Establishment of a national level political party on the basis of cadre-based units in the grass-root level of the immense majority people by the immense majority servile-classes of the lowest stratum of the society was a unique phenomenon in Indian political history. The dream and mission of Guruchand was fulfilled eventually a century after his demise through the struggle of Kanshi Ram.

Kanshi Ram told his followers initially when they flocked for tickets to contest election to send their representative in the Legislature that he had been issuing his cadres 'Platform Tickets' only. With these tickets, they could enter the platform of politics. However, he assured that candidates of his party very soon would be able to travel in the train but won't be able to reach to the destination. In the next stage, he confirmed that his party candidates would be in a position to damage and defeat the winning horses of the Brahmin parties. At this stage, the Bahujan Samaj as well as their candidates would start gaining value socially as well as politically. At the outset, they would acquire nuisance value to disturb sure winning candidates and even successfully defeat important personalities of the ruling class. Finally, the BSP will be in a position to issue tickets by which the candidates would be in a position to enter in the Assemblies and Parliament. He never visualised any short-cut as there was no royal road for achieving the goal of liberty. Indeed, the BSP gained its target even sooner than they calculated.

So long, after the ceasing of the Guruchand's political movement for becoming rulers of the motherland, the movement of the untouchables became a movement of gaining charity of social justice and for securing constitutional safe-guards like reservations in political and executive arena. It was a movement of the 15 per cent untouchables only. Tribals, Sudras and their proselytes Muslims, Sikhs and Christians were not taken in the camp. Kanshi Ram made it much broader, higher and straight battle for power-politics. It became a great leap from a movement of 15 per cent to 90 per cent of the country. It was a direct departure from Schedules caste or Hindu movement to the secular movement of the immense majority irrespective of caste or creed. It became an uncompromising move of the Oppressed India against the Oppressors. From fractional or provincial movement it jumped in the arena of entire nation. It became a movement for becoming rulers of own country and nation instead of begging justice from the hereditary ruling class. He differentiated the 'social-justice' movement with the 'social-transformation' movement. It resorted to the establishment of the rule of the immense majority, the producing lowest stratum of the society. He clearly said 'I do not want 'social-justice' I want to see the social atrocities in its original form so that the members of the *Bahujan Samaj* can realize the need to capture the instrumentalities in their own hands.

The motto of the agitation of the Untouchables or Scheduled Castes in earlier social-justice movement was to lodge their grievances of injustice, exploitation, discrimination and atrocities before the ruling class's machinery and seek redresses and justice from the oppressors. After hard-hitting struggles they got in many cases their grievances redressed and justice secured, wrong undone. With this success they happily went home back by shouting, "Jai Ho!" for the hereditary Masters. The organizers of the social-justice and constitutional movements never had a drive or appetite to take the ruling rod of their own country in own hands and to redress all grievances and do justice for the immense majority subjects. Kanshi Ram made it a struggle for freedom for the immense majority, the 85 per cent to 90 per cent of the total population of India by capturing political power through the BSP. He resorted to establish *Raja* from amongst the countrymen through the democratic process.

Kanshi Ram took up the movement fundamentally of freedom of the oppressed and exploited masses that started in the grass-root level in the rural Bengal and amongst the Untouchable peasantry in collaboration with their proselyte brethren under the leadership of Guruchand during 1880 to 1930. They struggled for becoming the 'Raja', the King through the voting rights and do justice. Kanshi Ram also abandoned the movement of submitting representation and begging justice social or political, mercy from the powerful Hindu Rulers. He raised cadres from grass roots level; created awareness amongst them to identify the friends and foe to gain liberty and establish political rights. He imparted practical and field training in joining electoral politics. Not social justice from the oppressors; he establish the Bahujan Samaj Party to replace the *Brahmin-Raj* with '*Bahujan-Raj*' to end the roots of the system of social injustice.

Democracy is, indeed, the '*Bahujan-cracy*' '*Ganatantra*' is '*Bahujanatantra*'. The Bahujan Samaj Party targeted to establish people's democracy, democracy of the immense majority. He picked up the self-conscious independent movement for self-emancipation and interest.

Therefore, he chalked out the blue print of his democratic country where every group and sub-groups, caste and tribe, creed and faith must get their share on the basis of equity distribution in the handling and enjoying the privileges and duties for the nation. He encouraged *jati sanmelon* or caste festivals to imbibe pride for own caste at the same time when he struggled for '*Jati Todo Samaj Jodo*' abolish caste create a consolidate society.

Kanshi Ram could not lay his hands on the legislation, 'Proportional Representation of the Communities in Public Jobs, Assam Bengal Government Act of 1907', that was yielded out of Guruchand's movement. But when his turn came, he delivered the same ideals of justice, '*Jiski Jitna Sankhya Bhari Uski Utni Bhagidari*' 'proportional representation of the communities as per their numerical strength in all the three wings of power politics i.e. Legislature, Executive and Judiciary. Participation of each and all the subjects in the governance of the country is the essence of democracy and liberty. Representation of each individual and every section of social groups from all economic strata in the instrumentalities of the Government only can ensure the liberty, happiness and pursuit of profession of each and all.

As a logical corollary, on the controversial issue of job reservation he added the new dimension. He questioned as to how those who form microscopic minority (The Brahmins and their allies) gives 'Job Reservation' to those who form immense majority. Why should not the 10 per cent of the compatriots, the creamy-layer of the privileged element of the country get reservation instead of the chunk that consists of 90 per cent of the citizens of Socialist Democratic Republic of India? He argued, that the Brahmins form less than 4 per cent of total population but enjoy more than 70 per cent privileges of all sectors. He will consider their problems only when they come below 4 per cent privilege mark. This great-leap in conceptual and organisational sphere from an 'Untouchable-movement' to 'Bahujan-movement', from elitist-reservation-movement to self-conscious and independent grass-root level people's mass-movement is the unique contribution of *Manyawar* Kashi Ramji. This fulfilled the mission of Dr Ambedkar in implementing his doctrine of democracy that "Democracy is a form of Government where the ruling class fails to capture power."

Kanshi Ram very carefully avoided the Brahmins' association in his party. He once met with Abudulla Bukhari, the Imam of Delhi Jama Masjid for a friendly discussion in regard to forging Dalit-Muslim unity and pre-poll alliance. After a protracted happy discussions, the Imam told Kanshi Ram that the BSP is all-good but there was only one lacuna in it. 'What was that?' Kanshi Ram inquired. 'Your party does not have any Brahmin', Imam *Sahab* expressed. 'Can you suggest any good Brahmin who can be taken in?', asked *Manyawar.* 'Yes, Hembati Nandan Bahuguna is there', concluded the Imam. '*Imam Sahab! Hamlog Brahman Ka Ek Gun Se Paresan Hain, Our Up Bahugun Brahmin Dekhla Raha Hai!*' 'Imam Sahab! We have been tired of One-*Guna* Brahmins already and now you suggest for *Bahuguna*!'. There ended the prospect of furthering the alliance between Muslims and BSP there. But this attitude never stood on the way to proportional representation to be given by the majority. He feared that the entry of a Brahmin in his party for total change will surely be spoiled by the stetusquist Brahmin.

A Mazbi Sikh, Kanshi Ram even denied to wear turban of a Sikh. Clean shaven Kanshi Ram led his life as a true secular man above all religious ritualistic bond. Kanshi Ramji who never indulged in any Hindu ritualistic function or festivals challenged the Hindu *Shakti* in the battle of ballots in the practical power game. He defeated them soon after the Hindu fascist fanatics dwindled the Babri Masjid down to dust. '*Mile Mulayam Kanshi Ram, Haoa Ho Gai Jai Sri Ram*' the unity between Mulayam (the Backward Sudras) and Kanshi Ram (the Untouchables) will drive away (*Jai Sri Ram*) the Hindu Brahmanical force from the helm of affairs. The Hindus destroyed Babri Masjid on 6th December 1992 when the Prime Minister of India was as usual a Brahmin, P. V. Narasimbha Rao. Kanshi Ram declared that we the untouchable families of India do not need to build any more temples. The

Sudras and the Untouchables do not have their latrines and schools. They need those things on priority basis. He assured the Muslims that 'Ram' is not their problem; they have many Rams amongst them; even Ramji Ram is one of their leaders. Moreover, Ram Lala from the Babri Masjid would disappear no sooner than the Untouchable Kanshi Ram touches the idol. No Hindu god can sustain a touch of an untouchable.

Before the expiry of one year of extinction of Babri Masjid the Sudras and the Untouchables unitedly assumed the ruler-ship of the heartland of the so-called holy '*Aryavarta*' the Oudh. Defying the comments of Babu Jagjivan Ram that in this wretched land a Chamar can never become a Prime Minister, in the post-Babri era, a *Chamarni* (a woman of Cobbler Caste) had become the Chief Minister of Uttar Pradesh from the Bahujan Samaj Party. The process of formation of the Bahujan Samaj was hastened due to the closeness of the Sudra Yadav community and the Untouchables at a time when the Muslims alienated from the Brahmanical forces in Uttar Pradesh. The Brahman Muslims rift became the catalyst force in the process.

Impact of the Bahujan Samaj Party

In a recent study conducted in the Lal Bahadur Shastri National Academy of Administration, Mossuri, (Puspendra, 1995-6) it has been analysed, "Till the formation of the RPI in 1958, the Dalit politics in UP kept swinging between the accommodative politics of the Congress and the revolutionary politics of Federation." These two tendencies of integration and separatism were to remain within the SC movement in the post-colonial India.[19] The phase of RPI lasted merely a decade. The influence of the party was confined to UP only because of its considerably heavy percentage of Untouchables and the Muslims. The party won 3 Parliamentary seats and 10 Assembly seats from the constituencies where concentration of Muslim population was big and the Muslims voted for the RPI. In Maharashtra where the Untouchable population never crossed double digit in percentage the untouchable leaders there simply enjoyed a big share of the cake by claiming that Dr Ambedkar contemplated the RPI. The Muslims also were less than 10 per cent in Maharashtra. RPI leader Buddha Priya Mauriya of UP is alleged to have betrayed his Muslim friends after the victory. B.P. Mauriya won the general seat of Aligarh Parliamentary constituency in 1962 election with the thumping support of the Muslims under the leadership of Md. Basir Khan, the Proctor of AMU and a close friend of Mauriya. Jyoti Prakash won the SC reserved seat of Hatras where the concentration of Muslim population was very high. Md. Basir Khan became MLA. B.P. Mauriya did not attend the funeral ceremony of his friend Md. Basir Khan even though the Muslims of Aligarh waited for his arrival for a long period of seven eight hours. This became the parting point. Consequently, when Mauriya came to address the election meetings in the second round, eggs and tomatoes are reported to have flown towards him from the crowds. In 1966, Chandra Paul became MP from 'Secendra Rao' reserved constituency. By 1969 election the RPI won only 2 Assembly seats and was assimilated in the Congress. B.P. Mauriya became Union Minister in Congress Government. Another RPI leader Sangh Priya Guam joined BJP and in course of time became Union Textile Minister in the BJP Government during 1987-89. The decade of 1970 is described by Sudha Pai as, a phase of integration and a hiatus between two periods of separatist political activities by the SC in UP." The Congress was able to co-opt both of them." It is found to have the repetition of Bengal movement (Dalit-Muslim Unity) in a miniature form in the divided India.

The phenomenal success of the Dalit movement through electoral politics in UP was due to obvious unity between Untouchables and the Muslims. The Republican Party of India (RPI) challenged the dominance of Congress in the most part of the sixties, but its influence was restricted only to UP zone, that too only in a few districts, however, control of the party policy and functioning remains in the hands of Maharashtra leadership. By the end of the sixties, even the RPI lost its attractions. Its leaders, like Dr Ambedkar, drifted towards the Congress party. The SC voters remained loyal to the Congress even on face of the troubled times of 1967 and 1977 (the percentage of the SC voters polled by the Congress was 45.2 per cent in 1967, 47.8 per cent in 1971, 82.8 per cent in 1980. It was only in 1977 that the Congress could barely manage 35.7 per cent of the SC votes while 53.0 per cent of the SC votes went to the non-Congress Party). Notwithstanding, never in the past the Congress faced any serious threat to the 'captive' vote-banks except in a few states under the Left-Rule. However, signs of decline in its SC vote share became the order during the elections held in the late 80's (1989) and the early 'nineties (1991) after the advent of BSP.

But 'Bahujan Samaj Party, the independent political party exclusively of the oppressed Indians established after the experimental exercise on BAMCEF, DS4. and Buddhist Research Centre (BRC) brought fundamental change in the electoral scenario of Uttar Pradesh in particular. He on the basis of political philosophy (not on the basis of ad-hock policy of convenience) of two diametrically opposite or hostile phenomenon the 'Oppressed' and 'Oppressors' the 'Victims' and 'Beneficiaries' emerging out of the same system awakened a big section of the oppressed India. Social consolidation was built on conscious understanding of social engineering and its political impacts. It had its definite impact on the voting pattern. The phenomenal change and tangible effects have been mentioned in the study report referred to earlier. The BSP had emerged strong in states where the concentration of SC population has been very high. Though it was not the party of the Scheduled Castes the ruling class propagated so. Besides, the OBCs who sided with the ruling class with the expectation for getting proper share of political power and other privileges from them, though disillusioned, took time to respond the reasonable call of the BSP. This dilemma of the

Sudras has delayed the formation of the Bahujan Samaj. The Scheduled Caste voters hold the key in many of the constituencies. For example, in four constituencies in Mariana, the percentage of SC voters to the total votes is 20 to 25 per cent while in 2 constituencies it is 25 to 30 per cent According to the 1991 Census, in UP the percentage pf SC population to the total is 21.05 per cent in the Punjab 28.31 per cent in MP 14.5 per cent and in Mariana 19.75 per cent. All India SC population is 16.48 per cent. Other states with SC population above the all India average are H.P. 25.3 per cent, Rajasthan 17.3 per cent, Tamil Nadir 19.2 per cent West Bengal 23.6 per cent and Delhi 19.1 per cent. In the first two states Congress sits comfortably over SC votes. In the last two DMK TMC and CPI(M) respectively enjoy their strong hold....." 'The BSP shared 59.5 per cent of SC votes in U.P., 22.9 per cent in M.P. and 12.2 per cent in Mariana..... The Election Commission data show that in the four constituencies (Gurudaspur, Phillur, Hoshiarpur, and Firozpur) of the Punjab where BSP contested, it won 5.8, 48.01, 39.50 and 36.83 percent of total polled votes.... In Hariyana on the 6 seats that it contested, its vote share varied from 5.01 per cent to 20.58 per cent. On Jammu seat, the party got 16.14 per cent of total votes. In Madhya Pradesh the party polled more than 20 per cent of votes in as many as 6 seats and between 10 to 20 per cent votes in 7 seats.'

The strengthening of the BSP has been a remarkable feature of this Election. This is a typical case of assertion of the SCs in electoral politics through a party, which was mainly based among the Untouchables. 67.4 per cent of its votes came from the SCs alone. The remaining came from Muslims, Sikhs and the OBCs. Kanshi Ram once even challenged the Brahmins that he had neither solicited their votes nor the Brahmins had given a single therefore, his party was not committed to special priority to look into their grievances. In the state of UP, Hariyana, Madhya Pradesh and the Punjab the party performed very well. Particularly, in UP it performed exceedingly well in terms of vote share and the number of seats it won. The all India figures show that the party contested 201 seats won 11 seats and was able to get 3.8 per cent of the total valid votes. Of the 11 seats, the BSP won 6 seats in UP, 3 in Punjab and 2 in MP. Of these seats only 3 seats belonged to the reserved and the rest belonged to the General seats. Of the SC vote all over India, its share was 13.7 per cent. The party in contest on 21 seats and on 64 seats the vote secured by the party has been more than the margin of victory. Election Commission data show that the party secured 20.16 per cent of total votes polled in UP. There were 52 seats in the states where the party polled more than one lakh votes. The Party stood 2nd on 17 seats and secured more than 20 per cent of the polled votes on 46 seats. Its vote share has shown steady increase in time. In 1985 Assembly election the party got 4 per cent of total votes which went up to 9.4 per cent of total votes in 1989 Assembly election, 9.9 per cent in 1991 *Lok Sabha* Election and 10.8 per cent in 1993 Assembly election. In W. Bengal particular, Kanshi Ram tired personally to build up popular base as he rightly considered that the roots of the Brahminism is watered in the province of W. Bengal. Here (undivided Bengal) the Bahujan freedom movement started a century back and at present in W. Bengal (actually) more than 39 per cent of the total population belonged to the SCs and STs and another at least 30 per cent proselyte Muslims. His industrious mission could yield little due to hellish and bloody torture on the untouchable population by the CPI (*Manuwadi*).

The BSP's rise in the four states seems to be linked, as a logical concomitant, with the decline of the Congress. In UP the Congress has been reduced to a peripheral party due to its losing the party's traditional vote bank of the Harijans. BSP, SP and BJP have now become the main party in UP. The BSP is found to have got firmly rooted amongst the *Jatav-Chamars*, the largest SC caste group in UP. More than 73 per cent of its votes in UP belong to this caste. And the Pasis constitute 45.7 per cent votes.

The figures presented above also display the commonly held belief that the BSP has a powerful electoral appeal only among the urban educated middle-class of the SCs. The voters' background of UP reveal that the BSP draws 62.7 per cent of its votes from non-lettered voters though they constitute only 44.8 per cent of the sample of respondent. The next large share to BSP votes come from the voters having education up to middle level constituting 27.4 per cent of total BSP voters. Voters having completed graduation or above constitute only 2 per cent of BSP voters though their representation in the sample has been 5.6 per cent. In fact, only 6.3 per cent of the graduates preferred to vote for the BSP where as this figure is as high as 51.3 per cent for the BJP. More are dependant for privileges, alienated from the society and Hinduised more they avoid freedom movement. Educated and privileged lot of the Dalits safely prefer to go for save and guard movement than fighting for the ruling rod. Earn privileges by *Chamchagiri* is their motto. Occupation wise BSP's voters mainly belong to the unskilled workers, agricultural and allied workers and artisans and small and marginal farmers. Persons engaged in business and white colour job constitute only 2.6 and 1.6 per cent respectively of the BSP voters. The all India figures also resemble the trends as observed in UP. For example, the all India figures reveal that 85.3 per cent of BSP votes came from the lower class alone. Table 3 (refer to the study report) also suggests, the BSP is primarily a party of the rural and poor.

The only other party known for representing mostly the SCs is the Republican Party of India. In 1996 parliamentary elections, the party emerged as obvious choice of the SC voters wherever it contested election in Maharashtra. Of the 11 seats it contested in the state, though without a win, in 5 seats its vote share is more than 20 per cent (the highest being 33.19 per cent in Akola constituency) and in 4 constituencies between 10 to 20 per cent of the polled votes. The party could poll more than 2 lakhs of votes in the two constituencies". The reason of sudden shine of the RPI after two and a half decade in Maharashtra seems to be to thwart the progress of the BSP, the party primarily of rural and poor in Maharashtra. In the province the untouchable and Buddhist population is less than 12 per cent. The Chamars and Mangs who compose 50 per cent of the untouchable population traditionally remains with the Congress. Ambedkarites are found to have opposed the growth of BSP in Maharashtra. Therefore, the glitter of the RPI in post 1995 election era confuses more than it directs. This appears to be the bubble burst, six decades after the ILP of Dr Ambedkar in 1937 Bombay election.

The study report also has disclosed the truth that with the emergence of their own political party the *Dalit-bahujan* who were merely used by the Brahmanical parties as their stored votes in their Vote-Banks, refused to be used as mere ballot in favour of the Brahmanical Social Order and in the detriment of the lower stratum of the society.

After independence the Dalit lagged behind the Upper castes in terms of exercising their franchise for various reasons. The most important aspect is the denial of voting opportunity by the upper caste men whenever their preference seems to come in conflicts with the SCs and fear of backlash. Voting is rigged in favour of the casteists who have less number of votes but more power, money, media and mafia. Besides, the ruling party always without fail has got themselves elected to the throne of power but miserably neglected those who elected them to power.

The best example can be sited from W. Bengal where Comrade Jyoti Basu and Buddhadev Bhattachariya ruled as CM in the name of Marxism for a long period of 34 years without break or facing meaningful or strong opposition. Com. Jyoti Basu was elected from Santgachia constituency of South 24 Parganas successively for four terms. Around 90 per cent of the voters in the constituency belong to untouchables and Muslims alone. The area, needless to say, is matchlessly backward being in blinding darkness of illiteracy, poverty and ill communication system. Those people voted Jyoti Basu to the CM's chair with mechanical repetition. However, even today when Mamata Banerjee has become the Didi CM a local train from South 24 Parganas nicknamed "JHIR TRAIN" (train of maids) carrying maidservants travels daily to Sealdah railway station. That is the first daily morning train studded with laboring class mainly the maidservants. They are dropped in the morning at 5 a.m. daily to be absorbed in the kitchens and Karkhanas of Kolkata *babus* and Marwaris. Other gentry avoid the train because unimaginable rush and bad smell. All tsunamis of changes come and go without altering the nameplate of 'Jhir Train'.

Fundamentally Indian democracy has remains hereditary, high-tech affair of the old royal families and big spiritual shrines. Poor has become pauper, illiterates have become ill informed, helpless have accepted their fate as a result of the deeds of their past lives. The 'Oppressed India' lay prostrate leaderless.

References

1. Dr B.R. Ambedkar, W and S, Vol. 17 (1) pp. 3-10.
2. Dr B.R. Ambedkar, W and S, Vol. 17 (2) pp. 506-10.
3. Dhananjoy Keer, B.R. Ambedkar: Life and Mission, p. 440.
4. Dr B.R. Ambedkar, W and S, Vol. 17 (1) pp. 409-19.
5. *Ibid,* p. 425.
6. Jagadish Chandra Mandal, Mahapran Jogendra Nath Mandal, Vol. 1, p. 7.
   Sekhar Bandhyopadhay, Caste, Politics in Colonial India.
8. Jagadish Chandra Mandal, Mahapran Jogendra Nath Mandal, Vol. 1.
9. *Ibid,* Vol. 1, p. 81 and quoted by N.B. Roy, A People in Distress, Vol. 2, p. 230.
10. Bahujan Nayak Kanshiram Sahib Ke Bhasan, Vol. 2, pp. 62-63.
11. Patrick French, India: A Portrait An Intimate Biograpgy of 1.2 Billion People; Out Look: January 17, 2011.
12. Dr B.R. Ambedkar, W and S, Vol. 10, p. 37 (Broadcast speech from Bombay. All India radio of Labour Minister Dr Ambedkar, on 1st January, 1943).
13. *Ibid*, Vol. 10, p. 107 and Vol. 9 (Let not Tyrants have freedom to Enslave).
14. Dr B.R. Ambedkar, W and S, Vol. 10, pp. 107-109.
15. N.N. Vorah Committee Report.
16. Dr Ambedkar W and S, Vol. 10, p. 495.
17. *Ibid,* Vol. 17 (1), p. 359.
18. *Ibid*, Vol. 17 (3), p. 298.
19. Sudha Pai, From Harijan to Dalits: Identity Formation, Political Consequences and Electoral Mobilisation.

10

We Can Change, Yes We Can

The new millennium, the third millennium echoed with the reverberating sounds of 'Change'. The 'Change', as has already been mentioned earlier, that was demanded in the Indian Parliament by *Manyawar* Kanshi Ram while discussing the disease of caste system on the 28th of may 1996. The morning 11.30 O' clock of the year 2009 January 20, witnessed the change in the amazing oath taking ceremony of Barack Hussain Obama as the President of USA. The audacity of hope, the incredible reality was observed in a palpable demonstration by millions of people assembled on the steps of the United States Capital in Washington DC in the cutting winter-chill of America. The most unbelievable incident came to reality with the fulfillment of the dream from his father. It burst into the spectacular sight of super nova sonic-bang in the universe. The direction of the Prophet *Hazarat* Muhammad came true. The Prophet asked Bilal, the sed-black Habsi-slave to say the first *Namaz* from the pulpit of Caba, in Mecca. From amongst the hundreds of 'Masters' and 'Fair-skinned', 'White' men, Bilal took his gracious stand on the pulpit to inaugurate the Islamic world, the reign of equality and universal fraternity. With one stone the Prophet is found to have indicated to dwindle down the 'Master's mastery and the White-Aryan's supercilious supremacy. "I have a dream" proclaimed Civil Rights fighter, Martin Luther King on 28th of August, 1963 in his broadcast to the American nation, ". . . . that one day this nation will rise up and live out the true meaning of its creed . . . . that one day even the state of Mississippi, a desert state, sweltering with the heat of injustice and oppression, will be transformed into an oasis of freedom and justice." The world celebrates the act of transforming the 'White-House' into a black Palace by one Kenyan Obama, the most powerful personality of today's world. A black, once upon a time, not very long ago, who had no voting right; no entry in schools, hotels, parks and clubs etc. became the President of America. Without any fundamental change or transformation of the structure and system of the society a change was celebrated with tears of joy.

In the USA, percentage of black population is less than 14 per cent. The tribes of Uncle Tom's Cabin were not having voting rights only a few decades back. They had to stone the Los Angeles High Court a few years back to make it fair to the black people of America. The Blacks were called contemptuously as Niger. Despite their poor numerical strength, they got spectacular entry into the White House because of their determination for freedom. They were solidly united to fight out their cause. They were mistake less to identify their enemy, and their black brothers fought the self-conscious movement independently. They voted en-mass for Barack Hussain Obama. The consolidated force of the black community earned great esteem from other people in the USA known by the term 'coloured' humanity (other than Dalits, Indian Hindus in general did not support Obama). Though Obama faced defeat in the White dominated pockets and provinces the victory crowned Obama comfortably. The black Americans never deterred to shed their blood as the price for liberty and never accepted the wise white race as their liberator or deliverer so they finally won the most precious object of human life. They declared black is beautiful; God is black.

The same situation was created in India in 1937 election by the Untouchables under the leadership of Mukunda Bihari in Bengal and Mangoo Ram in the Punjab. However, other oppressed castes did not show solidarity with them. Even Dr Ambedkar opposed Mukunda-Mangoo Ram's independent stand as it differed from Gandhian Hindu Nationalist stand and the stand adopted by the ruling classes of England. With a view to leading a freedom movement against the European colonial power, as in Vietnam and other countries there was the necessity to exist an Independent and self-conscious strong and militant middleclass desirous to shed blood and lives. Freedom from colonials rule, in India was arranged by the Colonial power. It was a freedom-fixing. So is the case with the immense majority servile class. Around 91 per cent of the population in the country formed the middle class in America. This picture is diametrically different in India. There is no middle class in India. The top 5 per cent are rich and super-rich. The remnant, 95 per cent are poor and below-poverty level subjects. What the Americans freely could decide cannot be expected to be done by the Indians therefore.

These 5 per cent upper class of India is composed of the creamy-layer upper castes headed by the Brahmins. Their traits of character and mental condition is rightly recorded as follows: "However much you may parade your descent from Aryan ancestors and sing the glories of ancient India day and night, and however much you may be strutting in the pride of your birth, you the upper class of India, do you think you are alive? You are but mummies ten thousand years old! It is among those whom your ancestors despised as "walking carrion" that the little of vitality there is still in India is to be found; and it is you who are the real "walking corpses". In this world of Maya, you are the real illusions, the mystery, the real mirage in the desert, you the upper class of India. You represent the past tense, with all its varieties of form jumbled into one. That one still seems to see you at the present time, is nothing but nightmare brought on by indigestion. You are the void, the unsubstantial nonentities of the future."[1]

The population below the poverty line though it faced better than China on this account in 1990, according the World Bank. In its report, 'Global Economic Prospects for 2009', said a quarter of India's population will be living in extreme poverty, on less than $ 1.25 a day in 2015. Further, it said the poverty line, measured at $1.25 in 2005, represents the average of the poverty line of 15 poorest countries, for which there is data. According to the report, the number of Indians living in extreme poverty were 43.6 Crores/ Billions (51.3%) in 1990 and will be 31.3 crores (25.4%) in 1915."[2] According to the report, 77 per cent of the people of India live in below poverty line (BPL) and in distressing condition. Again, Nancy Birdsall revealed the startling fact to be published for the Centre for Global Development in the World Bank Publication, Equality in globalizing World. In April 2010, that there is no Middle Class in India. According to the standard, a person having four members in the family, who earn $10 a day and above belongs to the Middle Class in a country having uniformly top 5 per cent of the citizens as rich. In India the entire population earning $10 and above a day come within the top 5 per cent of the country's population.[3] That is, India had not shifter, economically even an inch from the condition that prevailed in the 17th Century. Frachaoan Barnier, the Court physician of Great Mughal Aurangjeb, in his Travels' Account had recorded that there was no middle class in India. Today the top 5 per cent of the country is composed of the Super Rich, Rich and Petty-Rich. The immense majority 85 per cent are the BPL people and the remnant 10 per cent are poor. The subjects are equally illiterate and ill-informed.

Can there be any type of Democracy in such a country? Can these immense majority who are traditionally engaged all the time to earn their basic subsistence by any means; who fail to get a square meal a day and remain dependent on the mercies of the ruling class have any say over the governance of the country? Can such humankind fulfill its destiny without a fundamental revolution in the social state of the country?[4] Guruchand in the 90's decade of 19th Century prophetically commented:

> *"Dhana Hin Vidyahin Jahara Aei Bhahabe;*
> *Rajniti Kshetre Tara Shanti Nahi Pabe.*
> *Aattwonnoti Agrabhage Proyojan Tai*
> *Vidya Chai, Dhan Chai, Rajkarya Chai*"

'Those who are economically so poor, educationally so illiterate can never get satisfied or success in political field. In political life, in a parliamentary democracy preponderance of education, economy and executive jobs in the Government'[5] is never gainsaid. In the blinding darkness of commanding influence and control of spiritual superstitions from the ever expanding number of small and big temples all over the territory it has become almost an impossible phenomenon for causing social revolution against the Hindu Theocracy. In the age of super-computer, this has turned to be a Hindu Hereditary Democracy. This is what Gandhiji achieved in 1932 through the Poona Pact. The Ruling Classes, therefore, fancifully called him *Mahatma* and designated as the father of this modern Indian nation. Dr Ambedkar in his last speech in the Constituent Assembly finally appealed, 'If this constitutional disparity in the economic and social structure of Indian society continues those who suffer or victims of disparity will blow up the Parliamentary structure so laboriously built.' Disparity between the haves and have-nots, rich and poor, Brahmins and Shudras has gone up many hundred folds since then. The reign of divine contentment, yet continues. Can such a 'semi-barbarian and semi-civilised'[6] constitutionally fragmented society that exists without senses and interrelation, interaction of a civil society, muster courage and strength to blow up the repressive structure and establish a Government by the people? Can they blow up a government, merely of the people? Let us not forget that more than 50 per cent of the world's illiterate are Indians; completely bereft of any human aspirations. People are not only pauper and illiterate they are heavily drugged with the opium of religious rituals and superstitions. Can such a nation without nationality and social democracy avoid its destiny to be the pray of the brute and powerful creamy-layer ruling families of the 'eternal colony'[7] of the Earth? Hereditary Parliamentarians, today, after six decades of freedom, rather transfer of power in the hands of the Brahmins and their associates, have captured the Parliament of India. Indian Democracy is a Hereditary Democracy.

The Hereditary Parliamentarians are empowered to enact laws whatever they think or wish necessary for protecting and perpetuation their sovereignty. They are free to declare any dog, a mad dog that they want to kill. The present government has decided to pass students up to VIII standard in the Government schools without any examination. They are feeding the students with mid-day meals and not with learning. This is the best and calculated way to perpetuate the darkness of illiteracy amongst common subjects of the country and to nip their sense of self-respect in bud. Technically literate but without education this section of country people finally got pushed into economic distress. Such people in a mechanical process use their ballots to elect hereditary rulers to rule over them. Blind or the half-blinds remain debarred of political rights to be the ruler.

The Charter of Human Rights, drawn by the UNO and ratification by all its member nations protect fundamental rights of human beings of the Globe. Article 30 declares that 'no man on the Earth can remain without citizenship of a country.' The right to citizenship rests on the principle of self determinations. The Indian Hereditary Parliament, very courageously declare more than one billion Indian citizens 'No-citizen' by enacting a Citizenship Amendment Bill, 2003. This lot belongs to the lowest strata of the immense majority society. They have been snatched off their franchise right by declaring them no-citizen. This lot started demanding 'Vote Hamara Raj Tumhara Nahin Chalega' of the Bahujan Samaj Party. The target for this enactment is simply to disenfranchise the inconvenient and politically aspirant Bengalee Untouchable voters who are considered the most potential force to bring fundamental change in political movement of the servile class once again. The Bill was tabled in the House of the Parliament by the then Hon'ble Home Minister L.K. Advani who belonged to the BJP party. The Bill was jubilantly endorsed by all party leaders and policy makers of India. It was passed unanimously. Not even a single member in position or in opposition opposed it. In the polity structure of Hereditary Democracy many such methods are the natural concomitant of the system. It is not a system failure. Till 1987, with the enactment of a new citizenship Act a person born in India was a citizen. But the new law made it a condition that both of the parents of the new born must also required to be a citizen for the baby to be a citizen of India. Such laws became necessary to disenfranchise once again, the citizens of the lowest stratum who started a political party called BSP in 1984 with blue flags in hand, to capture political power and establish people's democracy. The inadequate law has been supplemented with guarding clauses in the citizenship amendment Bill 2003.

Swami Vivekananda, in his third speech in the Chicago Parliament of Religion, on 20th September 1993, cried out and appealed, "You erect churches all through India, but the crying evil in the East is not religion they have religion enough but it is bread that the suffering millions of burning India cry out for with parched throats. They ask us for bread, but we give them stones. It is a insult to a starving people to offer them religion; it is an insult to a starving man to teach him metaphysics. I came here to seek aid for my impoverished people, and I fully realised how difficult it was to get help for heathens from Christians in a Christian land."[8] But the ruling classes of India in post Vivekananda era and in post 'Transfer of Power' period have come up with erecting Temples and Maths on each street corners. The number of spiritual spots have increased even in greater speed than of Malthus population theory. Religious activities have gone multi-fold. The 'Opium of Religion' is extremely proficient and effective in every respect to perpetuate the poor in perpetual ignorance poverty and out of governance. Indian ruling classes use this poison freely and profusely. The modern Indian democratic State-sponsored activities from the spiritual institutions founded on vulgar display of public wealth and pomp have robbed off the gullible subjects their sense of right to govern their country. The servile classes have been taught to take care of the life after death in the other world and remain indifferent towards the prosperity of a life in this world. They have reduced to irresponsible on-lookers in the country having little concern over the political affairs of the country. It has become the monopoly of the microscopic minority creamy-layer elite class or castes. With a view to strengthening the situation innovative schemes of Free Economic Zones, Tiger Projects, Narmada Project come up under the beautiful slogans of ecological balance and development. In the name of civilisation, the servile people are being appropriated, uprooted, their socio-political consolidation is disrupted and eventually *Jal, Jamin* and *Jungle* (Water spots, Land, and Forests) that belong to them, the autochthons are grabbed through the necessity laws passed by the Hereditary Parliament in the land of Hereditary Democracy.

Manyawar Kanshi Ram in the Golden Jubilee Year of Indian Independence had circulated a pocket book with a caption; "*Swadhin Bharat Mein Bahujan Samaj Gulam Keun*?" i.e. "Why in Independent India Bahujan Samaj is Dependent?" He did not question the veracity of the freedom that India achieved as has been negated by the CPI leaders, "Ye Azadi Jhuta Hai, Mehanti Janta Bhukha Hai" 'This freedom is false, the laboring class is hungry'. But according to Kanshi Ram, the immense majority of the Indians did not get freedom. Independence is the exclusive privilege of the microscopic creamy-layer ruling section of the society. They are rich and free; they are powerful and independent to do or undo anything. They are independent and free to create any number of Godhras, Singur, Netai, Lalgarh or Kakrajhor anywhere any day. They are free to use 'Joutha Bahini' or Military forces on any sections of the dependent Indians. They have freedom really. Can in such circumstances the credulous, impulsive and blind people or the subjects behave in a democratic fashion?

In modern India too, the victims of the Brahmanical socio-political system though form the immense majority and the lowest stratum of the country, they continue to remain in the state of abject servitude. Further, the ninety percent of the total population remains fragmented into thousands of parochial and caste-racial groups. They have doggedly accepted their tormentors, the Brahmins only as their ultimate saviour and liberators. The religion of the exclusive victims and exclusive beneficiaries cannot be the same. Still in India, the victims of the Casteism have accepted, from the core of their hearts, the Hinduism as their spirituality. The '*Dalitbahujan*' are not at all ready to shed blood for their liberty even though they sacrifice their useless lives at the call of the Brahmin Gurus and Political leaders. Consequently, the servile classes or castes continue to be in the servile and deplorable condition. In the so-called Parliamentary democracy, the Dalit-Bahujan Samaj comes to vote for their masters and go home back to be ruled or miss-ruled for the next few years. The autochthons 'Bahujan Samaj' have developed a deep sense of analgesia and thereby do not feel the pinch of salt of humiliation of being in servitude for millennium. They hardly want to be the rulers of their own country. They rather prefer to be ruled.

All the traditional, national or regional political parties are found to have been launched by the spiritual rulers of India, the Brahmins at the cost of their coffers and perseverance, naturally to protect their own interests. No anger against the oppressors and exploiters for all types of acts of discriminations disturbed their sleep at night nor the slumber due to the absence of socialisation process amongst them, created an iota of appetite for ruling their own country by themselves. The slaves enjoy slavery and let the ruling class, the privileged 'Gurus' to enjoy their privileges in peace. It is a question of individualism and self-respect, equality and authority in the Democratic structure of polity for all. Bahujan Samaj is doggedly contented without all these. Instead of 'divine contentment', a sense of ceaseless 'celestial discontentment' or insatiate ambition is to be aroused amongst the *Dalit-bahujan Mulniwasi Samaj*. Some thinkers are in quest of 'anger'; anger is conspicuously missing amongst the oppressed. Anger is to be exhumed of the Indian immense majority and lowest stratum of the society so that they can 'stir, can raise their obstacles up, with the whole superincumbent strata of official society being sprung into the air.' In India this process of class-struggle for replacing one class by another either through the evolutionary process or through forceful revolutionary method created and organised consciously by the particular class has never been taken place. In the British India Depressed Class started taking its firm and palpable entity. However, that move was suppressed and Scheduled Castes resurrected in its place in the Poona Pact. Class consciousness shuttered since then. It is, as discussed earlier, due to non entity of class strata in the Indian society class struggles in the form of civil-wars has never taken place. In other countries, the history of their society is nothing but the history of successive civil wars. That is the pivot of their developed state. Indian society is yet to see such a civil war for the liberation and change. India cannot avoid her destiny without preparing for such a phenomenon.

The major, thinking and the elite element of the Indian Muslims have gone away with large landmasses in the Western and Eastern sectors of India as separate and sovereign nations. Remnants of them are weak section of Indian Muslims who remained as Indians. The vulnerable groups are condemned as pro-Pakistani, Pakistan-agents, terrorists and anti-national. The reign of anti-Muslim sentiment works speedily because of pampering of Hindu-chauvinism. In the post-partition era, therefore, Indian Muslims who form not less than 20 per cent of the total population has become totally isolated and subservient to the so-called Hindu majority society. It has become so because of the swelling of Hindu population after hijacking the helpless Untouchables and Tribals, who form not less than 35 per cent of the total population. This condition was predicted by the leaders of

Untouchable-Bengal, ". . . . That the division of the province into Hindu and Muslim Bengal (was) no solution of the Communal problem.... (it would) check the growing political consciousness and ruthlessly crush the solidarity of the Scheduled Castes of Bengal.... While the Scheduled Castes of Eastern Bengal (would) be at the mercy of the majority community (Muslims) the Scheduled Castes of Western Bengal (would) be subject to the perpetual slavery of the caste-Hindus. Hence the Scheduled Castes of the province (could not be a party to such a mischievous and dangerous move."[9] When the Bengalee Scheduled Castes were forced to accept 'the perpetual slavery' could the Scheduled Castes of India of remaining parts remain out of the purview of the slave Dom? The Indian Muslims consequently, like the Untouchables have got equally a type of analgesia and lost the spirit to be the rulers in the country. The developed a state of amnesia that during the entire medieval period they were the ruling class in India. They now feel comfortable in playing the role of the 'King-maker' rather than contesting to be the King. They add the burden of illiterate and BPL of the country.

Such a non-human mental set-up keeps human beings far from getting liberty and prosperity by advancing in the battles of ballots or democracy. This is the age of 'Ballots' not of 'Bullets'. Bullets may be required only to protect the 'Ballots' as rightly said by *Manyawar* Kanshi Ram when his votes were being rigged by the w Creamy-layer Ruling class who had little number of Ballots in their pockets. Until and unless, the votes of the 'Oppressed India' unite solidly behind the cause, as blacks behind Barak Hussain Obama, change is not possible. Change is a far cry until the disdained people resort fearlessly for great sacrifices. The 'Immense majority' *'Bahujan Samaj'* which include the number of the Oppressed and exploited Sudras (modern name Backward classes) get consolidated in a considerable number behind the united forces of the Muslims and the Untouchables they have no hope for freedom. There is no hope for rule of the servile class or democracy. Must they have to win the democratic battle through the self conscious independent struggle under the their own leadership at the first instance. But for a long drawn, relentless battles in tactical democratic way has no alternative for them. To reach to the Nom Chamski's goal for the future Government they are to strengthen first their knowledge of government, warfare, economy and strengthen their organisational solidarity. It may take long time. There is no royal rod for freedom. Like Guruchand, the leaders must show patience and be ready to be injured while advancing through different stages.

Kanshi Ram, the founder and the president of BSP disclosed his determination for change and the nature of change the nation needed in his speech on the floor of parliament on 28th May 1996 and gave the formula of 'change' in a meeting on 13th June 1996, at Mavalankar Hall, New Delhi. For 'change' we need to understand three factors i.e. N x D x S = Change.

'N' stands for need, 'D' stands for desire and 'S' stands for Strength. When needs for change of the society are inspired or ignited by the fire of desire of the needy subjects of the society to execute those, and that desire to change is mobilised by the strength of the society, the desirable change takes place. The organisations like BAMCEF, DS4 etc had been working to strengthen the *Bahujan Samaj* which is composed of Scheduled Castes, Scheduled Tribes, More Backward castes, backward Castes and the Proselytes of them. Change is a process; it is not an end. It takes place only when the protagonists of orthodoxy are over powered.

Cadre-based web of consciousness in regard to the social-history and political history of the entire country and of the world is the basic point. There is the indispensible need to create determination to pay back to the society, to push towards integrity of the disintegrated society in the first instance. This is to be maintained as the primary plank for achieving the goal of Change, the freedom, and to establish the statue of liberty. Democracy is the basic structure of Liberty. Yes, We can. We can bring Change whatever time it may take.

References

1. Complete Works of Swami Vivekananda, Vol. 7, p. 326.
2. *Times of India*, 13.5.2009.
3. *Hindusthan Times*, May 6, 2010.
4. Marx and Engels, Selected Works, Vol. 1, (Moscow Publication, 1977) p. 493.
5. Mahananda Haldar, Guruchand Charit, p. 573.
6. Karl Marx and Fredrick Engels, Selected Correspondence, Vol. 1, p. 492.
7. S.K. Biswas, Hindu Raj, Today-Yesterday and Tomorrow, p. 78.
8. The Complete Works of Swami Vivekananda, Vol. 1, p. 20.
9. S.K. Biswas, Hari-Guruchand, Banglar Chandal and Bharater Bahujan Abhuthan, p. 178 : (Resolution of 14th may 1947, All India Scheduled Caste Federation).

Index

I

W

Y

Z